The Complete Getaway Guide to Oklahoma

Sarah L. Taylor, Editor

Inprint Publishing, Inc.
306 S. Bryant, Suite C-152 • Edmond, OK 73034
(405) 340-1404 • e-mail: explore@oklahoma.net

Inprint Publishing, Inc.
306 S. Bryant, Suite C-152
Edmond, OK 73034
(405) 340-1404
e-mail: explore@oklahoma.net
Web site: www. exploringoklahoma.com

ISBN number 0-9645685-1-9
Library of Congress Catalog Card Number: 97-071984

Editor: Sarah L. Taylor, President, Inprint Publishing, Inc.

Design and production:
David, Randall & Yates Graphic+Design, Oklahoma City.

Editorial assistance provided by Donald E. Hines and Pam Pittman.

Contributing authors and their assignments:

Deborah Bouziden (Oklahoma City area); Susan Hollingsworth (Panhandle, Northeast Oklahoma); Sarah Kobos (Northwest Oklahoma); Taprina Milburn (Southcentral Oklahoma); Sarah Taylor (parts of Northwest Oklahoma); Elaine Warner (Southwest and Southeast Oklahoma, Guthrie, Norman).

Writers of special articles:

Deborah Bouziden, Shana Marlow, Jay Porter, Trena Thomas, Elaine Warner.

Cover Models: Rick Harper and Shawn Cochrane.

Front cover background photo by Jim Argo; **Front cover portrait** and **staff photo** by Whitaker Portrait Design.

To order *Exploring Oklahoma Together* and *Exploring Oklahoma with Children* (revised), contact Inprint Publishing, Inc., 306 S. Bryant, Suite C-152, Edmond, OK 73034, (405) 340-1404.

Dedication

This book is dedicated to my family—to my husband, John, who has supported me in countless ways through the process of compiling, editing, and writing this book, and to my precious children, Kathryne, Reed, and Zane, who have been more than patient and understanding.

Foreward

I love Oklahoma—not just because Oklahoma is my home but because it is a special place with special people. The state's history, bio-diversity, cultural diversity, urban areas with world-renowned attractions and events, small towns with character and pride, pristine rural areas, outdoor adventure opportunities, and more, make Oklahoma a wonderful place to live or visit. I even find Oklahoma's notoriously-unpredictable weather exciting at times but, more often than not, mild and pleasant. From the stark high plains of the Oklahoma Panhandle to the surprisingly-dense forests of Southeastern Oklahoma, the state has much to offer the casual visitor and the lifelong resident.

The goal of this book is to provide travelers with the most complete getaway guide to Oklahoma. We have worked diligently to uncover the state's most unique places to stay, tour, dine, shop, golf, relax, and have fun! By reading this book and by exploring the many Oklahoma sites listed, you will undoubtably gain a much better understanding about Oklahoma and its people.

The other element of this book is that it was written to encourage "togetherness" between couples, families, and friends. It is our family's experience that when we get away from home, whether for a day or a week, we're able to distance ourselves from the distractions of everyday routines. This provides the perfect opportunity to reconnect with each other, opening ourselves to better communication, thus enriching our lives and our relationships. Our perspectives change; we allow ourselves to focus on the more important things in life and to simply enjoy time together.

My sincere hope is that you enjoy all the facets of "Exploring Oklahoma Together." God bless!

Sarah L. Taylor, editor/publisher
Exploring Oklahoma Together and *Exploring Oklahoma with Children*
May, 1997

Acknowledgements

This book would not have been possible without the help, support
and guidance of the following special people:

Exploring Oklahoma Together **crew and writers:**
Randy Yates, Elaine Warner, Taprina Milburn, Sarah Kobos, Susan Hollingsworth,
Deborah Bouziden, Melba Prior, Martha Jacobs, Jay Porter, Trena Thomas,
and Shana Marlow.

Our most sincere appreciation to our corporate sponsor and our many advertisers.

Corporate Sponsor:
Children's Hospital of Oklahoma
All Advertisers (see page 277 for an index)

Friends and Advisors:
Pam Pittman, Donald Hines, Melba Prior, Roy Page, Richard Bedard, Jake Lowrey, the staff
of A Child's Garden, Kay Hunt, Teresa Brown, Julie Jones, Sandy Price, Tina Smith, Jeanette
Graves, Jeanette Henderson, Carla Hill, Elise Marrs, Jenny Johnston, the staff of the Oklahoma Department of Tourism, particularly Sandy Pantlik and Barbara Palmer, and from
the staff of Oklahoma Parks and Resorts, Kelly Newsom and Lisa Grant, the staff of *Oklahoma Today* magazine, particularly Joan Henderson and Brian Brown, Allison O'Rear, Jill
Bradshaw, Jeff and Diana McCown, and Robbie Scott.

A very sincere thank you to my entire family, especially my parents, Harold and Virginia
Lowrey, and my mother-in-law, Mildred Taylor, for helping when I needed it!

Invitation
You are encouraged and invited to provide suggestions for additions and changes to
subsequent editions of *Exploring Oklahoma Together*. We want to hear from you! Please
send your ideas to Inprint Publishing, Inc., 306 S. Bryant, Suite C-152, Edmond, OK
73034, (405) 340-1404, e-mail: explore@oklahoma.net.

Disclaimer
The information in this book has been thoroughly researched and tested to be as accurate as
possible. However, the travel industry is dynamic, and the contents of this book are subject to
change. Readers are advised to call ahead to verify information whenever they travel. Neither
the authors nor the publisher can be held responsible for the experiences of travelers.

Book Resources used for *Exploring Oklahoma Together:*
Footsteps through Tulsa, by Marilyn Inhofe, Kathleen Reeves, and Sandy Jones published
by Inhofe, Reeves, and Jones, 1995; *Oklahoma Travel Handbook* by Kent Ruth, University
of Oklahoma Press, 1985; *Oklahoma Historical Tour Guide* by Burnis Argo and Kent Ruth,
Crossroads Communications, 1992; *Oklahoma, A History of Five Centuries* by Arrell Morgan Gibson, University of Oklahoma Press, 1981; *The Oklahoma Land Rush of 1889* by
Stan Hoig, Oklahoma Historical Society, 1989; *Guthrie, A History of the Capital City 1889-
1910* by Lloyd C. Lentz, Logan County Historical Society; *The Sooner Story* by Charles F.
Long and Carolyn G. Hart, University of Oklahoma Press, 1980; *Historical Atlas of Oklahoma* by John W. Morris, Charles R. Goins, and Edwin C. McReynolds, University of Oklahoma Press, 1970; *Oklahoma: Off the Beaten Path* by Barbara Palmer, The Globe Pequot
Press, 1996; *Oklahoma Treasures and Treasure Trails* by Steve Wilson, University of Oklahoma Press, 1988; various articles from *Oklahoma Today* magazine.

Contents

Contents

Southeast Oklahoma

Southcentral Oklahoma

Southwest Oklahoma

Central Oklahoma (Frontier Country)

Using this Book

This book has been designed for ease of use. Here are some helpful guidelines that will help you find your way around.

- The book is arranged geographically by section, beginning with the Panhandle, going clockwise around the state, and ending with Central Oklahoma. Within each geographic section, the major towns or areas are in alphabetical order, and smaller towns or areas that are located nearby are listed as "In the Vicinity" to these towns.
- Within each city or area, the information is arranged as follows: **Attractions** (what to see and do), **Golf, Dining, Shopping, Accommodations,** and **Events**. Only unique accommodations such as B&Bs, guest ranches, or luxury hotels were included in this book. Only public or semi-private golf courses were included.
- The major geographic areas of Oklahoma are highlighted using a small corner map on each right-side page to help identify the entry's general location and for quick reference.
- Icons are used to help identify those places and attractions that are particularly outstanding and/or have placed advertisements or valuable coupons in the book. The icons and their meanings are as follows: ★ = Outstanding Attraction; ⑤ = Coupon; ⓘ = Advertisement.
- Handicapped accessibility is noted on most entries. Please call ahead if there is a concern about a particular venue.
- A Calendar of Events is provided in the back of the book.
- A map is included in this book for general reference only. Written directions are provided for most entries. Travelers will need an official state map, available free from any Tourist Information Center, most Chambers of Commerce, and the Oklahoma Department of Transportation.

Traveler Resources

Fishing Information (800) ASK-FISH
Frontier Country Marketing Association (405) 842-3232; (800) FUN-OKLA
Governor's Office (405) 521-2342
Highway Patrol/Emergency (405) 682-4343 (*55 on cellular phones)
Hunting Information (405) 521-2739
Oklahoma Arts Council (405) 521-2931
Oklahoma Community Theater Association (405) 236-0788
Oklahoma Department of Transportation (405) 521-2541
Oklahoma Department of Wildlife Conservation (405) 521-3851
Oklahoma Historical Society (405) 521-2491
Oklahoma Museums Association (405) 424-7757
Oklahoma Resorts, Parks, and Cabins (800) 654-8240
Oklahoma Restaurant Association (405) 942-8181
Oklahoma Scenic Rivers Commission (918) 456-3251
Oklahoma Tourism Department (800) 652-6552 (In Oklahoma City area 424-0473)
Red Carpet Country (800) 447-2698
Road and Weather Conditions (405) 425-2385

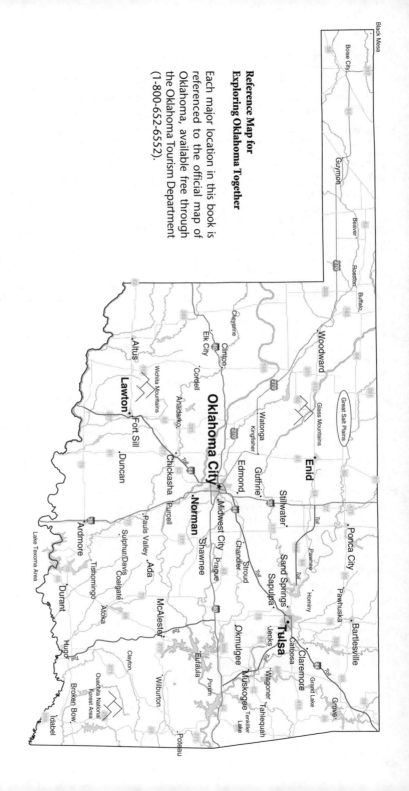

Reference Map for Exploring Oklahoma Together

Each major location in this book is referenced to the official map of Oklahoma, available free through the Oklahoma Tourism Department (1-800-652-6552).

Black Mesa
Boise City
Guymon
Beaver
Rosston
Buffalo
Woodward
Cheyenne
Elk City
Clinton
Cordell
Altus
Wichita Mountains
Anadarko
Lawton
Fort Sill
Duncan
Chickasha
Watonga
Kingfisher
Guthrie
Edmond
Oklahoma City
Midwest City
Norman
Purcell
Pauls Valley
Sulphur/Davis
Ada
Coalgate
Atoka
Ardmore
Tishomingo
Durant
Lake Texoma Area
Hugo
Broken Bow
Idabel
Great Salt Plains
Glass Mountains
Enid
Stillwater
Chandler
Stroud
Prague
Shawnee
McAlester
Wilburton
Clayton
Ouachita National Forest Area
Poteau
Sand Springs
Sapulpa
Okmulgee
Eufaula
Porum
Muskogee
Tenkiller Lake
Tahlequah
Tulsa
Jenks
Catoosa
Claremore
Wagoner
Ponca City
Pawnee
Hominy
Pawhuska
Bartlesville
Grand Lake
Grove

Defining Oklahoma

by Jay Porter

One Christmas when I was just a wee Okie, someone in my family gave me an instructional wooden puzzle with fifty state-shaped pieces. Each piece was painted brightly and emblazoned with a little star and the name of that piece's capital. I played endlessly with the puzzle, which to this day serves as my most concrete and reliable mental reference on the geography of America. In addition to that very useful knowledge, some other memories stick as well; I am sure that Texas was yellow, as were Florida and California. However, I cannot recall what color was used to represent Oklahoma.

Until I went away—1,600 miles away—to college, that map answered most of the questions I'd ever thought to ask about Oklahoma's place in the world. It was home, right there in the middle. What could be easier?

Away at college, I suffered through my self-imposed exile in a cold, wet, and dreary New England city. My homesickness for the

Elaine Warner

red earth and open skies of Oklahoma was made even worse by a growing sense that perhaps the question of where Oklahoma fits in the puzzle could not be so easily answered after all. People had many odd images about what Oklahoma must be like– all cowboys and Indians and oil wells–none of which was wholly true or false. They wanted simple answers and easy categories, but I had none to offer.

It was my French-German friend Christoph who finally provoked a real crisis of identity—not about my identity, but about Oklahoma's. In his mind, Oklahoma bordered Ohio. To make matters worse, he carried a suite of stereotypical visions of each region: the Midwest with its State Fairs, the West and its cowboys, the South and its mint juleps. He wanted to know where Oklahoma fit in.

With just a few words, he managed to strike a sore nerve. It's little wonder that a son of a state as young as Oklahoma should feel a bit intimidated by a friend who hails from two countries whose roots reach back twenty-five centuries. His question was unsettling, though, not so much because of who was asking it, but because I couldn't give him an unequivocal answer. Even given multiple choices, this was a test that I couldn't pass. Western? Midwestern? Southern? Southwestern? None of the above? Should I tell him about the hills that dip down to the Red River, or the flat expanse punctuated by Black Mesa, or the western range, or the eastern forests? I think I rambled on about all of it until he lost interest. Just talking about it made me miss home even more.

For the rest of my time in college, and even more since I've moved back, I've spent what many of my friends consider an inordinate amount of time trying to figure out exactly where our puzzle piece of prairie fits.

I can't imagine another state whose residents have as much trouble fitting neatly into one list or another. New Englanders and residents of the mid-Atlantic states have it easy. The Northwest, so trendy these days, has no problem defining its borders. However, Oklahoma lies on a fault line of sorts between regions and cultures that have histories in which Oklahoma arrives a bit too late to play an integral role. After all, our borders mark more where the other states stopped than where our state begins.

Oklahoma itself is routinely rocked by little earthquakes of internal dissent that have spawned something of a mythic geography. With its "back East" ethos, Tulsa is the capital of the shadow state of Eastern Oklahoma; folks in the Panhandle talk idly about joining with surrounding areas to make a new state; and Little Dixie believes itself seceded from everything else altogether.

To be fair to the would-be rebels, the state's terrain and lifestyles vary widely from Frederick to Miami and Beaver to Idabel. Only giant Texas has as many different ecological habitats as Oklahoma. Even today, it can still take much effort to convince folks that "the farmer and the rancher should be friends," as Rodgers and Hammerstein so shrewdly observed. However, until further notice we remain Oklahomans together, with Oklahoma City literally at the crossroads of the entire state and the point of conver-

gence of its mini-regions. The state remains landlocked, but its identity seems strangely at sea. Which way should we look to find the *terra firma* of a regional identity?

As I see it, my family has a representative from most of the six possibilities for our regional status. I'll start by demolishing the only one that I will not tolerate. Oklahoma is simply not midwestern. My father is from Iowa; after twenty-seven years here, he now drawls and would rather I say "was from Iowa." Iowa is definitely deep in the "heartland" of the midwest, although you'd be hard-pressed to find a pulse there. The people there are decent, honest folks, but they eat lots of boiled food with very few spices and speak in an accent with all the same charms. I can see some similarities between Northeastern Oklahoma and the definitely midwestern state of Kansas, though I would rather ignore them. But Minnesota, Michigan, Indiana, Iowa... these are not our regional neighbors.

The next candidate, the sentimental (though politically incorrect) favorite, is that Oklahoma is part of the Old South. This theory does have some merit, although society matrons in Savannah and New Or-

Tulsa's skyline.

Ouachita National Forest, Southeastern Oklahoma.

leans would gasp at the sheer audacity. They were holding cotillions when there weren't any white folks out here. However, Cherokee Stand Waitie was the youngest fighting Confederate General, and the Battle of Honey Creek was fought in what is now Oklahoma. Certainly Oklahoma accents lilt toward the Southern, albeit less drawn-out and with a broader and more nasal slant. Also, native Oklahomans' family recipes suggest a strong link with the traditions of the Deep South. (I will admit that I harbor a secret dream to see the state renamed Okrahoma in honor of my favorite vegetable.)

Certain Oklahomans, my grandmother among them, cling stubbornly to this vision of a gracious and warm Oklahoma; as their strongest evidence, they brandish their copies of magazines like *Southern Living* and *Southern Accents*. Who wants to argue with publications that can cover the memory of Simon LeGree, Jim Crow, and Orval Faubus with a "light and fluffy lemon chiffon icing" or a "do-it-yourself winter garden of hardy pachysandra"? Rather than contradict my sainted grandmother with the evidence that we are only Johnny-Rebs-come-lately, I'll just look away, look away.

On the other hand, my grandfather, with his 1948 Oklahoma High School Rodeo Champion saddle and his boots and white Stetson, convincingly represents the Oklahoma of the Old West. His Oklahoma is one of oil wells and herds of cattle, dusty and romantic. He even looks a little bit like Will Rogers, especially when he does rope tricks. Unfortunately, these images are romantic precisely because they are fading. The symbols of the Old West feel much too old for a young state. However, we must keep in touch with our Western heritage as preserved by entities like the National Cowboy Hall of Fame in Oklahoma City.

The New West, or Southwest, or whatever, offers a slightly more upbeat vision of our identity, but I can't quite see Oklahoma City (or Tulsa) as part of the New Mexico-Arizona-Southern California continuum. However, western magazines like *Sunset* claim us proudly. (Oklahoma seems to be a low-circulation pinch-hitter for these regional magazines.) I think most Oklahomans are probably less than comfortable with being lumped in with California. I certainly wish we were far enough away from Santa Fe to avoid all the embarrassing interior-design accidents with lime green and chili pepper red; however, blue corn chips never really caught on here, either–which I think is the true litmus test. So we're not Southwestern.

As I write, I can imagine the hordes of indignant Sooners who would storm my house if I came down solidly in favor of this next possibility. Oklahoma and Texas seem—except for one weekend in October—to share a reasonably common culture. I should own up right away to a slight flaw in my "Sooner Born, Sooner Bred" credentials: my family lived in Arlington briefly during my formative years and, worse yet, one of my sisters was actually born there. As the Sooners were losing the 1980 Texas-OU Game, I even told my grandfather that, since I was living in Texas, I could be happy with either outcome. I can still see the look on his face, an appropriate memory as I make the unfathomable suggestion that our arch-rivals are actually our closest kin.

The last possibility is the most romantic of all, the most self-congratulatory, the most intriguing. Perhaps we as Oklahomans don't know where we are because there is no valid point of reference. Perhaps we don't fit into any region because Oklahoma is absolutely its own animal—*sui generis*, as the Latin goes—a type unto itself. The creators of the "Native America" advertising campaign certainly understand this.

To believe this answer, all we really need are a few flashes of a fascinating history, including a knowledge of who was here before the whites came and an understanding

of what was done to them, and a few assorted tableaux of covered wagons, settlers planting their stakes and their first crop, teachers founding schools on empty plains, a gushing well, a football, I suppose—and yes, a rescue worker. Run through the images in your mind and indulge the impulse toward the mythic and the singular.

Indulge that impulse, but don't trust it. It can only be a starting place, like the jigsaw geography of my childhood. The past and the future demand of us a thoroughly soul-searching answer to the question of where and how Oklahoma fits in the puzzle. We can take pieces of each of the possible Oklahomas, but we cannot look for any one to provide a solution by itself. After all, Oklahoma's relative youth explains much of the difficulty in defining it. The challenge–and the thrill–of finding such a definition lies with us. As voters, citizens, and parents in a state less than a century old, our actions carry the weight of a history still very much in the making.

By reading this book and planning your own paths across our great state, you are taking the first steps along an important journey of discovery. Do your own research, your own exploring. Whether or not you find an answer, you are sure to find beauty, wonder, and excitement along the way.

After graduating from Yale University in 1995, Jay Porter happily fled the East Coast to return to his native Oklahoma City. He serves as Director of Development and Communications at the Oklahoma Foundation for Excellence, a group devoted to promoting academic excellence in Oklahoma's public schools. Jay is also an active freelance writer and editor; he currently writes a weekly food and drink column for the Oklahoma Gazette. This essay is based on a piece that appeared in the Oklahoma Gazette in November, 1995.

Romantic Weekend Tips

by Deborah Bouziden

Life is busy for most every family in Oklahoma. The pressures and everyday routines of work, parenting, household needs, shopping, and other activities may leave partners feeling alienated from each other. According to Ann Benjamin, a licensed marriage and family therapist from Edmond, Oklahoma, being a couple means taking on another identity separate from ourselves. "When we are so busy that we don't nurture that 'coupleness,' the relationship suffers greatly." The prescription? Take time away from the routine to restore your relationship. "Taking time off together as a couple is nutritional in nature; it provides the opportunity to build intimacy and celebrate your coupleness," Benjamin adds.

Oklahoma offers many wonderful opportunities for you and your spouse to get away and spend a weekend together, building and strengthening your relationship. From the luxury of a bed and breakfast, to the adventure of camping, from activities such as touring museums to canoeing the Illinois River, Oklahoma has something for everyone. This book is designed to give couples and groups of travelers all the information they need to spend time "reconnecting" with one another while exporing the unique state of Oklahoma. Here are some ideas to help you as you plan your getaway.

• Plan ahead. Discuss and decide in advance where, when, and how long you want to be away. Keep informed about attractions and events in your area, or refer to this book for ideas.

• Talk about why you need to get away and plan your activities accordingly. You may want to experience new activities together; maybe you desire to do nothing. Plan activities that you both enjoy.

• Purposely plan time to do nothing. Perhaps both of you have been working too hard and have not had time to rest. Cuddling in bed, ordering room service, visiting, strolling, and reading and sharing books do much to restore rest and to open communication.

• Stay within a budget; financial stress causes marital stress. Ask about special packages at bed and breakfasts or hotels. Fortunately, Oklahoma has numerous low-cost vacation options. With a little research, you can plan a weekend for any budget.

• Stay close to home. A short drive to your destination leaves more time for "doing nothing" and having fun together, and you'll feel more secure about leaving your children if you know that you're close enough to help if there's an emergency.

• Spend time and effort to find a reliable babysitter that both partners can trust. Consult family and friends for their ideas; interview each candidate extensively. Leaving children with a babysitter can be a traumatic experience, particularly for new par-

The view from Mount Scott near Lawton.

Elaine Warner

ents. Leave phone numbers and feel free to call if you need assurance while you are away. It's important to remember that children benefit and grow by experiencing another caretaker and from learning that you will return. Even more important to a child's well-being is the strong and happy relationship of their parents. Keep in mind that everyone benefits when mom and dad take time to renew their "coupleness."

• Be flexible; inevitably, there will be a "hitch" in the weekend. Don't let little problems get in the way of your purpose of the trip. Be prepared with alternative dates for your weekend and perhaps have another trusted babysitter as a backup.

• Relax, slow down, don't be in a hurry to do anything. Couples hurry enough in their everyday lives; no need to hurry when you've planned an intimate weekend. Enjoy each other's company. When you return home, the pace will pick up!

• Leave anything work-related at home. The point of the trip is to be alone with your significant other. Make spending quality time with your partner a priority–even more of a priority than your career goals.

• Limit packing; there's no need to add extra work and stress to your life.

• Spend time listening to one another; be open to each other's opinion. Talk about your individual and family goals. Take a

Beautiful Honor Heights Park, Muskogee.

book of questions (available at most book stores) to stimulate conversations. Laugh together. Try new techniques for conversing, such as active listening, ensuring that you have thoroughly understood your partner before you respond. Use the time away to be creative in solving problems.

• Every now and then, surprise your partner with a weekend away. With all the cares and concerns of job and family, a surprise weekend is an endearing gift for your spouse. Even if the weekend is not a surprise to either of you, plan some surprising "extras" such as soothing bath oils for a luxuriously-long soak. You might include a special book to share or a box of chocolates. A bit of surprise can make the weekend together even more special.

The London House, Edmond.

Oklahoma's Route 66!

by Trena Thomas

Route 66: just the mention of the name invokes a feeling of nostalgia, adventure, wanderlust. No other stretch of pavement has been more documented, photographed or captured on video than America's Main Street. Dubbed the "Mother Road" by John Steinbeck during the 1930s, this asphalt ribbon stretches 2400 miles, through eight states and three time zones. Route 66 begins at Grant Park in Chicago and deadends in Santa Monica at the corner of Ocean Avenue and Santa Monica Boulevard. Along the way, it embraces the states of Illinois, Missouri, Kansas, Oklahoma, Texas, New Mexico, Arizona, and California.

Dedicated November 11, 1926, Route 66 was officially known as U.S. 66. It began as a dream of Oklahoma State Highway Commissioner Cyrus Avery. Affectionately known as the Father of Route 66, Avery was a Tulsa businessman recruited by the Bureau of Public Roads to develop a system of uniformly-marked highways. With his strong persuasion skills, Avery convinced the powers that be to construct the road across his own state, passing through both Tulsa and Oklahoma City. The portion of the highway that crosses through Oklahoma remains the best preserved and most-well-used portion of U.S. 66 in existence.

Many a bustling business was born along Route 66 and, during its heyday, especially in Oklahoma, classic enterprises such as hamburger stands, filling stations and motor courts with air-cooled rooms lined the highway. Many of the original businesses or recreations of the era are in operation today across Oklahoma. You won't be at a loss for a place to grab a bite to eat or to bed down for the night along the way.

For those ready to venture the Mother Road, Oklahoma is the best place to start. Winding from the Kansas border at Quapaw to the Texas line at Texola, there are plenty of sites to see along the way; fillerup, grab the camera, and let's go!

Quapaw

Quapaw is home of the famous Spooklight. On a clear dark evening, you may see the Spooklight appear as a dancing, bobbing, rolling ball of light. Seen about 1.5 miles east of town on a bluff near the Spring River called Devil's Promenade, the Spooklight has been appearing regularly for years. Midsummer is the best time for viewing; there are many theories but no clear explanation for this strange phenomenon.

Commerce

With the Spooklight behind you, head to Commerce, home of baseball great Mickey Mantle (aka "The Commerce Comet"). Commerce is an old mining town;

Route 66 bridge near Sapulpa.

Elaine Warner

take time to check out The Rock Shop, an exhaustive outdoor display of rocks and minerals. It's located on–you guessed it– Mickey Mantle Boulevard.

Miami

Pronounced "My-am-uh" after the Miami Indians, this bustling town is home of the Coleman Theater, a beautiful art deco structure located at 103 N. Main. Touring is free. If your vehicle is up to it, it's worth the effort to travel at least one of the two nine-foot-wide stretches of original Mother Road that zigzag between Miami and Afton. To locate the road near Miami, heading eastbound, turn right one mile north of Narcissa. Westbound, stay on Main until it turns into E. Street SW and Highway 125. One mile after Highway 125 veers to the left, you'll come to a "T" intersection. Turn right, and you'll begin to see the narrow road peek through.

Afton

Hope you're hungry by now, because it's time for buffalo burgers! There are none better than those found at the famous Afton Buffalo Ranch, where bison roam out back along with a few turkeys, peacocks, and a collection of cats. Check out the Trading Post for some "can't-live-without" Oklahoma trinkets.

Foyle

This town is home of a ninety-foot totem pole, the world's largest; it was built by Industrial Arts teacher Ed Galloway. Galloway built many folk art creations and totem poles at totem pole park, four miles east of Foyle on 28A. After Galloway's death, the park was unattended for over twenty years until a grassroots art association, joined by local heritage and historical societies, began restoration. The interesting collection is well worth the short detour. Admission is free.

Claremore

Claremore is Will Rogers' town, and your trip is not complete without a visit to this famous historian and humorist's memorial and museum, located on a beautiful twenty-acre site one mile west of U.S. 66. A popular nickname for U.S. 66 is "Will Rogers Highway," another indication of the importance of this man's contribution to Oklahoma history. While you are in Claremore, don't miss the J.M. Davis Arms and Historical Museum, home of over 20,000 firearms and related items. (Find more information in this book about these two attractions.)

Catoosa

No, that large blue whale rising out of the water is not your imagination. At one time, the Blue Whale Swimming Hole located along the highway was a flurry of activity on summer afternoons. The swimming hole is in the process of renovation and is no longer in operation; you are welcome to stop and take photos of this piece of Route 66 nostalgia.

Tulsa

Staying on the original Route 66 is a challenge as you travel through Tulsa, but it can be done. Take 193rd Avenue south out of Catoosa and turn west again on 11th Street in Tulsa. This street will take you through the city to the Arkansas River and Southwest Boulevard. In downtown Tulsa, 11th Street meanders and alternates from 10th to 12th; just stay on the road until it deadends at the river. Turn left and follow Southwest Boulevard across the river and into Sapulpa.

While there are many places to eat in Tulsa, among them are several restaurants that promote the Route 66 theme. The Metro Diner is located on 11th Street near the University of Tulsa's Skelly Stadium. In downtown Tulsa, try the Route 66 Diner at the corner of 2nd and Elgin, just a few blocks north of the original route. To get to the diner, turn right at Lyon's Indian Store at the corner of 11th (where it turns into 10th) and Elgin. Lyon's contains an endless array of Tulsa memorabilia and Native

American gift items, and it is located in the old Warehouse Market, a beautiful and historic art deco structure. In southwest Tulsa, try Ollie's Restaurant at 41st and Southwest Boulevard. Railroad enthusiasts will enjoy the running model trains and displays in this restaurant.

Sapulpa

As you travel through Sapulpa, be sure to stop at the Frankoma Pottery Plant northwest of town, home of the famous native Frankoma pottery. The factory's gift shop sells a variety of dinnerware and serving items. All items are made from Oklahoma clay. Free factory tours are available Monday-Friday from 9 a.m. to 3 p.m. If you missed the restaurants in Tulsa, try Norma's Diamond Cafe, 408 N. Mission, a longtime Route 66 tradition.

Stroud

Heading down the highway to Stroud, be sure to schedule a rest stop at the Rock Cafe, first opened in 1939, and now known for its unique American and Swiss fare. If shopping entices you, there's none better than at the Tanger Factory Outlet Center with over fifty stores, located north on SH 99 along the Turner Turnpike.

Chandler

In the charming town of Chandler, check out the Lincoln County Historical Society Museum of Pioneer History. Admission is free. Also, keep your eyes open for authentic old signs that

The historic Round Barn at Arcadia.

remain painted on the sides of brick buildings, as well as an historic Phillips 66 cottage-style gas station. If you're looking for an authentic "Route 66" place to stay, try the Lincoln Motel. Still as neat and comfortable as it was when opened in 1939, the motel features a series of cabins, each complete with an American flag and canary yellow lawn chair. Dine at P. J.'s Bar-B-Que for dinner, then head back to the Lincoln for an evening of traffic watching in front of your cabin.

Arcadia

Arcadia is the home of the renovated and famous Round Barn, built in 1898 and prized for its acoustics. There have been many a jig danced and fiddle played in this interesting place. Visitors are welcome.

Oklahoma City

Like Tulsa, Oklahoma City is difficult to pass through on the original highway. Take heart–there are detailed maps outlining the route available, and signs are posted that indicate the original highway. One "must-see" attraction along the route is the National Cowboy Hall of Fame and Western Heritage Center, a cultural mecca of art and artifacts of Western history. Restaurants along the OKC area route include the Oklahoma County Line Bar-B-Que, famous for mouthwatering ribs.

El Reno

El Reno is the proud home of the world's largest onion-fried burger, now up to 650 pounds and gaining. Onion fried burgers were invented in El Reno, and they are now a standard across the state. If you want to see the monster burger, plan your visit for the first Saturday in May. No matter what date you visit, you may order your own at Johnny's (301 S. Rock Island, 405-262-4721), Robert's Grill (300 S. Bickford, 405-262-1262), and Sid's Diner (300 S. Choctaw, 405-262-7757).

East of town, pay attention to the sign at the Big 8 Motel. Your eyes aren't deceiv-

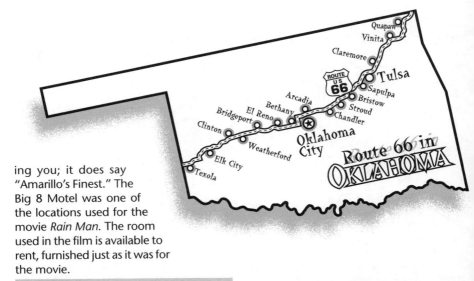

Route 66 in OKLAHOMA

ing you; it does say "Amarillo's Finest." The Big 8 Motel was one of the locations used for the movie *Rain Man*. The room used in the film is available to rent, furnished just as it was for the movie.

Clinton

It's "Route 66 Mania" in Clinton, primarily because the town is home to the Oklahoma Route 66 Museum, the first state-sponsored Route 66 museum in the nation. Located on Gary Boulevard just north of Interstate 40, the museum shows the history of the "Mother Road" by decade. There is even an exhibit of a shiny diner from the 1950s. After leaving the museum, stop to experience another Route 66 tradition; enjoy homemade pie and coffee at Pop Hicks Restaurant down the street.

Elk City

When you are traveling through Elk City, watch for the green dinosaur holding the Route 66 shield in the window of one of the Elk City buildings. There are more history lessons to be learned at the Old Town Museum on the west side of town. Found here are a turn-of-the-century gingerbread-style home, a pioneer church, a one-room school, a railroad depot, a Native American teepee, and much more. Soon it will be the home of the National Route 66 Museum. For a glimpse of a days-gone-by original Route 66 business, drive slowly by the Cozy Cabins and the old Red Ball station. Both are closed, but they are preserved for Route 66 travelers to enjoy.

Sayre

More history is to be found at the Short Grass Country Museum/Historical Society located in the Rock Island Depot at 106 E. Poplar, and the RS and K Railroad Museum at 411 North 6th. The railroad museum features twelve model trains of different gauges, together with over 350 feet of track. Children of all ages will enjoy a milkshake at the Owl Drug Store, 101 W. Main. Built in the 1920s, the store features a 1950s soda fountain.

Erick

If the milkshake at the drug store in Sayre didn't satisfy your sweet tooth, visit the OK Honey Farm, located two miles west of town on Highway 66, then one mile north under I-40. A working honey farm open March through December, the farm is open Monday-Saturday, 8 to 6, and Sunday, 1:30-5:30. Admission is free, but many tempting gift items are available.

Texola

One block north of Main on Highway 66 is the Old Territorial Jail. It had no window or door coverings; people said that in winter, crime dropped to zero, just like the temperature!

By now, the Texas border should be looming on the horizon, and your Route 66 tour of Oklahoma is complete. Here's hoping that you enjoyed the ride. No doubt you've made plans to return to more than one of the many stops you experienced along the way. Route 66 is like that, always beckoning your return to recapture the spirit of life along Oklahoma's stretch of the "Mother Road."

Recommended Oklahoma Route 66 reading (compiled by the Oklahoma Route 66 Association):

The Official Oklahoma Route 66 Association Trip Guide by Kathy Anderson is excellent. It is a wonderfully-detailed newspaper guide complete with photos, trivia, games, and roadside facts. Don't attempt a trip down the Mother Road without it. It is available through the Oklahoma Route 66 Association.

Another fine publication is *The Route 66 Cook Book* by Marian Clark. This book covers all eight states, but from the yummy vantage of past and present eating establishments. There are many mouthwatering recipes (along with Route 66 history) provided by original cooks and owners.

Oklahoma Route 66: A Cruiser's Companion by Jim Ross. This is the definitive guide book to Oklahoma's 396 miles of Mother Road. This book is documented and researched with meticulous detail regarding the older alignments of the Road and how to navigate through the towns.

Route 66: The Map Series by Jim Ross and Jerry McClanahan. This is a set of eight fold-out maps that are indispensable for those planning to travel all eight states. This is a simplified driving guide of the entire Route.

Route 66: The Mother Road by Michael Wallis. Covering all eight states, this book is considered to be the best on the subject. It contains wonderful photos, complete with stories of the road. This book was the catalyst for the Route 66 renaissance.

Route 66 World News. A newspaper based in Elk City, Oklahoma, each issue is heavily researched and deals with a single Route 66 state. Appropriately enough, the premier issue featured Oklahoma. Copies of their Oklahoma edition (as well as other issues) are available through the World News office at 204 N. Main in Elk City (405-243-0437).

Trena Thomas is a native of Tulsa who currently resides in Jenks, Oklahoma, the Antique Capital of the World. She holds a bachelor's degree in Fine Arts from the University of Tulsa and a Masters of Arts degree in Journalism/Mass Communications from the University of Oklahoma. In addition to free-lance writing and numerous volunteer activities, she is the Area Business Manager for Public Service Company of Oklahoma, an electric utility. Trena lives with her son Dylan, age seven, and their dog, Beau.

For "R&R," Try a "B&B"

by Elaine Warner

Few people are as focused as Martha Hall of the Arcadian Inn in Edmond. She has gone so far as to write a mission statement for her establishment: "To provide the perfect accommodations for guests to bond physically, emotionally, and spiritually." As a nurse, Martha knew that she had a nurturing personality. She had also dreamed of fixing up an old home. She found the perfect combination of nature and desire in turning the 1908 Ruhl home into a "bed and breakfast." In the process, she and husband Gary have provided such a delightful place to stay that it has become more a destination than simply a stop on the way to somewhere else.

"Bed and breakfast" seems self-explanatory, but the term covers a lot of territory. The renting out of rooms has probably been around since an early Egyptian found an extra room in his tomb, but the concept is fairly new to Oklahoma. The first "official" Oklahoma bed and breakfast establishments were opened in Guthrie in 1986. There are now close to one hundred B&Bs in Oklahoma, ranging from three-bedroom bungalows and western ranch houses to historic mansions. The diversity is staggering, but there is a unifying theme: you will rent a room with breakfast included in the price.

The theme seems simple enough, but the uses of the word "inn," and the term "bed and breakfast" sometimes create confusion. Many B&Bs call themselves "inns";

owners are typically called "innkeepers." The industry defines a "country inn" as one with several rented rooms and which serves meals other than breakfast. Bed and breakfasts are usually smaller, and they typically serve only breakfast. For semantic simplicity in this book, the word "inn" will be used interchangeably with B&B.

Bed and breakfasts are popular for a number of reasons, but primarily because they are a departure from the plastic every-room-in-every-city-looks-alike syndrome. Even within the same B&B, every room is different. Some differ simply in the choice of color or furnishings. Some inns, like the Montford Inn Bed and Breakfast in Norman, have chosen unique themes for each room; the Montford's "Legends of the Game" room celebrates the glory of baseball and other sports. The "Chickasaw Rancher" room is decorated with items from the early days in Indian Territory, while not neglecting such modern comforts as a jetted tub with separate shower.

Many times, bed and breakfasts are located in small towns which lack other accommodations yet offer interesting shopping and attractions. In large cities, the rates are frequently less expensive than hotel rates. They are usually located in quiet areas away from interstates and traffic. Best of all, B&Bs offer personal contact–a chance to meet special people and become better acquainted with a locality through the experience of a host who knows the area well. They often offer more pampering than even your mother would give you. At the Arcadian Inn, you can have a massage therapist come to your room for a relaxing treatment, or you can have dinner served in your room from one of many local restaurants.

Arcadian Inn

The romantic Arcadian Inn in Edmond.

The Grandisson at Maney Park in Oklahoma City offers many amenities for guests.

Some B&Bs provide extra entertainment. Several inns in Guthrie belong to the Stone Lion group, giving their guests a chance to participate in the Murder Mystery Evenings for which the Stone Lion has become famous. The Bed and Breakfast in the almost-100-year-old Stuart Hotel in Stuart, Oklahoma, presents occasional melodramas or their own unique "street theater" presentation about former guest Pretty Boy Floyd.

Breakfast is a culinary experience at a B&B. Although a few places offer only a continental breakfast, that is, juice, coffee and rolls or cereal, most pride themselves on setting an excellent table. Many hosts have specialties which have enhanced the reputations of their inns. Jo Meacham at the Holmberg House in Norman often serves her guests French Toast stuffed with cream cheese and fruit. At the Lauren Danielle in Guthrie, guests enjoy Debbie Judd's Hot Gourmet Raspberry Cocoa with a dip of white chocolate ice cream with their breakfasts.

Rates at B&Bs can be as little as $40 and as expensive as $200. Rates vary for a number of reasons: location, historicity, number of rooms available, popularity, and amenities; price alone will not tell you what to expect. Some B&Bs take credit cards, others do not. Some places offer special discounts for seniors, businesspeople, etc., so always ask.

A sense of adventure and a willingness to be flexible are the keys to enjoying the B&B experience. If you want to meet interesting people, be treated as a family friend, and enjoy different types of accommodations, try a B&B. If you want predictability, try a motel chain.

Over forty of Oklahoma's B&Bs belong to the Oklahoma Bed and Breakfast Association. Many fine B&Bs are not members; this is the personal choice of each innkeeper, not a reflection on the quality of the establishment. However, those who do belong have allied themselves with an organization which promotes professionalism in its membership. All member inns have been inspected for cleanliness, services and safety. For a list of Oklahoma Bed and Breakfast Association members, call (800) 676-5522.

The Panhandle of Oklahoma

Once called No Man's Land, the Oklahoma Panhandle belonged to no one for many years during the 1800s. Originally part of Spain and later Mexico, this strip of land thirty-six miles wide and 168 miles long came into the United States as part of Texas. However, as the boundaries of Texas, Kansas and New Mexico were established, this long, narrow portion of land was left unclaimed—and untamed. As part of the public domain of the United States, the land was open for settlement, but few laws protected area residents. This was No Man's Land, a rough, unruly country until it was established as part of Oklahoma Territory in 1890.

Since No Man's Land became part of Oklahoma Territory in 1890, it has retained its rugged, individualistic character. The people here are united by their determination to carve a living from the land. They are tied to the land through their heritage; here, generation after generation remains on the family ranch—keeping alive a way of life that's quickly vanishing along with our rural heritage. Here they live a lifestyle only dreamed about by "city slickers."

Beaver

Located in the eastern part of the Panhandle and settled as early as 1883, Beaver once contributed to the wild and unruly characteristics of "No Man's Land." Afraid of the prevalent lawlessness, and concerned about the physical distance from any established law and order, residents tried to create an independent Territory of Cimarron. Although this attempt failed due to the decisions of the territorial legislature in 1900, the citizens of Beaver still display this proud and independent spirit—a spirit once essential for survival in the harsh high plains.
Beaver is approximately 223 miles northwest of Oklahoma City on U.S. 270, and about 290 miles west of Tulsa. Beaver County Chamber of Commerce (405) 625-4726.

Beaver River Wildlife Management Area

Located six miles west of Beaver, (405) 259-6281.

This area offers some of the state's best hunting. Deer, quail, pheasant, and other game are abundant. Primitive camping is permitted at designated sites along the Beaver River.

Beaver State Park

Located one mile north of town on U.S. Highway 270, (405) 625-3373.

This 550-acre state park has a fifteen-acre lake with a bridge for fishing, a 1.5 mile hiking trail, picnic and play areas, pavilions for special events, and R.V. and primitive camp sites. Two hundred eighty acres of sand dunes have been set aside for off-road vehicles. Adjacent to the park and nestled in the foothills of the sand dunes is the **Pioneer Park Golf Course**, (405) 625-3633, a challenging and well-kept nine hole course open to the public.

Jones and Plummer Trail Museum

Located at the Beaver County Fairgrounds, (405) 625-4439. Wednesday-Friday 1-5:30, Saturday 1-5, Sunday 2:30-5. Free; donations are appreciated.

Visitors can explore the area's colorful history at this museum that depicts pioneer life in the Oklahoma Panhandle. Also available for touring is the Presbyterian Church, circa 1887, the first church built in No Man's Land.

Events

Cimarron Territory Celebration

Usually held the third week of April. For more information contact (405) 625-4726. Free.

This unique event draws international attention. The week-long celebration includes barbecues, foot and bicycle races, a chili cook-off, coin and hobby show, talent contest, concert, parade, dance, and other activities for the entire family. The climax of the week is the **World Championship Cow Chip Throwing Contest**. In the mid-1800s, buffalo hunters found that dried buffalo chips could be burned with good results. By the time settlers came to the area, most of the buffalo were gone; consequently, settlers relied on cow chips for fuel. When dry, the chips emitted no odor, gave a clear bright flame, burned with intense heat (6400 BTU's), and left no soot. Thus, in the fall, each pioneer family collected cow chips for winter fuel. The entire family collected chips, throwing them into the wagon. It became a contest to see who could throw the chips with the greatest accuracy.

To commemorate the fortitude of the early settlers, the festival began its first "Cow Chip Throwing Contest" in 1969. Now the contest has reached international proportions. Participants come from every state in the United States and many countries around the world such as Scotland, South Africa, and Australia–just to throw a chip. Wherever held, sanctioned Cow Chip Throwing Contests must use the arena layout and measurements used in Beaver to be officially recognized. This uniquely-Oklahoma event should not be missed!

Black Mesa

Rising 4,973 feet above sea level, Black Mesa towers over the rest of the state's great plains. At the top, a native granite obelisk marks the elevation, and an ammunition box at the base of the monument preserves the written accounts of travelers who have ascended the mesa to enjoy the view. Approximately forty-five miles long, the mesa extends from the southeast corner of Colorado, through the northeast corner of New Mexico, and into the northwest tip of Oklahoma. Ranging from one third of a mile to six miles wide, the mesa was formed by the flow of an ancient volcano. It is here that the Rocky Mountains meet the short grass prairie, and many species reside, either at the extreme eastern or extreme western portions of their range. Two areas help visitors experience and appreciate this unique area: Black Mesa Preserve and Black Mesa State Park.

Black Mesa Preserve

Take Highway 325 to the extreme northwest corner of the state. Look for the blacktop road marked "Colorado" and turn north. Drive five miles to the preserve parking area. The preserve is open sunrise to sunset.

The Nature Conservancy manages a 1600-acre preserve that protects most of the top of the mesa. A hike to the top of the mesa and back is about eight miles and takes four to six hours to complete. Bring at least a quart of water per person and wear a hat and other sun-protective clothing. Hiking boots are recommended; terrain is rough, and the hike to the top is strenuous. As a final precaution, be alert—this is home to many rattlesnakes.

Driving through the mesa area, travelers often amuse themselves by visualizing images out of the eroded rock, much like children make pictures out of clouds. Three prominent rock formations are the Wedding Party, the Old Maid, and Castle Rock, where it is said Coronado once passed in his search for the "Seven Cities of Cibola."

Not without its local lore, Robber's Roost stands nearby. Once the hideout of a local bad guy, Captain William Coe, this mesa camouflaged a rock building 16 x 30 feet, with walls three feet thick. Although there are no windows, the building contains 27 portholes, four inches wide on the outside widening to 18 to 20 inches inside. Gunmen within could direct their fire over a fairly wide range. Local legends vary about where Coe came from and how long he stayed. However, most agree that he was eventually caught, tried, and hanged.

Nearby, but still within the preserve, are three sets of **dinosaur tracks**. Made millions of years ago, the tracks are reminders of an earlier time and different climate. It's hard to believe that the mesa area was once a swampland.

Traveling through the mesa area, be sure to stop in Kenton at **Kenton Mercantile** for refreshments, souvenirs, or a bit of local lore. Being the only Oklahoma town on Mountain Time isn't the only thing that makes Kenton special. Every Easter, area residents perform an annual **Easter Pageant**. Started in 1952 as a cooperative effort of the Methodist and Baptist churches of Kenton, the pageant has grown into a regional event. Contact Monty Roberts at the Roberts Ranch for more information, (405) 261-7443. The pageant is free.

While you are visiting in this area, please respect the land and the people who own it. Drive carefully; since much of this land is open range, cattle may be on the road. If you open a gate, close it. Do not hunt, camp or fish on the preserve or private lands. Do not remove any natural features or artifacts, and pack out all litter. Restrooms are available at Black Mesa State Park, about ten miles away.

Black Mesa State Park

The park is located approximately ten miles south of the preserve off Oklahoma Highway 325. (405) 426-2222.

Visitors may camp, fish, and picnic at this park that features tall trees (a rarity in western Oklahoma) and a small lake. There is also a visitor's center where maps and brochures of the surrounding area are available.

Boise City

Boise City, a quiet, friendly little town, was established in 1908 by the Southwestern Immigration and Development Company of Guthrie, Oklahoma. The three men who started this company platted the town in the center of the county, with the hope it would be chosen as the county seat. Lots were sold to residents of Illinois, Indiana, and Missouri for $45 each, with promises of a developed town and prosperous farms already in existence. It was soon discovered that the three founding fathers not only exaggerated their claims of the town's existing prosperity, they did not have clear title to the land. In 1909, they were arrested for mail fraud and, in 1912, began to serve their two-year prison sentences. Despite this questionable beginning, Boise City has grown into a respectable little town.

Among the attractions in this town is the **Boise City Bomb Memorial**, located near the county courthouse on the main square. This memorial stands in recognition of Boise City as the only city in the continental United States that was bombed during World War II. In a good-humored tribute to the constant wind, a local gas station boasts the local "wind meter," (a large rock hanging from a heavy chain). Local residents will readily tell you, "The wind's not really blowin' until that meter hangs straight out!"

Boise City is located in the farthest west county in Oklahoma. Boise City Chamber of Commerce (405) 544-3344.

Cimarron County Golf Course

Located northeast of Boise City (call for directions), (405) 544-2589. Green fees are weekday $8, twilight $4.25, weekend $11, carts $8 (prices subject to change).

Try this new nine-hole public course. Amenities include a driving range, practice green, clubhouse, and a snack bar. No tee time reservations are required.

West End Roping, Inc.

Address: HCR Box 21, Boise City, OK 73933, (405) 426-2723. Call or write for cost and details.

For true cowboy adventure, plan to participate in a real cattle drive, hosted by West End Roping. Spend three days with an authentic, old-fashioned cattle drive through No Man's Land. Sleep under the stars, breathe the crisp clean air, and satisfy your hunger with the grub from Old Gus's chuckwagon. Several drives are held each year from May through September.

Guymon

Established as a small provisioning point along the Rock Island Railroad, the little village of Sanford soon became the hub city of the Panhandle. E. T. Guymon established a grocery store here, and later he opened a lumber yard. Because there was some confusion on the rail line between the names Sanford and Stratford, Texas, farther south, the freight agent, in frustration, suggested that Sanford be renamed Guymon, since "Mr. Guymon is the only one who ever gets any freight anyway."

Now a city of approximately 10,000 and growing, Guymon boasts a number of attractions and special events for visitors, among them the Line Rider Museum and the award-winning Pioneer Days Celebration. A scarcity of motels east or west of Guymon makes it a popular overnight stop; be sure to call ahead for motel reservations.

Guymon is centrally located in the Panhandle, about 275 miles northwest of Oklahoma City and 332 miles west of Tulsa. Guymon Chamber of Commerce (405) 338-3376.

Hitch Enterprises

Call ahead for tour arrangements and directions, (405) 338-8575.

To learn more about the cowboy life, visit Hitch Enterprises, the oldest business in the area. Established in 1884, the family-owned-and-operated Hitch Enterprises offers tours of their area feedyards and an overview of their entire operation to those in the cattle business.

Sunset Recreation Area

Located at South 4th and Sunset Lane. From Highway 54 and South 4th, go west two blocks. Follow the signs.

The 32-acre Sunset Lake is a favorite fishing spot; catfish are plentiful and trout are available seasonally. A handicapped-accessible dock is provided as a convenience to the physically challenged. Picnic areas are nearby with two pavilions available for reunions and large gatherings. Other features of the park are paddle boats, an operating miniature train, and playgrounds.

Sunset Hills Golf Course

(405) 338-7404. Open daily sunrise to sunset. Weekday green fees are $9, weekend and holiday fees are $12. Cart fees are $8 for nine holes, $16 for eighteen holes. Tee times are typically available without advance notice.

Sunset Hills is known for its outstanding bentgrass greens. Built in 1946, the course has water and tree hazards. The course has 6236 yards and is par 71, with a slope of 115 and a USGA rating of 70.1. Pro shop and food service are available. Rumor has it that one of the best burgers in town can be found at the pro shop.

Events

Pioneer Days Celebration

Held the first weekend in May. For more information, contact (405) 338-3376.

Possibly the best representation of early settlers' lives is found at the annual Pioneer Days Celebration. Scheduled to coincide with the May 2nd anniversary of the passage of the Organic Act of 1890 (the legislation that made the Panhandle part of Oklahoma Territory), this award-winning event draws thousands. Visitors enjoy western fare at the cookouts, barbecues, and a cowboy breakfast. For exercise, they participate in the 5K Run or Fun Walk. Spectators enjoy the parade, as well as the Tumble Weed Toss and the third largest PRCA rodeo in the nation, where steer roping is the highlight event. Amateurs try their luck at the carnival games, shoppers browse the arts and crafts extravaganza, dancers kick up their heels at the nightly hoedowns, and "Old Timers" reminisce with others who remember the "Good Ol' Days."

If you can't make it to Pioneer Days, try to

Fred Marvel/Oklahoma Tourism

Watching the parade in Guymon.

schedule your arrival around one of the other annual events: the **Five State Quilt Show** in January; **Antique Show** in April; **Gun, Coin and Hobby Show** in August; **Fall Cattle Festival** in August; **Panhandle Exposition** in September; **Oil and Gas Show** in October; **Dolls and Toys Show** in October; **Rod and Custom Car Show** in October; **Pumpkin Patch Festival Craft Show** in November; and the **Christmas Festival** in December. Before leaving the area, be sure to check the activities and attractions of nearby Liberal, Kansas, and Elkhart, Texas. United in spirit, geography, history, and economics, these towns often schedule events at coinciding times.

Dining

Eddie's Steak and Seafood *$$*, *$$$*

421 Village Shopping Center, (405) 338-5330. Highway 54 and East Street. Monday 4-10, Tuesday-Saturday 4-midnight.

Eddie's has some of the best food in town. Specializing in steak, seafood, and the traditional side orders of salad and baked potatoes, Eddie's offers diners hearty and delicious meals, served in a comfortable atmosphere.

LeAnn's Restaurant *$*, *$$*

205 Southeast 2nd, (405) 338-8025. Located at Highway 54 and S.E. Second. Daily, 11-9.

This restaurant offers diners a little bit of everything: burgers, sandwiches and a very special chicken fried steak. Daily specials are offered for both lunch and dinner. The dinner special consists of an entree (the pepper steak is highly recommended), salad, two vegetables, homemade bread, and dessert. LeAnn's is known for delicious homemade pie.

In the Vicinity

Cattle Country Inn

Located 38 miles west of Guymon, or 24 miles east of Boise City, (405) 543-6458. From Four Corners, travel southwest. The inn is off Highway 64/3. Call for rates and check-in times. Credit cards accepted. Plan to eat dinner before arriving, or bring the fixings for sandwiches and snacks. A small kitchen area is available for guests.

Lane and Karen Sparkman are two of the nicest people you could ever hope to meet. Both were born and raised in the area and their family ties run deep. Married for over thirty-five years, the Sparkman's raised three children on the ranch. Encouraged by her son to start a bed and breakfast, Mrs. Sparkman runs one of the cleanest, friendliest inns ever visited. The Sparkmans offer six guest rooms with shared baths. A hearty country breakfast is served each morning, and it includes eggs, homemade bread, nut breads, homemade jams and jellies, fresh fruit, and cereal.

The innkeepers are quite knowledgable about local attractions and they provide brochures and information about the surrounding area. Despite their initial fears that "no one would drive the dirt roads to get here," the Sparkmans have truly created a loving home away from home for travelers.

Goodwell

Goodwell is located ten miles southwest of Guymon on Highway 54.

No-Man's Land Museum

Located at 207 W. Sewell, just off Highway 54, (405) 349-2670. Tuesday-Saturday 9-5. Free.

Created through the combined efforts of concerned citizens and the Panhandle Agricultural and Mechanical College (now Panhandle State University), this 10,000-square-foot museum has four galleries which depict the lives and lifestyles of Oklahoma's early pioneers. Visitors can also witness the developments of agricultural devices and developments, including plows and barbed wire collections that helped modernize farms around the country. Two other galleries display items from Oklahoma's more distant past—Native American artifacts

and geological exhibits. The Museum contains a small library and an art gallery. Exhibits show how Oklahoma's early settlers survived both the Depression and the Dust Bowl during the 1930s, and how they emerged with a stronger, more modern Panhandle.

Northwest Oklahoma

Enid

Now an attractive city park, Government Springs was once a popular camp site along the Chisholm Trail where thirsty men and cattle stopped to enjoy the reliable water supply. It was not until 1893 that the Land Run of the Cherokee Outlet (sometimes referred to as the Cherokee Strip) transformed Enid—essentially overnight—into a tent city. Today, museums, historic buildings and organizations such as the Enid Arts and Sciences Foundation celebrate the city's colorful past and present. **Leonardo's Discovery Warehouse and Adventure Quest** is Enid's hands-on museum and playground focusing on arts and sciences. Don't miss it if you have children in tow (or if you just want to relive your youth and learn something in the process).

Hundreds of thousands of youth from a three-state area have participated through the years in the annual Tri-State Music Festival. Begun in 1932, the festival is held in early May and involves much of the community. Enid is also home of Vance Air Force Base and Phillips University. *Enid is located 84 miles north and west of Oklahoma City; take I-35 north to Highway 64/412 west. From Tulsa, travel west on the Cimarron Turnpike approximately 124 miles. Enid Chamber of Commerce (405) 237-2494.*

Robert Bartunek Winery

(405) 233-6337. From the intersection of Highways 412 and 81, go south one mile to Rupe, then west one mile to Cleveland. The winery is located just west of the intersection of Cleveland and Rupe, on the north side of the road. Open Friday and Saturday 1-5 or by appointment. Wine tasting and tours are free. Handicapped accessible; call ahead to make special arrangements to park near the building.

Each year, this small vineyard just outside of Enid produces 5000 gallons of top-quality wines. Every grape is hand picked and every bottle hand corked and labeled. (No, they don't crush the grapes by foot.) Stop by the winery for a tour and a lesson in wine making. Afterwards, enjoy a little wine tasting at the bar. You'll gain an appreciation for Bartunek's diverse varieties, which include Claret, Merot, Sauvingnon Blanc, Cabernet Sauvingnon, and Blush. The winery's store is the only place Robert Bartunek wine is sold. Prices are very reasonable ($10.50 per bottle), and the wine is excellent. Also available at the store are jellies, jams, sauces, T-shirts, gift baskets, and more. Looking for a unique gift for a wine connoisseur? Personalized labels are available by special order for an additional $2 per bottle.

Midgley Museum

1001 Sequoyah Drive, (405) 234-7265. At the corner of Van Buren and Sequoyah (one block south of the intersection of Highway 412 and 81) is one of the most intriguing houses in Oklahoma. Summer (April 1-October 31), Tuesday- Friday 10-5; Saturday-Sunday 2-5; closed Monday. Winter (November 1 - March 31), Wednesday-Saturday 1-5. Admission is free. Not handicapped accessible.

Dan and Libbie Midgley moved to Oklahoma as newlyweds in the late 1800s. Almost immediately, they began developing hobbies, among them rock collecting. Today, the rare fossils, rocks, crystals, and petrified wood collected by the Midgleys are not only displayed inside the museum, they ARE the museum. Thousands were used in the construction of the Midgley's former home. This house is a work of art! A beautiful, bizarre, and fascinating shrine to stone, the Midgley Museum includes the rock collection, antiques, a trophy room, and several outdoor displays.

Museum of the Cherokee Strip and Humphrey Heritage Village

507 South 4th Street, (405) 237-1907. Located one mile east of the intersection of Owen K.

Garriott Boulevard (Highway 412) and Van Buren (Highway 81). The museum is on the northeast corner of Garriott and South 4th. Tuesday-Friday 9-5, Saturday-Sunday 2-5. Closed Monday and holidays. Handicapped accessible.

The Cherokee Strip Museum celebrates the Land Run of 1893 with exhibits of pioneer and farm life, personal accounts, and photographs. Just north of the museum are several restored buildings comprising the **Humphrey Heritage Village**. Among the buildings are the Turkey Creek Schoolhouse, a 1902 Episcopal church, the Victorian-style Glidewell house, and Enid's original land office. Exhibits in the land office show what homesteaders faced after the run—from staking a claim to "proving up." You just thought bureaucratic red tape was a recent invention!

Railroad Museum of Oklahoma

702 North Washington, (405) 233-3051. Turn north at the intersection of Owen K. Garriott (Highway 412) and Van Buren (Highway 81), then turn east at Walnut Street. The museum is one block north at the corner of Washington and Chestnut Streets. Tuesday-Friday 1-4, Saturday 9-1 and by appointment. Free. Handicapped accessible.

Railroad buffs will enjoy this museum full of railroad memorabilia. Climb aboard a caboose, see a demonstration of Morse code on a telegraph machine, view railroad safety videos, and watch the large model train. Not a recommended stop for those in a hurry; be prepared to spend much time learning about a bygone era.

Dining

High Voltage $$, $$$

3205 S. Van Buren (Highway 81), (405) 237-3224. Friday-Saturday 5:30-10. Handicapped accessible.

The specialty of the house is steak, hand-cut to your specification and cooked on a grill in the center of the dining area. Seafood, pasta dishes, and Chateaubriand are also popular. The decor includes glass blocks and neon, and the ambiance is reminiscent of a New York bistro. High Voltage has one of the largest "wine by the glass" selections in Oklahoma.

Louisa's Ristorante Italiano $$

220 N. Independence, (405) 233-8707. Go north from the intersection of Highways 81 and 412 to Maple. Turn east to Independence. Tuesday-Thursday 5-10, Friday-Saturday 5-11. Limited handicapped accessibility.

Louisa's offers intimate dining in an Old World atmosphere. A favorite among the pasta dishes offered is the Seafood Primavera with Garlic Sauce. Louisa's lounge opens at 4 p.m., Tuesday-Saturday.

Philly's Sandwich Shop $

115 W. Maine (near the downtown square), (405) 233-5999. Monday-Wednesday 11-3; Thursday-Friday 11-7; Saturday 11-2; closed Sunday and holidays. Not handicapped accessible.

Try Philly's Sandwich Shop when you yearn for a genuine Philly cheese steak sandwich. The owner is a native Philadelphian who thought that Oklahomans would enjoy a taste of the City of Brotherly Love. Philly's also serves hamburgers and other sandwiches. For something a little out of the ordinary, try the Molokai sandwich, invented by a local postman. The Molokai is a quarter-pound hamburger with a slice of ham, BBQ sauce, raw onion, and American cheese. Philly's is simple, clean, fast, friendly, and conveniently located for downtown antique hunters.

Port Lugano $

813 S. Van Buren (Highway 81), (405) 233-6012. Monday-Thursday 7 a.m.-7 p.m., Friday and Sunday 7 a.m.-2 p.m. Closed Saturday. Handicapped accessible.

With its beamed ceilings and eclectic decor, this small coffee shop is making a big impression with its fabulous baked goods. Soups and sandwiches made with homemade bread are favorites, especially when topped off with a piece of baklava and a flavorful cup of coffee.

Richill's Cafeteria $

221 W. Randolph in downtown Enid, (405) 237-4005. Daily 11-1:30; Tuesday-Saturday 5-7:30. Handicapped accessible.

Casual atmosphere and great home cooking make Richill's a favorite stop in Enid. Their chicken pot pie and batter-dipped fish are among their most popular offerings.

The Sage Room $$, $$$

1927 S. Van Buren, (405) 233-1212. Located north of the intersection of Highways 412 and 81 (Van Buren). Monday-Thursday 5:30-9:30, Friday-Saturday 5:30-10:00, closed Sunday and major holidays. Reservations accepted for parties of six and more. Expect a short wait on Friday and Saturday nights. Handicapped accessible. 🖫

Romance is in the air at The Sage Room. During its twenty-five years of serving steak to Enid residents and visitors, The Sage Room has been the place of choice for marriage proposals and other special occasions. White tablecloths, candles on each table, and a unique collection of antique clocks add to the ambiance. Enjoy a piano player every night (except Monday) from 6-8 p.m. Dining specialties include award-winning steaks, seafood, and Italian and stir-fry dishes.

Sneakers $

1712 W. Willow, (405) 237-6325. Go north from the intersection of Highways 81 and 412 to Willow Road and turn west. Monday-Saturday 11-11. Handicapped accessibility limited by stairs.

The eclectic decor which includes antique chandeliers is a big draw, but the food is just as interesting with a variety of sandwiches, salads and burgers on the menu.

Shopping

Downtown Historic District

From the intersection of Highways 412 and 81, go east on 412 to Independence. Go north on Independence to Maine. The downtown "square" is bordered by the following streets: Maine on the south, Independence on the west, Randolph on the north, and Grand on the east.

An antique shopper's paradise, Enid's historic district is a wonderful place to find relics from the past. The downtown area is built around the Courthouse Square. Park near the square and walk to a half-dozen antique shops nearby. You will find furniture, dishes, toys, collectibles, and much more.

Cherokee Strip Mall, 124 S. Independence, (405) 234-7878. **Down Memory Lane**, 101 S. Grand, (405) 242-2100. **Mini Mall**, 129 E. Broadway, (405) 233-5521. **Olden Daze Mall**, 117 N. Grand, (405) 242-5633. **Tommy's This & That**, 424 S. Independence, (405) 233-5642.

Pride of Oklahoma is a shop worth noting. Here shoppers find a wide selection of Oklahoma-made products and food items. Make your own Oklahoma-shaped gift basket! Located at 216 W. Randolph (405-237-6440), the store is open Monday-Friday 9:30-5:30, Saturday 10-3.

Oakwood Mall

4125 West Owen K. Garriott (Highway 412), (405) 237-9177. Monday-Saturday 10-9, Sunday noon-6.

The mall includes over sixty stores, a movie theater, and a food court.

Accommodations

Worthington House Bed and Breakfast

1224 W. Maine, (405) 237-9202. Go north on Highway 81 past Highway 412 to Maine Street then turn west. $75 plus tax. Ask about special rates. Member of the Oklahoma Bed and Breakfast Association. Not handicapped accessible.

Owned by Gary and Cindy Worthington, this 1906 three-story house is furnished with period pieces and is dedicated to the owners' families. The Worthington Memory room is decorated with the flowers and frills loved by Gary's mother. The Worthington Love room honoring Cindy's folks is decorated in hunter green and burgundy. The rooms are accessorized with family memorabilia and have queen-size beds and private baths with showers. Breakfast is a three-course gourmet delight guaranteed to please. Cindy's French Toast Sundae, a breakfast banana split, is a favorite.

In the Vicinity

Glass Mountains

As you travel along Highway 412 just west of Highway 60, be prepared for some of the most surprising and beautiful topography in the state. The landscape's sudden transformation from wheat fields to red mesas will surprise any traveler unfamiliar with the area. If you didn't know better, you'd think it was Utah.

Early explorers referred to them as the "Glass" or "Gloss" Mountains because of the shiny gypsum deposits which crown the formations. However, the Glass Mountains are not mountains at all, they're mesas. Spanish for "table," a mesa is a plateau-like formation which remains after the less-resilient surrounding area has eroded away.

These red formations are at their photographic best when the sun is low, during early morning and late evening. To learn more about the geology of the Glass Mountains, visitors should stop at the turnout located approximately eight miles west of Orienta on the north side of the road.

Island Guest Ranch

Located near Ames, approximately thirty-five miles southwest of Enid. Call Carl and Mary White at (405) 753-4574 for more information. Cost is $100 per day per person which includes three home-cooked meals, horseback riding, fishing, swimming, and entertainment. A weekend special is offered for groups of five or more ($70 per day per person). Children welcome.

You'd never guess it, but Big Island Guest Ranch really is an island! Surrounded on all sides by the Cimarron River (which forks and later rejoins itself), the ranch consists of 2300 acres of rolling wooded hills and grasslands. This is the perfect place to "leave it all behind."

While daily activities allow guests to experience the Old West, living accommodations are modern, clean and comfortable. Each room has two double beds, a private bath, air conditioning, and daily maid service. Activities may include horseback riding, fishing, chuck wagon breakfasts, hiking, attending a Native American Powwow, or even visiting a recreated ghost town.

Fairview

From Enid, continue west on Highway 412 approximately thirty-five miles to Orienta. Follow Highway 60 south from Orienta about six miles to Fairview. From Oklahoma City, take I-40 west to Highway 281. Go north approximately twenty miles to Watonga. Continue north approximately thirty miles on Highways 51A and 58 to Fairview. ⬛

National John Deere Two-Cylinder Tractor Show

Held in July at the Major County Historical Society, located about one mile east of Fairview on Highway 58. Be sure to call (405) 227-2265 for more information.

Billed as a salute to America's most famous tractor, this show features demonstrations of plowing, bailing, threshing, and combining (harvesting)—everything you wanted to know about the "good old days" of farming in Oklahoma.

Oklahoma Mennonite Relief Sale

This festival and benefit auction is held the Friday and Saturday after Thanksgiving at the Major County Fairgrounds, 200 E. Bellmon Drive, Fairview, OK 73737. For information, call (405) 227-2701

Don't miss the chance to bid on hundreds of items such as wall hangings, furniture, toys, antiques, and over one hundred handcrafted quilts at this special sale. The quilts, afghans and comforters are handmade by Oklahoma Mennonites. A variety of ethnic and traditional foods are for sale. Forget the leftover Thanksgiving turkey and feast instead on Kielbasa, liverwurst, German stuffed sausage, homemade bread, pastries, and Russian pancakes.

The festivities begin Friday night with music, a grilled chicken dinner, and craft and food booths. The auction begins on Saturday morning. Proceeds support the worldwide hunger relief and community development programs of the Mennonite Central Committee.

Great Salt Plains Region

Located about thirty miles northwest of Enid. Take either Highway 45 or 412 a few miles west of Enid to Highway 132. Travel north to Highway 64, then west to Jet. To reach the Salt Plains observation tower and the Selenite Crystal Digging Area, go west on Highway 64 approximately six miles and follow the signs. To reach the Jet Recreation Area, Great Salt Plains Reservoir and State Park, and Wildlife Refuge Headquarters, go north on Highway 38. Entrances to the various locations will be to the west of Highway 38, and all are clearly marked by signs.

From a distance, the Great Salt Plains appears to be a large lake. The bright white expanse of the Salt Flats creates the illusion of water—until you realize people are walking and driving on its surface! In fact, what you are seeing is a perfectly flat, 11,000-acre expanse of salt-covered mud and quicksand, completely devoid of vegetation.

Millions of years ago, the Salt Flats were formed by the repeated flooding of an ancient sea. Cut off from the main body of the sea, salt water evaporated—each time leaving thick layers of salt deposits behind. These deposits were later covered by eroded sand and soil. The salt crust visible on the surface is a result of ground water percolating up through the salt-saturated sand. When it reaches the surface, the water evaporates, leaving a thin crust of salt.

Long before "discovery" by white explorers, the Great Salt Plains were considered a vital resource by the area's Native American tribes. In addition to salt, the plains provided rich hunting grounds. Many animals, including deer and bison, were drawn to this natural salt lick. Later, the Salt Plains were equally important to white settlers, who traveled long distances to collect the precious salt crust. Wagons were sent from as far away as Kansas and Texas to haul back great loads of salt from the area.

Today, visitors enjoy numerous activities at the Great Salt Plains area. From bird watching, to crystal digging, to boating, this place has something for everyone.

Great Salt Plains Observation Tower and Selenite Crystal Digging Area

To reach the observation tower from Jet, go west on Highway 64 approximately six miles and follow the signs to the Selenite Crystal Digging Area. The observation tower is located at the entrance to this area, and it offers a view of the immense salt plains.

Visitors to the Great Salt Plains can dig for selenite crystals from April 1 to October 15 each year. These crystals are formed when gypsum combines with concentrated saline solution in the soil. The selenite ranges in size from individual crystals a few inches long to large clusters weighing many pounds. Look for the characteristic "hourglass-shaped" inclusions of sand and clay in the crystals. The Great Salt Plains is the only place in the world where these unique inclusions occur in selenite crystals.

Visitors should dig only in designated areas. These sites are rotated annually to allow crystal regeneration. Because of quicksand danger in some areas and possible disturbance to the nesting habitat of endangered birds, visitors should drive only on designated roads. Brochures on crystal digging are located at the Wildlife Refuge Headquarters and near the Selenite Digging Area.

The **Crystal Festival** is held in late-April or early-May in Cherokee. Experienced selenite hunters help beginners uncover the crystal "treasures." Prizes are awarded to those who unearth the best crystal specimens each day. For more information, contact the Cherokee Chamber of Commerce weekdays from 9-noon at (405) 569-3053.

Great Salt Plains Lake

From Jet, go north on Highway 38. Boat ramps are located at various sites in the Great Salt Plains State Park and in the Jet Recreation Area. 🛉

Located within the Great Salt Plains National Wildlife Refuge, this shallow lake is famous for its channel cat fishing. Stocked with channel cat, hybrid striped bass, and saugeye, the lake offers year-round fishing opportunities. However, since the lake is encompassed by the Great Salt Plains Wildlife Refuge, boating is restricted to certain areas of the lake during different times of the year; contact the Refuge at (405) 626-4794 for complete information. Because the entire lake is very shallow, always check water depth before diving.

Jet Recreation Area

The Jet Recreation Area is on the southeastern shore of Great Salt Plains Lake, just north of Jet on Highway 38. Primitive camping, swimming, fishing and a boat launch are available from April 1-October 15.

Great Salt Plains State Park

Adjacent to the Great Salt Plains Lake and Wildlife Refuge, the Great Salt Plains State Park is eight miles north of Jet on Highway 38, (405) 626-4731.

The park makes a great headquarters for fishing, boating, swimming, bird watching, and picnicking. There are 171 designated campsites ranging from semi-modern hookups (electric and water) to primitive campsites. Also available are six clean and cozy **cabins** that each have a kitchen, bedroom, bathroom, and living area; they sleep up to six. There are no telephones or televisions in the cabins, so bring a deck of cards and a good conversationalist.

No group camping facilities are available, but there is a community center with basic kitchen facilities available for reunions and large group gatherings. The community center may be rented year round.

Great Salt Plains National Wildlife Refuge

From Jet, go north on Highway 38. Look for a sign on the west side of the Highway approximately two miles south of Highway 11. Follow the dirt road to the Refuge Headquarters, (405)626-4794.

Established in 1930 as a "breeding ground for birds," the Salt Plains Wildlife Refuge Area encompasses over 32,000 acres of non-vegetated salt flat, open water, marsh, woods, grasslands, and cropland. The refuge provides habitat for approximately 300 species of birds and thirty species of animals. Winter is the best season to spot ducks, geese, cranes, and bald eagles; summer offers prime viewing of endangered least terns, egrets, herons, and pelicans.

The **Eagle Roost Nature Trail** is a 1.25-mile loop trail which introduces visitors to a variety of wildlife habitats found in the refuge. Another way to learn about the wildlife refuge is to drive the 2.5 mile **Harold F. Miller Auto Tour Route**. Both the auto tour and nature trail begin near the Refuge Headquarters. While at the headquarters, be sure to pick up informational brochures to get the most from these self-guided tours.

The Salt Plains Refuge maintains a 1200-acre area for **public hunting** of migratory and upland game birds. Deer hunting is by permit drawing only. All other hunting is prohibited, and hunting is strictly prohibited in all other areas of the refuge. Contact the Wildlife Refuge office for details.

Byron State Fish Hatchery

From the corner of State Highways 38 and 11, go north two miles on Highway 38, then west one mile. Visiting hours are Monday-Friday 8-5, and by appointment on weekends. (405) 474-2663. Handicapped accessible.

HOW TO DIG FOR CRYSTALS:

For best results, come prepared. You will need a shovel, a bucket or jug of water, and a container in which to carry the crystals, which are fragile until dry. Since crystal hunters spend most of their time on hands and knees, an old towel is handy, both for kneeling and wiping hands. Sunglasses and sunscreen are essential; bright sun combined with glare from the white salt surface can quickly result in sunburn.

Use a shovel to dig a hole about two feet deep until you reach wet sand. Allow two or three inches of water to seep in from the bottom. Use your hands or a cup to splash water gently against the sides of the hole. (Some people bring a container of water, so they have plenty of water to splash...and to drink when it gets hot!) This washes the soil away and exposes the crystals. When you find a crystal, continue splashing it with water until it is mostly exposed. Newly-exposed crystals are fragile and will break if you try to pull them from the soil. After removing the crystal, place it where the sun and wind will dry it. Egg cartons are useful for drying and carrying smaller crystals. You are permitted to remove up to ten pounds of crystals, plus one large cluster each day.

If the fish at the lake aren't biting, you should consider a tour of the Byron State Fish Hatchery. This hatchery is responsible for producing and stocking sport fish throughout the state of Oklahoma. From spawning to harvest, the hatchery nurtures thousands of catfish, bass and saugeye each year. They supply the "little ones" that become the "big ones that get away." The best time to see eggs hatching is from mid-March to late May.

In the Vicinity

Heritage Manor Bed and Breakfast

Near the Sod House Museum and Highway 8, (800) 295-2563. $75 per couple, $55 single, suite $150. Handicapped accessible. No credit cards accepted.

Owners A.J. and Carolyn Rexroat moved two pre-statehood houses onto their property, consolidated them, and turned them into a large, lovely home decorated with period furniture. The Rexroats have four bedrooms—one with a queen-sized bed, the others with double beds. Though the rooms don't have baths, there are three bathrooms available making them easier to share. Guests choose their breakfasts from an extensive menu which includes a house specialty, Heritage Eggs. The house is situated on eighty acres with walking paths through groves of trees.

Sod House Museum

From the Great Salt Plains Area, travel south on State Highway 8. Tuesday-Friday 9-5, Saturday-Sunday 2-5, closed Monday and all state holidays. Free admission. Handicapped accessible.

When Marshal McCully staked his claim near present-day Aline in 1893, wood was scarce. Fortunately for him and thousands of other homesteaders, the abundant grasslands provided an alternative building material—sod.

Thousands of settlers in the plains used special plows to cut strips of sod and dirt from the virgin prairies. The dense root systems of the native grass held the soil together as it was cut into bricks and stacked to form walls. Supported by precious wooden poles, more sod formed the roof. If possible, the walls were then plastered. Although the thick sod provided exceptional insulation from both cold and heat, "soddies" were notorious for allowing rain, dirt, snakes, and insects into the home. Most settlers lived in them only long enough to build a more permanent structure.

The Sod House Museum now shelters the original sod house built by McCully in 1894. It is the last existing sod house built by an Oklahoma homesteader. Visitors can walk through the authentically-furnished soddie and admire the ingenuity of Marshal McCully and thousands like him who settled Oklahoma Territory a century ago. As an added treat, McCully's granddaughter is among the museum staff.

Kingfisher

Before the Land Run of 1889, Kingfisher was not a town; it was a stage station operated by a man named King David Fisher. When the Land Run started at noon on April 22, thousands flocked to the town site (originally called Lisbon), claiming all available lots within an hour! A second town, Kingfisher City, was established just north of Lisbon. The two communities finally merged a year later. Home of the second Territorial Governor, Kingfisher was once a serious candidate to become Oklahoma's capital. Although Kingfisher did not become the capital, the town played a major role in Oklahoma's formative years. Today, that history is celebrated at the Chisholm Trail Museum and the Seay Mansion.

Located twenty-five miles northwest of Oklahoma City. From Oklahoma City, travel northwest on Highway 3 (the Northwest Expressway). This road becomes Highway 81 and leads straight into Kingfisher. From Tulsa, take Highway 51 west approximately ninety miles to I-35, then go south twenty miles to Guthrie. Take State Highway 33 west to Kingfisher. Kingfisher Chamber of Commerce (405) 375-4445.

The Chisholm Trail Museum

605 Zellers Avenue, (405) 375-5176. From the intersection of Highway 81 and Seay Avenue, go west five blocks on Seay to 11th Street. At this point, you are actually behind the museum. To reach the front, go north one block to Zellers Avenue, and then turn left. Tuesday-Saturday, 9-5. Sunday 1-5. Closed Monday and all legal holidays. Free admission. Handicapped accessible.

The Chisholm Trail Museum is a treasure chest of Americana. The main building houses varied collections ranging from Native American artifacts to agricultural implements, antique household and personal items, and even an original telephone operator's switchboard. However, some of the most fascinating history is located behind the museum where several restored buildings are located. The Bank of Kingfisher, built in 1889, is one such exhibit. As you walk into the bank, notice the elegant teller's windows made of carved oak and etched glass. Other historic buildings such as the Gant Schoolhouse, a church and two log cabins (circa 1889) allow visitors to step back into history. One of the log cabins was the last home of Adaline Dalton, mother of thirteen children; five of these children later comprised the infamous Dalton Gang.

Seay Mansion

605 Zellers Avenue, (405) 375-5176. Located across the street from the Chisholm Trail Museum. Tuesday-Saturday, 9-5, and Sunday, 1-5. Closed Monday and legal holidays. Admission is free. Not handicapped accessible.

The Seay Mansion was built by the second Territorial Governor of Oklahoma, Abraham Jefferson Seay, in anticipation that Kingfisher would be named the capital of Oklahoma Territory. The 1892 home is elegantly decorated. Especially note the beautifully-carved oak molding used throughout the house.

Shopping

Kingfisher Antique Mall

1109 S. Main, (405) 375-3288. Located on Highway 81 between Enid and El Reno. Tuesday-Saturday, 10-5:30, Sunday, 1-5:30.

The Kingfisher Antique Mall is actually a former residence filled with collectibles. Treasure hunters will delight in wandering through its many rooms, all brimming with antiques of every kind.

Events

Annual Gas Steam Engine Show

Hosted every June on the grounds of the P & K Equipment Co. just outside of Kingfisher; call (405) 375-4445 for information.

The Annual Gas Steam Engine Show offers a rare chance to see vintage agricultural equipment in operation. Activities include threshing, baling and rope making. Discover how steam engines transformed the farmer's life in the days before diesel.

In the Vicinity

Eischen's Bar $, $$

Located at 2nd and Oklahoma in Okarche, next to the bank, (405) 263-9939. Okarche is just eighteen miles northwest of Oklahoma City on Highway 3 (aka Northwest Expressway). Monday-Saturday, 10 a.m. to midnight, closed Sunday. Chicken is served until 10 p.m.

The tiny town of Okarche is home to one really huge tradition—fried chicken at Eischen's, the oldest bar in Oklahoma. Established as Eischen's Saloon in 1896, it has been owned by the same family ever since. Although destroyed by fire in 1993, the bar was rebuilt; the Eischen tradition continues—right down to the sawdust on the floor. Their philosophy? Keep it simple and cook the best fried chicken in the state. There are no two-piece dinners, no coffee, no iced tea, no plates or utensils. $8 will buy you a whole fried chicken served in a paper-lined basket. You eat it with your hands, and wash it down with beer or a soda.

Come early on Friday and Saturday nights, when Eischen's is always packed; lines typically extend out the door. Children are always welcome.

Ponca City

Like many of Oklahoma's towns, Ponca City was born as the result of a 1893 Cherokee Strip Land Run. Though growing, the town was relatively quiet from the date of its incorporation until the 1920s, when oil was discovered in the area. Various "wildcatters" appeared to try their luck in the oil fields, but none was more successful that E.W. Marland. He, and the others like him, have left a lasting legacy in the town: their homes, their gifts, and the fine arts they sponsored are still here for Poncans to enjoy.

While in Ponca, check out the **Poncan Theater,** located downtown. This renovated theater hosts many entertaining productions and performances. Call (405) 765-0943 for a schedule of events and to schedule a tour.

Located approximately ninety miles from Oklahoma City and Tulsa. From Oklahoma City travel north on I-35, exit on Highway 60 and travel east for fifteen miles. From Tulsa, take the Cimarron Turnpike west approximately seventy miles to the Ponca City exit (Highway 177), then travel north about twenty-two miles. Ponca City Chamber of Commerce (405) 767-8888 or (800) 475-4400.

Marland Mansion

901 Monument Road, (405) 767-0420 or (800) 532-7559. From 14th Street (Highway 77) and Highland, take the circle drive north around the Pioneer Woman statue to Monument Road which leads directly to the mansion. May-September, Monday-Saturday 10-5, Sunday noon-5. October-April, daily noon-4. Closed Thanksgiving, Christmas and New Years Day. Guided tours are available Monday-Friday at 1:30, Saturday and Sunday at 1:30 and 2:30. Mansion tour: adults $4, senior citizens $3, students $1.75. Self-guided tours of the grounds and museums in the guest house are free. Tours last approximately one hour. Call at least one week ahead to schedule tours at a different time, or for group tours. ★

Once referred to as the "Patriarch of Ponca City," E.W. Marland was one of the state's most colorful characters. Athough already well-off financially, he "struck it rich" in May of 1920, when he discovered oil at Burbank (about sixteen miles east of Ponca). The next year he opened the successful Tonkawa field. By 1923, he was rich and living in stately style. In 1925, he commissioned John Duncan Forsythe to design a "castle." The structure, completed in 1928 by European artisans, had 55 air-conditioned rooms, a 2500-acre game refuge, stables, gatehouses, an art gallery and studio, a nine-hole golf course, polo grounds, and elaborate gardens.

Visitors to this mansion are often awed by its splendor. Hand-carved wood paneling, elaborate grill work, imported stained-glass windows, and stone staircases blend to create the air of an Italian renaissance palace. Gold leaf ceilings and Waterford Crystal chandeliers grace the ballroom. Marland's mansion featured the best that money could buy. By 1930 and the beginning of the Great Depression, Marland was broke. The oilman turned to politics, serving as one of Oklahoma's governors from 1934-38. The guest house at the estate includes exhibits on petroleum, E. W. Marland, and the 101 Ranch. A Conference Center and hotel are also on the property.

Pioneer Woman Statue and Museum

701 Monument Road, at the intersection of Highway 77 (14th Street) and Lake Road. (405) 765-6108. Tuesday-Saturday, 9-5, Sunday 1-5. Closed Monday and state holidays. Free. NOTE: Currently closed for renovation and expansion, the museum should reopen in the spring of 1998. Advance reservations are required for groups. Call after reopening to confirm hours.

"Behind every successful man is a good woman," or so the saying goes. This seventeen-foot **bronze statue** pays tribute to the heroic pioneer women who survived hardship and danger to create new homes on the frontier. The idea for the monument was E.W. Marland's. He announced and financed a competition among twelve of the country's best sculptors. The three-foot-high bronze models were taken on tour, and the public selected the winning entry. Bryant Baker's creation won; the third largest bronze statue in the world was dedicated in 1930, and it is now listed on the National Register of Historic Places.

Adjacent to the statue is the **Pioneer Woman Museum.** Everyday life on the frontier is the theme of the exhibits. Visitors can view a pioneer kitchen and bedroom, as well as an old-fashioned beauty shop. Artifacts and antiques intrigue guests of all ages, but exhibits are not limited to the lifestyles and living conditions of the women on the prairie. The expansion will feature displays on women everywhere who have been (and are currently) pioneers in their fields. This expansion will update Marland's image of pioneering women to include the hardworking and adventurous personalities of the twentieth century. Schedule at least an hour to view the statue and to wander through the museum.

Ponca City Cultural Center and Indian Museum

1000 East Grand Avenue, (405) 767-0427. From 14th Street (Highway 77) and Grand Avenue travel west to the southeast corner of 10th Street and Grand. Plan to spend about an hour at the Cultural Center. (405) 767-0427. Monday-Saturday 10-5, Sunday 1-5. Closed Tuesday and some holidays. Adults ages 16 and over, $1. Children free.

E.W. Marland's first home is host to cultural exhibits depicting the area's history. Built in 1914, the home is an attraction in itself. With twenty-two rooms, a hanging staircase, and the state's first indoor pool, this Italian Renaissance home reflects the style of its flamboyant original owner. Inside, more than 4000 artifacts and pieces of memorabilia bring to life the region's past. On the lower level, visitors can view Indian artifacts from many tribes throughout the United States; special attention is given to items that come from the Ponca, Kaw, Otoe, Osage, and Tonkawa tribes, the primary tribes of this region.

Many visitors are interested in the western relics from the 101 Ranch. Started in 1871 by George Miller and his three sons, this ranch covered 101,000 acres and was the most famous ranch in the country. With its own tannery, dairy, and dry goods store, the Ranch was self-sufficient; it was also home to the 101 Ranch Wild West Show which toured the world at the beginning of this century.

Also on display is the studio of Bryant Baker, the Brooklyn sculptor who designed the Pioneer Woman statue. The Daughters of the American Revolution Memorial Room is located here and features a thirteen-star U.S. flag recovered from a Revolutionary War battlefield.

Standing Bear Native American Memorial Park

Located at the intersection of Highways 177, 60 and 77 on the south edge of town. Free.

Sculptor Oreland C. Joe's magnificent twenty-two-foot bronze statue of Ponca Indian Standing Bear rises amid the grasses and wildflowers of his native prairie. Dedicated in October, 1996, the monument honors Chief Standing Bear as an early civil rights leader. Visitors can follow the circular trail to a sixty-foot diameter plaza which offers dramatic views of the statue and the sixty-three acre site. Plaza features include the story of Chief Standing Bear, tribal seals of the six Native American tribes closest to Ponca City, a reflecting pool, and an eternal flame. An American Indian-inspired design in the plaza surface encloses the names of the eight Ponca tribal clans.

Walking Tour of Downtown Ponca City

Downtown Ponca City, beginning at 5th and Grand. Call the Chamber of Commerce for a brochure detailing the tour. There are actually two tours visitors may take: the one mile tour, or the longer 3.2 mile tour. Plan at least an hour for this activity.

Founded on September 16, 1893, with the opening of the Cherokee Outlet, Ponca City experienced steady growth during its early years. The city took on grand proportions in the 1920s, due to the oil boom. Walking the downtown streets, one can see the history of the town in its architecture. The tour includes both public buildings and private residences, with construction spanning the years from 1900 to 1934. Visitors can compare the functional simplicity of red brick business buildings with the elaborate facades of personal homes. Included on the extended tour is the **Ponca City Library**, an excellent example of Art Deco architecture, and the **Soldani Mansion**, which now houses the Ponca City Art Center. Take your time on this walking tour; feel free to step inside any of the public buildings that are open on the day you are touring. Food and drink is available from several restaurants along the route.

Ponca City

Golf

Lew Wentz Memorial Golf Course

L.A. Cann Drive, (405) 767-0433. From Highway 77 and Lake Road, go east to Kyger. Go north on Kygar to L.A. Cann Road. Follow this road around Lake Ponca to the golf course. Eighteen-hole play is $12 on weekdays and $13 on weekends; cart rental is $16.

Situated along the north bank of Lake Ponca, Lew Wentz Memorial Golf Course is dedicated to the memory of one of Ponca City's favorite oil men. The manicured, 6261-yard course is par 71, with a slope of 125 and a USGA rating of 70. Amenities include a pro shop and fast food service. Tee time reservations are recommended two days in advance.

Dining

Crown and Rose English Pub and Restaurant $, $$

731 N. 14th, (405) 762-8489. Located on Highway 77 (14th Street), just north of Lake Road. Weekdays 10 a.m.-11:30 p.m., Saturday 10 a.m.-12:30 a.m., closed Sunday.

This cozy restaurant serves a variety of English specialties, all with appropriate British names. A variety of sandwiches and burgers are available, as well as Shepherd's Pie, Scotch Eggs, and the traditional fish and chips. Light entrees are available, as are delicious desserts. Cheers!

Godfrey's $, $$

200 N. 2nd, (405) 762-7280. From Highway 77, turn west on Grand. Go to 2nd Street and turn north. Lunch Monday-Saturday 11-3, dinner served Monday-Thursday 5-9, Friday-Saturday 5-10. Closed Sunday. Handicapped accessible.

Scheduled to open in June, 1997, Godfrey's describes itself as "an American grill with a taste of the Great Southwest." One of the specialties is Green Chili Chicken Chowder. The restaurant offers both indoor and outdoor dining plus upstairs banquet facilities.

Head Country Bar-B-Q Restaurant $, $$

1217 E. Prospect, (405) 767-8304. Located at Highway 77 (14th Street) and Prospect. Monday-Saturday 11-8, closed Sunday.

This restaurant has earned several awards, the most prestigious being the American Royal/ KC Masterpiece International Invitational in Kansas City. Now bottled and sold throughout the region, Head Country Bar-B-Q sauce is the number one selling sauce in Oklahoma. Stop by the original restaurant and sample this renowned taste sensation for yourself!

J.W. Cobb's $, $$

3200 N. 14th Street (Highway 77 and Prospect), (405) 762-8525. Monday-Saturday 10:30 a.m.-9 p.m. Closed Sunday and major holidays.

This is a family restaurant, serving homemade food in an old movie atmosphere. Diners enjoy daily specials such as pot roast and turkey and dressing. Patrons enjoy the television and movie memorabilia from the 1950s and '60s that adorns the wall.

Accommodations

God's Little Acre

Six miles east of Ponca City on Lake Road. Call for directions. (405) 765-6036 or (800) 519-3461. $60.

This secluded bed and breakfast offers two rooms to guests, one with a private bath and the other with a shared bath. Reservations are required.

The Homestead Bed and Breakfast

Located at the G.T. Ranch, three miles east of I-35 near Billings (about 25 miles south and west of Ponca City), (405) 725-3400. Call for directions. $65-100. Reservations are required. The B&B is a non-smoking facility and is for adults only. Member of the Oklahoma Bed and Breakfast Association. Major credit cards accepted.

Marvel at the bright stars and the wide open prairie at The Homestead Bed and Breakfast. Built as a B&B, the new log cabin is situated on a longhorn cattle ranch in big sky country. Owners Ted and Glenda Riddle have a reputation for gracious hospitality. With prior arrangement, guests can also enjoy an outstanding longhorn steak dinner whether they are staying overnight or not.

For those fortunate enought to stay the night, four guest rooms are available, each with a private bath and a Western theme, quilts and antiques. The honeymoon suite includes a sitting room and a jacuzzi bath. The Cherokee Room has a queen-sized log bed, hand-built by Ted. The great room features a cathedral ceiling and a fireplace made of native rock. Ponca City, with its many attractions, is located nearby. However, the owners report that most of their guests stay at The Homestead for rest and relaxation. Enjoy Oklahoma's wheat and cattle country at The Homestead!

Marland Estate Conference Center/Hotel

901 Monument, (405) 767-0422, (800) 532-7559, 35 units plus two suites, $39-45, suites $90. Amenities include nonsmoking rooms, an outdoor pool, a restaurant, and a meeting room.

The Conference Center and Hotel not only share the grounds, they actually connect with the Marland Mansion. Originally built in 1961 by the Felician Sisters as their living quarters, the hotel is tastefully decorated and maintains a tranquil, resort-like atmosphere.

Rose Stone Inn

120 S. 3rd Street, (405) 765-5699 or (800) 763-9922. $60. Children are welcome. Credit cards are accepted. Smoking is not permitted.

David and Shirley Zimmerman have turned this former savings and loan into an intimate inn. Each of the twenty-five rooms is named after an Oklahoma person, place or thing. Decor ranges from baronial to colonial to Victorian. Guests can choose to work out in the exercise room or check out a movie from the film library. Special attention has been given to the needs of business professionals visiting the area. Breakfast features homebaked goods and is often served on linen tablecloths set with china and silver.

Events

Iris Festival

Typically held the first weekend in May in downtown Ponca City, (405) 763-8082. Free.

Enjoy the beauty of spring when you visit the Iris Festival in downtown Ponca City. Visitors can peruse a flower show and fine arts, shop for arts and crafts, or enjoy a tasty treat at the Victorian Chocolate Festival. What a great way to celebrate spring!

101 Wild West Rodeo

Held the third weekend in August (Wednesday-Saturday) at the intersection of Ash and Prospect Street, (800) 475-4400. Adults $6-$8, children $3, under age six are free.

Re-live the excitement of the original 101 Wild West Show! Created by the Miller brothers at their famous 101 Ranch, the show toured the world during the early 1900s. Now the PRCA-sanctioned rodeo attracts more than four hundred of the country's best rodeo performers who participate in events including steer-roping, bull-riding and barrel racing to name but a few. Other activities affiliated with the rodeo include a dance, arts and crafts booths, and food vendors.

Octoberfest

Held the first weekend in October on the grounds of the Marland Mansion, (405) 767-0420. A nominal fee is charged.

When they visit the Marland Mansion on this special weekend, visitors feel that they've been transported back to the Old World. With over 100 booths to browse through, visitors enjoy shopping for arts, crafts, and food. Live entertainment, much of it with a German flair, features bands, singers, local gymnasts, and dancers.

Festival of Angels

Held throughout the city from Thanksgiving through New Years Eve. Special lighting displays are open from 6 to 10 p.m. Contact Ponca City Tourism at (800) 475-4400 for a calendar of events and tour maps. Special activities during the holiday season include a tour of historic homes, a downtown parade, and "The Nutcracker" at the Poncan Theater. Most events are free.

Angels grace the entire town during this Yuletide holiday event. A thirty-foot lighted angel near the Pioneer Woman Statue greets visitors to the festival. Other displays highlight the Cann Gardens, Cultural Center, Centennial Plaza, Poncan Theater, and numerous residential areas. On weekends children can visit Santa in his house at the park, or guests can enjoy a holiday ride in a horse-drawn wagon. New this year is the exhibit at Lake Ponca Park. Here angel hosts greet visitors, directing them to the animated angel and animal lighting displays. For those who can't bear to leave the angels behind, there's a gift shop at Angel Central where visitors may purchase handmade gifts and Angel souvenirs. All proceeds from the Festival go towards purchasing more displays for future festivals.

In the Vicinity

Blackwell

This clean, bustling small town was planned, platted, and promoted by A.J. Blackwell before any non-Indian pioneers could settle the area. As part of the Cherokee hunting grounds, this land was not available for settlement without permission of the Cherokee tribe. After the Civil War, however, the tribe was required to provide territories for the Kaw, Ponca, Tonkawa, Pawnee, and Otoe-Missouria tribes. Excess lands were opened to other settlers in the land run of the Cherokee Outlet in September 1893. Mr. Blackwell, who had been promoting the town prior to the Run, was chosen president of the town council, and he became the first mayor. *Blackwell is located about fifteen miles west and north of Ponca City along I-35. Blackwell Chamber of Commerce (405) 363-4195.*

Top of Oklahoma Museum

Electric Park Pavilion, 303 South Main, (405) 363-0209. Monday-Saturday 10-5, Sunday 1-5. Free; donations are appreciated.

The history of Blackwell and its residents is displayed in the Top of Oklahoma Museum. Visitors will find exhibits depicting home and family life, local industries, Native American lifestyles, and much more. All exhibits are housed in the Electric Park Pavilion, a remarkable building constructed in 1912-13. The building is listed on the National Register of Historic Places.

White's Factory Outlet

Located along I-35 (exit 222), (405) 363-4545. Monday-Saturday 9-9, Sunday noon to 6. Winter Hours: January-March, Monday-Saturday 10-7.

Those who love to shop should search for bargains at White's Factory Outlet. Over a dozen brand name retailers provide merchandise such as cookware, outerwear, and footwear.

If "old" is more enchanting to you than "new," visit one of Blackwell's many **antique shops**. Located in the red brick buildings of downtown Blackwell, these stores are brimming with the treasurers and trifles of the past. Hours vary by business.

Watonga

Founded in 1892, Watonga was named after Arapaho Chief Wa-Ah Dan-Ga-Ah, meaning Black Coyote. Although in its early years Watonga was noted for being a "wild" frontier town, the town is now known for its historic downtown, scenic beauty (particularly around the Roman Nose State Park area), and the Watonga Cheese Factory. Watonga is the boyhood home of Clarence Nash, the voice of Walt Disney's cartoon character Donald Duck. Watonga has not forgotten its past—a street is named in Nash's honor, and several local buildings have been restored for the public's enjoyment.

Located approximately 75 miles northwest of Oklahoma City. From Oklahoma City, take I-40 west to Highway 281. Go north approximately twenty-two miles to Watonga. Another possibility is to take Highway 3/81 to Kingfisher then take Highway 33 west approximately thirty miles to Watonga. From Tulsa, take State Highway 51 west to I-35. Go south approximately twenty miles to Guthrie, then take Highway 33 west to Watonga. Watonga Chamber of Commerce (405) 623-5452. 🛈

T.B. Ferguson Home

519 N. Weigle, (405) 623-5069. From Highway 33 and Highway 8 (Clarence Nash Boulevard) go north to 4th Street. Go east on 4th to Weigle Avenue, then take Weigle north one block. The T.B. Ferguson Home is located at the corner of E. 5th and N. Weigle. Wednesday-Saturday, 10-4, Sunday, 1-5. Closed Monday, Tuesday, and all state holidays. Admission is free. Not wheelchair accessible.

The sixth Territorial Governor of Oklahoma and founder of the Watonga Republican newspaper, T.B. Ferguson built this stately home in 1907. Filled with beautiful furnishings, period pieces, and historic photos, the Ferguson home is perhaps best known for its famous guests. Edna Ferber, a close friend of Mrs. Ferguson, stayed here while researching material for her novel Cimarron, a story about Oklahoma's tumultuous territorial days. Another well-known guest was President Theodore (Teddy) Roosevelt, who enjoyed hunting trips with Mr. Ferguson. Although not officially part of the tour, ask to see the museum office. This tiny room served as the Ferguson's guest bedroom. Imagine a president sleeping there now!

In addition to the home, see the first Watonga city jail and an 1870 U.S. Cavalry remount station, both relocated behind the Ferguson home.

Old General Store and Prairie House Museum

122 W. Main, (405) 623-2444. Monday-Saturday 1-5, or call for appointment. Admission $2, no charge for children under six. Handicapped accessible.

When Ed and Doris Neufeld "retired" and moved back to Ed's hometown of Watonga, they brought their occupations with them. For eleven years, the Old General Store and Prairie House Museum was part of the Shepherd of the Hills complex in Branson, Missouri. Now it's been recreated in western Oklahoma. Containing over 10,000 items, the **general store** represents retail merchandising from 1880 to 1940. The wood-floored store with its tin ceiling has a dairy department, candy shop, butcher counter, post office, and many more features. The **prairie house** depicts early-day living in the plains states. All of the items in the house are between one and two hundred years old.

The Place to Be

110 N. Noble (near the Noble House), (405) 623-2451. Monday 10-2, Tuesday-Friday 10-5. Call for appointments and prices. Handicapped accessible with some difficulty.

Want to be queen for a day? This is "the place to be." Cheryl Wolfe and Diana Pavlu provide massages (one hour for $35), facials, footials, reflexology, and all kinds of pampering. To be king for a day, you must be accompanied by a lady.

Roman Nose Resort Park

Located seven miles north of Watonga on Highway 8A (turn west off State Highway 8). For Resort Lodge reservations and information, call (800) 654-8240. For information about camping, call the Roman Nose Park Office at (405) 623-7281. 🅂

Named after Chief Henry Caruthers Roman Nose, a Southern Cheyenne who lived in a tipi in the canyon from 1887 to 1917, the park is one of the most beautiful in Oklahoma. With its natural springs and abundant wildlife, Roman Nose Canyon was once a favorite refuge of the Cheyenne and Arapaho tribes. Later it became a favorite hideout for outlaws. Today, golfing, horseback riding, swimming, camping, hiking, fishing, and the Roman Nose Lodge make this the perfect getaway spot—no matter your interests.

The **Roman Nose Resort Lodge** offers forty-seven guest rooms, ten one-bedroom kitchenette cottages, cabins, campgrounds, and tipis (complete with electricity).

No visit to Roman Nose is complete without exploring the extensive **trails** that wander through red shale canyons and gypsum hills. Hikers will appreciate the solitude and spectacular views, especially along the canyon rim. Interpretive **horseback rides** are another way to enjoy the park. Trip leaders in period costume recreate the history of the canyon, recounting stories of outlaws, cavalry and cattlemen in the 1800s. Offered are one, two, and three hour interpretive trail rides, as well as weekend dinner rides which include a steak dinner cooked over an open fire. Call the **Roman Nose Stables** at (405) 623-4354 for information.

The first Oklahoma state park to host a sanctioned mountain bike race, Roman Nose offers plenty of rugged terrain for **mountain biking**. While on the trail, bikers should remember that they must yield to both hikers and horseback riders.

Roman Nose Golf Course. Designed by Floyd Farley, this 3035 yard, par 36 course offers nine of the most unique holes in the state. Nine more holes are being built beginning in 1997. Unusual canyon terrain and frequent wildlife sightings make this an extraordinary golf experience. Narrow sloping fairways bordered by thirty to forty foot drop-offs and elevated greens will challenge any player. A second set of tee boxes allow for a par 70, eighteen-hole course. Call the Pro Shop at (405) 623-7989 for more information. Weekday Green Fee, $8.50, weekend Green Fee, $10.50. Senior and junior discount given. Cart Rental, $9.

Watonga Cheese Factory

314 E. Second Street, (405) 623-5915. From Highway 33 and Burford Avenue travel north five blocks to Second Street. The Watonga Cheese Factory is on the southeast corner of Second and Burford. Monday-Friday, 8:30-5, Saturday, 9-1:30, closed Sunday.

In 1941 (before the days of low-fat diets), local dairy farmers faced a common problem: what to do with the skim milk that remained after the cream had been separated and sold? The solution was simple: make cheese. That's what the Watonga Cheese Factory has been doing ever since.

Unbelievably, this tiny factory produces from 2000 to 8000 pounds of cheddar cheese each day. Visitors can watch this process through the factory's viewing window. The cheese is still made from local milk, and it may be purchased at the factory in two or thirteen pound blocks.

Dining

Hernandez ⑤

303 S. Noble, (405) 623-2631. Monday-Saturday 11-9.

This it the place for lovers of Mexican food. Their fajitas and quesadillas are particularly popular. A south-of-the-border decor carries out the theme. People-watching is a sport here, with a diverse clientele which includes oil field roustabouts and local attorneys. Handicapped accessible.

Noble House Restaurant ⑤, ⑤⑤

112 N. Noble, (405) 623-2559. From Highway 33 and Noble travel three blocks north. Look for the restaurant on the east side of the street. Monday-Wednesday, 11-3, Thursday-Friday, 11-3, 5-8:30, Saturday, 1-2, 5-8:30, Sundays, 11:30-2.

The Noble House Restaurant is one of the best kept secrets in the state. Built as a rooming house in 1912, this historic building was saved from oblivion by an innovative group of locals who purchased and renovated it. The investors completed much of the restoration work, and they remain an integral part of the restaurant. Don't be surprised if the "bus boy" is a shareholder; he probably also helped refinish the baseboards.

That's only half the story; the food is fantastic. Everything is made from scratch—from homemade sandwich breads to mouth-watering desserts. The house specialty, Watonga Cheese Soup, is an absolute must. Prices are very reasonable, and the menu includes everything from soup and sandwiches to steaks to grilled salmon.

An easy drive from Oklahoma City, the Noble House Restaurant is a gem of an eatery–a "don't miss" Oklahoma dining experience.

Shopping

Many shops are located along Watonga's Main Street. The following are among the more unique: **Antiques and Art**, 108 W. Main, (405) 623-2600, antiques and collectibles; **Ice House**, 103 E. Main (405) 623-2599, antique items, refinishing and repair; **Temptations**, 113 W. Main, (405) 623-8367, gifts from fine china to collectibles such as Precious Moments.

Accommodations

Kennedy Kottage

1017 N. Prouty, (405) 623-4384 or (800) 511-0141. From Highway 33, take Highway 8 (Clarence Nash Boulevard) north to Highway 51a (Eleventh Street). Go four blocks east on 11th to Prouty. Take Prouty south about a block; look for a small sign that identifies the Kennedy Kottage Bed and Breakfast. Guest rates are $65 per night for a double, plus $10 for each additional guest. Member of Oklahoma Bed and Breakfast Association. Personal checks accepted. Reservations are required. No smoking. Outside accommodations are provided for pets. Handicapped accessible.

Jerry and Ruth Kennedy stayed at their first bed and breakfast while traveling in Arkansas several years ago. Inspired by the experience, they have turned their own residence into the Kennedy Kottage B & B. Guests who like to travel but not to leave home will look forward to a stay at the Kennedy Kottage. Ruth and Jerry welcome guests into their home like family.

Built in 1948, the Kennedy Kottage offers guests a "just like home" atmosphere. The two guest rooms include private bathrooms and TVs. If you are traveling with children, the "Victorian Room" offers an additional sitting room/nursery. Also included is Ruth's home-cooked breakfast. If requested, Ruth will entertain you with her musical talent as she plays the piano, accordion or antique pump organ.

Redbud Manor

900 N. Burford, (405) 623-8587. From Highway 33 (Russworm Drive), go north on Burford Avenue to 9th Street. Redbud Manor and its grounds take up the entire 900 block of North Burford. $65 per night. Member of the Oklahoma Bed and Breakfast Association. All rooms are nonsmoking. Rooms are available by reservation only. No children, no pets, no credit cards accepted. Handicapped accessible.

Redbud Manor was originally built in the 1930s by Charles and Clella Rook. As owners of two local movie theaters, it was not uncommon for the Rooks to entertain stars of the silver screen who would come to town for opening nights. Redbud Manor was built with entertaining in mind, and it served for many years as the Rook's home. Although later abandoned, the house was resurrected by Peggy and Geoff Alexander, the owners and proprietors of Redbud Manor.

The first thing you will notice about Redbud Manor is the unique brickwork. Bricks which are deformed during firing and take on unusual shapes are known as "klinkers." They were intentionally chosen by Mrs. Rook to give the house's facade its whimsical look. Inside, the home is beautifully decorated—classy and comfortable with tall ceilings, hardwood floors and antique furnishings throughout. Once you move in, you may never want to move out. Served on Depression Glass dishes, breakfast may be eaten in the formal dining room or in the round breakfast nook, a bright and cheerful room that is part of the home's two-story turret.

The main guest room is the Garden Suite, which includes an exterior door to the terrace and a full bath and shower. Two additional rooms are located upstairs and share a common bathroom.

Events

Watonga Cheese Festival

Held the first Friday and Saturday in October. Call (405) 623-5452 for more information. ⚀

In honor of the Watonga Cheese Factory, this festival includes such "cheesy" events as a mouse walk, rat race, food contests (one ingredient must be Watonga Cheese), and of course, cheese tasting. Other activities include a parade, flea market, Made-in-Oklahoma exhibits, and arts and crafts. Winning recipes from the food contests are published annually in the

Watonga Cheese Festival Recipe Book which is made available at the festival.

In the Vicinity

Rattlesnake Roundup and Festival

Held the first weekend in May near Okeene. Call (405) 822-3005 for more information. Okeene is located approximately twenty-two miles north of Watonga on Highway 8. NOTE: Other rattlesnake festivals are held in **Waynoka** *during the first weekend after Easter, (405) 824-4741; in* **Waurika** *in March, (405) 228-2147; in* **Mangum** *in April, (405) 782-2434; and in* **Apache** *in April, (405) 588-3257.*

Quite possibly the most memorable type of festival you will ever experience, the Okeene Rattlesnake Roundup and Festival is a celebration like no other. During the festival, the tiny town of Okeene becomes the Rattlesnake Capital of the World. The roundup itself takes place outside of Okeene. The snakes are then brought into Okeene where they are sold for their meat and skin. A prize is awarded to the person capturing the largest rattler.

Okeene celebrates the rattlesnake in everything from folk art to food. This is your chance to try rattlesnake steak and decide for yourself if it really tastes like chicken. For a $1 donation, you can watch snake handlers in the "Snake Pit," or see the snakes being skinned and cleaned. Handlers welcome questions and are very knowledgeable about this fascinating reptile. Not all of the snakes are killed. To maintain a healthy snake population, many are returned unharmed to their natural habitat.

Woodward

Throughout its history, Woodward has survived and thrived against the odds. Whether it has been the many droughts through the years, the devastating 1947 tornado, or the oil boom and bust in the 1980s, Woodward residents have maintained their "can-do" attitude and have worked to make their town a thriving retail center for Northwest Oklahoma. It has been reported that Woodward has the friendliest people in the state. Besides good, old-fashioned hospitality, visitors will experience numerous recreational, cultural and historic attractions and events that showcase Woodward's independent spirit and desire for excellence, and the city's distinctive past.

Woodward is located 140 miles northwest of Oklahoma City on Highway 270, and 207 miles west of Tulsa on Highway 412. Woodward Chamber of Commerce (405) 256-7411 or (800) 364-5352. 🛈

Boiling Springs State Park

Northeast of Woodward, (405) 256-7664. For cabin reservations call (800) 654-8240. Travel north from Woodward on Highway 34. After crossing the North Canadian River, turn east on Highway 34C and travel four miles to the park entrance. 🅂

Long before white settlement, Native Americans came to the Boiling Springs area for its reliable source of clear spring water. Later, cowboys and then settlers would also discover this oasis on the plains. Built by the Civilian Conservation Corps (CCC) in the 1930s, Boiling Springs is one of Oklahoma's oldest state parks.

Don't come to Boiling Springs today expecting to be dazzled by the natural springs. Over the years, ground water depletion from irrigation has robbed the park's namesake of its famous bubbles. During dry seasons, nary a trickle is left.

Fortunately, there's much more to this park than the springs. Camping, swimming, and picnicking are just a few of the activities to be enjoyed here. Golfing is popular at the Boiling Springs Golf Course next to the park, and wildlife-watching is often a success as deer and turkey are prevalent throughout the area.

The pool and its pool house, a beautiful legacy of CCC craftsmanship, are two of the oldest structures in the park. The swimming pool is open from Memorial Day through Labor Day. Check with the park office for hours and rates.

Four one-bedroom **cabins** are available. Each sleeps up to four people and includes a living area with fireplace, furnished kitchen and televisions, but no telephones. RV sites with electric and water hookups are available, with some also having sewer hookups. Unimproved tent sites are also available. Each campground area has its own shower facility.

Plains Indians and Pioneers Museum

2009 Williams Avenue, (405) 256-6136. Located on Highway 270 (Williams Avenue) one mile south of the intersections of Highways 15/412 and Highways 34, 3,183, and 270. Admission is free; donations are appreciated. Handicapped accessible. ★

Nationally-recognized for its outstanding exhibits and known statewide as the best small history museum in Oklahoma, the Plains Indians and Pioneers Museum is a must for any visitor in the area. Visitors first notice the beautiful murals by noted artists Paul Laune and Pat "Kemoha" Patterson depicting scenes of the area's history. Two award-winning exhibits give an overview of the history of the Northwest Oklahoma area, from the Plains Indians to the early development of Woodward. Historic photos and numerous quotes make the history become more personal and real. The economic impact and development of agriculture is explored in the Agriculture Building located on the museum grounds.

Of special interest to visitors are the outstanding photo displays of the 1947 Woodward tornado and the Temple Houston exhibit. Youngest son of Sam Houston, Temple was a flamboyant and brilliant attorney during Woodward's early years. Although only on display during May of each year, the Federal Eagle Quilt has been noted as one of the best quilts ever made in the United States. Like many prized possessions, the quilt was brought to the area by early settlers in the area.

With its changing exhibits and monthly art shows featuring local talent, contests, and nationally-known artists, this museum offers something new and different for each visitor. Call ahead for information on special programs such as lectures on historical topics or artist receptions. The museum also hosts a special afternoon of activity for families each year on Mother's Day.

Woodward Arts Theater

818 Main Street, (405) 256-7120. From the intersection of Highways 270 and 15/412, travel two blocks north to Main Street. The theater is located just east of this corner. Box office hours are Monday-Friday 9-5, and ticket prices vary by performance.

Considered a cultural "gem" for the Woodward area, the Woodward Arts Theater was built in 1929. At the time, the theater's primary investor, a well-known rancher, thought that "talkies" were a fad and insisted the elaborately-appointed building be equipped for live theater, particularly vaudeville. Woodward residents are grateful for his mistaken belief because, after a long run as a popular movie theater, the building has been returned to its splendor and serves as the area's premier performing arts center. Residents and visitors enjoy a full repertoire of performances at the theater, from plays and musicals by local performers, to concerts by noted orchestras and groups such as Riders in the Sky.

Call ahead for a schedule and to get tickets. Some performances sell out quickly. Next door to the theater is the **Cultural Center** that serves as a place for visual art shows and art classes. Handicapped accessible.

Golf

Boiling Springs Golf Course

(405) 256-1206. Located at the entrance to Boiling Springs State Park; for directions see the park's information above. This "extra-value" course has green fees of $16 for all-day-play from Friday-Sunday and $11 from Monday-Thursday. Senior fees are $8 Monday-Friday. Cart fees are $16 for eighteen holes, $8 for nine holes.

Play eighteen holes of challenging golf surrounded by the beauty of native woods and plenty of wildlife at Boiling Springs Golf Course. This Don Sechrest-designed course is consistently rated as one of the top Oklahoma public courses. A wooded native rough, rolling bermuda fairways, varying elevations between tees and greens, sand, and water add to the fun and challenge. The signature holes are numbers nine and seventeen; at hole seventeen, golfers enjoy a spectacular panoramic view.

The course has par 71, with a length of 6511 yards, a USGA rating of 69.6, and a slope rating of 117. Call ahead for weekend tee times at least one week in advance, and call ahead for weekday play, especially to determine if the course is closed due to a tournament. Closed every Monday until noon. A golf pro shop and snack bar are available.

Dining

Rib Ranch *$, $$*

2424 Williams Avenue, (405) 256-6081, located on Highway 270 (Williams Avenue), just south of the Plains Indians and Pioneers Museum. Open Tuesday-Friday 11-2, 5-9; Saturday 11-9; Sunday 11-7. Closed Monday. Handicapped accessible.

A tradition in Woodward since the 1960s, the Rib Ranch has survived a succession of owners with its basic, well-known, and well-loved recipes for barbecue and all the fixings. Most long-time patrons recommend the ribs and beef and beans as their favorites. The log cabin exterior and antique-heirloom interior add to the western flavor of the Rib Ranch.

Wagg's Bar-B-Q *$, $$*

7th and Oklahoma Avenue; (405) 256-6721. Located one block east of the intersection of Highways 270 and 412. Open Monday-Thursday 11-8:30; Friday and Saturday 11-9. Smoking and nonsmoking rooms available. Handicapped accessible. 🖮

Unique decor and mouth-watering food along with a good dose of fun are the prescription at this establishment. Formerly Workman's Machine Shop and Garage, the building itself provides an interesting atmosphere at this warehouse-style restaurant. Car parts dangle from the ceiling, a vintage car serves as the pickle bar, antique signs add to the ambiance, and domino tables provide stable furniture for the heavy meals that are served. Traditional barbecue such as ribs, chicken, brisket, sausage, and outstanding steaks (cooked like those at the Oasis Steakhouse, a former Woodward landmark) are complemented by fried onions and the usual barbecue sidekicks such as cole slaw and beans.

Shopping

Downtown Shopping and Eateries

The Woodward Main Street Project (405-254-8521) has dramatically changed the face of this important economic area. The oil bust of the 1970s and '80s left parts of Main Street empty. Now visitors enjoy a return of numerous thriving gift and specialty shops, men's, women's and children's clothing and shoe stores, mini-malls carved from older buildings, and antique and craft malls. A stroll down Main Street between 7th and 12th Streets is a nostalgic and pleasant experience, and a sweet one as well if you stop by the local candy store.

Enjoy an old-fashioned burger and the latest town news at the **Polly Anna Cafe** at 902 Main Avenue, (405) 256-9037, a tradition in Woodward since 1928. The cafe is open Monday-Friday 6-4 and 5-8, and Saturday 6-2. Or for lunch, **Chicken Roscoe's** is a local favorite and features outstanding food and a friendly waitstaff (be sure to say hello to Roscoe). It is located at 11th and Main and is open Tuesday-Saturday 11-2. If a cookie for dessert sounds good, try **Mary's Sweet Shop**, located in the same mini-mall. The **Mercantile** at 809 Main (open Monday-Saturday 10-6) has been renovated into a mini-mall with mostly small clothing shops; it also includes a small restaurant where a gourmet chef serves savory chicken salad, spinach salad, and daily specials.

Accommodations

Adams Farms Bed and Breakfast

South of Woodward near Sharon, (405) 866-3344. $65 per couple. Not handicapped accessible.

Good hospitality, quaint quarters, and peaceful quiet are what you'll find at this log cabin B&B. Formerly a small grocery store, the cabin is decorated with antiques. Interestingly enough, the walk-in meat cooler is now the bathroom, and an old outhouse door opens to a closet. This comfortable place sleeps up to six, and children are welcome. In the morning, a full breakfast, including home-baked bread, is brought to your cabin. An added attraction is the stocked fishing pond.

Anna Augusta Inn

2612 Lakeview Drive, (405) 254-5400 or (800) 864-8320. From Highway 270 going north into Woodward, turn east at the first traffic light (Downs Avenue). Turn left at Lakeview Drive and the Inn is the first house on the right. Rates range from $54.95 to $84.95 for regular rooms, and are $150 for a two-bedroom family suite. Children are welcome here. Not handicapped accessible.

The Anna Augusta house was originally built in 1904 as a showcase for a prominent Woodward lumberyard owner and was located on Oklahoma Avenue (Highway 412). In the 1930s, it was a men's boarding house. Moved to its present location across from the city's Crystal Beach Park, the inn provides Victorian-style rooms and excellent hospitality thanks to innkeeper Joyce Spurgeon. Three of the rooms have claw-foot tubs and sinks in the rooms, with the commode down the hall. In addition, there are three suites with full baths, two of which would be ideal for families or long-term stays. The innkeeper serves hot breakfasts of the guest's choice in the Dining Room. Romantic dinners for two, or dinners and lunches for parties of eight or more may be arranged through Joyce.

The location of the Inn allows guests the benefits of golfing (nine holes), fishing, walking, picnicking, swimming, and more at the city park across the street. The innkeeper will also arrange a golf package weekend for those interested in the beautiful Boiling Springs Golf Course.

Three Sisters Inn

609 S. Laird, Mooreland, (405) 994-6003. From Woodward, travel approximately ten miles east on Highway 412 to Mooreland. At South Laird, turn south. House is the second on the right. Scheduled to open in June, 1997. Rates are $45-59. Children are welcome; in fact they may be greeted by the innkeeper's own children, the "three sisters." No smoking allowed. Not yet handicapped accessible.

Listed on the National Register of Historic Places, this B&B was built in 1930 as the home of the superintendent of the U.S. Department of Agriculture Woodward Research Station. Named the Chilcott House, it was recently moved to the nearby small town of Mooreland by innkeeper Tammy Smith and her husband. The inn features four rooms, each with a full bath and Colonial Revival decor. An overnight stay features a full breakfast; guests will also enjoy the gift shop. Be sure to ask about their special arrangements if interested in the excellent hunting located nearby.

Events

Blue Grass Festival

Third weekend in May at Boiling Springs State Park. (405) 256-3409. Admission ranges from $6 for Friday only to $12 for both days ($8 in advance). Handicapped accessible.

Started in 1991, this small, friendly festival is sponsored by the Northwest Oklahoma Blue Grass Association and the Arts Council of Oklahoma. Several major blue grass groups play each year, but impromptu "shade tree picking" adds even more musical entertainment. Bring your own seating material. This event will be cancelled in case of rain.

Woodward Elks Rodeo

Held in mid-July at the Woodward County Fairgrounds grandstand in Crystal Beach Park. Call (405) 256-3549 for information; (405) 256-8202 for tickets. Admission is $7-12.

Started in 1929, this event just keeps getting bigger and better. Activities associated with the rodeo include a hamburger feed on Wednesday, "best ball" golf tournament on Friday, an old-fashioned, Main Street rodeo parade on Saturday, and of course, the "toughest of 'em all!" rodeo each night from Wednesday through Saturday. This is a rodeo tradition you will really enjoy!

Crystal Christmas

Held from the Friday after Thanksgiving through December 31st at Crystal Beach Park. From the intersection of Highway 270 and Downs Avenue, turn east and travel a to First Street. Turn north and the park entrance will be on the east side of the road. For more information call (405) 256-7411. Open Sunday-Thursday 6-10 p.m., and Friday-Saturday 6-11 p.m. Free, but donations appreciated.

Crystal Christmas was a big hit for the Woodward area during its inaugural year of 1996. Over 20,000 cars full of interested spectators were treated to beautiful Christmas-themed lighting displays. Area organizations and businesses sponsor the various displays. Among the most popular are the thirty-foot Wise Men and a Stagecoach Santa. Visitors are encouraged to walk the grounds and to enjoy the lighted bridge across Crystal Beach Lake. Family nights are held on Thursdays, complete with visits from Santa, prizes and giveaways, and entertainment. Bring the family to enjoy over two million twinkling lights and much good cheer at Crystal Christmas.

In the Vicinity

Dewey County Great Western Cattle Drive

Held on the first Thursday, Friday and Saturday of June each year. Organized by the South Canadian River Cattle Company, the drive is always held in Dewey County. Call (405) 995-3120 for more information. Adults $145, children under age 17 $85. Receive a $25 discount for paying early, and a 10% discount for groups of ten or more.

Approximately 200 cattle are driven eight to ten miles each day of the "drive." Participants can help drive the cattle, or simply ride along and enjoy the scenery. If you don't have a horse, you can still enjoy the adventure and camaraderie of the drive by riding in a wagon. Either way, come prepared to camp out at night. Prices include two and a half full days on the trail, three meals a day, and nightly entertainment. The event raises money for scholarships and historic renovation in Dewey County.

Fort Supply-Cooper Wildlife Area

Travel north of Woodward on Northwest Highway 270 (412/3) approximately twelve miles. The refuge's main entrance is located on the east side of the road, across from the Ft. Supply Lake entrance. (405) 256-7119 or 766-2162.

Owned by the Oklahoma Department of Wildlife Conservation since 1992, this 16,000-acre ranch provides seasonal hunting opportunities. Hunters should check the information provided by the Oklahoma Department of Wildlife Conservation for any controlled hunting regulations and deadlines and to determine any other special regulations at these public hunting areas. The area is most noted for its quail, deer and turkey hunting, and it is located close to the 5000 acres of public hunting near Fort Supply Lake.

Proven by archeological finds to be an ancient hunting ground, the land also has a few points of interest for hikers, including the confluence of the Beaver River and Wolf Creek and the headwaters of the North Canadian River, and the probable original site of Camp Supply, established in 1868. Call to get directions to the closest entrance to these sites and to determine about hunting seasons; hiking is obviously not advised during hunting season. Also ask about the Custer's Springs area where George Custer supposedly claimed the fresh water source for the troops at Camp Supply.

The **Oklahoma Department of Wildlife Conservation** is the best source for those interested in hunting, fishing, and non-game wilderness areas. Call (405) 521-3853 to inquire about low-cost publications on public hunting and fishing, Oklahoma's biodiversity, observing wildlife, and much more.

Fort Supply Military Park

Located approximately thirteen miles northwest of Woodward on Highway 3/270. As you enter the town, look for the "old fort" sign and turn north, or enter the main entrance of the correctional facility and follow the signs. (405) 766-3767.

Explore a developing history park and discover a fascinating history of the U.S. Cavalry, the Plains Indians, famous and infamous military men, and early life on the plains. The few original buildings that remain on the fort's grounds tell an interesting story. Visitors will enjoy a replica of the original stockade made from cedar logs and a visit to the in-progress restoration of the Guard House and four other buildings. The "kiosk" exhibit is very informative; it shows a map of the area and features many flyers that explain the fort's history. If at all possible, stop by the Visitor Center (a small white house), view the pictorial displays, and get any questions answered by the park's curator.

Although the fort was closed in 1894, it was later converted to Oklahoma's first mental hospital. The grounds and most of its buildings now house the William S. Key Correctional Facility for nonviolent offenders. Inmates have contributed greatly to the restoration of the old fort which is a joint project of the Correctional Facility and the Oklahoma Historical Society.

Plan to spend about thirty minutes to an hour, depending on your interest. The best time to visit the fort is during its annual living history **Cavalry Days** event held the first weekend in October on Saturday. Call ahead to verify date and time of event.

Located just south of the old fort is **Ft. Supply Lake and Dam**. Picnicking, boating, and hunting at the nearby wildlife areas are popular activities at this Corps of Engineers project lake. Partially handicapped accessible.

Freedom: Alabaster Caverns State Park

(405) 621-3381. Located about thirty miles northeast of Woodward. From Woodward, go east on Highway 412 approximately ten miles to the junction of Highway 50. Go north on Highway 50 about eighteen miles to the turn off (Highway 50A) to Alabaster Caverns. Tours begin on the hour. Rates are adults $5, children ages 6-17 $2.50, ages five and under are free. Open from May 1-September 30, 8-5, October 1-April 30, 8-4.

Where do you go in Oklahoma when it's a hundred degrees in the shade? Head for Alabaster Caverns, where cave temperatures remain a blissfully-constant 50 degrees year round. Formed millions of years ago by an underground stream carving its way through massive gypsum deposits, Alabaster Caverns offers visitors a chance to see many different minerals and crystals, including rare black alabaster and isinglass.

Five species of bats may be found in Alabaster Caverns. Though often vilified in popular culture, the bat is a fascinating and beneficial animal. Each night these bats will eat approximately forty percent of their body weight in insects! As you wait to begin your tour of the cave, look carefully around you—especially in the small crevices of the cave's ceiling. If you're lucky, you might see a sleeping bat. Give thanks to the little creature as you notice there's not a mosquito in sight.

The world's largest gypsum cave open to the public, Alabaster Caverns is almost half a mile long. Tours last from forty-five minutes to an hour. Don't let the outside temperatures fool you—you'll want a light jacket or sweater inside the cave. Also, because smooth rock surfaces are frequently damp and slippery, you need shoes with good traction. For the more experienced "spelunker," there are five undeveloped caves in the park which may be explored by permit only. These caves are open from March to September.

Alabaster Caverns State Park is also a great place for **hiking**. Several trails wind through Cedar Canyon, which was once a cave, now long collapsed. Enjoy the many species of birds and wildlife in the area as you walk through the craggy gypsum canyon. Interpretive brochures (available at the park office) will help you identify many of the natural features along the way.

Primitive and semi-modern camp sites are available. All have picnic tables and cooking grills. Other facilities include picnic areas and a **swimming pool** (open Wednesday-Sunday during the summer for a low fee).

Selman Bat Cave/Bat Viewing

Located in Woodward County. This site is open during a few July and August weekends to a limited number of viewers, and you must have preregistered with the Oklahoma Department of Wildlife Conservation to attend. Request a registration form be sent to you by calling (405) 521-4616. Upon receiving your registration, they will mail a confirmation letter which will explain the *details of the bat viewing. Tickets are $4 per person. Handicapped accessible.*

Imagine viewing a cloud of about one million small bats rising from the caves to seek their daily diet of insects, then imagine the benefit to local landowners as these bats consume 1.25 tons of insects every night they stay in the area. Although participants will only see them exiting the caves, plenty of information about the bats and their habits will be discussed by the Wildlife Department guides during the viewing.

This cave is for mother and baby bats only. Most all of the approximately 500,000 migratory Mexican Free-Tail Bats who arrive in May or June every year have one "pup." By early July, the young are ready to feed themselves. Viewers to the first viewing weekend may notice the babies' rather clumsy attempts at flying. The bats will begin leaving the area by mid- to late-August.

All ages will enjoy the bat viewing, but keep in mind that being as quiet and unnoticeable as possible is important so as to not disturb the bat colony. Crying or rambunctious children may have to spend time at the parking area. Flashlights, pets, or lawn chairs will not be allowed, but bring binoculars and video and still cameras (without flash). The walk from the parking area to the viewing sites is not difficult. The bat viewing will take place despite the weather conditions.

Rosston: Lotspeich Cattle Company

Route 1, Box 117, Rosston, OK 73855, (405) 533-4718. Located near Laverne, approximately 45 miles northwest of Woodward. Call for rates and directions to the ranch. Discounts available if you provide your own horse.

If you enjoy horses and the wide open countryside, and you're looking for a decidedly different vacation experience, consider the Lotspeich Cattle Co. This is no dude ranch; R.A and Rosalee Lotspeich run a working cattle and wheat operation of over 10,000 acres. Guests will experience the life of a real ranch hand at this guest ranch. Depending on the season, guests can drive cattle, brand, vaccinate, or dehorn calves. Some guests may even try their hand at baling hay or driving a tractor. Each day brings new challenges and new chores that need to be done. Although the typical guest enjoys the hard work, you can always languish in the swimming pool if you need a break.

While R.A. coordinates the day's work and supervises the guests, Rosalee fixes all the meals, which are usually served in the Lotspeich's own dining room. R.A. and Rosalee are excellent hosts, making their guests feel instantly at home.

The bunkhouse used to be the home of one of the ranch hands. Don't expect cutesy Hollywood western decor—there are no split railings here. However, the house is comfortable with bedrooms, living room, dining area, bathroom, and kitchen. This ranch is not recommended for families with young children.

The Lotspeich Ranch offers guided quail and pheasant hunting trips in season. Bird dogs are provided and birds are cleaned and bagged. All hunters must have a valid hunting license, and a deposit is required to confirm reservations. Contact Troy Lotspeich for information at (405) 921-5813, Route 1, Box 67, Rosston, OK 73855.

Shattuck

Originally called Norice but renamed Shattuck for a railroad official, this small town was once known as the Broomcorn Capitol of the World and boasted several other industries., including a well-known hospital begun by Dr. O.C. Newman in 1907. Many Russian-Germans settled the area to farm. Shattuck residents honor their heritage with a new Windmill Museum and a community-wide Heritage Festival in October.

Shattuck is located 29 miles south and west of Woodward on Highway 15. Shattuck Chamber of Commerce (405) 938-2818.

Jim Powers Junk Art

Located at the intersection of Highways 15 and 46 in Gage, a small community between Shattuck and Woodward. Call ahead for hours; the museum is most likely to be open in the afternoons from mid-May to mid-September. Free. Handicapped accessible.

Though folk art is the focus here, Jim Powers himself is a big attraction. This is a man who loves life, loves people, and loves expressing himself through art. It's more than the hobby it started out to be. After having run a salvage yard for many years, Jim had quite a collection of metal parts and pieces. With his imagination and welding skills, he began turning them into animals such as a dinosaur from tire rims and a bear from combine chains. Ripley's Museum got wind of his talent and began buying pieces from him. He also dabbles in abstract art. Jim's own favorite piece is a ton of iron balanced so that it appears to be floating in midair and can be moved with the touch of a finger. Don't miss this fun side trip!

Shattuck Windmill Museum and Park

Located near downtown Shattuck and the intersection of Highways 15 and 283. (405) 938-2818. Open anytime. Free; donations are appreciated.

An invention patented in 1854 by Daniel Halladay, the windmill made a significant contribution to the settlement of the Great Plains. With this invention, wells could be dug to provide essential water to pioneers and homesteaders. Windmills continue to play an important role in the agricultural development of rural Oklahoma and other areas. To honor the contribution of this important invention, the small community of Shattuck displays twenty-eight windmills of varying sizes, styles, age, and rarity. From wooden-wheeled models to early steel models, the windmills each have their own "story" to tell.

Also included on the grounds of the Windmill Museum is a reconstructed half-dugout sod house. The soddy is furnished as it might have been in 1904. Its hard to imagine that nine people once lived in this house!

Heritage Festival

Held the first weekend in October in and near downtown Shattuck. Call the Shattuck Chamber of Commerce at (405) 938-2818 for more information.

From Native Americans to railroad and agricultural influences, visitors will understand the history and culture of the Shattuck area as they enjoy the many activities offered during this two-day festival. Living history displays and exhibits such as Native American dancers and camps, trapper camps, and buffalo hunters add to the weekend event. Visitors are invited to participate in hands-on activities such as cow milking and making butter. Because of the influence of the German-Russians who settled Shattuck, special German foods are sold, including case noodles and butterballs. A popular event during the weekend is the **Cowboy Camp**. Held on Friday night, families join storytellers around the campfire at the Windmill Museum's dugout for entertaining tales of area folk lore.

Waynoka: Little Sahara State Park

Located about 40 miles east and north of Woodward, and about 70 miles west of Enid. From Woodward, travel east on Highway 412 to the intersection of Highway 281. From this intersection travel north about ten miles. The park is on the west side of the road. (405) 824-1471. For those providing their own ORV, dune entrance fees are $5 per day per vehicle or $10 per vehicle for a three-day pass.

This unique state park is aptly named, as huge sand dunes cover most of its 1,867 acres. Created when the Cimarron River flowed across this area some 11,000 years ago, the dunes range from 25 to 75 feet in height. Early explorers called the dunes "walking hills" because of their ever-changing formations. Today, however, the dunes are no place to be caught on foot!

Off-road vehicle (ORV) enthusiasts have found their Mecca in Little Sahara State Park. This is a great place for dirt bikes, four-wheelers, and dune buggies. The dune area is open 24 hours a day, 365 days per year for off-road vehicle operation.

For those who do not own their own ORV, the park offers dune rides in a **six-passenger dune buggy**. The ride lasts about 45 minutes and takes visitors to areas of the park accessible only by ORV. Although larger than the typical two-seat dune buggy, the park's multi-passenger vehicle still gives riders the excitement and feel of the dune buggy experience. Dune rides are available Monday-Friday, 9-5, Saturday-Sunday, 8 a.m.-10 p.m. Dune buggy rides are $6 for adults, $4 for children, and $3 for senior citizens. Children must be big enough to wear a seat belt.

Visitors who bring their own ORV should be prepared to meet park safety requirements. Check with the park in advance to make sure all safety requirements are met. During the summer, major holiday weekends are extremely busy.

The campgrounds at Little Sahara are all close to the highway, so if you're looking for an isolated wilderness area, consider staying somewhere else. However, if you're looking for a convenient headquarters for dune buggy adventures—a place to roast marshmallows and share the camaraderie of other off-road enthusiasts—the park offers primitive and semi-modern RV camp sites. Showers, picnic areas, and group campgrounds are available.

Northeast Oklahoma

Bartlesville

The small, crude settlement that grew up around the grist mill on the Caney River is now a thriving, prosperous town. Named for Jake Bartles who bought the grist mill in 1875, Bartlesville is one of Oklahoma's most attractive cities. Oil was discovered here in 1897, and petroleum and oil-related industries have been an important part of the community ever since. Famous names such as Frank Phillips, H.C. Price, and J. Paul Getty have left their mark on the town. Successful corporations such as Phillips 66 contribute to a healthy business climate. Beautiful community facilities promote the arts, and a number of cultural and historic attractions are found nearby. Bartlesville is a rewarding place to study the past, enjoy the present, and explore the future!
Bartlesville is located 161 miles northwest of Oklahoma City and 47 miles north of Tulsa on Highway 75. Bartlesville Chamber of Commerce (918) 336-8708. 🛈

Frank Phillips Mansion

1107 Cherokee Avenue, (918) 336-2491. Take Highway 75 north to Adams Boulevard. Turn west on Adams and follow it to Cherokee Avenue. Turn south; the Phillips' home is located between 11th and 12th Streets on the west side of the road. Wednesday-Saturday 10-5, Sunday 1-5. Closed Monday, Tuesday and major holidays. Ring bell at the front door for admittance. Free; donations appreciated. Maintained and operated by the Oklahoma Historical Society, the museum has no public restrooms, and it is not handicapped accessible.

Frank Phillips, founder of Phillips Petroleum Company, is one of Oklahoma's most colorful personalities. Here at the Greek Revival-style mansion, visitors can see how this famous man lived. Built in 1909, the 26-room home has a pink brick exterior and white wooden columns. Inside, the home has been preserved in the style of the 1930s, when extensive remodeling was done. Guests delight in viewing the tasteful appointments: the mahogany staircase, brocaded walls, crystal chandeliers, and gold and marble baths. The professional barber chair in Frank's quarters says a great deal about the barber-turned-banker-turned-oilman who built this home. Be sure to ask about the secret "hidey-holes" in the library, the custom built elevator which

Frank Phillips mansion.

was installed in 1947, or inquire about Frank Phillips Japanese butler, Henry Eignaga, a steadfast personal employee who secretly amassed a fortune in the stock market.

On the first floor, a twenty-five minute video about Frank Phillips and Phillips 66 is available for viewing. The self-guided tour takes another twenty-five minutes. If you prefer a guided tour, call one week in advance.Look for an interpretive exhibit scheduled to open in the fall of 1997 that tells the personal life story of Frank and Jane Phillips. The exhibit and a museum shop will be located in the mansion's luxurious six-car garage.

Johnstone Park

Hensley Boulevard and Highway 123 North. From Highway 75 take Hensley (Tuxedo) west to Highway 123 (Cherokee). Turn northwest onto Highway 123 (do not go over the bridge). Johnstone Park is open all year. The Kiddie Park is open summer evenings 7-9:30. Most of the fourteen rides are twenty-five cents each.

Johnstone Park pays tribute to one of the most significant events in Oklahoma's history—the drilling of the first commercial oil well. In 1897, on the banks of the Caney River, drillers struck oil on Nellie Johnstone's land. Once considered useless because of the black, scummy river that ran through it, this land now contains a replica of that first oil well, along with two other historic attractions, picnic grounds, and children's playgrounds.

Originally located on the Mullendore Ranch, a restored train depot has been moved here for public viewing. Displayed nearby is a Santa Fe train engine, donated to the City of Bartlesville by the Santa Fe Railroad in 1946. However, the highlight of the park is the Kiddie Park; here parents can let even little ones run free. Armed with a dollar's worth of tickets, youngsters have the time of their lives running from one small amusement ride to another. A Ferris wheel, airplanes, a carousel, bumper cars, and more are all available to ride for only a quarter! Plan to drive through the park's **Fantasyland Forest** in December when the entire park is ablaze with Christmas light. Johnstone Park is a treat for children and adults alike!

Keepsake Candles

Located 2 miles west of Bartlesville, (918) 336-0351. Go west on Frank Phillips Boulevard (Highway 60) to the small blue and white Keepsake Candle sign. Turn right and follow the road until it ends, then turn right. Monday-Friday 9-5:30, Saturday 10-5, Sunday 1-5. Extended hours between Thanksgiving and Christmas. Closed major holidays. The fifteen-minute tours are held Monday-Friday at 11,1 and 3. Free. ★

More than twenty-five years have passed since Alice Ririe's mother-in-law brought home a candle shaped like an old-fashioned toothpick holder; thousands of candles have been made since Alice Ririe first decided to try to create something similar. What has evolved since then is the Keepsake Candle Factory.

Housed in what was once a recreation building for an Air Force radar station, Keepsake reproduces "antiques in wax" with unique methods of wax blending and mold making. Visitors can tour the factory to see candles created and then browse through the display rooms to purchase a special souvenir or gift.

The best time of day to visit this unique candle factory is in the early morning or after 2 p.m. Special events include **Fall Harvest**, the last weekend in September, when special autumn candle groupings are displayed. A **Christmas Open House** is held the first weekend in November. Call ahead for group tours. This is one of Bartlesville's highlights—don't miss it!

Keepsake Candles.

Prairie Song

Located near Dewey, just north of Bartlesville, (918) 534-2662. Going north on Highway 75 travel through Bartlesville to Durham Road. Turn right and go east four miles. Prairie Song is on the right. Prairie Song is open to the general public for tours on Monday, Wednesday and Friday at 10 a.m. and 2 p.m. It's best to call ahead for reservations. Adults $6, children under eight free. Group events are priced on a per event rate. Call ahead for group arrangements and pricing.

Standing quietly in the middle of an Oklahoma wheat field, visitors can close their eyes and listen to the sounds of the prairie—a Prairie Song. On the Moore Ranch where co-owner Marilyn Tate was raised, the song of the prairie has taken on a new melody. Here, twenty-seven buildings depict life on the frontier of the 19th century. There's the Wildwood Chapel, the main house, a one-room school, a saloon complete with bordello, a barn, blacksmith's shop, trading post, and several outhouses. Built on land that has been in Mrs. Tate's family since 1894, the village has been hand-crafted by Mr. Tate and a few helpers. Each building is enhanced with period furniture and artifacts so that visitors get a "feel" for life in the 1800s.

Ken and Marilyn Tate started the village in the mid-1980s as a weekend retreat; ten years later, the village is still growing. They have hosted every type of activity, from group tours and church retreats to weddings and family reunions. Arrangements must be made in advance and can include a wide range of activities: tours, church services, saloon shows, and catered meals.

Price Tower and Bartlesville Museum

(918) 661-7471. Located between Fifth and Sixth Streets on Dewey Avenue. Open on Thursdays from 1-3 p.m., with public tours conducted at 1:15, 1:45 and 2:15. Call the Landmark Preservation Council at (918) 333-8558 for group tours which are conducted by appointment only. Donations appreciated.

Once called "The Tree that Escaped the Crowded Forest," the Price Tower is one of only two skyscrapers designed by Frank Lloyd Wright. An architectural wonder, the nineteen-story building with gold-tinted glass and copper enhancements looks different from every viewing direction and light condition. Originally designed for construction in New York or Chicago, the structure was built in Bartlesville as offices for the H.C. Price Company. Opened in 1956, Wright himself compared the structure to a tree: "A composite shaft of concrete rises through the floors, each slab extended from the shaft as a cantilever slab. . .similar to the branch of a tree from its trunk."

Frank Lloyd Wright's Price Tower.

The design of the building is based on a diamond module of thirty and sixty degree triangles. Some furniture, also designed by Wright, is displayed inside. Price Tower was placed on the National Register of Historic Places in 1974 and received the prestigious American Institute of Architecture "Twenty-Five Year" award in 1983.

Even if you don't get a tour, be sure to visit the **Bartlesville Museum** (918-336-4949) that is located in Price Tower. Permanent exhibits include "Bartlesville, the City that Oil Built," an architectural history of the city; "Shin'enKan Remembered" which includes photographs by Joe Price, owner of the famed Bruce Goff-designed home that was destroyed by fire in 1996; and "The Price Tower." Temporary exhibits change every one to two months. The museum is open Tuesday-Saturday 10-3, Sunday 12:30-3, closed Monday and holidays. Admission is free; donations are appreciated.

Woolaroc

Southwest of Bartlesville, (918) 336-0307 or (800) 636-0307. From Tulsa take U.S. 75 to Highway 20 and go west. Continue into Skiatook. At the light in Skiatook, turn north onto Highway 11. Enjoy this scenic twenty-mile drive to Highway 123. Turn northeast onto 123 and follow the signs to Woolaroc. From Bartlesville, turn off U.S. 75 to Frank Phillips Boulevard, and turn west to Highway 123. Turn south on 123 and travel approximately twelve miles to Woolaroc. June-August, daily 10-5; September-May, Tuesday-Sunday 10-5. Closed Thanksgiving and Christmas. Adult $4, Seniors $3, and children 16 and under free. Charges vary for special events. Handicapped accessible. ★

Here in the heart of the Osage Hills are 3500 acres of WOOds, LAkes, and ROCks which inspired the name Woolaroc. This land, which originally served as a place of retreat and entertainment for Phillips Petroleum founder Frank Phillips, now serves as a wildlife preserve for herds of American bison, longhorn cattle, elk, deer, and other native wildlife. Take your time driving through the **Wildlife Preserve**. If cars behind you are in a hurry, pull over on one of the paved turnouts and let them pass, or circle around the museum and begin your drive again. While in the preserve, you must remain in your vehicle; despite all appearances, the animals are wild and therefore unpredictable.

Woolaroc Museum relates the story of man's cultural development in the New World, with an emphasis on prehistoric civilizations, the first white pioneers, and cowboy and outlaw life.

The Lodge, where Frank and Jane entertained America's politicians, businessmen, and celebrities, is also open to visitors.

Stop at the **Y-Indian Guide Center** where Native American culture is highlighted with an audiovisual presentation "Arrows Skyward." If the outdoors is beckoning you, traipse the nature trail or visit the summertime petting zoo. Concessions, including barbecue buffalo burgers are available at the Buffalo Haunt, or pack a lunch to be eaten at the picnic grounds just inside the ground's entrance.

A number of special events are held throughout the year; call the office for specific dates. The last weekend of each June Woolaroc hosts **Kidfest**, a three-day event celebrating children. Special entertainment, art, nature exhibits, and games introduce children to the nature preserve and museum. **Family Day**, a more craft-oriented event, is usually held in August and features free admission. If you visit during the summer, be sure to travel out the North Road for a visit with Woolaroc's resident mountain man—a real treat for living history buffs, or attend the newest of Woolaroc's special events,

Woolaroc entrance.

the revival of **Cow Thieves' and Outlaw's Reunion** held in the fall. There's so much to see and do in this remarkable setting.....no wonder Frank loved it so much!

Golf

Adams Municipal Golf Course

6001 E. Tuxedo, (918) 337-5313. Open daily including holidays, sunrise to dark. Green fees are $15, cart rental is $16. Twenty-four hour notice is recommended to guarantee tee times.

Built in 1963, this well-kept, attractive course draws golfers from the local community and surrounding areas. The eighteen-hole, par 72 course has a total yardage of 6800, a USGA rating of 72, and slope of 119. Amenities include a driving range and snacks and beverages.

Dining

Dink's Pit Bar-B-Que $

2929 S.E. Frank Phillips Boulevard, (918) 335-0606. From Highway 75, turn west onto Frank Phillips Boulevard (Highway 60). Dinks is on the left, less than a mile down the road. Sunday-Thursday, 11-8, Friday-Saturday, 11-9 Handicapped accessible.

This popular restaurant has been serving great barbecue in Bartlesville since 1981. Here locals fill up on ribs, sausage, bologna, and beef, accompanied by all the regular side dishes.

Murphy's Steak House $$

1625 S.W. Frank Phillips, (918) 336-4789. From Highway 75, turn west onto Frank Phillips Boulevard (Highway 60). The restaurant is on the left, approximately two miles ahead. Tuesday-Sunday, 11 a.m.-11:30 p.m. No credit cards. Handicapped accessible.

Since 1946, Murphy's has served delicious steaks and hamburgers to loyal patrons. Be prepared for a wait on Friday and Saturday nights. This popular restaurant's specialty is the Hot Hamburger which consists of a hamburger patty served open face on toasted bread and topped with hand-cut fries and brown gravy.

Washington County Hamburger Store $

412 S. Johnstone, (918) 336-4440. From Highway 75, turn west on Frank Phillips Boulevard, go south on Johnstone for one block. Weekdays 10-3. Handicapped accessible. No credit cards.

Diners feel comfortable in this homey cafe decor. Although known for good burgers, guests can also enjoy a "Fred," french fries covered with chili, cheese and onions. Decadent and delicious!

Shopping

There are a number of excellent specialty shops and antique stores in the Bartlesville and Dewey area. For a listing and map of these, contact the Bartlesville Chamber of Commerce at (800) 364-8708. Also available for shoppers in the area is **Washington Park Mall**, located at U.S. 75 and Price Road. This indor mall has several major department stores and specialty shops.

ITIO Trading Post

101 S.E. Frank Phillips Boulevard. (918) 337-9292. Located at the southeast corner of Johnstone and Frank Phillips Boulevard (Highway 60). Monday-Saturday 10-5:30.

Shopping in this historic building is a treat. The ITIO building is actually a replacement for the original that was destroyed by fire in the 1930s. History buffs will be interested to know that the ITIO building was named for the Indian Territory Illuminating Oil Company, an early-day oil company that used the upper floors of the building for their offices, while the first floor was a department store. Today, the old department store on the first floor is a mini-mall featuring eight shops. Merchandise ranges from women's clothing and accessories to antiques, children's clothing, bath and body items, and gifts. As an added bonus, a coffee bar in the courtyard features Godiva chocolates.

Yocham's

From Highway 75, turn east on Highway 60 (Nowata Road). Yocham's is four miles east on this road on the left. (918) 335-2277. Monday-Friday 9-5:30, Saturday 9-4.

Despite the space-age technology of the 21st century, a cowboy's best tools are still hand made. Randy Yocham has been making custom saddles since 1974. This is a skill that takes years to master; superior saddles must fit the curves of a horse's back and be made with quality materials. Yet Randy seems to have the knack; he and his employees produce saddles with a starting price of approximately $1100. Randy also makes other leather items: belts, purses, bags, billfolds, portfolios, and picture frames. He even produces a line of western leather furniture.

Visitors can watch this craftsman in action: Randy and his employees are busy but friendly, welcoming guests and their questions. Much of Randy's work is displayed in the showroom where western gifts can be purchased. There's a little bit of everything here—from jewelry, to accessories, to furnishings. If you want to see real cowboys, call ahead to check the roping event schedule. Located behind the store, the arena is host to weekly roping activities. Reservations are requested for group tours.

Accommodations

Hotel Phillips

821 S. Johnstone, (918) 336-5600 or (800) 331-0706, $65-125. Handicapped accessible.

With a total of 207 tastefully-appointed guests rooms and suites, this is Bartlesville's only luxury hotel. Situated near downtown, the hotel is only three blocks from the Phillips Petroleum complex and the crowd-pleasing Community Center. Two restaurants located in the hotel provide guests with a range of dining choices, from casual breakfast and lunch entrees to elegant dinner dining. The hotel has a health club, and parks, shopping, and entertainment are nearby.

Events

Biplane Expo

Held during the first weekend in June at Frank Phillips Field at the Bartlesville Airport. (Signs along Frank Phillips Boulevard direct visitors to the Expo.) For more information contact the Bartlesville Chamber of Commerce at (918) 336-8708. Friday $3, Saturday $5.

The National Biplane Association Convention and Exposition attracts pilots and owners of these unique biplane aircraft from around the country. By number and variety, this is the largest gathering of biplanes in the world. Of the 400-500 aircraft present, approximately 200 are biplanes. Educational forums, static displays, and aviation product exhibits are featured here. Although not of an air show nature, flight activities are ongoing.

Sunfest

Held the first weekend following Memorial Day in Bartlesville's Sooner Park. Signs along Highway 75 direct visitors to the park. Shuttle buses carry visitors to the park from Eastland Center at the intersection of Highway 75 and Frank Phillips Boulevard. For more information contact Sunfest, Inc. at (918) 337-0999. Friday 4 p.m.-dark, Saturday 10 a.m.-dark, Sunday 10 a.m.-5 p.m. Free admission.

Look forward to a day of fun! Sunfest offers activities for every age and interest. Children can participate in free craft activities, or test their skills in games and contests. Adults can browse through booths of arts and crafts or displays by juried artists. Local clubs and organizations present demonstrations. Storytellers and skydivers create chills and thrills. Wandering clowns and jugglers delight the crowd. Musicians and dancers fill the festival's five stages with the sights and sounds of music. On Saturday festival-goers can board a three-car train at the old Santa Fe station for a one-hour trip through the countryside. (Nominal fee charged.)

Vendors at the fair offer an array of foods—Indian tacos, pork chop sandwiches, drumsticks, barbecue, corn on the cob, and a variety of ethnic favorites.

Bartlesville

OK MOZART Festival

Held for nine days in mid-June at the Community Center in downtown Bartlesville. Ticket office (918) 336-9800, Showcase events (918) 336-9900. The Community Center is located at Adams Boulevard and Cherokee. From Highway 75 take Highway 60 west to Cherokee. The Community Center is on the right. Some Showcase events begin as early as 6:30 a.m.; others begin on an almost hourly basis throughout the day. Concerts begin at 8 p.m. and conclude at 10 p.m. Some local establishments remain open to serve refreshments after the concerts. Ticket sales by mail begin in mid-March. This is the best way to obtain tickets to the performances of your choice. Telephone sales begin in mid-March. Don't procrastinate—concerts and Showcase events fill up quickly. Admissions vary; most evening concerts are $15-25. Showcase events range from free-$20, especially if meals or supplies are offered. Student and child tickets are usually available. If you find yourself on an impromptu trip to Bartlesville during the Festival, check the ticket office in the south lobby of the Community Center: Often tickets can be bought the night of the performance. ★ ▣

Expect an extraordinary experience as you enjoy this mixture of Old World music and New World charm. Recognized around the world as a major musical event, the Festival celebrates the music of Mozart and many other composers. There is so much to see, do and hear during the OK MOZART Festival that patrons need to write or call the Festival office in advance for brochures.

OK MOZART

Orchestral concerts featuring world-renowned guest artists and performed by the Solisti New York Orchestra, under the baton of festival artistic director Ransom Wilson, are held in the Community Center. Designed by the Frank Lloyd Wright Foundation, the curved center houses a 1700-seat concert hall known for its excellent acoustics; there's not a bad seat in the house. On Wednesday evening, Woolaroc hosts an outdoor orchestral performance on the banks of a lake in a natural amphitheater. Thursday's concert has traditionally been devoted to jazz, and classical concerts with guest artists round out the Festival's Friday and Saturday performances.

Festival cafes provide lunches, dinners and buffets as well as treats and desserts. Unique and beautiful gift items are found at the Salzburg Haus Shoppe and the Moz-Art Shoppe, the Festival gift shops. The Center Art Gallery features fine art by nationally-known artists. In 1997, New York artist Evan Wilson is featured.

Fireworks at an OK MOZART concert.

Pre-concert talks are offered by nationally-acclaimed lecturers. Daytime events include chamber concerts, mini-concerts, lectures, and a dazzling variety of Showcase events. More than eighty activities feature the area's architecture, history, homes, ranches, and corporations, as well as musical performances, equestrian events, and children's activities. A complete listing is available through the Festival office. Reservations are required for these tours and activities.

Inspired by a casual conversation between Festival Artistic Director Wilson and Nan Buhlinger, a Bartlesville resident and Festival Executive Director, the Festival is now entering its second decade of excellence. This is a "don't miss" event for music lovers from around the world.

Tulsa Regional Fly-In

Held in September at Frank Phillips Field at the Bartlesville Airport. (See Biplane Expo for directions.) Contact the Bartlesville Chamber of Commerce at (918) 336-8708 for more information. Admission is by donation.

Similar to the Biplane Expo held in June, the Fly-In attracts aircraft such as antiques, classics, biplanes, experimentals, and ultra-lights. It is the largest sport aviation event in this region. Between both of these aviation events, visitors can see some of the best the aviation world has to offer!

Indian Summer

Usually held in mid-September at the Bartlesville Community Center, in the heart of downtown Bartlesville. Call Indian Summer, Inc. at (918) 337-2787 for exact dates and a schedule of events. Free.

Members of the Delaware, Osage, Cherokee, and other regional tribes gather here to preserve and display their Native American heritage. Craft demonstrations in beadwork and leatherwork are presented. Traditional Indian fashions are displayed. Children can participate in art activities. Young and old alike enjoy the intertribal powwow. Honor our Native American heritage at this event.

In the Vicinity

Jarrett Farm Country Inn $$$

Located at Ramona, (918) 371-9868. From Bartlesville, travel south about thirteen miles on Highway 75, or from Tulsa, go north on Highway 75 for approximately thirty miles. Jarrett Farm is on the left, with signs directing visitors to the entrance. Rates for the bed and breakfast range from $135-195 per night.

Situated atop a hill halfway between Tulsa and Bartlesville is the award-winning Jarrett Farm Country Inn. Guests can't help but be impressed as they drive through the main gate and up the long drive to the traditional house. Overlooking the countryside, the home of Jerry and Shauna Agnew has been turned into a distinctive restaurant and bed and breakfast. On Thursday, Friday and Saturday evenings, guests enjoy delicious gourmet dinners served in a quietly-elegant atmosphere. Seatings are at 5:30 and 8 p.m. on Thursday; 6 and 8 p.m. on Friday and Saturday. Specialties include steaks, lamb chops, seafood, pork and veal, in addition to the chef's special offered on weekends. Guests are encouraged to save room for Jarrett Farm's delectable desserts.

Overnight guests retire to their special three-room suites. Four of the five suites are found in the guesthouses surrounding the comfortable patio and heated swimming pool. Here they enjoy beautifully-appointed rooms with private baths and awaken to a full gourmet breakfast that is often served on the patio. Reservations are required for both dinner and overnight stays, and they should be made two weeks to one month in advance.

Catoosa

This small town serves as a crossroads for three different transportation systems. As early as 1867, cowboys passed through as they herded cattle on the old Texas Cattle Trail. By 1882 this town was an important shipping center on the Frisco Railroad. With its terminus at Catoosa, the Arkansas River Navigation System has connected this inland Oklahoma community with the major ports of the country and the world.

Located approximately fifteen miles east of downtown Tulsa. Take I-44 or I-244 east to Route 66. This historic highway runs right through town. Catoosa Chamber of Commerce (918) 266-6042.

The Blue Whale

Located just north of Catoosa on historic Route 66. For information, call Catoosa Chamber of Commerce (918) 266-6042.

Imagine the perfect wedding anniversary gift—a big, blue whale! That's just what Hugh S. Davis gave his wife for an anniversary present many years ago. A collector of miniature whales, Mrs. Davis was more than surprised with the eighty-foot-long, grinning blue whale which her husband had constructed on their property. Built with sucker rod pipes and covered with cement, the whale was painted a bright turquoise and sported a pearly-white smile, red lips, and a red iris in his eye.

Although the whale was located on private land, children began to sneak in to swim, slide down the whale's sides, and sunbathe on its back. In response, Mr. Davis constructed concrete tables and chairs, hired a lifeguard, and began to charge a small fee, thus opening the area's first water park. That was years ago. For the past twenty-five years or so, the blue whale has sat beside the road with its paint chipping, and Route 66 drivers wondered about its history. Thanks to the efforts of local businesses and volunteers, the blue whale has been restored. The project, which also includes off-road parking, lighting, restrooms and a combination gift shop/souvenir/information building, is scheduled for completion during the summer of 1997. The Blue Whale has come to life again–a true, vintage roadside attraction!

Tulsa Port of Catoosa

5350 Cimarron Road, (918) 266-2291. From Tulsa, go east on I 244. Following the signs to the Port, exit at 193rd East Avenue and go north. Turn east into the entrance gate and follow the main drive to the Port Authority Building. Monday-Friday, 8-4:30. Free.

The Arkansas River flows fast and clear from the Rocky Mountains in Colorado to the plains of Oklahoma. A temptress, the river has always called rivermen to navigate her waters. However, more than most rivers, the Arkansas has proved unpredictable and difficult to manage. As early as the 1920s, men began to dream of making the Arkansas a major trade-bearing river but, with the devastating floodwaters of spring and the muddy trickle of water in the summer, the task seemed impossible. Even Will Rogers once remarked that the "only way to make the Arkansas River navigable was to pave it." Yet two men persisted in this dream—John McClellan of Arkansas and Robert S. Kerr of Oklahoma, both U.S. Senators. Together they worked to see their goal become a reality.

With seventeen locks spread over the 445 mile length, this system transports goods in the most economical way possible. It's possible to move as many as eight barges at a time; the combined load is equivalent to 480 semitrailer trucks!

Other details about the navigation system are disclosed at the Port Authority Building. Visitors can tour the **Arkansas River Historical Society Museum**, in which artifacts and photos of the river's development are displayed. Guests can watch a working model of a towboat going through a lock and watch a six-minute videotape on the Port. A map is available for those who wish to take a self-guided tour of the terminal area. Plan to spend at least thirty minutes at the Port Authority Building. Extra time is required if you wish to visit the terminal area. The nearest lock is the **Newt Graham Lock and Dam**, twenty-three river miles away. This lock is located seven miles south of Inola; visitors are welcome. The Arkansas River Navigation System is truly a dream come true!

Dining

Molly's Landing $$$

3700 N. Highway 66, (918) 266-7853. From Tulsa, take I 44 or I 244 to Highway 66. Continue through Catoosa, turning left at the Molly's Landing drive, located just before the Verdigris Bridge. Open Monday-Friday 11-10, Saturday noon-10.

Located along the bank of the Verdigris River, Molly's Landing offers excellent fare in a unique atmosphere. Once a riverside bar with a sand volleyball pit, the Landing is now a five-star restaurant serving steaks, seafood, chicken, and quail in a rustic log-cabin atmosphere.

Claremore

Claremore was originally named for an Osage Indian, Chief Clermont. Arriving from Missouri with his people in 1802, Chief Clermont created a settlement in the area that could boast of a trading post by 1842 and a post office by 1874. Legend has it that the postal clerk's illegible handwriting is responsible for the name change from Clermont to Claremore. In 1903, drillers looking for oil struck artesian water northeast of town. The uncapped well drained into nearby Dog Creek; residents claimed that water could peel the paint off houses and turn gold black. It smelled bad! However, the water was also rumored to have healing properties. Before long, five bathhouses were offering services using the "radium water." Today, Claremore is a friendly little town with some big city amenities. It is probably best known as the home of Will Rogers.

Claremore is located approximately thirty miles northeast of Tulsa on Route 66. From Tulsa take I-44 or I-244 east to the Will Rogers Turnpike where the road joins Highway 66, then travel the historic "Mother Road" through Catoosa to Claremore. Claremore Chamber of Commerce (918) 341-2818.

Claremore Daily Progress/Will Rogers Statue

311 West Will Rogers Boulevard, (918) 341-1101. Located in downtown Claremore. From Route 66, turn west onto Will Rogers Boulevard and look for the newspaper office on the left.

Pause from your busy schedule to enjoy Claremore's newest tribute to its favorite son—Will Rogers. Located directly in front of the Daily Progress newspaper offices, this bronze statue depicts the likeness of Will Rogers, reading a daily paper.

Seated on a full-size park bench, the character looks quite lifelike. Employees of the Claremore paper report that it's fun to watch the visitors. Some sit with Will, some read with him, some have their photograph taken with him, and some even talk to him! Created by Claremore-born artist Sandra Van Zandt, the bronze sculpture shows Will as the unassuming and friendly person that he was reputed to be. Older citizens delight in remembering Will, while younger ones can enjoy learning about him in this comfortable and informal way. "All I know is what I read in the papers." –Will Rogers

J. M. Davis Arms and Historical Museum

333 North Lynn Riggs Boulevard, (918) 341-5707. Upon arriving in Claremore continue through town on Route 66, locally named Lynn Riggs Boulevard. The J.M. Davis Gun Museum is located on the left, soon after intersecting with Will Rogers Boulevard. Monday-Saturday 8:30 a.m.-5 p.m., Sunday and holidays, 1-5 p.m. Closed Thanksgiving and Christmas. Free.

J.M. Davis was a true hobbyist. First kept in his home and then displayed on the walls of a local hotel lobby, his collection of guns and weapons grew until it needed a building of its own. Now operated by the state, a museum was opened to house and display Davis' various collections on the collector's 82nd birthday in 1969. Visitors find a wide assortment of weapons: pistols, rifles, and cannons are displayed, as is a collection of knives and swords. Military weapons and uniforms from several different countries are exhibited.

Several display cases are dedicated to outlaw history and their weapons. On the gentler side is a collection of steins and an almost complete collection of statuaries by John Rogers. A gift shop with moderately-priced items is located within the museum. Plan an hour for this stop, unless you have an avid weapons buff in your group. Be sure to read the information printed on the display cards; it's very informative, especially to those with limited knowledge of the subject. Groups are welcome here.

Rogers University Conservation Education Reserve

Located adjacent to Rogers University, (918) 341-4147. Take Route 66 to Will Rogers Boulevard and turn west. Follow the road up the hill to Rogers University. Enter the Reserve through the walk-in gate located at the log cabin near the radio tower. Vehicles are not permitted on the grounds. Open daily from dawn to dusk, and other hours by arrangement. Free.

A cooperative project of Rogers University and county and state conservation agencies, this 120-acre reserve provides visitors with a comprehensive overview of Oklahoma's natural resources and habitats. The reserve includes an outdoor amphitheater for group presentations, a butterfly garden and backyard habitat plot, ecosystem laboratories, self-guided education trails, a wetlands observation dock and tower, and over two miles of hard-surfaced pedestrian trails, making it handicapped accessible. Visitors enjoy birdwatching, outdoor photography, picnicking, and fishing (per state regulations). Special workshops, seminars and interpretive programs are offered frequently. With advance notice, group tours and special programs are also available.

Claremore

Swan Brothers Dairy

938 E. 5th Street, (918) 341-2298. From Tulsa, take I-44 to the Will Rogers Turnpike. Enter the turnpike, exiting at Claremore. This short jaunt costs fifty cents in tolls. Turn left at the T-intersection, following the signs to Swan's Dairy. From Claremore, take Route 66, turn right on Patti Page Boulevard (Highway 20) and go east to Maiden Lane. Turn left and go up the hill to the dairy. Monday-Saturday 8-6. Free.

Ruby and Harley Swan, Sr. started their dairy business in 1923 with one cow. By 1946, their business had grown considerably; they had a good-sized herd of dairy cattle and offered home delivery to Claremore residents. However, the labor-intensive nature of the business forced them to change their retail practices; from 1946 to 1951, they sold milk only to processors. In 1951, the Swan family began selling directly to the public, a practice they continue today. The black and white dairy cattle produce a "natural" product. No chemicals are used on the fields, nor are hormones injected into the cattle to increase their production. Visitors can watch the afternoon milking (usually begins at 3 p.m.) from outside the glass-fronted building. Dress appropriately for outside weather conditions.

The dairy store is located next to the milking area. Be sure to stop and taste some of the cheese samples that are offered on Friday and Saturday afternoons; better yet, purchase some of the milk or cheeses the Swan Dairy sells. Seasonal gifts baskets are also available. Call for a copy of their Christmas gift brochure. What a treat to see where milk actually comes from!

Will Rogers Memorial

1720 West Will Rogers Boulevard, (918) 341-0719 or (800) 324-9455. From Tulsa, take I-44 to Route 66. (I-44 continues northeast as the Will Rogers Turnpike, Route 66 leads through Catoosa to Claremore.) In Claremore, turn left on Will Rogers Boulevard and follow the road up the hill and around the curve. Daily 8-5. Closed Thanksgiving and Christmas Day. Free, by request of Will Rogers' family. Donations are accepted and are recommended at $5 per family, $3 per individual. ★

Here, younger generations can learn about a simple Oklahoman who captured the heart and earned the respect of a nation. Older generations remember the tremendous popularity and influence this man exhibited. Atop a high hill overlooking the city of Claremore, the Will Rogers Memorial displays the personal possessions, keepsakes, and tomb of this well-respected man from Oklahoma.

Exhibits within the Memorial highlight the various aspects of this cowboy philosopher's life. Dioramas explain Will's early life on his father's ranch in Indian Territory. Letters tell of his romance with his wife-to-be, Betty. Promotional posters and sequined costumes reveal the life that he led as an entertainer in the Follies. A theater shows the box office hits he starred in. If children are with you, stop at the interactive children's area. Plan to spend an hour and a half here, longer if you want to watch one of Will's movies. Films are shown daily at 2 p.m.; a morning showing is sometimes scheduled as well. Tributes line one hallway, expressing the nation's sorrow upon his death. It is said that only at Lincoln's funeral had there been a greater outpouring of grief.

A gift shop sells Will Rogers books, tapes and videos, as well as souvenirs with a western theme. Groups are welcome here, although tours should be scheduled in advance. This is a "must stop" attraction for all interested in an inspiring legend, Oklahoma's native son, Will Rogers.

Dining

Hammett House $$, $$$

1616 West Will Rogers Boulevard, (918) 341-7333. From Claremore take Route 66, turn left (direction) onto Will Rogers Boulevard. Following the road up the hill, look for the restaurant on the right, just before the curve. If you get to the Will Rogers Memorial, you've gone too far. Open Tuesday-Saturday, 11-9.

A Claremore institution, the Hammett House has a loyal following among Claremore residents and Tulsans. LaNelle and Jim Hammett opened the restaurant almost thirty years ago. Famous for home-cooked meals and homemade pies, the restaurant served as a place for food and fellowship until its closing in the late 1980s. Reopened in 1991 by Bill and Linda Biard, the restaurant still uses many of LaNelle's original recipes, including the ones for pies, the Hammett House specialty.

The Pink House $

210 West 4th, (918) 342-2544. Tuesday-Saturday, 11-3.

Housed in one of Indian Territory's Victorian homes is one of the area's nicest tearooms. Here guests can enjoy a light luncheon; menu selections include daily specials, soup and sandwiches. Desserts here are a treat. Small gifts with a Victorian theme can be purchased in the waiting area of the restored 1902 home.

Shopping

Due to the large number of antique and craft stores lining Will Rogers Boulevard and Route 66, Claremore has acquired the name "Den of Antiquity." For a brochure listing the stores and a map of their location, call the Claremore Chamber of Commerce, (918) 341-2818.

The Belvedere

121 North Chickasaw, (918) 342-1127. From Route 66 in Claremore turn right (east) onto Will Rogers Boulevard. Drive east through downtown Claremore, turning left one block past the tracks (there is no street sign), then right onto Chickasaw. Christmas at the Belvedere is open from mid-October through mid-December, Thursday-Saturday 10-5, Sunday 1-5. Free; donations are appreciated.

Do your Christmas shopping early in this beautifully-restored mansion, owned by the Rogers County Historical Society. Closed for most of the year, the home is open regularly for those who wish to purchase antique or handmade Christmas gifts. The home is available for event rental throughout the year. One room is also open on a limited basis for overnight guests.

Accommodations

Carriage House Bed and Breakfast Inn

109 E. 4th, (918) 342-2693. Rates range from $50-75, but they are subject to change. Reservations should be made in advance, and will be accepted by phone or mail. A one night's deposit is due at the time reservations are made, and may be paid by credit card or check. Children, pets and smoking are not allowed. Confer with the owners regarding cancellation policies. Credit cards accepted.

Enjoy a comfortable summer afternoon sitting in a rocker on the wraparound porch of this popular bed and breakfast. Built in 1906, the main house features beautifully-restored hardwood floors and two original oak fireplaces. Two guest rooms with private baths are located on the second floor of the main house. The smaller Paris Room is decorated with mementos from a trip to France, while Charlotte's Suite has a sitting room, bedroom and private balcony. Adjacent to the main house sits the Carriage House, originally built to hold a horse-drawn carriage. Now converted, this small house has a living room with gas fireplace, bedroom, and private bathroom with a whirlpool bath for two.

A full breakfast, prepared and served by owners Dean and Sara Selvy, includes their popular cinnamon rolls. The Selvy's have observed that most guests are too full to eat them, so they send the rolls home with their guests instead! Other amenities include a plate of fresh cookies as a bedtime snack, complimentary beverages until 8:30 p.m., playing cards, board games, and if requested, a television.

Country Inn Bed and Breakfast

(918) 342-1894. Located north and east of Claremore. Call for directions. Rates range from $37-64. No children, no smoking. Reservations and a deposit are required in advance.

Experience the serenity of country living when you visit this secluded bed and breakfast. The five acres of yard surrounding the Inn create an atmosphere of quiet tranquility. Hosts Leland and Kay Jenkins work diligently to maintain this wonderful country retreat. Guests stay in charming barn-style quarters, separate from the main house. Hidden in the silo on the side of the barn, a staircase leads to two guest rooms on the second floor. The Burgundy Rose Room is furnished with a queen size bed, two comfortable wing back chairs, and a color cable TV. The Country Lace Room is similarly furnished, and both rooms have private baths. Located below, the Country Suite is paneled with old barn wood for a rustic country look. Decorated with antiques, this cozy suite with private bath, sitting area, and private front porch, provides a great get away for busy city-dwellers or harried travelers. A country breakfast is served at the time of your choice, between 8:30 and 10:30 a.m. Amenities include an in-ground pool surrounded by wooden decking, bicycles available for touring the countryside, and horse-shoes for those wishing a little old-fashioned competition.

In the Vicinity

Totem Pole Park

Travel historic Route 66 through Catoosa and Claremore to Foyil, then take Highway 28A about 2.5 miles east of Foyil to reach the park. For more information, contact the Rogers County Historical Society, P.O. Box 774, Claremore, Oklahoma 74018. Open dawn to dusk. Free, donations accepted.

This park contains one of the state's best examples of true folk art. Once a woodworking instructor at the Charles Page Home in Sand Springs, Foyil resident Ed Galloway spent his retirement years creating a tribute to the American Indian. The result of his efforts is the "world's largest totem pole," a familiar Route 66 landmark. Composed of steel and concrete, the totem pole stands ninety feet above the surrounding countryside. Inside are nine rooms, ranging in size from 5' x 5' to 10' x 12.' Outside, the pole is painted with more than two hundred Indian symbols and depictions of American wildlife.

The totem pole is now recognized as an example of "grassroots" art—artworks created by untrained artists as a means of self-expression. Many of the country's grassroots art objects are now being preserved. It is exciting to witness the preservation of the other elements of Galloway's roadside park by his family, the Rogers County Historical Society, and the state. Most of Galloway's work has been restored, the parking area has been enlarged, and a new entrance has been built. Although artist Galloway has passed away, his dream has now caught the imaginations of local residents.

Oologah

Born when the railroad came through around 1890, Oologah is a small town whose name in Cherokee means "Dark Cloud." Originally part of the Cherokee Nation, it was claimed by Will Rogers as his home town, although his father's ranch predates the town by several years. Will told people in New York that he was born in nearby Claremore, because "no one but an Indian could pronounce Oologah." Proud of his heritage and his upbringing, Will Rogers was pleased to call this land home.

From Claremore, travel about twelve miles north and west on Highway 88. Located approximately thirty miles north and east of Tulsa. Take Highway 169 through Collinsville to Oologah. Oologah is about 142 miles from Oklahoma City. Oologah Area Chamber of Commerce (918) 443-2790.

Oologah Lake

Located approximately three miles east of Oolagah on Highway 88. Most lake access is from Highway 88, but locals occasionally use one of the smaller county roads that service the lake area. Follow the signs that direct visitors to camping areas, boat ramps, and day use areas. Oologah Project Office, (918) 443-2250.

Imagine cloudless blue skies, emerald green water, and taut, colorful sails skimming along the surface of the lake, and you can picture Oologah Lake. Originally built by the Corps of Engineers to control flooding and to enhance navigation, the lake is now well-known for the recreational opportunities it provides. With more than 29,000 acres of water running parallel to Highway 169, this is one of Oklahoma's best sailing lakes; regattas are held continually throughout the summer. Fishermen also visit the lake, catching several varieties of bass, catfish and crappie. Fourteen public boat ramps provide easy access to the lake, and a marina offers a fishing dock and boat rentals. Four public campgrounds offer water, electricity and shower facilities; seven smaller sites offer limited facilities. A nature trail, equestrian trail, and swimming beach are also located here. Contact the U.S. Corps of Engineers, Oologah Project Office for availability, fees and other information.

Walking Tour of Downtown Oologah

To reach downtown Oolagah, turn left from Highway 169 onto Cooweescoowee Avenue. Write or call ahead for the walking tour brochure offered by the Chamber office, (918) 443-2790.

Restored to its Indian Territory days' architecture, downtown Oolagah provides an interesting walking tour through history. Most of the restored red brick buildings were built about the time of statehood in 1907. Although occupied by a number of various enterprises, most of the buildings still contain elements of the original structures. The Bank of Oologah was the first building to be restored in the downtown area. With its completion, other buildings underwent the restoration process. All restoration projects have been undertaken by private individuals; no government funding has been used.

At the intersection of Maple Street and Cooweescoowee Avenue (at the very center of town) is the historic town pump. Listed on the National Register of Historic Places, the pump was extremely important to Oologah's development. A life-size bronze representation of Will Rogers and his horse Comanche entitled "The Cherokee Kid," has been placed at this location. The statue was created by local artist Sandra Van Zandt.

Will Rogers Birthplace (Dog Iron Ranch)

Located just east Oologah, overlooking Oologah Lake. From Tulsa take Highway 169 north to Oologah. Follow the sign, turning right on County Road East-West 38 to the Birthplace Ranch. Ranch gates open at dawn, and close at dusk. Free.

Visit this 1879 living history ranch, the birthplace of Oklahoma's favorite son, Will Rogers. Tour the large home known as the "White House," where Will and his family lived. Across the farmyard is the barn where sheep goats, ducks, chicks, and a pig live. Built during a traditional "barn-raising" by the Amish in 1993, the barn is a valuable addition to the restored ranch. Longhorn cattle roam the ranch lands nearby. Several picnic tables are scattered throughout the grounds. With its quiet atmosphere and beautiful view of the lake, this is a pleasant stop for visitors. Learn about Will's early life by exploring the country he called home.

Dining/Shopping

Goodies

150 Cooweescoowee, (918) 443-2323. Monday-Saturday 7 a.m.-2 p.m. Closed Sunday.

With a decor featuring country antiques, Goodies serves both breakfast and lunch. Cinnamon rolls are the morning specialty; sandwiches with homemade bread and delicious pies attract diners for lunch. Also served for lunch are soups, salads and a hot plate daily special.

Take time to explore Oolagah's **specialty shops** located downtown. Among the more unique shops is **Maple Street Emporium** carrying country crafts and unique gifts and **Visual Expressions Gallery and Frame Shop**, featuring the work of Sandi Dyer. This shop is located in the Old Rock Church.

Hominy

Once a subagency for the Osage nation, Hominy grew with the discovery of oil in the early part of this century. Shrewd in their business dealings, the Osage sold their land but retained the mineral rights. By the late 1920s, the tribe was considered one of the wealthiest ethnic groups in the world, and those members holding headrights were rich. Cattle also brought wealth to the area, evidenced by the large 1920s farmhouses built along the roads. The railroad came, bringing white settlers and goods from the east, along with hotel keepers and merchants. Hominy was a prosperous town in the 1920s; its population once reached five thousand residents. With the decline of oil and ranching in the area, the town has retained some of its original flavor. Slowly, quietly, people are coming back to see the town again; tourists are coming to see the "City of Murals."

Located approximately forty-five miles northwest of Tulsa at the junction of Highways 20 and 99.

Hominy

From Tulsa go west on Highway 412 to the Highway 99 (Cleveland) exit. Go north on Highway 99 nine miles to Hominy. Hominy Chamber of Commerce (918) 885-4939. ★

"City of Murals"

Murals can be viewed dawn to dusk. Free. Donations to the ongoing mural project are received at several locations and are greatly appreciated.

Drive slowly and look closely as you enter the town of Hominy. Painted on the sides of local businesses are some of the most beautiful and meaningful murals in Oklahoma. The first paintings were created by Cha' Tullis in 1990 as part of the Oklahoma Homecoming celebration. Now there are more than a fifteen large murals decorating the town. Write or call the Hominy Chamber of Commerce for a brochure describing the locations and interpretations of the murals at P.O. Box 99, Hominy 74035, or (918) 885-4939. The Hominy Arts Council, 108 W. Main, also has brochures available.

Most of the mural themes are grounded in the beliefs and teachings of Native American culture. Two of the murals, "Many Buffalo Journey" and "Three Bears Seven," depict the importance of hunting for the survival of the tribe. Several murals emphasize the importance of keeping and teaching Indian traditions and the application of these values to modern day life. Other murals pay tribute to the more spiritual aspects of Native American life. Cha' (Charles) Tullis, a Northern Blackfoot Indian, graduated from Hominy High School in 1975. An artist in many mediums, he owns a gallery shop on Main Street in Hominy that features painting, sculpture, jewelry design, and appliqued clothing. Visitors to his shop will find him friendly and willing to talk about the accomplishments of his past and of his plans for the future. As creator of the murals, he is often available as a guide for tour groups. This amiable artist has achieved personal acclaim by creating the murals, and he has revitalized a town in the process.

Drummond Home

305 N. Price, (918) 885-2374. Going west on Highway 20, turn right on Price Avenue. Go north three blocks to Elm. The home is on the corner of Price and Elm. Friday and Saturday 9-5, Sunday 1-5. Closed Monday-Thursday and legal holidays. Free. Donations are appreciated.

Restored to its original appearance of about 1915, the Drummond Home is a wonderful witness to a prosperous life on the prairie. Frederick Drummond, a Scottish immigrant in 1884, dreamed of life as a rancher. However, he was more aptly suited for life as a businessman, as evidenced by his success in the Hominy Trading Company. He also served as mayor, banker, and ranch investor.

In 1905, Fred and Addie Drummond built a three-story Victorian house featuring a central square tower, a second floor balcony, and false dormers. Stained glass surrounds the front door, and beautiful woodwork enhances each room. Because the home remained in the family until 1980 when it was deeded to the Oklahoma Historical Society, many of the original furnishings and household records had remained on the premises, making restoration easier. Paint colors have been faithfully matched, original wallpaper has been reproduced, and Drummond family furnishings and belongings have been displayed. Set in a small Oklahoma prairie town, this home offers an authentic glimpse of the past. Tour groups are asked to call ahead for arrangements.

Walking and Driving Tour

Call the Hominy Chamber of Commerce (918) 885-4959 for the brochure "A Tour of Historic Hominy." There is no fee for the brochure or for any of the sites listed.

Enjoy viewing some of the county's oldest buildings on this driving tour. Visitors start at the old MKT Depot building where they can pick up brochures from the Chamber of Commerce. (Be aware that Chamber of Commerce office hours may be irregular.) The **Silver Dollar Cafe**, reputed to have delicious cinnamon rolls and huge steaks, is also located here. Other attractions on the tour include an **Osage Round House**, the only surviving community round house in Osage County; the 1904 **Stone School House**, the first permanent school in the county; a **Marland Oil Company service station**, several downtown retail establishments, and the **Hominy Cemetery**. Located just north of town on Highway 99, the cemetery contains a unique assortment of monuments and flagpoles. Many of the markers display portraits, a tradition of Hominy's Osage Indians.

Events

I-Lon-Shka Dances

Held in June. For specific dates and times, call (918) 287-2495. Free.

These dances are different from the social powwows held in Oklahoma. More typical in Oklahoma, social powwows are similar to reunions. They provide the opportunity for fellowship, and they are held in secular settings. At these powwows, the audience can be invited to join in some of the dances. In contrast, the I-Lon-Shka dances are held in a quiet and respectful atmosphere, with an emphasis on the religious and spiritual aspects of Osage tribal life. Dancers from throughout the United States meet at Greyhorse, Hominy and Pawhuska for four days of dancing. Afternoon and evening sessions are held, with Sunday's afternoon session reserved for family songs and gift exchanges. Traditional clothing is worn and traditional customs are observed. Although welcome, visitors should observe the customary rules established by the tribe: visitors should not photograph the setting or the dancers without permission, and no video photography or alcoholic beverages are allowed.

Grand Lake O' the Cherokees

This massive lake covers a large portion of northeast Oklahoma. From Tulsa travel northeast on I-44, exiting at the towns that offer the attraction and recreational facilities you prefer. Grand Lake Association (918) 786-2289 or Oklahoma Tourism and Recreation Department (800) 652-6552 or (405) 521-2409.

Seventeen-year-old Henry Holderman first dreamed of harnessing the water power of the Grand (Neosho) River in 1892. However, his subsequent efforts (and those of other private investors over the next forty years), failed to accomplish much. It wasn't until 1935, when the Oklahoma Legislature created the Grand River Dam Authority, that this ambitious plan for a dam finally came to fruition. Completed in 1941, the Pensacola Dam is the longest multiple arch bridge in the world. Winding through more than sixty miles of Ozark foothills, the lake has 1300 miles of shoreline and 59,000 surface acres of water. After a century years, Henry Holderman's dreams for development have finally come true!

Grand Lake is known as much for its beauty as it is for its many recreational opportunities. Visitors may fish, boat, water ski, camp, and much more at the lake, and they can take advantage of the entertainment offered at many shoreline villages nestled among the fingers of the lake. The lake is generally divided into three areas: the northern part of the lake, served by U.S. 20; the middle section served by U.S. 59; and the southern area served by Highway 28. The most developed lakeside community, Grove is found along the eastern side of the central section of the lake. Disney, another popular lakeside community, is found in the southern area. Both public and private recreation facilities abound. For a complete, continuously-updated listing, contact the Grand Lake Association (405-786-2289) for a copy of the "Guide to Grand Lake Magazine."

Located in the extreme northeast corner of the state, Spring River Canoe Trail includes three separate state parks on Spring River. These three parks, **Bicentennial State Park, Josephine Smith State Park,** and **Moccasin Bend State Park** range in size from five to fifteen acres. Facilities at Bicentennial State Park include electric hookups; the other two parks offer only primitive camping.

Twin Bridges State Park is located at the northern end of the lake, six miles east of Fairland at the junction of U.S. 60 and Highway 137. This sixty-three acre RV park has electric hookups, a dump station, picnic shelters, a playground, restrooms with showers, motor rentals, an enclosed fishing dock, boat ramps, a swimming beach, and a concession stand.

Bernice State Park, covering eighty-eight acres, is located 1/2 mile east of Bernice off Highway 85A. Here visitors can camp in RV's or tents, enjoy restrooms with showers, a dump station, a playground, a boat ramp, and a swimming area.

Honey Creek State Park is located off U.S. 59 near Grove. This thirty-acre park has picnic areas and shelters, camping, RV electric hookups, a dump station, a playground, restrooms with showers, a boat ramp, boat rentals, and a city swimming pool and bathhouse.

Cherokee State Parks and Disney. Composed of three separate areas with a total of fifty acres, the parks are located at the southern end of the lake. Electric hookups, camping, picnicking, boat ramps, swimming beaches, and a playground are available at these three parks.

In the Vicinity

Grove

One of the oldest towns in northeast Oklahoma, Grove offers visitors a number of activities besides water recreation. A small, agricultural town until the development of the lake in the 1940s, much of its prosperity now comes from tourism. A wide selection of accommodations and restaurants in the Grove area make this a favorite vacation spot for state residents as well as out-of-state guests. Locals and visitors alike relish the quaint, small-town atmosphere of the community as well as the seasonal activities offered here.

Located approximately eighty miles northeast of Tulsa. From Tulsa take I-44 to the Will Rogers Turnpike. Exit at Afton and turn back south on Highway 59 for about ten miles. Grove is located 200 miles northeast of Oklahoma City. Grove Chamber of Commerce (918) 786-9079.

Cherokee Queen

Located north of the Sailboat bridge on Highway 59. If entering town on Highway 59 from Afton, continue driving through town until you come to Sailboat bridge. Lakeside Restaurant is located here–as well as the offices for the Cherokee Queen. (918) 786-4272. May and September, Wednesday-Sunday 2 p.m.; June, July and August, Tuesday-Sunday 2 p.m.; Dinner/dance cruises Saturday only, late May-September, dinner 6:30-8:30 p.m., dance at 9 p.m. Special cruises are offered Memorial Day weekend, July 4th, and Labor Day weekend. Sightseeing Cruise, adult $8.50, senior $7, ages 4-12 $5. Dinner cruise, adult $19.50, child $10.50. Dance cruise, adult only $6. Group rates for ten or more, $6.50 each. Please call ahead to confirm schedules and prices, as both are subject to change. ★

Experience the grandeur of a Mississippi riverboat as you tour Grand Lake aboard the Cherokee Queen II. Designed to resemble the great paddle-wheelers of the mid-1800s, the diesel-powered boat offers ninety-minute cruises daily. Guests can sit outside on the decks of the boat, or they can ride inside if the lake breeze proves too chilly. Refreshments are served from the snack bar. You may choose to turn this short cruise into a romantic evening by taking the dinner and dance cruise on Saturday night.

Featuring three decks, two dance floors and three snack bars, the Cherokee Queen II can accommodate 390 guests for dinner. Tours offer glimpses of beautiful homes, Shangri-La Resort, and Har-Ber Village, as well as the awe-inspiring countryside surrounding the lake. Reservations can be made in advance for the daily sightseeing cruises, and they are required for the Saturday evening dinner/dance excursions. Plan to arrive at least fifteen minutes before the scheduled departure time; it takes a few minutes to park, purchase tickets, and board the boat. Cherokee Landing, where the boat docks, has a large waiting area with a snack bar and gift shop. Groups are welcome. The riverboats are also available for charter service. This riverboat ride is one of the area's most popular attractions!

Har-Ber Village

Located 3.5 miles west of Grove on Har-Ber Road, on the shores of Grand Lake. From Highway 59 in Grove turn south at Main Street. Take Main Street to the light at Har-Ber Road and turn west. Follow the signs to the entrance. (918) 786-6446. Open from March 1 to November 30, Monday-Saturday 9-6, Sunday 11-6. Free. ★

In 1968, Harvey and Bernice Jones began what is now known as one of the nation's largest antique museums along

Har-Ber Village.

the shores of Grand Lake. In an effort to pay tribute to the early settlers who created this country and to teach youngsters about this heritage, Mr. and Mrs. Jones set about to construct a nine-teenth century village. With over a hundred buildings, the museum is now quite large, and their mission has been accomplished. Comfortable walking shoes are required for the recommended three-hour tour of the village. Be sure to pick up the brochure with a map at the entrance. The map locates points of interest, collections, and restroom facilities; the text of the brochure provides information about the buildings and their exhibits.

Here visitors find a turn-of-the-century courthouse, a post office, dentists's office, drug store, jewelry store, schoolhouse, bank, beauty shop, pioneer home, and a chapel. The buildings house collections of china, household equipment, furnishings, dolls, glassware, and more. Antique farm equipment is displayed throughout the grounds. A handmade watering trough, windmill and waterwheel can also be seen here.

When your feet grow tired, rest on one of the benches and refresh yourself with a view of Grand Lake or spend a few quiet moments at the Church of the Vale, where a statue of Christ overlooks the lake. Sidewalks make the walking easy; the museum is handicapped accessible, and wheelchairs are available at no charge. Picnic areas are also available to visitors. Everyone, the very young to the very old, is welcome, "as long as you conduct yourselves as ladies and gentlemen." Enjoy Har-Ber Village where scenery and heritage have been combined to create a most unique museum!

Kountry Kuzins Jamboree

The Kountry Kuzins theater is located northwest of downtown Grove on Highway 59. (918) 786-9458 or (800) 292-1974. Call ahead to confirm show dates and times. Reservations are helpful, but walk-ins are welcome. Weekend performances are scheduled on both Friday and Saturday nights in June, July and August; Saturday night shows are held in March, April, May, September, and October. Special holiday performances are conducted in November and December. Doors open at 7:15, shows begin at 8:00 p.m. Adults $10, children ages twelve and under $5.

Expect a little bit of everything when you visit the Kountry Kuzins. As they have done for over a dozen years, the twelve "Kuzins" play, sing, and kick up their heels as they lead their audience in some old-fashioned fun. Homespun humor is a big part of the show; but none of it is negative or comes at someone else's expense. Another important component of the production, music ranges from country/western to gospel. Owned and operated by the Case clan, family members not only perform, but they sweep and pop popcorn as well.

Golf

Cherokee Grove Golf Course

Located two miles west of Main Street on Har-Ber Road, and 1/2 mile north on Quail Run Road, (918) 786-9852. Fees are $8.50 per nine holes, $15 for eighteen. Carts rent for $9 per nine holes; pull carts are $2.

This 3240 yard, par 36, nine-hole public course winds through a housing addition. Cherokee Grove offers lessons, a driving range, a pro shop, and a newly-renovated club house. Reservations are recommended, but not required.

Dining

Rheingarten Restaurant $$, $$$

911 S. Main Street, (918) 786-8737. Monday-Thursday 4-8, Friday and Saturday 4-9, Sunday 11:30-3. Closed Tuesday.

This quaint German restaurant offers diners some of the best in German fare. Located in an older, remodeled home, guests feel transported to the "Old World" when they walk through the door. German music delights the ear, and the aroma of schnitzel fills the air. Paricularly recommended for lunch is the French Onion Soup and the Reuben sandwich. Delicious dinner entrees are served in the small, stein-adorned dining rooms.

Grand Lake Area/Grove

Other restaurants with loyal followings include **Lupe's Mexican Restaurant**, 918-786-8723, located 1/2 mile south on Highway 59 past Sailboat Bridge; **Lakeside Restaurant**, 918-786-2212, on south Main near Honey Creek Bridge; and **Stony Point Supper Club**, 918-786-6221, north on Highway 59 past Sailboat Bridge.

Shopping

Grove has a variety of small specialty shops and antique stores. Most of these are located in the downtown area and along Highway 59, just south of Sailboat Bridge. Gift shops, a Christmas store, a wild bird supply store, and a thread shop are here, as well as Native American arts and crafts, and a store featuring hand-forged decorative items. There are numerous antique stores and craft malls. For more information, contact the Grove Chamber of Commerce at (918) 786-9079.

Accommodations

Candlewyck Inn Bed and Breakfast Cottages

59600 E. 307 Lane (same as Har-Ber Road), (918) 786-3636. Rates range from $99-139 per night, with the special Dogwood Suite costing a bit more.

Situated on seven acres overlooking Grand Lake, Candlewyck is the perfect place for a getaway weekend or a special celebration. Each of the twelve suites has a sitting room with a fireplace that can be enjoyed from the sitting room or from the bedroom. Balconies overlook the lake. All suites have TV/VCRs discreetly hidden in entertainment armoires. Several of the rooms also have whirlpool tubs. A full breakfast is served each morning. Monthly specials are also offered–from romantic Valentine weekends to St. Patrick's Day celebrations and quieter "curl-up-with-a book" getaways. Reservations are required. Call the friendly innkeepers, Ken and Karen West, for more information.

Oak Tree Bed and Breakfast

1007 S. Main, (918) 786-9119. $50-60 per night. Personal checks accepted.

Mack and Mary Oyler will greet you with a warm welcome when you visit them in Grove. Built by one of the area's prominent early families, their homey B&B is traditionally and comfortably decorated. In the morning, awake to a hearty breakfast before going out for the day's activities. There are three rooms, with two shared baths.

Events

Grovefest

Held the first weekend in May at the Grove Community Center in downtown Grove. Sponsored by the Grove Area Chamber of Commerce, (918) 786-9079. Free.

What do music, chili and bar-b-cue all have in common? The answer is an appearance at the annual Grovefest! Visitors can enjoy a car show, browse through booths of arts and crafts, and taste their way through the food fair. If you wish to taste the entries in the chili and bbq contest on Saturday, you must purchase a tasting kit, usually available for two dollars. Music rings through the air–from toe-tapping bluegrass to sing-along gospel. Entertainment begins around noon on the Community Center Lawn; bring a blanket or lawn chair to sit on. Face painting, sand art, and a petting zoo are planned especially for children; and the classic car show, with over 100 entries, draws young and old alike. The Antique and Classic Car Show begins at noon on Sunday, with winners announced later in the afternoon.

Annual Quilt Show

Held during a weekend near July 4th at the Grove Community Center in downtown Grove. Sponsored by Linda's Quilt Shop (918) 786-2046; you could also call (918) 786-5167. Free.

The talents and treasures of America's seamstresses come alive in this annual display of handiwork. Beautiful as well as practical, quilts have been important household possessions since first being stitched by American pioneer women. Originally created from leftover sewing scraps or recycled garments, the quilts were composed of numerous small pieces. If necessity dictated the small size of the pieces, then creative talents were needed to put the pieces together in eye-pleasing and artistic designs. Visitors to this show view a variety of quilts, both old and new. Here they can appreciate the practicality, resourcefulness, and ingenuity of our stitching forebears, as well as the artistic talents of current quilters.

Pelican Festival

Held in late September (Friday-Sunday) at Grove Community Center in downtown Grove, Grand Lake Association (918) 786-2289. Free; a nominal fee charged for tours.

This festival features one of the area's fine-feathered friends, the pelican! Stopping briefly at Grand Lake on their migratory route south, the American White Pelicans can be seen from mid-September until late October. The Festival features educational materials about the bird. Films, lectures, maps, books, and photos are all available. The Grand Lake Association and Grand Lake Audubon Society offer guided field trips to watch the birds. With motors quieted, boaters may drift near the pelicans while landlubbers can view them with telescopes or binoculars. Everyone is encouraged to be careful; these unusual and entertaining birds are an endangered species. Other activities include a fair, parade, arts and crafts, food, children's activities, and live entertainment. It's hard to imagine having so much fun while learning about our native wildlife.

Langley/Disney

Langley, located at the west end of Pensacola Dam, and Disney, located at the east end, first began as construction camps in 1938. Workers building the dam rested here each evening after a long day's work. Now Langley/Disney merchants provide supplies for fishermen, campers and sportsmen, instead of for weary laborers.

Located on Highway 28, approximately sixty miles northeast of Tulsa. Take I-44 (Will Rogers Turnpike) to the Adair exit, Highway 28. Go east through Adair and Pensacola to the Langley/Disney area.

Pensacola Dam

Traveling east on Highway 28, the Grand River Dam Authority Lake Patrol office is located on the left, just before you cross the dam, (918) 782-9594 or (918) 782-3382. Tours are offered May 1st-Labor Day, Wednesday-Sunday, 8:30-4. Free.

Spanning the Grand (Neosho) River between the towns of Langley and Disney is the Pensacola Dam. Completed in 1940, the dam stretches 5680 feet, from one side of the river to the other. Visitors wishing to tour the dam may do so. GRDA employees conduct the tours that take visitors inside and outside this amazing structure. It's best to take the thirty-five-minute tour in rubber-soled shoes, as there are several sets of stairs to climb and some wet pavement to cross. Interesting to older children and adults, this visit conveys valuable information about water power and the generating of electricity.

Picture in Scripture Amphitheater

The amphitheater is located three and one-half miles east, and one mile north of Disney, off Highway 28. (918) 435-8207. Performances run Friday and Saturday evenings from mid-June through Labor Day. Gospel singing begins at 8 p.m. An introduction to the city of Nineveh begins at 8:45; the performance begins ten to thirty minutes later, depending on the sunset. Waterfront, $10, General seats, $9; children ages 4-11, $4; children three and under free if held by an adult. Meal prices vary.

Experience first hand the dramatic story of Jonah and the Great fish and other Bible stories through the performance of "The Man Who Ran." Each evening, the ancient city of Nineveh comes alive as performers act out the Biblical story of Jonah, set in the ancient Assyrian city of Nineveh.

Staging includes actors in period costumes, live animals, and dramatic special effects. The audience experiences the terror of a storm at sea as lighting flashes, thunder rolls, and Jonah is thrown overboard and swallowed by a great fish. The outdoor, waterfront amphitheater seats 1000. Dinner is served each evening before the show; a number of menu options are available, including catfish, hamburger, chicken sandwich, and barbecue.

Groups are welcome, and a $25 nonrefundable deposit must accompany the request. Reservations for individuals and groups are required; individuals should call about one week in advance, groups should call as early as possible. A number of specials are offered throughout the season; check with the box office, or pick up a current brochure to see if there's one you wish to take advantage of.

Be sure to take a sweater and some insect repellant–the breeze off the lake can bring cooler temperatures and mosquitos. Proceeds from the presentations help support the New Lifehouse Girls Home, an outreach of Picture in Scripture Ministries, Inc.

New in 1997 is the **Christmas Caravan**. Scheduled for the first two weekends in December, visitors will view a live nativity scene while taking a camel-led walk through the city of Bethlehem. Dress for the weather; this is an outdoor activity. Admission $3.

Monkey Island

With the largest number of guest accommodations in the Grand Lake area, Monkey Island is a beautiful vacation destination. Several resorts here have their own restaurants, recreation facilities, and marinas. Specialty stores and restaurants line the road leading to the retreats. Art galleries and clubs lend an air of sophistication to this popular resort district. Beautiful private residences grace the shores, indicating to all who pass by that this is no ordinary lakeside community.

From Tulsa, take I-44 to the Will Rogers Turnpike. Go northeast on the turnpike to the Afton exit. Take U.S. 59 south from Afton to Highway 125. Follow the signs leading to Shangri-La which is located on Monkey Island. Contact the Grand Lake Association for a current listing of resorts, condominiums, and accommodations at (918) 786-2289.

Monkey Island Trail and Hay Rides, Inc.

From I-44 take the Afton exit, and then go south on U.S. 59. Turn off onto Highway 125. The stables are located on Highway 125, 3/4 mile south of 85A. (918) 257-5186. Wednesday-Monday, closed Tuesday, 10 a.m.-dusk. Cost is $20 per person for one hour trail ride, $10 per person for a 1/2 hour trail ride, and $10 per person for a one-hour hay ride.

Experience Grand Lake from a new perspective–atop the back of a horse. Here in Oklahoma horses are part of our history. What better way to combine two of the state's best resources–water and western heritage! At Monkey Island Trail and Hay Rides, guests take thirty-to-sixty-minute trail rides. This activity is available for every level of horseman, from beginner to experienced; horses are saddled and awaiting your arrival. Guides take groups of no more than ten riders over the varied terrain that comprises the 100-acre ranch. Riders pass through pastures, woods, and along the lake shore. Reservations for trail rides are not necessary; however, reservations are taken for specific ride times. No one may ride double; children under ten must have a parent or guardian accompanying them on the ride.

In addition to trail rides, visitors also enjoy a traditional hayride, or visit the farm petting zoo where goats, geese, horses, a hedge hog, and a potbellied pig reside. Hayrides must have a minimum of six participants, and reservations are required. No smoking or drinking is allowed for either activity. Payment must be cash or travelers checks only.

Owned and operated by Nancy and Val Saamer, the ranch is beginning its third year. Originally from Illinois, the Saamers moved here in 1994 after vacationing at Grand Lake for a number of years. Avid riders themselves, they realized a need for this type of service, and consequently opened this new and growing business. Come see them, and you will get a new perspective on Oklahoma!

Shangri-La Resort

From Tulsa, take I-44 to the Will Rogers Turnpike. Go northeast on the turnpike to the Afton exit. Take U.S. 59 south from Afton to Highway 125. Follow the signs leading to Shangri-La. Room rates range from $80 to $215 for suites. (918) 257-4204, (800) 331-4060.

Perched on the tip of a peninsula, Shangri-La looks out over beautiful Grand Lake. The largest resort on the lake, it began a quarter-century ago as a fishing lodge. With over five hundred guest rooms, a conference center, and multiple recreation facilities, Shangri-La now offers more than a quiet fishing retreat. Two well-designed and beautifully-maintained golf courses challenge players to do their best. Non-golfers can participate in a number of other physical activities, from tennis on full-size indoor or outdoor courts to a workout in the fitness center and water sports in the beach area. For those who prefer pampering to perspiring, a spa is available for massages, facials, pedicures and foot reflexology; guests enjoy shopping in the resort's seven stores or dining in one of the three restaurants. Families can enjoy spending time together on a pontoon lake cruise or bowling in the resort bowling alley. Shangri-La is a welcome retreat from the workaday world.

Shangri La Golf Courses. Both the Blue and the Gold courses at Shangri-La challenge golfers to exciting games. Situated along the shore of Grand Lake, the two courses offer lovely views of the water. With 7012 yards, and a par 72 the Blue Course is the longer of the two; playing to 5932 yards, and a par 70, the Gold Course has more water holes. Players not staying at the lodge should make tee time reservations two weeks in advance; resort guests may make reservations upon their arrival. Amenities include a pro shop and a driving range. "Halfway Houses" on each course provide snacks, light lunches and beverages to hungry golfers.

To contact the golf courses, call (918) 257-4204 or (800) 331-4060. Winter hours 8-5. Summer hours 6:30 a.m.-dark. Winter rates are $39, including cart rental; summer rates are $75 for the Gold and $80 for the Blue, including cart rental.

Dining

The Shebang $$

Located on the corner of Main Street and Highway 125 on Monkey Island, (918) 257-5569. Open nightly at 5 p.m., the restaurant closes when they "get tired."

This fun-filled place offers a little bit of everything–dining, dancing, drinking, and shopping! With a reputation for quality food, this restaurant has served pizza and delicious handmade pastas since 1984. Seafood fettucini is a favorite, along with prime rib and babyback ribs. Prime Buns, the owner's creation, is actually the end of the prime rib, stuffed in the middle of a fresh roll.

The Roadhouse $$, $$$

Located on Highway 125 on Monkey Island, (918) 257-8185. Open nightly 5-10 p.m. from spring through fall; during winter it is open Wednesday-Sunday from 5-10 p.m. Call to verify hours.

This comfortable restaurant provides vacationers with some of the area's best food. The steaks, prime rib, and smoked ribs are favorite entrees. The Roadhouse is known for the whiskey pepper sauce that tops its steaks. Fresh seafood is also on the menu, and it may be served alone or with one of the restaurant's steaks.

Muskogee

Historically known as Three Forks, the Muskogee/Fort Gibson area has played an important part in the development of northeast Oklahoma. Here, the Verdigris, Grand (Neosho) and Arkansas Rivers meet. Established at this junction in 1824, Fort Gibson provided protection for the Indian tribes and settlers living in the area. The town of Muskogee was created when the original Creek Indian Agency located here. Later, the Agency of the Five Civilized Tribes was located here, thus assuring Muskogee's growth. Now a bustling town of 37,000, Muskogee offers a variety of attractions and activities to residents and visitors alike!

From Tulsa take Highway 51 to the Muskogee Turnpike; there are five exits serving Muskogee. From Oklahoma City, travel west on I-40 to Highway 69 and go north. Located approximately 52 miles southeast of Tulsa and 138 miles east and north of Oklahoma City. Muskogee Area Chamber of Commerce (918) 682-2401.

Ataloa Museum/Bacone College

Bacone College Campus, 2299 Old Bacone Road. (918) 683-4581, ext. 283. From the Muskogee Turnpike, take the Shawnee Bypass to the Bacone College entrance and follow the road until you see the museum. Monday-Friday 10-4. Adults $2, children free. Group rates are available.

Bacone College is named after Almon C. Bacone, a New Yorker who came to Indian Territory to teach young Indian men in Tahlequah. Dreaming of a Christian school to educate Indian leaders, he persuaded both the Creek Indians and the Baptist Home Mission Board to support his idea. Started in 1880, the school is the oldest continuing center of higher education in Oklahoma. Along with academics, the school emphasizes Indian arts. Through the college, ancient Indian artifacts are preserved, and contemporary Native American art styles are studied and expanded. The Ataloa Art Lodge contains a small but impressive collection of Indian art, crafts and artifacts. In addition to other outstanding art works, the museum contains a collection of distinctive black-on-black pottery by Maria Martinez. Baskets and blankets woven by Indians of the Southwest are on display. A collection of more than eighty Kachina dolls, donated to the school in 1990, receives much attention from visitors. The Ataloa gift shop offers visitors arts and crafts items made by Bacone students and faculty. The gallery in **McCombs Hall** (Bacone's Art Department) has exhibits of student, faculty and alumni work, including Acee Blue Eagle, Woody Crumbo and Dick West. Individuals may view this interesting collection during the weekday hours; group tours of both the Ataloa Lodge and McCombs Hall are available with prior arrangement.

Five Civilized Tribes Museum

(918) 683-1701. From the intersection of Highways 62 and 69, travel south on Highway 69 to Broadway. Turn west and watch for the sign for Honor Heights Park on the north. Monday-Saturday 10-5, Sunday, 1-5. Closed Thanksgiving, Christmas and New Years Day. Adults $2, children $1, seniors $1.75.

Overlooking Honor Heights Park is the Five Civilized Tribes Museum. Originally built in 1875 as the Union Agency for the Five Civilized Tribes, the building now houses a museum displaying the art and artifacts of the Cherokee, Chickasaw, Choctaw, Creek and Seminole tribes. In 1875, the purpose of the Agency was to consolidate the affairs of the Indians of the five nations. Clothing items, documents, jewelry, photos, a reference library, and trading post are found in this historic building. Through the exhibits, visitors can compare the clothing, beadwork, and pottery of each of the tribes, or the branding irons of nearby ranches. Upstairs, a collection of art work, pottery and sculpture by some of the state's most famous Native American artists such as Jerome Tiger and Dana Tiger are displayed.

Art Under the Oaks Exhibition, Market and Sale is held for three weeks during April to coincide with the Azalea Festival. The exhibition features the sale of traditional and nontraditional pottery, basketry, beadwork, and textiles created by contemporary artists from the Five Civilized Tribes. During the third weekend, the festival features a two-day event that allows visitors to meet noted American Indian artists, experience American Indian traditions, and taste traditional Indian food. Booths sell handmade items. A program featuring Indian storytelling, flute playing, and ceremonial dancing is usually scheduled, and stickball games and blow gun skills are demonstrated. A devotional service is scheduled on Sunday morning.

Honor Heights Park

48th Street, on Agency Hill. (918) 684-6302. Follow the directions to the Five Civilized Tribes Museums. As visitors pass the museum, they enter Honor Heights Park. Open dawn to dusk. During the month of December the park is locked during the day, but opens from 5-10 p.m. for the Garden of Lights. Free; donations are appreciated.

Honor Heights Park.

Voted one of the nations's top ten parks, Honor Heights Park offers visitors a chance to hike, picnic and paddleboat in one of the state's loveliest areas. Laid out as a "Wreath of Honor," the park was dedicated in 1920 by the people of Muskogee as a tribute to those who served in World

War I. Covering 113 acres, the park climbs up the side of Agency Hill. During the month of April, thousands of visitors traverse the park, admiring the brilliant and abundant blooms of over 35,000 azaleas (see more below). Summer offers visitors a chance to visit the park in less crowded circumstances. Fall brings the dazzling colors of turning leaves. Winter is highlighted by an astounding Christmas light display, **Garden of Lights**. Honor Heights is a park for all seasons!

Thomas-Foreman Home

1419 W. Okmulgee, (918) 682-6938. From the intersection of Shawnee Highway (U.S. 62) and Business 62, turn left on N. Main and travel south to Okmulgee. Turn west on Okmulgee. The historic home is on your left, just past the Chamber of Commerce and Civic Center. Open Saturday and Sunday 1-4, and on weekdays by special arrangement. Free.

Built in 1898 by Federal Judge John Thomas, this house eventually became the home for his daughter Carolyn and her husband Grant Foreman. Known professionally for their historic writings about the state, the Foreman's spent much time enjoying extensive worldwide travel. The home reflects more of their personal life, with pictures and souvenirs of their travels prominently displayed. Photos capture the couple riding horses, elephants, and camels as well as meeting royalty and heads-of-state. By the time Carolyn died at age of ninety-four, she had written twenty-seven history books and visited every country in the world–except for four. Visit this historic home to learn about one of Oklahoma's most interesting couples.

U.S.S. Batfish

Port of Muskogee, (918) 682-6294. From the Muskogee Turnpike, take the Hyde Park/Harris Road exit and travel north. Follow the signs to the U.S.S. Batfish. Open mid-March through mid-October, weekdays 9-5 (not Tuesday), Sunday noon-5. From Mid-October through November open Friday-Saturday 9-5 and Sunday 12-5. Closed December-mid-March. It is advisable to call prior to arrival to verify that it is open. Adults $3, children $1. Adult groups of ten or more, and senior citizens are $2.50 each, and children's groups of ten or more are fifty cents each. Children under six are free.

Return to the drama of World War II as you tour this vintage submarine. Imagine you are the ship's skipper as you take hold of one of the wheels. Put yourself in the role of a crewman as you view the tiny quarters where these men lived. Named for a ferocious fish of the West Indies, the Batfish was commissioned in 1943 and served in the South Pacific; she sank three submarines in less than four days! Responsible for sinking eleven additional vessels, the Batfish earned nine Battle Stars. In the park adjacent to the submarine is a memorial to the fifty-two subs and their crews who were lost during WWII. Veterans and war buffs will also enjoy the display of war guns exhibited here. Picnic tables are available for those who wish to pack a lunch.

Golf

Eagle Crest Golf Course

40th and Border, (918) 682-0866. From Highway 69, go south through town to Border and turn west. Continue for approximately one mile; the course is on the corner. Open daylight to dark, seven days a week. Green fees are good for the whole day if the course is not crowded. Green fees are $12 on weekends, $10 on weekdays, ($10 and $8 respectively for junior and seniors).

Eagle Crest is Muskogee's only public eighteen-hole golf course. Wooded, with water on fourteen holes, this 6269-yard, par 72 course is challenging but fun. Tee time reservations are recommended a few days in advance for weekends and holidays. A smaller nine-hole course sits adjacent to the larger course. Driving range, pro shop and food service are available.

Dining

Muskogee has a number of excellent barbecue restaurants. **Slick's**, one of the oldest and best known spots in town, is located at 2329 W. Shawnee, (918) 687-9215, Monday-Saturday 11-8, Wednesday 11-2, closed Sunday. **Al's Barbecue** has its own following. Located at 1306 S. 32nd St., (918) 683-0910, Al's is open 11-8 daily, closed Sunday. Other popular stops include **Cowboy's Bar-B-Q**, (918) 682-0651, at 401 N. York. Open Monday-Saturday, 10:30 a.m.-9 p.m. **Log**

Muskogee

Cabin Bar-B-Q at 2840 S. York (918) 6887- 6252, is open Monday-Thursday 11-7, Friday 11-8. Closed Saturday and Sunday. All offer reasonably-priced food; most meals are priced under $10.

Harmony House Eatery and Bakery $

208 South 7th Street, (918) 687-8653. From Shawnee Bypass (Highway 62), turn south on Main to Okmulgee. Turn west on Okmulgee to 7th and then south on 7th for two blocks to the restaurant. Open Monday-Friday for breakfast and lunch from 7 a.m.-3 p.m.

Located in a renovated home decorated with antiques, this bakery and eatery has been said to have the best cookies in the state! Lunches consist of soup and sandwich fare, or the popular hot lunch daily special. Baked goods include breads, cinnamon rolls, cakes, pies, and cookies. The award-winning, made-from-scratch cookies come in several varieties: chocolate chip, snickerdoodle, oatmeal raisin, lemon krinkle, and chocolate crinkle.

Jasper's $$, $$$

1702 West Okmulgee, (918) 682-7867. Open Monday-Wednesday 11-10, Thursday-Saturday 11-11. Closed Sunday.

Jasper's offers diners a varied menu, with items ranging from burgers to shrimp, steak, lobster, and swordfish filet. Also highly recommended is the pepper steak. This comfortable restaurant, with its classy but casual decor, provides patrons a pleasant dining experience. Two banquet rooms provide seating for 125 and 65, respectively. Also try the Jasper's in Tahlequah, located at 2100 S. Muskogee Avenue, (918) 456-0100.

Miss Addie's Tea Room $, $$

821 W. Broadway (corner of Ninth and Broadway), (918) 682-1506. Lunch is served here from 11-2 p.m.; afternoon tea is served 2-4 p.m.

Miss Addie's features homemade entrees, soups, sandwiches, and desserts. Located in turn-of-the-century Smith's Drug Store, the tea room is furnished with antiques and offers specialty gifts for sale.

Okie's Diner $, $$

219 South 32nd Street, (918) 683-1056. From Highway 62 go west to 32nd Street (Highway 69) and turn left. Open Monday-Saturday 11-10.

A family restaurant, Okie's offers a wide variety of entrees for diners. Steaks, seafood, prime rib, shrimp, and chicken are served, as well as sandwiches. Chopped sirloin dishes, bearing colorful local names, such as Okie Mash, Okie Pride and Okie Special, all feature a distinctive sauce or topping. Fried zucchini is a local favorite.

Shopping

Arrowhead Mall

501 North Main, (918) 683-0683. From the intersection of Highway 62 and Main, turn south. Open Monday-Saturday 10-9, Sunday noon-6.

With fifty-seven stores, a food court, and a movie theater, this is one of Muskogee's busiest shopping areas.

Downtown Shopping and Antiques

A variety of specialty shops can be found in downtown Muskogee. Antiques, gifts, clothing, and sporting goods stores are available. Ask the Chamber for a copy of their Antique Country brochure. Two antique malls to try include **Main Street USA Antique Mall** (918-687-5517) at 2426 N. 32nd Street (Highway 69). Open daily from 9-6, this mall has over 200 dealers; and **Old America Antique Mall** (918-687-8600), located on Highway 69 at 24th Street. This mall is open daily from 10-6. Another interesting store is **J&E Feed Distributors** at 1509 N. Main, (918) 687-7111. Take Highway 62 to Main, then turn south. Look for the store on the west side of the street. Open Monday-Saturday 9-6, J&E Feed offers western wear to locals and tourists alike. Choose from boots, hats, belt buckles, and clothing.

Accommodations

Graham-Carroll House Bed and Breakfast, Dining Room $$, $$$

501 N. 16th Street (also known as "Silk Stocking Avenue"), (918) 683-0100. Rates begin at $80. It is reccommended to make reservations a few weeks in advance.

This beautiful nineteen-room Victorian-Gothic mansion dates back to Oklahoma's early oil-boom years. Built in 1912, the home offers the ultimate in lodging and dining. Five rooms, each with a private bath, are available for guests. The Silk Stocking Room has an 1890 French Bedroom suite, fireplace, and a whirlpool tub for two set beneath antique stained glass. This room adjoins a rooftop garden. The Honeymoon Suite has many of the same amenities, but also boasts its own private elevator. The Carroll Suite, with its four-poster bed, fireplace and sitting room is a treat—as are the Cedar Tower and Magnolia Rooms.

Offered on Friday and Saturday nights, dinner is an elegant and romantic event. Guests are treated to a full course, candlelight dinner, arranged when guests make their reservation.

Miss Addie's Bed and Breakfast

821 W. Broadway in downtown Muskogee, (918) 682-1506. Traveling east into town on Highway 62, turn north on Main then turn east on Broadway. $65 per night.

Housed on the second floor of the restored Smith's Drug Store, Miss Addie's Bed and Breakfast has three guest rooms. Each tastefully decorated and with its own private bath, these rooms are conveniently located above Miss Addie's Tea Room and are close to other downtown attractions. Complete breakfasts are served on the weekend, continental breakfasts during the week.

Queen's House

525 North 16th Street ("Silk Stocking Avenue"), (918) 687-6767. Call for room rates and directions.

Built in 1927, this beautiful mansion has been restored to its original charm and elegance. Five guest rooms are available, some with fireplaces and all with private baths. Furnished with exquisite antiques, guests can experience the elegance of the Oklahoma oil era as they sit in the living room or stroll the gardens. A full gourmet breakfast is served each morning.

Events

Azalea Festival

Honor Heights Park, 48th Street on Agency Hill. During the Festival, access to the park may be diverted for better traffic flow. Watch for signs telling directions. For more information and a much-needed brochure with a list of all activities, contact the Muskogee Parks and Recreation Department, (918) 684-6302. Free; donations are appreciated.

Multitudes of white, yellow, orange, scarlet, crimson, pink, and vivid purple blossoms greet visitors as they enter the park for this glorious display of spring color. Built on land given to the city by the Creek Nation, the park was designed by English gardener George Palmer and dedicated in 1920. Following the traditional style of old English estates, the park contains roads, walks and flower beds curved along the sides of Agency Hill. Planted throughout the park are several thousand tulips which add to the riot of spring color. The park also boasts an All American Rose Selection Garden which blooms from May through October. The highlight of the park are the azaleas—more than 35,000 plants of 625 different varieties. Visitors to the Festival may drive or walk through the park as well as participate in a number of Festival activities, ranging from an Azalea Mardi Gras Ball, to a parade, to a hot air balloon fly-in. This is an excellent time to visit colorful Muskogee!

Muskogee Air Show

Usually held the second weekend in October at Davis Field Airport (take Highway 64 to Davis Field Road). Call the Muskogee Area United Way at (918) 682-1364 for information and current ticket prices. Tickets can be purchased four to six weeks in advance through all area Git 'N Go stores and other locations. The show usually begins in early afternoon and lasts for about three hours.

This popular air show has something for everyone; civilian, experimental, and military planes are on ground display as well as in aerial exhibitions. In addition to the planes, spectators can enjoy the Bedouin Shrine Temple Classic Car Show, or they can stroll past the souvenir and food vendors. Since spectators actually sit on the airport tarmac, they should bring their own seating. Sunglasses or ball caps with visors and sunscreen are also recommended. Proceeds benefit the Muskogee Area United Way and the Bacone College Student Scholarship Fund.

Renaissance Faire

Usually held the first and second weekends in May at The Castle of Muskogee, 3400 Fern Mountain Road, (918) 687-3625. From the Muskogee Turnpike take the Highway 69 exit and go south to Fern Mountain Road. Turn right and follow the signs. 10 a.m.-dusk. Adult three-day pass $13, student/senior citizen three-day pass $11, child three-day pass $7; adult per day $7, student/senior citizen per day $6, child per day $4. Children five and under free. The Masked Ball and other activities cost more.

For those fascinated by history, the Renaissance Faire offers a unique opportunity to revisit the distant past. For three magical days, the hills of Oklahoma become the enchanted forests of the Old World. Villagers in medieval garb and knights astride thundering horses provide entertainment and excitement for all. Visitors can shop the booths of artisans and merchants, dine on medieval fare, and interact with scores of dashing nobles. Jousting tournaments are held, medieval weddings are presented, and a "living chessboard" illustrates the classic game. Children have fun in their own "realm" where storytellers, puppeteers and ventriloquists entertain them. Several activities relating to the Renaissance Faire and with a medieval theme are held throughout the year, including the Boars Heade Feast, Haunted Castle, and the Renaissance Christmas Festival. Contact the Castle of Muskogee for information about the Renaissance Faire and other seasonal events. What a surprise–finding Camelot in Oklahoma!

In the Vicinity

Fort Gibson

Shortly after the Louisiana Purchase was made in 1804, trappers and traders entered this area, then known as Three Forks. Named for the place where the Verdigris, Grand (Neosho) and Arkansas rivers meet, this area was easily accessible by water. The Osage Indian tribe was already here, claiming much of the land drained by the Arkansas River. Cherokees, who had settled in western Arkansas, began to move into the area, creating conflict between the two Indian nations. Military troops at Fort Smith tried to control these confrontations, but by 1824 it was clear that a post would have to be established farther west. With only a brief interruption prior to the Civil War, Fort Gibson was active from 1824 until 1890. The influence of the fort lives on in the national cemetery located nearby and in the town that grew up around it. *Fort Gibson is about seven miles east of Muskogee on Highway 62. Fort Gibson Chamber of Commerce (918) 478-4780.*

Fort Gibson

110 East Ash, (918) 478-3355. Located approximately eight miles east of Muskogee. Take Highway 62 east to the Highway 80 turnoff; drive north through the town of Ft. Gibson to the end of Lee Street. The Historic Site is open seven days a week from 9-5. The site is closed New Years Day, Thanksgiving Day and Christmas Day. The days and hours of special events vary. Call the fort for a listing. Free, but fees are charged for special events.

It is especially advised to visit this fort during special events. Now owned and operated by the Oklahoma Historical Society, the Fort stages several historic reenactments throughout the year. Although regular visits are interesting, special events make the history seem to come alive. Usually held the last Saturday in March, **Public Bake Day** gives visitors a chance to bake bread in the Fort's wood-burning Army oven. An average of 200 loaves a day were baked by Army cooks, fifty loaves at a time. On Bake Day, the public can bring their own dough to bake; those without dough may purchase baked goods. Each year in mid-May, the Fort hosts an

Armed Forces Day Military Timeline which depicts soldiers from every war from 1812 through Desert Storm of the 1980s. Another special event is the **Candlelight Tour** of the Fort. ★ Held in December, the tour offers guests a glimpse of an 1800s military Christmas. Dress for the weather; all tours are conducted outside.

The original fort was built closer to the waters of the Grand River. Considered indefensible and unhealthy because of frequent flooding, the first location was abandoned when reconstruction by the WPA began in the 1930s. Constructed of unseasoned timbers, the original buildings had begun to deteriorate before the post was even finished; the stockade built by the WPA has fared much better. Although smaller than the original post, the stockade replica allows visitors a glimpse of military life in the 1800s.

Fort Gibson National Cemetery

(918) 478-2334. From the Muskogee Turnpike take Highway 62 east approximately eight miles. Turn left at Wiley Road. Travel one mile north and then turn east onto Cemetery Road. The gates to the cemetery are always open; office hours are 8-4:30. Free.

This cemetery was created in 1866 when the federal government began to establish National Cemeteries. The cemetery comprises seven acres of land donated by the Cherokee Nation to the federal government. Many of the 3000 soldiers buried here have been relocated from other forts and, of these, over 2200 are graves of unknown soldiers. Other markers reveal that there are soldiers buried here from every war since the War of 1812. While some graves are shrouded in obscurity, others bear legends and tales. John Reese, recipient of the Medal of Honor, is buried here, as is Captain John P. Decatur. Talahina (Tiana) Rogers Houston, Sam Houston's second wife, is also buried here. Another interesting character in military history, Vivia Thomas, is buried here; legend states that, disguised as a man, she joined the service to be near a former love. A Memorial Day Service is held annually at 2 p.m. on the observed Memorial Day. Veterans Day Ceremonies are held every November 11th, beginning at 11 a.m. A walking tour is available; make requests in advance, or inquire at the office. A computer listing of names and maps are available outside the office. Every grave is important; from the distinguished Officer's Circle to the farthest corner of the cemetery, each marker stands for an individual who gave his life for our country.

Wagoner

Historic Wagoner was created when two railroad lines converged in 1886. Thought to be named for a local train dispatcher, Wagoner became a major agricultural shipping center. Now the town also caters to the needs of fishermen and vacationers enjoying nearby Fort Gibson Lake. Wagoner's main street (Cherokee) is lined with specialty stores housed in turn-of-the-century buildings. Large homes, once belonging to ranchers and businessmen, can be found along residential streets. Many of them restored and occupied, these homes are often open for special tours.

Located seventeen miles north of Muskogee on Highway 69, Wagoner is only 41 miles southeast of Tulsa. The town is 153 miles from Oklahoma City. Wagoner Chamber of Commerce (918) 485-3414.

Magnolia Garden Chapel

507 East Cherokee Street, (918) 485-8101. Located on Wagoner's main thoroughfare, at the corner of Cherokee and State.

Magnolia Garden Chapel is Wagoner's newest romantic retreat. Here, couples can stage their wedding or renew their vows in a building that was once known as the Holy Cross Catholic Church. Erected in 1910, the mission-style structure served as Wagoner's Catholic church until recent years. Now it is a wedding chapel and more. Open by reservation for a variety of special events, the Magnolia Garden also has a suite available for overnight stays by honeymoon couples or those who want to celebrate a special occasion. Owner Billie Inbody is friendly and accommodating, willing to help with almost any request that guests might make.

Oklahoma Historical Fashion, Inc.

Currently located at 810 N. State Street, the museum is in the process of relocating. Call (918) 485-2484 or 485-2513 for more information. Open by appointment.

Ladies enjoy viewing the fashions of the past one hundred years at this unique museum. Visitors at this small house are often found admiring the beautiful styles and fabrics of fashion worn throughout the years. The intricate details of pleated and beaded party dresses and the durable simplicity of daily clothes are noteworthy. Visitors also notice the small sizes of the clothes; the waists of our ancestors were often quite small, especially when cinched up in a corset. Equally delightful are the ladies who run the museum. Obviously enchanted with the subject they preserve, these guides are knowledgeable and friendly. Women enjoy this glimpse of the past–while wearing (and more fully appreciating) the casual styles of the present!

Western Hills Guest Ranch/Sequoyah State Park

Located on State Highway 51, between Wagoner and Tahlequah. The park is 52 miles east of Tulsa. Resort Ranch (918) 772-2545, Park Office (918) 772-2046. For reservations or more information, also try Oklahoma Parks and Resorts general number at (800) 654-8240.

Nestled in the foothills of the Ozarks is **Fort Gibson Lake**. Created in the 1940s with the completion of Ft. Gibson dam, this popular 19,900-acre lake offers a wide variety of recreational opportunities. Situated on a peninsula, **Sequoyah State Park** has both campsites and a lodge for those who wish to stay overnight. The state park has six camping areas with 339 campsites and a large group camp. Located within the park, **Western Hills Guest Ranch** has 101 rooms and suites and 54 cottages. Entertaining guests with a western theme, the Guest Ranch offers horseback riding, hayrides, stagecoach and covered wagon rides, and a "Cowboy Adventure" package. A **nature center** and **nature trails**, a swimming beach, paddleboats, marina, and grocery add to the fun and convenience of the area. Ask about the many **special events** held in the area throughout the year. Music festivals, eagle watches, and pelican tours are a few of the park's offerings.

Sequoyah State Park Golf Course (918-772-2297) has eighteen holes. The often-narrow and tree-lined fairways and elevated tees and greens add to the beauty and difficulty of the course. The par 73 course has a USGA rating is 66.7 and slope is 109. Open daily 7 a.m.-8 p.m., the course has a putting green, driving range and Pro Shop. Green fees are Monday-Friday $9.50 for eighteen holes and $7 for nine holes; Saturday-Sunday and holidays $12, nine holes $9. Twilight, junior and senior fees are lower. Carts are $10 for nine holes and $17 for eighteen holes.

Okmulgee

This historic town, whose name means "bubbling water," sprang up around the Creek Council House in the late 1800s. This town is a "must" for students of Native American history.
Located approximately thirty-eight miles south of Tulsa on Highway 75, and 104 miles east-north-east of Oklahoma City. Okmulgee Chamber of Commerce (918) 756-6172.

Creek Council House Museum

106 W. 6th, (918) 756-2324. Located in downtown Okmulgee. From Highway 75 turn west onto 6th (Okmulgee's main street) and continue about 1/2 mile to the town square. Enter the building through the south doors. Tuesday-Saturday 10-4:30. Free.

Built in 1878, the Council House was constructed to serve as the Capitol of the Muscogee (Creek) Nation. Separate chambers were constructed for the Executive, Legislative and Judicial branches of the Creek government, and all tribal business was conducted here. Preserved as a museum, The Creek Council House Museum is now the historic and cultural center of Okmulgee. Permanent exhibits inside trace the history of the Muscogee (Creek) people both before and after removal from their tribal homes in the southern United States. A booklet available to visitors explains the displays and offers informative narratives on Creek culture and social structure. The Red Stick Gallery Gift Shop offers beautiful gifts, including handmade baskets and Native American tribal dolls by Raven Star Creations. Docent tours are available by arrangement.

Creek Nation Tribal Complex

Located on Highway 75 at Loop 56, (918) 756-8700. Bingo sessions are held Monday, Wednesday, Thursday and Friday at 5:45 p.m.; Saturday games begin at 1:00, 2:00, 5:45, and 7:00 p.m.; Sunday sessions are also offered. To verify session times, call (918) 756-8400.

All Creek Nation tribal government activities are now conducted at the Tribal Complex. A distinctive building in the complex is the Mound Building. Visible from the highway, it is patterned after the types of earthen lodges that were built and used by the Creek people more than a century ago. The **Creek Nation Okmulgee Bingo Hall** and **Creek Nation Rodeo Arena** are nearby.

Dining

Coleman's *$, $$*

1015 Wood Drive, (918) 756-8983. Located north of Main on Highway 75 (Wood Drive). Open Tuesday-Saturday 11-10, closed Sunday and Monday.

Since 1950, Coleman's has been an Okmulgee tradition. Noted for their hamburgers, fries and chicken fried steak, Coleman's is always busy. Don't forget to top off dinner with a piece of their delicious pie.

Kirby's *$, $$*

219 W. 6th, (918) 756-8480. Located in downtown Okmulgee. From Highway 75, turn west on 6th and continue for about 1/2 mile. Monday-Friday 6 a.m.-8p.m., Saturday 6 a.m.-3 p.m. Closed Sunday.

Kirby's is conveniently located for downtown workers and visitors. For about the past twenty years, Kirby's has offered diners delicious daily specials as well as chicken fried steak and veal.

Nelson's Restaurant *$$, $$$*

3499 N. Wood Drive, (918) 756-7717. Located on Highway 75 (Wood Drive) south of Main Street. Monday-Saturday 7 a.m.-9 p.m., closed Sunday.

Featuring everything from steak to Mexican food, Nelson's offers diners a vast array of dinner choices. For special occasions, plan to dine here on Thursday, Friday or Saturday night when the Argentina Steak Room is open. Featuring custom-cooked steaks and fajita platters, the meats are kept warm on a small portable broiler that is brought tableside.

Shopping

Surrounding the Council House is Okmulgee's bustling downtown. Shoppers can browse through a number of retail establishments, including specialty and antique shops. Old-fashioned ice cream treats are served at the **Fountain on the Square**, a small soda shop tucked in between two stores, directly west of the Council House. Visitors may take in a movie at the **Orpheum Theatre**, a restored vaudeville theater built in the 1920s. Surrounding the retail area are neighborhoods featuring elegant homes built during Okmulgee's oil and mining boom. During the 1920s, Okmulgee was the commercial and cultural center for the entire area and boasted more millionaires per capita than New York City.

Events

Okmulgee Main Street, an organization dedicated to maintaining the downtown area as the commercial and cultural center of the city, hosts and co-hosts a variety of special events throughout the year. In April, classic cars, hot rods, and customized show cars line the downtown square during the annual **"50's Bash."** In June, the **Creek Nation Festival** sponsors events for Native Americans–softball games, track and field activities, and the **Creek Nation Rodeo**. In October, the **Oklahoma Indian Art Market** features original Native American arts and crafts, dances, fashions, and foods around the Creek Council House Square. However, the most famous Okmulgee event is the **Pecan Festival** in June. Okmulgee holds the world record for the largest pecan pie, the largest pecan cookie, the largest pecan brownie, and the biggest ice cream and cookie party. Faculty and students at OSU-Okmulgee help concoct these delicacies. The festival also includes entertainment, carnival rides, and arts and crafts. For specific dates on any of these events, contact the Okmulgee Chamber of Commerce at (800) 355-5552 or (918) 756-6172.

In the Vicinity

Henryetta

Founded in 1900 when the railroad arrived, Henryetta was named for a local Creek Indian, Hugh Henry, and his wife Etta. Today, **Territorial Park**, on the corner of West Moore and South 4th Streets, is a source of civic pride. Here citizens can gather for picnics or reunions under the gazebo, or visit the **Territorial Museum**, housed in the town's first school house. Fans of "America's Team," the Dallas Cowboys, know that this is the hometown of the current Cowboy quarterback, Troy Aikman. Displays about Henryetta's hometown hero can be found at the local McDonalds on the main thoroughfare through town.

From Tulsa travel about fifty-one miles south on Highway 75, and from Oklahoma City travel about eighty-nine miles west along I-40. Henryetta Chamber of Commerce (918) 652-3332.

G&H Decoys, Inc.

U.S. 75, north of I-40, (918) 652-3314 or (800) 443-3269. Monday-Friday during regular business hours.

When laws were passed in the 1930s prohibiting the use of live decoys by waterfowl hunters, John J. Gazalski started manufacturing lifelike waterfowl decoys. For over sixty years, the family-owned-and-operated business has made quality products for hunters. Their duck decoys are made of high density, molded plastic and look very realistic. Recently, the Gazalski's added new items to their product line, such as hand-crafted game calls and hunting blinds. Visit the showroom to see the amazing products this company has to offer.

J.W. Hunting Preserve

Located eleven miles east of Henryetta. Call (918) 466-3299 for more information and a brochure.

Sportsmen participate in fully-guided exotic game hunts at this private preserve. Hunters may stalk boar, sheep, deer, antelope, turkey, pheasant, or quail. Cabins are available for those who wish to remain overnight.

Pawhuska

Serving as headquarters for the Osage Tribe and county seat for Oklahoma's largest county, Pawhuska is a busy but charming small town. Named for the Osage Chief Pa-Hu-Scah, "old grey-haired man," the town still retains the flair of the Osage nation and the atmosphere of the 1920s.

Pawhuska hosts two interesting events. A forty-two year tradition, the **Ben Johnson Memorial Steer Roping** is held in June at the Osage County Fairgrounds. Don't miss the **Osage Ceremonial Dances** held the same month.

Located approximately 160 miles north and east of Oklahoma City and approximately 57 miles north and west of Tulsa. From Oklahoma City take I-35 north to U.S. 60. Follow U.S. 60 east to Pawhuska. From Tulsa take Highway 75 north to Highway 60 and travel west to Pawhuska. A more scenic route is available by traveling from Skiatook west on Highway 20 to Highway 99. Pawhuska Chamber of Commerce (918) 287-1208.

Constantine Center

Located on Main Street (Highway 60). For information about tours and performances, contact the Pawhuska Chamber of Commerce (918) 287-1208. Performance hours and admission vary. Purchase tickets in advance; many of the performances sell out.

Charles A. Constantine made Pawhuska his home during the Osage "golden age." During the early 1900s, oil flowed plentifully throughout the county, and oil lease bidders were company founders like Frank Phillips, Thomas Gilcrease, and W.G. Skelly. Knowing that big business would bring profit to the local community, Constantine bought the local hotel in 1911 and converted it into an elaborate theater. The finest architects, craftsmen, and decorators were brought in to transform the hotel. The lobby floor featured a Greek mosaic star; the decorative area surrounding the stage curtain (the proscenium) was made of ribboned terra cotta with hand-carved details. The seats were oversized, the curtains handpainted. No expense was spared in creating this magnificent playhouse. However, the changing economies of time eventually took their toll on the theater. Converted in 1927 to a movie theater, the Constantine was finally closed in the 1970s. Since then, concerned citizens have reopened the Constantine. With the dedicated efforts of almost every segment of the local community, the theater now reflects much of its original glamour. Performances are held on a regular basis, and tour groups visit often to hear the story of the theater's rebirth. Group tours are available and feature a slide presentation. Visit this historic site; the story of its renewal is a tribute to the residents of this small town.

Immaculate Conception Catholic Church

1314 Lynn Avenue, (918) 287-1414. From Highway 60, turn north on Lynn Avenue. Travel nine blocks to the church. It is imperative to call Father Higgins to make tour reservations; parish events are scheduled at the church on a regular basis. Mass is celebrated Monday-Friday at 7:30 a.m. and 6 p.m., Saturday at 6 p.m., Sunday at 9 a.m. Tours are free; donations are appreciated.

Rising out of the Oklahoma plains is one of the most elaborate and expensive Catholic churches in the state. Started while Pawhuska was still in Indian Territory, the church was completed in 1915. Because of World War I, the stained glass windows (made by the Bavarian Art Glass Co. of Munich, Germany) could not be immediately installed. Consequently plain glass was set in the church windows until the German manufacturer was able to send the million-dollar stained-glass panes and the artisans to install them.

The church and its windows were paid for by donations from parish members, 82 per cent of them members of the Osage tribe. There are twenty-two stained glass windows in the church; two of them are 12 x 36 feet. The most unusual window is valued at more that $250,000, and it depicts members of several Osage families who were living at the time the window was commissioned. Church members had to receive special permission from the Vatican to install the window because it included people who were alive at the time. The window is not meant to memorialize specific individuals, but to depict the coming of the Catholic faith to the Osage people. This unusual church shows the blending of New World peoples with Old World traditions.

Osage County Historical Museum

700 N. Lynn Avenue, (918) 287-9924. From Highway 60 turn north at the light and travel one block to the museum, located in the Santa Fe Railroad Depot. September-May: Monday-Friday 9-5, Saturday-Sunday noon-5. Admission is free. Donations are appreciated.

Tucked into the confines of the old train depot, this museum houses the history of the largest county in the state. Visitors can see exhibits featuring Indian artifacts and western memorabilia. A pioneer area contains old photographs, clothing and furniture. Other displays illustrate the area's profitable oil industry. In contrast to the exhibits of the rough-and-tumble west, there is a small area featuring two of Oklahoma's famous Indian ballerinas—Marie and Marjorie Tallchief. Visitors can also see artifacts from the nation's first Boy Scout troop. Organized in 1909 by Rev. John Mitchell, an English priest sent here as a missionary, the troop had nineteen charter members. A marker listing the names of the original members and a bronze statue commemorating them stand outside the museum. Also outside are two Santa Fe railroad cars, an 1890s gazebo, and an authentic one-room schoolhouse. Plan to spend at least an hour here; although it looks small, this museum has a great deal to see and enjoy.

Osage Indian Tribal Complex

819 Grandview, (918) 287-4622. From U.S. 60 go north on Grandview. The museum is on top of the hill and at the end of the complex on your left. Monday-Friday 10-5, occasional Saturdays 1-5 p.m. Closed Sunday and holidays. Call to confirm. Free; donations are appreciated.

Immediately north of downtown Pawhuska atop Agency Hill sits the Osage Indian Tribal Complex. All Osage business is conducted at the agency; tribal decisions are made in the council chambers. For a better appreciation of the Osage culture, visitors to the complex are invited to walk through the **Tribal Museum**. Opened in 1938, this museum is the oldest continuous tribal museum in the U.S. Displays include historic treaties, costumes, beadwork, and authentic clothing. Seminars in moccasin making, finger weaving, ribbonwork, and the Osage language are periodically held here to revive and preserve the Osage culture. Don't miss the site of the "Million Dollar Elm," where Osage oil leases were auctioned to some of the biggest names in the oil business: Skelly, Phillips, and Marland, to name only a few. In order to learn the most from your visit, call at least two weeks prior to your arrival to request a personal tour of the complex. The guide will tell you about the Osage tribe while you are walking through this very small museum. Take in the view of the town beneath the Agency, or better yet, traipse down the stairs that traverse the hillside for lunch in downtown Pawhuska.

Tallgrass Prairie Preserve

Pawhuska office, 100 W. Main, (918) 287-4803. To get to the Preserve from Main Street (Highway 60) in Pawhuska, go north on Osage Avenue. This road becomes the Tallgrass Prairie Preserve Drive. Open daily, dawn to dusk. Free. Donations appreciated. The Preserve has few services. It is wise to gas your car, pack your ice chest, grab the bug spray, and go to the restroom before leaving home for the Prairie Preserve.

The prairie existed long before Indians explored the land and built their mounded cities. Stretching over nearly half the continent, the sea of tall grasses created a habitat where small birds nested in the midst of roaming bison, and wildflowers lured butterflies to pause and rest. Deceptive in its diversity and awe-inspiring in its immensity, the prairie existed.....only to be plowed and planted by modern man. However, the Nature Conservancy is trying to turn back the hands of time. Here the tall grasses are growing again, the wildflowers are blooming, and the bison are grazing. Visitors from the crowded coasts are coming here to experience the gently rolling hills and wide-open vistas of the Oklahoma plains. With only 10% of the original tallgrass remaining, many in America realized the need for a national prairie park. However, the efforts of the National Park Service, Congress and private organizations failed. In 1989, the Nature Conservancy purchased the Barnard Ranch—29,000 acres that comprise the heart of the Tallgrass Prairie Preserve.

To experience the preserve, visitors should drive the gravel road that crosses it. Drive slowly; maximum speed is only 35 miles per hour, and guests may wish to stop at one of the scenic turnouts along the way. Those determined to see buffalo should travel the seven-mile Bison Loop and hope for the best. (Take binoculars to improve your odds.) However, don't get out of your car to view the buffalo at close range; part of this animal's historic mystique is its unpredictability. Located seventeen miles inside the preserve, the bunkhouse for the Barnard Ranch has been converted into a small visitor's center. The only restrooms in the Preserve are located here, as is a small gift shop. One- and two-mile hiking trails are nearby. A nineteen-page "Trail Guide" is available for self-guided tours along the Preserve's hiking trails. Here you may see some of the tallgrass' native wildlife, or you may enjoy the overwhelming sound of silence.

Please respect the "laws of the land"; stay only on the road marked Tallgrass Prairie Preserve Drive; do not smoke or discard cigarettes outside your vehicle; do not drive into smoke; do not litter; and do not remove any natural features, plants or artifacts. This is a most beautiful and unusual place; please help keep it that way. Your visit to the preserve is like a trip to the long distant past—a place where few from the twentieth century have had an opportunity to visit. Thanks to the Nature Conservancy the prairie is still here.

Dining

Bad Brad's Bar-B-Q $-$$

Highway 60 West, (918) 287-1212. Monday-Thursday 11-8, Friday-Saturday 11-9, closed Sunday.

Bad Brad's offers Pawhuskans some of the best barbecue around. Using blackjack and pecan wood, Bad Brad's smokes the ribs, brisket and sausage to perfection. Unusual for a bar-bcue restaurant is the prime rib that is on the menu daily. Rib eye steaks are served on Satur-day evenings. Situated in an old stone house at the edge of town, this cozy diner is decorated with pictures of rodeo stars and country singers. In fact, Bad Brad's is so good, the owners have built their second restaurant in Stillwater!

Shopping

Downtown Pawhuska offers a unique shopping experience. There's a little bit of everything here, from antiques and art work, to gifts and primitives. The **Osage Emporium**, (918) 287-2600, is a good example of the types of stores found here. A unique combination of small town charm and uptown inventory, this store sells everything from Kiva ladders to cappuccino. There are also several locally-owned restaurants where visitors can grab a bite to eat before venturing out to the Tallgrass Prairie Preserve.

Accommodations

The Inn at Woodyard Farms

(918) 287-2699. From Highway 60, turn north on Lynn Avenue. Travel approximately four miles north to the Inn. Open all year, the Inn welcomes children and is a member of the Oklahoma Bed and Breakfast Association. Credit cards accepted.

Let Innkeepers Nancy Woodward and Carol Maupin welcome you to this lovely, country-style farmhouse set amid 77 rolling acres of Oklahoma prairie. Relax on the wide porch that overlooks grazing cattle and horses, or retire to a room, one of four with private baths, each named for a different Oklahoma wildflower. In the morning, enjoy a full breakfast, including homemade biscuits baked by Carol. She once won the Texas' "best biscuit" contest.

In the Vicinity

Biven Garden

Located 1/4 mile west of Shidler on Highway 11, (918) 793-4011. From Pawhuska, travel twenty miles west on Highway 60/11, then travel north nine miles on Highway 11 to Shidler. Weekends, May-September. Other times by appointment with 24 hour notice. Adults $2.

Amid the rolling plains of north central Oklahoma blooms a garden—the Biven Garden. In 1982, Ray and Mollie Biven began their garden with the goal of having color visible from every window in their home. Fifteen years later, their house is surrounded by spacious lawns, colorful flower beds, and ornamental ponds. Rock gardens feature specimens from as far away as South America and West Africa. Bird houses, feeders and baths have been interspersed in the gardens—to the delight of birds and visitors alike. Aviaries house peacocks, pheasants, pigeons, and para-keets. The **Cottage Gift Shop**, situated in the west garden, offers a variety of unusual gifts, English teas, handmade ornaments, and perennial plants. If possible, make arrangements to visit the gardens in June or July, when the foliage is at its peak. Created out of a love for nature, the Biven Gardens are an oasis of color on Oklahoma's high plains.

Osage Hills State Park

(918) 336-4141. Located sixteen miles east of Pawhuska and eleven miles west of Bartlesville, just south of Highway 60. Reservations can be made in advance by calling (800) 654-8240 or the park office. ⑤

Osage Hills State Park is comprised of 1199 acres of beautiful scenery. Visitors can enjoy traipsing along marked hiking trails or driving winding roads to enjoy the views. Other activi-ties include tennis, swimming, boating, and fishing. Eight native-stone, one- and two- bed-room cabins are available for rental. Open April through October, the group camp provides quarters for up to 120. Two campgrounds are available; one has electric and water hookups for RVs, and the other contains primitive campsites. Both campgrounds have modern bath-room facilities. Call ahead to confirm availability.

Pawnee

This Native American community was created when the Pawnee Nation was relocated to Indian Territory in the early 1870s. A trading post was established to serve the Pawnees; an agency, school and several small businesses soon followed. Ranching became important here, as it was throughout the rest of the territory. In 1882, seventeen-year-old Gordon W. Lillie, an Indian interpreter and frontier scout, moved here to start his own ranch. Much of the town's flavor has been determined by these two influences: the Pawnee Indians and their friend Pawnee Bill, as Lillie came to be called. Visitors can delight in this local charm at several shops in Pawnee or at the various attractions and events held throughout the year. Don't miss the distinctive mural painted in memory of Pawnee native Chester Gould. As creator of the world-famous "Dick Tracy" comic strip, Gould entertained millions.

Located approximately 55 miles west of Tulsa and 91 miles north and east of Oklahoma City. From Tulsa, take Highway 64/51 west to the Cimmaron Turnpike (Highway 412). From Oklahoma City, travel north on I-35 to Highway 51. Go east to Highway 18 then north to Pawnee. Pawnee Chamber of Commerce (918) 762-2108.

Pawnee Bill Ranch and Museum

Located on the west side of town. From downtown Pawnee, go west 1/2 mile on Highway 64 to the outskirts of town. (918) 762-2513. Tuesday-Saturday 10-5, Sunday-Monday 1-4. Free.

Stroll through the comfortable atmosphere of a ranch house and grounds when you visit Pawnee Bill's home. Gordon W. Lillie built a cabin of native logs while attempting to make a living at ranching. A showman at heart, Lillie soon decided that the excitement and intrigue of the West were more marketable than a tasty side of beef. In 1883, he went on the road with the first of his Wild West Shows. The shows featured authentic cowboys and full-blood Indians displaying the skills that had once been required to survive in the untamed West. Costumed and choreographed, these "reenactors" traveled the globe, showcasing their abilities and portraying the animosity that sometimes erupted between Native Americans and whites.

By 1908, the Lillies returned to the ranch to build a large brick home where the paintings, tapestries, and memorabilia of their travels could be displayed. They remained here until their deaths: May's in 1936, Pawnee Bill's in 1942.

Today, visitors tour the house and museum, visit the blacksmith shop, and walk the nature trails. Guests can drive through the ranch for a close-up view of buffalo, longhorn cattle, horses, and elk. A picnic area is provided. Owned and operated by the Oklahoma Historical Society, the Ranch offers various classes and seminars throughout the year. Students of the West can participate in scheduled primitive arts classes such as arrowhead making and buckskin tanning. Call OHS at (918) 762-3614 for more information.

Pawnee Bill's Wild West Show

Held on the grounds of the Pawnee Bill Museum (see directions above) for six consecutive weeks beginning in late June. For information and reservations, visitors should call the Pawnee Chamber of Commerce (918) 762-2108. Barbecue dinners are served at 6:30 p.m. The Wild West Show begins at 7 p.m. Dinner is $6 for adults and $3 for children. The show is $8 for adults, $2 for children 7-12, free for children six and younger. Local merchants sell advance tickets for $7 per person; group rates are $6 each for thirty or more.

Sharpshooters, trick riders, buffalo hunters, trick ropers, cowboys, Indians, and horse thieves appear each Saturday night in Pawnee for the weekly Wild West Show. Staged on the grounds of Wild West entrepreneur Pawnee Bill, the show plays host to almost one thousand spectators each week.

The entire community seems to be involved in this newly-emerging tourist attraction. Local volunteers provide the entertainment, labor, and expertise. A few performers, those with special skills, are paid for each performance. Others have perfected their riding and roping abilities for the purpose of participating in this show. Doctors, lawyers, educators, and counselors are among the cast of cowboy sharpshooters and Indian dancers, while skilled craftsmen and local law enforcement personnel work side by side dishing up barbecue dinners before each show.

Bleachers provide the seating for the show. Visitors are encouraged to bring blankets or lawnchairs. On Saturday afternoons, visitors can watch the Wild West performers parade through downtown Pawnee, or they may visit the stores and craft booths that appear along the parade's route. A party atmosphere pervades Pawnee every Saturday night!

Events

Oklahoma Steam and Gas Engine Show

Held the first weekend of May at the new Steam Engine Park in the Pawnee Fairgrounds on the north side of town. For information contact the Pawnee Chamber at (918) 762-2108. Held the first full weekend in May. Adults pay $5 daily admission; children pay a nominal fee. A senior citizen discount is also available on Friday. Parking is free.

Once hailed as the progressive way to generate power, steam traction engines were popular in the late 1800s. The engines were more efficient than horses, allowing farmers to raise crops on larger areas of land. By the mid-1930s, gasoline- and diesel-powered engines replaced those powered by steam, making the earlier steam engines obsolete. Relatively few of these remain in operation today; most of those are owned and operated by the men and women fascinated by the engine's properties. Visitors see antique tractors, cars and trucks, browse arts and crafts booths, or watch demonstrations of early farm, home, and industrial tasks. Working exhibits include corn grinding, lathe turning, clothes washing, water pumping, spinning, weaving, cream separating, and toy making. A parade and entertainment add to this yearly event that brings our technological past alive!

Pawnee Indian Powwow

Held on a weekend near July 4th, 1/2 mile east of Pawnee at Memorial Stadium. Call (918) 762-2108 for more information. Activities are held throughout town, many of them on the Square in downtown Pawnee. Free.

First started in 1946 as a way for older Indians to honor and welcome home World War II servicemen, the Pawnee Indian Homecoming has grown into one of the country's largest free Indian powwows. Several hundred dancers, representing more than a dozen tribes, compete for four evenings in snake dances, eagle dances, and costume events. Held in downtown Pawnee, a parade begins Saturday at noon. Independence Day activities add to the event. Contests include sack races, egg throwing contests, turtle races, and the famous boot throw. In the evening, a street dance is followed by a giant fireworks display. While some seating is available, guests are encouraged to bring lawn chairs for the various activities.

Sallisaw

Established as a trading post and camp site between Fort Smith, Arkansas and the military's Fort Gibson, Sallisaw derives its name from French hunters who traded in the area. Situated in one of the first-settled areas of the state, the town is filled with the history of the Cherokee people. Dwight Mission, founded by the Presbyterian church to meet the needs of the Indians, is located nearby. Standing at the crossroads of I-40, two railroads and the Arkansas Navigation System, Sallisaw is now best known as a transportation hub.

Located on I-40 approximately 100 miles southeast of Tulsa, and 159 miles east of Oklahoma City. Sallisaw Chamber of Commerce (918) 775-2558.

Blue Ribbon Downs

Located just north of I-40, follow the signs to one of the state's best known racetracks. (918) 775-7771. Open throughout most the year, the race track offers seasonal racing. Call to verify dates and hours. General admission $2, club house seating $3.50, parking $1.

Thoroughbred racing is the ticket to excitement at Blue Ribbon Downs. Built at the edge of

town and visible from I-40, the racetrack offers first-time visitors and experienced track followers a chance to enjoy Oklahoma horse racing. Now in its thirty-fifth year of quarterhorse racing and its fourteenth year as a pari-mutuel track, Blue Ribbon Downs is known throughout the state for its competitive races. Food service is available. This is a great place to "place your bets!"

Sequoyah's Home Site

Northeast of Sallisaw, (918) 775-2413. Take U.S. Highway 59 north from Sallisaw for three miles. Turn east on Highway 101 for seven miles. Tuesday-Friday 9-5, Saturday and Sunday 2-5. Closed Monday and state holidays. Free.

Sequoyah was born in the Tennessee Appalachians around 1770 to a Cherokee Indian mother and white father. Abandoned by his father, the boy grew up with his mother's family, eventually becoming a skilled blacksmith and silversmith. However, Sequoyah tried his hand at a number of occupations, including as a clerk at a trading post. Here he became familiar with the white men's use of written language, and he began to dream of creating a similar tool for the Cherokee. During the next twelve years, Sequoyah experimented with a number of alphabets, eventually creating a syllabary–a system in which there is a symbol for each sound. Sequoyah's syllabary was completed in 1821. His daughter Ahoyka was the first to learn to read using this particular system, and together they demonstrated its use and practicality to skeptical tribal leaders. Soon after, the syllabary was being taught throughout the Cherokee Nation, and the tribe became literate within a very short time.

The small, one-room log cabin, maintained by the Oklahoma Historical Society, was built in 1829 when Sequoyah and his family moved to what is now Oklahoma. Through the cabin and interpretive exhibits, visitors understand the contributions Sequoyah made to his people.

Dining

Lessley's Cafe $

220 E. Cherokee (the town's main street), (918) 775-4788. Open daily 6 a.m.-7:30 p.m.

Lessley's is old-fashioned, small-town cafe eating at its best. Started in 1947, the storefront property overlooks Sallisaw's older section of town. Local residents come here as much to visit as to eat. The fare includes menu items typical of many Oklahoma diners: breakfast features egg dishes, while lunch choices include hamburgers and sandwiches. Reputed to have delicious home-style hamburgers and pie, this restaurant is clean and the prices reasonable.

Wild Horse Mountain Barbecue $, $$

Located three miles south of Sallisaw on Highway 59, (918) 775-9960. Tuesday-Saturday 10-8; Monday 10-6.

Started by Hubert and Betty Holman, this well-known, rustic barbecue restaurant has satisfied the hunger of local cowboys and international celebrities since 1964. Only the most choice cuts of meat are roasted over the open pit behind the small building. Created by Betty, the sauce drew loyal patrons back time and again. Now operated by the second generation of Holmans, the restaurant has maintained the quality and friendliness for which it is well known. Patrons continue to make their way to Wild Horse Mountain to taste the barbecue many say is the best in this part of the state.

In the Vicinity

Stilwell

Stilwell is a small, quiet community tucked into the hills of eastern Oklahoma, where the scenery is as beautiful as the people are friendly. Just north of town, the Old Baptist Mission marks the end of the Trail of Tears. The town, like many in the area, boasts of a large Cherokee population.

Strawberry Festival

Held for the past fifty years in downtown Stilwell on the second Saturday in May. Sponsored by the

Stilwell Area Chamber of Commerce and the local Kiwanis Club. Call (918) 696-6400 or 696-7845 for more information. Free.

Each year the harvest of Stilwell's crop of strawberries is celebrated at the annual Strawberry Festival. Strawberries have been grown in this hilly, rocky country for the past fifty years. The soil and climate of eastern Oklahoma are especially suited to strawberries and other specialty crops. The strawberry season usually starts about the first of May and ends a short four weeks later. Berries must be picked just as they ripen. Picked too soon, the berries are hard and sour; picked too late, they're mushy and moldy. It's reported that good pickers can harvest about one hundred quarts of berries a day, but it's hard, hot work; the berries grow close to the ground and legs and backs soon grow tired. For this reason, most folks prefer to buy their berries at the Strawberry Festival.

Although the main event is the enjoyment and purchase of strawberries, the festival features a run, parade, arts and crafts, and entertainment, as well as formal opening ceremonies, a luncheon and guest speaker. Berries are sold near the bandstand, and for best berries, buyers should plan to make their purchases early in the day.

One of the most interesting events of the afternoon is the auction of championship berries, submitted by local growers and purchased by buyers from as far away as Tulsa, but the highlight of the festival follows, when everyone is served free strawberries and shortcake. Young and old alike sit along curbs and tree-lined streets, enjoying this delicious spring treat. Later in the evening, a rodeo completes the day's activities. This is one of eastern Oklahoma's best ways to welcome spring!

Tahlequah

O-si-yo! Cherokee "Greetings" from Tahlequah, the Cherokee Nation's capital! Tahlequah is rich in history and beauty. Removal of the eastern Indians was talked about even at the time of the Louisiana Purchase in 1804, but it wasn't until the 1830s that Indian Territory had been created and the Indian Removal Bill signed into law by President Jackson. The Cherokees, along with the Creeks, Chickasaws and Choctaws, began forced marches to their new homes. In 1839, the Cherokees settled here at Tahlequah, the end of the "Trail of Tears." An organized and educated people, the Cherokees brought their language, government, and customs with them. Government buildings were erected; newspapers, printed in both Cherokee and English, were circulated; schools equivalent to academically-challenging high schools in the East were created for both young men and women.

With the legally forced demise of all Indian governments in 1906, the Cherokee Nation ceased to exist. Not until the mid-1970s did the federal government allow Indian tribes to rule themselves again. The W.W. Keeler Cherokee Nation Tribal Complex (south of town) currently houses the administrative and legislative offices for the tribal government. The old capitol building downtown serves as the Cherokee Nation Tribal Court offices. The Cherokee Supreme Court building and old National Prison are located here as well. What a treat it is to visit this town–steeped in history and set in some of Oklahoma's most beautiful country!

Located 66 miles slightly south and east of Tulsa and 167 miles east/northeast of Oklahoma City. Travel east from Tulsa on Highway 412 to Locust Grove. At Locust Grove travel south on Highway 82 to Tahlequah. From Oklahoma City, travel east on I-40 to the Highway 82 exit. Go north on "scenic route" Highway 82 to Tahlequah. Tahlequah Area Chamber of Commerce (918) 456-3742.

Blueberry Picking Farms

Beaverson's Blueberry Farm, owned by Ron Beaverson consists of eight acres and is located two miles north of Tahlequah off Highway 82. (918) 456-9522. Blueberry Acres, owned by Coker Denton, consists of seven acres and is located five miles north of Tahlequah off Highway 82. (918) 456-5407.

Treat yourself to one of the most fun and delicious outings there is! The area surrounding Tahlequah has long been known for high quality specialty crops. Strawberries, apples, and vegetables are grown in abundance. New to the area are blueberries. There are several "u-pick-it" blueberry farms scattered throughout the area. If you choose to pick your own, go prepared. Wear closed-toe shoes, take your own berry containers, and be prepared for insects.

Prices for blueberries are less than in the grocery store, and the quality of the fruit is much better. Call first to verify directions and to confirm the crop's availability.

Cherokee Heritage Center

Located three miles south of Tahlequah on Willis Road. (918) 456-6007. From the main street in Tahlequah (Muskogee Avenue), go south to the edge of town. Turn east onto Willis Road at the Cherokee Heritage Center/Park Hill signs. Follow the road as it turns right. The Heritage Center is just ahead on the left. Tsa-La-Gi Ancient Village and Adam's Corner Rural Village are open Tuesday-Saturday 10-5 (last tour 3:30). The Cherokee National Museum is open Tuesday-Saturday from 10-5, Sunday 1-5. Closed January, February, and March. Admission to the Cherokee Heritage Center, Ancient and Rural Village is adults $5, children (ages 6-12) $3. Children ages five and under are admitted free. Trail of Tears drama show tickets are: Monday-Friday adults $9, children $4.50; Saturday adults $10, children $5. Dinners for adults are $8, for children under twelve are $5. ★ ⚊

Travel back in time to the United State's East Coast, prior to the white man's arrival. Here you'll find Native Americans living a civilized and productive lifestyle. At the Cherokee Heritage Center's **Tsa-La-Gi Ancient Village,** this lifestyle is revisited through living history demonstrations of the skills and practices used by Native Americans for survival, hundreds of years before Europeans discovered America. Demonstrations include flint-knapping, basket weaving, pottery making, cooking, and hunting. At **Adams Rural Corner**, visitors observe the Indians as they lived in the American frontier period of the 1800s. The **Cherokee National Museum**, complete with welcome center, genealogy department, and display honoring Cherokee leaders, also has rotating exhibits pertaining to current Cherokee culture. The **grounds** have recently been re-landscaped, and they now include a self-guided walking tour of herb gardens. Natural healer Donna Chinosa Lenon, designer of the gardens, is a Cherokee herbalist who knows the ancient medicinal uses of the various plants. Labels help explain the herbs to visitors.

The **"Trail of Tears" drama** teaches about the Trail of Tears and the Cherokee's resettlement in Indian Territory. First opened in 1969, the play has recently been revitalized and restaged. A traditional Cherokee dinner has also been added to the Center's evening activities. A pre-show buffet of fried pork, baked chicken, Indian fry bread, corn bread, coleslaw, brown beans, and wild berry cobbler is available. Dinners are served Monday-Saturday from 5-7:30 p.m. Reservations for dinner are required when making show reservations and are advised about one week in advance. Presented from mid-June through mid-August, the Trail of Tears Drama begins at 8 p.m. Monday-Saturday. Audience members should bring a sweater and spray themselves with insect repellant before arrival. To see everything here, plan for a long day. Day visitors might wish to bring a lunch; picnic grounds are available, and no refreshments are available at the Center. The Cherokee Heritage Center shares the history and culture of its people in an exciting and entertaining way!

Murrell Home

Located just down the road from the Cherokee Heritage Center, (918) 456-2751. Wednesday-Saturday 10-5, Sunday 1-5. Closed Monday, Tuesday and state holidays. Free; donations are appreciated.

One of Oklahoma's oldest towns, Park Hill was the location of a Presbyterian mission in 1836. The settlement became a religious and educational center, and prominent members of the Cherokee tribe soon began to build their homes in this area. John Ross, principal chief of the Cherokees, and his family lived here in a southern plantation mansion named Rose Cottage. A social center for the Cherokee Nation, the elite Park Hill community was burned during the Civil War, leaving the home of George and Minerva Murrell as its sole survivor. Married to the niece of John Ross, George Murrell had a thriving mercantile business. He built his home in about 1845, primarily with slave labor. The southern plantation-style home was almost self-sufficient, and it provided southern hospitality to visiting officers from Fort Gibson. Be sure to walk through the grounds as well as visit the house–it's hard to imagine the sophistication found here in antebellum Indian Territory. Although there are a number of fast food restaurants located nearby on Muskogee Avenue, this is a nice place for a quiet picnic lunch. Owned and operated by the Oklahoma Historical Society, the home's curator is a direct descendant of the Ross family.

River City Players

From Highway 51 turn left on Muskogee Avenue and go north several blocks. The Northeastern State University Playhouse is located on the corner of Muskogee Avenue and Downing Street, (918) 456-5511, Ext. 2789. Performances are held from the first week of June through the first week of August, Tuesday-Saturday, at 8 p.m. Reservations are recommended. Ticket prices are adults $10, children under twelve $4.50.

During this high-energy, fast-paced musical presentation, talented students from Northeastern State University and the surrounding areas sing and dance their way into your heart with spirited performances of "oldies but goodies," as well as current chart-busters. Staged in a reproduced nineteenth-century opera house, the show draws sellout crowds throughout the summer. Although seating is reserved, the theater is small and intimate; there's not a bad seat in the house. A variety of musical entertainment is offered in Tahlequah. Listen carefully during intermission as one of the cast members recites the special discounts available to ticket-stub holders seeking late night entertainment. A variety show for all ages, this is family entertainment at a reasonable price.

Self-guided Tour of Historic Tahlequah

Request a brochure detailing their self-guided historic tour from the Tahlequah Area Chamber of Commerce. Map in hand, begin at Cherokee Square, located at the corner of Water Street and Muskogee.

Much of town's unique history is described in the self-guided tour available to visitors. Beginning at the **Old Cherokee National Capitol Building**, the tour includes many of the structures important to the tribe's early self-government. The Cherokee Council first met here in an open shed in 1839; log buildings followed until a more permanent structure was completed after the Civil War. The grounds of the Capitol Building are now filled with monuments, some honoring veterans of different wars, other paying tribute to the history of communication.

Located nearby, the **Cherokee Supreme Court Building** and the **Cherokee National Prison** are also on the tour. Dating back to the mid-1800s, these structures are testimonies to the Cherokee's ability and desire to effectively govern themselves. Several private, historic homes are included on the tour.

Another stop on the tour is **Northeastern State University**. Started in 1846 when the Cherokee National Council authorized the establishment of the National Male and Female Seminaries, this university has grown into a four-year institution offering a wide variety of degree options. Contact the University for a complete listing of special activities. You might wish to conclude the tour by visiting the new Cherokee capital complex, completed in 1978, just south of town. Ask about tours of the facility at the receptionist's desk, Monday-Friday 8-5.

Golf

Cherry Springs Golf Course

700 E. Ballentine Road, (918) 456-5100. Open seven days a week, 7 a.m.-8 p.m. Green fees are weekdays $8, weekends $10, seniors $6. Summer twilight fees are $5 Monday-Friday after 5 p.m. Rental carts are available for a cost of $7.50 per nine holes, $15 for 18 holes.

This nine hole, par 36 course has a restaurant and a driving range.

Cross Winds Golf Course

Six miles south of Tahlequah on Highway 62, (918) 458-4294. Open daily, 8 a.m. to thirty minutes before dark. Green fees are $7, seniors (fifty and over) $5, juniors (18 and under) $5. Summer twilight fees (Monday-Friday) are $4 after 5 p.m. Carts rent for $8 for nine holes, $14 for eighteen holes.

This challenging course has nine holes.

Tahlequah City Golf Course

Located three miles west of town on Highway 51, (918) 456-3761. This nine-hole course is open daily 8 a.m. until dark. Green fees are $5.

A snack bar is located in the pro shop.

Dining

Kelly's Tea Room $, $$

210 W. Keetoowah Street, at the corner of College and Keetoowah, (918) 456-0059. From Highway 51, turn north on Keetoowah and travel one block. Open Monday-Saturday 11-3.

Occupying one of Tahlequah's antique-filled older homes, Kelly's Tea Room serves delicious lunches. Tasty homemade sandwiches, quiche, pasta, soup, and daily specials are offered at a reasonable price.

The Peppermill Restaurant $, $$

4th and Bertha Parker Bypass, (918) 456-3200. If coming from the south on Highway 82, turn east at the first major intersection. Look for the restaurant next to the Holiday Inn Express on the right side of the road. Sunday-Thursday 6:30 a.m.-9 p.m., Friday-Saturday 6:30 a.m.-10 p.m.

This log cabin, western-style restaurant has quickly become a favorite with locals. Featuring American cuisine, breakfast consists of a complete buffet, and lunch and dinner items include specialty salads, sandwiches, homemade soups, and hand-cut steaks. Reasonably-priced country dinners each come with vegetables, potato and roll. To complete your special dinner at the Peppermill, try the Cherries Jubilee prepared tableside!

Shopping

Cherokee Nation Gift Shop

Located in the Cherokee Tribal Complex, 3.5 miles south of Tahlequah on Highway 62. (918) 456-2793, (800) 256-2123. Call to inquire about hours.

Shoppers will find a wide selection of authentic, hand-crafted Native American items at this interesting store. Locally-produced baskets and beadwork, artwork by both local and nationally-known talents, and traditional artifacts such as turtle shell shakers and buffalo grass dolls are featured here. There are also educational materials such as books, tapes and videos.

A number of specialty and antique stores line the main thoroughfare, Muskogee Avenue. Those desiring a mid-morning break from shopping should consider a stop at Morgan's Bakery, a long-standing Tahlequah establishment.

Accommodations

Bed and Breakfast of Tahlequah

215 W. Morgan, (918) 456-1309, or (9180 456-3377. Call for directions. Rates start at $40 per night

Bill and Mary Geasland greet their guests in the home where Mary spent her childhood. Guests stay in the home's upstairs garage apartment, built in 1932. The separate quarters provide a comfortable and private retreat. Trimmed with bright yellow shutters, the apartment is furnished with a double bed and a sleeper sofa. The fully-furnished small kitchen has a microwave. The tiny bathroom contains a 1929 claw foot bathtub. Each morning, a full breakfast is delivered to the apartment door by the gracious hosts. Beverages are available around the clock. Reservations are required and are recommended about one week in advance.

Glenn's Bed and Breakfast

340 Bailey Boulevard, ten miles north of Tahlequah, (918) 456-4451 or 456-9423. Call for directions. Rates are $20-36, two night minimum stay.

Guests looking for a quiet retreat will enjoy this bed and breakfast, located within walking distance of the Illinois River. Two rooms are available, each with its own bath. Guests may choose either a continental or full breakfast. Reservations should be made about one week in advance.

The Lord and Taylor's Bed and Breakfast

Located in historic Park Hill and directly across from Lake Tenkiller. Call for specific directions. (918)

457-4756 or 696-3147. Rates are $40-60.

This cozy bed and breakfast offers guests a choice of four bedrooms, two with private baths and two with a shared bath. Guests are treated to a continental breakfast featuring fruit plates, homemade breads and cinnamon rolls, juice, coffee, or tea. Ask the Taylor's about their facilities for special events such as receptions and weddings. Reservations requested at least one week in advance.

Events

Illinois River BalloonFest

Usually held the third weekend in August from Friday to Sunday afternoon. Due to this event's popularity, the location and logistics have undergone some changes; be sure to contact the Tahlequah Chamber of Commerce at (918) 456-3742 for the latest information. The grounds are located three miles east of Tahlequah, just across the Illinois River Bridge on Highway 62/51. $3 per person for a three-day pass. Daily gate admission is $2 per person.

Spirits soar as visitors watch these lighter-than-air craft rise above the Illinois River. Visitors delight in watching every aspect of hot air balloon flight–from the early morning ride preparations to the landing efforts of the chase crew. The event starts on Friday evening with the Balloon Glow, and Saturday morning's activities begin with an early morning mass ascension of as many as forty colorful balloons. Balloon races are held daily. Ongoing entertainment at the Fest include music, arts and crafts booths, and a kiddie carnival. Food is always plentiful. Special activities include a vintage fire engine and classic car shows, and an old-fashioned tractor pulling contest. Join thousands of others as they watch this colorful and breathtaking spectacle!

Cherokee National Holiday

Held on Labor Day weekend at various locations throughout the city. (918) 456-0671 or (800) 850-0348. Contact the Tahlequah Chamber of Commerce for a calendar of events. Available several months in advance, this calendar will specify site locations, times and fees for the various activities. Many of the National Holiday activities are free; some charge admission.

Native American traditions and culture are celebrated at the Cherokee National Holiday. Approximately 50,000 visitors from around the world attend this festival that commemorates the 1839 signing of the Cherokee Constitution. Activities include a cornstalk shoot (a bow and arrow event), a blow gun shoot, a marble game, and a rodeo. Competitions are also held in softball and golf. A parade featuring floats and regional school bands is held along the main thoroughfare downtown. A powwow and dance competition are held, Miss Cherokee is chosen, and authentic hand-crafted items are offered for sale.

HELPFUL HINTS FOR RIVER FLOATING

A canoe may be the traditional means of floating the Illinois, but first-time floaters and those with children may opt for a raft or a "ride on top" kayak, offered by several of the outfitters. Canoes, especially if manned by untrained paddlers, tend to tip over. To many, this is part of the fun. Although difficult to tip, rafts are also difficult to paddle. It's best just to sit back and relax if you're in one of these. Kayaks are new to the river and are considered more stable and maneuverable than canoes. The kayaks at the Illinois River have back and leg rests molded to fit around the bodies of riders.

Float trips vary in length, from two to three hours to two days or more. Rates vary slightly from one outfitter to another. Floaters usually choose an outfitter by availability, location, service or some special amenity. Check with your outfitter about the rules and regulations regarding children, pets, and alcoholic beverages. Float participants are encouraged to bring their own refreshments. Glass and styrofoam containers are prohibited on the river; floaters in violation can be fined up to $250. Ice chests should be tied into rafts and canoes so they don't float away if the boat tips. Valuables should not be taken on the river. Most suppliers provide a car key check-in service. Anything that you wish to remain dry should be kept in zip lock bags. Sunscreen is a must; many a floater has come home looking like a boiled Maine lobster and feeling miserable. Similarly, shoes are a must; this rock-bottomed river is painful to tender feet!

Illinois River

Illinois River

Located east of Tahlequah. From Tahlequah, turn left onto Muskogee Avenue and go north to Downing Street. Turn right on Downing (U.S. 62/Highway 51) and go east three miles to Highway 10. Winding around hills, between the Illinois River and overhanging bluffs, Highway 10 is designated as a scenic route. Public access to the river is provided at four areas. Several resorts along the highway offer float trips and camping facilities. Contact the Oklahoma Scenic Rivers Commission at (800) 299-3251 for a Floater's Guide with complete listings for outfitters. Call ahead in early spring to see when the suppliers will open. Both the beginning and end of the float season depends on the weather and condition of the river. Most outfitters are open daily between Memorial Day and Labor Day, and on weekends in May and September, with a few offering services year round. Reservations are strongly recommended. Rates range from $7 per person for a two to three hour float to $30 per person for a three-day trip. Rates are higher for those renting rafts and kayaks. Some suppliers offer family rates or reduced rates for children.

For a day of unsurpassed fun, float this scenic river. Flowing into the state from Arkansas, the river winds its way through some of the most beautiful scenery in Oklahoma. Fed by springs, the water offers excellent fishing and floating opportunities. More than ten outfitters are located along the river's banks. They offer float trips from a few hours to several days in length. Accommodations along the river range from primitive camping to campgrounds and cabins offered by the outfitters. The Illinois is designated as a "Class II" river, defined as having easy rapids with waves up to one foot and channels that are wide and clear. Some maneuvering is required, but typically the river is easy enough for novice rafters and families with children as young as four. Rafts are easier than canoes. With more than 60,000 visitors each year, the Illinois River is one of Oklahoma's most popular outdoor attractions!

Suppliers

Arrowhead Camp, (918) 456-1140 or (800) 749-1140. Canoes, cabins, camping, play ground, play area, and store. **Diamondhead Resort**, (918) 456-4545 or (800) 722-2411. Canoes, rafts, kayaks, motel, bunkhouse, camping, play area, game room, and store. **Eagle Bluff Resorts**, (800) OK-RIVER. Canoes, rafts, lodge, campground, play area, snack shop. **Falcon Floats**, (800) OK-FLOATS. Canoes, rafts, bunkhouse, play area, and camping. **Hanging Rock Camp**, (918) 456-3088, or (800) 375-3088. Canoes, rafts, motel, camping, and cafe. **Peyton's Place**, (918) 456-3847. Canoes, lodge, cottages, kitchenettes, camping, picnic supplies, and deli. **Riverside Camp**, (918) 456-4787, or (800) 749-CAMP. Canoes, rafts, kayaks, lodge, cabins, camping, play area, and store. **Sparrow Hawk Camp**, (918) 456-8371, FAX (918) 458-0124. Canoes, rafts, paddle boats, innertubes, bunkhouse, camping, play area, playground, and trampolines. **Thunderbird Resort**, (918) 456-4747 or (800) 749-4700. Canoes, rafts, lodge, camping. **War Eagle**, (918) 456-6272 or (800) 722-3834. Canoes, rafts, kayaks, motel, bunkhouse, camping, play area, game room, swimming pool for lodgers, and water slide.

Tenkiller Lake

Located approximately seventy miles southeast of Tulsa between the towns of Tahlequah at the northern end, and Gore at the southern end. From Tulsa travel southeast on Highway 51 to the Muskogee Turnpike. If you wish to visit the northern part of the lake, exit at Coweta and follow Highway 51 through Wagoner and Hulbert to Tahlequah. Turn right onto Highway 62 (Muskogee Avenue) and stay on this road until you reach Highway 82. Turn left on Highway 82 to Keys. To travel down the western side of the lake, turn right onto Indian Road. If you wish to tour the eastern side, remain on Highway 82. To reach the southern end of the lake, remain on the turnpike until you reach the Gore/Webber's Falls exit. Traveling north on Highway 100, follow the signs to the dam. Call or write the Lake Tenkiller Association for a current vacation guide (918) 457-4403. Information in-

cludes camping and resort information and a directory of local goods and services.

Enjoy the pristine beauty of this crystal clear lake. With its tree-covered banks and high rocky bluffs, this is one of Oklahoma's most magnificent reservoirs. The lake winds for 34 miles through the Ozark-like Cookson Hills, and it has over 130 miles of shoreline. Construction on the dam was completed by 1952. The dam was created for flood control and hydroelectric power as part of the comprehensive development plan for the Arkansas River basin. However, the opportunities it provides for water recreation are extremely important to visitors and local residents alike.

The lake has ten marinas and fourteen parks managed by the state of Oklahoma or the Corps of Engineers. Camping facilities range from primitive tent sites to comfortable cabins. Most marinas rent various types of boats; twenty-four ramps are available for those who have their own. Three **floating restaurants** feed hungry fun-seekers: one at Pine Cove Marina, one at Sixshooter Marina, and one at Barnacle Bill's Marina. Anglers fish for black bass, white bass, crappie, catfish, perch, and walleye. Rainbow trout are stocked in the river below the dam. Scuba divers come from miles around to dive in some of the most clear waters in a five-state region. Ranging from eight to twenty-five feet, visibility affords excellent views of the underwater world and its inhabitants. Scuba lessons are taught at **Gene's Aqua Pro Shop** at the south end of the lake. While learning about the skill of scuba diving, students explore a shallow underwater playground, complete with car, boat, swing set, school bus, and "shark." Wildlife in the area is abundant: deer, turkey, quail, rabbit, squirrel, and various waterfowl are often spotted by visitors. Tenkiller has much to offer those seeking relaxation or adventure!

Cherokee Princess

This paddlewheel tour boat docks at the Burnt Cabin Marina, (918) 457-5421. From Tahlequah take Highway 62 to Highway 82 and turn left onto Highway 82. Follow this road to Keys. At Keys, turn right on Indian Road, traveling down the west side of the lake. To reach Burnt Cabin Marina, turn left off Indian Road, following the signs. Seasonal hours of operation. Call to confirm hours and prices.

Fin and Feather Resort

From Muskogee, take Highway 62 east across the north edge of Muskogee, then Highway 10 south approximately eighteen miles to Highway 10A. Turn east and go five more miles to reach the resort. From Oklahoma City, travel east on I-40 to Highway 100 (Webbers Falls) exit. Travel north on Highway 100 to Highway 10A and go west to the resort. (918) 487-5148.

Call ahead for the Fin and Feather guest newsletter. The newsletter describes the resorts facilities and prices. This guide is especially helpful to those wishing to plan a retreat or family reunion at the resort. Rates range from $56 per night to $285 for the houses which sleep up to twenty guests. When making reservations, check the minimum stay requirements. Deposits equal to one night's lodging are required; a cancellation policy is in effect. Some early-bird special rental rates are available on certain dates; call to verify these dates, particularly if you're interested in visiting during the early spring or late summer. Reservations are taken starting January 1; cabins usually open in late March, and they close in late October. The dining room is open for breakfast, lunch, and dinner between Easter and late September. The snack bar is open only during the summer months.

Perched high atop a hill, Fin and Feather Resort overlooks the south end of scenic Lake Tenkiller. To travelers, the resort offers comfortable accommodations, entertainment, easy access to the lake, and a wide array of group facilities. To local residents, the resort offers great food, served buffet style. Started in 1960 by Les and Jerrie Manns, the "resort" originally consisted of twenty rental cabins and a small cafe. The first improvement made by the Manns was to build a fence "to keep the cows out." Many improvements later, the resort has 82 rental units and a dining room that seats 250. Units range from one-bedroom cabins to five-bedroom houses. Guest facilities include an indoor pool and whirlpool spa, tennis and basketball courts, a small movie theater, a fully-equipped game room, a playground, and a grocery store. Guests and local residents enjoy the delicious buffet meals served in the dining room. Each night, diners can sample a different fare, from Hawaiian to the Roaring '20s. Visitors can even take some of their favorite recipes home in the second edition of the Resort's cookbook. For those who prefer a lighter meal, the Veranda offers hamburgers, hot dogs, and ice cream. Shopping is available in the resort's gift shop, which features a little bit of everything, from swimming gear to gifts, all reasonably priced. Arts and crafts lovers will want to take advantage of the resort during the last weekend in September for the **Annual Fall Festival**.

Parks and Additional Private Resorts

Corps of Engineers camping: Two of the most popular Corps of Engineers camping areas are Cookson Bend and Pettit Bay. **Cookson Bend** is the largest Corps camping facility on the lake. Located on the eastern side, the 175-acre area has 132 campsites (68 electric) with showers, shelters, a dump station, boat ramp, grocery store, and a marina. Covering 280 acres and located at the northern end of the west side, **Pettit Bay** has 98 campsites, 65 or them with electric hookups. Modern restroom facilities are provided. Boat ramps, marina, heated fishing dock, grocery store, and restaurant are also located here.

Corps facilities usually open around mid-April. Campsite reservations are taken for the group camping areas only. Electrical sites are $12-14 per night, nonelectrical sites are $8. There are a number of smaller, primitive camping areas along the lake. For a complete listing, call the Tenkiller Project Office at (918) 487-5252, or request a copy of the Tenkiller Lake Vacation Guide.

Private Resort Areas: Sixshooter, Barnacle Bill's, and Elk Creek are **private resort areas** that offer a number of facilities to patrons. For information, call the Tenkiller Lake Association or each of the resorts directly.

Sixshooter (mid-lake, east side), (918) 457-5152. Located two miles south of Cookson on Highway 100/82. **Barnacle Bill's** (mid-lake, west side), (918) 457-5438. Located 5.5 miles south of Keys on Indian Road. **Elk Creek** (north end, east side), (918) 457-5142. Located six miles southeast of Keys on Highway 100/82.

State Parks: The popular **Tenkiller State Park** 🛈 (918-489-5643) offers a wide variety of amenities to campers. This 1188-acre park is located near the southeast section of the lake and has 279 campsites (112 of them electric). Amenities include modern restroom facilities, a dump station, boat ramps, a marina, a grocery store, and two restaurants.

Fees for camping in state parks are as follows: Water, electricity and sewer, $14 per night. Water and electricity, $11 per night. Tent camping, $6 per night. The state parks do not take reservations for tent camping.

In the Vicinity

Gore

One of Oklahoma's oldest towns, the Native American settlement first appeared on a French trader's map of the area in 1718. Later, the community served as a stopping place for the Cherokee Indians as they moved west in 1828. The Cherokees established their first capital, council ground, and courthouse here. The Cherokee capital was moved to Tahlequah in 1843. *Located south of Tenkiller Lake and three miles north of I-40 on Highway 10. Gore Chamber of Commerce (918) 489-5663.*

Briarbrush Art Gallery

Three miles north of Gore on Highway 100. (918) 489-5317. Open during regular business hours and by appointment.

Witness the creative talents of Deane and Delbert Stuart when you visit their art gallery that adjoins their home in Gore. Both of them senior citizens, the Stuarts are creative people. Mrs. Stuart paints; her pictures of dew-kissed roses are extremely lifelike. Mr. Stuart sculpts everything from wildlife to modern pieces. He learned the art of wax bronze casting at Bacone College in Muskogee, long after he retired from business. Together, they stock and maintain this small, private gallery. Stop by for a visit or to browse!

Cherokee Courthouse–Tahlonteeskee

From Gore, turn east on Highway 64. The Cherokee Courthouse is three miles east of town on the north side of the highway. (918) 489-5663. April-September, Monday-Saturday 9-5, Sunday 1-5. October-March, Wednesday-Saturday 9-5, Sunday 1-5. Other times by appointment. Closed state holidays. Free.

The log-hewn buildings at this site are all that remain of the Cherokees' original settlement in Oklahoma. As early as 1809, Chief Tahlonteeskee had led a group of about 300 tribal members westward into Arkansas Territory. Here they settled, recreating the homes and communities they had left in the eastern United States. With the expansion of Arkansas Territory, the "western" Cherokees were forced to move again in 1828 into what was later known as Indian Territory, near present-day Gore. They were joined by recent emigrants from the east, those who had traveled the Trail of Tears. Under the leadership of Chief John Ross, the "eastern" Cherokees won control of the tribe, moving the capital to Tahlequah. The buildings contain art work and drawings of significant events and personalities within the Cherokee tribe. There are also Indian artifacts, tools, and photographs.

MarVal Resort

From Gore, take Highway 100 about 1.5 miles north of town. Turn right at the MarVal sign on Gore Landing Road. Keep following signs to the entrance. (918) 489-2295.MarVal is open from late spring (usually March) through November. To help ensure the safety of the campers, security gates are locked each night, and trout fishermen must sign in each morning. Fees range from $12 for tent camping to $75 for cabins (based on four occupants). MarVal is also open to those who just want to play on the river for a day. Day-use fees are quite reasonable: $2 for adults, $1 for children.

Campers delight in this well-developed, private campground; here guests can fish, float and splash to their heart's content. The Illinois River, flowing south-southwest through Oklahoma from Arkansas, is one of the state's most scenic rivers. With an abundance of fish both native and those released by the state Wildlife Department (especially trout), it is also one of the state's best fishing rivers. MarVal, located above the confluence of the Illinois and the Arkansas, provides river access to campers and fishermen alike. In the river, guests splash, float or compete in tube races; restroom facilities and bathhouses are nearby. Those who wish to dry off can play basketball, mini-golf or volleyball in one of two sand courts. Youngsters can walk the 2.5-mile nature trail, or visit the recreation room to enjoy a variety of arcade games.

Guests with their own camper trailers can reserve RV sites, most with water and electric; seventeen are with sewer. Tent campers have a choice of twenty-five tent sites. For those who prefer to "camp" inside, the resort offers a variety of accommodations from cabanas with no toilet facilities of their own to cabins with decks and grills that sleep up to eight. All accommodations are furnished with small appliances, dishes and eating utensils; guests are encouraged to bring their own linens. A small store is located on the premises for those campers who find they've left something behind, and a snack bar provides youngsters with some of their favorite treats.

MarVal mails a quarterly newsletter, as well as a calendar of their many events to any who are interested; call and ask to be added to their mailing list. After you receive MarVal's calendar of events and activities, call ahead to make reservations. This family campground has a loyal following, and reservations are often made months in advance. Deposits are required at the time reservations are made; check with the office regarding their cancellation policy.

Tulsa Area

A cosmopolitan city with the friendliness of a small town, Tulsa is a wonderful place to spend a day, a week, or even a lifetime! Created out of the determination of its early settlers and enhanced by the fortunes of its famous oilmen, Tulsa is a city with many fine attractions.

Permanent settlers began to arrive in the area around the 1830s, when Indians from the eastern seaboard straggled in from the Trail of Tears. Relocated to Indian Territory by the Indian Removal Act of 1830, these resilient Native Americans turned "wilderness" into home. Council grounds were established, local governments created, and social structures and customs reinstated. Some Indians became businessmen; many others became farmers and ranchers. So successful were the Indians at creating "something from nothing" that, after the Civil War, the railroad came. Enterprising residents shipped cattle and prairie chickens east on the rails; once a small Creek settlement, Tulsa became a cow town, complete with cattle drives and rowdy cowboys.

By the turn of the century, this lifestyle was waning–in Tulsa and the rest of the West. In 1901, another force began to shape the town–oil! Discovered in nearby Red Fork in 1901, this slick, oozing liquid shaped the content and character of Tulsa for the next sixty years. Known as the "Oil Capital of the World," Tulsa had more oil companies and oil-related industries located here than did any other city on the globe. A unique combination of public and private development took hold, led by the oilmen of the day; Skelly, Phillips, and Sinclair, to name but a few.

Early-day leaders in business and in real estate built structures in the latest style–**Art Deco**. Business was good, and the creation of buildings, especially skyscrapers, was one of the economy's best indicators. "Zigzag" art deco, with its vertical emphasis, terra cotta facade, and symbolic embellishment dominated the landscape. Even religious structures (Boston Avenue Methodist Church and Christ the King Catholic Church) were built in this modern format. Today, Tulsa is ranked in the top five cities of the nation of the number of buildings erected in this popular architectural style.

On the dawn of a new century, Tulsa prides itself on being a clean city, dedicated to family values and economic diversity. Its history is evident in the many attractions and events that are here. But it's the spirit of Tulsa that makes the town unique; as Will Rogers said more than seventy years ago, "Tulsa...which would have been a real town, even if its people weren't greasy rich with oil, for it is founded on the spirit of its people."

Tulsa is located in the center of the beautiful, green hills of Northeast Oklahoma. From Oklahoma City, travel approximately 115 miles northeast on the Turner Turnpike (I-44), or take the more scenic "backroads," and relive history on Route 66. Tulsa Conventions and Visitors Bureau (918) 585-1201. 🗓

Tulsa Chamber of Commerce

Tulsa skyline.

Attractions

Bell's Amusement Park

3900 E. 21st Street, (918) 744-1991. Located on 21st Street, halfway between Harvard and Yale Avenues. Turn north at the appropriate sign for parking and park entrance. Open from April through September; days and hours vary depending on the month. Call for exact information. Park entrance $1, ride coupons are $1 each (rides require 1-3 tickets). All-you-can-ride wristbands are $13.75 for adults, $8.75 for children under forty-eight inches. Checks are not accepted, but major credit cards are. Senior citizens ride free with gate admission. A 5% tax is charged on all ride coupons and wristbands.

Enjoy old-fashioned fun at this traditional amusement park. Founded in 1951 by Robert K. Bell, Sr., the park sits adjacent to the Tulsa Fairgrounds and offers excitement for all ages. Small children enjoy the motorized cars, airplanes, and the ever-popular carousel. Teens enjoy the more active rides like the Tilt-a-Whirl, the Himalaya, and the Scrambler. Phantasmagoria, the haunted house, provides scary thrills for participants. The White Lightnin' log ride is a great place to cool off on hot summer days. The most popular ride at Bell's is Zingo, one of the nation's largest wooden roller coasters. The line moves quickly for this exciting combination of inching-uphill climbs and plunging-downhill races. For those with more sedate interests, there are two miniature golf courses, as well as a number of concession stands. When planning your trip to Bell's, be sure to check the local paper and coupon books for admission specials and discount coupons. One of the park's best bargains is the Family Four Pack: admission for four, with unlimited rides, Monday through Thursday evenings. Birthday parties, company parties, and group rates are all available with advance notice. Bell's is a wonderful place for summer fun!

Chainsaw Sculptures of Clayton Coss

The sculptures are scattered throughout the city. A listing of several easily-accessible sculptures follows. For more detailed information, pick up the local guide, "In the Trees of Tulsa," available at area bookstores for $18.95.

If you're unfamiliar with Tulsa, pick up a Tulsa street map at a local car rental agency, bookstore, or in the Tulsa telephone directory. Remember that streets running east to west are numbered; streets running north to south are in alphabetical order. North-south streets east of Main are named after cities east of the Mississippi River; streets west of Main are named after cities west of the Mississippi. Carvings owned by individuals are on private property, and they should be regarded as privately-owned works of art. Please do not enter the yards for a closer look or to take photographs without the owners' permission.

Tulsans are continually surprised and delighted by the talents of Clayton Coss, local chainsaw artist. Once an employee of Rockwell who dreamed of becoming a pilot, Coss turned to sculpting when his other plans didn't pan out. After ten years of carving, Coss has created sculptures depicting all types of wildlife: bears, eagles, songbirds, raccoons, dolphins, and dogs. He's carved boys with baseball bats, men with fishing poles, and children with their favorite pets. Mother Teresa, Babe Ruth, St. Francis of Assisi, and a Vietnam veteran have all been given lasting impressions by this talented sculptor. With Tulsa's abundant trees, Coss has an almost unlimited market; he schedules his work more than six months in advance. Each piece is special to its owners and to Coss, and there's a story to match each one. Watch carefully–that topped-out tree that you pass each day may be a new Coss creation tomorrow!

Sculptures in public places: Christ the King Church, 16th and Quincy; Utica Square, 21st and Utica; River Parks, 41st and Riverside; Veteran's Park, 18th and Boulder; Expo Square (inside the Expo Building), 21st and New Haven; Letter Carrier's Union meeting hall, 1st and Denver; Gilcrease Museum, 1400 Gilcrease Museum Road; Tulsa Zoo, Mohawk Park

Sculptures on private property, to be viewed from the street: 36th and Atlanta; 36th and Florence; 36th and Delaware; 38th and Toledo; 42nd and Jamestown; 31st and Woodward; 44th Place and Columbia; 39th Place and Delaware; 31st and Woodward; 31st and Peoria; 37th Place and New Haven. Sculptures located out of town: Sapulpa City Hall; Sapulpa High School; Jenks East Elementary; Will Rogers Memorial, Claremore; Honor Heights Park, Muskogee

Elsing Museum

University Village, 8555 South Lewis, (918) 299-2661, ext. 628, or 298-3628. From I-44 take the Lewis exit and go south on Lewis to 85th Street. Turn east into the ORU housing complex for retirees. Take the first right, following the road around the curve to the back of the complex. Turn right at the small white "Museum" sign. The collection is house in Cottage 28-A. Wednesday-Sunday, 1-4. Free, donations appreciated.

Diamonds, emeralds and rubies await visitors at this small but outstanding museum. At age 84, Willard Elsing has amassed a collection of minerals and gem stones that dazzle the ordinary visitor and excite students of geology. Exhibits trace the earth's history through millions of years. Individual rock specimens reveal the unique characteristics of the materials from which they're made. Florescent minerals glow eerily under black light; others bend and sway because of their composition. After sixty years of collecting, Mr. Elsing has also acquired artifacts from early civilizations and valuable Chinese art. One of his most unusual pieces is a three-foot long ship, carved from a single piece of jade. Older students and adults will enjoy a visit to this museum; Mr. Elsing, owner and curator, is present to answer questions and to provide commentary. Reservations for group tours should be made in advance.

Fenster Museum of Jewish Art

1223 E. 17th Place, (918) 582-3732. Located at 17th Place and Peoria, in the B'nai Emunah Synagogue. From I-44 take the Peoria exit and go north on Peoria to 17th Place. Parking is located on the west side of the building. Sunday-Thursday 10-4. Closed Friday, Saturday and all Jewish holidays. Free, donations gratefully accepted. Handicapped accessible. ★

The treasures displayed here span 4000 years of Jewish history, and they comprise the largest collection of Judaica in the Southwest. With artifacts from the Iron Age to the present, this museum shows the diversity of Jewish culture. Many exhibits contain sacred items marking the ceremonial events in a person's life; other articles are simple expressions of faith incorporated into everyday objects. The most revered items in the collection are the Torah scrolls. Some of the most moving items are those returned from the Holocaust. The exhibits at this museum are well maintained and explained. The staff is knowledgeable and helpful; they readily answer questions and provide explanations of the Jewish culture and heritage. Tours can be arranged by calling two weeks in advance. With advance notice, docents can be provided for even very small groups. The goal of this museum is not only to preserve Jewish culture but to encourage understanding between people of all faiths.

Gilcrease Museum

1400 Gilcrease Museum Road, (918) 596-2700. From Highway 51 West take the Gilcrease Museum Road exit and go north to Pine. (Or go north on the Osage Expressway from I-244 or Highway 75 to Pine. Go west on Pine to Gilcrease Museum Road.) The museum is located just south of the intersections of Pine and Gilcrease Museum Road (formerly 25th W. Avenue). Tuesday-Saturday 9-5. Also open Monday from Memorial Day-Labor Day. Thursday evenings until 8 p.m. Sunday and federal holidays 1-5. Closed Christmas Day. Admission is by donation, suggested at adult $3.00, family $5. Memberships are available. ★

Experience Gilcrease Museum, one of the nation's leading collections of western art and artifacts. Amassed by oilman Thomas Gilcrease, who received his first oil well as a gift at the age of fifteen, the collection contains Native American artifacts and a vast array of western art. In an attempt to provide educational opportunities for generations to come, Gilcrease opened his private collection first to scholarly study; later, he opened it to the public. The collection spans the period from 500 B.C. to the present, documenting man's development on the North American continent. The permanent collections at Gilcrease Museum are diverse, well-displayed, and very interesting. A number of galleries feature exhibits that are rotated on a regular basis. One gallery hosts an interactive exhibit of the museum's Mexican collection; another recreates an artist's studio. Of particular interest is the downstairs open storage area with glass coverings, where visitors can view many of the artifacts collected by Gilcrease. Free, docent-led tours are available daily at 2 p.m. or by special arrangement. Gallery tours for the hearing and sight-impaired are available by appointment. Please make all tour arrangements through the tour coordinator at (918) 596-2705.

The museum also offers a panoramic view of the scenic Osage Hills. Outside the museum are 23 acres of landscaped, **historic-theme gardens**. The remainder of the 440-acre grounds includes natural meadows and woodlands, **Thomas Gilcrease's home**, and **Stuart Park**. Visitors are welcome to stroll through the gardens and Stuart Park, and to visit Gilcrease's home which is now the headquarters for the Tulsa Historical Society. Tours of the gardens are also available. The museum and gardens are accessible to the physically challenged; wheelchairs and strollers are available.

Located on site, the **Rendezvous Restaurant** offers a lunch menu of sandwiches, salads, soups, daily specials, and desserts. The restaurant is open Tuesday-Saturday 11-2. Sunday Brunch is also served. Call (918) 596-2720 for information or reservations.

Each spring, the museum grounds come alive with the sounds of the annual **Rendezvous**. Originally a gathering of mountain men for the purposes of trading and socializing, the Rendezvous now provides an opportunity for historic "reenactors" to display period lifestyles and skills. The camp-like atmosphere is recreated when Indians pitch tepees, mountain men shoot muzzle-loading guns, storytellers capture the attention of listeners, and traders sell their wares. Other special events include lectures for adults and children's classes that are offered throughout the year. Most are limited in class size and require a small fee; registration is required. A Speakers Bureau is available year-round to make slide presentations to groups.

The **Museum Shop** features a unique selection of quality gifts and souvenirs. A wide variety of merchandise is available, from children's trinkets to handmade silver jewelry. Some of the best finds are art prints from the Gilcrease Collection and a wide assortment of books. A free catalogue is available upon request. With a balanced assortment of activity and art, the beautiful Gilcrease Museum depicts the significance of the American west.

Ida Dennie Willis Museum of Miniatures, Dolls and Toys

628 North Country Club Drive, (918) 584-6654. From Highway 51 west, take the Gilcrease Museum Road exit and turn right. Go north to Edison and turn right again. Go east on Edison past the golf course at Tulsa Country Club, and turn left onto Country Club Drive. The museum is in a renovated mansion on the left. Wednesday-Saturday 10:30-4:30 p.m. Closed Sunday, Monday and Tuesday. Adults $3; children ages seventeen and younger $2. Memberships are available.

Revisit your childhood as you tour this amazing collection of dolls and doll houses. Featuring every kind of doll from handmade folk dolls to dainty porcelain figurines, this museum celebrates dolls and the special relationship that girls have with them. Pop-up storybooks sit open beside character dolls who look as if they've stepped from the pages. Baby dolls lay in bassinets and strollers, awaiting the loving hands of a "mother" to take care of them. Especially fun are the promotional dolls from the past that were marketed to promote a particular product; Coke and Green Giant vegetables are both represented. Doll houses abound; from the inexpensively mass-produced to the painstakingly handmade, all of them are works of art.

Plan to spend about an hour at this museum. Reservations are required for groups. Mrs. Willis runs the museum. Visitors can often tour the museum with her, listening to her stories and enjoying her elementary-school-teacher style of explanation. With advance notice, Mrs. Willis will prepare a presentation featuring dolls and information on a particular subject. Mrs. Willis has a wonderful way of imparting knowledge of her subject and a love for collecting.

LaFortune Park

5501 S. Yale, (918) 596-8627. LaFortune Park is located between 51st and 61st Streets, Yale and Hudson Avenues. From Yale, parking is available in the lots at 52nd, 55th Place, and 58th Street. Smaller lots provide limited parking off Hudson Avenue. The park is open daily, 7 a.m.-11 p.m. Hours of operation for each facility within the park change seasonally. Admission to the park is free.

J.A. LaFortune was one of Tulsa's early citizens. Arriving in town around 1918, LaFortune tried his hand at several occupations. At that time, a man with intelligence, a small bankroll, and a willingness to take risks could make his way in the oil business, and that is just what

LaFortune did. Forty years later, Mr. LaFortune purchased a 270-acre tract of land to be developed as a park for the city of Tulsa. Today residents can play golf, tennis or baseball, and swim, jog or picnic at this beautiful park.

Two golf courses are located within the park. The **LaFortune Park Championship Golf Course** with 6970 total yards, is designed to provide a challenge for both novice and experienced golfers; in fact, LaFortune wanted the course to be "nothing less than perfect." This course has a par of 72, a slope of 123 and a USGA rating of 72.8. The other course is the only eighteen-hole, lighted **Par 3 course** in the region. This course is always busy. Call (918) 582-6000 for tee times at any of the public courses, up to a week in advance. For same-day tee times, call the Pro Shop at (918) 596-8627. A driving range, putting area, club house, pro shop and restaurant offer golfers traditional amenities. Green fees are $16.19 for the Championship Course and $11.87 for the Par 3. Carts are $19.43, pull carts are $3. Twilight, senior and junior fees are also available; call the Pro Shop for complete fee information.

The 3.2-mile **running path** that encircles the park is always busy. Along the path, runners can watch small children feeding ducks at the "big pond," located next to the Community Center. Those desiring a more leisurely stroll can visit **The Gardens**, where a flowering arbor and sensory garden are located. The sensory garden features aromatic plants with unusual textures. Braille identification plates have been placed for the visually impaired. An exercise course for those confined to wheelchairs is nearby. Also located in the Gardens is a **croquet and lawn bowling green**. Call the Community Center at (918) 596-8620 to reserve this area for a group or for more information. A **tennis complex** is located along Hudson Avenue.

The **Community Center** offers a variety of classes, from cooking to karate. Offered on a quarterly basis, these classes are described in a regularly-published newsletter. Day camps, home school activities, and special children's events are also offered. The Community Center can also be rented for private events during special hours. Call (918) 596-8620 for more information.

Most noticeable at LaFortune Park are the children. With several playgrounds throughout the park, this is a favorite picnic place for families with small children. The nearby rocks and creek provide ample opportunities for climbing, exploring and frog-watching. Families and children will also enjoy the large swimming pool and the batting cages. Family gatherings, church outings and high school reunions are held here on a regular basis. Shelter reservations are taken for weekends and holidays as much as a year in advance. Shelters can be reserved by calling (918) 596-5990.

Mac's Antique Car Museum

1319 East Fourth (Fourth Street and Peoria), (918) 583-7400. From Highway 51 (Broken Arrow Expressway) take the Peoria exit and go north on Peoria to 4th Street. The antique cars are housed in the white brick building with bright red letters, one block east of Peoria. (Look for the antique car at the corner of this intersection, advertising the museum.) Saturday-Sunday, noon-7. Adults $3.75, children ages 6-12 $2. Group tours are available on weekdays by appointment. Group rates are available.

Vintage cars, clean and shining, await your inspection at Mac's. A car collector for over twenty years, Mac McGlumphy has restored and assembled a collection of classic automobiles ranging from a 1912 Model T to a 1960 Mercedes hard top. The successful owner of Mac's Electric Supply Company, he decided about five years ago to open his collection to the public. Housed in a 2000-square-foot building only a few blocks from his business, the collection features thirty-seven classic cars. Although Mac enjoys all his cars, his personal favorites are the five Packards, one of which is valued at more than $400,000. From the sleek exterior paint jobs to the detailed, hand-worked interiors, these cars are classics. Appreciate the craftsmanship of a bygone era as you stroll through Mac's extensive collection.

Mohawk Park (Oxley Nature Center and Tulsa Zoo)

36th Street North and Sheridan Road, (918) 596-7275 or (918) 425-6871. From I-244 or Highway 11, take the Sheridan Road exit and go north to 36th Street North. Turn right onto 36th Street North and then immediately left into the park entrance. Daily, 5 a.m-9 p.m. $1 seasonal parking fee.

Drive through Mohawk Park to get a feel for all it has to offer. With over 2800 acres, the well-developed park has many things to see and do. Included in the park is the Oxley Nature

Center, the Tulsa Zoo, two golf courses, and a polo field. There are horseback riding trails, a hiking trail, playgrounds, and picnic shelters. A variety of special events (from powwows to rock concerts) is staged here each year.

Golfers enjoy playing at both of the eighteen-hole golf courses. The longer course, **Woodbine**, is par 72, with 6577 total yards, a slope of 115 and USGA rating of 71. The shorter course, **Pecan Valley**, has 6499 total yards and is a par 70 course (slope is 124 and USGA rating is 71.6). Green fees: weekdays $13.60, weekends $15.61. Twilight rates are available. Carts rent for $19.43, pull carts are $3. Tee times can be reserved by calling the Tulsa Automated Tee Time Reservation System at (918) 582-6000. Same-day tee times can be arranged by calling the Pro Shop at (918) 425-6871. A practice green, pro shop, and full service restaurant are also located here.

Oxley Nature Center

(918) 669-6644. Upon entering Mohawk Park, drive on the main road, past the zoo to the Oxley Nature Center entrance. Turn right and pass through the gate to the parking area outside the center. Trails: daily 8-5; Nature Center: Monday-Saturday 10-4:30; Sunday noon-4:30. Free.

For your best chance to observe wildlife, try to visit this unique retreat early on a spring morning or at dusk on an autumn day. Located in the northeast section of the city, this 800-acre wildlife refuge allows visitors to observe wildlife in its natural habitat. Start your tour in the Nature Center, where visitors view interesting and educational exhibits that introduce them to the area. Pick up a Trail Guide and hike along one of the center's seven nature trails to discover for yourself the beauty and mysteries of nature. The Red Fox and Blue Heron Trails are more developed; they feature printed trail guides and are handicapped accessible. Named for elements that can be found on each hike, the other, more primitive trails are Green Dragon Trail (named for a wildflower), Blackbird Marsh Trail, Beaver Lodge Trail, Coal Creek Trail, and Lake Trail. There are also trails to the Wildlife Study Area and to the North Woods.

Call ahead to inquire about special tours and events, or you may ask to be included in the Center's mailing list. The best way to enjoy the trails is by a group tour led by one of the center's naturalists. Tours are held on a regularly-scheduled basis (see the newsletter for listings), or form your own group of six or more and call for reservations. Special classes are offered on a periodic basis. They require advance registration; some may charge a small fee. Keep in mind that what you see will depend in large part upon the season and the time of day you visit.

Tulsa Zoo

(918) 669-6600. Located inside Mohawk Park. Once inside, follow the main road through the park. The zoo is visible on the left, with parking and the entrance well marked. Daily 10-5. Closed Christmas Day and the third Friday in June. Adults (ages 12-61) $5, senior citizens (ages 62 and over) $4, children ages 5-11 $2, children four and under free. Reduced admission is offered on several holidays and during Polar Bear Days, declared in January and February when the temperature drops to thirty-two degrees or below. Tulsa Zoo Friends, a support and promotional organization of the zoo, offers yearly memberships which include free admission to the zoo, quarterly newsletters, and preview nights for special events. For more information regarding membership, call (918) 669-6603. Handicapped accessible. ★

Everyone loves the zoo! Young and old alike delight in watching the animals and their antics. The Tulsa Zoo is just the place to go for a day of fun. Enter the zoo through the new entrance gate. To the left is the new gift shop; to the right is the train station and sidewalk leading to exhibit buildings. Directly ahead is a small plaza, paved with engraved bricks. Take a minute to read the inscriptions–some are humorous, many are touching, but they all have helped provide funds for the zoo's extensive renovation. Also located here is an events board, telling visitors about special presentations, animal feedings and training sessions. This is the place to rent a stroller or a wagon to carry your lunch, sweaters and camera. Covering seventy acres, the zoo takes at least two hours to visit, and it's easier if you don't have to carry items in your arms. Strollers are available for $2, wagons for $3. Feel free to pack a picnic lunch (a shelter and tables are located on the grounds) or eat at the Safari Grille. Other concessions are available on a seasonal basis.

Starting the tour to the right, patrons can first visit the Chimpanzee Connection. Visitors can see the chimps "up close and personal"; they are separated from these intelligent creatures only by thick panes of glass. The chimps roam freely inside and out to take advantage of their two playgrounds. Take a trip across the continent as you enter the Robert J. LaFortune North American Living Museum; four different buildings represent four different regions of our country: Arctic tundra, Southwest desert, Eastern forest, and Southern lowlands. Inside are exhibits about the land, the native culture, and the indigenous wildlife of each region. The next area is the Children's Zoo, where children can watch those cute little groundhogs or watch educational presentations in the amphitheater. Weary adults can rest here while their children are easily entertained at the playground area nearby. Restroom facilities are also close at hand. As you walk through the zoo, be sure to read the exhibit labels; they contain information about each animal's natural habitat and its current status in the world.

Inside the Main Zoo Building are aquariums, birds and reptiles. The reptile incubator and nursery are also located here. Properly identified by species and projected due date, eggs are prominently displayed, and baby reptiles can often be seen. Directly in front of this building are the sea lions. Daily feeding and training sessions are at 2 p.m. The big animals, lions, tigers, and bears, are located in cliff-type enclosures set in a large circle. A recent addition to the zoo is the new playground, located between the rhinos and lions. Children enjoy the climbing, running, hanging, and sliding that they can do here. Not far away is the station marking the halfway point for the train. Weary sightseers can board the train here (one way tickets are $1, round trip $1.50) and return quickly and effortlessly to the main gate. As visitors begin their stroll back to the entrance, they pass the African Savannah where giraffes, zebra, wildebeests, and other African animals live. Next, guests can visit the recently-completed Elephant Encounter. After viewing these huge animals at close range, go inside to enjoy interactive exhibits that explain, among other things, how elephants use their ears to stay cool. Visitors can even try to maneuver a mechanical elephant trunk!

The Zoo sponsors a variety of special events. **ZooFari**, an event especially for children, is held each April. In May, the Tulsa Philharmonic comes to the Zoo. **Sunset Safaris** are held on Tuesday and Friday evenings in July. On these special nights, admission is reduced after 6 p.m. and special entertainment is provided. **HallowZooeen** is held at the end of October. During this event, ghosts and goblins traipse along the Trick or Treat Trail, visiting booths to collect treats or play games. **Zoolightful**, a holiday light extravaganza, closes out the year. During the month of December, the zoo is open nightly for visitors to stroll among the beautiful lighting displays. The Zoo also hosts special overnight events, birthday parties, Spring Break activities, and summer workshops. Reservations are required. Group discount rates and after-hours picnics are also available. Call (918) 669-6600 for details..

Oklahoma Jazz Hall of Fame

322 N. Greenwood, (918) 582-1741. From I-244 take the Cincinnati/Detroit exit and turn north onto Detroit. Turn east on Haskell and circle the University Center at Tulsa, turning south on Greenwood. The red brick building is plainly visible from I-244. The Oklahoma Jazz Hall of Fame is open weekdays 9-5, and on Saturday from 10-1. Group tour arrangements should be made in advance. Free. Handicapped accessible.

Tulsa–the birthplace of American jazz. Many people are surprised when they hear this but, given the number of jazz musicians from the state and the caliber of their talent, this phrase could well be true. Early in the century, segregation made this part of downtown Tulsa a prosperous part of the black community. Neighborhoods prospered, businesses thrived, clubs and music halls lined the streets. Business on Greenwood was so good that the street became known as "America's Black Wall Street." Ernie Fields, Clarence Love, Cab Calloway, and Dizzie Gillespie all played here. As a tribute to these talented Oklahoma musicians and others like them, the Oklahoma Jazz Hall of Fame is now open. One exhibit shows the development of jazz from its earliest beginnings. Photographs of jazz greats line the walls. The Musical Library holds video, audio and photographic materials about featured artists. An art gallery completes the museum with sculptures depicting musical themes and performers. Musicians are inducted into the Hall of Fame each June in ceremonies that coincide with the annual observance of **Juneteenth**. This celebration of the Emancipation Proclamation of 1863 features jazz artists playing to crowds of more than 35,000. The documentation and preservation of this musical style may well make Tulsa the birthplace of American jazz!

Oral Roberts University

7777 South Lewis, (918) 495-6807. From I-44 go south on Lewis to the university entrance, the Avenue of Flags. Follow the drive to the right and park in the Mabee Center parking lot. Monday-Saturday 10:30-4:30, Sunday 1-5. Free. Handicapped accessible.

Started in 1963 with only three small buildings, ORU is now considered to be one of the most architecturally-unique campuses in the world. Driving down the avenue of flags, visitors see banners representing the countries from which students have come. Dominating the entrance to the university are the Praying Hands. Once the focal point of the sixty-story City of Faith medical complex located to the south, the hands represent the hand of medicine and the hand of prayer, raised together in healing. The hands were moved from their original location when the medical complex was sold. The shapes, colors, and materials of all the buildings have symbolic meanings. The Prayer Tower, which houses all visitor information services, sits in the middle of the campus. This two-hundred-foot tall structure is a modern representation of a cross; the vertical axis represents man's relationship to God; the horizontal axis represents man's relationship to man. Christ's Chapel, located nearby, is representative of Oral Robert's early tent revivals. The white of the buildings represents clean living and purity; the blue represents truth; and the gold represents the riches of heaven. The mirrors covering the buildings reflect man made in God's image, and they remind students that they are to be a reflection of Christ.

If you're touring the campus, be sure to stop at the **Visitor's Center** in the Prayer Tower. The Visitor's Center hosts two presentations for visitors. The slide presentation "ORU Excellence" explains the school's mission. This show runs every thirty minutes. "Journey Into Faith" is a multimedia presentation of Oral Roberts' call to the ministry. This thirty-six minute presentation begins every fifteen minutes, on the quarter hour. Both presentations are free. There is a small gift shop located on the same level, and an observation deck is on the floor above.

With over 4000 students, there are a number of activities and performances that are open to the public. For an events calendar, call 495-6400, or call the Student Activities Office or the School of Arts and Sciences for information about upcoming events.

The University sponsors **varsity sports** at the NCAA Division 1 level. Basketball, baseball, tennis, golf, soccer, track, and women's volleyball are offered and open to the public. Ticket prices ranges from $1-10, depending on the sport and the age of the spectator. Tickets to all sporting events can be purchased at the athletic ticket office or at the gate.

An accredited institution, ORU offers almost seventy undergraduate majors and four graduate and professional schools. Students from the United States and around the world attend this university, proving that, with his vision, Oral Roberts has had an impact on his world.

Performing Arts Center

Located at 3rd Street and Cincinnati, ticket office (918) 596-7111 or (800) 364-7111. From I-244 take the Cincinnati exit, and go south on Cincinnati to Third. Parking is available in several lots around the theater and in the underground parking lot located west of the building and accessed from Second Street. Tickets are available by calling the numbers above or at all Carson Attractions Select-A-Seat locations. $1.25 surcharge is added to all phone orders. Major credit cards are accepted. Group discounts are available.

Tulsa's unique Performing Arts Center (PAC) has just celebrated its twentieth birthday. Like many other entities in the city, this institution was erected through an unusual combination of private and public funds. Now a department of the City of Tulsa, the PAC is home to a variety of performing arts groups. Designed by Minoru Yamasaki, who was also the designer of the World Trade Center in New York, the PAC contains four theaters, with separate lobbies, dressing rooms, and work and rehearsal spaces, all located in a compact, one-half block area. **Chapman Music Hall**, with 2400 seats, is the largest theater in the complex. The **John H. Williams Theatre**, with 200 seats, is much more intimate. The two remaining studio theaters are smaller. Performances for a number of local arts companies are held here including the Tulsa Opera, Tulsa Ballet Theatre, Tulsa Philharmonic, Theatre Tulsa, American Theatre Company, Celebrity Attractions, Theatre North, LocalMotion, Tulsa Town Hall, CityArts, Tulsa Indian Actors Workshop, Theatre Pops, Theatreworks, and the Center for the Physically Limited. Forty-five-minute tours of the Performing Arts Center are offered free of charge by prior arrangement.

American Theatre Company

1820 South Boulder, (918) 747-9494.

As Tulsa's only resident professional theater company, ATC offers a variety of entertainment options throughout the year. From dramatic presentations to musical reviews, American Theatre Company has kept Tulsan's entertained for the past twenty years. Contact the company or the PAC ticket office for a calendar of scheduled performances.

Celebrity Attractions

(918) 254-1069, www.celebrityattractions.com.

Sponsors of the Best of Broadway series, Celebrity Attractions brings nationally-touring Broadway theater to the Tulsa stage. The upcoming 1997-98 season features five musicals, from "A Chorus Line" to "Peter Pan." Each production will have eight performances, with dates to be announced. Enjoy Broadway theater without traveling to New York!

Oklahoma Sinfonia/Tulsa Pops

6022-A South Sheridan, (918) 488-0396.

Each year, this forty-plus member ensemble performs a series of pop, jazz and classical concerts at the historic Brady Theater (call for directions). A number of special performances are also scheduled and held at various locations throughout the city. Less formal than the Philharmonic performances, the classically-trained musicians of the Sinfonia/Pops ensemble stage outstanding concerts. Call the administrative offices or the PAC ticket office for performance information.

Theatre Tulsa

207 North Main, (918) 587-8402.

Considered the oldest continuously-running theater company west of the Mississippi, Theatre Tulsa, once dubbed Tulsa Little Theatre, has won numerous awards for the quality of its work. Each season, the company presents eight productions, including a summer musical and two family-oriented plays. Contact the company or the PAC for upcoming performance information.

Tulsa Ballet Theatre

Performances held at PAC, offices located at 4512 South Peoria, (918) 749-6030. From I-44 take the Peoria exit and go south on Peoria to 45th Street. Continue south, just through the light and turn west into the parking lot. This is the home of Tulsa Ballet Theatre. Located here are the ballet company's studios, wardrobe rooms, scenery storage areas, administrative offices, and guild gift shop. Tulsa Ballet Theatre offices Monday-Friday 9-5. Ticket prices range from $11 to $57. Discounted tickets are available for children under age twelve, students, senior citizens, and groups of ten or more. ★

Oh, the beauty and intrigue of a live ballet performance! Tulsa Ballet Theatre was founded in 1954 by Roman Jasinski and Moscelyne Larkin, both principal dancers with the Ballet Russe de Monte Carlo. Although their school and civic ballet grew slowly at first, the company now includes thirty professional dancers with a full time staff of support personnel. The company's repertoire includes full-length classic ballets, as well as entertaining variations and contemporary performance pieces. For the best choice of seats, reservations should be made several weeks in advance. Although Chapman Music Hall at the Performing Arts Center seats 2300 patrons on three levels, most audience members prefer to watch the performance from the orchestra or front mezzanine seats.

Tours of TBT's facility are also available; call the office in advance to schedule. The home season of TBT includes two fall productions, two spring shows, and a series of Nutcracker performances. You can receive program information and make reservations by calling (918) 749-6006.

Tulsa Philharmonic

2901 South Harvard, (918) 747-PHIL. Ticket prices range from $10 to $35. Call for a schedule. ★

Tulsans have enjoyed excellent performances of classical music since 1948, when the Tulsa Philharmonic was founded. The Philharmonic offers a variety of series and special performances, including classics, pops, a series of young people's concerts, and family concerts. The orchestra also presents free concerts on special occasions, such as an annual Christmas concert and a concert at the Zoo. The 1997-98 Masterworks Series features several well-known performers, from violinist Elmar Oliviera to Tulsa's own Rodney Ackmann playing the bassoon. All concerts begin at 8 p.m. Open to all ticket-holders, a pre-concert discussion is held by Edward Dumit at 7 p.m. on concert nights.

Tulsa Opera

1610 South Boulder, (918) 587-4811. Call the Opera's administrative office or the PAC ticket office to inquire about upcoming performances. Tickets range from $5-13.50; discounts are available for students and groups.

Tulsa Opera is ranked among the top ten regional opera companies in the nation. Entering its 50th year in 1997, the company typically offers three operas each year.

Philbrook Museum of Art

2727 S. Rockford Road, (918) 749-7941 or (800) 324-7941. Located one block east of Peoria Avenue at 27th Place. Free parking in the museum lot. Tuesday-Saturday 10-5 (open Thursday evenings until 8 p.m.), Sunday 11-5. Closed Monday and major holidays. Guided tours are available to the public at 2 p.m. each Sunday and by appointment during regular hours. General adult admission is $4 plus tax; free to members and children ages 12 and under; admission for students with I.D. and seniors ages sixty-two and over is $2 plus tax. No admission is charged to those who only visit the museum shop, restaurant or grounds. Memberships are available; members receive a host of benefits including free admission. Group tours can be arranged by calling (918) 748-5309 at least two weeks in advance. A wide variety of art classes for young and old is offered through the Floyd Museum School. Call (918) 748-5374 for specific class information. Call the regular number for information on Philbrook's special events, held throughout the year. Handicapped accessible. ★

Tour beautiful Philbrook for a "window on the world." Waite Phillips was one of Tulsa's most successful oilmen and one of the city's most generous philanthropists. In 1928, he commissioned the building of Villa Philbrook, his new Italian Renaissance home situated on the outskirts of town. After residing at the Villa for eleven years, the Phillips donated their home to the citizens of Tulsa to be used as an art museum.

The home-turned-museum is beautifully appointed, and many of the furnishings are original. Villa galleries house Philbrook's diverse permanent collections of European, Ancient, Asian, Afri-

View of the gardens at Philbrook.

can, Native American, and twentieth-century American art and artifacts. Philbrook's exhibits help visitors understand not only the art but the culture of the countries whose art is represented.

Each year, special exhibitions from around the world are shown in the 150,000-square-foot **new wing**, completed in 1991. For example, three exciting special exhibitions are scheduled for 1998, Philbrook's "Year of Europe"; call the museum for details and ticket information.

The twenty-three acres of **landscaped gardens** and grounds include a terraced garden, a rock garden, and a reflecting pond. Plaques throughout the grounds provide visitors with information about the gardens; audio tapes for self-guided tours are also available for rent. The **Museum Shop** offers beautiful gifts and souvenirs, as well as a guide to the collections, the villa and the gardens. Overlooking the sculpture garden, **la Villa Restaurant** offers lunch and Sunday brunch. Call (918) 748-5367 for reservations and updated information on expansion of the restaurant hours.

Philbrook is one of only three museums in America with the unique combination of historic home, collections and gardens. With its beautiful collections, scenic gardens, and emphasis on multi-cultural understanding, Philbrook is truly a "window on the world."

Redbud Valley Nature Preserve

Approximately 161st East Avenue and Pine, (918) 669-6460 or 669-6644. From I-244 go west to 161st East Avenue. Turn left under the expressway and left again at the stop sign. Find 161st East Avenue and travel north for 3.5 miles. Watch for the signs. Maintained by Tulsa Parks and Recreation. Wednesday-Sunday 8-5; Visitor's Center open 11-3. Closed Monday, Tuesday, and holidays. Free.

The uniqueness of Oklahoma is experienced here, where three of the state's major land forms converge. Fertile bottomlands, limestone bluffs, and western prairie meet in this eighty-acre preserve. Hiking along the primitive one-mile trail, visitors see cottonwoods, maples, elms, and oaks growing in the fertile bottomlands. In the transitional zone between the bottomlands and bluffs are redbuds, whose red-purple flowers brighten the Oklahoma hills in early spring. The bluffs themselves contain caves, reminding hikers that these caverns have hosted a variety of visitors in the past. From a vantage point atop the bluffs, guests can look out over the vast expanse of prairie. This small preserve is a microcosm of the larger Oklahoma environment.

Choose a day of beautiful weather to visit Redbud Valley. Visitors should dress for an outdoor excursion; jeans, sweatshirt and hiking boots are recommended. Small children and pets should stay at home. Restrooms and a picnic area are located next to the Visitors Center at the entrance to the park. No food should be taken into the preserve itself; picnicking in the park is not permitted. Wildflower lovers might wish to take along a guide book to identify the many different varieties that grow here; but remember to stay on the trails and look, don't pick! Part of the beauty of the preserve is the pristine quality of the park.

River Parks

Located along both banks of the Arkansas River, River Parks Authority (918) 596-2001. The east side of the park runs from 11th Street on the north to 81st Street on the south, with playgrounds at 19th and 41st Streets. The west side begins at 11th Street on the north and runs south to 31st Street; the Old West playground is located about halfway between these two points. A curfew is enforced from 11 p.m.-5 a.m. Free. Restrooms are available at the Model Parks area at 19th Street, at the Pedestrian Bridge at 31st Street, and at the pavilion at 41st Street.

The Fountains at River Parks.

Concessions are usually sold at the pavilions during the summer months. Benches and picnic tables are scattered throughout the park, and they are available on a first come-first serve basis.

When you are standing on the bank of the Arkansas River, it's difficult to picture the majestic mountains where this river originates. Flowing eastward out of the Rockies as a crystal clear stream, the river finds its way to the southern plains. On more level ground, the river's flow is slowed, it's channel widened. It's along the banks of this river that the city of Tulsa grew.

Used only briefly as a source of water for the city, the river now provides abundant recreational opportunities. Fisherman cast their lures along the banks or from the bridge, hoping to catch the huge fish that feed below the low-water dam. Runners, walkers, bicyclists, and skaters travel the trail that runs along the water's edge. To reach the other side, park visitors cross the Pedestrian Bridge. Built by the Frisco Railroad in 1895, this was the first bridge in the area to span the Arkansas River. Upon its demise as a railroad bridge, it was donated to the city of Tulsa. The bridge and subsequent developments nearby are now the focal point of the park. A low-water dam has been constructed just under the bridge to create a small lake upstream. Here, water activities, such as rowing, canoeing and sculling are practiced. Illuminated during the summer months, Blair Fountain shoots a jet of water high into the sky.

The **West Bank** features the Old West playground, perfect for children. With seating for 2,000, the park's amphitheater is also located on the West Bank. Here, music lovers can hear big name entertainers perform on the floating stage. On Tuesday evenings during the summer, Tulsa's own **Starlight Band** performs free concerts under the stars.

Tulsa's River Parks Authority sponsors a number of activities along the banks of the Arkansas River. The Easter Bunny makes an appearance each spring during the annual **Easter Egg Hunt**. In July, aspiring artists try their hand at creating sand sculptures at the Arkansas River **Sand Castle Building Contest**. For almost fifty years, Tulsa's community-organized Starlight Band has held free **concerts** with music ranging from show tunes to pop music; these are now staged at the park's amphitheater and floating stage. For a calendar of events or more information, call (918) 596-2001.

Spotlight Theatre–"The Drunkard"

1381 Riverside Drive, (918) 587-5030. Located on the edge of downtown, the theater is on the corner of Riverside Drive and Houston. Parking is available on adjacent streets. Saturdays only; singing at 8 p.m., curtain at 8:15. $8.50 per person. Group tickets (available at a discount) must be purchased at one time, at least twenty-four hours in advance. Make reservations in advance for this fun-filled evening. While tickets are sometimes available the day before the show, the theater is small and often filled with tour groups and company parties, especially around the holidays. Plan on a late evening; if you stay for the Olio it may be midnight before you reach home. This fun-filled evening is most appropriate for children ages ten and up. The show donates all proceeds to various Tulsa charities.

Old-fashioned fun is served at "The Drunkard," Tulsa's longest-running, continuous production. A melodrama about the evils of drinking, this show has a villain worth hissing and a hero worth cheering, and the audience is encouraged to do both!

Overlooking the Arkansas River, the Spotlight Theatre was once the residence and musical studio of an early-Tulsa piano teacher. Designed by Bruce Goff, the building is a classic example of Art Deco architecture. The entrance is marked by rectangular windows faced with black panels (piano keys to those who notice as they enter the building). The show's pianist leads the singing of old-fashioned songs; then the lights go down, and the curtain goes up on one of Tulsa's oldest traditions. Audience participation is strongly encouraged and makes the production more fun for the actors, too! Patrons are served complimentary pretzels; soft drinks, beer, malt coolers, and sparkling water are available for purchase. After the show, enjoy free coffee and sandwiches before you witness the Olio, Tulsa's own version of vaudeville. Featuring local entertainment, the Olio is filled with some of the area's most unique acts.

Tulsa Drillers Baseball

Driller Stadium, 4802 E. 15th Street, (918) 744-5901. From 15th and Yale, turn west and go approximately one block. Parking lots are located inside either entrance. Attendants will direct traffic to

The Drillers.

the appropriate parking areas. Season runs from April to August. Games begin at 7:05 or 7:35, depending on the time of year. Sunday games begin at 2:05 or 6:05. Ticket prices range from $4 to $7. Occasional $1 discounts are given to children ages fourteen and under and seniors. Children ages three and under are admitted free if they do not occupy an individual seat. Tickets may be purchased in person at the ticket office, or by phone or mail. Drillers tickets are also available in advance at any of the four Tulsa Dillard's locations. Call the Driller office for a schedule and details about the games.

Tulsans have long enjoyed the thrills of baseball. From the city's earliest days, baseball has been one of the city's favorite sports. Because of the influence of oil on Tulsa's economy throughout the years, Tulsa's professional baseball teams have carried oil-related names, and they have worn oil-related logos on their uniforms. Now the Tulsa Drillers are the Double A Affiliate of the American League Texas Rangers. In addition to the game, other crowd-pleasing activities are often held. Promotional giveaways, laser light shows, and fireworks displays, a speed-pitch machine, Hornsby the mascot, and more are all part of the "extras" at the ball game. New amenities at the ball park are a "no-alcohol" section and backs on every seat. Engage in America's favorite pastime as you watch the Tulsa Drillers! Handicapped accessible.

Tulsa Oilers Hockey

Maxwell Convention Center, 100 Civic Center, (918) 596-7177. To reach downtown take either I-244 or Highway 51 (Broken Arrow Expressway). If approaching Tulsa from the east on I-244, follow the signs for the Downtown-7th Street exit. If taking Highway 51 west into town, follow the signs to Bartlesville, then immediately take the 7th Street exit which curves up and around into downtown. Go west on 7th to Denver. Turn right on Denver and go north to 6th Street. Turn west. The convention center is on the right, in the middle of the block. Paid event parking is available in lots north of the Convention Center. Some fee-based parking is available in lots adjacent to the arena. A skyway connect the Convention Center with parking and the Doubletree Hotel across the street. Monday-Saturday games start at 7 or 7:30, Sunday games start at 2:30. Adults $11 and $7, children ages eleven and under $9 and $5; children ages three and under are free if they don't occupy a seat. Tickets may be purchased at the Oilers office on Sheridan Road, at any of Tulsa's Dillard's Department Stores, or the Brady Theatre, 10 Southwest Brady Street. Phone reservations can be made by calling (800) 654-9545. Season tickets are available; 10% discount if paid in full by July 1. Ticket prices are subject to change. Handicapped accessible.

"Keep your eye on the puck" the announcer says each week, as the Tulsa Oilers host the other teams from the Central Hockey League. One of Tulsa's most popular sports teams, the Tulsa Oilers can boast one of the league's best records. Pick up a season schedule by visiting, calling or writing the Tulsa Oilers' office at 4528 South Sheridan, Suite 212, 74145, (918) 663-5888. While there, you can also check the promotional schedule–a number of hockey-related items are given away on various nights throughout the season. Concessions and souvenirs are on sale in the concourse encompassing the arena. If you're looking for fun and excitement, don't miss Tulsa Oilers hockey!

University of Tulsa

600 S. College, (918) 631-2307, (800) 331-3050, internet: www.utulsa.edu. Located between Delaware and Harvard, 4th Place and 11th Street, the college is easily accessible. Parking is at a premium. Some spaces are reserved for visitors in each of the lots. Additional parking is available on side streets. Dates and hours of activities vary from school to school and season to season. Contact the appropriate department for specific information. Handicapped accessible.

This school, which had its humble beginnings as a church school for Indian girls, has grown into one of the region's major universities. Originally named Henry Kendall College and located in Muskogee, the school moved to Tulsa in 1907. It was renamed the University of Tulsa in 1921. TU offers more than 54 major fields of undergraduate study to more than 3000 students. Masters degrees are offered in 27 programs, and doctoral degrees in nine programs. Nationally-recognized programs include English, psychology, finance, energy law, and mechanical and chemical engineering. The undergraduate and graduate programs in petroleum engineering are ranked in the nation's top five. TU is a leading research center for Native American law and history, and the College of Law offers special classes and programs in energy and environmental law.

Nestled in the heart of the city, the campus is quite pretty. It's appropriate that a walking tour of the campus should begin at Kendall Hall, the site of the University's first building. The first Kendall Hall sat majestically in the center of the campus. It served a variety of purposes until 1972, when it was razed for construction of the new **Kendall Hall**. This building now houses the theater department, the administrative office for the School of Music, and KWGS, the campus radio station. KWGS, whose call letters are the initials of W.G. Skelly, a prominent Tulsa oilman and university benefactor, is the local affiliate of National Public Radio. The **Theater Department** usually stages three to four performances each year. Tickets are $7 for adults and $5 for students and senior citizens. Tickets may be reserved by calling the box office at (918) 631-2567 or 631-3857. The **School of Music** offers free concerts and recitals throughout the year. For information on music events call 631-2262.

Guests will also want to visit Phillips Hall that now houses the School of Fine Arts and the **Alexander Hogue Gallery**. Alexander Hogue, himself an artist, directed TU's School of Art from 1945 until 1963. The gallery exhibits work by faculty, graduates and undergraduates; exhibits are rotated monthly. The Gallery is open weekdays 8-5, Saturday 1-4, closed Sunday and university holidays.

The University of Tulsa offers a wide variety of **varsity sports**: basketball, football, golf, soccer, softball, tennis, and volleyball. Football and soccer games are held in Skelly Stadium, the forty thousand seat arena partially funded by W.G. Skelly. Seasons and admission vary from sport to sport. Call the Ticket Office at 631-4688 for more information.

Student's spiritual needs are met in **Sharp Memorial Chapel**. This small, white chapel with pointed spire was named for one of Tulsa's oil men, Roger C. Sharp. The services offered here reflect the University's ties to the Presbyterian church. The appointments here, as well as the stained glass windows, are beautiful. The Chapel may be rented, and it is a popular place for weddings.

Perhaps most interesting to visitors is **McFarlin Library**. The building, completed in 1930 and expanded in 1979, houses a number of special collections. As a research center for Native American law and history, the library contains one of the nation's most complete sets of laws, constitutions, and regulations involving Indian tribes. Alice Robertson, Oklahoma's first female Congressional representative during the early 1900s, donated her collections of correspondence, photographs and books. There are distinguished author collections from major writers including William Faulkner, James Joyce, D.H. Lawrence, Gerturde Stein, and Walt Whitman. The university's Academic Publications Office publishes the world-renowned *James Joyce Quar-*

terly that provides more information about the collection.

The University of Tulsa campus has recently been declared an affiliate garden of the Oklahoma Botanical Garden and Arboretum. This designation requires that the garden have at least 250 species of flowers, shrubs, and trees; it also requires that the garden be available to the public. Other Oklahoma gardens sharing this designation are Honor Heights Park in Muskogee and the Kirkpatrick Center Botanical Gardens in Oklahoma City.

The University of Tulsa, started as a religious mission and built by oil men's fervor, offers students an excellent education. At the University of Tulsa, "education means the world."

Woodward Park/Rose Garden

21st Street at Peoria, (918) 746-7877 or 596-7275. From Peoria go south of 21st Street approximately one block and turn east to drive through or park. Daily, 6 a.m.-9 p.m. Free.

Once accessible only by wagon, this land was considered too far out in the country for a city park. When the city paid $100 per acre for the land, Tulsans were outraged. Now landscaped with more than 15,000 azaleas along the sloping creek bank, this park is the pride of the city. Enjoy a leisurely stroll along the trails that wind through the blooming azalea beds. Benches provide seating for quiet, reflective moments. Rock ledges and edgestones help create picture perfect settings for family photos. Picnic on the lawn in the shade of majestic trees. This is a perfect place to spread a blanket, stretch out, and read a book. Others enjoy soaring on the swings, playing catch, or hiking along the trails.

Several small gardens invite visitors to stroll their rock-hewn paths. Just east of the azaleas is a rock garden boasting beautiful seasonal plantings. Water trickles from a fountain through the garden. Children climb over the boulders and around the small pools that form in the crevices of the rocks. A visit here on Easter morning resembles an Easter parade, as families pose for pictures amid the flowering foliage. Just south of the rock garden is a circular herb garden, where visitors may pinch and smell the herbs that are grown.

From May through October, guests delight in visiting the **Municipal Rose Garden**. Built in Italian Renaissance style in 1935, the garden contains approximately 9000 plants of over 250 varieties. Fountains and pools reflect the beautiful colors of roses in bloom. Squirrels dart

Tulsa Chamber of Commerce

Scenic Woodward Park.

along the pathways; birds sing overhead. The rose garden offers a welcome respite from the busy and often chaotic lives we lead.

Just south of the rose garden is the **Tulsa Garden Center**. Once a private residence, the building is now headquarters for the Tulsa Garden Club. Inside are restrooms and an excellent gift shop offering garden-related treasures. The club sponsors various types of activities, and the home is available for rental. Behind the Garden Center is the **Conservatory** and **Arboretum**. The Conservatory showcases seasonal displays. The Arboretum contains unusual examples of trees and shrubs that will grow in this climate.

Don't forget your camera! The park provides perfect photographic backgrounds for family pictures. Favorite poses are staged along the creek, atop the log bridge, or in the nooks and crannies along the trails.

Dining

Albert G's Bar-B-Q $, $$

2748 S. Harvard (918) 747-4799. From Highway 51 (Broken Arrow Expressway), take the Harvard exit and go south (right) to 27th Street. The restaurant is on the west side of the street. Monday-Saturday 11 a.m.-8:30 p.m. Closed Sunday.

Albert G's owner, Chuck Gawey, was one of the city's first entrepreneurs to convert a closed-down gas station into a small, quaint eatery. Now diners order at the cash register and eat in the clean, white sitting area that used to be the garage. Mouth-watering ribs, brisket, and chicken are served daily. A special delight to health-conscious barbecue lovers is the delicious smoked turkey. Truly a family business, the traditional side dishes, potato salad, and cole slaw are made by Gawey's mother. His father helps with the cooking and catering deliveries. This restaurant offers "Smokin' to please bar-b-q." Enjoy!

Atlantic Sea Grill $$, $$$

8321-A E. 61st St. (918) 252-7966. From Highway 169, take the 61st Street exit and go west 1.5 miles to Eaton Square at the corner of 61st and Memorial. Lunch: Monday-Friday 11:30-2:30 p.m. Dinner: Monday-Thursday 5:30 - 10 p.m., Friday-Saturday 5:30-11:00 p.m. Handicapped accessible.

The Atlantic Sea Grill has long been a favorite of Tulsans, as evidenced by the many years the restaurant has been selected in Tulsa People's annual "Reader's Choice" awards. The Sea Grill offers diners exquisite decor, fine service and delicious food, including steaks, veal and pasta. However, the restaurant's specialty is seafood. Salmon, halibut, shrimp, lobster, and King crab legs are all featured items. Because of its elegant decor and quiet atmosphere, the Sea Grill is known as one of Tulsa's most romantic places to dine. During warmer months, loving couples may dine at candle-lit tables on a terrace under the stars. The Atlantic Sea Grill offers a memorable dining experience.

Avalon Steakhouse $$, $$$

6304 S. 57th W. Ave. (918) 446-9917. Located in west Tulsa. From I-44 take the Route 66 exit, making an immediate left U-turn in front of the large car dealership. Two right turns (follow the signs) will deliver you to the restaurant.

Known since 1968 for their outstanding steak, the Avalon is one of Tulsa's favorite restaurants. Diners can even choose their own steak from the meat case. The expanded menu offers seafood, pork chops and chicken, all served in a comfortable atmosphere of antiques and stained glass.

Big Al's Subs and Health Foods $

15th and Harvard, (918) 744-5085, FAX 744-5080. From Highway 51 (Broken Arrow Expressway), take the Harvard exit, going north on Harvard to 15th Street. Monday - Friday 11-8, Saturday, 11-4.

Big Al's was one of Tulsa's first health food restaurants. Started almost 25 years ago as a submarine sandwich shop, the restaurant began to expand its menu in the early 1970s. Smoothies were offered, and a juice bar was added. Salads, burritos (now popularly known elsewhere as "wraps"), vegetarian sandwiches, and burgers are also on the menu. Sandwiches come on white or whole wheat submarine buns, pita bread, or sliced bread, and white or whole wheat flour tortillas are used to make burritos. The salad menu includes spinach, taco, turkey and avocado, tuna, and veggie salads. Tabouli, potato salad, brown rice salad, and bean and cheese nachos comprise the side orders and snacks. Vegetarians can order from a customized menu. Parking at this popular eatery is limited. Call or fax ahead for carry-out orders.

Bourbon Street Cafe $$

1542 E. 15th Street, (918) 583-5555. From Highway 51 take the Utica exit, turning south on Utica. At 15th Street, turn west. The restaurant is a few blocks west, on the south side of the street. Limited parking is available in the lot next to the restaurant. Valet parking is available during the evening hours. Patrons may also park along nearby side streets. Open 11 a.m.-1 a.m. daily.

Tulsans no longer have to travel to New Orleans for delicious cajun food; they'll find it at Bourbon Street Cafe! Located in the trendy Cherry Street area and winner of *Urban Tulsa's* Best New Restaurant award, this restaurant combines savory cuisine, excellent service, and a stylish atmosphere. The used-brick walls, cement floor, exposed ducts, and arched doorways create an air of casualness. The white tablecloths and fresh flowers lend an air of sophistication. The extensive menu offers cajun specialities, with frog legs, alligator, and oysters as appetizers. Blackened and grilled steak, seafood, and chicken are available as entrees. Pastas, gumbos and salads are lighter alternatives. A well-stocked bar and a variety of delicious desserts complete the restaurant's presentation. A trip to Bourbon Street Cafe is a trip to New Orleans—without having to pack your bags!

Bravo! Ristorante $$, $$$

100 East 2nd Street, (918) 582-9000 or (918) 560-2254. Located in the Adam's Mark Hotel at the Williams Center. From I-244 take the Cincinnati exit and go south on Cincinnati to 1st Street. Turn west on 1st until reaching the Williams Center. Parking is available in the lot just west of the Williams Center. The Adams Mark is just across the street to the south. Sunday-Thursday 5:30-10 p.m., Friday and Saturday 5:30-11 p.m. Handicapped accessible.

"Bravo!" is what you'll want to shout after listening to some of the restaurants' singing waiters and waitresses! Guests here enjoy a pleasant, upscale atmosphere while they dine on delicious Italian cuisine. The menu features pesci (seafood), carni (beef) and pollo (chicken), as well as everyone's favorite pasta dishes. However, the most delightful aspect of the evening is the singing! Servers occasionally serenade diners at their individual tables; performing en masse, they delight the entire restaurant with excerpts from famous musical scores. Bravo!– for excellent dining and lighthearted fun! Reservations suggested.

Cafe Ole $, $$

3509 S. Peoria, (918) 745-6699. From I-44, take the Peoria exit and go north on Peoria to 35th. Cafe Ole faces 35th Street, not Peoria. Parking is available on the street or in the lot behind the cafe. Monday-Saturday, lunch 11-3, dinner 6-9, closing at 10 p.m. Friday and Saturday. Brunch Saturday and Sunday 9-1:30 p.m.

Tucked into the corner of a small Brookside-area mall, Cafe Ole caters to a leisurely, food-loving crowd. The cafe serves creative Mexican dishes, featuring both blue and yellow corn tortillas, black beans, and rice. Cervesa, chips and salsa, are popular appetizers that are enjoyed inside the small cozy restaurant or outdoors on the covered terrace. Subtly flavored and appealingly presented, the food is deliciously different from the usual Tex-Mex offerings of other restaurants. Brunch, served Saturday and Sunday, is a casual, leisurely affair.

Coney Islander $

Five locations in the Tulsa area: 7462 E. Admiral Place (918) 836-2336; 1614 N. Lewis (918) 587-4800; 3919 S. Peoria (918) 742-7259; 2838 E. 11th (918) 592-3113; 7825 E. 71st (918) 252-1711. Hours vary by location.

Here you find the absolute best hot dog in town! Started in 1926 by Christ D. Economou, the original store was located in downtown Tulsa. Busy office workers, judges, celebrities,

Tulsa Night Life

by Shanna Marlow

Tulsa's night life is as diverse as the city itself and your entertainment options are limited only by your own imagination. Listed below are a few of Tulsa's hottest new and favorite traditional night spots. The establishments listed below are for adults 21 years and older, unless otherwise noted.

Blue Rose Cafe

3421 S. Peoria, (918) 742-3873. Daily 11 a.m.-2 a.m.

Don't let the row of Harley Davidsons parked outside discourage you from enjoying this Tulsa landmark! The Blue Rose offers a festive, casual atmosphere. During warm months, the outdoor deck is a great place for people watching or enjoying special events such as the Mayor of Brookside Contest, the Herb Festival, or the Halloween Boo Ha Ha. The Blue Rose also has a small menu of appetizers and burgers. Live entertainment from folk music to jazz or cajun can be heard every evening except Friday, and sometimes even then. There is no cover charge. Handicapped accessible with some difficulty.

Cain's Ballroom

423 N. Main, (918) 584-2309.

No cruise through Tulsa's night life would be complete without Cain's Ballroom. Cain's is a world famous landmark for Western Swing culture and it reigns supreme as "Tulsa's Timeless Honky-Tonk." Cain's was once the home of Bob Wills and the Texas Playboys and has remained virtually unchanged during the past seventy years. Now on any given night, bands ranging from The Village People to Lyle

Lovett to Arlo Guthrie visit Cain's. Admission prices vary and the Ballroom is only open on show nights. Though there is an occasional outdoor event in the summer, the lack of air conditioning cuts the summer schedule way back. Call for show schedule, prices, and questions about handicapped accessibility.

Caravan Cattle Company

7901 E. 41st Street, (918) 663-5468. Tuesday, Thursday, Friday, Saturday nights. Cover charge $3.

Want to scoot a boot? This is the place. Boasting one of the state's largest wooden dance floors, Caravan is a two-stepper's paradise. The music is nonstop popular country music, sprinkled with disco and rock n roll. The club also offers a smaller "cabaret" area featuring live bands on weekend nights. Call ahead for specials such as free dance lessons and adies nights.

The Elephant Run Restaurant and Club

3141 E. Skelly Drive, (918) 749-5561. Open daily. Located inside the Trade Winds Central Inn.

The Elephant Run is one of Tulsa's hottest Karaoke bars. Crowds are heavy as people wait for their chance to be stars and enjoy the free hors d'oeurve buffet. Karaoke plays from 5-8:45; happy hour buffet is available from 5-7 p.m. Live music starts at 9 p.m. Though the full-menu restaurant is open daily, there is no entertainment on Sunday. Handicapped accessible.

Full Moon Cafe

Two locations: 6151 S. Sheridan, (918) 492-1551; 1525 E. 15th Street, (918) 583-6666.

Full Moon Cafe offers two kinds of fun under one roof. By day, you'll find a casual restaurant featuring a full menu of soups, salads, sandwiches, and entrees. By night, Full Moon becomes a favorite spot to hear Tulsa's most popular bands. Before 9 p.m., all ages are admitted to the restaurant. After 9 p.m., Full Moon admits ages 21 and over only. Be sure to catch the Full Moon Party every month on the night of the full moon. No cover charge.

Sideline Sports Bar & Grill

5936 S. Lewis, (918) 742-3499. Open daily 11:30 a.m.-2 a.m.

Looking for a great place to watch the big game? Filled with sports decor, Sideline Sports Bar features big screen television, multiple monitors, and a lively atmosphere. Check out the grill menu for munchies and burgers. Sideline features live music Wednesday-Saturday nights with an occasional cover charge. Handicapped accessible.

Tulsa City Limits

2117 S. Garnett, (918) 438-3263.

Tulsa City Limits is the venue for live country music concerts. It features two floors of seating, with dance floors located on each level. Performers such as Mark Chesnutt, Little Texas, Pam Tillis, and many more play at the Limits. It's no surprise the club is featured in the video version of Brooks & Dunn's "Boot Scootin' Boogie." Call ahead for concert schedules and cover charge information.

Tulsa Comedy Club

6906 S. Lewis, (918) 481-0558. Tuesday-Thursday and Sunday 8 p.m., Friday-Saturday 8 and 10:30 p.m. Tickets are about $4 for Sunday, $8-10 for other shows plus a minimum food or drink order.

This is one of Tulsa's newest and most popular night spots. Tulsa Comedy Club features nationally-known ("A" list) comedians from clubs such as the Improv. As many as three comedians typically perform during each show. Adults eighteen years of age and older are admitted. The Comedy Club also offers a great menu of appetizers and entrees. Reservations are required prior to show time and you should arrive early for best seating. Doors open at 7 p.m.

oilmen, cowboys, and street people all waited in line outside the steamed-up windows for a taste of that delicious frankfurter, wrapped in a steaming bun and covered with chili. Sitting in old school desks under slowly turning ceiling fans, the variety of patrons all enjoyed what has now become a Tulsa trademark. The original restaurant closed in 1995; a new one has opened just across the street, featuring the same grill that has cooked over sixty million hot dogs. The vintage school desks have also been moved, as has the 400-pound vat used to cook the chili.

Jamil's Restaurant $$$

2833 E. 51st St. (918) 742-9097. From I-44 take the Harvard exit (which actually puts you on 51st Street) and turn west. Jamil's is immediately ahead, on the north. Sunday-Thursday 4-11, Friday-Saturday 4-midnight.

In a part of the country known for great steak, Jamil's is one of Tulsa's oldest and most popular steak houses. For the past fifty-two years, diners have enjoyed some of the best hickory-grilled steaks, chicken and seafood in town. Jamil Elias opened the restaurant in 1945; his son Tyrone and granddaughter Jennifer now work here. Each meal begins with Lebanese appetizers: iced vegetable sticks and hummus dip, cabbage rolls, barbecue ribs, and bologna. Unwary patrons often fill up on the hors d'oeuvres, leaving little room for steak; however, the baked potato and steak, grilled to order, are the highlights of the meal. Fillet, ribeye, Kansas City Strip, and T-bone steaks are all available. Fish and chicken dishes have been added to keep up with trends.

The decor hasn't changed much in the 39 years Jamil's has been at this location. Located at the back of the building, the entrance faces Skelly Drive. Diners walk past the kitchen on their way to one of four dining areas. The dark rooms are cozily lit by candles; the tables are draped with plastic burgundy cloths; the walls are covered with pictures of sports and entertainment personalities. The service is friendly; several of the wait staff have been with the restaurant for years. All menu items are available for carryout; a Jamil's meal in the privacy of one's own home is a real treat!

Knotty Pine Barbeque $

3301 W. 5th, (918) 584-0171 or 71st and Lynn Lane (918) 258-1544. W. 5th directions: From I-244 take the Gilcrease Museum Road exit and go south to Charles Page. The restaurant is located at the corner of 33rd W. Avenue and Charles Page. Monday-Thursday 11-10, Friday-Saturday 11-11:45, closed Sunday.

Visitors to the original Knotty Pine on W. 5th are always surprised to see judges, lawyers, and businessmen sharing tables with construction workers, laborers, and railroad engineers. This is a great place to "people watch," because everyone appreciates Knotty Pine's tasty barbeque, a tradition in Tulsa for several decades. Especially good are the ribs. Enjoy this special BBQ in this no-frills, old-time eatery.

Nelson's Buffeteria $, $$

514 S. Boston in downtown Tulsa, (918) 584-9969. From Highway 51, take the Boston exit and go north to 6th. The restaurant is located on the west side of Boston. Metered street parking is often available. Especially convenient for the weekday lunch crowd and the after-church crowd, lunch is served daily from 10:30-2. Handicapped accessible.

This is one of Tulsa's oldest and best-loved eating establishments. Founded by Nelson Rogers in 1929, Nelson's has served businessmen and congressmen, Tulsa natives, and visitors some of the best home cookin' around. Famous for chicken fried steak, mashed potatoes and cream gravy, the restaurant also serves other favorites: meatloaf, chicken and dressing, pot roast, chicken fingers, and macaroni and cheese. A variety of seasoned vegetables is also served. Order your pie with your meal; if you wait until dessert time, it may all be gone. No reservations are accepted.

Polo Grill $$, $$$

2038 Utica Square, (918) 744-4269. From I-244 take the Utica exit and go south to 21st Street. Turn east on 21st to Yorktown. From Yorktown enter Utica Square shopping center. The Polo Grill faces Yorktown Avenue. Lunch: Monday-Saturday 11-5 p.m. Dinner: Monday-Thursday 5-10, Friday-Saturday 5-11. Occasionally open later for the after-theater crowd. Handicapped accessible.

Rest and relax in this cozy atmosphere. Located in one of Tulsa's most exclusive shopping areas, the Polo Grill offers diners some of the city's finest cuisine. Lighter fare consists of soups, salads, and sandwiches; specialities include salmon, shrimp, and trout. Chef's specials are also featured. Key lime pie and cheesecake are favorite desserts. Serving excellent food in a classy but casual atmosphere, the Polo Grill is an excellent choice for a business lunch. Live piano music lends a pampered feel to the special evening dinners. Reservations are recommended.

Queenie's Plus $, $$

1834 S. Utica Square, (918) 749-3481. From Highway 51 (Broken Arrow Expressway), take the Utica exit and go south on Utica to 21st Street. Turn east onto 21st and then into Utica Square. Queenie's is located near the center of the Square. Monday- Friday 7-7, Saturday until 6 p.m., Sunday 9-2.

This restaurant, deceptive because of its small size, does a tremendous amount of business. Located in upscale Utica Square, Queenie's is a popular place for breakfast, lunch and afternoon treats. Serving soups, sandwiches, quiche, toasted cheese sandwiches, salads, and hamburgers, this dining establishment offers a little bit of everything–all of it exceptional. The desserts are particularly appealing. The outdoor sidewalk seating provides a perfect place for shoppers to rest or for weekend diners to linger over coffee. During the summer months, patrons enjoy the setting as they listen to the sounds of the Square's Fifth Night celebrations. Great food, served in a classic atmosphere, makes Queenie's a Tulsa favorite.

Ron's Hamburgers and Chili $

Six locations in the Tulsa area, all family-owned and operated. 3239 E. 15th St. (918) 744-9016; 416 W. 6th St. (918) 584-8729; 2170 S. Garnett (918) 437-5717; 7119 S. Mingo (918) 250-7667; 6548 E. 51st St. (918) 664-5688; and 5239 S. Peoria (918) 749-7887. Monday-Saturday, 11-8.

Not-so-old locals remember when Ron's Hamburgers opened on 15th Street in the mid-70s. The counter-only restaurant's delicious smells were intoxicating as diners, with mouths watering, lined up outside, waiting for one of the ten counter stools. Twenty years later, Ron's original restaurant has spawned a family chain. Winner of *Tulsa People's* 1996 Reader's Choice "triple crown," Ron's received winning votes for Best Greasy-Spoon, Best Hamburger, and Best Chili. The menu features a variety of burgers and sandwiches. The old-fashioned hamburger has a thin meat patty and a soft bun that has been flipped on the grill to coat it lightly with grease. Specials include a cheeseburger topped with ham, bacon bits and fried onions, a half pork/half beef burger, and a locally-famous chili-cheeseburger. Grilled cheese, ham and chicken sandwiches are also available. Burgers can be smothered with chili, or chili can be ordered by the bowl. Three-way chili, another local favorite, is also on the menu. French fries, Spanish fries, chili fries, fried okra, and coleslaw are offered as side dishes. As a writer for the *Tulsa Tribune* once remarked in his review, "I'd stand up and applaud, except I'm afraid I'd lose my seat."

Savoy Restaurant 𝑆

6033 S. Sheridan, (981) 494-5621. From I-44 take the Sheridan exit, traveling south to 61st Street. The restaurant is located in the strip center on the east side of Sheridan. Monday-Friday 6 a.m.-3 p.m., Saturday 6 a.m.-noon. Handicapped accessible.

City businesses can seldom boast of a kinship with their clients, but the Savoy is an exception to this rule. A longtime Tulsa establishment, the Savoy was originally located in downtown Tulsa, where businessmen, construction workers and truck drivers all stopped for a delicious meal and friendly service. Opened in the mid-20s by Nick Kelamis, a Greek immigrant, the restaurant served tasty breakfasts, hot plate lunches, and steak and lamb dinners. Urban renewal forced the closing of the restaurant in the early 1970s; Mrs. Kelamis and her son Bill reopened the restaurant in 1975 at its current location. The restaurant does a booming breakfast business, serving everything from eggs, biscuits and gravy, pancakes, and oatmeal, to cinnamon rolls that boast a city-wide reputation. Plate lunches are still served; the daily special includes an entree, hot rolls and three vegetables, or two vegetables and a salad. Call for the weekly special schedule. Don't be surprised if your visit to the Savoy puts you in touch with long-lost friends–this homey restaurant is a great place to gather.

Ursula's Bavarian Inn 𝑆𝑆

4932 E. 92nd Street, (918) 496-8282. Approximately 91st Street, 1/2 block east of Yale. From I-44 go south on Yale to 91st Street. (From the Creek Turnpike, exit at Yale and turn left. Go north to 91st Street and turn right.) Ursula's is on the south side of the street. Tuesday-Thursday 5-9, Friday and Saturday 5-10. Closed Sunday and Monday. Reservations are suggested.

Ursula's offers excellent German fare and gracious service. Although Ursula's is an enjoyable place to eat any evening, Thursday nights are especially fun. On this night, performers Carl and Shirlee Stoops liven things up when they play the accordion and sousaphone. There are other instruments for would-be musicians to play: bells, tambourines, and little German whistles. The highlight of the evening is the "Chicken Dance," when everyone sets down his or her fork and joins in the fun.

Warren Duck Club 𝑆𝑆𝑆

Located in the Doubletree Hotel at 61st and Yale, (918) 495-1000. From I-44 take the Yale exit and go south to 61st Street. Weekdays 11:30 a.m.-2 p.m. and 6-10, Friday and Saturday 6-11 p.m. Closed Sunday. Handicapped accessible. Reservations are recommended.

The Warren Duck Club is Tulsa's premier restaurant. A four-diamond restaurant according to AAA ratings, the Duck Club offers diners delicious food and great service in an elegant setting. Diners enjoy American specialities including rotisseried meats and fowl, while they are seated in elegant surroundings overlooking the complex's parklike grounds. The unique appetizer bar features a number of favorites, including duck. The dessert bar is a delight, with pecan diamonds, fudge cheesecake, tortes, chocolate-covered strawberries, and chocolate mousse. For a romantic evening or special celebration, the Warren Duck Club is one of Tulsa's favorites.

White River Fish Market and Seafood Restaurant $$

1708 N. Sheridan Road, (918) 835-1910. From I-244 take the Sheridan exit and go north (left) on Sheridan approximately 1.5 miles. White River is on the west side of the street. Open Monday-Thursday 8:30 a.m.-8 p.m., open thirty minutes later on Friday and Saturday. Closed Sunday.

The White River Fish Market is one of Tulsa's few restaurants to have survived the Great Depression. The market actually began in the early 1930s as a vegetable stand which brought in fish from the White River in Arkansas. When the owners, S.M. Fallis and his son Oran, began selling more fish than vegetables, they converted the stand to a "fish only" establishment. Originally located near the bus station in downtown Tulsa, the market moved east in the early 1960s. Purchased by Garry Cozby in 1981, the fish market and restaurant has a large and faithful clientele. The market, with a counter inside the restaurant, sells several varieties of fish including catfish and buffalo. Crayfish, shrimp and lobster tails are also available. The restaurant features many of the same items, as well as seafood gumbo, the house specialty. Created by Cozby about two years after he purchased the restaurant, the gumbo is famous city-wide. The gumbo spices are mixed by Cozby himself, 100 gallons at a time. While much of the gumbo leaves the restaurant with his customers, a great deal is also donated to different benefit events each year. This clean, no-frills, community-minded restaurant is a long-standing Tulsa favorite!

Wilson's Bar-B-Q $, $$

1522 E. Apache, (918) 425-9912. From I-244 take the Bartlesville/Highway 75 N exit. Exit at Apache and turn left. Wilson's is ahead about one mile, on the south side of the street. Monday, Wednesday, Thursday 11 a.m.-midnight; Tuesday 11 a.m-7 p.m.; Friday, Saturday 11 a.m.-3 a.m. Closed Sunday.

It's hard to build a reputation for good barbecue in a town with so many excellent barbecue restaurants, but Wilson's has done just that. J.B. Wilson, who learned the barbecue business from his father, started the eating establishment in 1974 after dabbling in several other restaurant ventures. Now customers from across the city visit this comfortable cafe to enjoy some of the city's best smoked cooking. Now in his seventies, Wilson is still active in the business, mixing the secret spices for his meat rubs and sauces. His advice to at-home barbecuers? Smoke the meat slowly for the best flavor and tenderness. With the slogan "You need no teeth to eat our beef," Wilson has proven he has some of the tastiest, tenderest barbecue around!

Shopping

Brookside

Located along Peoria between 33rd and 51st. Hours vary by store.

In the 1950s, the Brookside area was one of the first shopping districts to be developed away from downtown. During the last several years, the Brookside area has undergone a renaissance. Shoppers will find stand-alone stores, strip centers, and mini-malls in this area, now offering a wide variety of stores, including art galleries, clothing stores, a frame shop, model train stores, gift shops, antique shops......the list goes on! Also located here are some of Tulsa's finest restaurants, serving scrumptious breakfasts and delicious lunches on shady outdoor patios. The merchants' association hosts several annual events, including a recently revived Shorts Day Parade, originally held to emphasize casual attire while shopping.

Cherry Street

Located on 15th Street, between Peoria and Utica. From Highway 51, take the Utica exit and go south to 15th Street. Turn west.

Originally called Cherry Street, Tulsa's 15th Street has blossomed into an area of quaint specialty stores. Here shoppers stroll through antique stores or browse in music stores. Several clothing merchants and gifts shops are also located here. However, Cherry Street is most famous for its many fine restaurants. From casual to sophisticated, small and intimate to crowded and noisy, Mexican to Chinese, Cherry Street has much to offer!

Drysdale's Western Wear

3220 S. Memorial, (918) 664-6481. From Highway 51, take the Memorial exit, turning left on Memorial. Monday-Saturday 10-9, Sunday noon-5:30

Drysdale's is Tulsa's premier store for western wear. Choosy shoppers can find that perfect pair of jeans when they have over 100,000 pair to choose from! The same is true for boots. With over 20,000 pair of boots, Drysdale's has the largest selection in the state. Western hats, Indian jewelry and Oklahoma souvenirs can also be found here.

Eastland Mall

Located on 21st Street between 129th and 145 E. Avenue, (918) 438-3400. From I-44, take the Highway 169 exit, then the 21st Street exit, turning east on 21st. Monday-Saturday 10-9, Sunday 12-6.

Opened for business in 1986, Eastland Mall has three major department stores, a wide variety of specialty stores, a General Cinema movie theater, and a food court. The Customer Service desk, located on the upper level just inside the main north entrance, has an informative newsletter which lists all stores and offers discount coupons. Strollers and wheelchairs may be rented at this desk.

The Farm Shopping Center

51st and Sheridan, (918) 622-3860. From Highway 51 take the Sheridan exit and go south to 51st. Hours vary by store.

Promoting itself as "The Only Country in Town," the Farm has over forty specialty shops in an open, "country" decor. From the Storehouse furniture store set in an old country barn, to Harold's apparel with a rustic facade, this center offers product variety with front-door parking convenience. Other amenities include restaurants, including an Ozark smokehouse, a German deli, a cafeteria, and a bistro, to name only a few.

Southroads Shopping Center

Scheduled to open in the summer of 1997, Southroads Shopping Center will have over 540,000 square feet of retail space and many major retailers. Also located in the center will be AMC's second largest movie theater complex in the United States. The twenty-screen, 4000-seat theater features stadium seating, highback chairs with dual armrests and cupholders, a new curved state-of-the-art screen and the most advanced digital sound system available. Call (918) 587-1700 or the Chamber of Commerce for more information.

Tulsa Promenade

On the southeast corner of 41st and Yale, (918) 627-9224. From I-44, take the Yale exit, turning north on Yale. Monday-Saturday 10-9, Sunday 12-6.

Originally called Southland when built in the mid-1960s, the shopping center was enclosed and redecorated in Art Deco style in 1986. Tulsa Promenade is a comfortably-sized mall. With four major department stores and over seventy specialty shops, the Promenade offers a great variety of shopping. The concession area is pleasant and offers a variety of choices. A four-screen movie theater is also located here. Strollers are available for rent.

Utica Square

On 21st Street between Utica and Yorktown, (918) 742-5531. From Highway 51, take the Utica exit and turn south. Hours vary by store.

One of Tulsa's first suburban shopping centers, Utica Square officially opened for business in May of 1952. The center is built in a series of small blocks, much like a village or community, with several shops on each block. Over three hundred trees have been planted throughout the square, adding to the comfortable village atmosphere. Over sixty upscale retailers add to the classy ambiance of the area. Shops include clothiers Renberg's, Miss Jackson's, Sak's, and Laura Ashley, and a wide variety of specialty and gift shops, including Williams-Sonoma and Pier One Imports. Some of Tulsa's most sophisticated and unique restaurants are located here. Dance in the streets every Thursday evening between Memorial Day and Labor Day from 7-9 p.m., when the shopping center sponsors "Summer's Fifth Night." Live music is presented for outdoor dining patrons, and the streets of the Square are cordoned off to provide a fun, block-party type event for Tulsans and visitors.

Woodland Hills Mall

Located at 71st and Memorial, (918) 250-1449. Monday-Saturday 10-9, Sunday noon-6.

When built in 1976, Woodland Hills Mall was considered "out in the country." Now the shopping center is a major attraction in the largest retail area of Tulsa. Woodland Hills Mall has four major department stores, over 150 specialty stores, as well as a food court. The Customer Service desk is located on the lower level, just west of the glass elevator. Here shoppers can rent strollers or pick up a directory of stores.

Accommodations

Adams Mark Hotel

100 E. 2nd, (800) 444-ADAM for reservations. Regular rates (double) $125, but packages and discounts are often available; their B&B package includes a room on the premier level and a full breakfast for $86

Comfortable rooms, 24-hour room service, indoor/outdoor pool, fitness center, and shuttle service to shopping in upscale Utica Square are just a few of the amenities available in this top-notch downtown hotel. Diners enjoy the Bravo! Ristarante with its singing waitstaff.

Doubletree at Warren Place

6110 S. Yale, (918) 495-1000. Regular rates (double) are $152; a special "Dream Deal" offers a double room with breakfast for $79. Inquire about availability.

Meticulous service and beautifully-landscaped grounds helped earn this hotel the AAA four diamond award. Among its other attributes are a state-of-the-art fitness center, lighted jogging trails, an indoor pool with sauna and steam room, and an executive level with private lounge and a 24-hour business center. Their premier restaurant is the Warren Duck Club. Sunday brunch is served overlooking the grounds in Greenleaf on the Park.

Gasthous Zum Nurnberger

1238 South Elgin, (918) 583-4043. Call for directions. Dinners are about $25 per person; guest room is $75 per night; reservations are necessary. No credit cards accepted.

Enjoy true German hospitality and outstanding German fare at the home of Alf and Sally Zellmer. The home has one guest room; guests awaken to a full gourmet breakfast featuring German sausages, homemade bread and other delicacies. The Zellmers also entertain dinner parties of ten or less in their almost one-hundred-year-old, handsomely-decorated home. Dinners feature outstanding seasonal German fare: venison, pheasant, quail, duck, turkey, and wild boar. The hosts provide "gemutlichkeit," an atmosphere of warmth and fellowship in the old German tradition.

The Lantern Inn of Brookside

1348 E. 35th Street, one block east of Peoria, (918) 743-8343. $70-75 per night. Call early for reservations, particularly for weekends. Handicapped accessible.

This cozy, English-style cottage is perfectly situated near upscale shopping and restaurants. The bedroom features a queen-sized bed complete with handmade quilts and down comforters. The clawfoot tub is big enough for two and velour robes are provided. In addition, guests enjoy the beautifully-landscaped yard. No breakfast is served; instead, guests receive vouchers to nearby eateries.

Sheraton Tulsa

10918 E. 41st, (918) 627-5000. Regular rates are $110; weekend packages range from $69 up. For $99, you will get a club-level room with breakfast; the Honeymoon package ($189) also includes dinner and champagne. Ask about their other packages.

This hotel has recently changed names and undergone a four million dollar renovation. There is an indoor/outdoor pool, a health club, and a wonderful Sunday brunch.

Events

Eagle Watch

Held the first two Saturdays of January by the Tulsa Audubon Society. Call Randy and Nyla B. Woody for information at (918) 455-6376. Free. Situated on the north bank of the Arkansas River, below the dam and east of the project office. Take Highway 51 west to Keystone Dam and enter the parking lot below the dam. Volunteers will assist with parking, and Audubon Society members will accompany observers to viewing sites.

View the majestic eagle at one of its winter feeding site. Each year, these impressive birds fly south in search of a more hospitable climate; many find it in Oklahoma. The state's mild winters and numerous lakes provide the birds with suitable habitat. Many of the birds roost along local rivers, including the Arkansas, just below Keystone Dam. For the watch, Audubon Society members provide several high-powered telescopes to help participants better spot the beautiful birds that typically nest or feed along the riverbanks. Dress for the weather; it is often quite cold in January. The winds blowing across the water can generate a temperature difference of up to twenty degrees. Don't forget your own binoculars. The event is cancelled only when there is ice on the ground.

Avid birdwatchers will enjoy the overnight adventure offered in conjunction with the Eagle Watch. Lodging and seminars are offered to couples or families who desire more in-depth study of the Bald Eagle and its habitats. Call (918) 865-4991 for more information or reservations.

Indian Powwows

A number of powwows are held throughout the year; these are three of the most popular. Each is held at the Tulsa County Fairgrounds, 21st Street and Yale. From Highway 51 take the Yale exit and go north on Yale to 21st Street. Turn west and travel to the first stoplight. Turn north into the Fairgrounds and proceed to the appropriate building, as listed below.

Tulsa Indian Art Festival

Held in February in the Expo Building at the Tulsa Fairgrounds. Call (918) 583-2253 or 744-1113 for more information.

This powwow features a major art show as well as special dance performances, historical exhibits, workshops, and artist demonstrations. A celebration of art, education and dance, this three-day event begins on Friday with demonstrations for children. On Saturday and Sunday singers, dancers and storytellers showcase their talents.

Annual Tulsa Powwow

Held in early June in the Fairgrounds Pavilion. Contact the Tulsa Indian Club for information at (918) 622-7147 or (918) 838-3207.

This is Tulsa's oldest powwow. Founder Kenneth Anquoe was born near Anadardo, and he moved to Tulsa in 1941. After winning the state Golden Gloves championship that year, he entered the Marine Corps and fought in World War II. After his return to Oklahoma, he organized the first Tulsa Powwow in 1951. The first powwow to be held in an urban setting, it was so successful that it became an annual event. The Anquoe family is still very involved in planning this powwow.

Intertribal Powwow

Two events are held at the Fairgrounds annually, one in August and one in December. Call (918) 744-1113 or (918) 836-1523 for information.

Hosted by the Intertribal Indian Club of Tulsa, this powwow has over 180 arts and crafts booths in addition to the traditional dancing. Over five hundred dancers compete for prizes and awards in twenty-four categories. With a reputation for being particularly well-organized, this powwow attracts participants from approximately twenty-five states.

Tulsa Walk

Held in historic areas of the city on a Sunday afternoon close to the end of April. Sponsored by the Tulsa World, (918) 583-2161. Free.

Join hundreds of happy walkers as they stroll through some of Tulsa's most historic neighborhoods. Once each spring, residents don their tennis shoes and, with guide in hand, traipse the streets of Tulsa, learning about the families and businesses that built the city. Four routes of various lengths are offered, with all routes beginning and ending at a central location. All routes are marked with color-coded arrows; signs are posted along the routes so that walkers won't lose their way. Some buildings along each route may be open to the public; however, private residences along the way usually are not. Walkers should register by filling out the entry form that is published in the paper. Registrants will receive a map booklet, which traces each route and offers narratives of each site. If it's cloudy out, come prepared; the walk is held even when there's an afternoon spring shower. This free, self-guided walking tour is one of Tulsa's most fun and educational spring activities!

Designer Showcase

Usually held the last week of April and the first three weeks of May. For more information call the Tulsa Philharmonic Ticket Office at (918) 747-7445. Tickets may be purchase for $8 in advance at the Philharmonic Ticket Office, 2901 S. Harvard. Tickets are $10 at the door. Senior citizens pay $8, children under 10 are not admitted.

Tour one of the city's most elegant houses! Each year the Volunteer Council of the Tulsa Philharmonic sponsors the Designer Showcase. A home, often historic and in need of renovation, is selected, and electrical and plumbing systems are brought up to code and structural repairs are made. Then thirty local designers, interior decorators, and landscape artists donate their time and talents to "re-do" this remarkable home. When the Showcase opens in late April, guests are delighted with the beautiful decor of this historic setting. The Showcase is usually open one weekend before work begins for those who wish to see the house in its "before" phase. Call the Philharmonic office or watch the local paper for details on this special showing. The official opening is in April. Provided by one of Tulsa's restaurants, lunch is usually available on-site; reservations are required for groups of ten or more. Depending on the vendor, desserts and tea are often available in the afternoon. Offering unusual craft and gift items, A Boutique is also located on the grounds. You won't want to miss the elegance of Tulsa's Designer Showcase!

Mayfest

Held downtown on Main Mall from Thursday through Sunday during the third weekend in May. For more information call Downtown Tulsa Unlimited, (918) 583-2617. The festival is held from the Williams Center Green at 3rd Street and Boston Avenue, to the area at 6th and Main. Park on side streets near Mail Mall or in one of the fee-based lots. Free.

"I Love Downtown!" That's the new slogan that many Tulsans agree with when they visit the city's spring celebration, Mayfest. Enjoy the quality art of both local and national artists when you visit the Invitational Art Gallery or shop the aisles of arts and crafts booths that line the downtown streets. Listen to both local and big-name entertainment on any one of three festival stages. Watch performances of local school organizations, dancers, cloggers, singing groups, and other entertainers. Sample some of the city's best festival food available. The Family/Kidzone area provides engaging entertainment for the younger set.

Participate in one of the special activities offered in conjunction with Mayfest. Past offerings have included a Big Band Dance, 5K Mayfest Run, and a guided tour of downtown Tulsa. Throughout the festival, special demonstrations of quilting, woodworking, beading, and various other crafts are held for older adults. Celebrate spring as you stroll the streets of beautiful downtown Tulsa!

FYI: Downtown Tulsa Unlimited, an organization dedicated to the promotion and growth of downtown Tulsa, hosts a number of other activities and events throughout the year. Each March, city residents recognize Ireland's patron saint by celebrating St. Patrick's Day with the **"Luck of the Irish" Restaurant Crawl. Junteenth**, a four-day festival which historically has celebrated the end of slavery, features jazz performances and cajun-style food. In July, the group sponsors **"Summer in the City"**, a '50s-style street dance. The **Hispanic Fiesta**, held each September, offers tasty Mexican cuisine, clothing, arts, and crafts. A highlight of the fiesta is the music played by mariachi bands, and acoustic guitarists. Each December, Santa takes time out from his busy schedule to ride in Tulsa's Christmas **"Parade of Lights."** Call Downtown Tulsa Unlimited for a complete calendar of events. (918) 583-2617.

Reggaefest

Held at the River Parks Festival Stage the last weekend of June. Travel west on 21st Street across the bridge to Jackson. Turn right on Jackson, and travel two blocks north to the paid parking area. Parking is also available south of 21st Street adjacent to the festival grounds. Call the River Parks Authority for information (918) 596-2001, or visit their home page on the Internet www.reggaefest.com. Tickets for adults and children are available at all Oklahoma Git N Go stores for $12.

"The best party around!" That's how one enthusiastic reviewer described Tulsa's Reggaefest. (*Tulsa World*) Now in its twelfth year, the festival features the music, food and art of Jamaica and other countries. Reggae takes center stage here, although a variety of music is showcased on the festival's multiple stages. Jamaican cuisine is featured, including the popular specialty "jerk chicken." Those desiring a taste of other cultures can visit booths offering Italian and American food. Even the health conscious can enjoy guilt-free indulgences at a booth offering vegetarian cuisine. More than thirty-five vendors offer ethnic arts and crafts for sale. Craftsmen from such faraway places as Jamaica and Africa provide jewelry, clothing, and decorative items to interested buyers. Parachutists and wandering jugglers entertain the crowd, as music lovers relax on blankets brought from home, and children enjoy many activities just for them. Revel in the festive atmosphere at Reggaefest!

Boom River Celebration

Held July 4th at River Parks, along the banks of the Arkansas River. Call (918) 596-2001 for more information. Parking is available in several lots along Riverside Drive, on some streets adjacent to Riverside and from some residents along the thoroughfare. The fireworks display can be seen from many different locations throughout the city. Free.

Enjoy a flag-waving good time at Tulsa's Boom River Celebration. Festivities begin at 4 p.m. and conclude with a giant fireworks display later in the evening. Celebrants should bring lawn chairs, blankets, coolers, and picnic baskets if they want the comforts of home. Vendor refreshments and novelties are also available. The 1997 celebration has a Centennial Theme, in recognition of the city's 100th Birthday. Local entertainers perform for the crowds. Beginning at 8 p.m., Tulsa's own Starlight Band hosts a patriotic salute on the amphitheater's floating stage. Fly-bys of various aircraft and demonstrations by parachutists fill the air prior to the fireworks. At 9:45, Oklahoma's largest free pyrotechnical display begins. Staged from the 21st Street Bridge, the aerial salute lasts twenty-five minutes. The music for the fireworks program is simulcast over a local radio station.

Balloonfest

Typically held the first weekend in August from Friday through Sunday. For more information, contact the Gatesway Foundation, (918) 251-2676. Held in the southwest corner of 41st Street and 129th East Avenue. Parking is available for $5 per car. Shuttle service is $2 per person, children under age five are free. No alcoholic beverages are allowed on the grounds; pets and ice chests should be left at home. For safety reasons, a no-smoking policy is enforced on the balloon field. Shuttles regularly depart from Expo Square at the Fairgrounds and Broken Arrow High School. Parking and shuttle fees are an important source of funds for this nonprofit organization that helps children and adults with developmental disabilities.

Nothing is more beautiful than over seventy-five colorful hot-air balloons floating in a blue Oklahoma sky, and that's just the sight that visitors delight in at this annual event. The balloons are of every variety: solid color or striped, standard design, or custom built. Character balloons, such as Smokey the Bear, Hagar the Horrible, and Noah's Ark add fun and whimsy to the festival.

The colorful Balloonfest.

A balloon glow, in which tethered balloons are illuminated against the night's sky, is held on Friday evening. Special balloon races are held on Saturday. Festival-goers are treated to live entertainment on two different stages and a display of antique and collectible cars. Sky-divers "drop in" throughout the day, and more than one hundred booths offer arts, crafts and refreshments to visitors. This family-oriented festival has one of the best activity areas for children; young ones can participate in most activities at no additional charge. Enjoy the colors and activities at Balloonfest!

Jazz on Greenwood Celebration

Held downtown, between Archer and Haskell Streets on Greenwood. Call (918) 584-3378 for information. This four day event is traditionally held the second or third weekend in August, Wednesday-Saturday. Free.

Listen to some of the country's best jazz artists when you visit this music celebration. Held in the historic Greenwood business district, this event draws an estimated 80,000 jazz enthusiasts. Once known as "America's Black Wall Street," Greenwood was a thriving commercial center for Tulsa's black population. In the 1920s, musicians were often found improvising in the clubs and on the streets, creating a truly American form of music called Jazz. The Jazz on Greenwood Celebration recognizes the contributions of these artists with this annual music festival. Started in 1988, the festival has hosted jazz greats Lou Rawls, Natalie Cole, Cab Calloway, and Dave Brubeck. Concerts by more than forty local and regional bands begin at 6 p.m. nightly on the festival's three stages. All headline acts begin nightly at 9 p.m. on the Dreamland Stage. Music lovers are encouraged to bring their lawnchairs. Some of the area's best vendor food is available here. Visit Jazz on Greenwood–perhaps you'll be convinced that Tulsa is the birthplace of jazz!

Bluegrass and Chili Festival

Usually held the second weekend in September on the downtown Main Mall. For information, call Downtown Tulsa Unlimited at (918) 583-2617. Main Mall is located along Main Street, a brick street, between the 2nd and 6th Streets. Free.

Savor the sights and smells of the Bluegrass and Chili Festival. At this festival, the aroma of simmering chili blends with the sounds of country music entertainment for one of the area's most fun fall festivals. More than ninety entrants in the Mid-America Regional Chili Cook-Off try to outdo each other in several different categories of competition. "Best Chili" is the coveted prize, but awards are also offered in booth decoration and presentation. Chili lovers in the crowd can sample the various recipes by purchasing a tasting kit. Just as much fun as tasting the delicious chile is visiting with the often-flamboyant chefs and competitors. Originally started as a small bluegrass festival in 1979, this event now draws nearly 60,000 visitors each year. In addition to the chili and music, entertainment includes exhibition dance teams who perform clogging and two-step routines. Arts, crafts, and food booths line the sidewalks of Main Mall. The Kiddie Korral offers special activities for children.

Tulsa Scottish Games

Usually held on a weekend in mid-September at Chandler Park, 6500 West 21st Street. For more information or to order tickets call (918) 241-6399 or (405) 525-6070. From I-44 take the Riverside Drive exit. Go north on Riverside to 21st Street. Turn west, going over the Arkansas River on the 21st Street bridge. Follow the road as it curves to the right, then left. Continue going west approximately three miles to Chandler Park. Adult one day ticket, $4 in advance, $6 at the gate; Adult two day ticket $8 in advance, $10 at the gate. Senior and children rates are also in effect.

Scotland comes to Oklahoma each year during the annual Scottish Games. Hundreds gather to celebrate their family heritage, and others come to learn more about life across the sea. Participants compete in traditional Scottish athletic events, and sheep dogs demonstrate their special skills. Highland dancers compete amid the stirring sounds of "pipes." Guest artists entertain with their dancing and bagpipe playing. Overnight packages are available through the Oklahoma Scottish Games and Gathering and a local hotel. Celebrate the wonderful and intriguing Scottish heritage! FYI: A similar Scottish Games festival is held in March in Midwest City near Oklahoma City. Call (405) 739-1293 for more information.

Tulsa State Fair

Held the last week of September to the first week of October at the Tulsa Fairgrounds. For information call (918) 744-1113. From Highway 51 take the Yale exit and go north to 21st Street. Turn west onto 21st to Pittsburgh. The entrance to the State Fair is on the north. Parking is available on-site, along adjacent streets, and in the yards of residential entrepreneurs. A tractor-drawn shuttle service is available to fairgoers who use outlying on-site lots. Gate admission is adults $5, youth $2, children under six are free. A variety of promotions and gate discounts are offered. Watch the local media for details. Handicapped accessible.

Start planning early to attend this all-American cultural event! Begin watching the *Tulsa World* in mid-September for information outlining the entertainers, what's new, and where to eat at the fair. Each year a special pullout section, featuring a ten-day calendar of events, is made available to subscribers, or you may pick up one of the booklets distributed at the fair, and begin your trek. Walk through the livestock barns located along the perimeter of the fairgrounds. As you observe the cows, horses, sheep, and pigs, remember that much of our early history is tied to farms and to the raising of livestock. Children enjoy visiting the Children's Barnyard, where cats, dogs, goats, chickens, ducks, and donkeys can be seen with their young. Stroll through the educational displays of the Oklahoma Wildlife Department and tour the trade buildings where the latest gadgets are demonstrated. Witness educational displays, explore new products and services, collect campaign literature, and sign up for sweepstakes. There's a little bit of everything displayed at the Fair. Then stroll down the Midway. Try your luck at one of the many games, or enjoy watching the attempts of others. Sample the tremendous variety of food—from sweet treats to full-course meals. Ride the carousel or ferris wheel, or one of the other amusements brought in for this event. On opening night, special ride passes can be purchased for a substantial savings over other ride/gate packages. An all-you-can-ride bracelet, good for the duration of the Fair, can also be purchased. Watch for details in the Tulsa paper, or call the Fairgrounds for purchasing information.

Rest your weary legs at one of the many daily shows. With two stages in the Expo building and several more located throughout the grounds, there's ample room for the singers, dancers, musicians, high divers, sky divers, magicians, jugglers, and other entertainers that frequent the Fair. Special events include concerts, rodeos, and the sensational Ice Capades. Tickets for these special performances can be purchased at the Pavilion Ticket Office (918) 747-0001, or the Grandstand box office. Other services include a post office, first aid station, and automatic teller machine. Strollers and wheelchairs are available for rent at the Pavilion. Sundry items are sold at the Comfort Zone on the Midway.

Oktoberfest

Usually held the third weekend in October along the west bank of the Arkansas River. Call the River Parks Authority at (918) 596-2001 for more information. From 21st Street, travel west across the 21st Street bridge. Turn south, following the signs to the Oktoberfest parking and entrance. Free. Parking is somewhat limited at the festival site; shuttle service is available for $1 from several convenient locations.

What do accordions, sausages, and beer have in common? Tulsa's annual Oktoberfest! Ranked as one of the top ten German celebrations in the country, this festival offers some of the most authentic German food and music around. Visit Der Bier Garten tent, the center of activity during this four-day festival. Visitors can purchase food and beverages, listen to a German band, and perform the popular Chicken Dance. Other tents, with colorful names such as Das Ess Zelt und Garten, host food vendors, beer sellers, juried arts and crafts, and hands-on children's activities. Souvenirs can be purchased in the outdoor Kunst Markt and Der Floh Markt. Enjoy Tulsa's version of "Germany on the Arkansas!"

Tulsa Chamber of Commerce

Tulsa's Octoberfest.

In the Vicinity

Broken Arrow

Situated just southeast of Tulsa, Broken Arrow provides the tranquility of a small town with the conveniences of a larger city. Originally a Creek Indian settlement, the town derives its name from the scouting activities of its early founders. When Indians were gathering materials with which to make arrows, branches were broken off the trees instead of cut off. Consequently the site became known as "Thlikachka" or "Broken Arrow."

Located adjacent to Tulsa, visitors can reach Broken Arrow by travelling southeast on the Broken Arrow Expressway, Highway 51. Broken Arrow Visitors Bureau and Special Events (918) 251-1518.

Battle Creek Golf Course

3200 N. Battle Creek Drive, (918) 259-8633. Take the Broken Arrow Expressway to 145th, exit north and take the first right (Granger); follow Granger to the top of hill. Open daily, dawn to dusk. Monday-Thursday $26, Friday-Sunday $35; carts are $10. Yearly memberships are available and they provide cost savings to frequent users of the course.

This challenging course opened in March of 1997. A links-style, par 72 course with water and bunker hazards, its slope is 130 and USGA rating is 75.4. It has 7237 yards. A driving range, pro shop, and putting and chipping practice areas are other amenities.

Forest Ridge Golf Club

7501 E. Kenosha, (918) 357-2282. From Highway 51 (Broken Arrow Expressway), take the 71st Street exit and turn east. Travel east on 71st until you see the course on your right. Open dawn to dusk, the club offers a two-tiered fee structure. Fees (including cart rental) are Monday-Thursday $50, Friday-Sunday and holidays $60. A player's card can be purchased that provides green fee discounts and other privileges. Tee-time reservations are accepted four days in advance.

A beautiful course opened in 1989, Forest Ridge offers golfers a challenging game. This eighteen-hole course, with its carpet of cool-season grasses, has been ranked among the highest in the state. The championship course is 7069 yards, par 71, with a USGA rating of 74 and a slope of 134. The club includes a 12.5 acre driving range, an elegant club house, a pro shop, a full service restaurant, and a grill. In addition to the golf course, Forest Ridge Swim and Tennis Club offers a swimming pool, kiddie pool, tennis course, volleyball pit, and playground. With golf, swimming and tennis available on a daily fee/use basis, Forest Ridge is comparable to a private club, without the initiation fee or monthly dues. Forest Ridge is your "Country Club for a Day."

The Peach House $, $$

12500 S. 129th E. Avenue, (918) 455-5404. From Highway 51, take the exit for 129th E. Avenue. Travel through Broken Arrow; look for the restaurant on the west side of the street. Monday-Saturday 9-9, Sunday 11-9.

Once a roadside stand for the nearby orchard, the Peach House has bloomed into a gift shop and restaurant that draws guests from the big city to this comfortable rural setting. The log building, which sits is front of the orchard, once served as the headquarters and retail store for the peaches from the orchard and the peach ice cream and dumplings that were sold as orchard by-products. The building now houses a gift shop and restaurant with seating for 55. Guests can enjoy a pleasant lunch, browse the gift shop and, in season, purchase peaches by the peck or by the bushel. Meals feature sandwiches, salads, and soups that are often served in unique ways: sourdough bread becomes a bowl for delicious soups, and perfectly ripened and quartered pineapples hold ham, crab or chicken salad. Daily specials are recited by the friendly waitresses. Several of the items served at the restaurant are available for purchase. Children especially enjoy the homemade-tasting peach ice cream. Eaten on the porch or under the shade of a parking lot tree, this treat alone is worth the drive, particularly on hot summer days.

Tea for Two $, $$

804 S. Main, (918) 251-8305. Take Highway 51 to 161st, exit and turn south. At 71st Street, turn east and go to Main. At Main Street turn south. Open Tuesday-Saturday 11-2:30.

Nestled inside an old home decorated with antiques and knickknacks, Tea for Two serves delicious homemade lunches to hungry diners. Daily specials, particularly the lasagna and chicken enchilada, are favorites. Sandwiches, made on homemade wheat bread, are also served—as are soups, salads and quiche. Diners may choose pie or cake for dessert. The 1927 home still has hardwood floors and other quality, old-home features. The built-in shelves are full of original art works, home accessories, pottery, and tea sets; all are for sale. Before you leave, pick up some of their homemade pies, rolls and bread to take home.

Rooster Days

Held for four days, usually during the second weekend in May. For information or a schedule of events call (918) 251-1518.

More than 100,000 visitors line the streets to watch the exciting festival parade. A Miss Chick contest is held each year, along with a carnival and rodeo. Booths feature trade exhibits, arts and crafts, and delicious foods. Continuous on-stage entertainment delights both children and adults.

Jenks

The Jenks townsite was created when the route for the Midland Valley Railroad was laid out. Originally part of an allotment made to Nathan Spring, a Creek freedman, the land became a stop on the Midland Valley line. With the discovery of oil at Glenpool in 1905, Jenks experienced fairly rapid growth; however, the bulk of the new business went to nearby Tulsa. A number of promotions were staged to attract businesses and residents to Jenks. One of these promotions centered around a steamboat that was built to carry passengers between the newly-founded town and Tulsa. Unfortunately, the steamboat couldn't always run because the river had "it's bottom too close to the top." With the completion of a bridge spanning the Arkansas in 1910, Jenks became dependably linked to Tulsa, and it has experienced steady growth ever since. Now home to one of the state's best school districts, Jenks boasts big city conveniences and a small town charm all its own.

Jenks is located ten miles south of downtown Tulsa on US Highway 75. From Highway 75, take the Jenks Road exit and drive east into Jenks. Jenks Chamber of Commerce (918) 299-5005.

McLean Historic Home

123 E."A" Street, (918) 446-2745 or (918) 299-8634. From Main Street in Jenks, turn north on 1st and go one block to "A" St. The McLean home is on the corner. Monday-Friday 9-noon, 1-4. Public tours are scheduled for Saturday afternoons at 3 and 4 p.m. or by appointment. Adults $2, children $1.

Step into the past as you visit Dr. McLean's home. Built in 1913 by Dr. McLean's father-in-law and brother-in-law, the home was constructed for a total cost of $869.74. This house was not only a home for the doctor and his wife Maude, it was a medical office as well. Built with a small waiting room and examining room, Dr. McLean treated many patients here. However, his practice ended abruptly when he died in an automobile accident on his way to a medical convention. Mrs. McLean boxed up his belongings and stored them in a shed behind the house, where they remained until her death in 1967. Family members have since inventoried the boxes, finding thorough records and complete sets of medical supplies. Realizing the importance of their discovery, they have spent several years restoring the house and displaying the tools of Dr. McLean's medical craft. Also on display are furnishings and reminders of daily life in the 1930s. The home's curator is Melinda Bennett, the doctor's great niece. Feel free to call her for information about the home or to arrange a tour appointment. Groups are welcome.

Perryman Wrangler Ranch

11524 S. Elwood Avenue, (918) 299-2997. From Tulsa go south on Highway 75 to 111th St. south. Turn east on 111th and continue to Elwood. Turn south onto Elwood and go to the ranch entrance. Hours by appointment, priced by event.

Enjoy visiting this true "home on the range." Established by Mose and Lulu Perryman, this 280-acre ranch was once part of the extensive holdings of the Perryman family. Arriving in this area in 1848, the Perrymans were one of the largest and most prominent families in this frontier settlement. The ranch is now operated by Mr. and Mrs. Wes Dickinson, descendants of the Perrymans. Company outings, group dinners, hayrides, and birthday parties are all scheduled here on a regular basis. A variety of entertainment is also available for large gatherings. Call Wes several weeks (or even months) in advance to schedule your activity. A deposit is required; inquire about refund policies. Experience history as you visit the historic Perryman Wrangler Ranch.

Trails End Blues (Blueberry Farm)

9422 S. 53rd West Place, (918) 224-7587. From Highway 75 south, take the 81st Street exit, turning west onto 81st. Continue to the stop sign and turn south onto Union. Go one mile to 91st Street. Turn west onto 91st and follow the road until it ends at 49th West Avenue. The paved road turns back to the north, but Trails End is to the south; turn left and follow the signs. Call before venturing out; even during the picking season (early- to mid-June), the field is periodically closed to allow the berries to ripen.

Grab your bucket, tennis shoes and insect spray for some good old-fashioned fun–picking vine-ripened blueberries. You'll pay less for the berries here than you will at the store, and the berries are a great deal fresher. The Hall family is well organized, and the grounds are clean and well-kept. The best thing about picking berries? When you get home you can enjoy the tasty "fruits" of your labor! Plan for the dangers of the hot sun by picking berries in the morning, wearing a hat and sunscreen, and drinking plenty of water.

South Lakes Golf Course

9253 S. Elwood, (918) 746-3760. From Highway 75 south take the 81st Street exit and turn east. At Elwood (look for the stop sign), turn south and go one mile. Green fees are $16.19 for 18 holes, seven days a week. Twilight rates are available. Carts rent for $19.93.

South Lakes is one of the area's newest golf courses. Opened in 1989, it features an eighteen-hole championship course. Situated on 130 acres with seven interconnected lakes, this 6340-yard course keeps golfers challenged. Southlakes is par 71, with a slope of 113, and USGA rating of 68.6. To reserve a tee time call the Tulsa Automated Tee Time Reservation Service at (918) 582-6000. Tee times are recommended one week ahead. A driving range, putting greens, pro shop, and restaurant complete the list of services available.

Auntie Em's Victorian Village and Ice Cream Parlor $

1st and Main, (918) 299-7231. Monday-Saturday 10-5, Sunday 1-5.

This nostalgic ice cream parlor offers fountain treats to shoppers, after they've had a chance to browse through the furniture, glassware and collectibles that are offered for sale.

Back Street Bistro $$, $$$

1st and "A" Streets, (918) 299-0689. Monday-Thursday 11-9, Friday-Saturday 11-10. Closed Sunday. Reservations recommended.

This is one of Jenks' newer and classier restaurants. Serving steaks and cedar-plank salmon, the Back Street Bistro offers diners more than the usual restaurant fare. The Bistro is also known for its daily specials and delicious desserts. If you're not watching your diet, treat yourself to the baked fudge with walnuts and whipped cream or one of the other special desserts prepared on a daily basis.

El Potosino Mexican Restaurant $

2nd and Main, (918) 298-0881. Tuesday-Saturday 11-2:30, and 5-8.

This ethnic restaurant offers homecooked Mexican food, prepared from scratch by the Manzo family.

Jenks Restaurant $, $$

215 E. Main Street, (918) 299-9329. Open Monday-Friday 6:30 a.m.-8 p.m., Saturday 8:30 a.m.-2:30 p.m. Closed Sunday.

This is an authentic small town cafe serving typical diner fare: eggs for breakfast, sandwiches for lunch, and old-fashioned entrees for dinner. Specials are offered on a regular basis. Here since 1952, this restaurant is a Jenks tradition.

Tea Cup Tea Room $

4th and "A" Street, (918) 299-8204. Monday-Saturday 11-3.

The Tea Cup offers light lunches of salads, sandwiches and pastries. The Victorian-decorated restaurant is also available for private dinners in the evening, when homemade casseroles, salads, breads, and tasty desserts are served.

Antique Shopping

The antique and craft shops are located along Main Street. Municipal parking is located one block north of Main at 2nd and "A" Streets. Most stores are open Tuesday-Saturday 10-5. A few shops are open on Sunday and Monday. Some stores are open by appointment. Call the Chamber of Commerce or The Guild Shops at (800) 886-8115 for more information and/or a brochure. ★

Go bargain hunting in one of the area's most popular antique haunts, Jenks, America. Locally known as the "Antique Capital of Oklahoma," Jenks downtown is full of crafts and antiques. Awaken old memories as you browse through items reminiscent of your grandmother's era. Discover treasures you can't live without. Visit with shop owners about the special qualities of their pieces, the services they offer, or the best way to display the trinkets they sell. Specialty shops are as plentiful as antique stores. With wares ranging from paintings to spices, visitors are sure to find something of interest.

Five Oaks Ranch

528 E. 121st Street, (918) 298-6405, FAX (918) 299-6495. From Tulsa, take US 75 south to Highway 117, also known as 121st Street. Turn east 2.5 miles to Five Oaks Ranch. Overnight guests: Sunday-Thursday, $95 per couple; Friday-Saturday $140 per couple. Overnight stays include breakfast. Fees are charged for some day-use activities.

Imagine your own private, 185-acre retreat, complete with woods, pond and cozy log cabin, then find this place for yourself at Five Oaks Ranch. Built by Claudia and Randy Imel on land that once comprised the Skyline Amusement Park, Five Oaks is an exclusive getaway for individuals, couples or families. A lodge-pole pine structure, the oversized cabin has a king-sized bed, whirlpool bath, and a fully-equipped kitchen and utility room. A partially-covered rock porch hugs the cabin, and it provides room for the large barbecue grill and smoker. The cabin's use is not limited to individuals or families. Groups may also use the facility for activities ranging from weddings, to company picnics and teenage slumber parties. Guests are welcome to explore the entire ranch by walking or paddling about in one of the canoes or paddleboats available. Fishermen can try to hook one of the largemouth bass stocked in the pond. Costs are variable, depending on the activities chosen and the number of people participating. Deposits are required, and a cancellation policy is in effect. Whether you're looking for a private retreat or a place to host a private party, Five Oaks provides a beautiful and serene setting.

Trinity Farm Bed and Breakfast

Located near Haskell, thirty miles southeast of Tulsa, (918) 482-5655.

Scheduled to open in the fall of 1997, this B&B is situated on sixty-three acres with wildflowers, fruit trees, and a vineyard. Guests will enjoy sitting on the big porch, soaking up the rural beauty. Three rooms with private baths will be available. Call for more information.

Jenks Events

A number of special events are held throughout the year in Jenks. The **Jenks Country Fair**, held each June, provides visitors with an opportunity to view and purchase antique quilts. Live craft demonstrations are staged among the various craft and food booths, and a street dance on Saturday evening caps the activities. In November, the town hosts the annual **Teddy Bear Convention**. Held in the school's central campus gym, 205 E. "B" Street, this event places special emphasis on stuffed bears, both old and new. A $3 admission is charged for the convention. Also in November, shopkeepers host an annual **Christmas Open House**. During this special weekend, shoppers can purchase seasonal antiques and crafts, and they are treated to the nostalgic sights, smells, sounds, and tastes of Christmas.

Sand Springs

Charles Page, handyman, lumberman, miner, railroader, real estate broker, and finally oil man, set about creating a town in the early part of this century. Successful at a number of ventures, Charlie Page earned the reputation of being a "soft touch" for those who needed a helping hand. While living in Tulsa, he often assisted stranded or down-on-their-luck families whose husband/

fathers were working in the oil fields. In 1908, Indians offered to sell him land west of Tulsa: sand hills filled with springs of water and covered with tangled briars and undergrowth. Page bought the land with the intention of creating a home for children. By mid 1908, the Sand Springs Home was operational, with tents housing those in need of immediate aid. The numbers of those served at the home increased rapidly; by 1916, a Widows' Colony was created. In his business dealings, Page built his own railroad, offering service from Tulsa to Sand Springs. He constructed an electric power plant and a water company; he enticed companies to the area with free building sites and promises of cheap utilities. He then arranged for the Home to be self-supporting through the income from his business interests. The Sand Springs Home is still raising children and helping families today. It takes nothing from any of its residents, their families, the state, the federal government, or any charitable organization. Originally created in an effort to bring new life and hope to the sand hills, Sand Springs is now one of Oklahoma's most successful and prosperous towns.

Located just ten minutes west of downtown Tulsa. Take Highway 51/64 west to Sand Springs. Three exits serve this town of 16,000. Sand Springs Area Chamber of Commerce (918) 245-3221.

Discoveryland's "OKLAHOMA!"

Located ten miles west of Tulsa on West 41st Street, (918) 245-6552. Take I-244 or I-44 to the 51st Street exit and go north to 41st Street. Turn west and continue approximately ten miles, passing through a part of Sand Springs locally known as Prattville. Turn right at the big Discoveryland! sign. The show opens in mid-June and usually closes in mid-August (in 1997, June 12-August 23). The park opens at 5:30 p.m. Dinner is served from 5:30-7:30; Native American Dancing at Discoveryland's Indian Teepee Village begins at 7; the Western Musical Revue begins at 7:30; "OKLAHOMA!" begins at 8. Monday-Saturday: Adults $14.95, Senior Citizens $13.95, Children under twelve free if accompanied by a parent. Ranch-style dinner: Adults $7.95, Senior Citizens $7.50, children $4.95. Group rates are available for both the dinner and show. Call ahead for information and reservations. ★ ⓢ

Spend an entire evening in Oklahoma's great outdoors, enjoying outstanding family entertainment! Arrive at 5:30 for a country barbecue dinner in Discoveryland!'s Circle-D Ranch Barn and shaded picnic area; afterwards, browse the several small gift shops for Oklahoma souvenirs. Visitors can find everything from western arts and crafts to Native American jewelry. Enjoy the pre-show entertainment featuring traditional western singers and high-stepping dancers. The highlight of the evening is when Discoveryland's cast of fifty talented singers, actors, and dancers performs the great musical masterpiece, "OKLAHOMA!" Originally created for Broadway by Rodgers and Hammerstein, the show is spectacular in the great outdoors! Live horses, real wagons, and a surrey with fringe on the top bring excitement and realism to the earthen stage. Snacks and desserts are sold during intermissions. Audience members should bring a camera; the cast and crew gather on stage after each performance for autographs. The show concludes around 11 p.m. Discoveryland! has recently been named the official "National Home of Rodgers and Hammerstein's "OKLAHOMA!" by the children of the musical's creators. Don't miss the opportunity to see the beloved musical "OKLAHOMA!" under the stars!

Try to plan this outing at least a week in advance. Tickets are available throughout the season, although most shows in late July and early August are sellouts. Reservations are required for both the musical and the barbecue dinner which is served beforehand. To be prepared, audience members should bring a light sweater, insect repellant and an umbrella. The show is rarely cancelled due to weather.

An Herbal Affair

Typically held the third Saturday in April in downtown Sand Springs. Visitors should take Highway 51/64 west to the Adams Road exit, and then take 2nd Street to Main. Parking is available on the streets. Call the local Chamber for the exact date or (918) 246-2560 for more information. Free. ★

Celebrate spring by strolling the streets of downtown Sand Springs, listening to folk music and learning about herbs. Only six years old, this is one of the area's fastest growing festivals. With ninety-five vendors from Oklahoma and six surrounding states, 25,000 guests visited the Festival last year. Vendors sell many different products, including live plants, herb-related products, and lawn and garden ornaments. All products sold must be herb-related and earth friendly. Children participate in turn-of-the-century games in Peppermint Lane, and interested adults listen to free lectures in Lavender Hall. Entertainment is provided in the Basil Street Theater, where visitors enjoy performances by harp, guitar, and dulcimer players. Area cloggers kick up their heels to the toe-tapping music of the hills. Food vendors sell tasty treats to those who wish to sample them. Downtown comes alive with the sights and sounds of an old-time springtime celebration!

Sapulpa

Sapulpa residents credit three major forces with creating their town–Indians, railroads and oil. Jim Sapulpa, the first permanent settler in the area, was a Creek Indian Chief and farmer who established a trading post at his home. When the railroad came through in 1886, it established a stop at "Sapulpa Station," so named to honor Chief Sapulpa. By 1901, the station had become a major division point on the line and a leading agricultural shipping center. When oil was discovered at the nearby Glenn pool oil field, just few miles southeast of Sapulpa, the town "boomed." By the mid-1920s, the city boasted a population of almost 20,000. Now home to two glass plants, a pottery factory, and several small manufacturing concerns, Sapulpa displays a delightful small town charm to visitors.

Sapulpa is located on Route 66, just twenty minutes southwest of Tulsa. From Tulsa take I-44 west to the Route 66 Sapulpa exit. Route 66 is a "free" road. From U.S. Highway 75 South, take Highway 117 west. Sapulpa Area Chamber of Commerce (918) 224-0170.

Frankoma Pottery

2400 Frankoma Road, (918) 224-5511. From Tulsa take I-44 west to Route 66. Go west on Highway 66 to Sapulpa. Turn right at the first light onto Frankoma Road. Follow this road for one mile to the factory and showroom, located on the right. Monday-Saturday 9-5, Sunday 1-5. Free. ★

Sense the uniqueness of Oklahoma when you visit Frankoma Pottery. John Frank, the creator and founder of Frankoma Pottery, came to Oklahoma from Chicago in 1927. An art instructor at the University of Oklahoma, he strove to develop a durable pottery from local clays. In 1936, he resigned his teaching position at O.U. to devote his full attention to the creation of pottery. Using clay mined from Sugar Loaf Mountain in Sapulpa, Frank was able to devise an inexpensive, yet durable product, decorated in a western motif. Offered on weekdays from 9:30-2, factory tours allow visitors to see pottery being made by a combination of hand-crafting and modern technology. Tours last approximately twenty minutes, and they can accommodate twenty people. This pottery (both ovenproof and dishwasher safe) is sold in the gift shop, where a wide variety of styles and colors is displayed. Reasonably-priced small gifts and souvenirs are also available for purchase. If you have time to "dig," bargains can be found in the "seconds" section of the store. One of Oklahoma's most well-known products, Frankhoma Pottery is sold worldwide.

Historic Walking Tour

After stopping at the Chamber of Commerce (101 E. Dewey) to pick up your Historic Walking Tour brochure, begin your walk at the corner of Hobson Avenue and Main Street in downtown Sapulpa. Stroll the streets anytime. Free.

Walk the avenues of Sapulpa to learn about Oklahoma in the early part of this century. The detailed tour brochure informs visitors about current buildings and businesses, as well as those historically housed in the buildings. With architectural styles dating from 1898 to 1922, the downtown area provides visitors an excellent view and understanding of an early oil town. Allow plenty of time for this tour; intermingled with the old buildings are new enterprises where visitors can browse or stop for a bite to eat. Of special interest is **Sara's Country Corner** at 1 S. Main Street, open Monday-Saturday 8:30-5:30. Menu items range from hamburgers and sandwiches to old-fashioned sodas and sundaes. By recreating the atmosphere of a 1925 drug store, the owners have developed the perfect stop for tour-takers.

While walking, be sure to notice the "ghost signs"; advertisements painted on the brick buildings' facades. Restored and repainted with funds raised by elementary school children, the signs are reminders of early Oklahoma entrepreneurship. Six of fifteen possible signs have already been restored: two Coca Cola signs, a Quality Ice Cream sign, a sign for Mentholatum, and two signs for local businesses. Repainted by A.J. Cantrell, a "wall dog" (someone who paints signs on walls), the advertisements resemble early billboards. The project was created to help teach local history, to involve students in the community, and to help foster a sense of civic pride. Allow at least an hour for this tour, with extra time allotted to stop to eat. Stroll the sidewalks of Sapulpa to see civic pride on display!

Sapulpa Historical Museum

100 E. Lee Avenue, (918) 224-4871. Located in downtown Sapulpa. Take Route 66 (Dewey Avenue) to Water Street. Turn south for one block. The Museum is on the southeast corner of Lee and Water. Monday-Thursday 10-3. Closed Friday, Saturday, Sunday and holidays. Free.

The Sapulpa area's history, from Indians to oil, is preserved and presented for all to see and enjoy. Housed in a three-story building covering a half block, the museum is quite extensive and interesting. A 1939 fire truck and other large and in-progress exhibits are housed in the museum annex. Of particular interest in the main museum building is the exhibit featuring World War II memorabilia. Since September 1996, the museum has displayed a Route 66 Satellite Exhibit. Designated by the Oklahoma Historical Society as one of nine locations to house Route 66 exhibits, the museum offers educational exhibits about the "Mother Road."

Sapulpa Golf Course

West of Sapulpa on historic Route 66, (918) 224-0237. Open dawn to dusk. Green fees are $12 weekdays, $14 weekends; twilight, junior and senior discounts are given.

This par 70, tree-lined course was redesigned and reopened in August, 1994. All holes have water hazards, and the greens are small and fast, creating challenges for golfers. The course has 6565 yards, a slope of 123, and a USGA rating of 71.3. Call at least two days in advance to reserve a tee time. Pro shop and snack bar available.

Freddies Bar-B-Q Steak House and Banquet Facilities $$, $$$

1425 New Sapulpa Road (Route 66), (918) 224-4301. Open weekdays at 11 a.m. and Saturday at 4 p.m., closed Sunday.

Freddies is known for Lebanese-style dinners; hungry diners come here for salads, cabbage rolls, ribs, steaks, lobster, and more! Freddies has expanded to Stillwater and Mannford.

Hickory House $, $$

626 N. Mission, (918) 224-7830. Located on Route 66, just past the Liberty Glass factory. Open Monday, Tuesday and Wednesday 11-9, Thursday, Saturday 11-10, Friday 11-11.

Another of Oklahoma's great barbecue restaurants, the Hickory House offers daily lunch and dinner buffets. The Hickory House specializes in smoked brisket, ribs, bologna, and sausage.

The McManor Bed and Breakfast

706 S. Poplar Street, (918) 224-4665. From I-44 take exit 215, Highway 97 and follow this through town to Taft Street. Turn west on Taft and then north on Poplar. Call for rates; ask about their extended stay discounts. Reservations are required at least five days in advance.

This 1920s Tudor home has a two-bedroom, two-bath apartment available for travelers looking for a homey, private atmosphere. The apartment has a small living area with an adjacent kitchen, and it overlooks a grassy lawn and water garden. Children and pets are welcome here; the apartment is especially suited to families because the two bedrooms connect.

Route 66 Blowout/Juried Art Show

This nostalgic celebration is held in downtown Sapulpa during a weekend (Friday-Sunday) in June. Call the Chamber of Commerce at (918) 224-0170 for more information. Free.

Hundreds of classic cars, parked along Sapulpa's Main Street, bring back memories of life in the fast lane....or at least life along Route 66. Car clubs meet here before leaving for their cruise along the "Mother Road," that grey ribbon of highway that once connected the Midwest with the California coast. Sights, sounds and smells delight visitors of all ages. The gleaming colors and finishes of restored automobiles bring gasps of admiration. The toe-tapping sounds of live entertainment fill the air. Prepared by street vendors, the mouthwatering smell of food tempts those on the strictest diet. Local artists sell their creations or demonstrate their skills. Along with the nostalgic folk celebration of Route 66, the city hosts a three-day juried art fair. Approximately 300 works from seventy-five local artists are on display. The best time to see the juried art show is at the Friday evening opening reception. If you're interested in seeing the classic cars, try to go Friday evening or early Saturday morning before cruise participants depart. There's something for everyone at this blowout!

SapulpaFest

Held in downtown Sapulpa on a Friday and Saturday in August. Free.

All kinds of exciting things happen in Sapulpa during this annual town festival. As many as 150 local artists sell their wares during this popular downtown activity. Some booths offer carnival-type games; others provide hands-on craft activities for those who wish to try them. Three different beauty pageants are held; nearby, entertainment keeps festival-goers amused. With much to see and do, this is one celebration families don't want to miss!

Southeast Oklahoma

Atoka

Atoka, which was once part of the Choctaw Nation, was named for Captain Atoka, a Choctaw sub-chief. Reverend J.S. Murrow, a Baptist missionary, established a settlement here in 1867. During the Civil War, nearby Boggy Depot was the major supply depot for Confederate troops operating in Indian Territory. The Battle of the Middle Boggy, February 13, 1864, took place when Major Charles Willette and three troops of the 14th Kansas Cavalry came upon the encampment of Captain Nail's Company "A" of the First Choctaw and Chickasaw Cavalry, a detachment of the 20th Texas Cavalry, and a group from the Seminole Battalion of Mounted Rifles. The Union scored a decisive win.

To get to Atoka from Tulsa, take U.S. Highway 75 (Indian Nation Turnpike) to the U.S. Highway 69 exit south of McAlester. Take U.S. 69 to Atoka. From Oklahoma City, take I-40 east to the Shawnee-U.S. Highway 177 exit going south. When the highway splits just south of Asher, take S.H. 3W through Ada into Atoka. Atoka is about 130 miles from Oklahoma City and about 140 miles from Tulsa. Atoka Chamber of Commerce (405) 889-2410.

Atoka Confederate Memorial Museum and Cemetery

(405) 889-7192. One mile north of Atoka on U.S. Highway 69. Tuesday-Saturday 9-4. Closed Monday and national holidays. Free. Handicapped accessible.

The most interesting exhibits in the museum are bits and pieces of military gear found in the area. These include buttons, buckles, bullets, musket balls, a bayonet, silverware, and metal pieces from saddles or bridles. There is also a Civil War physician's medical bag and amputation kit. Many of the Indian tribes were important to the Confederacy. There were at least fifteen Indian regiments and battalions, with the best-known being the 1st Cherokee Mounted Rifles. Native American artifacts are prominent in the collection with pipes, arrowheads and tools on display. Other exhibits pertain to early-day Atoka.

In the cemetery, eight Confederate soldiers have now been identified. Their deaths in the spring of 1862 remained a mystery until early 1996, when a gentleman from North Carolina sent a copy of a letter written by one of his ancestors describing a measles epidemic which struck members of Dawson's 19th Ark Infantry as they travelled from Fort Smith to Fort McCullough. Thirty minutes is sufficient to see the exhibits and walk through the cemetery. There is a rest stop with picnic tables on the property.

Atoka

Boggy Depot State Park

(405) 889-5625. From Atoka, travel eleven miles west on State Highway 7, then four miles south on Park Lane, the first road west of the bridge over Clear Boggy Creek. Free. There are no handicpaped restrooms.

This 630-acre state park is shaded by giant oaks and other hardwoods. Though little is left, historical markers indicate the sites of buildings in this old community, which saw its first settlers in 1837. For over thirty years it was one of the most important settlements in Indian Territory; it was situated on the military route from Ft. Gibson to Ft. Washita. Travelers to Texas and gold seekers headed for California often passed through the area. In 1858, Boggy Depot became a stop on the Butterfield Overland mail route from St. Louis to San Francisco. Boggy Depot's decline began in 1872 when the railroad bypassed the town for a spot two miles south. Chief Allen Wright, principal chief of the Choctaw Nation, lived here, and he is buried in the nearby cemetery. In 1866, it was Wright who suggested the name "Oklahoma" for the proposed Indian Territory. In 1907, the name was adopted as the official state name.

This is a quiet little park with nice picnic facilities. Camping facilities range from unimproved to sites with water, electricity and sewer hookups. Individual family camping is first come, first served. Large groups can make advance reservations. There are no handicapped accessible restrooms. There is a reason this area has so many features named "Boggy." Don't plan to go after there's been a big rain; Park Lane may be under Clear Boggy Creek!

Cimarron Cellars

(405) 889-6312 (Winery), (405) 889-5997 (Tasting/Salesroom) The tasting/sales room is located near the tiny town of Caney, twelve miles south of Atoka on U.S. Highway 69. Watch for the blue sign that says "Cimarron Cellars." The tasting room is on the east side of the highway. The winery is five miles east of the highway. The winery is open by appointment. The tasting/sales room is open Monday-Saturday from 12-5. Free. Handicapped accessible.

Dwayne and Suze Pool were living in California's Napa Valley when they heard about a vineyard for sale in Oklahoma. In a reverse Okie-type migration, they moved to Oklahoma, bought the vineyard, and began selling grapes to Texas wineries. In 1983, they decided to open their own winery, Cimarron Cellars. They now produce about 2000 cases of wine a year from their twenty acres of mature grapes. The winery specializes in French-American hybrids and produces ten varieties of red and white, dry, semi-dry, and sweet wine. One of the Pool's favorite wines is a 1988 red wine which they call "Vin d'Ok." They have since lost the vines which produced the grapes for this wine, making it even more special.

Activities vary during the year at the winery. Harvest is between mid-July and mid-August. There is more to be seen at that time; however, throughout the year there may be short periods of bottling activity. Call ahead if you want to see the winery. Even if nothing is happening, you can still see the equipment and hear an explanation of the process. The road to the winery is not paved, so avoid the trip during bad weather. The tasting room is open year-round.

In the Vicinity

Clarita

The little agricultural community of Clarita was originally named "Kittie," but was later renamed to honor the wife of the president of the Missouri, Kansas and Gulf Railroad. At the peak of its prosperity due to peanut and cotton farming, Clarita boasted twenty businesses, including a bank, two hotels and two cotton gins. Now it is best known for Amish farmers who live in the area. *Clarita is about 25 miles west-northwest of Atoka.*

Amish School Consignment Auction

Held the second Saturday in September. For information, call The Little Country Store (405) 428-3403. The sale is held on a farm just east of State Highway 48 between Tupelo and Wapanucka, one mile north of State Highway 31. Look for signs. Parking $1.

Here is a unique opportunity to learn about an interesting group of people. The Amish have a strong sense of community; Amish folk come from as far away as Ohio to help with the auction that raises funds for the Clarita School. The day begins with a pancake and sausage breakfast served from 6-10 a.m. The auction starts at 9 a.m. All sorts of things are auctioned, from antiques, collectibles, and quilts, to buggies and livestock. There are many arts and crafts booths as well as food booths offering a variety of taste treats. It's best to go early; homemade apricot pies are a big seller.

Attending this event takes some planning. For greatest enjoyment, you need to arrive early, but the question is, "from where?" Nearest towns with a selection of places to stay are Atoka and Ada. You'll still have to drive 30-45 minutes to get to the Auction. The key is to make your reservations early. It's helpful to read about the Amish before going. *Oklahoma Today* magazine (September 1996) has an excellent background article. Leave your camera at home; photography is not permitted. Handicapped accessible with difficulty.

Coalgate

Coalgate was born from the coal mining activity in the area. By 1885, three railroads came through here. The town was originally called "Liddie," but at a meeting of M.K.&T. directors, it was suggested that the town be named after railroad president Coalgate Hoyt. The obvious tie-in to the local industry influenced the city organizers, and the name was changed in 1898. *Coalgate is approximately fifteen miles northwest of Atoka on S.H. 3. Coal County Chamber of Commerce (405) 927-2119.*

Coal County Historical and Mining Museum

212 S. Broadway, (405) 927-2360. Tuesday-Wednesday 9-4, Thursday 9-11:30. Free. This small, volunteer-run museum is dedicated to preserving pieces of the most significant years in the town's history—the coal boom. Some of the exhibits are self-explanatory, some remain a mystery as there are no labels. Genealogists looking for Coal County connections will find a number of old records here. Handicapped accessible with some difficulty.

A visit to this museum is an example of mining; you'll have to do some digging, but there's rich material here. The hours may change, so check ahead. If you're looking for a nice picnic spot, there's a lovely little park with a duck pond on the south side of town.

Memories Bed and Breakfast

120 West Queen, (405) 927-3590. Located on S.H. 3 on the west side of town, north side of the highway. The gift shop is open Tuesday-Friday 10-5. $27-32 plus tax. Reservations are necessary, no deposit required. No credit cards accepted. Not handicapped accessible.

When Sandy and Jim Anderson retired, they moved back to their hometown and bought an old building which had once been a rooming house. The two-story white house, with charming Wedgewood blue shutters and gingerbread trim on the porch corners, is now Memories Bed and Breakfast. There are four bedrooms available for rent—three with double beds, one with two twin beds. Baths are shared or private, depending on availability. Two of the rooms have sitting areas attached. Decor is cozy without lots of frills. On Sunday mornings, Sandy serves a continental breakfast in an upstairs sitting room. Other mornings, guests are given a voucher for a full breakfast at the cafe across the street. Sandy also runs a small gift shop where she carries a variety of craft items, dolls, baskets, and knickknacks.

McGee Creek Natural Scenic Recreation Area

Contact McGee Creek State Park (see below), (405) 889-5822. All visitors must check in at the permit station. To get there, go approximately five miles east of the Farris intersection (where you turn north to McGee Creek Lake), to the Centerpoint intersection where you turn north and travel thirteen miles to the permit station. McGee Creek NSRA is about twenty-three miles east-southeast of Atoka. The permit station is open from daylight to dark. Free.

Rolling hills, giant moss-covered boulders, tumbling swift streams, deer, river otter, bobcats and an occasional bear–what more could you ask for in a scenic area? Almost 9,000 acres adjacent to McGee Creek State Park have been set aside for wilderness-type recreational experiences; only backpack or equestrian camping is permitted. Fifty miles of well-marked trails crisscross the wilderness area. The trails are designated as multiuse, hiker/biker, or hiker only. Motorized vehicles are not permitted. Everyone entering the area must have a permit. Since a limited number of permits are issued, it is wise to call ahead for full-day or overnight camping permits. A maximum of forty half-day permits are issued daily on a first-come, first-served basis. Reserved permits must be picked up by 10 a.m. on the date of issue. There is a secure parking lot for overnight campers and a horse trailer unloading and parking area.

McGee Creek State Park

(405) 889-5822. The park is located about eighteen miles southeast of Atoka and three and one-half miles north of the town of Farris. The park is open 24 hours a day. Free. Check with the park office for camping fees. The fishing pier and the restrooms in the Buster Hight area are handicapped accessible.

This is one of Oklahoma's best fishing lakes; outdoor-sports writer Covey Bean lists it at the top of his "Top Ten Oklahoma Lakes" list. There's good news and bad news for bass fishermen: the good news is this lake is a hot spot for largemouth bass; the bad news is you can't eat them because of natural mercury contamination. This doesn't affect other kinds of fish, and the fishing for crappie, sunfish and catfish is also good. Camping accommodations include eight lake huts (nice wooden buildings with electricity, screened porches, and indoor picnic tables–much more luxurious than a tent), twenty-five improved sites, and over a hundred primitive sites. Reserve the lake huts in advance. All other camping is first-come first-served. There's a swimming beach, a fishing pier, picnic tables, and restrooms in the Buster Hight area. Three boat ramps are in the park. There are no boat rentals or concessions at the lake; bring what you need. However, there is a convenience store just outside the park's main entrance that carries groceries, bait, fishing licenses, etc.

Lake Eufaula

Anyone with any geographical sense knows that Oklahoma is landlocked. But water-lovers, take heart! Oklahoma has more shoreline than the East Coast, due in part to the many man-made lakes of Eastern Oklahoma. Lake Eufaula is a big contributor to the enjoyment of water in this part of the country; with over 151,000 acres of water and over 650 miles of shoreline, this is one of the largest lakes in the region and one of the largest man-made lakes in the country! Running almost eighty miles north to south and forty miles from east to west, the lake is known for good fishing and beautiful, sandy beaches.

The lake was created in 1964 when the Eufaula Dam, designed to control flooding along the Canadian River, was completed. Sportsmen enjoy visiting the Eufaula area. Hunting and fishing are popular outdoor pastimes as are summer water-related recreational activities. For hunters, several wildlife management areas are maintained by the Oklahoma Department of Wildlife Conservation. Open to the public, these areas have various seasons for rabbit, squirrel, deer, turkey, and quail. Appropriate stamps and /or tags are required to hunt most game. Fishermen enjoy catching bass and catfish, although Eufaula is best known for its crappie. Each spring a tagged **crappie fishing tournament** is held, with prizes ranging from $25 to $50,000 for the specially-tagged fish. Visitors also enjoy boating, water skiing, sailing, parasailing, and swimming. Activities ashore include shopping, horseback riding, hiking and entertainment. A number of private establishments offer rides and arcades; or for those interested in getting back to nature, camping facilities abound. Two companies even rent houseboats for that unforgettable, out-of-the-ordinary vacation. Lake Eufaula is one of eastern Oklahoma's favorite playgrounds.

Lake Eufaula is located about 120 miles east/southeast of Oklahoma City, and about 78 miles south of Tulsa. Oklahoma City residents may travel straight east on I-40, and Tulsans may choose to travel south on Highway 64/62 to Checotah, then drop further south to the lake on Highway 69. The Lake Eufaula Association at (918) 689-7751 is a good source of additional information about Oklahoma's largest lake.

With almost 2500 acres of grounds, **Arrowhead State Park** (918-339-2204) is one of eastern Oklahoma's most attractive parks. Campsites include eighty-five water and electric hookups, seven comfort stations with hot and cold water showers, two sanitary dump stations, and three group shelters. There are picnic areas, swimming areas, and playground areas for children. Two nature/hiking trails are located within the park. Amenities include a marina with rental boats, an enclosed fishing dock, a swimming pool, tennis courts, horseback riding (in season), and an eighteen-hole golf course. The park is located fifteen miles north of McAlester on U.S. Highway 69, and eighteen miles south of I-40.

Arrowhead Golf Course is located within Arrowhead State Park (follow the signs). Recently rated number one in Oklahoma, this golf course is located on a hill, providing elevation challenges and beautiful scenery. Par is 72 on this 6741-yard course; USGA rating is 71.4 and slope is 119. Amenities include a pro shop, a practice green, and rental clubs. Tee times are recommended a few days in advance for weekends and tournament days. Contact the course at (918) 339-2769. Open daily, dawn to dusk. Green fees are $10.50 weekdays, $12.50 weekends, Jr. and Sr. discounts given; All-Day play at any state-owned golf course such as this one is $35 (includes cart and green fees) on weekdays only. Carts are $17.

Owned by the Choctaw Nation of Oklahoma, **Arrowhead Resort and Gaming Center** (918-339-2711) offers eighty-four motel-type rooms ($50-55) and seventy cabins ($52 and $82 for one bedroom; $129-149 for two bedrooms; cooking utensils not provided). Other amenities include a bingo hall, restaurant, lounge, gift shop, and an outdoor swimming pool.

Fountainhead State Park is located seven miles south of I-40 on Highway 150, (918) 689-5311. Once the hunting ground of the Osage Indian tribe, this 3400-acre park now features camping, hiking, and golfing. There are 248 unimproved camp sites at Fountainhead, 84 modern and semi-modern hookups, seven comfort stations with showers, and a sanitary dump station. A **Nature Center** offers interpretive activities during the summer months; programs include hikes, crafts, slide programs, and lectures. A marina has rental boats and an enclosed fishing dock. Tennis courts, horseback riding (in season), and playground areas are also available. **Fountainhead Resort** is also located here. Call (800) 345-6343 for more information.

Fountainhead Golf Course is located within the state park, (918) 689-3209. This well-established par 72 course has beautiful greens and many trees. The front nine has tight fairways. Yardage is 6919; USGA rating is 71.3, and slope is 116. Call one week in advance for weekend and holiday tee times. Open daily, dawn to dusk. Green fees weekday $10.50 plus tax, weekend $12.50 plus tax; carts are $17 plus tax.

Join the ranks of wealthy yachtsmen when you take a houseboat vacation with **Getaway Cruises, Inc.** Their vessels offer the latest in marine design and safety, and vacationers are assured comfort, privacy, and ease of operation. Travel the entire lake in your boat, enjoying fishing, swimming, and water skiing, or stop at some of Eufaula's famous sand beaches for an afternoon swim or evening cookout. Each vessel is impressively equipped, including a full kitchen. Dinette seating accommodates eight to ten. The deck has a grill, swimming platform and water slide. Additional features include air conditioning and forced-air heat, custom-built couches and double beds, cassette stereo, and privacy curtains. Cooking utensils, pots and pans, and cleaning supplies are provided, as are life jackets, first aid kits and fire extinguishers. For an out-of-the-ordinary vacation, don your sailor's garb and charter your own private houseboat for a tour of Lake Eufaula. For reservations contact (918) 689-2200. Peak season is May 15th-September 15th. Peak season and off-season rates are available for both weekend and week-long cruises. Call for directions and rates. Open seasonally.

Eufaula

The town of Eufaula sits along the banks of Oklahoma's largest lake. Sportsmen and tourists alike are discovering that this once sleepy little lake town now has much to offer. Originally called North Fork Town, this small Creek Indian village was established at the crossroads of two westward migratory trails. The railroad arrived in 1872, linking this Indian educational center with the rest of the territory.

Eufaula Reservoir was completed in 1964, creating the nation's seventh largest man-made lake, and making Eufaula the gateway to water adventure. Shoppers enjoy the specialty and antique stores located along the town's Main Street. Others enjoy dining at one of several local establishments and the variety of events scheduled throughout the year. Whether visiting the lake to catch the biggest crappie, or just passing time en route to another destination, visitors will relish the fun and friendliness Eufaula provides.

Located at the junction of US 69 and Highway 9. Contact the Eufaula Chamber of Commerce (918) 689-2791.

Belle Starr Jamboree Village

Located four miles east of Highway 69 on Texana Road, (918) 689-2122. Open daily from Memorial Day through Labor Day. Other times the village is open for special events; call for a schedule. The craft business is open only on weekends. The music shows are staged each evening from 8-10; dinner is served from 4-10. Tickets to the variety show are $8, or with dinner $15.

Belle Starr Jamboree Village, named after the lady outlaw who lived nearby, is a rustic, old-fashioned town with twenty-six enclosed shops where crafters sell their wares on weekends. Add to this a musical variety show held nightly throughout the summer and you'll have nothing less than a grand old time! Shopping and singing...what could be more fun!

Wild Woman's

418 S. Main (Business Highway 69), (918) 689-5481. Open Monday, Wednesday through Saturday 10-6, Sunday 11-2. Closed Tuesday.

Guests to this unusual commercial establishment will first notice the beautiful and fragrant flower garden surrounding this 1914 Sears Roebuck mail order house. Inside, dried and live medicinal herbs (most of which are grown on the premises), specialty teas, gifts, and books are sold. The **Tea Room** serves only fresh, healthy delicacies; a selection of homemade soups, salads, and sandwiches on fresh-baked bread are offered daily. Jim and Sue Anglin are the owners, cooks, servers, and gardeners at their "wild" and interesting shop and tea room. Devoted to a healthy lifestyle, Sue has become an amateur herbalist and often lectures on natural medicines and herbal treatments. Her talents and interest in flowers has resulted in her garden being the only source of antique European roses in the state. You'll leave The Wild Woman feeling enriched and perhaps educated by the good conversation with your hosts. Also held at the shop is the **Wild Woman's Wild Herb, Wild Rose and Wildflower Festival**. Held each year on the Saturday before Mother's Day, the festival features vendors selling herb-related products, wildflower field trips, and demonstrations of turn-of-the-century crafts, everything from soap-making to furniture-making. This event is free to the public and is growing each year.

Accommodations

Cedar Creek Bed and Breakfast

Located a few miles west of Eufaula on Highway 9, (918) 689-3009. Call for directions. $70 per night. Reservations are necessary. Member of the Oklahoma Bed and Breakfast Association.

Built as a B&B, this new establishment complete with fishing pond is located on twenty acres in the hills surrounding Eufaula. Two rooms, each with private bath and jacuzzi tub, are available; one has a Native American theme and the other is decorated in country florals. Enjoy a hike or a bike ride on the trails surrounding the home, or relax in a porch rocker or on the hammock in the trees. Complimentary beverages and a TV/VCR are found in the great room. Owner Karra Sparks, a registered dietician, serves breakfasts guaranteed to please. Experience the country life and great hospitality at Cedar Creek!

Tolleson House Bed and Breakfast

201 Forest, (918) 689-2745 after 5 p.m. Call for reservations and directions. Member of the Oklahoma Bed and Breakfast Association.

The Tolleson House is one of the state's newest B&Bs. Built in 1920 by Dr. Tolleson and his wife, the brick home is graced with white pillars and has a large yard with a pool and Japanese garden. The B&B's decor is best described as "comfortable Oriental" and reflects the owner's interest in the Far East. Three rooms with private baths are available. Full breakfasts are served daily and include gourmet egg dishes with variety of fruits and breads.

Events

Whole Hawg Day

Held in downtown Eufaula on the Friday and Saturday of the last weekend of July. Contact the Chamber of Commerce at (918) 689-5481 for specific dates and more information. Free.

Have a rip-snortin' good time when you visit Eufaula's Whole Hawg Day. This fun-filled and unique event includes activities for the entire family. Friday evening begins with a parade and street dance. Arts and crafts, kiddie carnival rides, and food concessions are offered throughout the weekend. Saturday activities include a pancake breakfast, a car show, a banner competition, bake sales, sidewalk sales, and live radio broadcasts. However, the main event is the Hawg Cookoff Contest. Whole hogs are roasted, with winning cooks receiving cash prizes. There's even a trophy awarded for Best Showmanship. At 5 p.m., the Free Hawg Sandwich Giveaway begins. Visitors have an opportunity to enjoy the delectable taste of fresh-roasted pork at this old-fashioned pig party!

In the Vicinity

Checotah

Established in 1872 as a railhead along the Katy line, Checotah became an important shipping point for the territory's agricultural products. Over the years, the surrounding ranch lands have bred a number of world famous rodeo horses and five native Checotahns hold nine PRCA World Championship Bulldogging titles. This outstanding cowboy tradition has been acknowledged by a nationally-known jean manufacturer with the creation of their specialty line of western wear—Checotah. The town also provides services to hunters and fishermen, and it is the site of the **Battle of Honey Creek**, authentically staged every three years by the Oklahoma Historical Society (405)521-2491.

The town is located on Highway 69, just north of I-40. For more information, contact the Katy Depot Visitor's Center at (918) 473-6377.

Sharpe House Bed and Breakfast

301 N.W. 2nd, (918) 473-2382. Located two blocks west and two blocks north of the only stoplight in town. Rates are $35-50. Reservations are recommended.

This beautiful, four-column antebellum home was once a rooming house for female teachers. Converted to to a bed and breakfast in 1991, it has three rooms with private baths. Homebaked breads and muffins are served each morning; upon request, owner Kay Kindt will prepare her special Mexican breakfast. Breakfast is served either on the screened porch or in front of the fireplace.

Okrafest

Held on a Saturday in mid-September on Main Street in downtown Checotah. For more information contact the Checotah Chamber of Commerce at (918) 473-2070. Free.

In Oklahoma there's a festival for almost everything. Add the Okrafest to your list of the state's unique and fun events. Okrafest's approximately 6000 visitors will enjoy browsing the stores of Main Street or the booths set up by local artisans. Arts and crafts and entertainment abound. Food featuring this most unusual vegetable is available everywhere; you may even pick up many recipes to try at home.

Hugo

Hugo was named for French writer Victor Hugo. The town was important in early state-hood days for its connection with the railroad. Hugo still enjoys its railroad heritage with one of only two excursion trains in the state, its historic depot, and remnants of the Harvey House tradition. Its other claim to fame is as a circus winter home. Although most of the traveling shows are out of business, three traveling circuses still have winter headquarters in Hugo. *Hugo is 208 miles southeast of Oklahoma City (I-40 to the Indian Nation Turnpike, then south) and 168 miles from Tulsa (south on U.S. Highway 75, then continuing south on the Indian Nation Turnpike). Hugo Chamber of Commerce (405) 326-7511.*

Circus Winter Quarters

(405) 326-3173. Turn north from U.S. Highway 70 onto S.H. 93 and go about a mile to East Kirk Road. Turn west and go to the circus wagon. Weekdays 9-5. Free. Handicapped accessible.

Three circuses, the Carson and Barnes Circus, the Kelly Miller Circus, and the Chinese Imperial Circus, are in winter quarters here from mid-November until mid-March. The guided tour will focus on the animals. Animals from all three circuses winter with the Carson-Barnes outfit. You'll also see circus trucks and equipment and, depending on the schedule, you may be able to see various performers practicing their skills. Be sure to call in advance for an appointment; your reception will depend on the circus schedule and who is available to show you around.

Hugo Frisco Depot Museum

300 West Jackson, (405) 326-6630. Coming from the west on U.S. Highways 70 and 271, you will see the old depot on the north side of the highway immediately after you cross the railroad tracks. April 1 through mid-November, Monday-Saturday 10-4. Free. The downstairs portion of the museum and the restaurant are handicapped accessible.

Built in 1913 to replace an older structure, the depot now houses a large collection of items of historical interest only, a portion of which relates to the railroad. Hugo's circus heritage has an important part in the exhibits, a favorite being a miniature five-ring circus complete with animals and performers. Local industry of the past is saluted, including a recreation of the still where Rod Sanders made his ever-popular Three Star Whiskey. At the south end of the depot, the original Harvey House restaurant is being refurbished. In the past, it was open occasionally for sandwiches and light lunches. Current plans call for a full-service restaurant. In the 1870s, Fred Harvey made a deal with the railroad to provide food service on its western routes. The restaurants were famous for fresh, well-prepared meals served at lightning speed by young ladies of good reputation whose chaperonage and housing was arranged by the Harvey organization. Upstairs in the Hugo Frisco depot, you can see a typical Harvey dormitory.

Hugo Heritage Railroad

1-888-RR DEPOT or (405) 326-6630. Trains leave from the Frisco Depot. Hours and fares vary from trip to trip. Some trips leave as early as 8 a.m.; others depart at 2 p.m. Prices range from $15 to $26 for adult round-trip tickets. Calling ahead for specific schedules and reservations is absolutely necessary. The train is available for large group charters. Handicapped accessible.

This is a chance to relive history as you ride in comfort in one of two restored 1946 passenger cars pulled by a Kiamichi locomotive. Rides are scheduled each Saturday from April through November. Destinations include Ft. Towson, Antlers, Paris, Texas, or Idabel. Some trips involve special events such as Idabel's Dogwood Days or Octoberfest, dinner trips, or a Christmas theater trip.

Mount Olivet Cemetery

800 East Trice, (405) 326-9263 or 326-7511. From Jackson Street (U.S. Highway 70) turn south on Eighth Street. The cemetery is on the east side of the street past the railroad tracks. Daily, dawn to dusk. Free. Large groups need to call in advance. Visitors need to be sensitive to those people who are not here for sight-seeing. Particular courtesy needs to be exercised during funerals.

A monument with a dancing elephant and the inscription "A TRIBUTE TO ALL SHOWMEN UNDER GOD'S BIG TOP" marks the section of the cemetery known as "Showmen's Rest." This area has been set aside for circus folk. Many of the headstones tell stories; the circus wagon wheel with a missing wheel nut marks circus road manager Ted Bowman's grave. In the old days when the circus would come to town, the sheriff would take possession of the wheel nut from the office wagon. When all bills in town were paid, the nut would be returned. The circus expression "making the nut" referred to breaking even. Circus owner Jack Moore's stone is a circus tent, while animal trainer John Narfski has a hippo carved on his marker. Two of the most famous bull riders in the history of rodeo are buried in another part of the cemetery. Freckles Brown's monument bears his likeness and that of his belt buckle as 1962 Rodeo Cowboys' Association World's Champion Bull Rider. Lane Frost's stone is topped with the shape of a belt buckle and is inscribed "A CHAMPION IN THE ARENA, A CHAMPION IN LIFE."

Shopping

Fallon Road Emporium

(405) 325-3947. Travel four miles east of Hugo on U.S. Highway 70 to Fallon Road. Turn south two blocks to reach the Emporium. Thursday-Friday 12-5, Saturday 10-6, Sunday 1-5. Both buildings are handicapped accessible.

Unique, handmade treasures crafted by local artisans fill this restored 1932 farm house. This is also a place to find interesting antiques, handmade quilts, custom designed clothing for children and adults, and many other goodies. The shop has been so successful that mother and daughter-in-law Thersea and Earnesteen Allen have built another building next to the original to house more items.

Accommodations

The Old Johnson House Bed and Breakfast

1101 East Kirk, (405) 326-8111 or (405) 326-3103. Go east from downtown Hugo on Jackson Street (U.S. Highway 70) to Tenth Street. Turn north on Eighth, then east on Kirk. $55-65 (ask abou;t special weekday business rates and about required cancellation notice). Call at least a week in advance for reservations. No pets or smoking is allowed, but children are welcome "as long as they don't pull the heads off my daylilies," says Mollie. Credit cards are accepted. Not handicapped accessible.

Built in 1910 for the family of lawyer Tyree Johnson, the home remained in the family for close to ninety years, giving it the obvious nickname "The Old Johnson House." It was purchased in 1993 by Mollie and Wayne Higginbotham, who turned the 4000 square-foot, two-story house into a bed and breakfast. Each of the six bedrooms is decorated in a different style, from a Victorian room abloom with hundreds of cabbage roses to a country style room with two full-sized iron bedsteads, antique quilts and white eyelet accessories. There is also a guest cottage in the former servants' quarters. Breakfast is an ample repast, complete with farm fresh eggs from the Higginbotham's own chickens. Mollie makes her own jams and jellies that taste delicious with her homemade biscuits or muffins. Other items often found on the breakfast table include breakfast meats, casseroles, fruit and, during holiday season, a festive cranberry torte.

Gardeners particularly enjoy visiting in May and June when perennial peonies, daylilies and daisies, planted when the house was built, are in bloom.

Events

Bill Grant's Bluegrass and Old Time Music Festival

Held for five days in early August in Salt Creek Park. Call (405) 326-5598 for more information. Salt Creek Park is one mile east of Hugo on U.S. Highway 70 and one-half mile north on Bill Grant Road. Call or write Rt. 2, Box 74, Hugo, OK 74743 for more information and a full schedule of events. Adults $12 a day or $50 for the full five days, children ages 12 and under are admitted free with a parent.

This is the oldest bluegrass festival west of the Mississippi and, at five days, is one of the longest. Most days, the music goes from ten in the morning until midnight. About two dozen top groups and individuals keep toes tapping and the good times rollin'. Food is available, or bring your own picnic. No beer is sold or allowed on the grounds. Seating is on stationary benches, but you can bring folding chairs if you like. There are cold showers on the grounds ($0.50), and ice and water is available to help beat the August heat. Some twenty thousand people show up for this festival, thus overnight space is tight. There are several motels in Hugo, and more in Paris, Texas, located about thirty minutes away. Camping spaces are available in the park on a first-come, first-served basis.

In the Vicinity

Ft. Towson Military Park/Doaksville

(405) 873-2634. Located one and one-half miles east of the town of Ft. Towson on the north side of U.S Highway 70. Monday-Saturday 9-5, Sunday 1-4. Free.

Ft. Towson was established as Cantonment Towson in 1824 as a safeguard on the Mexican frontier and as a base for negotiations with the Plains Indians. As events unfolded in the area, the post was abandoned, reestablished as a fort, flourished and dwindled, until it was abandoned again in 1854. The remaining buildings were given to the Choctaws (whose removal from the eastern United States gave the fort prominence in the 1830s).

During the Civil War, the fort was commandeered by Major General Same Bell Maxey (CSA). It was here in 1865 that Brigadier General Stand Watie, with his Confederate Indian Brigade, became the last Confederate general to surrender. Today, you can see the remains of foundations of barracks and other post buildings. The original Sutler's Store (a civilian who sold provisions to the military) has been recreated, complete with merchandise. Interpreters are available for guided tours, and drop-in visitors are welcomed. If you want to bring a group, call ahead. Wear comfortable walking shoes. Slacks or jeans make walking through tall grass more comfortable. There is a nice picnic pavilion on the grounds. Partially handicapped accessible.

There are at least two reenactments held at the fort each year. The first weekend in March is the fur traders' rendezvous; later in the year is the military encampment. Call for specifics.

Nearby Doaksville was an important commercial, political and social center from the time of the Choctaw removal until the 1860s. Between 1850 and 1863, it served as the Choctaw National Capitol. Almost nothing was left of the town when the University of Oklahoma Department of Anthropology and the Oklahoma Historical Society began excavations. Thousands of artifacts have been found along with foundations and other structural evidences of the town. To view the site, which is about one-half mile from the old fort, call the Fort Towson number in advance. Doaksville is opened by appointment only. If you are interested in participating in an archaeological dig, inquire with Dr. William Lees, Director of Historic Sites Division at the Oklahoma Historical Society, (405) 522-5233. These are long-term projects with college credit available.

McAlester

In late 1869 or early 1870, trader J.J. McAlester set up a tent store at a spot known as the "Cross Roads" where Texas Road and the California Road intersected. It was a money-making proposition from the start. When the Missouri, Kansas & Texas railroad reached McAlester, more businesses started up in the area. In 1873, a post office listed as "McAllister" was opened; the obvious misspelling was corrected in 1885. In 1889, the Choctaw Coal and Railway planned a route through McAlester, but it wanted financial incentives from J.J. McAlester. He declined to pay, and the railroad went south of McAlester, founding a new town, "South McAlester." J.J. McAlester disputed the legality of the claims purchased in South McAlester and, when proved correct in court, bought up the judgements and became a large property holder in the new town. Ironically, his investment cost more than the $10,000 the railroad had demanded of him originally. Today, South McAlester is the thriving city we know as McAlester. North McAlester still exists and shows promise as an antique hunter's delight.

The **Pioneer Coal Miner Memorial** is located in Chadick Park and honors the coal industry prevalent in the McAlester area. It features a life-sized statue of a pioneer coal miner and a "Wall of Memories" that bears the names of over 1700 miners who were killed in pursuit of their trade. *McAlester is 132 miles southeast of Oklahoma City (I-40 to Henryetta, then south on the Indian Nations Turnpike to the U.S. Highway 270 exit), and 92 miles from Tulsa. McAlester Chamber of Commerce (800) 879-2550.*

McAlester Building Foundation, Inc.

200 East Adams, (405) 423-2939. Old McAlester High School is located two blocks north of Carl Albert Parkway (U.S. Highway 270) and two blocks east of Main Street. Monday-Friday 8-2. Free. All tours are guided. Drop-in guests are welcome, but groups should call ahead for an appointment. Plan at least an hour to see everything. The museum is handicapped accessible.

Fourteen rooms in this former school building are being used to house museum exhibits about the area's history. Displays include the Native American Room which honors local Native American tribes and the Coal Mine Room devoted to the history of the coal industry. Through period rooms such as the 1800s Historical Room, visitors find clothing and furniture typical of the era. Displays are well-organized, and the setting is unique. During the Christmas season, beautiful Christmas trees are decorated to carry out each room's theme.

Golf

Thundercreek Golf Course

Highway 270 West. (918) 423-5799. Sunup to sundown. Closed on Christmas Day. $12 daily, $8 seniors. Carts are available $16 for eighteen holes, $9 for nine holes. Senior rates available.

The signature hole on this course is number 17. It's a 485 yard, par 5 killer with three creek crossings. The real challenge is that the hole sits on a cliff thirty-nine feet above the last creek. According to pro Mark Cox, "If you can't get the ball in the air, it's just going to bounce back and laugh at you!" The eighteen-hole course (6840 yards, par 72), designed by Doug Tewell and built in 1994, takes advantage of the natural terrain. Slope is 135; USGA rating is 73.8. A summer junior program is available. From March 15 to Labor Day, weekend tee times may be reserved up to one week in advance. The rest of the time, it's first-come-first-served. There is a pro shop and a snack bar-grill, and practice putting range, chipping greens and a driving range.

Dining

Baker's Street Bistro $$

212 East Choctaw, (918) 423-3100. The restaurant is in downtown McAlester, one block south of Carl Albert Parkway (U.S. Highway 270) and two and one-half blocks east of Main Street. Lunch Tuesday-Friday 11:30-1:30, dinner Tuesday-Saturday from 5:30. Handicapped accessible; credit cards are accepted.

This is an upscale "linens and china" restaurant specializing in seafood and continental cuisine.

Gia Como's $$

19th and Comanche, (918) 423-2662. Located on the U.S. Highway 69 Bypass South on the east side of town. Comanche is about seven blocks south of Carl Albert Parkway (U.S. Highway 270). Tuesday-Saturday 11:30-9:30. Closed most major holidays. Handicapped accessible.

Like the three Italian restaurants in Krebs, all entrees come with plenty of extras. Gia Como's is particularly proud of its steaks, the excellence of which is attributed to "a special secret." Of course, there are Italian entrees to choose from including chicken florentine, veal parmigiana, and shrimp alfredo.

Janalynn's $

324 East Carl Albert Parkway, (918) 423-4183. Janalynn's is on the main east-west street (U.S. Highway 270) in downtown McAlester. Monday-Friday, open at 8:30, lunch is served from 11:30-2, with a 2:30 closing time. Handicapped accessible. No credit cards.

"Quiet and quaint" are two words often used to describe this combination tea room, bakery and antique shop. You can't miss the green-fronted building with its awning striped with rich plum and green. Janalynn's opens early with coffee, tea and fresh Danish pastries served until lunch. The lunch menu varies from day to day, but it always has soup, sandwiches, and both a regular and low-fat blue plate special. "From scratch" desserts are made fresh daily, with coconut cream pie being the number one seller.

Trolley's $$

21 East Monroe, (918) 423-2446. Monroe is five blocks north of U.S. Highway 270. Open Monday-Saturday, 5 p.m. to close.

It's a toss-up as to which is the biggest attraction at Trolley's, the food or the atmosphere. Fortunately, you get both! The restaurant is housed in an 1886 house which has been remodeled using some of the home's original features, plus other items of historical significance. The front sidewalk is made of bricks from the streets of old McAlester, and the tin ceilings in several rooms came from the old Bender Drug Store. The lounge is a New Orleans trolley repair car. While eclectic, the decor tends toward the romantic and elegant, with chandeliers and etched glass windows. The menu features seafood and steaks. Many of the entrees are prepared with a cajun twist, and all are served with tabouli, New Orleans-style gumbo, salad, homemade bread, baked potato, and vegetable. Partially handicapped accessible.

Shopping

North McAlester, between the 2600 and 2800 blocks on North Main Street, offers a number of antique stores. Visitors will find another interesting store further down the street at 2815 North Main. **Etudaiye** is a pottery studio with attractive bowls, pitchers, vases, and serving pieces for sale. The shop is open by appointment only by calling (918) 423-8808. Choctaw Street, one block south of Carl Albert Parkway in downtown McAlester, features a number of interesting and attractive shops including the **Yellow Gazebo** (109 East Choctaw), cooking items and gifts; **Pansy's** (200 East Choctaw), ladies' clothing and unique accessories; **Southeast Artisans** (215 East Choctaw), an arts cooperative; and **Long Branch Antiques** (514 East Choctaw). A walk down Choctaw will take you by a variety of clothing, gift and bookstores. This is old-fashioned downtown shopping at its best.

Events

Italian Festival

Held the Saturday and Sunday of Memorial Day Weekend at the Southeast Oklahoma Exposition Center (Pittsburg County Fairgrounds). (918) 426-4666. The Fairgrounds are east of the Indian Nations Turnpike on U.S. Highway 270 on the west edge of McAlester. Look for the fairground buildings on the south side of the road. Free. Handicapped accessible.

Begun in 1970, this festival celebrates the history, heritage and influence of Italian immigrants on the community. Festivities begin with an opening ceremony on Saturday at 10:30. A highlight is the crowning of the Re and Regina (King and Queen of the festival), a ceremony that is performed in Italian. What would an Italian Festival be without Italian food? No worries here: Italian sausage, meatballs, spaghetti, and garlic bread are consumed by the pound this weekend. While the food is the main attraction, other activities add to the merriment, including Italian games, traditional music and dancing, entertainment, an arts and crafts show, and carnival rides. Italian souvenirs for sale continue the theme. Call ahead to verify location after 1997.

Oklahoma Prison Rodeo

Held during Labor Day Weekend at "Big Mac," Oklahoma State Penitentiary. Call the Chamber of Commerce at (800) 879-2550 for more information and a schedule of Saturday activities. From the Indian Nation Turnpike, go east on U.S. Highway 270. The first road going north is West Street. It will take you to the prison gate, where attendants will give you parking directions. Rodeo performances are at 8 p.m. each evening. General admission tickets are $5, reserved and box seats are

$8-12. Reservations are taken after July 1. Handicapped accessible.

The focus is on the rodeos on Friday and Saturday nights, but other activities are held on Saturday, including a parade, the Inmates' Arts and Crafts Show, and tours of the prison museum. Begun in 1940, the rodeo draws competitors from both professional rodeo ranks and from a number of state correctional institutions. In addition to traditional events like calf roping and bronc and bull riding, there are fun events like "Money the Hard Way," an event in which inmates try to grab for money tied between the horns of a bull. Motels fill up fast; make early reservations if you want to stay over.

Southeastern Oklahoma Arts and Crafts Association Show

Held the first weekend in November at the J.I. Stipe Center. Call (918) 423-7429 for more information. The Stipe Center is located on Monroe (five blocks north of U.S. Highway 270) between Eighth and Ninth Streets (north and east of the center of town). Free. Handicapped accessible.

Artisans from a number of states exhibit at this show, which has grown larger each year. Although this is not a juried show, organizers say that the buying public acts as jury. The finest crafters are successful and return; each year the quality improves. Homecooked meals are available; you can shop, eat and rest, and shop again! The location of the show could change, so call ahead.

In the Vicinity

Hartshorne

Hartshorne is another coal mining town of Southeast Oklahoma. The town is proud to be the hometown of baseball great Warren Spahn.

Hartshorne is about seventeen miles southeast of McAlester on Highway 270, then Highway 63.

Saints Cyril and Methodius Russian Orthodox Church

Modoc and Third Street, (918) 297-2872 or 297-1122. Traveling west on Highway 270 into town, watch for Lindley's grocery on the north side of the road. Just west of the grocery is the sign for the church; turn south and continue 1/2 mile. Visitors are welcome at Vespers (Saturday at 4 p.m.) and at Sunday mass at 10 a.m.

The parish of Saints Cyril and Methodius was founded in 1897 by 75 families who brought their faith from the old country (Galicia in the Carpathian Mountains) as they sought work in the coal mines in Choctaw Territory. The present church with its onion domes dates to 1917. Inside, the chandeliers hold real candles, and antique icons glitter in the twinkling light. Father Joseph Nelson is most gracious about sharing the uniqueness of the church and its heritage with visitors; call ahead, and you may find yourselves enjoying a cabbage roll with the priest. The congregation sponsors a **bake sale** around Thanksgiving. Russian black bread, fruit rolls, pirogi, stuffed cabbage, and braided Easter breads are among the treats available.

Krebs

Krebs was founded in 1871 with the arrival of the Katy Railroad. The area was rich in coal deposits and became a prime destination for Italian immigrants looking for work in the mines. The mines are gone now, but the Italian heritage lives on in Krebs.

Krebs is about five miles east of McAlester just off U.S. Highway 270.

Lovera's Grocery

95 West 6th Street, (800) 854-1417. Monday-Saturday 7 a.m.-6 p.m. Handicapped accessible with some difficulty. Credit cards are accepted.

Lovera's Grocery has been in operation in this 1910 building since 1946. The first thing that hits you when you enter Lovera's is the wonderful smell of Italian spices. The second thing will be the variety of Italian products on the shelves. In the back of the store is the meat counter. Festoons of hanging cheeses and ristras of peppers add a carnival air to the store. Lovera's carries a number of homemade products from their great sausage and caciocavallo cheese to butter and cannoli. They also carry attractive hand-painted Italian bowls and platters. Their gift baskets are special. If you would like to see sausage or cheese being made, call ahead to find out the production schedule. Take a cooler with you so you can take home some of Lovera's products.

Lovera's Grocery.

St. Joseph's Catholic Church

290 N.W. Church Street, (918) 423-6695. Daily 9-5, with 7:30 a.m. mass on weekdays, 6 p.m. mass on Saturday and 11 a.m. on Sunday. Handicapped accessible.

Though this building dates back to 1903, the parish was established in 1885. Features of particular interest include the pressed tin ceiling and exquisite stained glass windows. The church is listed on the National Register of Historic Places. If you have a specific interest and want more detailed information about the building, call ahead about the possibility of a tour.

Isle of Capri $$

150 Southwest 7th Street. (918) 423-3062. Monday-Saturday 5-10:30. Closed Sunday and major holidays. Handicapped accessible. Credit cards are accepted.

In addition to Italian specialties, the Isle specializes in cornfed steer steaks prepared with a sauteed garlic and butter sauce. All entrees are served with antipasto, salad, spaghetti, ravioli, and garlic toast.

Pete's Place $$

8th and Monroe (Highway 270 East). (918) 423-2042. Monday-Saturday opens at 4 p.m., Sunday opens at noon. Handicapped accessible. Credit cards are accepted.

This is the "granddaddy" of the outstanding Italian restaurants in Krebs. Established in 1925 by Pietro Piegari (later anglicized to Pete Prichard), it is now run by grandson Joe Prichard. Family-style service includes spaghetti, meatballs, ravioli, salad, antipasto, and garlic bread with entrees. Their slogan, "If you haven't had "fries" at Pete's, you've never had fries," refers to Pete's famous lamb fries. You can wash these down with "Choc" beer, an old Choctaw Indian recipe for homebrewed beer.

Roseanna's Italian Food $, $$

205 East Washington (Highway 31 East). (918) 423-2055. Tuesday-Wednesday 11-8, Thursday-Saturday 11-9. Handicapped accessible. Credit cards are accepted.

Another longtime authentic Italian restaurant, Roseanna's has an extensive menu with 1/2 order dinners available. This is a great idea, since the portions are more than ample. Devotees declare the lasagne "awesome." Orders by the pint and quart are also available.

Krebs Ethnic Festival

Labor Day Weekend at the City Park. (800) 854-1417. Watch for festival signs. Free. Handicapped accessible.

This is one of Oklahoma's smaller, friendlier festivals; there's a real family atmosphere and an effort to provide food and fun that gives entertainment value without great expense to the festival-goer. Though Krebs is noted for its Italian roots, this festival salutes many nations. You'll find a variety of food items including Lovera's famous sausage sandwiches, Mexican treats, and German eats, among others. Entertainment is eclectic with blues bands and accordion players competing with Greek dancers for attention, and arts, crafts and games. There's no place to stay in Krebs, and this is the weekend of the Prison Rodeo in McAlester; make reservations well in advance if you plan to spend the night.

Stuart Hotel and Tea Room $

Located in Stuart, twenty miles west of McAlester on U.S. Highway 270., (918) 546-2591. The tea room is open Tuesday-Saturday 10-5, Sunday 11-3. B&B room are $40-65. The dining area is handicapped accessible, the guest rooms are not. Reservations are a must.

The three-story Stuart Hotel was built in 1899 with cypress siding and a tin roof. It served as a hotel until 1946, when it closed. In 1989, Jack and Shirley Emerson bought the old relic and, over the next two years, worked to restore it to more than its former glory. The original didn't have indoor plumbing! The eight second-story rooms are all named after Oklahomans, including Shirley's parents. Antiques and memorabilia decorate each room. The Emersons have equipped a sitting room with television and an extensive library of western videos. On the third floor is the Pretty Boy Floyd suite, named after the bank robber who once stayed in the old hotel. This is the honeymoon suite, complete with its own whirlpool bath, brass bed, and antique fainting couch. Most of the rooms are tiny and depend on a shared bathroom, just as original guests would have done, but Shirley has made good use of the small spaces with decorative touches that often qualify as still-life material.

Guests are served a full breakfast, which could include such specialties as Jack's jalapeno cheese grits, blueberry biscuits, sausage and eggs, juice, and fruit. The Emersons offer access to their 28-acre private fishing lake, but they encourage interested guests to bring their own tackle. There are several special weekends scheduled each year, with activities from murder mysteries and "mellerdramas" to a "street play" about Pretty Boy Floyd, complete with pre-1935 autos. Call for information.

The tea room is an excellent spot for lunch, whether you chose Shirley Emerson's own creation, "Shirl's Salad" (a combination of chicken breast, veggies, Parmesan cheese, and croutons with a French dressing), quiche, sandwich, or soup. Be sure to save room for dessert. On Sunday, Shirley serves a "cook's choice" meal which could be smoked turkey, ham, roast, brisket, or "whatever I feel like fixing." Seating is limited; therefore, for the Sunday lunch, parties of six or more should call for reservations.

Ouachita National Forest Area

*For information, contact the Choctaw Ranger District, HC 64, Box 3467, Heavener, OK 74937, (918) 653-2991. The primary roads into the northern (and more popular) portion of the Ouachita National Forest are S.H. 1 east from Talihina, U.S. Highway 270 south from Heavener, or U.S. Highway 259 north from Broken Bow. The southern portion of the Ouachita National Forest is located in far southeast Oklahoma. The **visitor information center** at the Oklahoma end of the Talimena Trail is open Friday-Monday 8:30-5 in the winter (mid-November-April 1). During the rest of the year, the center is open Friday-Monday 8:30 -5, plus as many additional days of the week as the budget will allow. To find out if the center will be open on a specific day, call (918) 653-2991.*

The best known attraction in the Ouachita Forest is the **Talimena Scenic Drive** which stretches 54 miles from Talihina, Oklahoma to Mena, Arkansas. Along the drive are a number of scenic vistas, historical sites, and camping or hiking opportunities. The **Robert S. Kerr Memorial Arboretum and Nature Center** is located at the midpoint of the drive. The exhibit shelter provides information on the interrelationship of living and nonliving things and man's role in the forest environment. Three short trails nearby offer insights into the struggle for survival in a living forest, the process of soil formation, and a chance to identify a wide variety of plants and trees growing in their natural setting.

Free maps are available at the Information Stations at either end of the Talimena Scenic Drive (on State Highway 1). The booklet," Talimena Scenic Drive Guide," by McWilliam, Lane and Johnston isn't expensive, but it will give you much more information on the history of the area and good descriptions of each overlook and point of interest along the drive.

Ouachita Forest Area

The **Cedar Lake Recreation Area** offers regular camping, swimming, hiking, fishing, and a boat ramp. One of the most unique parts of the area is the **Cedar Lake Equestrian Camp**, known as the best equestrian camping facility in the state. More than seventy miles of well-blazed trails, varying in length and difficulty, wind over mountains and down valleys. The camp is strictly BYOH (bring your own horse); there are no horses for rent in the park.

The equestrian camping area has nineteen campsites with both electric and water hookups and thirty campsites with centrally-located water. There are clean, heated restrooms with showers, and there are three horse-wash racks. There are five handicapped-accessible campsites and a large number of primitive sites. Rates run from $3 for day-use of picket poles to $12 a night for a double site with water and electricity. For reservations at the traditional campground areas in the Oklahoma portion of the National Forest (Winding Stair, Cedar Lake and Billy Creek), and the Cedar Lake Equestrian Camp, call (800) 280-2267.

There are a number of **hiking trails** throughout the forest, ranging from the 192-mile Ouachita National Recreation Trail (52 miles of which are in Oklahoma) to less-than-a-mile interpretive trails like the ones at the Kerr Nature Center. While there are no specifically-designated mountain bike trails, most of the hiking trails permit mountain biking (the exception being the long Ouachita National Recreation Trail). Since some of the other trails loop along the Ouachita Trail, determining a legal biking trail is a little tricky. Call for specific information about equestrian, mountain bike or ATV trails.

In the Vicinity

Broken Bow

Named for their Nebraska hometown, Broken Bow was established in 1911 by the Dierks brothers, pioneer lumbermen. Their business later merged with the Weyerhaeuser Company which was incorporated in Tacoma, Washington, in 1900. Broken Bow is best known for the beautiful scenery in the area, particularly Beavers Bend State Park and Broken Bow Lake.
Broken Bow is 228 miles southeast of Oklahoma City. Take I-40 east to the Indian Nation Turnpike, then drive south to Antlers. If you are coming from Tulsa, take U.S. Highway 75 to Henryetta, then take the Indian Nations Turnpike. At the Antlers exit, take S.H. 3 to Broken Bow. From Tulsa to Broken Bow is a distance of 188 miles. Broken Bow Chamber of Commerce (800) 52TREES.

Beavers Bend State Park

(405) 494-6300. The main entrance to the park is seven miles north of Broken Bow on U.S. Highway 259A. Three more entrances are located in the next four miles north on 259A.

Most Oklahoma parks try to offer something for everyone. Beavers Bend not only manages that, but whatever it is you like to do, you'll enjoy it more in the stunning scenery. Broken Bow Lake, adjacent to both Beavers Bend and Hochatown State Parks, is a rich blue color, inviting bass fishermen, scuba divers, swimmers, and boaters. Below the dam, the Mountain Fork River winds through Beavers Bend State Park. The river is regularly stocked with brown and rainbow trout, making it a mecca for fly fishermen. Boat, canoe, and jet-ski rentals are available. Other activities include horseback riding, eagle watches, fly fishing clinics, hiking, campfire talks, golf, camping; the list is just too long to cover completely.

The **Nature Center** has a schedule of daily activities available at no charge. These include hawk and owl feeding, nature walks and campfire programs. Nature Center hours vary, but in summer it is usually open from 10-4 Tuesday-Sunday. In the winter it is open Friday-Sunday.

A popular feature at the park is **Cedar Creek Golf Course** (405-494-6456). It may be an exaggeration to compare this course to Augusta, but the setting is certainly striking. Tall pines, oaks and hickories line the fairways with dogwood, redbud and wild plum adding colorful accents. "Eagle" here could refer to "bald," with birds and wildlife plentiful in the woods. Built in the seventies by course designer Floyd Farley, the front nine was complemented with an Art Proctor-designed back nine in 1993. Challenges are built into the course due to its rolling terrain. Four of the par five holes have elevated greens. Scattered quartz in the rough makes finding a ball a real treasure hunt. Several of the holes have lake views, with one hole having a peninsular green, the ultimate in water hazards.

Total yardage for the par 72 course is 6,724 yards, USGA rating 72.1, slope 132. PGA Pro Victor Pedrola is a gold mine of information and enthusiasm about his course. The pro shop can supply whatever you need, including snacks. During the week, tee-time reservations are unnecessary. The course is located thirteen miles north of Broken Bow at the Cedar Creek entrance. Open daily daylight to dark; green fees on weekdays are $9.50, weekends and holidays $12; carts are $10 for nine holes, $17 for eighteen.

Forest Heritage Center (405-494-6497) is open daily from 8 a.m. to 8 p.m. This combination museum, educational facility, and conference center was built by a group of concerned citizens in 1976. Its purpose is to inform and educate the public about forestry, to demonstrate proper natural resource management, and to explain how man has interacted with this environment in the past and what the future may hold. Exhibits include historical documents, antique tools, wood art, homestead memorabilia, and fourteen dioramas which illustrate the evolution of the forest. The facility is handicapped accessible.

John Taylor

View of Broken Bow Lake from Lakeview Lodge.

Reservations must be made well in advance for the forty-seven popular **Beavers Bend Cabins** ⑤ (405-494-6538). For the summer season, calling the first of the year is not unreasonable. Don't forget that winter is an interesting time to go. There are no crowds to contend with, and many of the cabins have fireplaces, making them particularly cozy. Rates are $38-94, depending on the cabin's size and the season it is rented.

The cabins (most with fireplaces) sleep from two to six people. Most popular choices are the cabins overlooking the Mountain Fork River. The facilities are showing their age, but the delightful setting makes any shortcomings minimal. Firewood is for sale at the Riverside Restaurant and Country Store in the park. They have a very limited supply of groceries and are closed in January and February. There are several stores just outside the park, including the Frontier General Store on U.S. Highway 259. About half of the cabins are wheelchair accessible. Others may have a small step or two, limiting accessibility.

The park's new **Beavers Bend Lakeview Lodge** (405-494-6179) is located ten miles north of Broken Bow. To find the lodge, turn east off U.S. Highway 259 at Stevens Gap Road. Rates are $110-175 ⑤. This beautiful lodge is for people who don't like to rough it! Each room offers a million-dollar view, from either a balcony or patio. The thirty-six rooms and four suites are attractive with dusty rose carpeting (blue in the suites) and pickled-pine furniture.

A commons area where a complimentary continental breakfast is served joins the two wings of the lodge and features a great room with a two-story beamed ceiling, game tables, comfortable seating, a television, and a huge rock fireplace. Like the rooms, it overlooks the lake and has a balcony and tables for al fresco breakfasts in nice weather. There are several rooms designed for maximum handicapped accessibility. This is a no-smoking/no pets facility. Reservations are a must during the busy seasons of spring, summer and fall.

Two festivals are held at Beavers Bend. The **Owa-Chito Festival** is a free, four-day celebration that is held around the third weekend in June. The festival celebrates the area's major industry with chainsaw events, lumberjack competitions, turkey calling, canoe racing, an art show, and children's activities. Entertainment includes a gospel concert on Thursday night, 50s music on Friday night, and a big-name country western entertainer on Saturday night. Food booths are available. Rooms in this area book up fast; call early for reservations. The art show is held at the Forest Heritage Center; the other festival activities are held in the Youth Camp area. Call (800) 52TREES or (405) 286-3305 for more information. Handicapped accessible.

Held the second weekend in November is **Beavers Bend Folk Festival and Craft Show**. This free festival is held when it is usually peak color time for the trees; the colorful site itself adds to the festival mood. Highlights include craft demonstrations, live folk music and dancing, a quilt show, and refreshments. About 7000 visitors attended the festival in 1995; if you want to spend the night, make reservations early. Call (405) 494-6497 for more information.

Gardner Mansion

Located six miles east of Broken Bow on U.S. Highway 70, (405) 584-6588. Summer hours, Monday-Saturday 8-6, Sunday 2-6; winter hours, Monday-Saturday 10-5, Sunday 2-5. Viewing the tree and museum, adults $2, children ages 6-11 $1; for the tree viewing only, $0.50. The house is not handicapped accessible. Privately owned, its hours may be erratic. Calling ahead is recommended.

The Gardner Mansion was built in 1884 for Jefferson Gardner, who was elected Chief of the Choctaws from 1894-1896. Owners of the home, Dr. and Mrs. Lewis Stiles, are in the process of rebuilding the antebellum-style house as it would have originally appeared. The property has been in the Stiles family since 1922, and the original structure has been modified since then. The house contains an eclectic assortment of fossils, Indian artifacts and antiques.

Also on the property is what is left of a historic landmark, a giant cypress tree estimated to be 2000 years old. Due to a lightning strike, all that is left is a stump, but a mighty impressive one it is. The ground level circumference is 45 feet. This tree was a well-known landmark on the Trail of Tears.

Riverside Restaurant $

Beavers Bend State Park, (405) 494-6551. Located just east of the Park Headquarters and the Forest Heritage Center. Monday-Thursday 11-8, Friday 8-8, Saturday 8-9, Sunday 8-2. A breakfast buffet is served on weekends. The restaurant is closed during the months of January and February. Handicapped accessible. No credit cards are accepted.

In good weather, the large deck overlooking the Mountain Fork River is a wonderful place to relax and enjoy a meal. If you are forced inside, David Richardson's collection of fishing lures adds interest to the room. The specialty here is hickory smoked ribs served in huge portions. Ask the Richardsons about their special smoker; they're justifiably proud of it. Other entrees include chicken fried steak, rainbow trout, and fried catfish. Top off your meal with made-from-scratch pie.

Tootie's Restaurant $ $

Highway 259 North /Stephens Gap Road, (405) 494-6791. Stephens Gap Road is the third road into Beavers Bend Park north of Broken Bow (or the second road, if you're coming from the north). Tuesday-Sunday 11-10, with a buffet on Sunday from 11-2. Closed Monday. Handicapped accessible.

Although not long on ambiance, Tootie's is a good place to eat. Owner Tootie Wilmouth is the epitome of a genial host. Portions are more than ample, with unusual side dishes, like beer hushpuppies and green tomato relish, adding interest to the entrees. Steaks are a specialty, but the fried catfish is a great buy and is hard to resist. The Friday night seafood buffet with its huge crab legs is a real crowd-pleaser.

Sojourner's Bed and Breakfast Inn

(405) 584-9324. Four miles south of Broken Bow, east of U.S. Highway 259. $55 per couple.

This is like visiting your aunt and uncle. The house is modern, clean, comfortable, and the price is right. Not for the seeker of the elegant, historic, or unusual, this is in keeping with the original concept of "bed and breakfast." The owners, David and Kristi Webb, usually rent out only one room; however, if couples are traveling together, they will rent two. Breakfast may consist of a casserole of eggs, cheese, and sausage served with homemade muffins, and juice.

Idabel

The area around Idabel had been occupied since the 1830s by the Choctaws, who had been forced to leave their ancestral lands in Mississippi. Under pressure from the U.S. Government, the Choctaws were persuaded in 1893 to give up sovereignty and accept individual allotments. In 1902, the city of Idabel was platted as a stop on the Arkansas and Choctaw Railroad. With statehood, Idabel was designated county seat of McCurtain County.

Idabel is 225 miles southeast of Oklahoma City and 185 miles from Tulsa. Idabel Chamber of Commerce (405) 286-3305.

Barnes-Stevenson Home

300 Southeast Adams, (405) 286-6314 or 286-3305. During the winter, the house is open by appointment only. From May 1-September 1, open Sundays from 2-4, other times by appointment. Free. Not handicapped accessible.

Judge and Mrs. Barnes arrived in what is now McCurtain county with little more than his law books. When Oklahoma became a state in 1907, Barnes was elected a county judge. With investments in banking and real estate, he had begun building the sixteen-room, three story mansion by 1911. The house was constructed with the conveniences of indoor plumbing, electricity, and central heat from a coal furnace. Woodwork of hand-finished oak and parquet floors of white ash added beauty to the structure. Many of the original leaded glass windows remain.

In 1987, the home was purchased by the McCurtain County Historical Society. It has been furnished with items appropriate to the early years of the home. The property is listed on the National Register of Historic Places.

Museum of the Red River

812 East Lincoln Road, (405) 286-3616. Located on the U.S. Highway 70 Bypass, just east of the Highway 259 south intersection. Tuesday-Saturday 10-5. Free. Handicapped accessible.

The museum started as the private collection of Quintus and Mary Herron. Mr. Herron's own Choctaw heritage influenced his interest in Native American culture. Items include Caddoan artifacts (found in the area) which date back to 700 A.D. Exhibits include pottery, basketry, and fabric crafts. A replica of a Choctaw house includes many items that were in daily use around the turn of the century. The museum is a member of the American Association of Museums. If you are touring with a large group, please call ahead for an appointment. The parking area will accommodate buses and RVs.

Blue Note Coffee Shop $

101 Southeast Avenue A, (405) 286-3221. In downtown Idabel. Monday-Friday 7:30 a.m.-2 p.m. Not handicapped accessible. Credit cards are not accepted.

Black and white tile floor, Louis Armstrong posters, and jazz music carry out the theme of the restaurant which specializes in fine coffees. They open early, serving cinnamon rolls, bagels, and biscuits or muffins with their gourmet brews. Lunch specials often include a pasta dish with Caesar salad and garlic bread. The atmosphere in this tiny eatery is intimate and friendly.

Ole Tid's Antiques and Storage

(405) 286-3733. Six miles north of Idabel on Highways 70 and 259. Monday-Saturday 10-5 (also open on Sundays during the summer).

Owner Jeff Tidwell buys, sells and trades such a variety of items; you just have to go see what's there. You'll find lots of glassware, furniture, vintage hats, toys, and antiques.

Dogwood Days

City-wide festival held the first Saturday in April. (405) 286-3305. Free.

Idabel has every intention of becoming known as the Dogwood Capital of Oklahoma. Each year, more Dogwood trees are planted, bringing the 1996 total to around 6000. Dogwoods are for sale during the festival, and maps are available for a driving tour around Idabel to see the trees in bloom. In addition to the dogwoods, the festival features crafts, entertainment, sidewalk sales, food booths, a 5K run, a soapbox derby, and a sanctioned barbecue cook-off. One of the special features of the festival is the chance to ride the excursion train from Hugo. Advance reservations are necessary. Call the Hugo Heritage Railroad for information (405) 326-6630. When you arrive in Idabel, shuttlebuses will be available to all the festival sites.

Octoberfest

Held the first Saturday in October at venues all over town. (405) 286-3305. Free.

This fall festival includes crafts, food booths, live entertainment, a chili cook-off, and special sales and promotions by area merchants. This festival also takes advantage of the Kiamichi Railroad out of Hugo. It should be a gorgeous trip–forty-three miles through southeast Oklahoma at a colorful time of year. For information about reservations, contact the Hugo Heritage Railroad (405) 326-6630. Shuttlebuses take train passengers to locations of various activities.

Octavia

Babcock's Store

Octavia and Babcock's Store is approximately fifteen miles south of Big Cedar and the Ouachita National Forest on U.S. Highway 259. Bill Babcock says normal hours are Monday-Saturday 9:30-5, Sunday 1-4, then adds, "But we're never normal!" If the gate is open, the store is open. The store is usually closed in January and February. Mostly handicapped accessible.

Babcock's Store was built in 1983, but the lumber is much older. It came from a Studebaker Wagon Assembly Plant built in 1882 in Wills Point, Texas. It doesn't seem possible to have amassed such a collection of stuff that decorates the lawn in front of the store. This is an unapologetic "tourist trap," and is loads of fun. You'll find all sorts of souvenirs, and you can enjoy a treat from the soda fountain while you're at it.

Eagle Creek Guest Cottages

Babcock's.

Located in Smithville, just a few miles from Octavia. (405) 244-7597. One mile west off U.S. Highway 259 in Octavia. Look for the firehouse (on the southwest corner) and turn west here. Drive about one mile; watch carefully for the sign pointing north to the cabins. Sunday-Thursday $65-95; Friday, Saturday and holidays $70-110. Reservations several months in advance are a must for these popular cabins (call between 8 a.m. and 8 p.m.). A deposit is required. Because nearby eateries and groceries are open seasonally, inquire about the supplies you may need to bring with you.

These new cottages are perfect for luxurious, private getaways. Enjoy fishing or hiking in this area, or just relax with a book by the picture window in your beautifully-appointed log cabin. Each cabin comes fully-equipped with fireplace, whirlpool bath, TV/VCR, kitchen, charcoal grill, and king-sized bed. Each cabin is a little different, and some have better views than others; ask for details.

Big Eagle Creek runs below the cabin area. This scenic stream is popular with smallmouth bass fishermen and with whitewater canoeists. A small lake on the property is stocked with catfish, bluegill and Florida bass. The fall foliage is outstanding; in the spring, dogwoods and redbuds are equally appealing. The cabins are located within close distance of both Beavers Bend State Park and the Ouachita National Forest.

Poteau

"Poteau," which is French for "post," was named for the nearby Poteau River. It had its first post office in 1888 and was incorporated in 1898. It is the site of "the world's highest hill," Cavanal Hill, which tops out at 1,999 feet. Poteau was listed in a 1992 Prentice-Hall book,

"The Top 100 Small Cities in America," by Norman Crampton.
Poteau is 189 miles east of Oklahoma City. Take I-40 east to the west Sallisaw exit, then turn south on Highway 59. To travel the 135 miles from Tulsa, take the Muskogee Turnpike south to I-40, then continue east to the Highway 59 exit. Poteau Chamber of Commerce (918) 647-9178.

Kerr Conference Center and Museum

1507 South McKenna, (918) 647-8221. Coming south from Poteau on Highways 271 and 59, turn right where Highway 59 heads straight south to Heavener. Almost immediately, you will cross the Burlington Northern Railroad tracks. The street parallel to the tracks is McKenna (there may not be a street sign). Turn right on McKenna and go south for four or five miles. You will see signs for the Kerr Conference Center. If you are coming from another direction, call for directions. The house is always open; however, it's best to call ahead. Museum hours: Monday-Friday 10-5, Saturday and Sunday 1-5. Free.

The Kerr Mansion was completed in 1960 at a cost of $650,000. U.S. Senator Robert S. Kerr lived in the ten-bedroom house for only two years before his death. The architecture combines native stone and wood, much of which came from other Kerr properties. Next door is a museum which contains displays relating to the Spiro culture, runestones, possible Viking exploration of the area, and items from pioneer days.

In the Vicinity

Heavener

Named around 1895, the town honored Joe Heavener, who owned the townsite. Said by some to be a Native American, by others a white man, Heavener had come from Virginia and settled among the Choctaws. The site was a stop on the Pittsburg and Gulf Railroad (later named the Kansas City Southern).
Heavener is located approximately ten miles south of Poteau, Heavener Chamber of Commerce (918) 653-4303.

Heavener Runestone State Park

Located just outside of Heavener, (918) 653-2241. Turn east at the intersection of Avenue C and Highway 59. Cross the railroad tracks and turn north on Main Street. Turn east again on Avenue A, then north on 7th Street until you come to the marked entrance to the road up Poteau Mountain. Daily 8 a.m. until dark. Free. Good walking shoes with nonskid soles are helpful. The path down to the runestone is steep and sometimes wet. Though there is some explanatory material at the interpretive center, the path to the runestone itself is not handicapped accessible.

The path meanders down into a secluded ravine; at the bottom is a rough wood and rock shelter which protects the twelve foot tall runestone. This giant slab of rock was probably once capstone atop Poteau Mountain. According to oral tradition, the stone was found by Choctaw Indians in the early 1800s. Later settlers assumed the carved characters in the rock were Indian glyphs and called the stone "Indian Rock." In the 1920s, the runes were identified as relating to Scandinavian runes. The first translation was a date. Later research indicates the letters are a boundary designation, "GLOME DAL," translating into "Valley of (or belonging to) Glome."

Though the truth may never be known, impressive evidence is being collected that the runes are authentic. At the least, the stone is an interesting oddity; at the most, it is an important piece of North American history.

Peter Conser House

Located four miles south of Heavener on Highway 59, (918) 653-2493. Wednesday-Saturday 10-5, Sunday 1-5. Closed Mondays and Tuesdays. Free. Not handicapped accessible.

The attractive two-story farmhouse is a testament to the industry and abilities of Peter Conser (originally Coinson). The son of a white trader and a Choctaw woman, Conser was born in southeast Oklahoma and came to the Heavener area after the Civil War. With little more than a sack of seed corn, he began farming and, with careful planning and hard work, became prosperous. He was well-respected and became a captain of the Choctaw Lighthorsemen. These men were the mounted police force for the Five Civilized Tribes. Conser also served as a representative, later a senator, to the Choctaw Council. In addition to his farm, he ran a blacksmith shop, grist mill, saw mill, and a general store with the post office. His home, built in 1894, remained in the family until its donation in 1967 to the Oklahoma Historical Society. It is furnished with period items.

Keota

About twenty miles northwest of Poteau on Highways 271 and 59.

Overstreet-Kerr Historical Farm

(918) 966-3396 or (918) 966-3282. Ten miles south of Sallisaw (I-40) on Highway 59 (from Poteau, travel north for a few miles on Highway 59), then 1/4 mile west on Overstreet-Kerr Road. Tuesday-Saturday 10-4, or by appointment. Adults $3, children ages 6-18 $2. The price may increase during special events or exhibits.

The two-story Overstreet-Kerr house, with its captain's walk on top, is a restored 1895 Choctaw pioneer home that is listed on the National Register of Historic Places. Maintained by the Kerr Center for Sustainable Agriculture, the facility is dedicated to educating the public on the lives of farmers and ranchers in Choctaw Territory during the late 1800s and early 1900s. Inside are only a few pieces of furniture which are original to the house; however, most pieces are true to the period. Almost all the woodwork is original, as are the gas lights. Attractive upstairs bedrooms are included on the tour. In keeping with the purpose of the farm, efforts here are ongoing to perpetuate historical breeds of livestock, including pineywoods cattle, the Choctaw horse, the Choctaw hog, Dominique poultry, and Gulf Coast Native sheep. A tour takes about an hour for the house and the grounds. Groups need to call for reservations. Ground floor rooms are handicapped accessible.

Held the second Saturday in October, the **Historical Fall Farm-Fest** is a wonderful time to visit this historical farm. The highlight of the day is the sorghum milling and cooking. The house and livestock areas are open for self-guided tours, and throughout the day there are demonstrations of 1800s-style crafts such as basket weaving, broom making and quilting. Live entertainment, food, and gift items add to the festivities. Admission is $5 for adults, $3 for children.

Lake Wister and Wister State Park

The park office is just west of U.S. Highway 270, two miles south of Wister. Poteau is eight miles northeast. (918) 655-7756. 🏕

Not as well known as some of Oklahoma's parks, Wister becomes a favorite with those who discover its charm. It offers many of the features of larger parks–without the crowds. The lake is noted for bluegill, channel cats, sand bass, crappie, and walleye. Boating, water skiing and swimming are also popular. Small boats, canoes, and bicycles may be rented, and a swimming pool is open during summer months. In addition to its attractive setting and abundant wildlife, Wister State Park is a good base for exploration of the area. Heavener and the Runestone are just fifteen minutes away, and not too much further is the Ouachita National Forest and the Spiro Mounds Archaeological Site. There are fifteen cabins which rent from $48-78 per night. The cabins have no televisions or telephones. All utensils are furnished. One of the two-bedroom cabins is equipped for complete handicapped-accessibility. Five camping areas are located in the park, with 172 sites ranging from primitive to modern (rates $6-17). For reservations, call (800) 654-8240 or the park number. A group camp with a community building and equipped kitchen is available, with reservations being accepted up to one year in advance.

Spiro

Incorporated in 1899 with the arrival of the Kansas City Southern Railroad, Spiro experienced an immediate growth spurt with the influx of a number of settlers from Scullyville who moved to Spiro because of the railway. Spiro is best known for its proximity to the Spiro Mounds. *Spiro is eight miles north of Poteau on Highway 271, then Highway 9.*

Spiro Mounds Archaeological Park

(918) 962-2062. The mounds are located two and one-half miles east of Spiro on State Highway 9, then three and one-half miles north on the W.D. Mayo Lock & Dam Road. Watch for signs. Wednesday-Saturday 9-5, Sunday 12-5. Free. Handicapped accessible.

The Spiro site is more significant for what isn't here than what is. Whether or not you enjoy it depends on your ability to use your imagination. Imagine a sophisticated society which existed for 600 to 800 years (from about 600 to 1450 A.D.), a trade confederation which encompassed thousands of square miles, and fabulous artifacts which included delicately-incised pottery, jewelry, and sculpture. While Spiro represented all these things, almost nothing is left here at the site; the vast majority of archeological artifacts were taken from the site in the 1930s by private owners of the land. What you will see is an eighteen-minute slide show which gives the history of the area and the archaeological activity through the years, a 140-acre grassy expanse punctuated by twelve mounds, and a small interpretive center with a few display cases, mostly housing replicas. It will help if properties manager Dennis Peterson is there. His enthusiasm can bring history to life, making up somewhat for the lack of artifacts.

Spiro was one of the most important centers of the Mississippian culture, and it is the site with the most artifacts that show the Spiro people as being leaders. Items taken from the Spiro Mounds can be found in museums from London to the Louvre. No Oklahoma education is complete without a knowledge and an appreciation of this tremendous society. Wear comfortable shoes for walking around the grounds.

Aunt Jan's Cozy Cabin Bed and Breakfast

(800) 470-3481. Call for directions. $95-115 a couple with reductions for additional nights stayed. Extra people are $10 per night. Member of the Oklahoma Bed and Breakfast Association. Reservations and a guarantee are required. Credit cards are accepted. Handicapped accessible.

This spacious, one-room cabin is panelled in knotty pine and decorated with quilts and other homey touches. The cottage can accommodate as many as five people, and has a queen-sized bed and a sitting area with television. Other amenities include an outdoor hot tub, a fully-equipped kitchen, and snacks. Jan even stocks the refrigerator with snacks and pop, and she provides a hearty breakfast for guests in the morning. Ask about the romantic package that includes fresh flowers, candy, fruit, and sparkling juice for special occasions.

Wilburton

The history of Wilburton dates back to the arrival of the Choctaw Coal and Railway line, but activity in the area goes back several thousand years to wandering hunters who camped along the Fourche Maline Creek. Later, cultures related to the Spiro civilization lived here. French traders and trappers traveled through the area, naming things along the way. After the Civil War, the area became known as an outlaw hangout. Some of the stories associated with the area make modern history seem tame.

Wilburton is 153 miles southeast of Oklahoma City and 123 miles south and east of Tulsa. Go to McAlester, then take Highway 270 east to Wilburton. Wilburton Chamber of Commerce (918) 465-2759.

Robbers Cave State Park

(918) 465-2565. The park is located five miles north of Wilburton on S.H. 2. To reserve a cabin, call the park office or (800) 654-8240. Cabins rent for $48-88. For traditional campsite reservations, call (918) 465-2562. Campsites rates are $6-17. For equestrian or group camping information, call (918) 463-2565. In the park, there's a small grocery store which is open year-round. ⑤

The main attraction in the park is the "robber's cave," the purported hideout of such villains as Belle Starr and the James boys. The trail up to the cave is not for weaklings or small children. It is 3/4 mile long and is described as having a moderate to steep grade; you'll need good hiking shoes. The cave itself is a bit anticlimactic, but the view from the top is superb. On the way down you pass the stone corral, a natural enclosure where the outlaws hid their horses. There are good hiking, mountain biking, and equestrian trails in the park. Three lakes located inside park boundaries provide visitors with excellent bass, catfish, and crappie fishing. From December 1 through March 15, try the trout fishing on the Fourche Maline below Carlton Lake. Located in a restored CCC bath house, the **Nature Center** is open year round, but the hours vary. The naturalist on duty leads a full schedule of activities. Call (918) 465-5154 for more information. Other activities that make this park particularly appealing to families is miniature golfing (when weather permits), swimming in either the lake or the pool, paddleboating, and canoeing.

Held in the park and in nearby Wilburton on a mid-October weekend, **Robbers Cave Fall Festival** offers as its biggest draw a rod and custom show. Other activities include an arts and crafts show, food booths, an old West show, gospel singing, and carnival rides. Get an early start to this popular festival; over 50,000 people attend this fun festival, and parking can be dificult to find.

There are twenty-six cabins and 117 campsites at the park. Another option for overnight guests is the new twenty-room **Belle Starr View lodge** ($78 per night). The lodge is an attractive one-story wooden building. Nineteen of the rooms have two double beds, one room has a king-sized bed, and all have televisions and coffeemakers but no telephones. Each room comes with another wonderful benefit: a great view of trees, the valley, and Coon Creek Lake. Two of the rooms are handicapped accessible. Non-smoking rooms are an option. For more information call (918) 465-2565. For reservations, call (800) 654-8240 or (918) 465-2562.

Dining/Accommodations

Windsong Inn and Windsong Inn Bed and Breakfast $$

100 West Cedar (918) 465-5174. Turn south from Highway 270 on Central Street. It is about three blocks to Cedar. Look for the inn on the southeast corner of Cedar and Central. Dining is available from Friday-Saturday 5:30-9:30, Sunday 11:30-2. Rooms cost $59-79 per couple, $10 for each additional person. Older children are welcome. Reservations encouraged. No credit cards. The dining area is handicapped accessible with assistance; the Inn is not handicapped accessible.

This imposing three-story Victorian Prairie House sits atop South Hill like a queen on her throne. Construction began on the home in 1907, with completion in 1911. All of the construction material, and even the workmen, were brought by train from Kansas City. The woodwork, fireplaces and stained glass are all original. The dark woods and rich colors are typical of the period. One can almost imagine the original owner, Mr. Lusk, leaning back in one of the heavy armchairs, smoking a cigar. Unfortunately, he probably never enjoyed the house much. Rumor has it that he embezzled funds from one of the local banks, and he had to hotfoot it to parts unknown!

The dining room overlooks a magnificent view of the Winding Stair Mountains. The menu is delicious but limited, with a choice of an Italian dinner or one of four flame-grilled items. Entrees other than the Italian dinner are served with spaghetti, Italian sausage, salad, and hot bread. If you have any appetite remaining, try one of Gayle Carnahan's wonderful desserts.

Upstairs are three comfortable bedrooms with private baths. A full breakfast is served at the guest's convenience. Afternoon snacks are provided.

In the Vicinity

Clayton

The town of Clayton is nestled between the Jack Fork Mountains and the Kiamichi Mountains. From Wilburton, travel south along the winding highway (Highway 2) for about thirty miles.

Sardis Lake

(918) 569-4131. Three miles north of Clayton on Highway 2.

This attractive blue-water lake with 117 miles of shoreline offers delights in all seasons. The dogwood and redbud add spring color, and summer brings its own palette with Indian paintbrush and gayfeather. The lake has a good reputation with bass and crappie fishermen, and 8000 surrounding acres are open for in-season wild turkey and wildfowl hunting. Camping, swimming, picnicking, and boating are popular at the lake. There are three boat-launching ramps, three fishing piers, three designated campsites, two group shelters, and one picnic area available. The six parks around the lake have ample restroom facilities (one with showers). This is one of Oklahoma's newer lakes, and it lacks concessions. Bring your own equipment, food, etc. Supplies can be purchased in Clayton, but not at the lake.

Clayton Country Inn and Dining Room $,$$

(918) 569-4165. One and one-half miles south of Clayton on Highway 271. Dinner served Monday-Saturday 5:30-9:30. Rooms cost $42-45 per night.

This small but charming dining room seats forty people; reservations are advisable on the weekends. Entrees of steaks, chicken and fish are served with salad, bread and potato. Desserts are special, particularly one chocolate concoction which is rich enough to live on for a week.

In the inn, there are nine rooms in the main building and two guest rooms with kitchenettes in a duplex cottage. With warm quilts and attractive furnishings, each cozy room has its own personality. The great room of the inn is grand, with a log-beamed ceiling and a natural rock fireplace. Here guests can read, dream, or watch television in easy chairs or on large sofas. Breakfast is continental style.

Tuskahoma

"Tushka Homma" means "Red Warriors" in the Choctaw language. Although not the first eastern tribe to move into the area, the Choctaws were the first to be assigned a territory in the Indian lands. They are also responsible for the first constitution to be written in what is now Oklahoma. Their first national capitol was close to Tuskahoma. When that building burned in 1849, the national meetings were held in other locations, until the capitol was established near Durant in about 1861. In 1883, a vote of the Choctaw Nation established the permanent capitol at a place they called Tushka Homma. By 1884, an impressive building was completed. A post office was established at Tushka Homma in early 1884. In 1891, the town's name was changed to its present spelling.

Tuskahoma is about six miles northeast of Clayton on Highway 271 and about thirty miles south of Wilburton on Highway 2.

Choctaw Nation Capitol

(918) 569-4465. From Highway 2, turn east on Highway 271. You will come to a crossroads with a sign pointing south to the town of Tuskahoma and north to the National Capitol. Go north two miles. Monday-Friday 8-4, closed holidays. Free. The main floor of the building is handicapped accessible.

The three-story French-style building with its mansard roof sits impressively on the plain. Built of brick with native sandstone trim, it features round, handcarved attic windows, and door frames which were hauled by oxen from Ft. Smith, Arkansas, and Paris, Texas. After statehood, the capitol fell into disuse and was sold. When tribal elders discovered that the buyer planned to raze the building, they bought it back. Visitors can see a courtroom which is still used, along with the rooms which once housed the Choctaw Senate and House of Representatives. A museum contains items which were brought over the Trail of Tears. Other exhibits feature vintage clothing, historical documents, and examples of craft work. There is a nicely-stocked gift shop.

Choctaw Labor Day Festival

Four-day fest on the grounds of the National Capitol. For more information call the Choctaw Tribal Complex in Durant at (405) 924-8280. Free.

This late summer festival has been a tradition since 1884. Games, dancing, entertainment, gospel singing, and food are important parts of this gathering. Monday is Traditional Dress Day with a powwow and a social dance exhibition. An arts and crafts show and a carnival continue all weekend. Participants generally camp overnight; there is a large campground with bathhouses, a cafeteria and a playground. Reservations for camping are taken after January 1, and they are usually filled by the end of that month.

Southcentral Oklahoma

Ada

Jeff Reed was one of the first non-Indian settlers in this area. In 1890, he and his family built a two-room log cabin on the location which is now 522 West 4th Street. Two years later, they built a small store next door. This became the trading center for the area, and Mr. Reed soon realized that a post office was needed. He submitted three names to the Post Office Department. The final submission, the name of his oldest daughter Ada, was accepted in 1893. The Frisco Railroad came through the town in 1890, assuring its continued growth. Ada's most famous citizen was Robert S. Kerr, Oklahoma's first native-born governor (1943-1947) and U.S. Senator from 1949 until his death in 1963. The log cabin where he is born stands at the bottom of the hill where he is buried on the south side of Ada.

Ada is 85 miles from Oklahoma City. Go east on I-40 to the Shawnee/Highway 177 exit. After crossing the Canadian River just south of Asher, take Highway 3W to Ada. From Tulsa, go southwest on I-44 to the Highway 377/99 exit at Stroud. Go south on 99 to Ada to complete the 122 mile trip. Ada Chamber of Commerce (405) 332-2506.

McSwain Musical Theater

130 West Main, (405) 332-8108 or (405) 332-1024 (ticket outlet). From Highway 3W, travel ten blocks east on Main. The theater is at the corner of Main Street & Broadway. Performances are held the first and third Saturdays of the month at 7:30 p.m. Adults $6, children $3. To obtain tickets, call at least one week in advance. If requested, a list of performers can be sent to you. Handicapped accessible.

Originally built in 1920 for vaudeville shows, McSwain Musical Theater was restored in 1992 by the Alford family as a country and gospel music theater. In addition to country and gospel groups which are the mainstay of the theater, groups also perform music from the Big Band era each quarter. Every October, an **awards ceremony** is held to honor the best performers who have entertained at the theater, and the Mae Boren Axton Award is presented to a celebrity. Past recipients include country music superstars Garth Brooks and Reba McEntire. The awards show usually sells out; call at least two to three months in advance to reserve tickets.

Dining

Folger's Drive-In $

406 E. Main, (405) 332-9808. From east Highway 3W (Main Street) travel straight ahead. The drive-in is on the north side, before the Mississippi Street intersection. Monday-Friday 10-7.

The Folger family has served up hamburgers for four generations. Drive in or enjoy the retro-50s diner atmosphere. For a change, try a chiliburger or barbecue burger with their own secret tangy sauce. Other menu items include chili and beans, hot dogs, and hamburger steak.

Events

AdaFest

Held at the end of May. For more information call (405) 436-3032.

Ada's biggest community event includes more than a hundred arts and crafts booths, live entertainment and food. Exercise enthusiasts may join the one-mile fun walk or the 5K run. A special attraction, KidsFest, provides a place where children can play games, take amusement park rides, and learn how to fish or milk a cow.

Ardmore

Once a railroad station on the Santa Fe line, Ardmore was named by a railroad official for his hometown of Ardmore, Pennsylvania. The town suffered through two disasters in the early days. In 1895, a large fire destroyed eighty-two homes and businesses. Twenty years later, a railroad car blew up, killing forty-four people and injuring 200. In the early 1900s, oil became the economic base for Ardmore, and it remains so today. Located halfway between Oklahoma City and Dallas, Ardmore offers a wide variety of activities for a weekend getaway, especially antique shopping and outdoor recreation.

Located 97 miles south of Oklahoma City on I-35. Ardmore is approximately 183 south and west of Tulsa. Ardmore Chamber of Commerce (405) 223-7765.

Charles B. Goddard Center for Visual and Performing Arts

D Street and 1st Street SW, (405) 226-0909. From I-35, take exit 31 to Highway 199 (Main Street), and travel east. Turn south onto D Street in downtown Ardmore, and travel one block to 1st Avenue N.W. The Goddard Center is on the northwest corner. Art Museum: Monday-Friday 9-4, Saturday-Sunday 1-4. The Art Museum is free; ticket prices for theater performances vary. Call ahead for information and tickets. Handicapped accessible. Parking is available on the south side of 1st Avenue.

The Goddard Center was dedicated to the memory of Charles B. Goddard, founder of Humble Oil Company, by his wife Ethel. The oil company later achieved worldwide acclaim under its new name, Exxon. At the center, four galleries feature the works of Western and contemporary artists. View the gallery's permanent collection or special exhibits of locally-owned art and traveling exhibits.

In addition to art work, performances by the Ardmore Little Theater, Community Chorale, and The Dance Center are held at the center. In September, the museum hosts the annual Ardmore Art Guild Show, a popular show featuring local artists. The in-house theater group performs three plays and one musical each year in the 300-seat theater.

Greater Southwest Historical Museum

35 Sunset Drive, (405) 226-3857. From I-35, take Highway 70 east. Turn north onto Sunset Drive (located just past the football stadium). The museum is on the west side of the street. Tuesday-Saturday 10-5, Sunday and holidays 1-5. Free; donations gratefully accepted. Call at least two days in advance to reserve a guided tour for large groups. Disabled accessible.

Housed in a 40,000-square foot building constructed under the old WPA public works program, this museum showcases more than 100,000 items from Indian Territory days of the 1890s to the 1930s. Start at the Sam Noble Hall to take a glimpse at artifacts that reveal pioneer lifestyles. Among the exhibits are an original log cabin, a general store, a drugstore, medical and dental offices, and a schoolhouse. Even adults will delight in the room filled with doll houses and children's toys.

In another wing of the building is the **Military Memorial Museum**, which pays homage to local veterans of several eras, from the Spanish-American War to the Persian Gulf War. Residents from the community donated many of the items on exhibit. The museum includes an impressive collection of uniforms, flags, archival materials, and field equipment.

Dining

Cafe Alley $

107 E. Main, (405) 223-6413. One block north of Main Street, with parking behind Walls Department Store. Monday-Friday 11-2.

Take a break from antique shopping on Main Street at this trendy lunch eatery, located in an elegant yet casual warehouse setting. For the past eight years, the house specialty at Cafe Alley has been buttermilk pie. Also try the Cobb salad (small portion is generous) or one of the pasta dishes.

Fireside Dining $$, $$$

From Lake Murray Resort Park, travel west one mile on scenic Highway 77 to Lake Murray Village. The restaurant is on the south side of the road. (405) 226-4070. Tuesday-Saturday 5-10. Reservations for large groups (up to fifty or so) should be made one week in advance. The restaurant does not overlook the lake, but a seat in the enclosed porch area affords a spectacular view of trees and seasonal flowers. 🍴

Over its twenty-year history, the award-winning Fireside has become beloved by local residents and vacationers alike. The interior (with its exposed cedar logs) has a mountain-like decor; even better, the food is delicious. Prime rib and steaks are always excellent. Feeling adventurous? Try the hickory-grilled salmon with teriyaki sauce. If requested, entrees are served with a rich, creamy potato casserole. All meals come with the "Fireside Salad Bowl," a heaping house salad, topped with fresh-baked garlic croutons.

Shopping

Just a few years ago, Ardmore's Main Street was quiet on Saturdays, with few shoppers. Then merchants tried a strategy to draw more people; they decided to cluster shops offering similar services and goods together on the same block. This move succeeded in reinvigorating Main Street. In fact, weekend business has blossomed so much that Ardmore's Main Street now qualifies as a must-stop on several bus tours. Most stores carry exquisite and exotic items, including many pieces imported from Europe. Other downtown streets that offer antique shopping are Broadway and Washington.

Antique and gift shops to enjoy in the area include the following. Hours vary by store. **Antiques Etc.**, 10 East Main Street, (405) 226-3490. **Peddler's Square Mall**, 117 West Main Street, (405) 223-6255. **Main Antique Mall**, Historic Masonic Lodge Building, on Main Street, (405) 226-4395. **Village Surplus**, 815 West Broadway, (405) 223-7223. **The Gallery**, 21 N. Washington, (405) 223-4033. **Watermark Antiques & Interiors** (18th & 19th Century English & French Country Antiques), 19 N. Washington, (405) 223-7900. **The Antique Sampler**, 15 Sam Noble Parkway, (405) 226-7643. **The House of Stuff**, 1105 E Street N.W., (405) 223-8999.

Accommodations

Blackberry Farm Bed & Breakfast

2715 Hedges Road, (405) 223-8958. From I-35, travel west at Exit 29. Turn right at the stop. The house is on the left. $75 per night. It is best to call two weeks in advance for reservations. No children or pets. A member of the Oklahoma Bed and Breakfast Association. Not handicapped accessible.

Built in 1996 on twenty-nine acres, Blackberry Farm sports a French Country design. This Inn is near Lake Murray and within minutes of the antique shops on Ardmore's Main Street. Two guest rooms are located on the second floor, each decorated smartly in Ralph Lauren decor with queen-size wrought iron beds. Besides bathrooms, televisions and telephones in each room, the second floor has a large living area equipped with a TV/VCR and a game table. An exercise room will satisfy the health enthusiast. Throughout the house, a tasteful selection of antiques complement the new furnishings throughout the house. Innkeepers Sara and Kenneth Wiley have scrumptious breakfasts cooked up for their guests, which include Belgian waffles and quiche. Linger with a cup of coffee on the covered backporch and enjoy the view.

Events

Ardmoredillo Chili Cookoff

Held in mid-April in downtown Ardmore. For more information, call the Ardmore Main Street office at (405) 226-6246. For $1 you can sample from as many chili, beans and salsa entries as you like.

Along three-fourths of a block downtown, chili cooks are ranged elbow to elbow. They dance and sing for you (while preparing their specialties, of course). Some twenty-five cooks and their teams vie for the title of Top Showman, or crowd pleaser. Other awards are given for the best chili, salsa and red beans recipes. The overall best group receives the coveted stuffed armadillo, which is passed on the next year. Wild West Shows and a parade also enliven the downtown celebration.

Art in the Park & A Taste of Ardmore

Held the last weekend of September in Central Park, downtown Ardmore. Contact the Ardmore

Main Street Project office for more information (405) 226-6246. Admission is free.

At this two-day festival, up to forty people display their fine art, crafts and pottery. Food booths and entertainment by local musicians and dancers are provided. At the children's area, young ones can get their faces painted and enjoy their own hands-on art projects. The event opens with A Taste of Ardmore: local restaurants cook up their specialties, including barbecue, trout and homemade pies.

In the Vicinity

Lake Murray Resort Park

Southeast of Ardmore, (405) 223-6600 or (800) 654-8240 for lodge and cabin reservations. From I-35, take Highway 70 east, then Highway 77S south to the lake. The park office is located at the intersection of Highways 70 and 77S. 🏖

A day at beautiful and popular Lake Murray Resort Park can be relaxing or adventuresome. Of course, the water is the main attraction. Enjoy it aboard a paddle boat, pleasure cruiser, or sailboat–or try water-skiing or windsurfing. If you just want to settle down with a good book or gaze upon a sunrise or sunset, visit the lodge's back lawn, which overlooks the water. You will always enjoy the scenery and, in summer, you will also appreciate the shade.

When you're ready to quicken your pace, take a guided two-mile **horseback ride** (call Lake Murray Riding Stables at 405-223-8172 for hours and costs) or enjoy a stroll on any of three easy-hiking **nature trails**, none of which is more than three miles long.

Don't miss **Tucker Tower** (405-223-2109), a landmark stone building with a grand view of the lake. It houses exhibits about the area's wildlife and ecology, as well as Lake Murray's meteorite, the largest of its kind known to exist. In the 1930s, the Civilian Conservation Corps (CCC), a public works program that put young men to work during the Great Depression, began construction on Tucker Tower which was to be Governor Murray's retreat home. It remained unfinished until the Park Service completed the project. In 1954, the Tower opened as a museum. Bring your camera when you visit; various flowers line the walks leading to the building, and the balcony offers a beautiful vista of the entire lake. Open Wednesday-Sunday 9-5. Closed Monday and Tuesday. Open holidays. Admission is $.50. Tucker Tower is not handicapped accessible.

The lake's swimming areas include a large beach near the boat marina and a smaller beach that happens to be near the lodge. Also near the lodge is a **swimming pool** and a **playground**.

For a little exercise on the water, try the **paddle boats**. They rent out each day at $3 per hour, 10 a.m. to dusk (weather permitting). **Miniature Golf** (405-223-6000, extension 163) is fun and can be played each day 10 a.m. to dusk (weather permitting). Cost is $3 per person for eighteen holes.

Reservations may be made for pavilions near the lodge that front the lake. They are ideal for hosting large gatherings.

The eighteen-hole **Lake Murray Golf Course** (405-223-6613) offers a scenic view of the lake. The course's signature hole is number 16, which is challenging because of the presence of a waterfall. The 6200 yard course has a par 70, a slope of 127, and a USGA rating of 71.6. For weekend play, make reservations on Wednesday. Snack bar is available.

Weekday fees for eighteen-hole play are $10.50. Weekend and holiday $12.50. Cart rental for eighteen holes is $16, for 9 holes $9. All-day play (Monday-Friday) $35 per person, which includes green and cart fees. Senior discounts are available.

The park also offers **seasonal events**, including a Thanksgiving Feast, Traditional Country Christmas, and an Easter holiday celebration. Call the park for more information.

Whether you're camping or staying in the lodge or a cabin, plan to have breakfast at the **Apple Bin ($, $$)**. Try the cinnamon French toast with sausage or sample from a wide selection at the breakfast bar. The restaurant has also won praise for its catfish dinners. The restaurant is open daily 7 a.m.-8 p.m.

For its **accommodations**, the park offers everything from tent camping to resort lodge rooms and large family cabins. Campsites are available on a first-come, first-served basis. The lodge has two-room suites and guest rooms with twin, queen or king-size beds. (Winter rates are $40-75;

summer $58-75; suites are $150 year round.) Cottages sleep two to four people, and they include a small kitchenette with a microwave and small refrigerator. (Winter rates are $43-68; summer $53-78.) Cabins sleep four to six people and have small kitchens. A larger-sized family cabin ($128-225) sleeps up to 14 people and includes such amenities as a full-sized kitchen. Also available are a Cottage Suite ($98 year round) and Villas (winter $63-130; summer $78-130). Cabins and cottages lack cooking utensils; bring your own. Bedding and towels are provided.

It's wise to call ahead at least one year for summer reservations; for winter reservations, call one to two weeks ahead.

Houseboat cruises are offered year round on a 42-foot twin engine boat through **Charter Houseboat and Sailboat Services** (405-223-0088). The boat comfortably holds twenty people for a party ($13 per person, $130 minimum; catering is extra), or can be used as a "bed and berth"– a floating lake cabin. The houseboat sleeps six people and rents for $125 per night Friday through Sunday, $100 per day on weekdays. It has a full-size bath and kitchen with a stove and microwave. A continental breakfast is provided free.

Durant

Durant was born in a boxcar; when the "Katy" railroad reached the site, a boxcar was placed beside the tracks to serve as a depot. Named for Dixon Durant, who came to Oklahoma with his Choctaw-French family on the Trail of Tears, Durant is now known for being the "Home of the World's Largest Peanut." However, an equally descriptive and more attractive name is "City of Magnolias" for the many flowering trees in the city.

Durant is 148 miles southeast of Oklahoma City and 172 miles southwest of Tulsa. From Oklahoma City, go south on I-35 to the Highway 70/Madill exit, then go east. From Tulsa, take Highway 75 south and southwest. Durant Chamber of Commerce (405) 924-0848.

Shopping

Fairchilds Art Gallery

401 Denison Street, (405) 924-2399. On Highway 75 travel east into Durant. Highway 75 becomes Main Street. Turn north on Denison and travel twelve blocks. The art gallery is on the south side of the street at the corner of Grant and Denison. For a tour, call a day in advance; or for a group tour, call two to three days in advance. Handicapped accessible.

Career school teacher Mrs. Berenice Fairchilds opened the gallery eighteen years ago, and she operates it to this day. Her objective is to impress upon people of all generations the importance of understanding other cultures, particularly those of Native Americans. This gallery features a collection of authentic Navajo oil paintings, Kachina dolls, Navajo rugs, jewelry, sand paintings, beadwork, and crafts.

Events

Oklahoma Shakespearean Festival

Hosted by Southeastern Oklahoma State University and held from the end of June through July. For more information call (405) 924-0121, ext. 2944. Ticket prices for the performances are $4 for workshop performances and $20 for dinner theater performances, which includes the cost of the meal. Dinner theater tickets should be reserved 72 hours in advance. Season ticket buyers receive discounts, as do groups of thirty or more. This festival has been a tradition in the area for over eighteen years. Handicapped accessible.

Actors bring to life such works as *Macbeth*, *The Sound of Music*, and a *Midsummer Night's Dream* in dinner-theater shows. Along with the musicals and dramatic plays staged by more accomplished student and professional actors, the summer lineup includes workshop productions by children and teens. The Oklahoma Shakespearean Festival also offers an Elderhostel in which approximately twenty people throughout the United States come to study theatrical crafts.

Fort Washita

Located fifteen miles east of Madill on State Highway 199 or fifteen miles north of Durant on SH 199. From Lake Texoma, take Highway 70 east to Silo Road (three miles west of Durant), and turn north. Travel approximately seven miles to the stop sign, and turn left. Drive one mile, and turn left on State Highway 199. Travel three miles. (405) 924-6502. Monday-Saturday 9-5, Sunday 1-5. Free.

This 300-acre historic fort once protected the civilized Chickasaw and Choctaw Indians from the Plains Indians. It was the first fort ever built for such a purpose. When the Civil War began, Fort Washita was abandoned by federal troops and then occupied by Texas Confederates who used it as a supply depot. Acquired by the Oklahoma Historical Society in 1962, the barracks were reconstructed, and they are now open to the public–along with a museum and the remains of military buildings.

Hundreds of shade trees fill the grounds of Fort Washita, making for pleasant picnics. Bring a quilt or use one of the tables placed around the site. Not handicapped accessible.

In late March or early April, the **Fur Trade Rendezvous** ($2 per car) is held. The living history program highlights life before the 1840s. Included are 150 camps of fur traders and pioneers who demonstrate for visitors the skills required for survival on the frontier. They also participate in axe, rifle, pistol, and knife competitions.

Lake Texoma Resort Park

Located approximately fifteen miles west of Durant, halfway between I-35 and Highway 75. The lake is also surrounded by the communities of Kingston and Madill on the west and Tishomingo on the north. (405) 564-2311 or (800) 654-8240 for lodge reservations. 🅢

Lake Texoma is not only the second largest lake in Oklahoma, but it is also the Striper Capitol of the World. Guides take individuals or groups on exciting, world-class fishing expeditions for this fish. Seagulls lead fishermen to the striper; gulls dive for shad, which happen to be the striper's food of choice. If you want to fish but aren't much of an adventurer, try the indoor/outdoor fishing marina.

Lake Texoma is the winter home to many migratory Bald Eagles. The **Two Rivers Nature Center** sponsors Bald Eagle and Wintering Waterfowl tours each Saturday from November through March and other events throughout the year.

Adjacent to the Lodge is **Lake Texoma Golf Course** (405) 564-3333, a popular eighteen-hole golf course complete with putting green and driving range. The par 71, 6128-yard course has a USGA rating of 67.8, and a slope of 112. The most-used course of all the state-operated courses, it is noted for its scenic beauty and water difficulties; the course is situated along Lake Texoma and has many ponds.

Golf fees for eighteen-hole play are Monday-Friday $10.50, weekend and holidays $12.50. Carts for eighteen holes are $17, for nine holes $10. All-day play (available daily except for holidays) is $35 per person, which includes green and cart fees. Twilight, Senior and junior discounts available. Call ahead after noon on Wednesday for weekend tee times.

The **Lake Texoma Lodge** is within walking distance to the golf course, and it offers a variety of guest rooms, cottages and cabins. The Bayview building alone has twenty bedrooms, a large kitchen, and a large living area. The facility sleeps up to forty people and is ideal for corporate retreats and family reunions. The lake beach and swimming area is a short drive from the lodge, but there is a pool at the lodge. It's wise to make reservations at least one year in advance for summer months and one month in advance for winter months.

Rates for guest rooms without kitchenettes range from $40-80 in the winter, and from $58-91 in the summer. Cottages with kitchenettes range from $50-85 in the winter, and from $63-99 in the summer. Bayview (sleeps forty) costs $350 per night in the winter, and $650 in the summer. 🅢

Camping is also available on a first-come, first-served basis. Of the 580 campsites, most are tent sites with water and electric; others are RV sites with water, electric and sewer ($14) and primitive sites.

Lake Texoma Area

Events abound in the area, but the biggest are the Sand Bass Festival held during the first week of June in downtown Madill, and the Striper Festival held in mid-July in Kingston. The **Sand Bass Festival** features educational presentations on fishing, nightly entertainment, a craft fair, 5K fun run, basketball tournament, and a talent search add to the fun. For more information, call the Madill Chamber of Commerce (405) 795-2431. The **Striper Festival** features a fishing tournament as its major event. Other activities include nightly entertainment, arts and crafts booths, and a car show. For more information, call (405) 564-9512.

Other accommodations in the Lake Texoma area

Alberta Creek Resort, P.O. Box 9 Kingston, OK 73439, (405) 564-2552. Mobile homes with maid service to change sheets and towels; no pets, $65-80. **Bridgeview Resort**, Route 2, Box 117 Madill, OK 73446, (405) 795-3979. Cabins that sleep four to eight people, $36-50. **Buncombe Creek Resort Marina**, HC 71, Box 521 Kingston, OK 73439, (800) 636-2543. Two mobile homes with full-size kitchens, $42-48. **Caney Creek Resort**, 6.5 miles south of Kingston on Highway 70B, (800) 772-4927. Sixteen motel rooms with refrigerators, $40-80. **Little Glasses Resort**, Route 3, Box 108 Madill, OK 73446, (405) 795-2068. Cabins and mobile homes, $50-70.

Willow Springs Marina (Houseboat Cruises) is located between Durant and Kingston, one mile south of Highway 70. (405) 924-6240. Call at least two months ahead to reserve a houseboat. Choose from either a forty-foot boat that sleeps six or a fifty-six foot boat that sleeps fourteen. Off-season and midweek rates are less. Rates range from $645 to $1,795 for a weekend, three days during the midweek, or a full week.

Dining

Sanford's *$$, $$$*

Located 1/2 mile east of Lake Texoma Resort Lodge on Highway 70. (405) 564-3764. Tuesday-Thursday 4:30-9, Friday-Saturday 4:30-10. Closed Sunday and Monday. Handicapped accessible.

Family-owned and operated, this restaurant has been serving outstanding cuts of steak for thirteen years. Filet mignon steak is a favorite, but the menu also includes dishes featuring frog legs and catfish. Order an entree, and help yourself to the salad and soup bar.

Accommodations

Deer Run Lodge

Located a few miles east of Caddo, north and east of Durant, (405) 367-2687 or (405) 924-4402. From Oklahoma City take I-35 south to Ardmore. Turn east on Highway 70 to Durant and take Highway 75/69 to Caddo. In Caddo, travel east about seven miles on Highway 22 to a sharp right curve. At the Deer Run Lodge sign, turn left and then follow the signs for eight miles. From Tulsa take Highway 75 south to Henryetta. Take the Indian Nation Turnpike south to Highway 69 into Caddo. A package retreat (four-five days) includes food and all your activities. Adults $87 per day, plus tax; children $48 per day, plus tax. Children two and under are free. Make reservations one to two weeks in advance. Handicapped accessible.

Get out of the city and saddle up at a real working ranch. Ride with cowboys to round up horses or, if you're less experienced, choose from a selection of steeds suitable for anyone from a beginner to an expert. If you prefer a little relaxation, sit back with a book on the large porch that overlooks a pecan meadow where longhorn cattle graze.

Deer Run Lodge is in its third summer as a guest lodge, but the ranch is three generations old. Owner Lena Clancy inherited the 7200-acre ranch from her parents. The rustic two-story ranch house has eight rooms, each of which sleeps as many as six people. In addition, the lodge has a conference room and a restaurant where guests eat all their meals. Deer Run Lodge is perfect for family reunions, getaways for families or couples, and retreats for businesses and churches. During the winter months, the ranch offers hunting packages for quail, wild turkey, pheasant, duck and dove, wild hogs, and whitetail deer.

Although the ranch is just a few minutes from the town of Durant, the canyons, ponds, pine groves, and bluffs give guests a feeling of seclusion. Bring a swimming suit and enjoy a dip in the canyon pond, or enjoy strolls and horseback rides through the river valley area. Indulge in the hearty southern cooking that features such menu items as fried chicken, pot roast, and brisket (lighter fare is available). At Deer Run Lodge, there's never a dull moment; activities include volleyball, soccer, softball, shuffleboard, fishing, hunting, hay rides, and cookouts.

The hosts will customize a vacation for your needs. Stay a day, weekend, or a week. Bring good shoes for horseback riding (boots or some type of high top footwear that will not get caught in the stirrups).

Pauls Valley

Pauls Valley takes its name from Smith Paul, who came to Indian Territory with the Chickasaw Indians in 1857. He worked for a man named McClure, who was married to a Chickasaw woman. Upon McClure's death, Smith Paul married his widowed wife and ended up farming over 5,000 acres of land in the western part of the Chickasaw Nation. In 1870, Smith Paul gave his land to the railroad. The town became Smith Paul's Valley, which was later shortened to Pauls Valley so the name would fit more easily on railroad signs.

Located about 58 miles from Oklahoma City and about 148 miles from Tulsa. From Oklahoma City, take I-35 south to Highway 19, then travel east into Pauls Valley. Pauls Valley Chamber of Commerce (405) 238-6491.

Santa Fe Depot

204 South Santa Fe, (405) 238-2244. From I-35 south, take exit 72 east onto Highway 19, which runs into Grant Street, also known as South Santa Fe. Open Tuesday-Sunday, 10-5. Closed on major holidays. Donations are accepted.

The aging depot was scheduled to be demolished in 1989; however, a group of Pauls Valley citizens banded together to refurbish the historic structure. The Santa Fe Depot, built in 1905, now houses significant items from the town's past. Along with local memorabilia, the depot has a number of artifacts from World War I. The town's founder, Smith Paul, is remembered with a collection of his personal belongings and commentary published about him. There is an original copy of a New York Herald newspaper dated April 15, 1865; the huge headline on the cover announces the news of President Abraham Lincoln's assassination. The depot holds many relics from the former Washita Valley Museum. These exhibits include early archeological findings of Native American life on the Washita River. Call one week in advance if you would like a guided historical walking tour of Pauls Valley by a member of the Pauls Valley Historical Society.

Dining

Bob's Pig Shop $

829 N. Ash, (405) 238-2332. From downtown Pauls Valley, travel eight blocks east on Highway 77 (Ash Street). Monday-Thursday 11-8; Friday, 11-9; and Saturday, 11-2. Handicapped accessible.

At Bob's Pig Shop, some like it hot. This mom and pop bar & grill is locally popular for its barbecue and spicy, authentic Mexican food. The stone-gabled restaurant is more than sixty years old, and it is decorated with antiques and memorabilia. Try the tamales or the pig sandwich (careful: the relish is rather spicy and hot). The pig sandwich comes with beans and, for a few extra cents, a pickle. Homemade peach and cherry cobblers are choice desserts, and they may be served a la mode.

Sulphur

Human occupation goes back as far as 7000 years when primitive nomadic bands camped in the vicinity of the numerous springs, both fresh and mineral, in this area. The springs' land was Indian land, but as more non-Indians moved into the area, the Indians became concerned for the preservation of this wonderful resource. In the early 1900s, they gave the area to the U.S.

Government to be made into a park. This site became Platt National Park, which had the distinction of being the smallest national park in the country. The town buildings which had been constructed inside the park boundaries were moved, giving the town its present location. In the 1970s, the park, along with the Lake of the Arbuckles and adjoining lands, were incorporated into the Chickasaw National Recreation Area, and Platt National Park ceased to exist.

Akia, a spa for women is located near Sulphur and the Chickasaw National Recreation Area. Call (405) 842-6269 for more information about this spa that teaches its guests how to live a healthier lifestyle.

Located 71 miles south of Oklahoma City off I-35. Take Highway 7 east into Davis, then drive nine more miles east to Sulphur. Sulphur is about 150 miles from Tulsa. Sulphur Chamber of Commerce (405) 622-2824.

Chickasaw National Recreation Area

(405) 622-3165. Travertine Nature Center Summer hours: Sunday-Thursday 8-7, Friday-Saturday 8-9. Winter hours: 8-5 every day except Christmas and New Year's Day. Free admission to Travertine Nature Center. Camping is $8 per night, per camp site.

A leafy canopy of trees shades the park, where it is always a bracing delight to dip your toes into the cold waters of one of the creeks. Years ago, nomadic Indians rested and recuperated in this area, which was respected by many tribes as a neutral zone. Water from the Buffalo and Antelope springs flows in to Travertine Creek, a popular spot for wading and swimming. Little Niagara, which is about seven feet deep, also draws its share of swimmers. Rock Creek is another pool worth visiting.

The **Travertine Nature Center** is a museum with displays of native wildlife. A nature movie shows hourly from 11 a.m. to 1 p.m. Ranger-guided nature hikes are scheduled each morning for 9:30 a.m. View the park's beauty at night on an evening nature hike that begins at 9 p.m. (bring a flashlight). Be sure to sign up early in the day. Night hikes are given only during the summer, on Fridays and Saturdays.

Dining

Quail Hollow Depot $

Highway 7 West (one mile west of Sulphur), (405) 622-4080. Antique Store: Monday-Saturday 10-5; Country Store: Monday-Saturday 9-5; Tea Room: Tuesday-Saturday 11-2:30. Handicapped accessible.

The 1890s Santa Fe depot from nearby Dougherty is now a combination of tea room, antique store and country store. The antique store sells an assortment of fine collectibles. The tea room, decorated in burgundy, forest green and beige floral, serves sandwiches, chicken salad plates, and desserts. The country store offers primitive antiques and country gifts. The Quail Hollow Depot features a working grist mill that grinds cornmeal and flour, which is sold at the store.

The Silver Turtle $$, $$$

Highway 7 West, 2 1/2 miles west of Sulphur. (405) 622-3500. Not handicapped accessible.

This seventeen-year-old restaurant is considered a wonderful place to dine. Best known for its steak and seafood, The Silver Turtle also has chicken on the menu. For an appetizer, try the fried green tomatoes. You'll leave with a pleasant memory of the food, and of the plush red carpet and elegant red velvet chairs. For groups of ten or more, call two to three days in advance.

Shopping

The Gettin' Place, 100 West Muskogee, (405) 622-3796. Monday-Saturday 9-5; Sunday 11-5. This 7000-square foot building is host to sixty-five dealers with various goods, from fine collectibles to primitive bottles and jars.

Memory Lane, 820 West 12th, (405) 622-2090. Monday-Saturday 10-5; Sunday 12-5. Memory Lane is known for its quality antiques, glassware and furniture.

The Dog Trade Flea Market, located on Highway 177, 1/2 mile north of Sulphur, (405) 622-5371, and held Sunday mornings from dawn to noon. Shoppers can find everything from real, live dogs to antiques here. The number of people who attend is large, but manageable; it is suggested that you arrive early. Open all year and most holidays.

Accommodations

The Artesian

1022 W. 12th Street, (405) 622-5254. From I-35 south, take the Davis/Sulphur exit east onto Highway 7. Travel twelve miles east into Sulphur. At the first stoplight, turn north and travel two blocks. The home sits on the west side. Rates for two adults are $45-$60; singles are $35-$50. It is best to make reservations one month in advance. No pets. No children under 12. Not handicapped accessible.

This lovely 1904 Victorian home has an L-shaped front porch that overlooks manicured, lush flowerbeds. Old-timers in the area say that the home was ordered from Sears & Roebuck, sent to Davis on the Santa Fe Railroad, and assembled on the lot. Every corner of the home is decorated with tasteful antiques and collectibles. There are two bedrooms, the Travertine and Bromide, each with a private bathroom. Guests may use the living room. Innkeepers Karen and Tom Byrd serve breakfast at 8:30 in the guest breakfast room or on the garden deck. The meal often consists of an egg casserole or a baked German pancake served with fruit and breakfast bread or muffin, coffee, and juice.

Four Sisters Inn

1307 Cooper Memorial Drive, (405) 622-4441. Take Highway 7 west to Cooper Memorial Drive (also known as Point Road), turn left and drive one and three-tenths of a mile. Look for a white pillared gate, which is the entrance to the Inn. The rate is $80 per night, with a two-night minimum stay. Make reservations one to two months in advance. No children. Not disabled accessible.

The decor in this bed and breakfast elegantly and accurately represents Oklahoma's cowboy and Native American history. The 1918 ranch-style home was renovated in 1994 by Shar Dodson, her family, and her three sisters, Brenda, Reggie and Penny (hence the name Four Sisters Inn). Large picture windows provide an awesome view of the surroundings. Guests often spot wildlife, including deer, wild turkey, and rabbits. Inside the inn, there are books to read; outside, guests enjoy walking trails, stocked fishing ponds, and a forty-foot lap swimming pool. Mountain bike trails have recently been added.

There are three bedrooms in the main house, including a honeymoon suite with a double jacuzzi. Guests have access to a sitting room with a coffee/tea bar and a TV/VCR. Opening to the pool are two additional rooms, the Cowboy Poet and the Native American. All rooms have private baths (robes are provided). Breakfast includes a choice of cereal, sweetbreads, and a hot entree. High tea is served at 4 p.m. Shar Dodson is an international flight attendant, and she brings back teas from all over the world. If guests stay during one of the summer holidays—Memorial Day, Fourth of July, or Labor Day—they're invited to join Shar's family for one of their old-fashioned family celebrations.

Olde Bathhouse/Hotel

1102 W. Lindsay, (405) 622-5930. From Highway 7 turn south on Twelfth Street. Continue to Lindsay Street then turn left. Room rates are $65 per night or $15 per person for a day visit. Bring a bathing suit and shower shoes. Spas are therapeutic in nature, and they are not intended for children. Make reservations two weeks to one month in advance.

In the early 1900s, there were several hotels in Sulphur that offered soothing soaks in mineral baths. Over the years, all the hotels have been torn down except for the Olde Bath. Recently it has gone through remodeling and modernization. Now it has returned to resemble its former glory, with

The Olde Bathhouse.

working mineral pools and seven guest rooms. Visitors may schedule an extended overnight stay or a day-visit at the Bathhouse. Innkeeper Roger Graham emphasizes that this is not a bed and breakfast, but rather an inn that serves a continental breakfast. Rates for overnight rooms and day visits include the use of two indoor mineral pools and use of the downstairs showers. Staff massage therapists provide full-body massages for $35.

In the Vicinity

Davis

Like so many Oklahoma towns, Davis traces its origins to the heyday of the railroad in the late nineteenth century. In 1887, it was built up on the west side of the tracks; however, patterns of construction and settlement have shifted the bulk of the town onto the east side. Davis is a small, attractive place with clean-swept streets. Antique stores intermingle with other businesses along Main Street. The town is well-situated for the tourist trade, as it happens to be near Arbuckle Wilderness, Chickasaw National Recreation Area, and Turner Falls.

Located 71 miles south of Oklahoma City on I-35. From the interstate, take Highway 7 east three miles to Davis. Davis is located approximately 155 miles south and west of Tulsa. Davis Chamber of Commerce (405) 369-2402.

Arbuckle Wilderness

From I-35, take exit 51 south of Davis. Travel 1/4 mile and follow the signs. (405) 369-3383. Open every day from 8 a.m. until one hour before sundown. The park is now open on Christmas Day. Safarian Lights, the park's Christmas season lighted drive, opens the day after Thanksgiving. Adult: $14.99, senior citizen $8.99, children age three through eleven $8.99. Group rates are $2 less than the regular admission price. Prices include the Fun Park and walk-through zoo.

Adults and children will take pleasure in driving through this nature park where literally hundreds of animals are seen peacefully grazing, sleeping, galloping along, or even scrambling up trees. Some will boldly welcome you by peering in your car window, or they may decide to plop down in the middle of the road, right in front of your bumper! It's all part of the fun. You may even have an animal or two that wants to join your party. Be ready to raise the windows!

The park is full of deer, elk, ostrich, giraffe, lions, tigers, buffalo, and zebras. Park officials say that the animals are active most of the day. After your drive, visit the walk-through zoo, where you will see exotic birds, alligators, and twin chimpanzees. The Fun Park area offers paddle boats, adult and child-size go-carts, and an arcade.

Make sure you have enough gas in the tank; you don't want to get stranded out among the park's wild creatures! Also, be aware that your car may get dirtied and, at worst, "bumped" by the animals as they approach to bury their hungry snouts and muzzles in the specially-prepared animal food bought before the tour ($2.25 for a small bucket and $3.50 for a large). The tour is only six and one-half miles long, but it usually takes an hour and a half to complete. To avoid a crowd, go on a weekday. During the winter, the Fun Park rides are open only on the weekends, weather permitting.

Pack a lunch or plan to enjoy a meal at one of the two restaurants at the park. Meals can be bought for less than $5. Arbuckle Wilderness is a day-long adventure; plan accordingly. Consider bringing drinks, towelettes, and other day-trip essentials.

The cost of admission includes the activities in the Fun Park area, including paddle boats, go carts, and the walk-through zoo. Arcade games cost extra. Group rates are available. For groups of thirty-five or more, park tour guides supervise guided hayrides and cookouts. Call for rates and menus.

Cedervale Gardens, Restaurant ($-$$$) & Mountain Cabins

From I-35, take exit 51, then Highway 77 south for 1/4 of a mile. Follow the signs. (405) 369-3224. The restaurant and gardens are open April through October daily from 11-9 from April through October. Garden tours are free for dinner guests; others pay $3 each. The two cabins rent for $75 and $85 per night.

For two generations, the Howell family has run Cedervale, where trails wind through beautiful gardens, and diners enjoy the house specialty, fresh trout, while gazing over the banks of Honey Creek. In this gorgeous setting, mountain cabins are available for overnight stays. Since 1976, Cedervale has been a treasured place to steal away for a few hours, or even a few days. The restaurant is handicapped accessible. Groups of more than eight must make reservations.

Most of the thirty or so varieties of plants and trees found in the manicured gardens are native to the Arbuckle Mountains. In May, tropical flowers are planted, adding stunning colors to an already scenic area.

Cedervale offers two mountainside **cabins.** The large cabin sleeps up to six people, and it has a full kitchen. The smaller cabin sleeps up to four people, and it has a kitchenette with a microwave. There are no televisions or telephones.

Turner Falls Park

South of Davis, (405) 369-2917 or (405) 369-2988. From I-35, take exit 51 and turn south on U.S. 77. The entrance is 3.5 miles south of Davis. Follow the signs. Swimming areas are open daily from May to September; camping is available all year. Park admission: adults, $6; children ages seven to twelve, $4.50; senior citizens,

Fred Marvel/Oklahoma Tourism

$4.50. Group rates available. Per night camping rates: adults, $7.50; children, $5.50; senior citizens, $6.50. Cabins, $45 per night.

Owned by the City of Davis, Turner Falls is Oklahoma's oldest park and is known for its 77-foot cascading water fall—the largest in the state. There are two natural spring-fed swimming pools, Blue Hole and Falls Pool, and several sandy beaches. In summer, lifeguards are posted on duty, but lifejackets are still recommended. Take an afternoon to spread out a picnic lunch amidst the many natural hiking trails and caves, or explore the area's natural rock formations. On your way to the waterfall, stop by the miniature English stone castle, built in the 1930s. Hamburgers are always hot and tasty at the outdoor cafe, Cactus Patch (open only in the summer). Trout fishermen have to wait for the cooler months; the season runs from November through March. Fishermen have to pay regular park admission, plus $1.25 per trout per person.

Two rustic camp **cabins** are available on the grounds. Each includes a refrigerator, with linens for the two double beds. Bring your own dishes. Grills and picnic tables are located outside the cabins.

Turner Falls

Turner Falls Park sponsors several events throughout the year, including Ron Alexander's Car Show in June and arts and crafts shows in early April and early October. During the month of December, the park hosts **Fantasyland,** a half-mile display of Christmas scenes.

Tishomingo

Cedar Green Bed & Breakfast

909 South Fourth Street, (405) 369-2396. From State Highway 7 (Main Street) turn south on Fourth Street and travel nine blocks. $50-60 per night. Two-night anniversary and honeymoon packages are available. It is recommended to call two to three weeks in advance for reservations. Cedar Green does accept children ages ten and older. No pets allowed. Not handicapped accessible. Member of the Oklahoma Bed and Breakfast Association.

This 1938 cedar and stone oasis is nestled in a sleepy neighborhood that feels as if it's worlds removed from the bustle of city life. The cozy guest rooms and upstairs suite each have private baths. The Walnut Room is a decorated Victorian style; the Pecan Room is decorated in contemporary floral. The colors of Sage Garden and Cactus impart a cooler tone to the Maple Suite. In the morning, innkeepers Miles and Pat Judkins whip up a big, satisfying country breakfast, including fruit and beverages. Their specialty is a country egg dish with plenty of peppers, onion, cheese, and potatoes, served with biscuits or muffins. Dine indoors or outside on the deck. Feeling a bit lazy and introspective? A front porch swing provides an ideal perch for enjoying a good book or, on a hot summer evening, contemplating the peaceful solitude while nursing a glass of iced lemonade. For the colder months, sip apple cider or hot chocolate in front of the fireplace. If you're a hopeless romantic, ride the Judkins' tandem bicycle with your mate around the town of Davis.

Chigley Mansion Bed & Breakfast

210 N. Fifth Street, (405) 369-3404. Just two blocks north of Main Street (SH 7) on N. Fifth Street. Look for the gates at the north end of the street. $55-81 per night. Reservations recommended one week in advance. Children are accepted. No pets. Not handicapped accessible.

The Chigley Mansion was built in 1891 by a civic-minded local man, Nelson Chigley. Originally a school for Indian children, the white, two-story, Southern mansion-style home sets on seven shaded acres. There is one bedroom with a full-size antique bed and a family suite that sleeps up to five people. Both rooms have private baths. Have your tea or coffee in the bright, warm, sun room. Breakfast may include a casserole or waffles, pancakes, bacon, sausage, and fruit.

Tishomingo

The first "official" capital of the Chickasaw Nation after their 1837-1847 removal from Mississippi was at Good Springs, a small settlement which they later named Tishomingo in honor of a respected chief. The Chickasaws moved willingly to the new lands which they shared with the Choctaws. Both tribes had been successful in farming large plantations in Mississippi, and they brought these practices with them to their new homes. Though this was technically "Indian Territory," there were a number of non-Indians who settled in this area. There were soldiers from nearby forts, slaves who worked the plantations, and merchants and manufacturers who supplied the needs of the community, making Tishomingo a hub of commerce in the area.

Evidence of Tishomingo's Chickasaw heritage can still be seen in the town. The impressive granite building on a hill above Main Street was built in 1897 as the third capitol of the Chickasaw Nation. It served as the Johnston County Courthouse from 1907 until 1992. The building is once again owned by the Chickasaws, who are in the process of restoring it. The 1902 **Bank of the Chickasaws** on Main Street now houses a small museum that is open by appointment (405-371-2175).

Tishomingo is 115 miles from Oklahoma City and 213 miles from Tulsa. From Oklahoma City, take I-35 south into Ardmore. Turn east on Highway 199 and north on Highway 1 into Tishomingo. From Tulsa, take I-44 west to Stroud, then take Highway 377/99 south into Tishomingo. Tishomingo Chamber of Commerce (405) 371-2175.

Blue River Public Fishing and Hunting Area

Located four miles east of Tishomingo on Highway 78 and six miles north into Johnston County, (405) 924-4087. Traveling on Highway 78 from Tishomingo, look for the Blue River sign; turn north and continue to follow the signs.

Besides its obvious beauty, Blue River is considered unique because of its limestone and granite rock formations lying in the stream, over which the water flows in lovely falls and ripples. The river runs for more than six miles through the Blue River Public Fishing and Hunting Area. Operated by the Oklahoma Department of Wildlife Conservation, this area covers roughly 3400 acres. Each year, an estimated 20,000 hunters and fishermen visit Blue River. Only those who fish and hunt on the grounds are permitted to use the primitive camping, and then only at designated campsites. At the **Carl R. and Ruth Walker Landrum Wilderness Area**, no camping is allowed, but there are some hiking trails and fishing areas accessible to the handicapped. The major fish species are catfish and largemouth bass. From October through March 31, the river is stocked with rainbow trout.

Visitors must arrive after 6 a.m. or before the closing of the gates at 10 p.m. Recreational users should be sure to have the proper state license (for fishing or hunting). A **Trout Derby** is held in early November.

Chickasaw Council House Museum

205 North Fisher, (405) 371-3351. Tuesday-Friday 8:30-4:30; Saturday 10:30-4:30. Closed Sunday, Monday and major holidays. Free. Handicapped accessible.

The museum has Chickasaw artifacts relating to their history after the tribe was relocated to Indian Territory. The collection includes photographs, clothing items, educational tools, baskets, and pottery. It also houses the first Council House, a log structure built in 1856. Another interesting area displays the private collection of internationally-famous actress and storyteller, Te Ata. This Tishomingo native was the first person to be named a "State Treasure" by the Oklahoma Arts Council. Several of her beautiful buckskin dresses and her drums and rattles are on display. Call two days in advance for reservations for a thirty-minute guided tour.

Tishomingo National Wildlife Refuge

Located a few miles south and east of Tishomingo, (405) 371-2402. Take Highway 78 east to Refuge Road, turn south, and drive three miles to the Refuge Headquarters. All visitors must stop at the headquarters building before entering the park. The refuge is open seven days a week, from sunrise until one-half hour after sunset, except for night fishing and camping.

Located in the upper Washita Arm of Lake Texoma, the refuge is the home of migratory waterfowl. Of its 16,000 acres, a full 13,000 are water. Other terrain features includes grasslands, wild plum thickets, and woodlands of oak, hickory and elm. Bring your camera. Picture-taking and sight-seeing expeditions are encouraged throughout most of the refuge from March 1 through September 30, and in limited areas during the rest of the year. At one time, there can be as many as 100,000 ducks and 45,000 geese here. During the winter, up to ninety endangered bald eagles nest at the refuge.

During summer, woodland birds, wood storks, nesting wood ducks, herons, and egrets are regularly spotted. Over the years, more than 250 different species of birds have been observed. If you want to see whitetail deer grazing, the best times to visit are early morning and late afternoon. You may also catch a glimpse of cottontails, raccoons, and squirrels. Groups or individuals may visit and take drive-through tours, or climb up the observation tower to view the birds.

At present, the refuge is not set up for walking tours, but school classes and other groups are welcome. Call one week in advance to have refuge personnel discuss the refuge's programs. Fishing and hunting are permitted in season.

Southwest Oklahoma

Altus

It wouldn't be surprising if Altus had an identity crisis; its first few years of existence were marked with changes. Altus started life in 1885 as Frazer, Texas, in infamous "Old Greer County."

Altus

The town was located on the Frazer River, now known as the Salt Fork of the Red River. In 1889, a flood washed away most of the town, and its inhabitants moved to a new site on higher ground. The name "Altus" comes from Latin and means "high." In 1901, the name of the town was changed to "Leger," then in 1904, back to Altus. In the meantime, the United States Supreme Court settled the long-running dispute over the Texas boundary and Altus (and the rest of Greer County) had joined Oklahoma Territory. At statehood, the southern portion of Greer County became Jackson County, and Altus became the county seat. Since the 1940s, Altus has been home of Altus Air Force Base (call 405-481-7700 or 481-7729 three weeks in advance for a tour).

Altus is 139 miles southwest of Oklahoma City and 263 miles southwest of Tulsa. Take I-44 out of Oklahoma City to Lawton, then go west on U.S. Highway 62 to Altus. Altus Chamber of Commerce (405) 482-0210.

Museum of the Western Prairie

1100 North Hightower Street, (405) 482-1044. From U.S. Highway 62, on the east side of town, look for the airplane in City Park. Turn on Park Lane (on the east side of the park) and go north. Watch for the left turn lane onto Falcon Road. Go west until you see the reservoir on the north. Look for Memorial Road going south. There are brown signs locating the museum. Tuesday-Friday 9-5, Saturday and Sunday 2-5. Closed Mondays and holidays. Free; however, a $1 donation for adults and $0.50 for children is suggested. Handicapped accessible.

The architecture of the museum itself is reminiscent of a half-dugout, a common housing structure in the area in frontier days. The above-ground portion is faced with native stone from nearby Creta. The need for shelter and a source of water were primary for area pioneers. Two of the museum's exhibits highlight these struggles. There is a lot of interesting material concerning the old Greer County controversy.

This is one of the newest and most attractive of the Oklahoma Historical Society's sites. Plan on about 45 minutes to see the inside and outdoor displays.

Quartz Mountain Adventure Tours and Guide Service, Inc.

Located near Altus and Quartz Mountain State Park. (800) 687-6243. (www.intellisys.net/users/advtours/) Cost varies from backpacking tours at $20 per person to five-day bicycling tours at $580, $730, and $900 per person.

Bike, hike, hunt, or fish in the rugged beauty of Southwest Oklahoma with experienced guides from Quartz Mountain Adventure Tours. In operation since March, 1997, this guide service is the ticket for those seeking adventure in Oklahoma. True "thrill seekers" should ask about their Southwest Oklahoma storm chasing tour; even if the weather is calm, you will enjoy fishing, rappeling, and cycling.

Scott Farms

Route 3, Box 1498, Altus, OK 73521. (800) 482-1950. Scott Farms is six and one-half miles north of downtown Altus on U.S. Highway 283. Look for the green awning. Monday-Friday 9-5. (Around the Christmas season, they are often open on Saturdays. Call ahead to be sure.)

Scott Farms is primarily a mail-order business specializing in their own spice mixes, dip mixes, a variety of popcorns and seasonings, gourmet beans, and Southwest specialties. Visitors have become so frequent that they have opened a small retail shop. In addition to their ninety-plus products, they carry Frankoma and Three Rivers pottery and Neighbors coffee.

Events

Shortgrass Arts Festival

Held the second Saturday in October in the Community Center. Contact (405) 482-7242 for a brochure. Take U.S. Highway 62 into Altus. Turn north on Veterans Drive to Falcon Road and turn left. The center is on the north side of Falcon by the reservoir. Free. Handicapped accessible.

This one-day festival includes painting and drawing, designer crafts, pottery, sculpture, and graphic arts. There is a children's activity center to encourage participation in and enjoyment of various art forms. Snack foods are available in the food booths. This is an indoor-outdoor festival, but most activities are inside.

Quartz Mountain Resort Park

Lone Wolf, Oklahoma, (405) 563-2424. The resort is seventeen miles north of Altus on Highway 283. Advance reservations for lodging are a must. ★ ⑤

A 1500-foot protuberance of pink granite, Quartz Mountain dominates the surrounding plains. Once part of a mighty mountain range, it lies like a fossil tailbone, the end of the spine of the Wichita Mountains. Quartz Mountain State Park is in a buffer zone between the eastern and western United States, providing an interesting mix of flora and fauna. A naturalist is on duty, and programs are frequently scheduled to take advantage of the geologic and biologic diversity of the region. Located on the shore of Lake Altus, the lodge is in the midst of reconstruction and expansion. The present lodge has 45 rooms, with 100 more scheduled for the new building. There are three duplex cabins and eight cottages with kitchenettes. Camping facilities include group camps, a dormitory, rustic camp sites, and an RV camp. The park offers fishing, miniature golf, paddleboats and canoes, tennis courts, volleyball, a waterslide, go-carts, picnic areas, an outdoor swimming pool, and an eighteen-hole golf course.

The resort is best known as the home of the Oklahoma Summer Arts Institute, a two-week-long institute where Oklahoma's best and brightest high school students are mentored by nationally- and internationally-known artists. The summer program has been so successful that adult programs are now offered during other seasons. Contact the Oklahoma Arts Institute at (405) 842-0890 for information.

The park is offering a number of programs even during the construction period. These include eagle watches, a wildflower festival, July Fourth celebration, and Christmas activities. Call the park for information.

Natural beauty is a big attraction at **Quartz Mountain Resort Park Golf Course** (405) 563-2520. Roughs with wildflowers and quail are part of the charm. The front nine was built in the late 1950s, the back nine, designed by Art Proctor, was added in 1994. The signature hole, the 600-yard Number 5 nicknamed "Forever," becomes increasingly narrow as you approach the green. There are no water hazards on the course, but sand and roughs add plenty of challenge. Golf pro Gene Abernathy is justifiably proud of the new pro shop. Cold sandwiches, chips, pop and beer are available in the clubhouse. The 6595-yard, eighteen-hole course has a par of 71.

Open sunup to sundown; green fees are Monday-Friday $9.50, Saturday, Sunday and holidays $12. Senior, junior and twilight reductions available. Carts are $16 for eighteen holes. Reservations for weekend tee times available after 11 a.m. on Wednesdays.

Anadarko

Anadarko is often thought of as the "most Indian" place in Oklahoma. The town is named for one of the Caddoan tribes, the Nadako clan, but the name was spelled incorrectly when it was sent to the U.S. Postmaster in 1874. Before the town was opened to non-Indian settlement in 1901, it served as the agency for several tribes which had been relocated to this area. The Apache, the Delaware and the Wichita tribes have their headquarters here. Downtown Anadarko with its many turn-of-the-century buildings is designated a historic district on the National Register of Historic Places.

Anadarko is sixty-five miles southwest of Oklahoma City, and about 242 miles southwest of Tulsa. From Oklahoma City, take the H.E. Bailey Turnpike (I-44) to the Highway 62 (#83) exit at Chickasha, then go west to Anadarko. One of the most informative items available is the annual "Guide," published by the Anadarko Daily News. It is available free at any of the major attractions in town or from the Anadarko Chamber of Commerce (405) 247-6651. Ⓤ

Indian City, USA

Two and one-half miles south of Anadarko on Highway 8, (800) 433-5661. Open every day (with the exceptions of major holidays) from 9-6 in summer and 9-5 in winter. Admission to the museum is free, but tours of the villages cost adults $7.50, children ages six to eleven $4, under age six free. All tours of the Indian villages are guided and last 45 minutes. The first tour starts at 9:15. Tours leave every 45 minutes, with the last tour beginning at 4:15. Handicapped accessible with some difficulty.

The Indian villages are the most important part of this attraction. Fifty thousand visitors a year from all parts of the globe come to tour the recreated Indian habitats. Indian City USA worked with the Department of Archaeology at the University of Oklahoma in planning and designing the villages. Southern Plains tribes represented include Arapaho, Caddo, Cheyenne, Comanche, Kiowa, Navajo, and Pawnee. Wickiups, tepees, hogans, and other types of housing are accurately recreated. The Native American guides are knowledgeable and interesting.

Indian dancers perform for each tour during the summer and on weekends during the school year. There is a fairly extensive Indian museum and a large gift shop. This attraction was started in the mid-1950s, and the facilities are showing their age. Still, the historical information they present is timeless, making this a good stop when you are in the area.

National Hall of Fame for Famous American Indians

U.S. Highway 62 E, (405) 247-5555. On the east edge of Anadarko on US Highway 62, north side of the road. Monday-Saturday 9-5, Sunday 1-5. Free. Handicapped accessible.

The most important part of this attraction, the sculpture gardens, is outdoors, making this is a good place to stop to stretch your legs. Copies of the self-guided tour newspaper are available inside the small visitor center. There are several large bronze animal sculptures, in addition to the busts of famous and not-so-well-known Indians who made significant contributions "to the molding of our American way of life." To get the most from the museum, allow thirty to forty-five minutes to read the biographies and background information on each honoree's tribe as you stroll through the gardens.

Philomathic Pioneer Museum

311 E. Main Street. (405) 247-3240. From U.S. Highway 62, turn north on N.E. Third Street. Main Street is three blocks north. Tuesday-Sunday 1-5. Free. Partially handicapped accessible.

The museum, whose name means "love of learning," was founded in 1935 by women of the Philomathic Club. It has been located in the renovated Rock Island Depot since 1976. The collection includes artifacts and outstanding beadwork from many of the Southern Plains tribes. Probably the most impressive piece on display is the war bonnet of Chief Apeahtone, the last recognized chief of the Kiowa tribe. The headdress dates back to the 1890s and is decorated with seventy-two eagle feathers. The rest of the museum contains a variety of exhibits relating to early days in Caddo County. Allow about thirty minutes to tour the exhibits.

Southern Plains Indian Museum

Located on the east edge of Anadarko, just past the Hall of Fame, (405) 247-6221. Summer: Monday-Saturday 9-5, Sunday 1-5; Winter: Tuesday-Saturday 9-5, Sunday 1-5. Free. Handicapped accessible.

A showcase of the richness and diversity of Indian culture, this museum is small, but well worth the stop. The museum features both permanent and changing exhibits. Finest of the permanent displays are the ceremonial garments which are exhibited on life-size mannequins. The Oklahoma Indian Arts and Crafts Cooperative which shares the building is an excellent place to purchase outstanding examples of Indian arts and crafts. The Arts and Crafts Cooperative carries a number of interesting books, pamphlets and catalogues in addition to the artwork. You won't be able to miss the wall display of brilliantly colored beaded medallions created by present and past members of the cooperative.

American Indian Exposition

Held during six days in early August at the Caddo County Fairgrounds, N.E. 7th and Broadway, two blocks north of Highway 62 on the east side of town. For a brochure and schedule of events, call the Anadarko Chamber of Commerce or write the American Indian Exposition, P.O. Box 908, Anadarko, OK 73005. Entrance to the fairgrounds and arts and crafts exhibits are free, but there is a charge for the dancing, pageants and racing.

Indian dance competitions, arts and crafts, games, pageant presentations, dog and horse racing, parades–all this adds up to a great opportunity to enjoy Native American culture! Try Indian tacos, fry bread, corn soup, or Indian stew at the food booths. The entire town supports the Exposition; even attractions which are normally closed parts of the week are open during the event.

Holiday Celebration

Held from dark to ten p.m. nightly beginning the Tuesday preceding Thanksgiving through New Year's Eve. Located in Randlett Park. Go west on Central (Highway 62). Continue west on Central several blocks past Mission Street (where 62 turns south), you'll see signs to the Celebration. For a brochure, call or write the Anadarko Chamber of Commerce. Free.

This Christmas light festival started in 1995 with thirty-five light displays, and it's growing. Many of the displays have special significance to the donors; some exhibit a Native American influence. Hot chocolate and coffee are sold in the park. You can drive through, park and walk, or hire a horse and buggy when available.

Shopping

In the downtown area, there are a number of stores featuring Native American arts and crafts. You'll also find antique shops and pawn shops where you can pick up some great buys if you know what to look for. **The Gallery of Art** (115 N.E. First) and **Susan Peters Art Gallery** (116 W. Main) are good bets. **Lacer's Indian Store** (109 E. Georgia) is a pawn shop worth trying.

In the Vicinity

Horn Canna Farm

(405) 637-2327. Go west from Anadarko on Highway 9, then north on State Highway 58. You will come to a small intersection with a little utility building on the southwest corner (this is about a mile south of the old Alfalfa School). Turn west. The cannas are about a mile and a half down this road. Free.

A riotous Peter Max palate of reds, yellows, oranges, and pinks paints 110 acres with glorious color. The cannas bloom from July until they are harvested the first of October. In addition to commercially-available plants, the Snows (owners of the farm) also have a number of plants which are being evaluated for future production. You can even fill out an order blank for bulbs (which will be mailed to you at planting time) of your favorite colors for your own garden. There are no scheduled tours, so call ahead to make sure it is convenient to visit. The best time to see the cannas is in the early morning before it gets too hot.

If you are looking for activities along the way to or from the farm, try the nice city park in Carnegie and the

Horn Canna beauty.

Cheyenne

Kiowa Tribal Headquarters located one mile west of Carnegie on State Highway 9. The headquarter's small museum is open Monday-Friday 8-4:30. Admission is free.

Cheyenne

Before the opening of the area to white settlement, the territory around Cheyenne was surveyed and designated "F" County, with the Cheyenne site chosen as the future county seat. The area was opened to white settlement with the Run of 1892. Fifty hardy souls staked claims in town. They named the town for the local Indian tribe and renamed the county for a Texas statesman, Roger Mills.

Cheyenne is approximately 150 miles from Oklahoma City and 231 miles from Tulsa; go west on I-40 to Sayre, then north on Highway 283. Cheyenne Chamber of Commerce (405) 497-3318.

Black Kettle Museum

U.S. Highway 283 and State Highway 47, (405) 497-3929. Located on Highway 283, just south of the intersection with Highway 47. Tuesday-Saturday 9-5, Sunday 1-5. Closed Monday and legal holidays. It is advisable to verify hours; call either the Oklahoma Historical Society (405-521-2491) or the museum. Free; donations are appreciated.

The focus of this museum is the story of the Battle of the Washita. This battle (sometimes referred to by historians as a massacre) was lead by the infamous General George Custer. A number of tribes were wintering in the broad valley of the Washita, but it was the camp of sleeping Cheyennes led by Black Kettle which was surprised early on Thanksgiving morning in 1868, under the cover of a heavy snowstorm. Black Kettle, who had been noted for his peace-making efforts, and his wife were among those who were killed.

Other exhibits at the museum feature local celebrities including Oklahoma's own "Grandma Moses," artist Augusta Metcalfe, and Ziegfield Follies star Mignon Laird. The museum has a good selection of books for sale on the area. This museum is a good introduction to the history of this part of Oklahoma. Plan on about forty-five minutes.

If you want to visit the **Battle of the Washita Site**, be sure to pick up brochures at the museum. To reach the Site, go almost a mile west of the intersection of Highways 283 and 47, turn north on Highway 47A and drive another mile. Once there, you'll find a small pavilion overlooking the Valley. A historical marker describes the massacre and maps indicate troop movements. The site is scheduled to become part of a national historic area and is currently undergoing an archeological survey to determine the precise locations of encampments.

Roll One-Room School

Cheyenne City Park, Highway 283 South. (405)497-2455 or 497-3318. Cheyenne City Park is located on the south side of Cheyenne. Open Memorial Day-Labor Day, Wednesday-Sunday 1-4. and during the fall and spring, 9:30-1:30 when "class" is in session. Free. Handicapped accessible.

This white clapboard building was built in 1903 and operated as a school until 1943. In 1990 it was moved to Cheyenne City Park where it is used for hands-on history and as a museum. Area school children are given the opportunity to relive a 1910 school day at the school. Classes use the McGuffy Reader, "cipher," and learn the games children played years ago. Class is often in session on spring and fall weekdays; visitors are welcome to observe. For information or to schedule a group visit, call Judy Tracy (405) 497-2106. Even when the school is closed, you can still enjoy looking through the windows and reading explanatory material which is posted.

Roger Mills County Courthouse

Highway 283, State Highway 47. (405)497-3395. Monday-Friday 8-5. Free. Handicapped accessible.

The first courthouse in Roger Mills County was a tent. This was followed by several wooden structures. In 1907, a sturdy sandstone vault was built to protect county records, a good investment, because the courthouse burned in 1916. This same vault stands in its original spot, now sheltered by an overhang of the current courthouse. Just inside the courthouse is a statue called "Washita" created by sculptor Ernest Berke in 1984. This moving, life-sized bronze sculpture shows a naked Indian woman clutching her baby and a blanket and running in terror through the snow. Though representative of the Black Kettle Massacre, it is dedicated by the artist to "all the women who agonized and were killed in all wars." It is worth the short fifteen-minute stop.

Accommodations

Coyote Hills Ranch

(405) 497-3931. To get to Coyote Hills Ranch, go four miles west of Cheyenne on Highway 47. Look for the Coyote Hills sign, go north two miles, then west two more miles. Current prices start at $40 per person for bed and breakfast. Accommodations, meals and all activities cost $75 per person per night. Mostly handicapped accessible.

Your day at Coyote Hills starts with a hearty western breakfast. From there you may choose to go trailriding, hiking, or just sitting in a swing on the patio enjoying the smell of fresh air. Sight-seeing trips to area museums or galleries can be arranged. In the evenings, guests can be found singing around the piano, reading or watching videos in the library, enjoying special entertainers, or, if they are lucky, seeing an Indian powwow.

Horseback riding is a primary activity, but many other options exist. Activities vary with the weather, so bring appropriate clothes, particularly footwear. You might even put your rollerblades in the car; in case of rain, the social hall has occasionally been turned into a skating rink! There's lots of nature to see here; bring your guidebooks for bird-watching, identifying wildflowers, or scanning the night sky. This area is so far from competing city lights that it is known as a "dark spot," great for astronomy buffs. If you want to herd cattle or go hunting, owner Kass Nickels can arrange it. With all of these activities, it's no wonder that the hot tub is a popular spot for saddle-weary guests.

Most guests choose rooms in the territorial style hotel-bunkhouse with air-conditioning and baths, but tepees are available if you really want to rough it. Reservations are a must! Ask about family and group rates and special packages. The Thanksgiving weekend package is one of the most unusual, including traditional Thanksgiving fare, a solemn Cheyenne ceremony in remembrance of the Black Kettle Massacre, and an Indian dance.

Events

Oklahoma Wildlife Heritage Festival and Street Fair

Held the first weekend following Labor Day. Sites include the City Park, Cheyenne High School, and downtown Cheyenne. Call the Chamber of Commerce for information. Free. Handicapped accessible.

This festival is sponsored by the Roger Mills County Sportsmen's Club to promote appreciation of the environment, hunting and fishing, and to teach young people the proper use of firearms. It features 3-D archery, sporting clays, bird dog field trials, coon dog bench show and hunt, and muzzleloader shooting. No personal firearms or equipment are permitted; everything for these competitions is furnished. To compete, just show up and stand in line! Currently there is no charge for participation but this could change. Exhibitors' booths offer hunting and fishing information, and displays of taxidermy, art, clothes and knives.

Reenactors set up a Mountain Man Rendezvous in the City Park. They cook, camp and give demonstrations of skills used by trappers and explorers in the mid-nineteenth century. The **Street Fair**, sponsored by the Chamber of Commerce, includes a craft show, sidewalk sales, a quilt show, matinee movies, and children's activities. Parking is available at the City Park on U.S. Highway 283 on the south side of town, with a shuttle bus which runs to the other locations.

In the Vicinity

Blue Bird Gallery

(405) 983-2215. From Cheyenne travel north eight miles on Highway 283 to Highway 33, turn west and continue for 1/2 mile. Open daily 9-7.

Neil Schmidt was well known on the rodeo circuit for his daredevil riding, particularly

Roman riding where he stood astride two galloping horses. An accident ended his career and sent him in another direction. Now he and his wife operate a small art gallery. Eileen Schmidt paints scenes of the Antelope Hills area, and their son makes gold and silver jewelry. The Blue Bird Gallery is off the beaten path, but makes an interesting stop.

Clinton

Clinton is best known for its location on Route 66. From powwows to picnics, Clinton is small-town Oklahoma at its best. Downtown has benefitted from much refurbishing, including new awnings, store fronts and attractive pocket parks. On summer Saturday nights, McLain Rogers Park Amphitheater rings with music from pops to classics. Five productions a year are held at Southwest Playhouse, a 1930s WPA native rock building.

Clinton is located eighty-four miles west of Oklahoma City on I-40. For more information, call the Clinton Chamber of Commerce (800) 759-1397, or locally 323-2222.

Mohawk Lodge Indian Store

(405) 323-2360. One mile east of Clinton on Route 66. From I-40, take Exit 69 and go south. This will put you on old Route 66 through Clinton. Monday-Saturday 9-5.

The oldest Indian store in Oklahoma, this place is part museum and part shop. It began in 1892 in Colony, Indian Territory, where it was situated next to the Indian Agency. Missionaries of the Dutch Reformed Church, anxious to provide opportunities for the Indians to sell their wares, started the store and even published a catalog. Back then, a pair of fully-beaded moccasins sold for $2, compared to $260 today.

In 1940, the store was moved to its present

History for sale at Mohawk Lodge.

location on Route 66. Owner Pat Henry still sells or trades materials to the Indians and retails their finished products. New merchandise sits side by side with antiques, making this as much a history lesson as a shopping expedition.

Route 66 Museum

2229 W. Gary Boulevard, (405) 323-RT66 (7866). From I-40, take Exit 65; the museum is about 1/4 mile north on the west side of the street. Winter hours (Labor Day through Memorial Day): Tuesday-Saturday 9-5, Sunday 1-5. The museum is closed on Mondays and the first week of January. Summer hours: Monday-Saturday 10-7, Sunday 1-6. Adults $3, children ages 6-18 $1, children under age six are free. Handicapped accessible.

In this monument to "America's Main Street," visitors are ushered through the golden years of America's romance with auto travel. Even the architecture recalls the jutting tail fins of the '57 Chevy. Inside, the nostalgia starts with "The World's Largest Curio Cabinet," a hodgepodge of collectibles and souvenirs from the road. Subsequent rooms feature the history and culture of each decade on the road, including a 1928 International truck, mattress on top and dust storm behind, representing the Okies of the dust bowl era, and, from the fifties, a shiny replica of a diner. Oklahoma's history and the history of the "Mother Road" are intertwined, making this museum a good (and fun!) Oklahoma history lesson.

Ticket price includes an audio cassette tour. The cassette tape adds information and plays music of each era. Although the audio tour lasts only twenty-seven minutes, plan to spend more time if you want to see everything. At the end of the tour, an hour-long video entitled "Route 66, An American Odyssey" is shown. It will add to your enjoyment and understanding. The museum gift shop has an excellent supply of sourvenirs, books and videos about Route 66.

The **Route 66 Festival and Car Show** is held at the Route 66 Museum and McLain Rogers

Park in late June. Activities at the festival include rod runs, entertainment, special museum activities, and food booths. The highlight is the car show which includes cars of all vintages and styles from Model Ts to muscle cars.

Dining

Cafe Downtown Clinton 💲

502 Frisco, (405) 323-2289. Monday-Friday 9-4:30, Saturday 10-4:30.

With light lunches, occasional specials, soups and sandwiches, and wonderful homemade desserts, this cafe provides an intimate atmosphere with hardwood furniture and the original 1907 parquet wood floor. Glass windows and French doors provide access to the Gift Gallery next door.

Pop Hicks Restaurant 💲

223 Gary Boulevard, (405) 323-1897. Take Exit 69 from I-40 and travel west into Clinton. This is old Highway 66, which becomes Gary Boulevard in town. Open 24 hours a day. The only time the restaurant closes is from 2 p.m. Christmas Eve until the morning of the 26th of December. Even then, if you come down on Christmas morning, chances are you can get a free cup of coffee and a doughnut and shoot the breeze with the local farmers. Be aware that smokers reign supreme and the restrooms are not handicapped accessible. 🚫

Pop Hicks Restaurant, in business on Route 66 since 1936, is the best known restaurant in Clinton, and it is a tradition for those traveling the "Mother Road." Here you can enjoy some of the best of traditional American road food. The chicken fried steaks are legendary, and the desserts are always fresh. The luncheon specials which include salad bar, entree, potatoes, two vegetables, and dessert are very reasonably priced.

Shopping

Downtown Clinton, particularly Frisco Street which is one block south of old Route 66 (Business I-40), offers a variety of stores featuring antiques and unique gift items. The following lists the better know shops; hours vary.

Antique Mall of Clinton, 815 Frisco, (405) 323-2486. With over 12,000 square feet and more than fifty booths, this shop specializes in high-quality merchandise, antiques and collectibles. **Gift Gallery**, 500 Frisco, (405) 323-2289. This store carries the top collectible lines, including All God's Children, Tom Clark Gnomes, Maud Humphrey, and Cherished Teddies. **Southern Expressions**, 511 Frisco, (405) 323-6388. Elegant gifts and home accessories. **Southwest Interiors**, 521 Frisco, (405)323-3050. Interior design and decorating items. **Wood'n Things**, 604 Frisco, (405) 323-1300. Antiques, decorating service, and wreaths.

In the Vicinity

The Kachina Gallery

705 Main Street, Bessie, (800) 367-4094. Bessie is on S.H. 183A, one mile west of Highway 183, eight miles south of Clinton. Monday-Saturday 10-noon, 1-5. 🚫

This could be one of the last places you'd expect to see a high-dollar Santa Fe-style gallery, but here it is. Catering to serious collectors and corporate art buyers, owner Paul Armstrong's establishment is "a museum where everything is for sale." Armstrong specializes in Indian artifacts and antiquities, and he claims ownership of the world's largest collection of Kachinas, sacred Hopi Indian statues. Even if you don't have thousands of dollars to invest (but especially if you do), a stop at the Kachina Gallery is a great idea!

Foss State Park

West of Clinton, Park office (405) 592-4433, Marina (405) 592-4577. Leave I-40 at Exit 53, go north seven miles on Highway 44. Handicapped accessible bathroom facilities are located at the Cutberth, Mouse Creek and North Side campgrounds.

Foss Lake was created with the construction of the world's largest earthen dam, 134 feet high and three miles long. The largest lake in Western Oklahoma, it has about nine thousand acres of surface water and sixty miles of shoreline. The surrounding land was originally the home of several Plains Indian tribes, and it was later part of the Cheyenne-Arapaho Indian reservation. In many ways, the landscape still looks much as it did in those days. The lake is home to catfish, crappie, blue gill, walleye, and bass.

In addition to fishing, the park offers camping, boating, and picnic and playground facilities. There is a swimming beach (no lifeguard) and two group picnic shelters which can be reserved in advance. The marina sells fishing supplies, bait, licenses, and groceries, and it operates a covered fishing dock. The gift shop in the park office sells souvenirs and other gift items. Bring your camera and binoculars for spotting wildlife. In addition to the deer, raccoons, beaver, geese, and other birds around the lake, there is a small herd of buffalo adjacent to the park office.

Christmas in July is held the Saturday closest to the 4th of July. This celebration was started to honor the veterans of the Persian Gulf War; there are usually some military displays, arts and crafts booths, food booths, and boat races. In the evening there is always a lighted boat parade and fireworks. Bring sunscreen, bug spray and folding chairs. It's usually a long hot day; some folks come early to see the displays, then come back before dark for the evening activities. For information, write L.C. Murphy, P.O. Box 222, Foss, OK 73647.

Portside Cafe ($, $$), is known for its catfish and steaks and offers both indoor and out-door dining. It can seat ninety inside with an additional forty on the deck, and has an attractive turquoise and white exterior and a nautical theme throughout. The restaurant is located at 1 Marina Road, (405) 592-4490. Go west on the road opposite the park office. Take the first road to the right and travel toward Cedar Point, then turn right again and go toward the marina. Summer, daily 8 a.m.-9 p.m. Winter, closed on Monday. The restaurant does not accept reservations, but call ahead to check hours.

Cordell

The town's official name, "New Cordell," dates back to its move from the original townsite settled in the Land Run of 1892. The water supply at Cordell soon proved unsatisfactory; the town moved to its present location one mile southwest and became "New Cordell." The land had already been platted; two developers donated parcels of land to be used for the county courthouse, a real exercise in optimism, since the county seat had already been established at Cloud Chief. Voters approved the change in county seat in 1899, but it did not become official until 1904. The first courthouse was a two-story wooden building, which burned in 1909. Its replacement, designed by state capitol architect Solomon Andrew Layton, sits solidly and impressively on Courthouse Square, presiding over one of the most charming downtowns in Oklahoma.

Cordell is ninety-three miles west of Oklahoma City. Take I-40 west to Clinton, then travel south on U.S. Highway 183 (Exit 66). For helpful brochures and other information, contact the Cordell Chamber of Commerce, (888) CORDELL.

Courthouse Square

One block west of U.S. Highway 183, in the middle of Highway 152.

With its lovely columns and cannas, the courthouse is the focal point of the square. It is constructed right on the section line which became state Highway 152. Around the square, fake fronts are coming off old buildings, revealing their antique charms. Don't miss the **drug store** on the southwest corner of the square. Since the building was built shortly after statehood, it has always housed a corner drug store with a soda fountain. If you're just passing through, allow yourself a

Elaine Warner

Cordell's stately courthouse.

couple of hours to take the walking tour, to explore interesting shops and buildings, and to enjoy a cool drink. Be sure you have a copy of the **walking tour map** from the Chamber of Commerce; it's full of interesting information and old photos of the buildings.

Dining/Shopping

Opera House Antique and Craft Mall

225 East Main, (405) 832-5557. Monday-Friday 11-5:30, Saturday 10-5:30.

In addition to many booths with a wide variety of antiques and collectibles, check out the original pressed tin ceiling in this 1907 building. The building originally housed a department store downstairs and an opera house on the second floor.

Grapevine Galleria and Tea Room $

114 East Main (405) 832-2200. Open Tuesday-Friday 10-2 or by appointment. No credit cards.

You will find antiques, gifts and a tea room in this 1902 building with its original tin ceiling. Light lunches and heavenly, homemade desserts are served in a charming setting. Note the attractive mural of old-fashioned ladies enjoying tea in an idyllic setting.

Accommodations

Chateau Du Rhe

(405) 832-5564. In Cordell, from Highway 183 and 14th Street, go west to Grant Street, turn north to the "private drive" signs on the west side of the road (about 3/4 mile). $75-100 depending on room. Ask about corporate rates. Call for reservations and deposit policy. No credit cards. Handicapped accessible.

Built in 1984, this large Country French-style home promises real comfort and quiet. Owner Chloe Du Rhe McLerran was talked into opening a bed and breakfast by her grown children. Their comments such as "Mom, coming home is like staying at a resort!" gave her the idea. You'll enjoy the hot tub and the other activities such as horseback riding and trap shooting. A typical breakfast consists of fruit, breakfast casserole and sweet rolls. Dinner can be provided if advance arrangements are made. There are even bedtime snacks, just like at mom's!

Grape Arbor Inn Bed and Breakfast

114 East Main, (405) 832-2200. $75 plus tax per night per room. Reservations are a must. A 50% deposit is required at the time of booking. Credit cards are not accepted; not handicapped accessible.

Conveniently located above the Grapevine Galleria and Tea Room, the Grape Arbor Inn has two rooms, the Rose Room and the Garden Room, each with a double bed. There is a shared bath. For an extra charge, a cot can be set up. The large living area provides a great view of the square. The kitchen is stocked with refreshments, and a full breakfast is provided in the tea room. Decor is traditional, with antiques, fine linens, and lace appointments.

Events

Rural America Celebration

Held in mid-April at the Courthouse Square. Contact Main Street Cordell (405) 832-5888 for information. Free. If you want to enjoy all the activities, you might want to spend the night. Lodging in town is limited; call early for reservations at one of the two local bed and breakfasts.

This is a celebration of small town America, past and present. Activities begin Friday night with a chuckwagon supper and live entertainment. On Saturday, new and antique farm equipment is on display, crafters are encouraged to demonstrate their skills, particularly old-fashioned ones like soap-making or rope-making, gospel choirs entertain, and 3-on-3 basketball is played on the square. Displays of modern telecommunication technology show how Americans can have big city jobs and small town life at the same time.

Pumpkin Festival

Held on the Courthouse Square in early October. For a brochure, call (888) CORDELL. Free.
    Celebrate autumn at the Pumpkin Festival which features a pumpkin cooking contest, giant pumpkins, arts and crafts, fun contests, a flea market, and new model auto displays. Start the day with a pumpkin pancake breakfast in the Community Center, located at the northwest corner of the square. Preregistration is required if you want to enter the Great Bed Race or the cooking contest. At night there is usually a rodeo.

Duncan

    Duncan is named after William Duncan, a tailor and trader, who settled in the area in 1879 with his wife who was a citizen of the Chickasaw Nation. In 1889, the Chickasaws were given allotments, and Mrs. Duncan chose hers where the Rock Island Railroad was due to come through. She later divided the land and sold lots. The official founding date of the town is 1893. Both the Chisholm Trail and the Old Military Trail came through the area. Earle P. Halliburton started his now-famous oil well cementing service here in 1924. Since then, the fortunes of the town and the company have been entwined.
Duncan is ninety miles south and west of Oklahoma City, and two hundred miles south and west of Tulsa. Take I-44 (H.E. Bailey Turnpike) to Chickasha, then U.S. Highway 81 south to Duncan. Duncan Chamber of Commerce & Industry (405) 255-3644.

Earthway Herb Farm

(800) 708-4372. By appointment only. No admission charge for individuals and small groups; larger groups need to inquire. There may be a charge for special events.
    This farm is five acres of display beds, with herbs, ornamental grasses, desert southwest plantings, a moon garden with all plants in silvers, grays, and whites, and a koi pond, a miniature rose garden, and a Jackson & Perkins rose garden. Though outstanding in summer, even in winter the grasses are attractive. To see the gardens or to find out about any of the occasional special events, call the toll-free number.

Simmons Center

800 N. 29th Street, (405)252-4386. If traveling south on U.S. Highway 81, turn west at Plato Street on the north edge of town. (Wal-Mart is on the southeast corner). Go one mile to 29th Street and turn south. The Simmons Center is about one and one-half miles south of the intersection of 29th and Plato. Indoor facilities: Monday-Friday 6 a.m.-10 p.m., Saturday 8-8, Sunday 1-6. The playground is open from daybreak until 11 p.m. Visitors can purchase day passes to the recreation area or temporary weekly memberships. Day-pass $5; no charge for Centennial Park. Prices for cultural events vary. Handicapped accessible.
    The Simmons Center complex contains both recreational and cultural facilities. The recreation area includes a fully-equipped health-club-type gym and swimming pool, and children's pool and recreation area. Centennial Park is a fantastic outdoor playground located nearby, which was designed with the needs of children of all abilities in mind. The **Theatre** is the home of the American Music Festival (see below) as well as other musical and stage events. Call (405) 252-2900 for a schedule of events.

Stephens County Historical Society Museum

U.S. Highway 81 and Beech, (405) 252-0717. Thursday-Sunday 1-5. Free. Handicapped accessible.
    Located in an old armory in Fuqua Park, this museum is larger than the average county historical museum. Through its extensive collection, visitors leave with a real sense of the personal history of the area. The Boomer Room showcases pioneer life from 1877-1920. Displays include Indian artifacts, Chisholm Trail memorabilia, and replicas of a covered wagon and a surrey. A schoolroom and a dentist's office have been recreated. The Sooner Room highlights the history of Halliburton and the oil industry.

Antique Marketplace and Tea Room $

726 W. Main, (405) 255-2499. Tea Room: Monday-Saturday 11-2:30; Antique Mall: Monday-Saturday 10-6. Handicapped accessible.

Tucked inside the Marketplace, the **Tea Room** is decorated in rich colors accented with white lattice. Table centerpieces change with each season. Specialties include homemade muffins, chicken salad and chocolate fudge cake. They also serve sandwiches and other items.

Over forty dealers carrying everything from furniture and jewelry to vintage clothing are housed in the **Marketplace**. The original occupant of this building was the Dixie Department Store. Present owners have saved the original wood floors and turned the mezzanine into a gift gallery.

Main Street in downtown Duncan is home to a number of antique and specialty stores including: **Antique Mall** (formerly Penny Farthing), 920 West Main, (405) 255-2552. This large, two-story shop features furniture, Fostoria, dolls, flow blue and Vaseline glass, and jewelry. **The Loft**, 916 West Main, (405) 252-3942. American and English antiques, accessories and interior design and furniture. **Serenity Day Spa**, 1205 W. Main Street, (800) 708-4372. Call for appointments. This spa offers facial treatments, aromatherapy facials, deep cleansing facial, body treatments including aromatherapy salt glo (sea salt and aromatherapy oils massaged over the entire body for exfoliation,) herbal body wraps, hand facials and foot facials, and theraputic massage with aroma therapy massage oil. Serenity staffers create custom-blended makeup foundations. They also carry essential oils. Call for brochure on treatments and prices, and a list of their essential oils. Clients are treated to specially-blended herbal teas which are for sale along with green and black teas. Other Duncan specialty shops include: **Brass Rail Antiques**, 5051 N. 81 Highway, (405) 252-7277. Antiques, collectibles, gifts, furniture, collectors' books, and refinishing shop. **The Ginger Jar**, 1609 N. 81 Highway, (405) 252-2329. Antiques, furniture, pictures, mirrors, and silk flower arrangements.

Lindley House Bed and Breakfast

Since this facility was not opened when this book went to press, it cannot be properly evaluated. The plans for conversion of this two-story, 1940 English Country-style house into a bed and breakfast establishment sound very promising. Owners and innkeepers-to-be Danny and Bonnie Talley hope to open in late summer 1997. Call (405) 255-1719 for information.

American Music Festival

Mid-July salute to American composers at the Simmons Center. For information, call (800) 255-0909. Evening performances $15-$20, afternoon performances $20, children's concert $2.50. Series packages are available at a discount price.

This four-day fest features classical and popular American music and premiers a newly-commissioned work each year. As the festival builds, it is attracting more concert-goers and more big-name entertainers. In the past, guest artists have included guitarist Mason Williams and trumpeter Al Hirt. Popular American classical works like Barber's "Adagio for Strings" share the stage with big band compositions or Rogers and Hammerstein favorites. There's something for everyone's musical taste at this exciting and growing festival!

Addington

Addington is listed in John W. Morris' book, "Ghost Towns of Oklahoma," but the 150 people who live there will argue about that. Building began in Addington in 1892, when the

Rock Island Depot was completed, and trains started coming through. Addington became the largest cattle shipping point in Oklahoma; cattle were lined up for six miles to be shipped to Kansas City or Chicago. A landmark on the Chisholm Trail and the highest point on the trail north of the Red River, Monument Hill is three miles east of the center of town. The Rock Island Railroad, which owned land in other areas, had little interest in the future of Addington, and the town eventually dwindled. Ruins of the old jail can be seen behind the pecan store. *Addington is the official Pecan Capital of Oklahoma and is located seventeen miles south of Duncan on U.S. Highway 81.*

Cow Creek and Company

(405)439-6489. On U.S. Highway 81. Thursday-Saturday 10-5:30, other times , by chance or appointment. Call ahead; the hours are erratic. It's hard to get good help in a ghost town!

Although many people stop to browse the antiques, the big draw is the fragrant "cow patty" Rosemary Price serves on lovely china. Don't misunderstand—these cow patties are light, moist, and chocolate, topped with chocolate syrup and pecans, a not-to-be-missed treat. Enjoy this special dessert in the Addington Room, an area decorated with the teller window from the old bank and other memorabilia.

Hastings

Founded in 1901, Hastings is another of those once-thriving little Oklahoma towns which have fallen on hard times. In 1904, Southwest Academy, forerunner of Oklahoma Baptist University, was located here. In 1905, an all-brick opera house was built, and by 1908, the population had grown to one thousand.
Today, 164 people live in Hastings, which is located eleven miles northwest of Waurika on State Highway 5.

Peachtree Plantation

Located on Highway 5, (405) 963-3311 or www.peachtreeplantation.com. Tuesday-Thursday 10-5, Friday-Saturday 10-8. The downstairs area is handicapped accessible.

Located in a 1906 building (the only original two-story business structure in Hastings), Peachtree Plantation is another example of Oklahomans' love of their homes and a desire to "bloom where we're planted." This philosophy makes it easier to understand the finding of a place like this in such a tiny community. Tanya and Clarence Shook, who refurbished the old building, carry fine art items, photo art, hand-thrown pottery, unusual crafts, collectibles, and hand-spun yarn and woven items. Tanya offers custom-designed handmade vests, coat vests and ponchos which she has prepared from the fleece to the finished product. Chickasaw, Osage, Cherokee, and Comanche items are available. Where else could you find stained glass stepping stones for your garden? Upstairs is an art gallery and studio for art classes.

Marlow

Named after the Dr. Williamson Marlow family, this town was originally a settlement known as Marlow's Grove. Dr. Marlow's five sons are the source of much controversy and legend in the area. Depending on one's perspective, they were either excessively spirited or just plain outlaws. An incident in Texas resulted in four of the brothers being accused of cattle rustling; this incident was the basis for a scene in the movie, "The Sons of Katie Elder." The brothers, having been jailed, were being transported for trial when they were ambushed. Two of the brothers were killed. The surviving brothers were leg shackled to the dead brothers and escaped by amputating the feet of their deceased siblings. The men were eventually exonerated, and the members of the ambushing mob were sent to prison. The Marlow football team is known as the "Outlaws" in honor of the Marlow brothers.
Marlow is ten miles north of Duncan on Highway 81. Marlow Chamber of Commerce (405) 658-2212.

Giuseppe's $$

201 W. Main, (405) 658-2148. One block east of U.S. Highway 81 on Main. Tuesday-Saturday 11-9. Handicapped accessible through a special entrance.

Denise and Brian DiCintio opened this wonderful Italian eatery in the spring of 1996. It is housed in the old State National Bank building (circa 1911) and retains the wood floors, some of the bank furnishings, and the vault, which is used as a gift area. Cloth napery and Italian opera music add to the ambiance. In addition to traditional Italian favorites, entrees featuring emu and ostrich are included on the menu.

Outlaw Days Annual Ambush

Next-to-the-last Saturday in September in Redbud Park. For information, call the Chamber of Commerce. Free. Redbud Park is four blocks east of the intersection of U.S. Highway 81 (Broadway) and State Highway 29 (Main) on Main Street.

Beginning with a parade and ending with a street dance, this is an all-day party; bring lawn chairs and plan to spend the day. The parade features everything but the kitchen sink: floats, horses, bands, pets, bicycles, and crammed Volkswagens! Continuous entertainment ranges from blue grass music to cow patty bingo. There's a reenactment of the Marlow Brothers Ambush, a farmhand Olympics, arts and crafts, and food booths.

Rush Springs

Originally located six miles east of the present town and called Parr, Rush Springs changed its name in 1892 and its location in 1893. The move was motivated by the location of the railroad line. The name came from one of the springs on the Chisholm Trail. The town bills itself as the Watermelon Capital of Oklahoma, a nickname adopted by thousands of people who come to the annual Watermelon Festival.

Rush Springs is nineteen miles north of Duncan on Highway 81.

Watermelon Festival

Held the second Saturday in August in Jeff Davis Park. For information about the festival, call (405)476-3277; for inquiries about the arts and crafts fair, call (405) 476-3255. From Highway 81, turn east on State Highway 17. The park is on the highway (which in town is known as Blakely or Main Street). Free.

Whether it's listening to music, taking part in the seed-spitting contest, looking at the entries for largest melon, riding carnival rides, or strolling through the large arts and crafts show, you'll enjoy much activity at the festival. There's free watermelon from noon to 8 p.m. Concession stands offer a variety of food and drink. With about 25,000 people converging on this tiny town on one day, you might want to park downtown and take the free shuttlebuses to the park; they stop at every corner and run every fifteen minutes. Bring your lawn chairs–there's plenty of shade, but seating is limited.

Waurika

Originally called Peery then Moneka, Waurika was established in 1890. In 1912, it wrested the county seat status away from the town of Ryan, ten miles south. During the years of the cattle drives, the lush buffalo grass around Waurika made it a welcome respite on the Chisholm Trail. When the Rock Island railroad arrived, Waurika became a busy rail center and crew-change point.

Waurika is twenty-six miles south of Duncan on Highway 81. For more information, contact the Chamber of Commerce, (405) 228-2081.

Chisholm Trail Historical Museum

Located just east of the intersection of Highway 70 and 81, (405) 228-2166. Saturday 10-4, Sunday 1-4. Free. Call ahead to verify hours or to make a special appointment. Handicapped accessible.

This museum contains a very focused collection highlighting the history of the famed cattle trail. Traced by the Delaware scout Black Beaver in 1861, the trail was originally a military trail; it was also the quickest route for driving Texas cattle to the railhead in Abilene, Kansas. Trader Jesse Chisholm was never a cattleman, but he was such a well-known figure on the trail that it eventually was called by his name. Expansion of the railroads south through Indian Territory in the 1890s spelled the end of the famous cattle drives. Artifacts and photographs in the museum tell the story of the trail, and they give a picture of life in the early days of Waurika.

Duncan Area/Elk City

Moneka Tea Room (\$) and Antique Mall

Located just west of the intersection of Highways 70 and 81. (405) 228-2575. Tuesday-Saturday 9:30-5:30; lunch is served between 11:30 and 2:30. Handicapped accessible on first floor only.

This is a real triple-play—a place of historic interest, a place to shop, and a place to eat—all in one. Constructed almost a century ago, the building is the only known structure of its kind still in existence. It was built as a boarding house for railroad crews. Rumors of ghosts cling to the old place; the rumors are fed by the story of a robber who was killed here while trying to rob the railroad men.

Several of the rooms are filled with antiques; upstairs is a small art gallery, and there is the tea room. Sandwiches, soups and salads are served, with portions available to suit the daintiest (or heartiest) appetite. If you're a real antique buff, allow plenty of time to see everything. In addition to this building, there is a 13,000 square foot building full of goodies next door.

Elk City

Lift a glass of frosty brew to Elk City, which, for a brief time, was named Busch. When the St. Louis brewery failed to build an expected plant in the town, the name was changed to Elk City after nearby Elk Creek.

Elk City is approximately 120 miles west of Oklahoma City on I-40. Elk City Chamber of Commerce (800) 280-0207.

Ackley Park

U.S. Highway 66 and Pioneer Road. Traveling from Oklahoma City, take Exit 41 from I-40 and go west through Elk City on old Route 66. The park and the Old Town Museum are on the west side of town. The only restrooms in the park are in the Aquatic Center, which is closed in the winter.

For years, travelers on Route 66 made this park a favorite stopping place, either for picnicking or just getting out of the car. With its attractive pond, old mill, playgrounds, and trees, this stop is still a good idea. The small pond offers fishing for children and senior citizens. There are ducks for feeding or watching and, on weekends and summer evenings, miniature golf and a mini-train are big attractions. There's also an aquatic center, tennis court, and fenced playground area.

Old Town Museum

U.S. Highway 66 and Pioneer Road (next to Ackley Park), (405) 225-2207. Tuesday-Saturday 9-5, Sunday 2-5. Adults \$2.50, children under age twelve are free. The main floor of the museum and several of the Cowtown buildings are handicapped accessible (others may involve several steps).

The main part of the museum complex is located in an authentic turn-of-the-century home. Several rooms are decorated in the style of the Victorian period. The toys in the child's bedroom are particularly appealing. Elsewhere in the museum, you'll find a variety of exhibits reflecting the lives and interests of the people in the area.

The Old Town Museum.

One resident contributed a campaign button collection. Former Miss America and Elk City native Susan Powell donated her crown, dress, trophy, and earrings from her 1981 triumph. Upstairs is the Beutler Brothers Rodeo Hall, housing memorabilia and equipment donated by the Beutlers, rodeo cowboys and producers of rodeo stock. Adjacent to the museum is the "Cowtown." Buildings include both original and replicated structures. You'll find a one-room school, livery stable, chapel, depot, and a one-room house (the first wooden home in Elk City). If the buildings are locked, please ask in the museum. Allow at least an hour to see the exhibits in the museum and to look around the old town.

Country Dove Gifts and Tea Room 🅢

610 West Third, (405) 225-7028. Located on old Route 66 on the west side of town. The gift shop is open Monday-Saturday 9-5, the tea room serves lunch from 11-2, but desserts and drinks are available after lunch hours. Not handicapped accessible.

If you're a chocolate lover, this place is for you! The tea room has gained an international reputation for its French silk pie, a concoction consisting of a pecan crust with a creamy chocolate middle topped with real whipped cream and chocolate shavings. Of course, you can order other items, from soup and sandwiches to a daily special. The chicken avocado sandwich is a particular favorite with many patrons.

The tea room and gift shop are located in a house which was built in 1924. The atmosphere is genteel with floral wallpaper, lace curtains, and fabric tablecloths. It could be described as "a ladies' place," but many a man will brave the decor for a piece of chocolate pie! The gift shop carries inspirational books, pictures, collectibles, and floral decor items.

In the Vicinity

Erick

"King of the Road" Roger Miller was born in Erick, the next-to-the-last town before the "Mother Road" leaves Oklahoma. Erick also boasts of actor, singer, and songwriter Sheb Wooley and songwriter Michael Smotherman. A museum focusing on the 100th Meridian boundary and other, more local interests is located in Erick's old National Bank building. Open by appointment only, the museum is intimate and interesting. For more information about the 100th Meridian Museum contact (405) 526-3433 or 526-3221. The annual **Honey Festival** is held on the second Saturday in November.

Erick is about thirty-five miles west Elk City. Erick Chamber of Commerce (405) 526-3505.

OK Honey Farm

(405) 526-3759. Take Exit 5 (Honeyfarm Road) from I-40. The farm is a quarter of a mile north. Monday-Saturday 8-6, Sunday 1:30-5:30. January and February open by chance or appointment. Free. Group tours are available if you call ahead. The facilities are handicapped accessible.

This is no slick tourist spot–it's an old-fashioned tourist spot. Although its history dates back to just before the end of the Route 66 era, OK Honey Farm is reminiscent of the kind of mom and pop shop you could have found on the old highway. The North family produces all flavors of honey from common clover to chocolate and pecan. They also make candles, lip balm, body lotion, and furniture wax from bee by-products! In her spare time, Alvina North writes books. Depending on the time of year, you may see bee activity, candlemaking, or some other product being made. There's a picnic area and playground under the trees.

Cal's Country Cooking 🅢

(405) 526-3239. On the northeast corner of I-40 and State Highway 30 at Exit 7. Daily 6 a.m.-10 p.m. Closed Thanksgiving and Christmas. Handicapped accessible.

Save your calories; this is better than when both your grandmas competed at Sunday dinner! Originally on Route 66, the restaurant moved to I-40 in 1979. The constant is Cal Rogers, owner and chef since 1946. Everything is made from scratch–no fudging by using the term "fresh baked"; Cal and his crew promise "homemade" from start to finish. Ham hocks and beans, fried catfish, roast beef, chicken fried steak–it's all here and it's wonderful. Don't leave without buying some of Cal's cinnamon rolls or bread.

Hinton

Early in 1902, the Chicago, Rock Island, and Pacific Railroad bought a plot of land to establish a new town on a spur of the railroad from Enid to Lawton. Handbills were distributed exclaiming, "WE WANT YOU AT THIS NEW TOWN!" On June 14, 1902, city lots went on sale. The first worship service in Hinton was held in an unfinished business on Main Street, and worshipers sat on planks furnished by the lumberyard, atop beer kegs loaned by a saloon keeper. This northern Caddo County town of 1233 people was named after the family of the wife of developer Ivan G. Combs.

Red Rock Canyon State Park

South of Hinton, (405) 542-6344. The park is about sixty miles west-southwest of Oklahoma City. Take I-40 west to the U.S. Highway 281 exit to Hinton. The park entrance is about a mile south of town on the east side of the road. Free; there are charges for camping, swimming, and reserved picnic facilities.

Driving across a flat section of Oklahoma, be prepared for a surprise as you enter the park. A steep, winding road takes you down into the canyon which, while probably not on the main trail, was historically a spot for repairing and regrouping for travelers on the California Trail. There are several walking trails, picnic facilities, and a pool in summer. The Rough Horsetail Trail should not be missed. The Rough Horsetail, which grows here, is also known as "Scouring Rush," and it is related to plants that originated before the dinosaurs. In addition, you're apt to see animal tracks, beaver-chewed trees, and a variety of birds. This short trail, less than a quarter-mile long, is located at the north end of the park and is one of the first things you'll see when you reach the canyon floor. Over thirty species of trees have been identified in the park, and, over the course of a year, at least forty-five different kinds of birds can be seen.

Red Rock Canyon is a good spot for picnicking and camping. For a wonderful time to spot birds or wildlife, plan a breakfast picnic. Rock climbers often practice rappeling on the canyon walls. Most facilities are first-come, first-served, but group facilities can be reserved. The park is a good place for fall "leaf peeping," but check with park headquarters for peak time. Some of the eastern species in the canyon peak up to two weeks earlier than native species on the uplands. On your way to or from the canyon, enjoy the scenic drive (particularly in fall) along State Highway 152 between Binger and Minco.

Lawton

August 6, 1901, was the birthday of Lawton, with 1,422 town lots being auctioned for a total of $414,845. Many of the people bidding for land were hoping to find gold in the nearby Wichita Mountains. Today, Lawton is the fourth largest city in Oklahoma. Lawton has an active arts council and a full slate of arts activities, including both community and university theater and the Lawton Philharmonic Orchestra. It is the hub of an area containing fascinating museums, natural beauty and wildlife, and places of historic importance and interest. Lawton Chamber of Commerce (800) 872-4540.

Lawton is ninety-eight miles southwest of Oklahoma City on I-44 (H.E. Bailey Turnpike); it is 214 miles southwest of Tulsa.

Fort Sill

Located just north of Lawton, (405) 442-5123. To see the post, look for the Key Gate Exit (Exit 41) from I-44. Daily 8:30-4:30. Closed December 25-26, January 1-2. Free. Partially handicapped accessible. ★

Construction of Ft. Sill was authorized by the Treaty of Medicine Lodge in 1869. There are actually three distinct posts at Ft. Sill. The earliest post was built around a quadrangle with limestone houses and cavalry barracks on the sides. There is a **museum complex** in the Old Post area (the largest assemblage in the Army's museum system) which includes the **Old Post Headquarters** (1870), the **Geronimo Guardhouse** and other historic structures.

The 1911 post featured brick and stucco construction, while the 1935-36 post was built in Spanish style. Prominent Native Americans are buried in two cemeteries on the post. People still bring tributes to the grave of Geronimo, who is buried in the Apache cemetery.

Several special events are held during the year, including the **Candlelight Christmas Stroll** through the Old Post Quadrangle, and **A Tea in Time**, a recreation of an old-time entertainment featuring authentic recipes of the chosen period. The biggest event is the **Heritage Fair**, held on Memorial Day weekend. This educational experience is designed to showcase traditional skills and lifestyles of the military, civilian, and Native American peoples of the nineteenth century. Occasionally, there are military parades and ceremonies. Call ahead for information on scheduled events.

You can pick up a map for a **self-guided tour** at the Visitors' Center in the Old Post area, or from one of the marked map kiosks. Souvenirs are available in the Gift Shop in the Old Post Corral. For unusual handicrafts, visit the Prairie Crafters Gift Shop just south and east of the Old Post Chapel. All items are made by military and DOD employees family members and retirees. The shop is open Monday-Saturday from 10-5.

There are so many interesting things here, plan at least half a day to see it all. There's a fast food restaurant on the post at the corner of Currie and Sheridan. (Sheridan is the road which passes through Key Gate. Continue west to Currie.) If you bring a picnic, check at the Visitors' Center for the location of appropriate picnic spots.

Mattie Beal House

1006 Southwest 5th Street, (405) 353-6884. From I-44, take Lee Boulevard west to 5th Street. Turn north onto 5th and proceed to Summit Avenue. The home is on the northeast corner. Open the second Sunday of each month, 2-4, and occasionally other Sundays. Adults $2, children ages twelve and under $1. Limited handicapped-accessibility.

Almost a year after winning her land in the 1901 lottery, Mattie Beal married lumberman C.W. Payne. In 1907, they began work on the Neoclassic Greek Revival mansion which was reminiscent of Mattie's grandmother's plantation home in southern Missouri. The house has an unusual curved door with beveled glass, impressive dark woodwork, and a stained glass window depicting the Wichita Mountains. As interesting as the house is, the most important reason to visit is to hear the story of Mattie Beal and her contributions to the city of Lawton.

Museum of the Great Plains

601 Ferris, (405) 581-3460. Approaching Lawton on I-44 from the north, watch for the museum signs. When I-44 turns west, do not turn, but continue straight ahead (on 2nd Street) to Ferris. Turn west to the museum. Museum is open Monday-Friday 8-5, Saturday 10-6, Sunday 1-6. Trading Post is open Wednesday-Friday 8:30-4:30, Saturday 10:30-5, Sunday 1:30-5. The trading post is closed on Mondays and Tuesdays. Adults $2, children ages seven to eleven $1, children six and under, free. The fourth Sunday of the month is free for all visitors. Handicapped accessible. ★

With its extensive exhibits and outside areas, this museum is one of the best in the region, and new construction is making it even bigger and better. Exhibits show a history of the area from 11,000 years ago into this century. The giant woolly mammoth skull complete with huge curled tusks and the information on the discovery of the Domebo Mammoth Kill Site are particularly interesting. Turn-of-the-century history is depicted through recreations of early shops and businesses.

The museum was fortunate to secure the Tingley collection, one of the largest collections of twentieth-century Plains Indians artifacts. This collection came from Tingley's Indian Store which operated in Anadarko for almost a century. The museum's expansion will give more display space to this 3200-item treasure trove.

On the grounds of the museum are farm tools and implements, a train engine, and a replica of a trading post. The museum's **Red River Trading Post** was built to illustrate the buffalo robe and fur trading activity which was important to the area in the 1830s and '40s. Over one thousand logs were used in construction, with every effort made to make the post authentic. One of the most unusual features is the fur press, a weighted log contraption which was used to compress bundles of hides into bales suitable for transport on pack animals.

Spring and fall encampments feature reenactors demonstrating skills and crafts of the mid-1800s, making this a special time to visit. Contact the museum for exact dates. Plan at least an hour to see everything; you could easily spend more time than that. The museum has a small, well-stocked, gift shop.

Percussive Arts Society Museum

701 Northwest Ferris, (405) 353-1455. The museum is west of the Museum of the Great Plains. Look for the sign; the building is tucked behind McMahon Auditorium. Monday-Friday 8-5, Saturday 10-6, Sunday 1-6. Adults $1, children eleven and under free. Handicapped accessible. ★

If you can bang it, shake it, or hit it together, you'll find it here. Over 250 musical instruments from at least fifteen countries are on display. There are six hands-on nooks where you can actually play instruments, from an African thumb piano to an ocean drum. In addition to unusual instruments, there are instruments belonging to famous percussionists, for example, a broken drumstick belonging to Buddy Rich and the xylophone played by Haskell Harr, author of the most widely-used percussion instruction series. There is also a research library which contains periodicals and books on the subject and copies of solos that are a good source of inspiration for percussion students. The museum also sponsors occasional concerts.

This is one of the most unusual museums in Oklahoma. Even if you don't think you're interested, go anyway. The displays are attractive, and the urge to strike the ten-foot wind chime which hangs from the ceiling is irresistible. Be aware that the noise can reach ear-shattering levels when the museum is crowded. During the school year, there are likely to be groups between the hours of 10 and 3 on weekdays. Plan accordingly! The time you spend will depend on whether you are a casual visitor or a serious percussion student, but allow at least thirty minutes for a visit.

Wichita Mountain Wildlife Refuge

Northwest of Lawton, (405) 429-3222. From I-44 (H.E. Bailey Turnpike), take exit 45 and drive seven miles west on State Highway 49. Refuge: daily, daylight to dark. Mount Scott Road: 9 a.m. until one hour after sunset. Visitor Center: Wednesday-Monday 10-5:30, closed Tuesdays and major holidays. Handicapped accessible restrooms are located in the Visitor Center and at several of the campsites, including the Doris Campground. ★

In 1901, the Wichita Mountain Wildlife Refuge (then called a Forest Reserve) was designated as a refuge for the almost-extinct American Bison (buffalo) and other wildlife species. Of the sixty thousand acres in the Refuge, approximately one-third is open to the public. There are self-guided tour maps available at map kiosks at park entrances. Entering from the east on State Highway 49, watch the signs for the road up **Mount Scott**. The panoramic view, which is especially dramatic at sundown, is more than worth the three-mile drive. Sighting herds of bison is one of the most popular activities for visitors. Texas longhorns, deer, elk, and wild turkey can also be seen. The flora and fauna of the area is diverse, as the geography shifts from prairie to high plains and mountains.

A new, twenty-two-thousand-square-foot **Visitor Center** is located at the intersection of State Highways 115 and 49. In addition to outstanding and informative exhibits, there is a map which gives current information concerning wildlife sightings. Located nearby, **Doris Campground** has a number of sites for tent, RV, or group camping. Several sites are designed specifically for handicapped-accessibility. Fees range from $6-10. A trip to the Refuge can consist of as little as a drive-through to longer stays for picnicking, hiking, fishing, and general or back country camping. Contact the park for specific

Sarah Taylor

View from Mount Scott.

areas and regulations. The Refuge staff also offers some wonderful programs and tours. These include an **eagle watch**, a **wildlife tour**, a **bugling elk tour**, and a **historical sites tour**. Stargazing, wildflower and fall foliage walks, an aquatic ecosystems walk, a wilderness hike, and a waterfall hike are also offered. Call the park for the full schedule.

Year-Round Volksmarch

Contact people with the Holy Family Walkers Volksmarch Club are Mrs. Margo Pulrang (405) 581-1244 and Mr. George Snyder (405) 357-2930.

The present start point is the Ramada Inn, 601 N.W. 2nd Street, (405) 355-7155. You may start anytime between dawn and three hours before dusk any day of the year; you must finish the walk before dark. Anyone may walk free; if you want an award or an award with IVV credit, there is a small fee. All walkers must have a start card which will go in the volksmarch box file upon completion of the walk. This is a ten-kilometer trail (6.2 miles) which goes through shaded residential areas and parks. The trail is mostly on relatively flat terrain. Do call ahead to make sure the course has not been changed. All you need are comfortable shoes and clothing. The Ramada offers corporate discounts to volksmarchers.

Dining/Shopping

Pisano's Italian Restaurant $$

1320 N.W. Homestead Lane, (405) 357-4033. The restaurant is one block south of Cache Road (U.S. Highway 62) on Homestead Lane west of Sheridan. Where NW 26th goes north from Cache Road (U.S. Highway 62), Homestead Lane goes south. Lunch 11-2, dinner 5-10, Sunday 11-9. Cappuccino/wine bar 4-close. This restaurant is smoke free and handicapped accessible.

The restaurant features an Italian menu, aged charbroiled steaks, and an Italian bakery. The chef's specialty dessert is cheesecake; he makes over sixty different kinds. The decor is elegant with white tablecloths, classical background music, and beautiful floral arrangements.

Volkssport—Activities for Everyone
by Elaine Warner

Looking for an inexpensive activity for the whole family—one that gets you outdoors, gives you a chance to see some interesting Oklahoma sights, provides exercise without exhaustion? Volkssporting could be the answer.

Beginning in Germany, volkssport (people's sport) came into being as an antidote to competitive athletics and as a way to promote health and fitness for everyone. Although many sports are included, the most popular form of volkssporting is walking. Also called volksmarches or volkswalks, they take place on ten to twelve kilometer courses (six to seven and a half miles). There are both scheduled walks, typically one-day events, and year-round walks.

Scheduled events usually allow participants to start anytime within a two to four hour time frame and travel at their own pace to finish before closing time. Year-round walks are even more flexible, being limited only by daylight hours.

Volksmarch courses may include historical areas, residential areas, or wilderness trails. Each course will be rated by difficulty and information on handicapped accessibility will be provided.

Though Volkssporting is noncompetitive, avid fans often try to attend as many events in as many places as possible. There are even companies which organize tours especially for volkssporters. Both a national and an international organization promotes the sport, with member clubs in Oklahoma City, Tulsa and Lawton.

For more information on volkssporting in Oklahoma, call Al Heberlein (405) 843-5731 (no collect calls, please). The American Volkssport Association has recorded information about upcoming events at (800) 830-WALK. The recording lists only events during the current month. For more information, including a list of area clubs, write AVA Headquarters, 1001 Pat Booker Road, Suite 101, Universal City, TX 78148, or call (210) 659-2112.

Volkswalking provides a good time for family interaction away from interruptions. This is a great way to explore Oklahoma—from the ground up and at your own pace!

Central Mall

200 C Avenue, (405) 248-1353. Monday-Saturday 10-9, Sunday 12-6.
This is a large indoor mall with major department stores, restaurants and an arcade.

Cache Road Square

38th Street and Cache Road, (405) 355-3020. Hours vary by store.
This outdoor shopping area includes a variety of stores and eateries.

Events

Arts for All Festival

Three-day fling in Shepler Plaza City Park held the first weekend in May. For more information call (405) 248-5384. The park is on the south side of Gore Boulevard between 4th and 5th Streets. Free. Handicapped accessible.

Arts for All, Inc. is a nonprofit umbrella organization which provides funding for five major arts organizations in the Lawton community. The Festival features a juried art show which includes painting, sculpture, jewelry, pottery, stained glass, and some fine crafts. Entertainment is ongoing and features both professional and amateur performers. Food booths offer a wide variety of choices, from international treats to good barbecue.

International Festival

September celebration in Library Plaza, 4th and B in downtown Lawton. (405) 581-3470. From I-44, take Business 281 into Lawton. Turn west on Gore, then south on 4th Street. Free. Call for a schedule of events.

The Festival is a delight for the senses, with sights, sounds and smells of artwork, and entertainment and food from all over the world. There are two stages offering entertainment and special concerts and street dances on Friday and Saturday nights. Ft. Sill has many visitors from other countries, enriching the local cultural scene. This is a chance to sample international cuisine and to visit with representatives from many nations.

Octoberfest

Held in early October at the Great Plains Coliseum, 920 S. Sheridan Road. For more information call (405) 353-3082. From I-44 to Lee Boulevard (State Highway 7), turn west to Sheridan Road, then north. The Coliseum is on the east side of Sheridan, just south of the railroad tracks. Adults $2, children under eighteen are free.

Beer and bratwurst, ja vohl! This event is sponsored by the German-American Club of Lawton to preserve and share traditions, fun and food. Expect lots of music, dancing, and great German food.

In the Vicinity

Apache

Like Lawton, Apache was born with the Lottery of 1901; it was named for the Apache Indians. Before the turn of the century, as the frontier was moving west, there were many clashes between the U.S. Army and the Apaches who lived in what would become Arizona. After the death of Chief Cochise in 1874, Geronimo became prominent in continuing the struggle to maintain a traditional way of life. With the surrender of Geronimo in 1886, the government began the Apache equivalent of the "Trail of Tears," first moving the Indians to Florida, then Alabama, and finally to Ft. Sill in 1894. The Apaches remained there until World War I, when they were given the choice of moving to a New Mexico military post or receiving land in southwest Oklahoma. About ten families chose to remain in Oklahoma. Known as the Fort Sill Apaches, the group has its headquarters in Apache.

Apache is about seventeen miles north of Lawton on U.S. Highway 281. Apache Chamber of Commerce (405) 588-2181.

Apache Historical Museum

Evans and Coblake (Apache's main intersection), (405) 588-3392. June and July, Monday-Saturday 9-5, the rest of the year, Monday-Friday 1-5. Free. Handicapped accessible.

The museum is housed in a 1901 building which was originally the First State Bank of Apache and is now listed on the National Register of Historic Places. The collection is a hodge-podge of items of local interest, including many items donated by Ft. Sill Apaches. Plan on twenty to thirty minutes for a quick tour.

"Mo" Betta Clothing Company

104 E. Evans, (800) 259-9222. Store: Monday-Saturday 9-5, Factory: Monday-Thursday 7:30-5:30.

Here's where you'll find those shirts that Garth Brooks has made famous. Buy one off the rack, or have one custom made. The store also carries some women's and children's items and accessories. If you call ahead, you can enjoy a walk-through, twenty-minute tour of the factory and watch the shirts being produced.

Medicine Park

The town was designed as a resort community in the early 1900s. At one time, it bustled with politically-prominent, fashionable, and even notorious visitors from Oklahoma and Texas. Most of its buildings were constructed of cobblestones, giving the architecture a fairy-tale twist. There are interesting changes taking place in Medicine Park. New places are opening, and a golf resort is in the planning stages, giving hope that Medicine Park will attract a new generation of visitors to this old town on beautiful Medicine Creek.

On the eastern edge of the Wichita Wildlife Refuge, Medicine Park is about five miles north of Lawton. From I-44, take the Highway 49 exit. Medicine Park Chamber of Commerce (405) 529-2825.

The Old Plantation 𝟓-𝟓𝟓𝟓

(405) 529-9641, located a block and a half north of the post office. Tuesday-Saturday 12-9, Sunday 1-7. Bring cash; credit cards are not accepted. Handicapped accessible. ⛔

The restaurant is in the old hotel which was built in 1906. The decor is an eclectic blend of historic memorabilia and knick-knacks. Owners "Grandma" and Rex Leath are best known for serving plate-covering steaks. Prices vary, depending on whether you want a sandwich or a full meal.

The Riverside Cafe 𝟓, 𝟓𝟓

(405) 529-2626. Located across from the post office. Thursday-Monday 11:30-2:30 and 5-9. Reservations are suggested. Handicapped accessible.

Owners Candace and David McCoy have big dreams for Medicine Park, and the Riverside Cafe is the beginning. The restaurant has a big patio and deck for summer outside dining overlooking Medicine Creek. Inside, the white walls, decorated with Candace's murals, and the Saltillo tile floors give one a feeling of summer year-round. The menu includes steaks, salmon, chicken, and some wonderful heart-healthy items like a pasta pizza and a fresh-steamed veggie platter. Occasionally, there is live entertainment.

Meers

At one time, three hundred people lived in Meers, most of them hunting gold in the Wichita Mountains. Now the population is four, and all that remains of the town is the conglomeration of buildings known as "The Meers Store."

From the intersection of I-44 and Highway 49 just north of Lawton, travel west to Highway 115 then go north a few miles to Meers. The "town" is located on the edge of the Wichita Mountains Wildlife Refuge.

The Meers Store.

Lawton Area/Weatherford

The Meers Store $

(405) 429-8051, Monday-Friday 8 a.m.-9p.m., Saturday-Sunday 7 a.m.-9:30 p.m. Handicapped accessible with some difficulties. Credit cards are not accepted.

The decor is early ramshackle, and the service is sometimes that way, also. The lines are often long, thanks to its popularity as a tour bus stop. In spite of these things, everyone needs to try a Meersburger at least once. There are other items on the menu, but the Meersburger is legendary. This plate-sized longhorn burger is big enough to share; splitting one also leaves you with room for delicious cobbler.

Weatherford

The land around Weatherford was opened to settlement in a land run in 1892. The town was established in 1898 with the arrival of the Choctaw, Oklahoma, & Gulf Railroad; it was named for U.S. Marshal William J. Weatherford, who came to the area at the opening. Weatherford is the home of Southwestern Oklahoma State University which was established in 1901 as a teachers' training school.

Weatherford is seventy miles west of Oklahoma City on I-40, and 179 miles southwest of Tulsa. Weatherford Chamber of Commerce (800) 725-7744.

General Thomas Stafford Museum

3000 Logan Road, (405) 772-6143. The museum is housed in Weatherford's airport, not-so-coinciden-tally named the Thomas P. Stafford Airport. Exit I-40 on Airport Road on the east side of Weatherford. Go west on the access road to Lyle Road. Go north to Logan Road, then east to the airport. Daily 8 a.m.-6 p.m. Free. Handicapped accessible.

Weatherford citizens are justifiably proud of astronaut Thomas P. Stafford, who grew up here. The displays at this museum focus almost as much attention on Stafford's personal history as on his glory days as an astronaut. It's interesting to see samples of his fourth grade penmanship, to read comments from his teachers, and to see how a little boy from western Oklahoma grew up to fly higher and faster than almost anyone in the world. In the room dedicated to his NASA career, there's a video which tells his whole story, including his space flights. Stafford commanded Apollo 10, the final dress rehearsal for the lunar landing. He and Gene Cernan left the mother ship and piloted the lunar module to within fifty thousand feet of the moon's surface. From this vantage point, they scouted for landing sites.

Stafford Museum.

Stafford honored our state by naming a range of mountains "Oklahoma Hills." His final flight was as commander of the Apollo-Soyuz program. It's fun to relive the glory days of the space program, and this museum does it well. The number of hours and days the museum is open make it easy to visit, just be sure to plan enough time to really enjoy the exhibits.

Central Oklahoma

Chandler

With its historic downtown district set atop a hill, Chandler is one of Oklahoma's most scenic towns. Founded in 1891, Chandler boasts a beautiful Main Street, with several attractions nearby.

From Tulsa drive west approximately sixty-six miles on I-44 (the Turner Turnpike), and from Oklahoma City travel about forty-eight miles east to the Chandler exit. A more scenic, leisurely route is enjoyed on Route 66 from either Tulsa or Oklahoma City. Chandler Chamber of Commerce (405) 258-0673.

Museum of Pioneer History

717 Manvel (the town's main thoroughfare), (405) 258-2425. Open Monday-Friday 9:30-4. Free.

The Museum of Pioneer History is housed in a beautiful, turn-of-the-century stone building with arched windows. Artifacts and exhibits include early-day drug store fixtures, a dentist's office, an old-time post office, and an early telephone switchboard. While at the museum, inquire about their interesting children's programming that includes history lessons using marionettes.

NOTE: **Antique shopping** and other stores are located near the museum. If you need refreshments after shopping, try the bakery located next to the museum. It is easily identified by its medieval-style banner showing pictures of baked goods.

Read Ranch

Located approximately five miles west of Chandler on Route 66. Well-placed road signs make the ranch easy to find. (405) 258-2999. Open Tuesday-Saturday at 10 a.m. and Sunday at noon. Admission is free; activity costs vary.

Opened in 1992 as a 240-acre guest ranch, Read Ranch includes a petting zoo, a pavilion, longhorn cattle, bison, ponds, bunkhouses, and RV sites with electrical hookups. Western activities abound, including individual guided trail rides and group hay rides. There are moonlight rides, breakfast rides, chuck wagon rides, and haywagon and trolley rides. The grounds are available for individual campers, or city slickers can participate in the City Slicker Special— two days of camping out; all you bring is a bedroll! Read Ranch will help with any kind of celebration–birthday parties, weddings, and company outings. Every Labor Day, Read Ranch hosts a **Talent Contest and Music Jamboree**. Musicians, trick ropers, fiddlers, cowboy poets, and others compete for prizes. Read Ranch offers the very "best of the old west."

Southern Ranch Hunting Club

Located east of town, just north of Highway 66. Call Dean or Terri Caton at (918) 377-4226 or (405) 258-0000 for more information.

At this hunting club, sportsmen shoot clay pigeons that are thrown over natural cover and through trees to simulate the flight of game birds, or shoot at clays bouncing over the ground, simulating the race of a rabbit. Guests can participate in organized European pheasant drives or hunt the game bird of the season over the 1500 acres that comprise the club. Certified instruction is available, and safety standards set by the National Sporting Clays Association are followed. This club is open only by reservation. Overnight guest accommodations are available in the lodge which sleeps sixteen. A restaurant and bar are also located on site.

Dining

P.J.'s Bar-B-Que $, $$

1420 S. Manvel, (405) 258-1167. Open Monday-Tuesday 11-4, Wednesday-Saturday 11-7. Closed Sunday.

A favorite of many Route 66 aficionados, P.J.'s has served BBQ for over eleven years. Try their ribs, beef brisket sandwiches, and famous potato salad as you enjoy the old gas station ambiance.

In the Vicinity

Davenport

Be sure to notice Davenport when driving scenic Route 66 between Chandler and Stroud. Settled in the land run that opened the Sac and Fox lands, the town is named for the community's first postmistress, Nettie Davenport. On the Saturday before Mother's Day in May, the town remembers Nettie and the other pioneer settlers of the area with **Nettie Davenport Day**. A parade, banquet, music, and an arts and crafts show are all part of the celebration. *Located on historic Route 66 between Stroud and Chandler. Davenport Chamber of Commerce, P.O. Box 66, Davenport, 74026 (918) 377-2241.*

Dan's Pit Bar-b-que

Located on Route 66, (918) 377-2288. Open Monday-Thursday 10-9, Friday-Saturday 10-10, and Sunday 10-3.

Hungry travelers can eat their fill at Dan's Pit Bar-b-que. Owned by John Vandever for the past fifteen years, this restaurant boasts some of the best food around. It is listed among the top ten BBQ establishments in *The Great American Bar-b-que Book*, written by Dr. Rich Davis of K.C. Masterpiece fame, keeping company with other famous BBQ restaurants such as K.C. Masterpiece in Kansas City and Angelo's in Fort Worth. House specialties include ribs and chicken fried steak, with most customers choosing their meals from the buffet. With a seating capacity of almost 100, Dan's welcomes groups, including bus tours.

Chickasha

Chickasha is a child of the railroad, the Rock Island to be precise. It started in 1892 when a shack town grew up around the tracks. The land for the town was later purchased from an Indian family, and Chickasha began to grow. By 1907, streets were paved, and substantial houses were being built. The establishment of Oklahoma College for Women in 1908 made Chickasha a center of learning and culture. The school, now called the University of Science and Arts of Oklahoma, has an enrollment of approximately 1,700 students and remains a source of pride to the community. This city is now well-known for its continuing fascination with transportation (namely automobiles), and the beautiful "Festival of Light," held during the Christmas holidays.

Learn more about the area at the **Grady County Historical Society Museum**, 415 Chickasha. Open limited hours on Saturday (2-4 p.m.) and on the third Sunday of each month or by appointment, the museum can be contacted at (405) 224-0442 or (405) 224-6480. *Chickasha is forty-seven miles southwest of Oklahoma City on the H.E. Bailey Turnpike (I-44). Chickasha Chamber of Commerce (405) 224-0787.*

Antique Automobile Club Museum of Transportation

18th and Chickasha, (405) 222-4222. From I-44, take Exit 83 west into town. Turn south on 8th to Chickasha (one block) then west until the street dead-ends in Borden Park. Saturday-Sunday, 2-4. Free. Handicapped accessible.

This is a small collection made up of the "pride and joy" autos of the club members. At any given time, there will be about twelve cars displayed, many of which are still driven in local parades. The oldest car, a Stanhope White Steam Carriage (circa 1900), was actually made by the White Sewing Machine Company. The rarest specimen is a 1942 Ford Super Delux Coupe. Not many were made because Ford shut down production in February, 1942 due to World War II. In addition to the cars, there are license plates, hubcaps, radiator badges, and other collectibles.

Golf

River Bend Golf Club

(405) 222-1995. Take Exit 83 off the H.E. Bailey Turnpike (I-44), then go east across the Washita River Bridge. Turn north on Arena Road, go one mile, then travel back west over the turnpike. Watch for signs. Call ahead for tee time. Pull carts are not available. All-day green fees are weekdays $12.14, weekends $15.64. Carts (eighteen holes) are $8.36/rider. A weekday senior discount is given. Tee times are accepted for holidays and weekends beginning on Tuesday mornings of the week before. No metal spikes are allowed.

Opened in 1995, this public course features an eighteen-hole South course and a nine-hole North course. The courses are bordered on three sides by water and have water hazards (ponds) throughout the course. The courses offer a combination of flat and hilly terrain with irrigated Bermuda fairways and bentgrass greens. The South course (6482 yards) has a par of 72, a slope of 126, and a USGA rating of 72.8; the North course (3125 yards) has a par 36 and is not otherwise rated. Golfers find these courses challenging, particularly when playing with a strong north or south wind. Amenities include a driving range, a practice green, a small pro shop, and a limited snack bar.

Events

Bob Lowe Memorial Toy Tractor Show

Held the second weekend in February in the Community Building at the Grady County Fairgrounds located on Highway 62, 1/4 mile west of I-44 (take Exit 83). Call the Chickasha Chamber of Commerce for more information. Adults $2, children under 12 $1.

About sixty vendors from all over the United States will display museum quality farm toys for viewing, sale and trade. Like garage sales, avid folks go early to grab the best deals.

Montmartre Festival

Held the first Thursday in April on the USAO campus. Call public relations at USAO (405)224-3140, for more information. Coming from the north on I-44, take the second Chickasha exit, Turn north on Highway 81, then west on Grand Boulevard. The entrance to the oval at the university is at 17th Street. Free admission. Handicapped accessible. Restrooms are available in nearby campus buildings.

Prepare to be amazed as sidewalk artists produce fantastic works in chalk, charcoal or pastel on 5'x6' squares of pavement. Artists have from 9 a.m. to 1 p.m. to complete their projects. Judging results follow. Recently over a hundred artists displayed their skills. Walk around and watch the beautiful works-in-progress. There is usually food available.

Check the weather before you go. If it is raining, the Festival will be canceled until the next year! This is an activity you can enjoy either as a spectator or participant. Anyone junior high age and up can enter. There are two judging categories: junior/senior high school students, and above high school level. Artists can use only temporary media such as chalk or pastel. Designs must be suitable for public display, with the proposed design being submitted for approval before beginning. To participate, meet with festival organizers in front of Trout Hall at 8:30. There is a $5 entry fee.

Fall Antique Auto Swap Meet

Held the first weekend in November at the Grady County Fairgrounds located a quarter of a mile west of I-44 on Highway 62 (I-44 Exit 83) For a flyer or other information, call (405) 224-OKLA between 6 and 10 p.m. The meet is open from dawn to dusk. Free.

Everything here is auto-related from complete autos–restorable autos, parts of autos, you name it. There are also booths with road memorabilia, diner memorabilia, drive-in theater memorabilia, and any kind of collectibles you can imagine.

This is the largest swap meet of the year, but Chickasha has several smaller ones including the Horseless Carriage Swap Meet (cars and parts from the first fifty years of the auto) and the Muscle Car Swap Meet. Contact the Chamber of Commerce for more information.

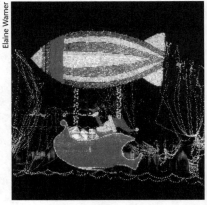

Festival of Light

Shanoan Park. Take Exit 83 from I-44 then follow the blue and white signs with candle symbols that are posted along the way. This roundabout way to get to the park is necessary to avoid traffic backups on the interstate. Call (405) 224-0787 for a complete schedule of events. Held Thanksgiving through New Years Eve nightly 6-11. Free.

The highlight of this spectacular Festival is the lighting display in Shanoan Park. Over a million

Festival of Light.

and a half twinkling lights adorn trees and create picture displays including fourteen-foot camels, Santa in a blimp, and the Grinch, among others. The bridge across the lake is turned into a glittering fantasy span; it has even been utilized for holiday weddings. There's a gift shop where hot chocolate, cider, dessert, and souvenirs are for sale.

Because of the popularity of this lovely festival, start early. Crowds are more manageable the first and last weeks of the Festival; weeknights are less crowded than weekends. Be sure to get a brochure ahead of time; there are many events such as concerts, plays, and home tours going on in town during the Festival. If you have a group of twenty-five or more, you can arrange for a home-style dinner in the historic bathhouse or at various churches. Call by August to secure a reservation.

Parking is scarce, but it is worth the effort to get out and walk around. Serious photographers should take a tripod and cable release for photos; flash just doesn't work. After seeing the park lights, use the map provided upon entry to the park to find Woods Lane and Maple Lane. These usually have some of the most fantastic home decorations in town, and they're close and easy to find.

Accommodations

Campbell-Richison House Bed and Breakfast

1428 Kansas Avenue (405)222-1754. Taking Exit 83 from I-44, come west on Choctaw (U.S. Highway 62) to 12th Street. Turn south two blocks to Kansas, then west to the home. Current rates are $35-55 not including taxes. This is a "no smoking" home and it is not handicapped accessible. Reservations and a deposit are required. No credit cards. Member of the Oklahoma Bed and Breakfast Association.

Personable hosts David and Kami Ratcliff will welcome you to their lovely three-story prairie-style home which was built in 1909. Kami is a registered dietician; be prepared for wonderful homemade breads and careful attention to any special dietary requirements you might have. She also loves gardening and fills the house with cut flowers during blooming season. The Ratcliffs currently have one large room with private bath and two smaller rooms with a shared bath. David is quick to point out the red oak pocket doors between the parlor and dining room and the stained glass, just two of the original features of the spacious old home. Breakfast is "Continental plus," served in the family dining room or on a tray in your room.

In the Vicinity

Ken's Steak and Ribs $$

215 East Main Street in Amber, (405) 222-0786. Amber is about eight miles north of Chickasha on Highway 92. Thursday-Saturday 5-9, Sunday 11-2. No credit cards accepted.

Known as one of the best steakhouses in Oklahoma, Ken's features great food, little atmosphere, no menus, lots of hospitality, and crowds! This "don't-miss" restaurant seats 120, but serves 400 to 500 people a night. Choices are limited to 8 or 10 ounce top sirloin grilled over an open-flame mesquite fire, three or five rib dinners, smoked chicken, and brisket. The salad bar isn't fancy, but is always fresh and includes Watonga cheese, fried okra and beans. Come early if you don't want to stand in line!

Edmond

Originally named Summit Station when established in 1887, Edmond was a coal and watering station for the railroad, due to its location at the highest point between the North Canadian and Cimarron Rivers. After the 1889 Land Run, Summit Station was renamed Edmond, after Edmond Burdick, a railroad agent. In that same year, the progressive town built the territory's first public school house and first church, St. John the Baptist Catholic Church.

Located at the edge of the crosstimbers, the thriving city of Edmond is growing at a phenomenal rate; the city offers shopping, golf, elegant and casual dining, live theater, and beautiful parks. Settled between Oklahoma City and Guthrie, Edmond is an excellent place to experience all that central Oklahoma has to offer. ⚠

Edmond is approximately fifteen miles north of Oklahoma City and may be reached by U.S. Highway 77 (Broadway Extension) or by I-35. If you are traveling the approximately 115 miles from Tulsa, exit north onto I-35, or continue on the turnpike (in Oklahoma City named the Kilpatrick Turnpike), and take the Edmond exit north. For more information contact the Edmond Conventions and Visitors Bureau at (405) 341-2808.

Arcadia Lake

9000 E. 2nd, (405) 396-8122. From I-35, exit onto 2nd Street and go east. Approximately three miles on the south side of U.S. 66 (2nd Street) is the entrance to Central State Park, and further east on U.S. 66 is the Project Office Building. Central State Park and its three campgrounds are open daily year-round. Edmond Park, Spring Creek Park and Scissortail Campground are open seasonally. Seasonal park operations hours and dates are subject to change. Check at the entrances for posted dates and times. Daily entrance fees are Pedestrian/Bicycle $1; Vehicle $6; Watercraft $6; Motorcycle $2. Camping fees range from $8-15.

Visitors enjoy hiking, camping, picnicking, boating, fishing, swimming, bicycling, skiing, bird watching, disc golfing, bird watching, or just lounging at Lake Arcadia. With 679 acres of developed park area and 1820 surface acres of water, there is plenty of room for fun.

At the lake, there are many shaded areas with tables near the water or in the woods for picnicking. Mountain-bikers may utilize a ten-mile multiuse trail, and hikers will appreciate not only the ten-mile trail but also many small, marked trails. Anglers use boats or the twenty-six miles of shoreline as they attempt to catch fish from the stocked waters. Among the fish species are bluegill, redear sunfish, channel or blue catfish, and largemouth bass. Swimming areas and beaches are located in Edmond Park, Central State Park, and Spring Creek Park. Children under the age of thirteen must wear a U.S. Coast Guard-approved flotation device of the proper size and fit when they are in the water. (No lifeguards are available, and beaches are open during daylight hours only.)

Edmond CVB

Arcadia Lake is ideal for sailing.

Watercraft is welcome on the lake. Jet skis, wet bikes, wave runners, and/or similar motorized craft are restricted to the water near Spring Creek Park. Sailing enthusiasts may participate in the annual **Arcadia Lake Regatta**, sponsored at the lake by the Edmond Area Chamber of Commerce during the first weekend in August.

The state's only thirty-six hole disc golf course is available in Spring Creek Park. The course works on a first come, first served basis, and no extra fee is charged.

For best viewing, wildlife lovers are encouraged to arrive early in the day. Of special interest to bird watchers is the Bird Watching Blind located in Central State Park and the migratory Bald Eagles that winter at the lake from about November until mid-March. For a special treat, join the park's naturalist and other bird enthusiasts at the annual **Eagle Watch**, held the first weekend after New Year's Day.

Camping throughout the park is on a first come, first served basis. RV camping with full hookup is available in Central State Park. Showers are available throughout the parks, with Central State Park's Cottonwood Campground showers being the most accessible. Seniors will appreciate the quiet Scissortail Campground with 38 wooded sites and no beaches and boat docks.

Of special interest to families are the playgrounds available in several park areas, and the popular nature programs offered for groups of children preschool aged and up. Call two weeks ahead to schedule.

Edmond Historical Museum

431 South Boulevard, (405) 340-0078. Take 2nd Street west from I-35 or east from Broadway Extension to Boulevard. Turn south on Boulevard. Follow Boulevard two blocks to the museum, which is found on the west side of street. Wednesday-Friday 10-4; Saturday 1-4. Free; donations are appreciated. Handicapped accessible.

This museum provides an historical overview of Edmond and surrounding areas through well-organized and interesting exhibits. Located in a 1936 armory building listed in the National Register of Historic Places, the museum also includes a comprehensive research library with much archival material about Edmond's early days.

In April, the museum offers an **89er Homestead Fair**. Through special hands-on exhibits, children and adults learn what life was like during Oklahoma's pioneer days. Admission for this event is $1. Traveling exhibits such as the world-acclaimed Anne Frank Exhibit and educational programs are offered periodically. Call ahead to get a schedule.

Hafer Park

9th Street and Bryant Avenue, (405) 359-4630. Exit I-35 at 15th Street and travel west to Bryant Avenue, or from Broadway Extension, turn east onto 15th Street and continue to Bryant. At Bryant, turn north and continue about 1/2 mile to 9th Street. The entrance to Hafer Park is on the east.

This lovely, tree-filled city park offers extensive walking trails, well-maintained playgrounds, a flower garden, a kids-only fishing pond, and pavilion rental for group gatherings. Many city events are held here, including the **Edmond Blues and Jazz Festival** on Memorial Day weekend and **summer concerts** featuring a variety of local and regional bands. Music ranges in style from big band to alternative rock. Call the Parks Department for a schedule.

Oklahoma Shooting Sports Complex

24100 N. Hiawassee, (405) 396-2661. Take I-35 to 2nd Street (Highway 66), travel east seven miles to Hiawassee Road. Go north on Hiawassee for 3.5 miles. The complex is on the east side of the road. Wednesday-Sunday (and Monday holidays) 10 a.m.-dusk. Monday and Tuesday are available for groups by reservation only. The cost for fifty targets is $14; for 100 targets, $26. Senior citizen discount is given. Ask about family and individual memberships. Dress as if you are going to play golf. Reservations required only for Saturdays. Call for information about guided upland game bird hunts.

The "birds" are always flying at Oklahoma Shooting Sports Complex. Begun in England, this sport simulates field bird hunting. Participants walk through woods and shoot at clay targets released from electric traps. Each station simulates a unique hunting situation. The course changes every month—occasionally twice a month. Although only three years old,

Oklahoma Shooting Sports has been ranked in the top ten sporting clay fields in the United States for the number of targets thrown.

No permits are required here, but eye and ear protection are. A pro shop offers not only protective gear, but also shooting accessories, ammunition, and loaner guns. Other amenities include a log cabin conference/meeting room available for groups, a snack bar, and practice ranges for shotgun, outdoor pistol, rifle shooting, and 3-D archery. Oklahoma Shooting Sports offers individual shooting technique instruction by appointment only.

Shakespeare in the Park

Held at Hafer Park, 9th Street and Bryant Avenue, (405) 340-1222. See "Hafer Park" entry above for directions. Once you enter the park, follow the signs to find the amphitheater. Season runs from May through August. All performances are held Thursday through Sunday beginning at 8 p.m. Season tickets may be purchased for $20 (for four tickets to be used for any performance); regular tickets may be purchased for $6 at the gate. Children ages twelve and under are free. Students and senior citizens are $5. Special rates are available for groups of ten or more.

Since 1985, Shakespeare in the Park has thrilled audiences of all ages with performances of classic Shakespearean stories. Held in a natural amphitheater, the plays are performed by semiprofessional actors. There is never a dull moment on stage as the classic plays such as *Henry IV* and *As You Like It* come to life under the trees of Hafer Park.

Expect to walk down the paved and lighted path to the theater area. Take lawn chairs or blankets to sit on, or rent chairs for a nominal fee; bring a picnic or purchase the snack items that are available. If you like to sit close to the stage, arrive early. However, no matter where you choose to sit, you will be able to hear the lines; a new speaker system has helped acoustics. Performances are held regardless of the weather, and they are cancelled only at the last minute because of extreme circumstances. A few of the troupe members perform around the state throughout the year; call for a schedule.

University of Central Oklahoma Theater

Mitchell Hall on the University of Central Oklahoma campus, (405) 341-2980, ext. 3375. Exit I-35 onto 2nd Street and travel west to University Drive, or from Broadway Extension go east on 2nd Street to University street. Go north and find Mitchell Hall on the east side of University. Show times vary; call ahead to request a schedule of events. Adults $8, senior citizens $3, students from any other school (college, high school, etc.) $2, UCO faculty and students free. Season tickets are available.

The UCO Theater offers everything from drama, dance, and opera performances to instrumental and vocal concerts by guest artists, students, and faculty of the university. *Fool for Love*, written by Pulitzer Prize-winning playwright Sam Shepherd, *Gypsy*, and *The Merchant of Venice* by William Shakespeare are a few of the plays and musicals presented in the past. It is advisable to call before taking children; productions may contain material suitable for adults only.

UCO is starting a new program called **Senior Adult Theater**, designed for interested seniors (with or without prior experience) to participate in drama courses and theatrical performances. For more information, contact Dr. Roberta Sloan at 341-2980, Ext. 5511. UCO also offers low-cost classes for seniors in their **"Summer at Central"** program held in June. Classes range from participatory art to an introduction to computers. In the past, day trips to interesting Oklahoma museums and areas have been included. Call (405) 341-2980, ext 2413 for a schedule.

Golf

Coffee Creek Golf Course

4000 N. Kelley, (405) 340-4653. From Oklahoma City, take the Broadway Extension to the Memorial West exit. Travel west a short distance, then turn north on Kelley and continue six miles to the southeast corner of Coffee Creek. Open daily from dawn til dusk. Green fees are $16.30 to walk and $25.95 to ride from Monday to Thursday, and $20 to walk and $29.65 to ride from Friday to Sunday. Call for tee time about one week in advance for weekdays and at 7:15 a.m. on Monday morning prior to the weekend you want to play. Be prepared; golf pros say that weekend play is often *booked within an hour of that time. Proper golf attire is required.*

Coffee Creek's front nine offers long, gently rolling hills; the back nine is more wooded. Two lakes and a creek add beauty and difficulty to the course. The course has tight, well-manicured fairways and excellent greens with few sand traps. This public course was voted one of the Top Ten Golf Courses in Oklahoma by Golf Digest.

The par 70 course has a length of 6,693 yards, a course rating of 71.5, and a slope rating of 129. Amenities include a snack bar and restaurant, a driving range, and a practice area.

Kickingbird Golf Course

1600 E. Danforth, (405) 341-5350. From I-35, travel west on Danforth, or from Broadway Extension travel east on Danforth to Bryant. The facility is located on the southeast corner of Danforth and Bryant. Open from dawn til dusk. NOTE: Kickingbird Golf Course will be closed for major improvements until about October, 1997.

Green fees: Daily until 4 p.m. $13.50 plus tax; from 4-6 p.m. $11. Twilight, junior and senior rates given. Cart rental is $17 for eighteen holes, $10 for nine holes.

Built in 1971, this eighteen-hole golf course owned by the City of Edmond is heavily wooded with scenic ponds and creeks. The par 71 course measures 6834 yards in length. USGA rating is 71.4; slope rating is 127. Facilities include a restaurant, snack bar, pro shop, clubhouse, driving range, bunker practice area, and more. Call one day in advance for weekday tee time and one week in advance for weekends.

Edmond is known for outstanding golf.

Dining

Bellini's $, $$

801 E. Danforth, (405) 348-8033. Exit I-35 onto Danforth. Go west for approximately 2.5 miles to Bellini's on the north side of the street. Open everyday at 11 a.m. Monday-Thursday, closes at 10:30 p.m. Friday and Saturday, closes at 11:30 p.m., and on Sunday, closes at 9 p.m. Sunday brunch is served from 11-2:30. No reservations are needed. Ample parking. Handicapped accessible. The original Bellini's is located at the Waterford Complex, 63rd and Pennsylvania Avenue.

At Bellini's, take a trip to Italy without boarding a plane. Dine inside in the casually-elegant atmosphere created by an open brick oven, granite-tiled floor, and wrought iron accents, or enjoy a beautiful Oklahoma evening outdoors on the tree-lined patio. Either way, you will savor the experience. Feast on Italian-specialty or traditionally-topped pizzas, sandwiches, salads, steaks, chicken dishes or Bellini's special recipe lasagne. Frittatas, omelets, and traditional breakfasts are available during their special Sunday Brunch.

Cafe 501 $, $$

501 S. Boulevard, (405) 359-1501. From I-35, take 2nd Street west to Boulevard. At Boulevard, turn south and travel three blocks to the restaurant. From Broadway Extension, turn east on 5th Street and go to Boulevard. Monday-Saturday 7 a.m.-10 p.m., Sunday 9 a.m.-3 p.m. Extra parking is available immediately across the street on the east side of Boulevard. Handicapped accessible.

Since opening in 1995, Cafe 501 has quickly become a "hot spot" and favorite of locals.

Before opening their cafe, the owners spent years researching and learning special food preparation techniques. Described as "California cuisine with a European twist," menu items are a unique blend of spices and ingredients; even the bread is made in classic European style with hard crusts and soft insides. From a breakfast of omelets and Belgian waffles, to lunch consisting of sandwiches, soups, and "out-of-this-world" salads and pizza, to dinner entrees such as pork tenderloin and chicken alfredo, guests will enjoy unique taste treats and excellent service. Specialties include the popular "501 Salad" made with Granny Smith apples, blue cheese, and pumpkin seeds and their Portobello sandwich made of spinach, grilled onions, portobello mushrooms, and balsamic vinegar.

If the food doesn't "transport" you to Europe, the decor will. The eclectic blend of tile, ethnic fabrics, old school desks, and a wall of bakery items add to the experience of a small French or Italian cafe. After enjoying the delicious breads and other specialties during your meal, you'll want to take home a few of their bakery items, including walnut raisin bread, cornflake cookies, German chocolate cookies, parmesan bread, or raspberry scones.

Cafe 501 is located near the Edmond Historical Museum and an interesting shop named Artifex with hand-crafted home accessories from old Mexico.

Dot Wo $-$$$

64 S.E. 33rd Street, (405) 341-2878. From I-35, travel west on 33rd Street, or from Broadway Extension, turn east at 33rd. The restaurant is located in the Edmond Crossing Shopping Center about a block from the southeast corner of Broadway Extension and 33rd Street. Open weekdays for lunch from 11 a.m. to 2:45 p.m. and for dinner, Monday-Thursday from 5 to 10 p.m. and Friday from 5 to 10:30 p.m. Saturday hours are 11:30 a.m. to 10:30 p.m., and Sunday hours are 11:30 a.m. to 10 p.m. Handicapped accessible. Another location is at 3101 N. Portland in Oklahoma City, (405) 942-1376.

Dot Wo's serves authentic Chinese cuisine at its best. Chef Denny Ha brings his seafood-preparation expertise to the business, and co-owner Andy Sheung brings his enthusiasm for fast and friendly service. Chinese seafood is the specialty of the house, and freshness is of utmost importance; Sheung goes to the airport each day to pick up fresh fish for his guests' enjoyment. From the standard Chinese fare such as chicken chow mein and sweet and sour pork, to shrimp egg foo yung, squid dishes, and lobster tail, this restaurant has something for everyone. Dress casually as you come to enjoy the freshly prepared food and relaxing atmosphere of this clean restaurant.

London House $$, $$$

One South Broadway, (405) 330-9045. Exit I-35 at 2nd Street and travel west to Broadway. Turn north and travel two blocks to the southwest corner of First and Broadway. Tuesday-Thursday, 11 a.m.-10 p.m. (lunch served til 3 p.m.); Friday-Saturday, 11 a.m.-10:30 p.m. Sunday, 10:30 a.m.-2 p.m. Handicapped accessible on first floor. ☐

Located in charming downtown Edmond, the London House restaurant is a perfect place to end a fun day of shopping or to celebrate a special occasion. Formerly a movie theater and hospital during Edmond's early days, the London House provides elegant dining in a relaxing, casual atmosphere. The front English Pub area located street-side has a full bar; the back rooms are more formal, with white linens and lace cafe curtains. Menu items range from tender London Broil sandwich with pasta salad for lunch to broiled filet mignon with blue cheese herb topping for dinner. Complete your dining experience with a decadent dessert and espresso or cappuccino.

Seller's Crab and Steak House $$, $$$

One North Sooner, (405) 340-4400. Take I-35 to 2nd Street. Go west across the interstate, then turn north on the first access road (Sooner Road) and travel about one block to the restaurant. Open Tuesday-Thursday, 5:30-9:30 p.m., Friday-Saturday, 5:30-10:30, Sunday Brunch 11-2. Handicapped accessible. Dress is "nice casual." Reservations are optional.

From first glance, guests of the Seller's Crab and Steak House know they are about to experience something special. Originally the headquarters of the O.A. Cargill Buffalo Ranch, the stone building was expanded and transformed into a restaurant in 1985. Now known as the Sellers Crab and Steak House, the restaurant features the elegance of etched glass, mahogany wood, burgundy accents, and white linens. Although the original ranch is now commercially developed, diners are still able to experience a magnificent view out the picture windows lining the west side of the restaurant. Menu items include steak, lamb, chicken, and fresh seafood of all varieties. Stuffed shrimp, crab cakes, and catfish are some of the standards. No matter what entree is chosen, diners will not leave hungry. This is a truly relaxing and enjoyable dining experience.

Twelve Oaks Restaurant $$, $$$

6100 N. Midwest Boulevard, (405) 340-1002.
From I-35, exit Waterloo Road north of Edmond. Travel east to the first stop sign (Midwest Boulevard). Turn south and take the first drive turning east. Monday-Saturday, 5:30-10 p.m. Closed Sunday. Valet parking is available. Reservations required. Call ahead about one to two days for weekdays (sometimes same day), and one week in advance for weekends. Handicapped accessible to first floor only.

This beautifully-restored Victorian house that was built before statehood invites guests to leave their cares behind and enjoy a refreshing dining experience. Surrounded by huge green pastures, this out-in-the-country restaurant has a decidedly uptown feel. Twelve Oaks Restaurant is a great place to relish a romantic dinner by the fireplace or in one of the private suites upstairs. Owner Bill Horn reports that many couples have become engaged in this elegant setting. Enjoy fresh and delicious entrees such as marinated quail, Norwegian salmon, shrimp scampi or filet mignon, but just as good are the salads and side dishes.

Shopping

The Angel House

203 E. Main, (405) 330-9ART. From I-35 travel west or from Broadway Extension travel east on 2nd Street to Boulevard. At Boulevard, turn north for two blocks. The gallery is within easy walking distance of downtown Edmond. Monday-Saturday 10-6. Not handicapped accessible. $

Named after former owners John and Daisy Anglea (pronounced Angel), this charming Victorian home is now the studio of nationally-recognized artist C. Butler Pendley. An art gallery and working studio for the artist, the shop features Pendley's watercolors, limited edition lithographs, and embossed etchings of angels, florals, landscapes, and birds. The collection even includes a selection of paintings featuring the people and places of the Southwest. Her work is displayed in over 400 galleries around the world, and is found in homes of such notable collectors as President Bill Clinton, Walter Cronkite, Ed McMahon, and Betty White.

Besides Pendley's work, the house is filled with other unusual items such as hand-crafted pottery, unique lamps, and angelic gifts in many forms and sizes. This intriguing gift shop invites visitors to slow down and spend time enjoying the atmosphere of Angel House, visiting with the artist, and examining the quaint and colorful English garden that graces the front of the house.

Edmond Antique Mall

907 South Broadway, (405) 359-1234. Exit I-35 at 2nd Street and travel west to Broadway. Turn south for seven blocks. The mall is on the west side of Broadway. Monday-Saturday 10-6. The mall has convenient parking and is handicapped accessible.

Fifty-five dealers fill this 12,000-square-foot nostalgic mall. Shoppers will find everything from complete bedroom suites to tin matchstick holders and glass collectibles, with most items dating from the 1800s to the 1950s.

NOTE: Other antique stores in Edmond are **Courtyard Antique Market** located on the southeast corner of 33rd and Broadway, and in downtown Edmond, **Broadway Antique Mall** just north of 2nd and Broadway and **Carriage House Antique Galleries** at 6 North Broadway. Hours vary.

Downtown Edmond

The downtown Edmond area begins at 2nd Street and Broadway and continues north for several blocks. Business hours vary with each business.

Whether you're looking for children's clothes, antiques, jewelry, or just having lunch with a friend, downtown Edmond is the place to be. This charming area is often decorated for the season and now includes quaint, old-fashioned street lights that add to the ambiance. Select gifts and home accessories at **Tis the Season** and **Ambiance**, buy upscale clothing for the entire family at **McCall's** or women's clothing at **St. John's**, pop into **Java Dave's** for a flavorful cup of coffee, then step into **Simply Southwest** for a unique selection of Southwest apparel and other items. Other specialty shops include an art gallery, a collectible doll shop, and more.

During the weekend before Mother's Day, the downtown merchants host their annual **Edmond Arts Festival**. Approximately 100 artists and vendors line the sidewalks and welcome guests to enjoy their beautiful art. Local entertainment and concessions add to the fun. For more information call (405) 359-9408.

Kickingbird Square

Bryant and Danforth, (405) 340-0020. From I-35, travel west on Danforth; from Broadway Extension travel east on Danforth to Bryant. The shopping center is located on the northwest corner of the intersection.

Upscale boutiques, gift and card shops, a travel agency, a pet shop, a sandwich shop, and an eight-screen movie theatre are just some of the twenty stores located in Kickingbird Square. From shoes to restaurants, clothes to books, you'll find everything you need in one area.

Accommodations

Arcadian Inn

328 East First, (405) 348-6347. Exit I-35 onto 2nd Street and head west; from Broadway Extension travel east. On University, turn north one block. The inn sits on the southwest corner of First and University. Rooms start at $85 with special midweek rates. Adults only. Reservations are required. Credit cards and personal checks are accepted. A cancellation policy is in effect. Smoking is not allowed. 🚭

The Garden Room at Arcadian Inn.

Built in 1908 as the home of Dr. A.M. Ruhl, M.D., and his family, the Arcadian Inn is now the hallmark of luxurious Victorian splendor. From the atmosphere to the food, gracious innkeepers Martha and Gary Hall make certain your romantic getaway is memorable. Seven Victorian-decorated rooms are available at the inn, including the Zeimer Master Suite with mahogany gas fireplace and whirlpool tub for two in front of the fire. Other notable rooms are "M'Lord's Chambers" with its more masculine decor and "The Garden Room" with brass bed, white wicker, and jacuzzi tub for two. Ask about the newest addition to the inn, the elegant "Captain's Quarters."

Rated by AAA (Automobile Association of America) and the winner of numerous prestigious awards, the Arcadian Inn is noted for attention to detail and a high level of service. All rooms have private baths and showers. Some rooms include a privately-served breakfast; others offer breakfast served in the sunlit dining room downstairs. Inquire about special touches such as a private candlelight dinner for two and therapeutic massages that can be arranged.

Events

LibertyFest

Held during the first week of July at various locations in Edmond. Call (405) 340-2527 for a schedule. Admission is free for most events.

One of the biggest Fourth of July celebrations in the state, LibertyFest celebrates freedom, family, and fun. Several events such as a **Kitefest**, a **Road Rally**, the **PRCA Rodeo**, the **Classic Bike Tour**, and others, lead up to the festival's exciting and colorful conclusion on Independence Day.

Edmond/Guthrie

Edmond holds its annual **parade** (one of the biggest and best in the state) with all the pomp and ceremony that Independence Day deserves. Starting at 10 a.m., the parade travels from the University of Central Oklahoma campus through downtown Edmond. Celebrities, drill teams, a brigade of Elvis-impersonators pushing lawn mowers, bands, floats, clowns, and more entertain the crowd for over two hours. The parade is free, but arrive early to get a good spot; it seems as though the entire population of Edmond and at least as many guests attend this parade. Shade is not easy to find; consider bringing your own. Lawn chairs and sunscreen are "must-bring" items.

After the parade, the celebration continues at Hafer Park (9th and Bryant). **Parkfest** begins at noon after the parade and features free watermelon for everyone, games, clowns, trolley rides, and a Kid's Talent Review and costume contest. The final event of the day is the **Fireworks Display** held at Wantland Stadium on the University of Central Oklahoma campus. Entertainment begins at 7 p.m.; the spectacular fireworks begin around 9:15 p.m. Refreshments are available at the stadium.

In the Vicinity

Round Barn of Arcadia

Located on Highway (Route) 66 in the town of Arcadia just a few miles east of Edmond's city limits, (405) 396-2398. Exit I-35 onto 2nd Street. Go east about six miles to Arcadia; you cannot miss the red barn on the north side of the road. Tuesday-Sunday, 10-5. Closed Monday. Admission is free.

The round barn was originally built for livestock in 1898 by farmer/educator William Odor. But why did he build a round barn instead of a conventional rectangular barn? The sentiment of the day was that a tornado would go around the barn and not hit it. To build the barn, lumber was sawed on site, then soaked in the river and curved to conform to the barn's design. In mid-1940, the barn was sold to Frank and Katie Vrana, who later donated the barn to the Historical Preservation Society. Luke Robinson, a retired builder and carpenter, began the daunting task of repairing the dilapidated barn and, with help from many friends in the area, restored the barn for all to enjoy. An important attraction along old Route 66, the barn is listed on the National Register of Historic Places.

Take thirty minutes to learn about the early days of the town of Arcadia, the Round Barn construction, and the "Mother Road" from the pictures on display on the first floor of the barn. The exhibits also include a pictorial display of round barns located around the nation and a twenty-minute video of the Round Barn's reconstruction. The spacious and architecturally-interesting second floor can be rented for special events, but it is advised to reserve the space many months in advance.

Guthrie

Guthrie is Oklahoma's own Sleeping Beauty. Planned as a capital city before the Land Run of April 22, 1889, Guthrie went quickly from a temporary tent town to a cosmopolitan city. The first brick building in the territory, the National Bank Block, was completed in May of 1889. By August, the city directory listed six banks, thirty-nine doctors, five newspapers, and forty restaurants. By the end of the year, electric street lights illuminated the growing city. Through the next years, Guthrie experienced the usual growing pains but was confident of the future. In 1906, an act was passed authorizing the organization of a state government and designating Guthrie as capital until 1913 when an election was to be held to permanently decide the issue. President Roosevelt signed the statehood proclamation, officially making Oklahoma the forty-sixth state on November 16, 1907.

Until statehood, local politics had reflected national control, with many Republicans being appointed to important posi-

Victorian Guthrie.

tions. Statehood brought about some changes, with the first governor elected in the state being Democrat Charles Haskell. Political maneuverings by Oklahoma City leaders and constant sniping from the Republican newspaper in Guthrie helped bring matters to a head. Governor Haskell decided not to wait until 1913 to hold a vote on statehood, but scheduled the election for Saturday, June 11, 1910. With the following day being Sunday, opponents had to wait an extra day before filing objections and injunctions. By then, it was too late.

There are several stories describing the manner in which the official state seal was smuggled out of Guthrie and taken to Oklahoma City where the Governor used it to imprint a document declaring Oklahoma City the official capital of the state. The legal wrangling ended in the United States Supreme Court; in 1911, the election decision was upheld. This signalled the beginning of the end for Guthrie. Economic growth ceased, as the business of government moved south. Guthrie languished for years until some shrewd citizens looked around and realized that Guthrie itself was a museum of turn-of-the-century America. Guthrie boasts the largest contiguous area of historically significant property in the United States. Like Sleeping Beauty, Guthrie has taken on new life, making it one of Oklahoma's premier tourist attractions.

Guthrie is located ninety-one miles from Tulsa and about thirty miles north of Oklahoma City on I-35. Convention and Visitors Bureau (800) 299-1889 or www.guthrie.com.

Byron's Music Hall

117 1/2 E. Oklahoma, (405) 282-6646. Admission is $7.50-15, "depending on who's in town, or if we're serving food," according to the owner. Not handicapped accessible.

A three-time national fiddle champion and two-time Grammy Award nominee, Byron Berline has played with many famous musicians (the Eagles, Alabama, the Rolling Stones, and Vince Gill, to name a few). His music hall is a wonderful surprise package that shouldn't be missed! The schedule is erratic, and the prices are varied. There are often concerts on Friday and Saturday nights and Open Mike Jams on Sunday. Occasionally the bluegrass music is accompanied by barbecue. Call for a schedule–Byron and his friends play excellent blue grass!

Dowart Custom Cowboy Boots

117 South Second, (405) 282-1258. Located north of the State Capital Publishing Museum in one of Guthrie's oldest buildings. Monday-Saturday 9 a.m.to "dark:30."

R.A. Dowart had been a ranchhand and cowboy for many years when he realized that his profession offered no retirement security. For that reason, he left the Wyoming ranch to apprentice with a boot maker and start a new career. Besides being able to order custom-made boots from materials such as calf, alligator, and ostrich skins, visitors will enjoy an interesting visit with a true gentleman. The visiting is free, but the boots will cost $675 and up. Credit cards accepted.

First Capital Trolley

(405) 282-6000. March-December weekdays and Saturdays 9-4, Sundays 1-4, December candlelight tours at 6, 7, and 8 p.m. January-February weekdays noon until 2, Saturdays 9-4, Sundays 1-3. All tours leave on the hour. Adults $2, children ages 12 and under $1, all seats for candlelight tours $2. Not handicapped accessible.

A trolley tour will give you a quick orientation to the town and a good history lesson with some humor thrown in. Catch the trolley for the forty-five-minute tour at the southwest corner of Second Street and Harrison.

Guthrie Scottish Rite Masonic Temple

900 East Oklahoma, (405) 282-1281. Guided tours Monday-Friday at 10 and 2, Saturday at 10 (schedule may vary during festivals). Adults $2, no charge for Masons or students. Call ahead for handicapped accessibility entrance information.

Prepare to be dazzled! A tour of the temple offers a good course in architectural history. There are thirteen "artistic" rooms, each designed to reflect a particular historical period. The Egyptian auditorium is patterned after the style of 3700 B.C. Egypt. The paint was prepared by hand in the Egyptian manner. The Crystal Room, with its massive Czechoslovakian chandeliers, is also called the Gold Room because all the hardware, even the screws in the door hinges, are triple-plated gold. Woven by hand in one piece in Ireland, the rug required two railroad flatcars for transportation. The Rose Room, decorated in eighteenth century English style, features Tiffany windows. These are just a few of the treasures you'll see in this most amazing building, the largest Scottish Rite Temple in the world. Self-guided tours are no longer permitted, so plan your visit accordingly. The guided tours take about ninety minutes.

Lazy E Arena

From I-35, take the Seward Road exit (Exit 155) and go east four miles to the ranch gate, (405) 282-7433 or (800) 595-RIDE. There is no charge for tours. Admission to events varies. For a schedule of Arena events, call (800) 234-3393. Be sure and ask if any special discounts are available for Arena events; there may be savings offered by sponsoring companies. The arena is handicapped accessible.

The Lazy E is a giant complex which encompasses the ranch with its breeding program, the Training Center where both Lazy E and other horses are conditioned and trained, and the Lazy E Arena, a massive entertainment facility which hosts not only rodeo and horse events but also such diverse programs as moto-cross competition and concerts. The forty-five minute tours of the ranch include the stallion and mare barns and breeding shed and involve much walking. Tours start at 1:15 Monday through Friday, except for breeding season (February 1-July 1), when they are available every other day. Call (405) 282-3437 for precise information or to arrange a tour at another time. The arena is open Monday-Friday from 8:30-5. You may take a self-guided tour of this facility.

Some of the most popular events at the arena include **Bullnanza** with top bull riders from the Professional Bull Riders Association, the **National Finals Steer Roping** in which the top fifteen steer ropers compete for the title and $90,000 in prize money, and the **O.C.A. Range Round-Up**. Competitors in the Range Round-Up come from some of Oklahoma's largest ranches and compete in such events as wild cow milking, team branding, and wild horse racing.

Love Is Carriages

(405) 282-0299. $30-35 per couple for a thirty-minute ride. The price variation depends on whether or not a reservation has been made, and on the equipment being used.

The Bowers family owns four surreys, three black and one white. They operate year-round and are not only available for Guthrie tours, but they can be booked for weddings or special occasions. Steve Bowers says a carriage ride is a real stress reliever and can be a very romantic experience. "People have time to talk at five miles an hour," he says. Though you'll occasionally find one of the surreys tied up in front of the Harrison House, most of their business is by appointment.

National Lighter Museum

107 S. Second, (405) 282-3025. Daily 10-6. Free; however, a $2 donation is suggested. Handicapped accessible with assistance.

Lighters date back 4500 years before the discovery of tobacco. The museum's owner, Ted Ballard, is a nonsmoker and is quick to point out that this museum is not about smoking, but "mechanical pyrotechnical apparatuses." Interest in these little devices is growing, and they are now among the top ten collectibles in the world. Only about one-third of Ted's 20,000 piece collection is on display at any given time; you'll find new things of interest each time you visit. Among the unusual items in the collection are a Kewpie lighter and a Godzilla flamethrower.

Oklahoma Frontier Drug Store Museum

214 W. Oklahoma, (405) 282-1895. Tuesday-Friday 10-5, Saturday 10-4, Sunday 1-4. Free. Handicapped accessible with assistance.

Prepare for a real time trip. More like a genuine drug store than a museum, the space is furnished with antique counters and cases. The floor is wood, and the ceiling is pressed tin. Liquids of ruby, sapphire and emerald hues sparkle in giant bottles. In the cases, samples of the remedies of yesterday testify to the difficulties of life in earlier times. Though the gleaming soda fountain is for display rather than service, you can get a bottle of sarsaparilla or creme soda.

This is an interesting and unusual museum; it is one that fits its location in historic downtown Guthrie. The museum is run by the Oklahoma Pharmacy Heritage Foundation, an outgrowth of the Oklahoma Pharmaceutical Association, and it is supported by pharmacists all over the state. If you get started reading labels on some of the old patent medicines, you're apt to lose track of time!

Oklahoma Sports Museum

315 W. Oklahoma, (405) 260-1342. Saturday 10-4, Sunday 1-4, or by appointment. Free. The museum is handicapped accessible.

Through the years, many sports heroes have been from Oklahoma or have had close Oklahoma ties. Names like Spahn, Bench, Mantle, Thorpe, Aikman, and Miller decorate exhibits which include programs, jerseys, paintings and, in the case of Shannon Miller, one of the torches carried in Olympic celebrations. Stars of basketball, golf, bowling, and rodeo are honored also. Opened in 1996, the museum now occupies one building, but will expand to others as funds become available. A goal of the museum's founders is to provide educational and motivational programs to encourage positive behavior in young people.

Oklahoma Territorial Museum

406 E. Oklahoma, (405) 282-1889. Tuesday-Friday 9-5, Saturday 10-4, Sunday 1-4. Closed Monday and legal holidays. The last entry is thirty minutes before closing. Free.

Operated by the Oklahoma Historical Society, this museum is furnished and the artifacts exhibited in the clean, uncluttered style for which OHS is known. You'll find an excellent explanation of land divisions since the Louisiana Purchase and exhibits on surveying techniques. Other displays relate to everyday life in territorial Oklahoma. One of the most unusual is a display of mourning materials with a chart describing in detail the proper dress for mourning. Levels range from the deepest mourning, that of a wife for a husband, which entails four levels which stretch over two and one-half years to the least restrictive mourning, that of a wife for her husband's first wife's parents, which only lasts three months.

Adjacent to the museum and accessed through it is the old **Carnegie Library** which was built in 1902. What fun it is to see its elegant rotunda with the dome soaring sixty feet above the floor! It is the oldest remaining Carnegie library structure in Oklahoma and probably the most elegant. The most important moment in the history of the Carnegie Library came on November 16, 1907, when the first governor of the state of Oklahoma was sworn in on the south steps of the building. Today the Carnegie's rooms are often used for meetings or parties. Plan on at least an hour in the museum. The museum is handicapped accessible. There is a small gift shop on the first floor and a research library which is open 1-4 p.m. weekdays or by appointment.

Pollard Theatre

120 W. Harrison, (405) 282-2800. Thursday-Saturday 8 p.m., Sunday matinee at 2. Ticket prices range from $12 to $16 with higher prices for musicals. Ask about senior or student discounts.

The building was built in 1901 as a furniture store and funeral parlor. In 1919, it was converted into a vaudeville house; later it became Oklahoma's first all-sound movie theater. The Pollard Company was formed in 1987 with a resident troupe, and has been providing quality entertainment since then. Plays vary from period farces to contemporary drama and musicals. During the Christmas season they perform the highly popular "Territorial Christmas Carol," an adaptation of the Dickens' classic and a recommended family attraction for the holidays. Call for a schedule. Reservations may be made by phone with a credit card guarantee.

The Preservation Playhouse

118 E. Oklahoma, (800) OK-BANJO. Tuesday, Thursday, Friday and Saturday, doors open at 5:30, buffet service begins at 6, entertainment at 7:30. Around $25 for dinner and show. Group rates are available. Reservations are encouraged. Handicapped accessible. ⚅

The Preservation Playhouse is billed as "Oklahoma's newest fun-filled family entertainment opportunity." The theater provides a full evening's entertainment which starts with a buffet dinner followed by a sing-along featuring banjo and ragtime piano accompaniment. The main attraction of the evening may be a melodrama, perhaps a mystery, but always a musical, and always guaranteed to make you laugh. The evening comes to a close with an old-fashioned olio–a variety of comedy, song and dance by the resident company. The playhouse produces four different shows each year, including a special Christmas show. Each show runs about ten weeks, with a few weeks off between shows and no shows during January.

State Capital Publishing Museum

301 W. Harrison, (405) 282-4123. Tuesday-Friday 9-5, Saturday 10-4, Sunday 1-4. Last entry is fifteen minutes prior to close. Closed Monday and legal holidays. Free; suggested donation adult $1, child $0.50. Handicapped accessible.

Completed in 1902, the Foucart-designed building housed *The Oklahoma State Capital*, a newspaper which was an important part of Guthrie's growth from 1889 to 1911. The Co-Operative Publishing Company used the building until 1974. It now belongs to the Oklahoma Historical Society (OHS), and it is one of very few turn-of-the-century printing plants still in existence. Exhibits educate about printing, binding and bookmaking. Downstairs is the composing and press room. The big front room is interesting in itself as a piece of the past. If you're lucky enough to be there alone, stand quietly; listen to the tick of the old clock; smell the must of a century; then picture gentlemen in bowlers and ladies with skirts which sweep the floor. You can imagine a foot resting on the brass rail at the subscription counter. However, you might want to stop imagining when you get to the brass spitoons! At Christmas, the museum is decorated with themed Christmas trees, a new one added each year. Current trees include a button tree, a patriotic tree, a musical tree, and many more.

Golf

Cedar Valley Golf Club

210 Par Drive, (405) 282-4800. Located eight miles west of Guthrie on Highway 33. Open daylight to dusk. Weekday green fees $11 for 18 holes, weekends and holidays $12. Senior discount given. Carts are $16 for eighteen holes. Tee times can be reserved one day in advance for weekdays, one week in advance for weekends and holidays.

Cedar Valley was built in 1972 and designed by Duffy Martin. Golf pro is Jeff Martin; owners are the Martin Family. They have two eighteen-hole courses; Augusta (6312 yards, par 70, USGA rating 70.3, slope 108), is the harder of the two, with the fairways being narrower. International is a 6205-yard, par 70 course with more water. Its USGA rating is 71.1 and slope is 112. A unique feature of the courses is that they are all natural with native vegetation, water hazards, roughs, and no sandtraps. There is a pro shop, driving range, two practice putting greens, and a chipping green. The restaurant serves a full breakfast and sandwiches for lunch and dinner.

Cimarron National Golf Club

(405) 282-7888. The club is located on Highway 33, three miles west of Guthrie. Open daylight to dusk. Green fees: weekdays $12; weekends and holidays, $16; carts weekdays $16, weekends and holidays, $18. Tee times for weekdays can be reserved one day in advance. For weekends and holidays, call up to a week ahead. Call for an exact schedule. There are some restrictions on Cimarron National; to speed up play on weekends during peak season, no walkers or fivesomes are allowed.

As with Cedar Valley, there are two eighteen-hole courses owned by Duffy Martin. The Floyd Farley-designed layout opened in 1992. Cimarron National is a 6045-yard, par 70 course. It has a USGA rating of 91.4 and a slope of 120 and is considered the tougher of the two Cimarron courses. The terrain is hilly, and it has many trees. Aqua Canyon (6132 yards, par 70, USGA rating 90.8, slope rating 114) is more open, but the greens are smaller. Both courses have lots of water, wonderful scenery, and no bunkers. The pro is Marty Colbert. There is a pro shop.

The restaurant is full service and equipped to serve everything from chili pie to a prime rib dinner. During the off-season, dinner hours are limited to weekends. A breakfast buffet is available during the busy season.

Dining

Daily Grind $

212 W. Harrison, (405) 282-4960. Monday-Friday 7:30 a.m.-2 p.m. Handicapped accessible.

This may look unassuming, but don't be fooled—locals have nothing but praise for the food. The menu is limited: basic breakfast items, soups, sandwiches, and a daily special for lunch. The prices are rock-bottom, but the quality is high.

George's $$, $$$

202 W. Harrison, (405) 282-7771. Thursday-Saturday 6-9 p.m. Handicapped accessible.

Elegant is the word to describe this restaurant. The large mural by artist Fred Olds on the west wall adds color and interest, as Guthrians point out friends and neighbors who appear in the turn-of-the-century scene. Originally known as the Sand Plum, the restaurant features continental cuisine, including appetizers such as stuffed mushrooms and main courses such as their popular steaks, pork and seafood. Piano music adds to the atmosphere at this special place.

Granny Had One $, $$

113 W. Harrison, (405) 282-4482. Monday-Saturday 11-9, Sunday 11-3. On Friday and Saturday nights, the bar is open until 2 a.m. Handicapped accessible.

With wooden floors, a pressed tin ceiling and brick walls, Granny's is a comfortable and nostalgic spot. This may sound like a "ladies place," but the sandwiches are gargantuan. Choose from soup, salad, sandwiches, or full meals. A buffet is offered weekdays and Sunday at lunch, and Friday and Saturday evenings. Everything's good here, and the desserts are "to die for." There's live entertainment on Friday nights and Karaoke on Saturdays.

The Stables Cafe $, $$

223 N. Division, (405) 282-0893. Sunday-Thursday 11-9, Friday and Saturday 11-10. Handicapped accessible. 🚹

The building started out in 1890 as the Tallman Livery Stables, but as the automobile became popular, Mr. Tallman began converting his business to serve the motoring public. The restaurant retains the building's history in its name and salutes its later love affair with the auto in its decor. However, the draws here are the steaks and the barbecue–huge, heaping plates of ribs and more! Bring a friend and plan to share. Burgers, spaghetti, salads, and south of the border favorites are also offered on the extensive menu.

Shopping

Shopping is a major activity in Guthrie. There are too many antique stores to begin to list and many other stores carrying attractive and unique gift items. Among the more unusual shops are: **Vic's Place** (124 North Second) specializing in gas station memorabilia (and, according to Vic's wife, "anything shiny or that Vic wanted when he was a kid!"); **Sandstone Gallery** (108 South First) featuring "earthly antiquities and art using all natural sources"; **The Fabric Shop** (115 South First) and **The Pincushion** (124 West Oklahoma) where you can find beautiful fabrics, period patterns, and Victorian clothing to buy or rent; **Boston House** (in the Victor Mall, Harrison and First) with New England country items, cross-stitch, primitive stitchery, and Indian art; **Woodcrafters Emporium** (105 West Harrison) which carries unfinished furniture, including wine racks and entertainment centers made in Guthrie at the Pioneer Millworks; **Byron's Double Stop Fiddle Shop** (121 East Oklahoma) where you'll find violins, banjos, guitars, mandolins, recordings, and music magazines; **Jim Carter's Classic Auto Showcase** in Elk's Alley Mercantile (210 West Harrison) which always has at least one classic car in the midst of the antiques; and **Miss Lizzie's Bordello** (114 1/2 West Harrison) which houses seventeen assorted shops carrying everything from cookbooks to clothing. Hours at the stores in Guthrie are decidedly casual. Normal business hours (10-5) are a good bet but, during holidays and festivals, they may stay open later. If the fish are biting, they may close down in the middle of the day. If you have a specific goal in mind, call ahead; otherwise prepare to succumb to the small town ambiance and take your chances!

Accommodations

Guthrie is the "Bed and Breakfast Capital of Oklahoma." Each of the following B&Bs have their own charms and emphases. Be sure to ask about special packages that may include dinner, a carriage ride, tickets to the Pollard Theater, and/or other special amenities. Because they are historic homes, most of the B&Bs are not handicapped accessible or are limited in their accessibility. Ask the innkeepers individually about their handicapped accessibility. Harrison House does have an elevator.

Arsenic & Old Lace Bed and Breakfast Cottage

223 S. 1st Street, (405) 282-0012. $95-105; Murder Mystery package $205. 🖫

In 1899, Harvey and Jennie Olds borrowed $600 and built their dream house, a little two-story brick home on the corner of First and Vilas. Both of their daughters were married in the house, and their first two grandsons were born here. In 1993, it was restored by the Logan County Historical Society as an example of how the average Guthrian lived during Territorial times. It now belongs to Mona Luker, who runs it as a bed and breakfast. She's added decorator touches that would have had the '89ers agog. It features two large suites, each with private bath. The downstairs suite features an ornate brass bed and a two-person claw-footed tub. The upstairs suite is furnished with an open canopy bed with crocheted side curtains. There is also a claw-footed tub in this room. You'll find coffee, tea, hot chocolate, and soft drinks in each suite. A full gourmet breakfast will be brought to your room in the morning. The location is prime, with just a short walk to all the downtown attractions.

The Byrd House Bed and Breakfast

315 N. Maple, (405) 282-7211. $60-90. 🖫

Linda Byrd caters to ladies and families in her 1905 light blue and white Dutch colonial nest. Guests will find a chocolate egg on their pillows at night, just one of many ways Linda pampers her visitors. The house is full of family heirlooms and treasures. Any one who loves the color blue will love the dining room with its collection of blue glass sparkling in the windows. Relax in a bubble-brimming claw-footed bath tub and, for a special treat (and an extra charge), enjoy a massage before bed. Linda is known as the "Waffle Lady" for her Belgian waffles, part of a full breakfast which starts with coffee and juice in the sun room. She has two rooms, both with double and twin beds and a shared bath. With ingenuity and doubling-up, The Byrd House can accommodate as many as eight people. This is perfect for "hen" parties or families. There is even a baby bed and high chair available.

Caretaker's Cottage Guest House

1009 West Warner, (405) 282-0012. $95 ($195 for the Murder Mystery). Two couples sharing the cottage for a Murder Mystery stay will get a reduced rate. 🖫

Across the street from the Stone Lion, this small cottage is usually rented by two couples. The rooms are spacious. The east room, with its wood floor and oriental rugs, is decorated with bird's eye maple furniture and has a queen-sized bed. The bathroom features side-by-side claw-foot tubs. The other room is furnished in oak, with a generous sitting area and a refrigerator. There is a connecting door between rooms. Breakfast is delivered hot and fresh to your door.

Harrison House Inn

124 W. Harrison, (405) 282-1000 or (800) 375-1001. $65-110. Ask about packages which include dinner and theater.

Located downtown, this is the largest of Guthrie's bed and breakfasts and one of the oldest, opening in 1986. Each of the thirty rooms is decorated with a different theme, some named for individuals with Guthrie connections, like Lon Chaney, Tom Mix, or Carrie Nation, or for occupations significant to Guthrie, for example, the Banker's Room, or the Gambler's

Room. Decor includes many items of historical interest. The inn is handicapped accessible. The full breakfast includes waffles or an egg dish, cereals, sweet breads, juices, coffee, and tea.

The Lauren Danielle

1403 W. Cleveland, (405) 282-4230. $75-95. Victorian Cottage is $95-125. Credit cards are accepted. Banquet/conference facilties are available. [$]

This faithfully-restored 1890 Eastlake Victorian home is the oldest home in Guthrie and is listed on the National Register of Historic Homes. The house is beautifully decorated with antiques, including a seventeenth-century French armoire and an 1850s parlor sofa. There are four bedrooms, two with private baths, two with a shared bath. The food is as appealing as the decor. Apple or cherry pie is always available if the "munchies" strike. Innkeeper Debi Judd is noted for her ample gourmet breakfasts, which include items like Belgian waffles, souffles, and crepes. A special favorite is her Hot Raspberry Gourmet Cocoa with a dip of white chocolate mousse ice cream.

Inquire about the one-hundred-year-old Victorian Cottage. Decorated with period antiques, the fully-furnished home includes a parlor, dining room, study, Victorian bed and bath, sun room, and kitchen; it is perfect for honeymoons and business trips.

Debi and husband Cliff host a **Victorian Christmas Ball** every December in which guests, attired in elegant turn-of-the-century finery, dance to the music of a string quartet and enjoy a seven-course candlelight dinner. Make your reservations at least a month in advance for this special evening. Victorian niceties such as dance cards and feather masks are included. The evening costs $75 per person and does not include an overnight stay.

Railroad House Bed and Breakfast

316 W. Vilas, (405) 282-1827. $69-99. There is an adjoining community room which could be used for meetings or retreats. Credit cards accepted. [$]

Solid, square, symmetrical. These words describe this classic, 1904 red brick home constructed in Federal style with Georgian overtones. When the Connolly family built the home, they planned to live downstairs and rent out the upstairs room to railroad men. Indeed, Santa Fe railroad workers continued to rent rooms for many years, giving the house its name. Owners Fran and Ralph Watkins normally use three of the eight upstairs rooms (each with private bath) for guests, plus the cottage; however, accommodations can be made for larger groups. One of the rooms, Number 5, is a two-room suite with a queen-sized brass and porcelain bed. Number 8 is a burgundy delight with a beautiful crocheted spread on the bed and a claw-footed tub. Number 4 has a deep-footed tub and shower and a queen-sized bed. The cottage in back is the original 1894 home where the Connollys lived during construction of the larger house. The decor is primitive country and it has two bedrooms, making it handy for families. The Railroad House is located a short block from downtown Guthrie. Gourmet breakfast is served.

Redstone Country Inn Bed and Breakfast

206 S. 2nd Street, (405) 282-0012. $95 (for Murder Mystery at the Stone Lion, add $100). [$]

At the turn of the century, this building was the home of the Coyle-Smith Wholesale Grocery Store. Through the years, it gained a reputation as a spot where laws concerning gambling and drinking were winked at, and "good company" could be found in the upstairs roo,ms. Times change and this shady lady has turned respectable. Now an English country inn-styled bed and breakfast, it caters to a more upscale clientele. Five second-floor rooms are all suite-sized with comfortable sitting areas and kitchens. The refrigerators are stocked with soft drinks and teas; coffee and hot chocolate are located on the kitchen counters. A gourmet breakfast is delivered to each room.

Rosewood Manor

401 E. Cleveland, (405) 282-8431. $69-85. [$]

This sturdy home, with its eighteen-inch thick walls (the original owner was afraid of tornados) is a prime example of the architectural skill of Joseph Foucart. Inside is some of the most beautiful woodwork in Guthrie. The flooring is striped with light ash and dark walnut woods;

Guthrie

interior doors are topped with spindlework. The master suite features a queen-sized sleigh bed, a beautiful round stained glass window, and a claw-footed tub. The suite and the other two available rooms all have private baths. A full breakfast is served.

Elaine Warner

Savannah Rose Bed and Breakfast and Tea Room

123 S. Capital, (405) 282-7497. $59-79. 💲

Located across the street from the Scottish Rite Temple, this 1904 Colonial Revival home is noted as much for its food as its accommodations. Gourmet breakfasts are a feature here with one of the specialties being French Toast stuffed with cream cheese and fruit. There are three attractively-decorated bedrooms upstairs. You can also arrange for lunch or dinner with one-day notice.

NOTE: Scheduled to open in October, 1997, the **Savannah Rose at the Swan** will feature

Rosewood Manor.

fifteen rooms, a restaurant, and a gift shop. Innkeeper Marcina Xanders, who also owns and operates the Savannah Rose, is well-known for her culinary talents and generous hospitality. The Savannah Rose at the Swan is located next to the Sports Museum which is at 315 W. Oklahoma. Call the Savannah Rose phone number for more information and reservations.

The Seely House Bed and Breakfast and Cottage

701 E. Mansur, (405) 282-8889. $59-125. 💲

This is literally a new house in an old frame. The home got a face and body lift when it was moved in 1987 from its original location to its present site. It was built in 1893 for lawyer Silas Seely and his family and is now the home of the Duffys. Eleven-foot ceilings give a feeling of spaciousness to the home, and touches such as handcut wallpaper panels and original and reproduction furniture add to the elegance of the decor. (A not-so-elegant, but amusing touch is the reproduction chain commode with its aerial flush box, a departure from boring contemporary fixtures!) All rooms have private baths, and the Honeymoon Cottage has its own two-person whirlpool tub and a fireplace.

Stone Lion Inn Bed and Breakfast

1016 W. Warner, (405) 282-0012. $75-120; add $100 for the Mystery package. 💲

While the Stone Lion Inn is probably best known for its Murder Mystery Weekends, it is just as popular for its decor and food. The 1907 Greek Revival mansion is decorated in the dark, ponderous style popular around the turn of the century. The Victorians were great collectors, and owner Becky Luker has saluted this custom with a number of collections of her own including shells, globes, and items representing the search for beauty. Murder mysteries are held on Friday and Saturday nights, with guests arriving in time for a cocktail party, dinner and dessert, interspersed with murder and mayhem as the mystery unravels. The next morning, surviving guests gather for coffee, a history of the house including ghost stories (yes, the house is haunted), and a gourmet breakfast. Guests at any of the Stone Lion group establishments can participate in the murder mystery, but guests wishing to stay in the Stone Lion will find it necessary to make reservations at least three months in advance.

Victorian Garden Inn

324 S. Broad, (405) 282-8211. $79-119. 💲

Listed on the National Register of Historic Houses, this 1908 Colonial Revival-style cottage was originally built for David Rainsburg, station agent for the Chicago, Rock Island, and Pacific Railroad.

During the restoration of the home, a 1911 signature by a paperhanger was uncovered as wallpaper was stripped. Present owners, Nancy Palmer and Tim Arbaugh, have put a frame around the find, making it a special part of the history of the home. The focal point of the parlor is the original Italian tile fireplace. The Wild Rose Room features an antique walnut double bed and armoire. The dark green and burgundy room is highlighted with floral prints and Battenburg curtains, giving it a Victorian flavor. The honeymoon suite, Amina's Secret Bower, is done in shades of cream and rose with floral fabrics. It has a queen-sized bed and oversized jet-spa tub. The full gourmet breakfast always begins with a fruit dish (sometimes a fruit soup!). Two additional rooms are planned to be available by Christmas, 1997.

Victorian Rose Bed and Breakfast

415 E. Cleveland, (405) 282-3928. $59-89. ⑤

The Victorian Rose Bed and Breakfast, built in 1894, is located just three blocks east of the downtown area. The Queen Anne-style home features a wraparound porch with gingerbread accents. Oak floors, original beveled glass, stained glass, and antiques grace the home. Foy and Linda Shahan offer friendly southern hospitality and a warm welcome to their Christian home. The Victorian Dream Room has its own balcony for morning coffee, and the other two rooms have a sun porch for quiet conversation or reading. Each of the rooms feature a queen-size bed and private bath. The wraparound porch with its swing and rockers and a small outdoor garden area with a fountain are pleasant places to spend time during pretty weather. Breakfast is a three-course gourmet meal which could include banana crepes or eggs in antique coddlers.

Ask about their special Victorian Package that offers a horse and buggy ride, dinner at Guthrie's best restaurant, tickets to the current play at the Pollard Theatre, lodging, and a full gourmet breakfast.

White Peacock

616 East Warner, (405) 282-0012. $125 (additional $100 to participate in the murder mystery at the Stone Lion). ⑤

Built in 1897 for Frank Greer, publisher of the first newspaper in Oklahoma Territory, the elegant Colonial Revival mansion's exterior doesn't begin to hint at the excitement inside. The public rooms are elegantly and attractively decorated but seem sedate compared to the suites. This is where owner Becky Luker has let her talent and imagination run wild. You could find yourself sleeping in the Egyptian Room, complete with murals copied from designs which adorned the throne of King Tut, whistling an Irish jig from a whiskey barrel bed, or visiting a Mediterranean garden in the Italian Gazebo Room. This grand old house has gone through some hard times, even being chopped up into tiny apartments; perhaps it's only fair to let it have some fun! Enjoy the luxury of a full gourmet breakfast delivered hot to your room.

Events

For information on all events, contact the Convention and Visitors Bureau at (800) 299-1889. There is handicapped parking in the downtown area. Handicapped restrooms are available in the Chamber of Commerce office and at City Hall.

'89er Celebration

Held the week of April 22nd in Downtown Guthrie and other venues. Free.

This almost-week-long celebration offers a lot of food, fun and history to commemorate the Land Run of April 22, 1889. Arts and crafts, a carnival, a chuckwagon feed, and live entertainment, topped off with Oklahoma's largest parade, make downtown Guthrie the place to be. Rodeo events at the Lazy E offer more possibilities for fun.

Jazz Banjo Festival

Memorial Weekend in May (Friday-Sunday) in downtown Guthrie

Jazz Banjo bands from all over the United States perform Dixie Land and other types of banjo music at various downtown locations. There are also impromptu jam sessions and workshops during the festival.

Sandplum Festival

Held the fourth weekend in June in Downtown Guthrie. Free.

The ripening of the tart, native sandplum was cause for celebration from earliest times. The weekend's activities include a juried fine arts show, children's activities, bed races, Victorian debates, a pet parade, and live entertainment daily.

Autumn Magic/Tom Mix Festival

Held the weekend after Labor Day in September (Friday-Sunday). Free.

Prepare to enjoy a variety of events highlighted by a Tom Mix Film Festival (he was once a bartender at Guthrie's Blue Belle Saloon). Other activities include a memorabilia market, an antique and collectibles show, and a car show. These events take place primarily in downtown Guthrie. There is usually a major event taking place at the Lazy E during this weekend.

Oklahoma International Bluegrass Festival

Held in mid-October all over town. $50-70 for the three day festival; advance tickets save money.

This is a new event for 1997 and is a real coup. It's starting big with major stars Vince Gill and Ricky Scaggs. In addition to lots of American performers, eight international groups from as far away as Czechoslovakia and Japan will attend the first year. In addition to performances, there will be workshops, crafts, music company displays, and food booths.

Territorial Christmas Celebration

Thanksgiving weekend through New Year's Eve all over town. Many activities are free, others charge admission.

There are so many things going on that you really must call for a schedule of events. Activities include home tours, downtown lighting, evening trolley rides, living window displays, caroling, a Christmas parade, a Christmas tree auction, and Pollard Theatre's annual presentation of "A Territorial Christmas Carol."

Norman

Although the town of Norman was once called "Dugout," the name "Norman" has been identified with the site since the early 1870s. Abner Norman was the head of the crew which surveyed the area for the U.S. Land Office. Crew members burned the words "Norman's Camp" into a tree near a watering hole, and the name literally and figuratively stuck. The Santa Fe Railroad came through the area by 1887 and planned a stop near the camp. On April 22, 1889, about five hundred people staked claims at the Norman site.

Today, over 87,000 residents call Norman "home," making it the third largest city in Oklahoma. Norman is now best known for the University of Oklahoma, one of the state's first institutions of higher education, but it is also gaining a reputation for its many tourism attractions and events.

Norman is nineteen miles south of Oklahoma City on I-35. From Tulsa, take I-44 west to I-35, then south to Norman for a total of about 130 miles. For more information, contact the Norman Convention and Visitors Bureau (800) 767-7260.

Bob Moore Farms/Broadacres Polo Club

Located near Norman, farm (405) 329-8571; polo club (405) 364-7035. From I-35, take State Highway 9 west one mile. Watch for the sign which will tell you to turn on Santa Fe. Go one mile north on Santa Fe to the ranch entrance. The polo club is open from mid-March through mid-October. Free.

Designed by architect Stan Gralla, Bob Moore Farms rivals the beauty and utility of the famous Kentucky breeding stables. This is a working ranch where broodmares and foals are kept; tours must be scheduled in advance. The best time to see babies is in the early spring, but because this is also the busiest time for staff, calling ahead is imperative. Bob Moore has been breeding champion quarter horses since the 1950s, and now he has fourth and fifth generations of Moore horses. Equine artist Oren Mixer designed the gates both for the farm and the polo club.

Broadacres Polo Club is located on the ranch grounds. During the season, there are matches almost every weekend. Often, polo horses are boarded here for the season. Tours can be arranged by calling ahead. Admission at the polo matches is free. There are bleachers, but spectators often bring lawn chairs or blankets and picnics.

Firehouse Art Center

444 S. Flood, (405) 329-4523. Take the Main Street exit from I-35. Go east to Flood, then south to the Firehouse. Tuesday-Friday 9-5, Saturday 10-4, Sunday 1-5. Admission to the gallery is free; fees vary by class. Mostly handicapped accessible.

This art center includes a gallery with changing exhibits and a school offering a wide variety of art classes. Classes include the usual drawing, watercolor and oil classes, but also more unusual subjects such as Chinese calligraphy, handspinning and lost wax casting. Call for a schedule of classes.

Sponsored by the Firehouse Art Center, the Chocolate Festival is a major event in the community (see below for more information). Another special event is **Mid-Summer Nights' Fair** held in mid-July on a Friday and Saturday evening from 6 p.m. until midnight. There are arts and foods booths, free entertainment, arts activities for children, a Dalmatian competition, and a ceramic auction. The Fair is held in the park next to the Firehouse; admission is free.

Jacobson House

609 Chautauqua, (405) 366-1667. Leave I-35 at the Lindsey exit. Go east to Chautauqua, then turn north. The Jacobson House is on the southeast corner of Chautauqua and Boyd. Tuesday-Saturday 1-5. Adults $1.50. Children 11 and under and members are admitted free. Handicapped accessible.

Born in Sweden, Oscar Jacobson was the first head of the School of Art at the University of Oklahoma. The house itself, built in the early 1920s, is unusual in its contemporary style and use of passive climate control. Jacobson was the sponsor of the "Kiowa Five," young Native American artists whom he supported artistically; Jacobson even housed them. It is fitting that his house is now a gallery which features Native American art in rotating exhibits. Special events held by the Jacobson House Foundation include an **Indian art auction** called "Horse Power" and an **Indian art market**, both held in October. Call for a schedule of events.

Little River State Park

*(405) 360-3572. From I-40 east of Oklahoma City, take Choctaw Road exit south eleven miles to Alameda Drive, then one mile east to Indian Point information center. The park has facilities for picnicking, camping, fishing, boating, swimming, and hiking. **Thunderbird Stables** rents horses for horseback riding (405-321-5768; reservations are recommended). This is one of a few state parks offering **lake huts**–essentially tent camping without a tent, only better. Attractively-constructed structures feature plank floors, pine paneling, ceiling fans, electricity, picnic tables, screened-in porches, and fireplaces. There are no kitchens, bathrooms, or running water, but grills and pumps are handy, and a new bathhouse with hot running water is nearby. The huts rent for $25-35 a night and need to be reserved in advance (reservations recommended several months ahead for busy weekends and holidays).*

The park has a naturalist who maintains a small **nature center** and organizes special programs including Bald Eagle Watches, firearm safety, Native American crafts, and fishing skills. A restaurant is open in the summer in the Clear Bay area. Call ahead for camping information and reservations. For boat rental or other marine information, call either the Little River Marina at Indian Point (405)364-8335, or the Calypso Cove Marina at Clear Bay (405)360-9846. Call ahead; hours are likely to be erratic.

Little River Zoo

(405) 366-7229, located east of Norman, eight-tenths of a mile south of State Highway 9 on S.E. 120th. Daily 10-5 by appointment. Adults $4, children 11 and under $2. Call for group rates.

Janet Schmid, who co-owns the zoo with her husband Bill, has always enjoyed being around animals. She never outgrew her interest, and she has now given up a career in the health field to become a zookeeper. The collection includes over 400 animals from domestic species like chickens to more exotic specimens like servals and caraculs. There is a petting zoo with more domesticated farm animals, but with the guided tours, visitors are allowed to touch several "wild" animals while Janet gives information about their histories. The Schmid's goal is to give visitors a deeper appreciation of the animals as individuals, not just exhibits. These are special people with an unusual interest and a desire to share it with others. It is imperative to call ahead for an appointment. Plan on a couple of hours spent here. The tour involves walking on unpaved paths; a dry day is best for visiting, particularly with wheelchairs. A concession stand, a picnic area, and a gift shop are located on the premises.

Moore-Lindsay House

508 North Peters, (405) 321-0156. If coming to Norman from the north on I-35, take the Robinson exit east; if you are coming in from the south on I-35, take the Main Street exit east. Go east to Peters. The Moore-Lindsay House is between Robinson and Main Street on the corner of Peters and Acres. Wednesday 10-12, 1-4; Saturday 10-4:30. Call to verify hours. Individuals and small groups are admitted free; large groups will be charged a small per-person fee. Donations are always welcome.

This 1900 Queen Anne-style house was the first built on what would later be referred to as "Silk Stocking Row." Cost of construction was $5000, over ten times the amount an average home of the time cost. The portiere (spindle) work in the doorways is particularly fine. There are some original furnishings and home accessories in the house, but the rest were chosen as typical of the period. If you visit in summer, you'll want to see (and smell) the old-fashioned roses in the yard.

Sooner Theatre

101 E. Main, (405) 321-9600. For recorded information about events, call 321-8091. Web site is http://members.aol.com/kyme3/stn.html. Monday-Friday 1-5. Tours are free; call ahead for an appointment. Admission is charged for performances. Handicapped accessible.

Designed by architect Harold Gimeno, the theater was built in 1929 in Spanish Gothic style and is listed on the National Register of Historic Places. The theater hosts many events during the year, from theatrical and dance performances to concerts. Visitors may enjoy a performance or a tour of this lovely building. Among the architectural features of the theater are the 256 Spanish Coats of Arms on the three-story vaulted ceiling and the lobby's stained glass windows.

University of Oklahoma

Visitor Center-Jacobson Hall, 550 Parrington Oval. (405) 325-1188,(800) 234-6868 web site http://www.uoknor.edu. From I-35, exit on Main Street. Go east to Flood, then south to Boyd. Turn east on Boyd to the light at the Parrington Oval. Jacobson Hall is on the northeast side of the Oval.

This must be your first stop on a visit to O.U. If you have a specific interest, or want to arrange a guided tour of the campus, call in advance. When you arrive on campus, you may park anywhere not designated as faculty, staff, or handicapped. Know your license number; you'll need it to get a visitor's parking permit. At the Visitor Center, you'll find maps and instructions for self-guided tours of the campus, receive your parking permit, get an overview of the place, and begin to get a "feel" of the campus. Jacobson Hall has undergone major renovation to restore its 1919 elegance. University president David Boren has taken a personal interest in this "front door" of the university. The reception

Homeward Bound *by Allan Houser at O.U.*

area is brightened with colorful Southwest rugs, Mission-style furniture, and Tiffany lamps. A thirty-one foot mural entitled "The Grand Entry" showing Native American dancers in ceremonial dress adds to the grandeur of the area. Upstairs is another mural which depicts the history of the University. The University Visitor Center has also been designated a Local Tourism Information Center by the Oklahoma Tourism and Recreation Department; you'll also find lots of information on local and state attractions here.

As you continue your tour of O.U., consider a stop at **Bizzell Library.** The Collegiate Gothic Style library was completed in 1930 at the unheard-of cost of over $500,000. It was due to the determination of O.U. President William Bennett Bizzell that the state legislature grudgingly approved the expenditure. A visit to the Great Reading Room, 185 feet in length with forty-foot high ceilings, is like a trip to Cambridge or Oxford. The handcarved woodwork of dark oak is particularly attractive in this impressive room.

The library is the home of several interesting special collections. The **History of Science collection** on the fifth floor holds over eighty thousand volumes. The goal of the collection is to include every edition, including translations, of every book that has been published on science since the inception of printing. The oldest book is Hrabanus Maurus' *Opus de Universo* (*Work about Everything*), printed before July 20, 1467. Galileo's own first edition copy of his *Dialogo*, with margin notes in his own hand, is part of the collection. Also on the fifth floor are the **Bass Business Collection** and the **Bizzell Bible Collection** which comprises 665 Bibles, the oldest being the 1479 Koberger Bible. To see these collections, please make prior arrangements through the Visitor Center.

Other special collections are housed elsewhere on campus. The **Carl Albert Congressional Archives** is located in Monnet Hall. It houses over fifty collections of the official papers, manuscripts and photographs of U.S. congressmen and congresswomen, including those of Carl Albert, Dewey Bartlett, Mike Monroney, and Robert Kerr. Step into a recreation of the office that Carl Albert used when he was Speaker of the U.S. House of Representatives. Also in Monnet Hall are the **Western History Collections.** Books and other research materials relating to the American West are here. Wrought iron doors and longhorn steer horns add to the western ambiance. One area of the room contains the **Henry B. Bass Collection** on the Civil War and Abraham Lincoln. Special exhibits are often on display. The primary purpose of all these collections is the preservation of vital historic material for scholarly research. However, they are a precious legacy which belong to all Oklahomans who are welcome to see them by making arrangements through the Visitor Center.

Burton Hall, on the west side of the campus, houses the Political Communications Center where the **Political Commercial Archives** are located. This is the world's largest collection of political commercials produced for radio and television, and it is used frequently by national media and others.

Fred Jones Jr. Museum of Art (410 West Boyd Street, 325-3272) was founded by Oscar Jacobson, the first director of the School of Art. He wrote "In 1915 there were no art museums or collections in the state available to the public....the nearest (art center) being St. Louis. Yet I felt that art students should have the opportunity to see good painting and sculpture as part of their cultural education." The collection has been housed in its present location since 1971. The permanent collection contains over six thousand objects, with particularly fine examples of American painting after 1945, photography and graphic arts, ceramics, Native American painting, and Oceanic art. The most recent acquisition (1996) is the Fleischaker Collection, one of Oklahoma's finest private art collections; it moves the museum to new level of excellence. It includes more than four hundred major pieces of art: paintings, sculpture, pottery, basketry, and Native American artifacts. Notable artists include Thomas Hart Benton, Marc Chagall, Henri Matisse, Joan Miro, and Pablo Picasso. Among the Native American artists represented are Maria Martinez, Allan Houser, R.C. Gorman, and Jerome Tiger. In addition to displays comprised of pieces from the permanent collection, there are a number of temporary exhibitions on display each year. Call for a schedule and to verify hours. School year hours are: Tuesday, Wednesday and Friday from 10-4:30; Thursday 10-9; Saturday and Sunday 12-4:30. On football Saturdays, the museum closes at kickoff. Summer hours are shorter. The museum is closed on Mondays. Admission is free.

Jimmie Austin University of Oklahoma Golf Course (1 Par Drive, 325-6716) is at the far southeast corner of the campus. Go south on Jenkins to Constitution and turn east to Par Drive. The eighteen-hole course was designed by Perry Maxwell, and it opened in 1951, with major renovation in 1996 (Robert E. Cupp, redesign architect). Bring your sand wedge; this championship layout course, host of the 1997 NCAA regional championships, has seventy-nine bunkers. Holes are labeled with picturesque names like "Finesse and Forgiveness," "The Grove," "Hidden Depths," and "Thread the Needle." The course has 7197 yards and a par of 72. Slope is 134, USGA rating is 74.9. There is a well-stocked pro shop and food service which includes everything from snacks to breakfast and burgers.

The course is open seven days a week, 8 a.m. until dark. Green fees for Fridays, Saturdays, Sundays and holidays are $30. Lower rates prevail the rest of the week, with reductions for O.U. faculty, staff, students, seniors, and juniors. Carts are $20. Yearly memberships are available. Tee time can be reserved up to three days in advance; the necessity of early reservations varies with the time of year and the weather.

The **National Severe Storms Laboratory** (web site www.nssl.noaa.gov) is part of the University Research Park, also known as the North Campus. From I-35, take Robinson Street east just over a mile to Halley Avenue. Go north on Halley to Westheimer Drive. NSSL is on the southwest corner of Westheimer and Halley. The NSSL is one of the National Oceanographic and Atmospheric Administration's internationally-known environmental research laboratories. In partnership with the National Weather Service, their goal is to improve the nation's severe weather warnings and forecasts in order to save lives and reduce property damage. Public tours, lasting 45 minutes to an hour, are given at 2 p.m. on Thursdays. Groups of ten or more may tour by appointment–with two weeks advance notice. The tours are suitable for ages ten and up, and they are educational and informational–not a lot of gee-whiz equipment or a "dog and pony show," but a serious explanation of the work that goes on here. For more information, call (405) 366-0437.

The **Sam Noble Oklahoma Museum of Natural History** is scheduled to open in the fall of 1999. It will be located on forty acres at Timberlake and Chautauqua. The magnificent new building replaces the old Stovall Museum which closed in the fall of 1996. When it is completed, it will house a collection of five million objects in its 190,000 square foot space. NOTE: Call (405) 325-4711 to find out whether the "old" museum location is open for exhibit viewing. Due to popular demand, a small portion of the museum may be open on a limited basis.

While touring the campus, you will have many opportunities to enjoy the landscaping and art works which enhance the University setting. One of the newest areas began almost as a joke. Back in the 1960s, when campus unrest was a fact of life, David Burr was named Vice-President of the University Community. He was opposed to overuse of space, and he campaigned to maintain green areas around student housing. He fought against turning every inch into parking, particularly a small area which he could see from his office in Walker Tower. Colleagues and students began to refer to the area as **Burr Park**. The name stuck, and eventually the small unimproved space became identified as Burr Park on university maps. President Boren noticed the area, inquired about it, authorized its landscaping as a memorial to the man whose name had become associated with it and officially named it the David A. Burr Park. The design of the park calls for canopied shade from London plane trees, sycamores, and other deciduous trees. Seating is provided, and the Borens donated an Amish gazebo which is becoming popular as a setting for weddings. Other areas named for prominent campus figures include the **Fisher Gardens**, east of Jacobson Hall, named for Dr. Ada Lois Sipuel Fisher, the first African-American student admitted to the OU Law School, and the **Elaine Bizzell Thompson Gardens** which surround the statue of Dr. Bizzell in front of the library. The garden in front of Evans Hall is a formal planting patterned after a Vatican courtyard called the "Villa Pia." The gardens between Adams Hall and the library feature an Allan Houser statue, "Homeward Bound." The beds on the south oval are a riot of color, with brilliant petunias blooming from late May until mid-July. They are then replaced with over twenty-thousand mums which bloom from mid-October until a hard freeze.

As with any major university, there is a full schedule of events which include concerts and theatrical and dance presentations. For information and/or tickets, call (405) 325-4101. Events

at the **Lloyd Noble Center**, the University's 12,000-seat arena, include university basketball, gymnastics, wrestling, and major concert events. In the past, Lloyd Noble Arena has hosted such greats as Elvis Presley, Pavarotti and the Barnum and Bailey Circus. For information, call (405) 325-3838. For information about varsity athletics, including football, call (800) 456-4668.

Year-Round Volksmarch

For information about this, or any other Volksmarch activity, call Al Heberlein (405) 843-5731 (no collect calls, please) or refer to the "Volksmarch" article on page 192.

This is an eleven kilometer walk (about 6.5 miles). Most of the route is on sidewalks and city streets with no significant obstacles. The walk begins through residential areas of Norman, then winds through part of the University of Oklahoma campus. Registration and starting point is the Thunderbird Lodge, 1430 24th Avenue S.W. Wheelchairs and strollers may find some of the curbs and grassed areas difficult to traverse. It is recommended that you complete the walk during daylight hours. Anyone can walk the course free. If you want IVV credit and/or an award, there is a small fee.

Golf

Westwood Park Golf Course

2400 Westport Drive, (405) 321-0433. From I-35, take Robinson east, turn south on 24th Avenue. Westport Drive is the first street on your left. Open sunup to sundown. Daily green fee is $13.98. Carts are $18.28 for eighteen holes, $9.68 for nine. Senior discounts given. Yearly memberships are available.

This eighteen-hole course, designed by Floyd Farley, was built in 1967. It is 6015 yards long, with a par of 70. The slope is 108, and the USGA rating is 67.7. The course is relatively flat, with nice fairways and greens. It is described as "a fun course for avid or high-handicap golfers." Tee times can be reserved up to one week in advance. Food service includes burgers and sandwiches, and breakfast (if the weather's good). There is a pro shop.

Dining

Cafe Plaid $$

333 West Boyd on Campus Corner across the street north of the O.U. campus, (405) 364-6469. Monday-Thursday 8 a.m.-9 p.m., Friday and Saturday 8 a.m.-10 p.m., Sunday 9-5.

To dismiss this as the ultimate in yuppiedom (which it is) would be a mistake. Owned by the famous Harold's clothing company, this eatery is a prototype for a marketing concept which provides a "total retail experience," something along the lines of shop til you drop, then eat. The decor is comfortable and relaxing, with terra cotta tile floors, lots of brick and dark wood. The food is an experience to be savored. The varied menu includes salads, pasta dishes, sandwiches, and pizza. A favorite dinner entree is the Rosemary Chicken: sauteed chicken with rosemary, tomatoes, and mushrooms in a white wine cream sauce. Top off a meal with one of Cafe Plaid's homemade desserts. Handicapped accessible.

Coaches, BBQ, Pizza and Brewery $$

102 West Main, (405) 360-5726. From I-35, go east on Main Street to the end of the main part of downtown Norman. Monday-Wednesday 4 p.m.-2 a.m., Thursday-Sunday 11 a.m-2 a.m. 🅣

There's no question about the theme of this restaurant as you step on an O.U. Sooners' emblem on the sidewalk and as you grasp the baseball bat handle doors. If sports are your thing, this is your place. Hickory-smoked barbecue and hand-tossed pizzas are the specialties here. Portions are generous; Coaches gives you options on sizes, a nice touch. Also known for unique, hand-crafted beers brewed on the premises and for its upscale billiards ballroom with eighteen regulation-size pool tables, Coaches is an excellent and entertaining restaurant.

Crispy's Produce Company $, $$

3720 W. Robinson Street in Brookhaven Village, (405) 360-3164. Exit I-35 at Robinson and travel west to the shopping center. Friday-Saturday 11 a.m.-midnight, Sunday-Thursday 11 a.m.-10 p.m. Handicapped accessible.

Crispy's features American food with an emphasis on "California light" cuisine. Their specialties are their salads. Try the giant Rancho California Salad which stars a cajun chicken breast on a bed of lettuce with cheese, avocado, scallions, sprouts, hard-boiled egg, black olives, and cucumbers.

La Baguette $

924 Main Street, (405) 329-5822. Monday and Saturday 7 a.m.-8 p.m., Sunday 10 a.m.-4 p.m., Tuesday-Friday 7 a.m.-9 p.m. Also located at 323 W. Boyd Street on Campus Corner (321-3424) and 3700 W. Robinson in Brookhaven Village (329-1101). Call for hours at these additional locations.

Each La Baguette is described as a "European bakery and coffee house." They all have soups, salads, pasta dishes, sandwiches, quiche, meat pies, and vegetarian items. All sell wonderful breads, cakes and individual desserts. At the Campus Corner location, the atmosphere is a bit more Bohemian. Students are often found lingering over coffee while reading or playing chess. The Brookhaven Village location has a more extensive menu, and the decor is more "dressed up" with lots of natural light and a forest of green plants.

Legend's $$

1313 W. Lindsey, (405) 329-8888. Monday-Saturday 11-11, Sunday 10-10 featuring a brunch from 10-4:30. Handicapped accessible. ⚑

This restaurant could have been named for the legends it is creating with its excellent food and service, but it isn't. Far from the elegant establishment it is today, it began life as a pizza delivery service called Lemuel B. Legend's, Ltd. It's come a long way, baby! The decor is eclectic and interesting, including items like the lockers from the old "bottle club" days, and chandeliers from Oklahoma City's old Huckins Hotel. The food is the big attraction, with owner/chef Rebecca Sparks offering entrees noted for the subtlety and complexity of flavors. The menu offers pasta, beef, veal, pork, sea food, fish and poultry items, plus a section of healthy or vegetarian dishes. If you're feeling self-righteous for choosing a low-fat entree, reward yourself with dessert. Rebecca's desserts have been featured in *Bon Appetit* magazine, and they are worth a trip to Norman, all on their own.

Liberty D's $

786 Asp on Campus Corner, (405) 321-7765. Monday-Saturday 11 a.m.-2 a.m. (kitchen closes at 11 p.m.). Cover charges for live band nights range from $3-5, depending on the group.

In 1942, Liberty Drug Store was a quiet, hometown pharmacy. Today its existence is saluted in the name and honored by a few old colored bottles on display. It still has the original pressed tin ceiling. Everything else is gone, including the quiet. This is one of the hot spots for music and night life in Norman. You can get burgers, sandwiches, and salads here, but things really start to swing after 9:30 Tuesdays through Saturdays when it becomes a "21 and over" club with live music.

Lovelight $

529 Buchanan on Campus Corner, (405) 364-2073. Monday-Friday 7 a.m.-9:30 p.m., Saturday 8 a.m.-9:30 p.m., Sunday 8 a.m.-6 with Sunday brunch served from 8 until 2. Parking on Buchanan is limited, but Lovelight has a good parking lot which is accessible from Asp.

This restaurant is the essence of college ambiance, a delightful combination of hippie and yuppie where pony-tailed guys in ragged jeans sit beside lady lawyers in classic suits. The food is for anyone who likes a good selection of healthy fare, both vegetarian and non, and wonderful fresh-baked goods. Located in a fairy-tale building with half-timbered gables, tall chimneys, and stucco with protruding bricks, the restaurant's interior decor is eclectic but uncluttered. There is a courtyard for outside dining in nice weather. While the atmosphere is usually casual, Friday nights are dress-up, with white tablecloths and live jazz. Tuesday night is "open mike" night for budding poets and the occasional musician.

However, the big draw is the food, which is good, fresh and interesting. Try a Julie Special for breakfast: toasted bagel, eggs, jack cheese, tomato, salsa, and olives; or for lunch, choose a custom-designed sandwich from a long list of ingredients on their "Sandwich Factory" menu. Their home-baked breads are for sale, and gift baskets and catering services are available.

Misal of India $, $$

584 Buchanan on Campus Corner, (405) 360-5888. Monday-Friday 11-3, Sunday-Thursday evenings 5-10, Friday and Saturday evenings 5-11.

The first thing you notice about Misal is the decor. A colorful tent-like awning, called a shamiana, is suspended from the ceiling. The tables have beautiful fabrics, often embroidered and trimmed with tiny mirrors, under glass. You're prepared for an exotic dining experience from the moment you walk through the door. While many restaurants use the word "tandoori" in describing their dishes, Misal is one of a very few Indian restaurants in the U.S. to actually use a Tandoor, a clay oven imported from India. The kitchen is glass-enclosed; you can watch the process. In addition to the attention to flavor, the chef at Misal is also health- conscious, using the freshest ingredients and lean meats. The curries are not seasoned with "curry powder," but with distinctive blends of spices which are prepared fresh daily. This is a "don't miss" dining adventure.

Shopping

Malls and shopping areas include: **Brookhaven Village**, corner of 36th Avenue NW and Robinson Street, with over forty businesses, most locally owned, and the site of a number of community activities; **Carriage Plaza**, 2001 W. Main, featuring locally-owned specialty stores; and **Sooner Fashion Mall**, I-35 and Main Street, with major department stores plus seventy other shops. **Campus Corner** rates high for its shopping opportunities, as well as its charm and diversity. Shops here include everything from the upscale, classic-style clothing at **Harold's** (329 W. Boyd) to the funk of **Deco Dence** (307 White), an unusual little shop which carries "vintage everything." Other unusual retailers include **Voo Doo Home** and **Voo Doo Clothing** (731A and 733B Asp) with futons, custom framing, and contemporary furniture in the Home store, and "an alternative women's boutique" with clothing from kinky to slinky, and **Cookies and Cards** which carries not only cookies and cards, but a multitude of things you didn't know you needed until you saw them. (Telescoping back scratcher, anyone?) The Corner is also home to more traditional businesses and some wonderful restaurants. Wandering around Campus Corner is always an adventure.

Gallery Nouveau

1630 W. Lindsey. Located in the Hollywood Shopping Center between McGee and Berry. (405) 321-8687. Monday-Saturday 10-6.

Gallery Nouveau specializes in "things with personality." You'll find the unusual, the unique and the eclectic here—from antiques, upscale decorative items, fine art, and period furniture to porcelain. Handicapped accessible.

Kiss of the Wolf Designs

(405) 364-8150. Call for address and directions.

As much an attraction as a shopping experience, this home-based business produces unique items. Beginning with white silk from China, artists Lori and Marshall Bacigalupi turn plain fabric into wearable works of art. Their hand-painted, quilted vests, jackets and coats have been exhibited at the Smithsonian Craft Show in Washington, D.C. and the New York Crafts Museum, among other prestigious venues. They work in their home and will show their wares by appointment.

Rose Rock Farms

705 Goodman Lane, (405)321-1863. Take State Highway 9 east from I-35 to 72nd Avenue S.E. Go one mile north, then east on Lindsey one-fourth mile.

For an old-fashioned Christmas, choose and cut your own Christmas tree. Rose Rock Farms is open from the Saturday after Thanksgiving until Christmas Eve. They grow Scotch and Virginia pine up to eight feet in height.

west to the shopping center. Friday-Saturday 11 a.m.-midnight, Sunday-Thursday 11 a.m.-10 p.m. Handicapped accessible.

Crispy's features American food with an emphasis on "California light" cuisine. Their specialties are their salads. Try the giant Rancho California Salad which stars a cajun chicken breast on a bed of lettuce with cheese, avocado, scallions, sprouts, hard-boiled egg, black olives, and cucumbers.

La Baguette 💲

924 Main Street, (405) 329-5822. Monday and Saturday 7 a.m.-8 p.m., Sunday 10 a.m.-4 p.m., Tuesday-Friday 7 a.m.-9 p.m. Also located at 323 W. Boyd Street on Campus Corner (321-3424) and 3700 W. Robinson in Brookhaven Village (329-1101). Call for hours at these additional locations.

Each La Baguette is described as a "European bakery and coffee house." They all have soups, salads, pasta dishes, sandwiches, quiche, meat pies, and vegetarian items. All sell wonderful breads, cakes and individual desserts. At the Campus Corner location, the atmosphere is a bit more Bohemian. Students are often found lingering over coffee while reading or playing chess. The Brookhaven Village location has a more extensive menu, and the decor is more "dressed up" with lots of natural light and a forest of green plants.

Legend's 💲💲

1313 W. Lindsey, (405) 329-8888. Monday-Saturday 11-11, Sunday 10-10 featuring a brunch from 10-4:30. Handicapped accessible. 🍴

This restaurant could have been named for the legends it is creating with its excellent food and service, but it isn't. Far from the elegant establishment it is today, it began life as a pizza delivery service called Lemuel B. Legend's, Ltd. It's come a long way, baby! The decor is eclectic and interesting, including items like the lockers from the old "bottle club" days, and chandeliers from Oklahoma City's old Huckins Hotel. The food is the big attraction, with owner/chef Rebecca Sparks offering entrees noted for the subtlety and complexity of flavors. The menu offers pasta, beef, veal, pork, sea food, fish and poultry items, plus a section of healthy or vegetarian dishes. If you're feeling self-righteous for choosing a low-fat entree, reward yourself with dessert. Rebecca's desserts have been featured in *Bon Appetit* magazine, and they are worth a trip to Norman, all on their own.

Liberty D's 💲

786 Asp on Campus Corner, (405) 321-7765. Monday-Saturday 11 a.m.-2 a.m. (kitchen closes at 11 p.m.). Cover charges for live band nights range from $3-5, depending on the group.

In 1942, Liberty Drug Store was a quiet, hometown pharmacy. Today its existence is saluted in the name and honored by a few old colored bottles on display. It still has the original pressed tin ceiling. Everything else is gone, including the quiet. This is one of the hot spots for music and night life in Norman. You can get burgers, sandwiches, and salads here, but things really start to swing after 9:30 Tuesdays through Saturdays when it becomes a "21 and over" club with live music.

Lovelight 💲

529 Buchanan on Campus Corner, (405) 364-2073. Monday-Friday 7 a.m.-9:30 p.m., Saturday 8 a.m.-9:30 p.m., Sunday 8 a.m.-6 with Sunday brunch served from 8 until 2. Parking on Buchanan is limited, but Lovelight has a good parking lot which is accessible from Asp.

This restaurant is the essence of college ambiance, a delightful combination of hippie and yuppie where pony-tailed guys in ragged jeans sit beside lady lawyers in classic suits. The food is for anyone who likes a good selection of healthy fare, both vegetarian and non, and wonderful fresh-baked goods. Located in a fairy-tale building with half-timbered gables, tall chimneys, and stucco with protruding bricks, the restaurant's interior decor is eclectic but uncluttered. There is a courtyard for outside dining in nice weather. While the atmosphere is usually casual, Friday nights are dress-up, with white tablecloths and live jazz. Tuesday night is "open mike" night for budding poets and the occasional musician.

However, the big draw is the food, which is good, fresh and interesting. Try a Julie Special for breakfast: toasted bagel, eggs, jack cheese, tomato, salsa, and olives; or for lunch, choose a

custom-designed sandwich from a long list of ingredients on their "Sandwich Factory" menu. Their home-baked breads are for sale, and gift baskets and catering services are available.

Misal of India $, $$

584 Buchanan on Campus Corner, (405) 360-5888. Monday-Friday 11-3, Sunday-Thursday evenings 5-10, Friday and Saturday evenings 5-11.

The first thing you notice about Misal is the decor. A colorful tent-like awning, called a shamiana, is suspended from the ceiling. The tables have beautiful fabrics, often embroidered and trimmed with tiny mirrors, under glass. You're prepared for an exotic dining experience from the moment you walk through the door. While many restaurants use the word "tandoori" in describing their dishes, Misal is one of a very few Indian restaurants in the U.S. to actually use a Tandoor, a clay oven imported from India. The kitchen is glass-enclosed; you can watch the process. In addition to the attention to flavor, the chef at Misal is also health- conscious, using the freshest ingredients and lean meats. The curries are not seasoned with "curry powder," but with distinctive blends of spices which are prepared fresh daily. This is a "don't miss" dining adventure.

Shopping

Malls and shopping areas include: **Brookhaven Village**, corner of 36th Avenue NW and Robinson Street, with over forty businesses, most locally owned, and the site of a number of community activities; **Carriage Plaza**, 2001 W. Main, featuring locally-owned specialty stores; and **Sooner Fashion Mall**, I-35 and Main Street, with major department stores plus seventy other shops. **Campus Corner** rates high for its shopping opportunities, as well as its charm and diversity. Shops here include everything from the upscale, classic-style clothing at **Harold's** (329 W. Boyd) to the funk of **Deco Dence** (307 White), an unusual little shop which carries "vintage everything." Other unusual retailers include **Voo Doo Home** and **Voo Doo Clothing** (731A and 733B Asp) with futons, custom framing, and contemporary furniture in the Home store, and "an alternative women's boutique" with clothing from kinky to slinky, and **Cookies and Cards** which carries not only cookies and cards, but a multitude of things you didn't know you needed until you saw them. (Telescoping back scratcher, anyone?) The Corner is also home to more traditional businesses and some wonderful restaurants. Wandering around Campus Corner is always an adventure.

Gallery Nouveau

1630 W. Lindsey. Located in the Hollywood Shopping Center between McGee and Berry. (405) 321-8687. Monday-Saturday 10-6.

Gallery Nouveau specializes in "things with personality." You'll find the unusual, the unique and the eclectic here–from antiques, upscale decorative items, fine art, and period furniture to porcelain. Handicapped accessible.

Kiss of the Wolf Designs

(405) 364-8150. Call for address and directions.

As much an attraction as a shopping experience, this home-based business produces unique items. Beginning with white silk from China, artists Lori and Marshall Bacigalupi turn plain fabric into wearable works of art. Their hand-painted, quilted vests, jackets and coats have been exhibited at the Smithsonian Craft Show in Washington, D.C. and the New York Crafts Museum, among other prestigious venues. They work in their home and will show their wares by appointment.

Rose Rock Farms

705 Goodman Lane, (405)321-1863. Take State Highway 9 east from I-35 to 72nd Avenue S.E. Go one mile north, then east on Lindsey one-fourth mile.

For an old-fashioned Christmas, choose and cut your own Christmas tree. Rose Rock Farms is open from the Saturday after Thanksgiving until Christmas Eve. They grow Scotch and Virginia pine up to eight feet in height.

The Cutting Garden Bed and Breakfast

927 West Boyd, (405) 329-4522. $65-85.

As the name implies, the gardens are an important feature of this comfortable B & B. In spring, hundreds of bulbs provide color; and in summer, over one-half acre of perennials add brilliance and scent, as well as supplying fresh flowers for the three bedrooms. All three rooms have queen-sized beds and private baths. "The Manly Room" in deep greens and wine offers comfort in a masculine setting. "Flo's Room" is more feminine, with floral prints and a wrought iron bed. "The Celestial Suite" overlooking the gardens is spangled with gold, bright against deep blue. This room has a whirlpool tub. Breakfasts are all made from scratch with ingredients as healthy or decadent as you choose. Those who love luxury will enjoy the baked French toast, dipped in a custard mixture, and topped with brown sugar and pecans.

Holmberg House

766 DeBarr, (405)321-6221. $65-85.

The house was built in 1914 by Professor Fredrik Holmberg, first dean of the University of Oklahoma's College of Fine Arts. Just a short walk puts you in the heart of the OU campus, making this ideal for enjoying university activities (and avoiding parking problems). Innkeeper Jo Meacham has preserved the integrity of the house, restoring the original oak woodwork and the attractive staircase. The main floor living area is warm and welcoming with dark wood floors, oriental rugs, and a gas fireplace. There are four bedrooms. "The Blue Danube Room" features a queen-sized antique iron bed, with a claw-foot tub in the private bath. There are two other rooms with queen-sized beds and a third room with both a queen-sized bed and two twins. All rooms have private baths. Full breakfasts are served at the guest's convenience. The house specialty is French toast stuffed with blueberries, cream cheese and bananas.

Montford Inn

322 W. Tonhawa, (405) 321-2200 or (800) 321-8969. $90-165. Inquire about commercial or other special rates. Handicapped accessible.

The Montford Inn was built as a B&B. With previous experience in the business, owners Ron, Phyllis and William Murray knew exactly what they wanted and, more to the point, what their guests would want. The result is a gracious, spacious home away from home for the traveler lucky enough to stay here. There are ten rooms in the main house and two suites across the street. Every room is beautifully decorated, with styles ranging from collegiate with historical photos of campus life and other college memorabilia to Victorian with antique furniture and a queen-sized bed with an eight-foot walnut headboard. The suites are really like townhouses, with nine hundred square feet in each. Whatever you want, the Murrays have already thought of it–from dual jacks for modems to a guest office with a fax machine and afternoon snacks. Breakfast, prepared by father and son, Ron and William Murray, features fresh fruit, homemade breads and an entree–perhaps the Montford Sunrise, a casserole of grits, cheese, corn, and green chilies.

Whispering Pines

7820 East Highway 9, (405) 447-0202. $75-145 (plus tax). Ask about special occasion packages, senior and military discounts.

Really get away from it all in this butter-yellow new Victorian-style home. Owner Nancy Harden loves antiques, and she has scattered them throughout the house. The "Victorian Rose Room" was designed with handicapped-accessibility in mind. It has a queen-sized bed and an extra-large bathroom. Vintage wedding attire is displayed in "Satin Splendor," an elegant room which has its own private balcony. There are two other rooms in the main house,

Whispering Pines.

Frontier Country

each with private baths. Pine Cone Cottage is decorated with an Oklahoma flavor. This roomy cabin has a king-size bed and a queen-size sleeper sofa. Several of the rooms have whirlpool tubs, and there is a hot tub in a plant-filled Florida room just steps away from the main house. Full breakfasts are served, usually with a choice of main dishes. Cottage guests may have their breakfast served picnic style in their own cabin.

Events

Chocolate Festival

Held on the second Saturday of February at OCCE Commons on the O.U. campus, (405) 329-4523. Take the Lindsey Street exit east from I-35 to Asp and go south to Kellogg. Watch for signs. Hours for tasting, 11-3 (last entry at 2:30), Gala-begins at 6 p.m. Tasting tickets are $12, Gala tickets are $30. Handicapped accessible.

Delicious desserts, entertainment, sculptures and paintings made of chocolate, chocolate competitions, and lots of chocolate to eat–what more could anyone want from a festival near Valentine's Day? A $12 ticket entitles you to ten samples; several people can share a ticket. The evening concludes with a Chocolate Gala, a dinner with an auction, entertainment, and judging of competition for most delicious entries. Entry for the tasting is limited, making advance tickets a must. Reservations can be made by phone and secured with a credit card. Proceeds benefit the Firehouse Art Center.

Medieval Fair

Duck Pond, (405) 321-7227. From I-35, exit at Lindsey Street and go east past the O.U. football stadium. The park is on the north side of Lindsey. Friday and Saturday 10-7, Sunday 10-6. Free. Parking is at a premium around the park. There are university parking areas on Jenkins which can be used. On Saturday and Sunday, a campus bus will run between the Lloyd Noble Arena parking lots and the Fair.

Join the fun in a fairy-tale kingdom where knights and ladies rub shoulders with jesters and

In character at the Medieval Fair.

Fred Marvel/Oklahoma Tourism

minstrels. The theme is the middle ages, with craft booths, entertainment from juggling to joust-ing, and food following the theme. The University of Oklahoma College of Continuing Education, sponsors of this event, also offers a one-hour course in Medieval Culture as an addition to the Fair. (For information and enrollment, call (800) 522-0772, ext. 5101 or (405) 325-5101.) This event draws over seventy thousand people, making it one of the bigger festivals in the state.

May Fair Arts Festival

Held the second Saturday in May in Reaves Park. From I-35, take the Lindsey exit east to Jenkins, then go south to Reaves Park, which will be on your left. Contact the Norman Convention and Visitors Bureau at (800) 767-7260 for more information. 10-6:30. Free. The site is handicapped accessible.

Over 125 artisans and craftspeople display their works in this juried outdoor festival. You'll find paintings, drawings, sculpture, pottery, photography, jewelry, stained glass, and at least twenty thousand art lovers at this one-day event. Local restaurants provide food booths, and two stages are venues for all-day entertainment. The festival is sponsored by the Assistance League of Norman, a philanthropic organization.

Jazz in June

Held the last weekend in June (Thursday-Sunday) at various locations around Norman. Call KGOU radio (405) 325-3388 or (405) 325-5468 for more information. All concerts are free to the public. All venues are handicapped accessible.

Jazz performances range from nationally-known artists to new and local groups. The logo changes each year, making T-shirts and posters collector's items. Food and drinks are avail-able. Events are held in several spots around town; call ahead for a schedule.

Summer Wind Festival

Held for six days in July at various locations on the O.U. campus. Call (405) 325-0711 for more information. Most events are free; however, workshops may have a charge. All events are handi-capped accessible and special needs, such as interpreters, will be provided on request, making it one of the most inclusive festivals in the state. Call for a schedule.

This festival offers arts-related fun for the entire family, from workshops to concerts. The O.U. Parrington (North) Oval is transformed into a fairyland with kites, pinwheels, banners and soft sculptures. Most of the activities are held outdoors, and 95% of the events are free. Many of the morning activities are planned for children, with performances, demonstrations and workshops for preschool through grade-school ages. Evening events include music, drama and dance under the stars.

In the Vicinity

Noble

This town of less than five thousand people was born the day of the Land Run, April 22, 1889. It was named after John W. Noble, Secretary of the Interior under President Benjamin Harrison. A community-wide celebration is held in May honoring the Rose Rock.
Noble is located about five miles south of Norman on U.S. Highway 77.

Timberlake Rose Rock Museum

419 S. Highway 77, (405) 872-9838. Tuesday-Saturday 10-6. Free. Limited handicapped accessibility.
Barite roses are unique configurations of barite and sand which resemble blooming roses. The state rock of Oklahoma, these unusual "roses" are only found in a small area of Okla-homa, a narrow band which stretches from Pauls Valley to Guthrie. Joe and Nancy Stine, museum owners, have a number of specimens on display, plus jewelry and decorative items which they have made using rose rocks and other materials.

United Design

1600 N. Main, (405) 872-7131. From I-35 at the south edge of Norman, go east on State High-way 9 for five and one-half miles, then turn south on U.S. Highway 77 and go two and one-half

miles. The plant is on the west side of the highway on the north side of town. Tours are held Monday-Friday at 10 and 1:30. The Gift Shop is open Monday-Friday 9-5, and the first Saturday of the month 10-4. Handicapped accessible.

Jeanie and Gary Clinton started their business in a chicken house, and they came out with the goose that laid the golden egg. They began producing standard pottery items, but somewhere along the line, they came out with a little animal that was such a hit that they knew they were onto something. That "something" is now a company which employs seven hundred fifty people producing as many as twenty-five thousand pieces a day–everything from little animals to picture frames, refrigerator magnets, large garden sculptures, and collector's Christmas figures. Plant tours will show you the whole process. Groups should call ahead, but families can just show up for one of the two tours held Monday through Friday. Tours last about thirty minutes. There is also a video tour which you can see in the gift shop at any time.

The gift shop is a real highlight where you'll see hundreds of items on display. Anyone who can leave without buying something can probably eat just one potato chip!

Kendall's Restaurant $

100 S. Main Street (U.S. 77), (405) 872-7158. Monday-Saturday 7 a.m.-9 p.m.

Down-home cookin' in a hometown cafe setting is what you can expect at this restaurant. This is chicken-fried steak country, but burgers, salads, Mexican dishes, and sandwiches are among the offerings. The outstanding thing about this place is its commitment to the community and to youth. The second Sunday of every month, the restaurant opens for a special Sunday brunch featuring chicken-fried steak, ham, veggies, biscuits and gravy, omelets, salads, desserts, and beverage for a truly reasonable price (around $6.95). The purpose of this brunch is to raise money for child-oriented projects within the community. Seventy-five per cent of the gross goes to charity, with over $40,000 raised in under three years. People from all over the state line up to enjoy the bounty and salute the generosity of owners Richard and Kim Lock and Dee Downer. Reservations for this meal are suggested.

All Cedar Birdfeeders

115 S. Main Street (U.S. 77), (405) 872-5212. Monday-Friday Noon-5, Saturday 10-5.

The three Snively brothers who own this store make over thirty-five items, from basic feeders to feeders in unusual shapes like trains, airplanes, or even the state of Oklahoma. In addition to the feeders and houses which they manufacture, they carry all sorts of items for bird lovers, bat lovers, and even butterfly lovers.

Purcell

In 1887, two early settlers, Robert Jeremiah Love and a gentleman named Sparks, decided to draw up plans for a town that would later become Purcell. They hired an engineer who made a sketch of four town blocks–on a piece of wrapping paper! Furrows were plowed to mark off streets and alleys. Upon application, Chickasaw Indians were given business lots. With the Santa Fe Railway came a switching yard. The town was named after a director of the railroad, E.B. Purcell.
Purcell is located about fifteen miles south of Norman. Travel south on I-35 to the Purcell exit. Purcell Chamber of Commerce (405) 527-3093.

Butler's Antique Shop

200 West Main, (405) 527-9592. From I-35 south take the Purcell/Lexington exit. Travel south to the third stop light and turn east onto Main Street. The shop is on the south side of the street. Monday-Friday 9-5:30, Saturday 9-6, and Sunday 1-6. If reservations are made one day in advance, the Butlers will give tours in period clothing from the 1890s. Handicapped accessible on first floor only.

Built in 1895 by Purcell's founder Robert Jeremiah Love, this brick hotel was once acclaimed as the finest in the area. The three-story, sixty-three room Hotel Love was once a favorite place for newlyweds to spend their honeymoon, and it was known in those days for having all the modern conveniences, steam heat and electric lights among others. Rooms rented at $2 a night.

Hotel Love was placed on the National Register of Historic Places in 1995. When the current owners, Jerry and Elaine Butler, renovated the elegant, century-old building, part of it became their home. Two stories are devoted to Butler's Antique Shop, which contains reasonably priced antiques. Items range from furniture and glassware to linens and books.

T's Antique Mall

116 West Main, (405) 527-2766. Located near Hotel Love (see above). Monday-Saturday 10-6, Sunday 2-6. Handicapped accessible on first floor only.

This building provides a renovation success story. First built in 1895 as an opera house, the building became a movie theater in the 1940s. After closing in the 1970s and sitting vacant for many years, it was purchased and renovated less than two decades later. In 1994, it was awarded the Best Building Facade Renovation from Oklahoma's Main Street Program. Inside are two floors of antiques and collectibles displayed in more than thirty booths.

Jo's Famous Pizza $, $$

1538 South Green Avenue, (405) 527-2379. From Highway 77 travel south past Lexington into Purcell. The restaurant is on the east side of the road, approximately three blocks past the Walnut Creek Bridge. Monday-Friday, 4-midnight, Saturday 11-11. Handicapped accessible.

Since 1964, Jo has been attracting customers from all over the state by making pizza with her secret sauce recipe. The staff also makes their own dough, and the toppings are fresh and plentiful. A few of the favorites include Canadian bacon, pepperoni, and combination pizzas. Sandwiches are also on the menu.

Cranberry Hill Inn

130 West Almond, Lexington, Oklahoma (405)527-7251. Travel sixteen miles on Highway 77 from Norman or two miles north of Purcell on Highway 77. At the stoplight, turn one block south on First Street and 1/2 block west on Almond. $55-75 per night. To stay overnight, make reservations two to three weeks in advance. Children are accepted. No pets. Not handicapped accessible. The owners host weekday lunches and afternoon teas for groups of ten or more. Call ahead for details; reservations should be made one week in advance. The cost includes a guided tour of the home. The Cranberry Hill Inn is also available for weddings, bridal showers, and birthday parties.

This 6000-square-foot inn has all the frills of a Southern Victorian mansion, including seven fireplaces, a garden room, and stained glass windows. Outside are flower-lined walkways. The home was built in 1901 by Morgan Abernathy, a local banker. The third floor once served as a ballroom. The marble in one of the fireplaces was imported from Italy. Innkeepers Luther and Barbara Dean, formerly of Louisiana, serve a generous country breakfast featuring their own homemade jams and jellies. At night enjoy their signature dessert, a cranberry-orange pound cake with warm butter-almond sauce, served with coffee.

The Inn has three guest rooms. The Lavender Lace room is a smaller room with an antique iron bed, an oak chest and dresser, and a dressing table with cabbage rose skirt. The walls of the Golden room are papered in yellow roses. Cozy up on the four-poster oak bed with a good book or, in the cold months, stretch out in front of the fireplace. The Golden room has an adjoining sitting room. The Bed of Roses room is large enough to sleep up to four people. It also has a sitting area with wicker furniture and a fireplace. Each room is on the second floor, and guests must share a bathroom.

Oklahoma City Area

On April 22, 1889, Oklahoma City was settled by 10,000 pioneers in the Land Run for the Unassigned Lands in central Oklahoma. At noon, men and women raced on horseback, by trains, on bicycles, or in wagons across the plains to stake their claims for town lots and farm land. In a single day, Oklahoma City went from being a small village with a Land Run office to a small tent town.

Two major events stand out that sealed the fate for the small town and its future. In 1907, Oklahoma achieved statehood, and Guthrie was named Oklahoma's capital. However, it wasn't

long until a vote of the people changed the capital from Guthrie to Oklahoma City. Stories abound about how, under the cover of night, the state seal was moved from Guthrie in a laundry basket in 1910. Then, in 1928, something happened that would cause Oklahoma City to grow quickly; a test well was drilled. The well hit oil and gushed over 110,000 barrels before it could be capped. That incident started Oklahoma City on its way to prosperity.

Oklahoma City has something for everyone with its world-class sporting events, festivals, performing arts, art galleries, museums, beautiful parks, and lakes.

Oklahoma City is located in the heart of Oklahoma. It is 115 miles southwest of Tulsa and 200 miles from Dallas. Take I-44 west from Tulsa or I-35 north from Dallas. Oklahoma City Conventions and Visitors Bureau, (405) 297-8912 or (800) 225-5652. ⓘ

Attractions

Ballet Oklahoma

Performances are held at the Civic Center, (405) 848-TOES. From I-40 East: Exit at Walker and go north. At Colcord, go west and look for the Civic Center on your left. From I-40 West: Exit at Robinson and go north. At Reno, go west to Walker and turn north. At Colcord, go west and look for the Civic Center on your left. The season runs from October through April. Each production is performed on Friday and Saturday evenings and Saturday and Sunday matinees. Ticket prices vary with each performance, and season tickets range from $20-100. Call ahead to be put on the mailing list for a season brochure. If you arrive early enough, you may be able to park free on the streets surrounding the Civic Center; otherwise, plan to spend a few dollars on paid parking nearby. ★

Celebrating its twenty-fifth season in 1996, Ballet Oklahoma continues to bring magic, artistry, music, and ballet to the community. Past performances include *Don Juan* and the world-premiere of *Svengali*. The Christmas season in Oklahoma City is more special due to the annual performance of *The Nutcracker Suite*. A performance by Ballet Oklahoma is a "don't miss" event in Oklahoma City!

Black Liberated Arts Center

Performances are held at the Civic Center Music Hall, (405) 232-2522. (See Civic Center directions under Ballet Oklahoma.) Office hours for more information are weekdays 9-5. Ticket prices range from $10-20. Call ahead for a season brochure.

This fine arts organization offers a full season of performing arts which includes music, dance, and drama. Guest artists sponsored by BLAC have included Alvin Ailey, Lena Horne, Eartha Kitt, Ruby Dee, Ossie Davis, the Boys Choir of Harlem, and nationally-touring theater groups performing dramatic and musical productions.

BLAC also sponsors a popular jazz and blues festival near downtown Oklahoma City. The **Deep Deuce Jazz Festival** is held at N.E. 2nd and Walnut Street and attracts thousands of music lovers who enjoy all-day music, delicious ethnic foods, and arts and crafts. Each year the festival features three or more headliner talents such as Joe McBride, Sonny Rhodes, and Jay McShann and the best local and regional jazz and blues musicians. The festival is held on Saturday and Sunday of the last weekend of July; admission is $3. Call BLAC for a festival schedule after June 1.

Canadian County Historical Museum

300 S. Grand in El Reno, (405) 262-5121. From I-40, take the I-40 Business Loop through El Reno. At Grand, turn south and travel one block. Wednesday-Saturday 10-5, Sunday 1:30-5. Closed Monday, Tuesday and some holidays. Free.

The museum's main building is the old Rock Island Railroad Depot, with exhibits inside tracing the history of the area from prehistoric times through pioneer days. Also on the grounds is the Red Barn, filled with antique automobiles and farm equipment. Other buildings include the Possum Hollow School (a one-room school), the original El Reno Hotel, the Darlington Indian Agency Jail, the first Red Cross Service Center from World War II, and General Philip Sheridan's cabin. Sheridan had served in the Civil War, and he commanded the Indian wars from 1874 to 1885. Every April, the Eighty-Niner Day Celebration is held on the museum grounds to celebrate the Land Run. Arts and crafts, games, food, and other activities make this an all-day event.

Located five miles west and two miles north of the museum is Fort Reno. It was established for the protection of the Darlington Agency during the Cheyenne uprising of 1876, and it is now home to a livestock research station branch of Oklahoma State University. Many original buildings remain on the grounds. The Fort Reno Old Post Cemetery is located nearby. (Tours are available Monday-Friday 8:30-4:30. Call ahead for tour reservations.)

Canterbury Choral Society

Offices are located at 428 W. California and concerts are held at the Civic Center Music Hall. (See directions under Ballet Oklahoma.) Call (405) 842-5387 for tickets or (405) 232-7464 for other information. Prices range from $18 to $45. Season Subscription saves 25% off single-ticket prices.

Through its concerts, the Canterbury Choral Society brings the very best in choral music to the community. Performances in the past have included notable works by such artist as Bach, Mendelssohn, Vaughan, Williams, Mozart, and Berlioz. In addition to scheduled performances, the Canterbury Octet and Canterbury Chamber Choir are available for community and private functions.

Carpenter Square Theatre

400 W. Main, (405) 232-6500. Westbound, exit I-40 at Robinson Street and continue west to Walker. Turn north to Main then turn east on Main and continue to Hudson. Carpenter Square Theatre sits on the southwest corner of the intersection of Main and Hudson. Eastbound, exit I-40 at Walker, travel north to Main, then turn east on Main to Hudson. Thursday, Friday and Saturday performances with Sunday matinees. Dates and time vary. Individual tickets range from $8-12.50 for a play, to $10-15 for a musical. Season tickets range from $65-85.

Carpenter Square Theatre is a nonprofit community theater which offers unique, uncensored plays performed by volunteer and professional actors. Plays performed in the past include *Six Women With Brain Death* or *Expiring Minds Want to Know, The Illusion,* and *Corpse.* Comic adventures, zany musicals, dramatic comedies, and madcap murder mysteries are key words to describe Carpenter Square's season events.

Enterprise Square, USA

2501 East Memorial Road, (405) 425-5030. Exit I-35 at Memorial Road and go west, or from Broadway Extension, exit Memorial Road and travel east. The museum is located between Eastern and Bryant on the Oklahoma Christian University of Science and Arts campus. Look for signs on the north side of Memorial. Tuesday-Friday 9-4, Saturday 9-5, Sunday 1-4. Closed Monday. Hours are extended during the summer months. Adults $6, senior citizens $4.50, students ages 6-18 $4; free for children ages five and under. Tours begin every fifteen minutes, and they last approximately two to three hours. Visitors may remain in the building two hours after the last tour begins. Children will enjoy the tour much more if they can read. Handicapped accessible.

A tour guide starts visitors on their journey through an in-depth study of our nation's economic system. Through creative video and technology, visitors observe and interact with the exhibits designed to help them understand such notions as supply and demand, the value of money, our nation's government and how it affects the economy, and more. This is an excellent place to learn about the excitement and perils of the American dream–owning and growing your own business. The history of the economy comes to life in the Hall of Giants, where influential American inventors and entrepreneurs such as Thomas Edison and Henry Ford are highlighted. Hands-on economic adventure is encouraged through thirty-two game stations in the Economics Arcade. The tour ends at the "Venture" exhibit, which uses touch-screen technology to help visitors learn to manage various types of businesses.

45th Infantry Museum

2145 N.E. 36th, (405) 424-5313. Exit I-35 at N.E. 36th Street and travel west. The museum is located ahead about one-half mile on the north side of 36th. Tuesday-Friday 9-5, Saturday 10-5,

Sunday 1-5. Closed Thanksgiving and Christmas. Free. Tours are given to groups of ten or more by reservation only; call at least one week ahead. Group tours can be tailored to fit different subjects such as the Civil War or the Vietnam War. Handicapped accessible.

The history of Oklahoma's citizen/soldier from about 1841 to the present is revealed at the 45th Infantry Museum. Weaponry dating from the Civil War, personal items from Adolf Hitler, Bill Mauldin's famous World War II cartoons, and more help interpret the history of wars and how they affected Oklahoma and the people of Oklahoma. The Dachau/Concentration Camp exhibits show the very dark side of war. A unique collection of the museum is the Jordan B. Reeves gun collection, said to be one of the finest in the nation. It includes military weapons dating from the Revolutionary War to Vietnam, as well as the famous Civil War-era Mosby Cannon. There is a large outdoor display of military vehicles, weapons, and aircraft, covering the twelve acres that surround the museum.

On the observed Memorial and Veterans Days, the museum hosts special ceremonies that honor Oklahoma's military men and women. Ceremonies begin at 10 a.m. and last about an hour. Call the museum for more information.

Frontier City

11501 N.E. Expressway, (405) 478-2412. Located off I-35 between 122nd Street and Hefner in northeast Oklahoma City. Open from April through October (weekends only in April, May, September, and October). Hours vary; call ahead for a prerecorded message. Pricing for the 1997 season is parking $4 per car, adults $20.99 plus tax, children under 48 inches tall $14.99 plus tax. Children under three are free. Special discounts are available for seniors and the physically challenged. ★ ⑤

Seventy-five rides, shows, shops, and attractions for the entire family are offered at this western-theme amusement park. Among the highlights at Frontier City are four exciting roller coasters, including the ever-popular Silver Bullet and the forward and backward Diamondback; both leave riders breathless. The Nightmare, an indoor, in-the-dark roller coaster, provides a different kind of thrill, and a classic wooden coaster makes guests want to try it again.

Thrill-seekers meet their match when they encounter the Geronimo Skycoaster: stepping off a 180 foot tower gives participants the feel of flying and bungee jumping all in one. An extra price is charged for the experience, and many say it's worth it. The Prairie Schooner is exciting, swinging higher than most expect, and the Time Warp will swing and stop, allowing riders the experience of being upside down. Tired of all the excitement? The Centennial Skywheel is a calm and relaxing ride, and the view is outstanding. Don't forget the many shows that are available. Pick up a brochure (with map) as you enter the gate.

The Kids Korral and the new Paul Bunyan Tiny Timber Town offer a variety of rides and exciting hands-on and interactive activities for children and parents to enjoy together. Included are Babe's Barnyard Buddies petting zoo, Teeny's Tea Time tea cup ride, and Tippecanoes at Tadpole Creek. The highlight of the area is the Buzz Saw Company, a four-story, interactive adventure set that is perfect for family participation and fun.

Around 9:30 p.m., a fireworks display is offered most nights from Memorial Day through Labor Day. For best viewing, reserve your spot early by the Log Flume Lagoon.

Restaurants are plentiful, offering fare such as pizza, Mexican food, hamburgers, hot dogs, barbecue, and deli sandwiches. Prices range from two to five dollars per entree. No outside food and drinks are allowed inside the park, but a picnic area is available outside the gates. For those seeking souvenirs, stop in at the Old Time Photography Studio for a family portrait or visit the well-stocked Frontier Trading Company.

Weekdays (particularly Mondays) before five are typically not as crowded; Saturdays and evenings are the most popular. Call ahead for information regarding hours, admission, and special events. A first aid office with trained EMT's is located next to the Silver Bullet Rollercoaster. Childcare areas and strollers are available. An ATM is located near the southeast corner of the Trading Post retail store.

Summer concerts are offered for guests at no additional charge. Upcoming performers include the Little River Band, Three Dog Night, and Lesley Gore and the Coasters. Call ahead for more information.

In addition to summer concerts, several outstanding events are scheduled at the park. On July 4th, Frontier City celebrates our nation's birthday with the **Old-Fashioned American Celebration**. Activities include a concert and an extended fireworks display. During **Oktoberfest**, held the first three weekends in October, guests enjoy a taste of German foods, decorations, theme music, and entertainment by local talent. A special low rate allows visitors to enjoy this event, but a ride pass is extra. Get spooked at **Hallowscream**, held during the last two weeks of October. Children ages twelve and under can travel the trick-or-treat trail from 7-9 p.m.; those twelve and older can experience the Trail of Terror after dark.

Harn Homestead

313 N.E. 16th Street, (405) 235-4058. Located south of the Oklahoma State Capitol, west of Lincoln Boulevard about two blocks on N.E. 16th Street. Look for the signs along Lincoln Boulevard. Tuesday-Saturday 10-4. Harn Home tours are conducted daily, at the top of the hour from 10-3. Adults $3, children under age twelve $1.50. Educational Programs and group rates are available. The Homestead is partially handicapped accessible. Visitors are always welcome to bring a picnic lunch to enjoy on the shaded grounds. ★

The Harn Homestead presents everyday life of the Territorial days between 1889 and 1907. Visitors will see a one-room schoolhouse, working gardens and orchards, a working barn, an exhibit barn, a furnished farmhouse, the Shepherd house, and the restored and furnished Harn home. The 3200-square-foot Harn home was ordered from the 1890 National Homebuilder's catalog. It cost $8,000, and it took six months to build. A replica of those found during Territorial days, one of the barns holds agricultural and household exhibits along with a surrey, a weaving loom, and a variety of items of the era. A dairy barn built in 1904 by the Shinn family is used for children's programs.

Call two weeks ahead for group tours and specially-arranged educational programs. Adult and youth workshops are available throughout the year. Held in October, the **Harvest Festival** provides an excellent opportunity for hands-on family fun. Spinners, weavers, blacksmiths, and storytellers gather to enlighten and entertain visitors. A petting zoo, farm animals, sack races, cake walks, and stilt walking are available for everyone to enjoy.

Jewel Box Theatre

3700 N. Walker, (405) 521-1786. Exit I-35 at N.E. 36th. Go west to Walker and turn north. At the bottom of the hill (about 1/2 block) turn right into the parking lot. Season runs from August through May, with performances held Wednesday-Saturday 8 p.m., Sunday 2:30 p.m. Adults $10, children (ages 18 and under) $5. Season tickets are available. Call Monday through Friday between 1 and 6 p.m. for tickets.

Quality, award-winning theater is what audiences find at the Jewel Box Theatre. Each year, the theater sponsors six productions in its theater, and it presents two musicals in an outdoor amphitheater. Presented with a Governor's Award for Excellence, Jewel Box Theatre proudly celebrates over two decades of quality live theater. Past plays and musicals have included *West Side Story, The Lion In Winter, Driving Miss Daisy, South Pacific, Guys and Dolls, Annie*, and two state premieres, *Crazy For You* and *The Will Rogers Follies*.

Lake Hefner

Located in northwest Oklahoma City, (405) 525-8822. Traveling north on the Hefner Parkway from Northwest Expressway, exit on Britton Road. Turn west and drive until the road ends at the lake. Parking areas are nearby. Open daily. Free.

Sailing, biking, hiking, skating, and more can be enjoyed at Lake Hefner. There are two paved trails that follow the shoreline of Lake Hefner; one is for skating and bicycling, the other for walking and jogging. Benches are available for those needing to rest from their activities. Picnic areas are available on the south side of the lake.

Located nearby is a **duck pond**. To find it, travel west on Wilshire from May Avenue until the road ends at Lake Hefner. This is a perfect spot for young children to feed the waterfowl or for adults to enjoy some quiet time.

For information on any water activities, stop at the Ranger's Station located on the south side by the boat ramp. A free map of the biking and hiking trails can be obtained from Wheeler Dealer Bicycle Shop, 2729 Northwest 50th, (405) 947-6260. Some of the trails offer no shade. Take plenty of water and, in the summer months, try to go early morning or late afternoons for your physical activities. Whether skating or bicycling, wear your helmet.

Lyric Theatre

2501 North Blackwelder. Performances are held in the Kirkpatrick Auditorium on the Oklahoma City University campus. For tickets call (405) 524-7111, or to be added to the brochure mailing list call (405) 810-9300. To locate the Kirkpatrick Auditorium, exit 23rd Street from I-235 (Centennial Expressway), exit 23rd Street and go west. At Blackwelder, turn north. Watch for the Kirkpatrick Fine Arts Building on the left. The season runs from late May to early August. Shows and hours vary with each perfor-mance. Single tickets (available after April 1) range from $13-25. Season ticket prices are $57.50-110. Call a week ahead to reserve tickets.

Outanding musicals at Lyric Theatre.

Since 1962, Lyric Theatre has continued to thrill audiences with outstanding musicals. Voted Best Live Theater in *The Daily Oklahoman's* 1995 Reader's Choice, and 1995 Best Performing Arts Group by the *Oklahoma Gazette*, Lyric utilizes professional musical theater actors and the best talent in the Oklahoma City area to perform in award-winning musicals such as *Jesus Christ Superstar, Will Rogers Follies, Damn Yankees, Evita*, and *Camelot*.

Martin Park Nature Center

5000 West Memorial Road, (405) 755-0676. Located in northwestern Oklahoma City. The park is on the south side of Memorial between Meridian and MacArthur. From April through November, open Tuesday-Sunday 9-6. Closed Mondays. From December through March, open Wednesday-Sunday 9-6. Free, although there may be nominal fees for guided hikes and special activities. The Nature Center is handicapped accessible, but the restrooms are not.

Rendezvous with nature at Martin Nature Park Center. No matter the season, this 140-acre urban wildlife park provides an interesting back-to-nature experience. Follow the trail signs or learn from a guided tour. While you are adventuring, watch for many species of birds, prairie dogs, waterfowl, turtles, owls, and snakes.

There is a hands-on Nature Center; recreation areas are available for picnics. For custom-ized nature hikes, call two weeks in advance to make reservations. Also call ahead for reserva-tions for the **family tour**, offered each Sunday at 2:30. The fee is $1 per person.

Educational programs are offered throughout the year at the Nature Center and at other OKC parks. For a seasonal program guide and map of Oklahoma City parks, call (405) 297-2211.

Myriad Botanical Gardens

100 Myriad Gardens in downtown Oklahoma City, (405) 297-3995. From the east, take I-40 to Robinson. Go north on Robinson, then west on Reno. Parking is on the right. From the west, take I-40 and exit on Walker. Go north on Walker to Reno. Turn east. Parking is on the left immediately past Hudson. Daily 9-6; closed Christmas Day. Admission, which is subject to change is adults $3, seniors $2, children ages four to twelve $1.25, children under four are free. (Admission subject to change.) Several "free" days are scheduled each year. Guests can get in free on March 25th, which is the Garden's anniversary date. Mothers get in free on Mother's Day and senior citizens on Senior's Day. Handicapped accessible. ★

Imagine going from the tropics to a desert in three minutes; it's possible at the **Myriad Botani-cal Gardens** and **Crystal Bridge Tropical Conservatory**. Conceived as part of a 1960s plan to revitalize downtown Oklahoma City, the gardens and conservatory are modeled to some degree after Tivoli Gardens in Copenhagen. Exotic plants, lizards, colorful butterflies, and a real waterfall delight guests of the garden. Located in a glassed "tube," the landscaping and ecosystems are thoroughly explained through labels.

Guided tours are available seven days a week; reservations need to be made at least a week in advance. Tours average thirty minutes ,and they can be geared to any age group. Special exhibits, nature classes, and celebrations are held throughout the year; call for a brochure. In the summer, it is very hot inside the Conservatory. The cooler days of fall and winter provide a more comfortable temperature and bigger, more colorful blooms from the plants.

Seventeen acres of native landscaping surround the Crystal Bridge. During nice weather, take a stroll and enjoy the Japanese Koi and Goldfish in the spring-fed lake. A visit to the gift shop is worth the effort. The environment and its protection are the theme in this well-stocked and interesting store.

The Crystal Bridge at Myriad Gardens.

National Cowboy Hall of Fame and Western Heritage Center

1700 N.E. 63rd Street, (405) 478-2250. Take I-44 to Martin Luther (M.L.) King Boulevard, exit and go north a short distance to N.E. 63rd Street then turn west. The museum sits on the south side of 63rd. Labor Day to Memorial Day 9-5. Memorial Day to Labor Day 8:30-6. Closed Thanksgiving Day, Christmas Day, and New Year's Day. Adults $6.50, senior citizens $5.50, children ages six to twelve $3.25, children under age six free. Handicapped accessible. ★ ⑤

Dedicated to preserving the history and legends of the West, the National Cowboy Hall of Fame and Western Heritage Center features a renowned collection of classic and contemporary Western art and artifacts. A heroic-size bronze statue of a weary cowboy facing the sunset welcomes visitors to the museum. Inside, James Earle Fraser's moving sculpture, The End of the Trail, and Gerald Balciar's marble masterpiece, Canyon Princess, grace broad corridors.

The vast permanent collections of the museum, considered a "national treasure," reflect the breadth of America's frontier past from cowboys and Indians to miners, soldiers and homesteaders. Breath-taking art works by famous Western artists such as Remington, Russell and Moran provide visitors an inspiring view of the Old West.

The Hall is home to the Rodeo Hall of Fame, the Hall of Great Performers, and the Hall of Great Westerners—as well as many other superb permanent and traveling exhibitions. The Sam Noble Special Events Center showcases Windows to the West, five monumental Western landscape paintings by Wilson Hurley. Visitors encounter beautiful outdoor sculptures and a variety of indigenous vegetation in the Hall's picturesque gardens.

The Hall annually hosts the **Western Heritage Awards** in February, **Chuck Wagon Gath-**

Frontier Country

National Cowboy Hall of Fame

erings and the **Howdy Pardner Children's Festival** in May, and the **Cowboy Christmas Ball** in early December.

Tour guides are available by appointment only. Call or write the tour coordinator two weeks in advance to secure reservations (adult tours, 478-2250, ext. 254; children's tours, ext. 224). The beautiful Sam Noble Special Events Center, with a fully-equipped stage and state-of-the-art catering kitchen, has become a favorite rental facility for banquets, workshops, receptions, dances, and trade shows. Call 478-6407 for information. The museum is handicapped accessible. An indoor snack bar and eating area is available, and "Trappings of the West," the beautiful museum **gift store** is a "must-do" shopping experience, with all items relating to the Western theme, from inexpensive souvenir items to beautiful art work and Native American jewelry.

Oklahoma City Art Museum

3113 Pershing Boulevard, (405) 946-4477. Located at State Fair Park. From I-44 take the Northwest 10th East exit and go

End of the Trail.

to May Avenue. Turn south on May to the first fairgrounds gate (Gate 25) and go west. The museum is the first building on your left. Tuesday-Saturday 10-5, Thursday 10-9, Sunday 1-5. Adults $3.50, seniors/students $2.50, children under age twelve are free. Guided tours are conducted by appointment only, and are available in five languages. Call two weeks in advance. Membership information is available upon request. Handicapped accessible.

Over three thousand works of modern art comprise the Oklahoma City Art Museum's collection. Each year, up to twelve rotating exhibits featuring works from the museum collection and on-loan pieces are displayed. A significant portion of the museum's more famous art pieces came from the former Washington Gallery of Modern Art, a Washington, D.C. gallery active from 1916 to 1968.

Quality educational programs provide opportunities for visitors of all ages to appreciate artistic abilities and traditions from across the world. Among the educational outreach programs of the museum are lecture series, film festivals, special exhibit openings, a Children's Art Festival, Family Days, and more.

Oklahoma City Blazers Hockey

Myriad Convention Center, (405) 235-PUCK. From I-40 exit at Walker. Go North to Sheridan. Turn east on Sheridan. Paid parking is available under the Myriad or in nearby paid parking lots. The season runs from October to March, with games usually starting at 7:30. Ticket prices range from $8 to $12, with children twelve and under receiving a discount. Season tickets are available; call for more information. ★

Wild and crazy fun is what you'll experience as you watch one of the top minor league professional hockey teams in the country! The Oklahoma City Blazers have earned numerous top honors throughout the past few years. A popular choice for entertainment in downtown Oklahoma City, each game is fast paced and exciting; the fans are about as interesting to observe as the game!

Oklahoma City Coyote Rollerhockey

Myriad Convention Center, (405) 236-HOWL. From I-40, exit at Walker. Go North to Sheridan then turn east. Season runs from late May to early August, with games usually beginning at 7:35 p.m. Ticket prices range from $5-12; discounts given for seniors, children 12 and under, and groups. Season tickets range from $65 to $165.

The newest professional sports team to come to Oklahoma City, the Coyotes bring high-scoring, hard-hitting fun and excitement to rollerhockey fans, both young and old.

Oklahoma City 89ers Baseball

All Sports Stadium, State Fair Park, (405) 946-8989. From I-44, go east on Northwest 10th Street to the fairgrounds. Follow the signs to All Sports Stadium. Arrive early or be prepared to walk a distance from the parking areas to the stadium. NOTE: The new ball field in downtown Oklahoma City's Bricktown is scheduled to open for the 1998 season. Season: April-August; call for game time. Admission ranges from $2 for general admission to $6 for lower box seats. Ages four and under are free. Ticket packages and season tickets are available. ★

The Oklahoma City 89ers (Triple A professional baseball) is the Texas Rangers' top farm club. A long-standing tradition in Oklahoma City, the 89ers celebrated their 35th season in 1996. Home games are special for 89ers fans. Activities such as premium giveaways, sumo wrestling, and celebrity appearances are held during most every game. In addition to regular stadium seats, there is a grassy hillside that is especially convenient and fun for families. Bring your own seating for this area.

Oklahoma City Philharmonic Orchestra

Concerts are held at the Civic Center Music Hall (see Ballet Oklahoma entry for directions), (405) TIC-KETS or (405) 297-3000. The season lasts from September to early May. Times and dates vary with each performance. Single tickets range from $9-32, season tickets from $43-245. Call for a season brochure. ★

From timeless masterpieces to familiar favorites, the Oklahoma City Philharmonic inspires and thrills audiences. Conductor Joel Levine, the orchestra, and featured guests provide variety throughout each season. Guest artists have ranged from Fred Penner for a family concert to Van Cliburn for the more sophisticated audience.

The Philharmonic season typically includes nine concerts, each featuring a different guest artist, six concerts in a **Pops Series**, and two **family** or **discovery series concerts**. Audiences enjoy a special Christmas treat when they attend the **Yuletide Festival** held in early December. Talented dancers, singers, headline guest artists, and even Santa use humor, song, dance, and witty skits to entertain even the youngest who attend. Don't miss the opportunities for great music and entertainment offered throughout the Philharmonic's season.

Oklahoma City Zoological Park

2101 N.E. 50th Street, (405) 424-3344. From I-35, exit N.E. 50th Street, travel west one mile and follow signs to entrance. From I-44, exit on Martin Luther King Boulevard, go south to Remington Place (N.E. 50th), turn east and follow signs to zoo entrance. April-September open daily 9-6. October-March open daily 9-5. Exhibit buildings close fifteen minutes before the zoo closes. Adults $4, children ages three to eleven and seniors ages sixty-five and older $2. Children under three are free. For groups of twenty-five or more, children $1.50, adults $3. Must pay as a group and no reservations are needed. Aquaticus show $2. Seasonal Sky Safari $1 per person one way, children under three free. Seasonal train guided tours $1.50 per person. Handicapped accessible. A $40 zoo membership provides free admission for one year for parents and children and the opportunity to visit about one hundred zoos nationwide free. ★

A number of adult educational classes are available throughout the year at varying costs. Call the education department (ext. 218) to get a brochure. The zoo's special events include the **Summer Season Celebration** in April, **Judy the Elephant's Birthday Party** in May, the **Annual Pumpkin Drive** and **Haunt the Zoo** in October, and **Deck the Zoo** and **Santa Delivers** in December. For details about these

The Great EscApe.

and other special events, call the zoo phone number for a recorded message.

One of the top zoos in the nation, the Oklahoma City Zoo is a top-notch facility that provides "edutainment" for all ages. Upon entering, purchase a twenty-five cent map and plan your visit. Several exhibits require special attention: Aquaticus, the Island Life exhibit building, the Herpetarium, the South American Aviary, the Great EscApe, and the Cat Forest/Lion Overlook.

At **Aquaticus**, the dolphins are the stars of the show, and the funny motions of the sea lions also amuse the crowd. After the show, visit the exhibits down the ramp at Aquaticus to view more fresh and seawater animal life.

The **Island Life** exhibit building features six Galapagos tortoises, parrots that hang upside down, ducks that whistle, many endangered species, as well as interactive educational exhibits (try lifting the tortoise shell).

In the **Herpetarium** are reptiles and amphibians from all over the world. Rattlesnakes, a boa constrictor, tree frogs, and eyelash vipers are just a few of the creatures you can observe up close and safely through the glass windows. Make sure you close both doors as you step into the **South American Aviary**. This is a free-flight environment which features some of the great and beautiful birds and mammals from South America.

The **Great EscApe** exhibit features a major collection of great apes (gorillas, chimpanzees and orangutans). It is the first exhibit in the United States to reproduce three and one half acres of tropical forest, meadows and streams. Visitors truly feel a part of a misty tropical forest as they view the gorillas through large glass windows. Mothers and baby gorillas are often within close view. Watch as mothers groom their babies and note how they interact with one another. Sometimes as visitors study these creatures, they find themselves the object of much scrutiny by the gorillas! Cool days will almost always insure good viewing because the gorillas crowd around the heated rocks near the windows.

The **Cat Forest/Lion Overlook** is the newest addition to the zoo. At a cost of $8.4 million, this exhibit covers more than four acres. Every effort has been made to simulate the natural habitats of the many cats living at the zoo. Sumatran tigers live in an area with bamboo, snow leopards enjoy rock outcroppings like those in the Himalayas, and the web-footed fishing cat wades through the exhibit's pool. Many other small and large wild cats can be seen in this extraordinary exhibit.

Don't miss the **butterfly garden** (most active from mid-spring to early fall) and the rides, the Sky Safari and train. The seasonally-available Sky Safari allows for a birds-eye view of the animals, and it runs from the front entrance to Aquaticus. The cost is $1 one way per person (children under three are free). The train runs from April through October. It will take you for a guided tour of the hoofed-stock animals. Regardless of whether you ride the train or walk, plan to enjoy this area; it features some of the rarest animals in the zoo.

The Butterfly Garden.

NOTE: Call the information line for complete updates on the zoo and its activities. Visitors also learn much about the programs at the zoo at kiosks in the Information Area, not far from the entrance.

You may bring your own picnic; but whether you buy or bring your own food, there are many shaded areas to enjoy. Strollers are available for $2, and wheelchairs are available (for a small deposit). From October-March, the dolphin show on weekdays at 11 a.m. is a free training show. The zoo is busier during nice weather and on weekends. Peak hours are 11-3. The animals are most active during early morning and late afternoon.

Oklahoma Firefighters Museum

2716 N.E. 50th Street, (405) 424-3440. Located halfway between Martin Luther King Boulevard and I-35 on the south side of Northeast 50th Street, just east of the Oklahoma City Zoo. Open daily from 10-4:30. Closed holidays. Adults $3, Children ages 6-12 $1.50, senior citizens $2. Group rates are one-half price for regular tours. Handicapped accessible. Call two weeks in advance to arrange tours. Tours last for approximately seventy-five minutes and are given to groups of twelve or more by appointment only.

The Oklahoma Firefighters Museum is the only firefighters museum that is owned and operated by volunteer or paid firemen. Through the museums' exhibits, visitors learn and appreciate the technological advances in firefighting over the past 150 years. Guests begin their tour with the first fire station in Oklahoma, built in 1869 at Fort Supply in northwest Oklahoma then continue with a viewing of over thirty restored fire trucks. Among the many unique items here is the 1919 restored Seagraves Rig that shines and sparkles under the museum lights. Also on display is an arm patch collection numbering close to 7000 and a large fire hat collection. Along tne south wall is an eight foot by fifty-eight foot mural by artist Lynn Campbell. It is a detailed, pictorial history of firefighting apparatus from the days of the horse-drawn steamer to vehicles of the 1950s. A gift shop is available. The staff enjoys answering questions; don't hesitate to ask.

Oklahoma Governor's Mansion

820 N.E. 23rd Street, (405) 523-4268 for group tours. From I-44 exit on Lincoln Boulevard and go south to 23rd. Turn east and continue about 1/4 mile. Parking is available just west of the mansions' west gate on North Phillips. Public tours are held from 1-3 p.m. on Wednesdays—but not in December and January. Tours of forty or more should call three to four weeks in advance.

The Governor's Mansion.

Oklahoma is blessed with a beautiful Governor's Mansion to complement its Capitol. This Dutch Colonial, three-story, twelve-room mansion provides visitors with a sense of history and a sense of pride. The mansion was completed in 1928. During the 1995 restoration of the Governor's Mansion, Oklahomans participated by giving gifts to furnish the Mansion. A huge Montgolfier crystal chandelier hangs over a new, heirloom-quality state seal rug. These are just two of the examples of the many new and elegant furnishings at the home. Other points of interest on the tour are the rotating artwork in the entry hall, provided from the collections of the National Cowboy Hall of Fame and Gilcrease Museum, and an elaborately-carved mahogany bed in the guest room (once owned by Emperor Maximillan of Mexico). The home was recently named an "outstanding attraction" by the Oklahoma tourism industry. Don't miss the opportunity to view the beautifully-restored Governor's Mansion.

Oklahoma Heritage Center

201 N.W. 14th Street, (405) 235-4458. Traveling south on the Centennial Expressway (I-235), exit at 23rd Street. At the stop light, go straight, and you'll be on Broadway. At 14th Street, turn west. The Oklahoma Heritage Center is two blocks ahead on the northwest corner. Monday-Saturday 9-5, Sunday 1-5. Adults $3, seniors $2.50, students $2, children ten and under free. Handicapped accessible.

The Oklahoma Heritage Center is a gift from State Supreme Court Judge Robert A. Hefner

and his family to the people of Oklahoma. The former residence of the Hefner family, the home was built in 1917 and is located on the edge of historic Heritage Hills. It was opened to the public as the Oklahoma Heritage Center in 1972. Within this lovely mansion, visitors will find beautiful collectibles of the Hefner family and much information about influential Oklahomans who have been inducted into the Oklahoma Hall of Fame. Photographs, biographical sketches, oil paintings, and bronze sculptures of these honored Oklahomans are on display. The most notable items collected by the Hefner family and on display in the home are Persian rugs, French and Italian chandeliers, and a hand-carved French clock (circa 1860).

In addition, the Oklahoma Heritage Center includes over ten thousand volumes of Oklahoma-related books and periodicals in the Shepherd Oklahoma Heritage Library. The Hefner Memorial Chapel and manicured garden areas on the grounds surrounding the house are lovely additions to a tour of this Oklahoma landmark.

Oklahoma Opry

404 West Commerce, (405) 632-8322. From I-40, exit at Robinson Street and travel south to 25th Street. Turn west; the Oklahoma Opry is about three blocks ahead on the south side of Commerce. (25th Street becomes known as Commerce after you turn west from Robinson.) Shows are held every Saturday except when icy. Doors open at 7 p.m. and the show starts at 8 p.m. Adults $8, senior citizens (65 or older) $7, children $4. No smoking or alcohol is allowed. A snack bar is available.

Oklahoma City residents say that the best country and gospel music in the region is found at the Oklahoma Opry. A showcase for up-and-coming country artists, the Opry features eight to ten different entertainers each Saturday night. Entertainers come from Oklahoma, other areas around the U.S., and from other countries such as Canada and Germany. This small-scale version of Nashville's Grand Old Opry boasts a full professional band, a barn-like stage, a seating capacity of eight hundred, and family-oriented entertainment. An awards show is featured in October.

Oklahoma State Capitol

Located at N.E. 23rd Street and Lincoln Boulevard, (405) 521-3356. From I-44, exit at Lincoln Boulevard and proceed south to Northeast 23rd Street. The easiest parking is on the south side of the building on the east side of Lincoln. Monday-Friday 8-4:30. Free. Tours last 45 minutes, and are they conducted every hour on the half-hour from 8-3 or by appointment. During the months the House and Senate are in session (February-May), visitors may observe House legislative sessions from the viewing gallery during business hours from Monday through Thursday. The Senate Chamber viewing gallery is open Monday through Friday. It is best to plan a tour during nice weather; the rotunda area is neither heated nor air-conditioned. The Capitol is handicapped accessible. A tunnel is located under the east side of the Capitol; it exits near the State Museum of History. A tourism information center is located on the first floor of the rotunda.

The Oklahoma State Capitol is the only capitol in the world surrounded by working oil wells. It is also noted for its Classic Greco-Roman architecture and for being one of only twelve Capitols without a dome. Completed in 1917 at a cost of $1.5 million, the building has six hundred-fifty rooms and eleven acres of floor space.

Besides seeing how our State Government works, visitors will delight in the beauty and history found in many murals and portraits at the capitol. Among the most noteworthy are four large portraits of famous Oklahomans located on the fourth floor rotunda's curved walls. Charles Banks Wilson, a native Oklahoman from Miami, was commissioned to paint the portraits in the 1960s. Murals above each portrait depict Oklahoma's early history. An especially intriguing mural is by Chickasaw Indian artist Mike Larsen. Entitled "Flight of Spirit," Larsen's mural honors

Elaine Warner

As Long As The Waters Flow

five world-famous Oklahoma Indian ballerinas. A hidden staircase, the elegant Supreme Court room, the Governor's Blue Room, and more add mystery and fun to the tour of the Capitol, where history is being made every day.

Omniplex

2100 N.E. 52nd Street, (405) 427-5461 or (405) 424-5545. Exit I-44 at Martin Luther King Avenue. Go south. The complex is on the left, just past Remington Park. Adults (ages thirteen to sixty-four) $6.50 plus tax, children ages three to twelve $4 plus tax, children under three free, senior citizens $4.50 plus tax. Labor Day to Memorial Day: Monday-Friday 9:30-5, Saturday 9-6, Sunday 12-6. Memorial Day to Labor Day: Monday-Saturday 9-6, Sunday 12-6. Closed on Thanksgiving and Christmas. Family memberships ($35-45) from any of the museums provides free admission and other amenities. The Planetarium is closed the first Monday of each month for maintenance. Ask at the desk for planetarium show times. Weekends and holidays are the busiest times for the complex; Mondays are the least crowded. After 2 p.m., it is less crowded than the mornings; call ahead if crowds are a concern. Omniplex is handicapped accessible. ★

Within Omniplex, visitors will find many museums and learning areas under one roof. In fact, the complex contains so many that most guests could not possibly experience all of the areas in one visit! The Kirkpatrick Science and Air Space Museum, the International Photography Hall of Fame, the Red Earth Indian Center, the Kirkpatrick Planetarium, and the Gardens and Greenhouse area comprise this educational wonderland.

The two major areas within the Kirkpatrick Science and Air Space Museum are the Hands-On Science Museum and the Air Space Museum. The **Hands-On Science Museum** contains over three hundred exciting and educational exhibits. Experience being weightless in the Aerotrim, travel back in time in the Geovator, or give your life extra energy with the 750,000-volt Tesla Coil. Forecasting the weather becomes a simple feat when one is inside the Weather Station/OmniStudio, and what could be better than experiencing an earthquake in a safe environment? These are but a few of the interactive exhibits available here.

Stargaze and wonder about our ever-changing universe in the **Kirkpatrick Planetarium**. Original presentations and educational shows about our galaxy and those beyond are offered daily. On busy days, free tickets to the planetarium are distributed to help with crowd control. These tickets go quickly; ask at the front desk upon arrival to see if tickets are still available.

From vintage aircraft such as a 1914 Parker Pusher to an actual Apollo Command Module Simulator, visitors at the **Air Space Museum** will find something fascinating, no matter their interests. Memorabilia from famous Oklahoma pilots like Wiley Post and Oklahoma's six astronauts are displayed proudly. Learn what astronauts eat and wear when they go into space, realize your dream of flying in one of the simulators, and marvel at the advancements that we have made since the early days of aviation. Exhibits also include full-scale models of Mercury, Gemini, and Apollo capsules. Young people may want to check out the Young Astronauts Program to become more involved in the study of space.

Omniplex offers classes for children and adults covering a variety of areas, including aviation, science, gardening, space, art, world cultures, Native American history, and photography. Classes are held during the week and on Saturdays. Call ahead for reservations and more information at (405) 424-5545 or for callers outside the 405 area code, (800) 532-7652.

The **International Photography Hall of Fame** (405-424-4055) is located on the second floor of Omniplex at the west end. Visitors experience life through the eyes and talents of photographers from across the world. Learn about photography, from its early equipment to master photographers such as Matthew Brady, and about contributions to photography by innovators Louis Daguerre and George Eastman. The Photography Hall of Fame hosts traveling exhibits regularly throughout the year. These special exhibits have included outstanding and intriguing works by photographic artists such as Mark Webber, Jan Watten, Christina Patoski, and Tim Ernst. Don't miss the world's largest photomural, a 360-degree laserscape of the Grand Canyon.

Learn how Native Americans lived, from their housing to the way they carried their children at **Red Earth Indian Center** (405-427-5228). This museum is located on the second floor and the east end of Omniplex. Of special interest at the center is an exhibit of cradleboards

from the Duepree collection. A stuffed bison stands in the center of the room, surrounded by information on supplies and weapons made from the animal's parts. The bison was all-important to the Plains Indians; it provided their housing, food, clothing, toys, medicine, and more. In fact, there were over a hundred ways the bison could be used; no part of the animal was wasted. Enjoy the Indian artwork lining the walls of the museum, try your hand at basket weaving, or listen by cassette to stories about Native American life.

A Kyoto Garden, a tropical garden, an orchard, and a working greenhouse are only a few of the pleasures enjoyed in the **Gardens and Greenhouse** area behind Omniplex. The Gardens' purpose is to offer ideas for gardeners. Visitors learn about the language of flowers, herbal teas, drought-tolerant plants, and much more. Pack a picnic lunch or grab something from the snack bar and refresh your mind in these small, information-packed gardens.

Located on the first and second floors throughout Omniplex, the eighteen historical, artistic and cultural collections that make up the **Kirkpatrick Galleries** provide brief but interesting glimpses into other areas of the world. Among the most notable exhibits is Admiral William J. Crowe's World Hat Collection. It features hats from over thirty nations, seven continents, two kingdoms and three navies. Former Chairman of the Joint Chiefs of Staff and current U.S. Ambassador to Great Britain, Crowe began his collection of hats in 1976 when he was presented with an Australian army bush hat. Artwork from Africa, Japan and Korea, a popular exhibit of Oklahoma's First Ladies Ball Gowns, the Navy Gallery, a Toy Train Collection, four complete sections of the Berlin Wall, traveling art exhibits, and more await visitors.

Several events, exhibits and festivals are held throughout the year at Omniplex. Two of the most popular include the Winter Expo and the Holiday Treefest. Native Americans demonstrate their customs at **Winter Expo** held in February and sponsored by the Red Earth Indian Center. Held from mid-November to December 31 and noted as one of the top yuletide events in the country, **Treefest** features beautifully-decorated trees highlighting Christmas traditions from around the world. Each summer, the Kirkpatrick Science and Air Space Museum hosts a traveling exhibit such as animated dinosaurs or the science of detective work. Call ahead for more information.

Be sure to take advantage of the well-stocked **Museum Store** offering a wide variety of gifts, toys, books, games, and more. Indoor or outdoor picnic areas and a snack bar are available.

OSU Horticultural Center

*400 North Portland, on the campus of Oklahoma State University Oklahoma City. (405) 945-3358. Exit I-44 at N.W. 10th Street. Go west to Portland and turn south. Look for the OSU campus on the east side of Portland. The **Farmers' Market** is open during any growing season, Wednesday and Saturday, from 8 a.m. to 1 p.m. The **gardens** are accessible at all times. However, during business hours (Monday-Friday 8-5), someone is usually available to answer questions; restrooms in nearby buildings are accessible. Free; donations are appreciated. Special tours for a minimum of fifteen people are available with advance notice. Handicapped accessible.*

The Horticultural Center has much to offer visitors, from the Sensational Garden to its Farmers Market. The **Sensational Garden** is a delight for the senses: listen to a waterfall, smell the delectable fragrances, feel various plant textures, see the colorful blends of plants, the floral dinosaur hill, topiary dinosaur, and butterflies. Those with handicaps will particularly appreciate the many sensory ways to enjoy the gardens. The peak time for floral display at the Sensational Garden is June.

Located just north of the Sensational Garden is one of twenty-eight nationally-sanctioned All-American Trial Gardens, with both vegetables and flowers. Featuring over 550 flowers and over 60 varieties of trial and display vegetables, the Trial Gardens are open for year-round public display and tours.

Check out the fresh fruits and vegetables offered at the **Farmers' Market**. With over twenty-five vendors present, the market offers produce, flowers, plants, herbs, fresh baked goods, and more. Vendors come from Oklahoma City and from communities such as Newalla, Choctaw, Guthrie, and Newcastle. Organically grown, these products are some of the finest in the state. In May, plan to attend the **Herb Fest**. Learn about herbs and their properties and choose from an extensive selection of herb plants for sale. Food and entertainment add to the event.

Oklahoma City

Overholser Mansion

405 N.W. 15th Street, (405) 528-8485. Tuesday-Friday 10-4:30, Saturday-Sunday 2-4:30. Closed Monday and state holidays. Free. Tours are conducted on the hour, with the last tour of the day beginning at 4 p.m. Tours are geared to adults, but they can be adjusted to appeal to older children (about age six and up).

This three-story, French Chateau-style home has attracted attention from Oklahomans since it was built in 1904. The first built in Heritage Hills, the home is a historical landmark for the area–as much for the history of the Overholser family as for the home itself. Henry Overholser came to Oklahoma during the Land Run of 1889. It was through his efforts that the Frisco Railroad decided to extend their line from Tulsa to Oklahoma City, thus insuring that the city would become and remain a commercial center of the newly-opened lands. His actions opened the door for the State Capitol to be moved from Guthrie to Oklahoma City in 1910.

The Overholser Mansion.

Overholser purchased the three-and-a-half acre lot north of Oklahoma City for $3700 in 1901. The mansion quickly became a focal point of Oklahoma City high society. Anna Ione Murphy, Overholser's second wife, was very active in social events. As the first treasurer of the newly-founded Oklahoma Territory, she cofounded such groups as the Modern Classics Club and the Chafing Dish Club.

Restored through the efforts of several historical groups, the Overholser Mansion offers turn-of-the-century decorative arts, English carpets, Brussels lace curtains, and stained glass windows from France. Furnishings reflecting European taste are prevalent throughout. This is a magnificent home, dedicated to the memory of a hospitable and influential Oklahoma City family.

Remington Park

One Remington Place, (405) 424-9000 or (800) 456-9000. Exit I-44 at Martin Luther King Boulevard. Travel south to Remington Park, located on the east side of the road. From I-35, exit at Northeast 50th Street (Remington Place) and go west to Martin Luther King. Turn north to the Remington Park entrance. Valet parking is available at Gate One on Northeast 50th Street. Call for information on the four seasons and hours. General admission $2.50, senior citizens $1.50, Clubhouse admission $3.50. Reserved seats are $2 extra. Infield Only: children ages 7-11 $1.50, ages 6 and under are free. Parking: general $1, preferred $3, valet $5. Handicapped accessible.

Remington Park is an elegant, ninety-seven million dollar horse racing showcase and is quickly making its mark in the horseracing industry. Thoroughbred and Quarter horse racing seasons are held during the year. Remington Park features indoor viewing of the live races, art galleries featuring Western art, restaurants serving food from hot dogs to prime rib, and year-round simulcast races from other tracks.

Guests are welcome at all track levels. Track Level includes the Grandstand Apron restaurant, free bench seating, two gift shops, racing information, Paddock Gardens (an area where jockeys saddle and walk the horses), and the Trackside Cafe. The Grandstand Level offers free bench seating and reserved seating. The Clubhouse area offers reserved seating, Club One private box seating, a lounge, three restaurants, and twenty private penthouse suites on the two upper levels.

Infield Park features a large family recreation area with playground, picnic tables, pavilions, concession centers, pari-mutuel windows, TV-monitors, and special events. Infield Park is open on weekends and holidays from mid-March to early November.

Softball Hall of Fame and Stadium

2801 N.E. 50th, (405) 424-5266. Exit I-35 at N.E. 50th and go west. Look for the gate on the north side of the road. Monday-Friday 9-4:30. Additional weekend hours are available from mid-May to October, Saturday 10-4, Sunday noon-4. Adults $2, children $1. Handicapped accessible.

Honor and learn about the nation's number one participant sport at the Softball Hall of Fame. The museum houses more than eighteen thousand square feet of memorabilia relating to softball and the people who have played the game. Exhibits include photos of national champions, slow pitch and fast pitch records, uniforms of the past and present, action photographs, player biographies, plaques, and trophies.

Through the Hall of Honor, visitors pay homage to the one-hundred-thirty inductees of the Hall of Fame, and they learn about others who have made contributions to the game. The newest area at the Softball Hall of Fame is the Olympic Gallery featuring four color murals that tell the story of softball's long road to the Olympics. Visitors can also view videotapes of Olympic and World Championship Softball Games.

Spencer's Farm

5528 N. Peebly Road in Harrah, (405) 454-3471. From I-35 and Memorial travel twelve miles east to Peebly Road. Turn south and go 4 3/4 miles to Spencer's. Fruit and vegetable season is from the end of May to the middle of September. The flower season is from October 1 to June 1. Summer Hours: Monday-Friday 7:30 a.m.-6 p.m., Saturday-Sunday 7:30 a.m.-5 p.m. Winter Hours (dependent on weather and flower availability) daily 8-3. Products are priced just above wholesale, and they are sold by the pound or bushel. Not handicapped accessible.

Savor the taste and freshness of homegrown and fresh-picked fruits and vegetables at Spencer's. Tomatoes, seedless blackberries and fourteen varieties of peaches are available for picking, either by Spencer's employees or by the customer. Free tasting is allowed, and all packaging and supplies are provided. Other produce available for purchase are potatoes, watermelons, cucumbers, onions, sweet and hot peppers, squash, honeydew melons, cantaloupe, and green beans; in the late summer, black-eyed and purple whole peas can be purchased. In the fall and spring, annual bedding plants such as geraniums and periwinkles are available.

State Museum of History

2100 N. Lincoln Boulevard, (405) 522-5244. Located just southeast of the State Capitol. From I-44 exit onto Lincoln and proceed south to N.E. 20th Street. Watch for signs. Park on the southeast side of the building. Monday-Saturday 8-5. Closed Sunday and holidays. Free; donations are appreciated. Handicapped accessible.

Walk through the state's colorful and unique past at the State Museum of History. Through well-organized exhibits, visitors will be able to piece together the many facets of Oklahoma history. The battles fought on Oklahoma soil and the Oklahomans who fought in wars across the globe are the theme of one area. The Native American exhibits show the differences between the many tribes who have called Oklahoma their home. Territorial days, a decade by decade look at Oklahoma since statehood in 1907, and oilfield wildcatters are other subjects at the museum that tell Oklahoma's story.

Archivists, historians and genealogical researchers will find much documentation in the museum's basement. Particularly noteworthy are the Indian Archives and the Photo Archives.

Stockyards City and National Stockyards Exchange

Located just south of I-40 on Agnew. (405) 235-7267. Monday and Tuesday are livestock sales days; sales begin at 8 a.m. and continue all day. If a holiday falls on Monday, the sale changes to Tuesday and Wednesday. Free. The Stockyards area is partially handicapped accessible.

For over eighty years, little has changed about Stockyards City except the name. Originally known as Packingtown, this area has contributed greatly over the years to the Oklahoma City economy. Thousands of cattle and other livestock are sold each week from Stockyards City. People from around the world come here to see how the livestock operations and auctions work and to buy western goods from a number of specialty shops.

To start your tour, climb the stairs of the catwalks to view the livestock waiting to be auctioned. Make your way to the auction building located near the far northwest corner of the catwalks. Little has changed in the way the auctions have operated in Stockyards City. Visitors can see how the cattle are prepared for the sale and, once inside, note how quickly the cattle sell. This process sets the standard for cattle prices around the country. On a limited basis, the company also auctions sheep and pigs.

After the auction, plan to visit the many interesting businesses located in the area. Many of the businesses such as Cattlemen's Steakhouse have been here for decades. Visitors get a feel for the Old West through retail stores such as Langstons, art galleries, and shops featuring craftspeople who make saddles, tack, hats, boots, and Western clothing. These professionals are happy to demonstrate their skills and to answer questions about their work.

Two noteworthy events provide opportunities to fully experience the area. Usually held the first Friday and Saturday in June, the **Stockyards Stampede** is designed for old-fashioned fun. Music, storytellers, reenactors, a Friday night dance, barbecue cook-off, western arts and crafts, and the **Bullistic Rodeo** (featuring some of the top bull riders in the country) are a few of the festival's events. All events are free except for the Bullistic event on Saturday. During the Christmas holidays, Stockyards City hosts **Cowboy Christmas**, complete with strolling carolers and a western Santa. This event is held on weekends between Thanksgiving and Christmas. Call (405) 235-7267 for more information.

White Water Bay Theme Park

3908 West Reno, (405) 943-9687. Exit I-40 at Meridian, traveling north to Reno. Turn east on Reno and watch for the sign on the south side of street. Open weekends in mid-May, then every day from Memorial Day until school opens. The park is open weekends only from the time school starts (mid-August) until after Labor Day. The park opens at 10 a.m. each day, with rides starting at 10:30. Closing times vary between 6 and 9 depending on the day; call for information. Adults $16.99, children (forty eight inches and shorter) $12.99. Group rates for fifteen or more people are available by calling 478-2412. On most days, Night Water is offered, with half-price admission after 4 p.m. Call ahead to determine when the park is open and when Night Water is available. For group sales, call (405) 478-2412. Season passes are also available. [$]

White Water Bay has something for every member of the family. Featuring over thirty slides, some more exciting than others, this twenty-five-acre water adventure park is the perfect place to keep cool in the summer. From the Wave Pool to the Big Kahuna and the Acapulco Dive, White Water Bay has it all!

Several concession areas and restaurants with typical fast food fare are located within the park. Adults meals cost around five dollars, and children's meals are about two dollars. Picnic facilities and a cooler station are provided. Enjoy the refreshing fun at White Water Bay!

Will Rogers Park and Arboretum

N.W. 36th and Portland, (405) 951-0108 or (405) 943-0827. From I-44 east, exit at N.W. 36th Street and go west on the overpass to Portland. Turn south (left), and the park is on the east side of the road. Horticulture Gardens open 7 a.m. until dark. Free. Mostly handicapped accessible.

The first tree in this arboretum was planted in the 1930s by Oklahoma City Horticulturist Henry Walters. Gathering trees from different sources and planting them in groups, he created an educational wonder. Many varieties of trees (all native to Oklahoma) are planted here including the Redbud, Oklahoma's state tree, and over sixty varieties of eastern red cedar. With over 2000 unique trees, this arboretum is considered one of the best in the state. Another area of interest is the rose garden located on the east side of the arboretum.

Wind Drift Orchards

19400 N.E. 63rd in Harrah, (405) 454-6635. Exit I-35 at Memorial Road and go east thirteen miles to Luther Road. Turn south and travel five miles to Northeast 63rd, then one half mile east. Wind Drift is on the south side. Look for signs posted along the roadside. Season runs from mid-June to late August. Open daily during season, 8 a.m. to 7 p.m. Products are sold by the pound,

peck or half bushel, and the produce typically costs less than that found in the grocery store. Farm tours are available at no charge; call ahead a week or so to make arrangements. Ten acres of wooded and picnic areas are available for customers.

Fifteen varieties of peaches from four thousand trees on fifty acres–what a delicious summertime treat! Call ahead to determine which varieties are ripened and ready to pick. In addition to peaches, two varieties of nectarines are available during the last two weeks in July. Wind Drift is a self-pick farm that supplies its customers containers and picking poles.

World Organization of China Painters

2641 N.W. 10th Street, (405) 521-1234. Exit I-44 at N.W. 10th Street. Go east about one and a half miles. The World Organization of China Painters is on the north side of the street, between May and Villa. Monday-Friday 10-4. Closed holidays. Free. Handicapped accessible. Call for information about classes and seminars held throughout the year on china painting. Special tours for thirty or more are available by appointment. Through prior arrangement, a luncheon can be catered in conjunction with a tour.

Dedicated to the preservation of hand-painted china, the China Painters Museum houses one of the finest collections of painted china by artists throughout the world. Porcelain painted by organization members and other noted and award-winning artists are displayed. Visitors are often astounded at the exquisite and delicate work of the porcelain artists.

Additional facilities include a library in which visitors may read and learn more about china painting, a gift shop where hand-painted china and artist supplies may be purchased, meeting facilities, and a guest apartment. In March, this organization hosts a china painters show.

Golf

Earlywine Park Golf Courses

11600 South Portland, (405) 691-1727. Travel south on I-44 and exit at Southwest 104th and continue on the west side service road. Go south about one half mile to the clubhouse. Open daily, daylight to dusk. Daily fee $14.63; twilight, junior and senior discounts given. Carts are $18.42 for eighteen holes, $9.75 for nine holes. Tee time reservations are recommended one day in advance for weekdays, one week in advance for weekends.

Earlywine offers North and South eighteen-hole municipal courses. Opened in 1976, the South course has rolling hills, but it is open for driving on most holes. This course has a total yardage of 6728 with par 71. Its USGA rating is 72.5, and its slope rating is 107.

The North course opened in 1993, and it is heavily wooded with rolling hills. Water hazards are present on almost every hole. Challenging to even the most seasoned golfer, the course has 6721 total yards, a par 72, a USGA rating of 71.9, and a slope rating of 121.

John Conrad Regional Golf Course

711 South Douglas Boulevard, Midwest City, (405) 732-2209. Take I-40 east to Douglas exit. From there go north one and a quarter mile. Look for the course on the west side. Open daily, daylight to dusk. Daily green fee is $14.50, senior and junior discounts given. Carts are $18.28. Call for tee times one week in advance for weekends, one day in advance for weekdays.

This eighteen-hole course opened in 1971. A tight course with trees, water, and sand traps, the course's total yardage is 6854, with a par 72. Slope rating is 115, and USGA rating is 124. Facilities include a putting green, driving range, snack bar, and a pro shop.

Lake Hefner Golf Courses

4491 South Lake Hefner Drive, (405) 843-1565. At N.W. Expressway and Meridian, turn north on Meridian for one mile. Open daily, daylight to dusk. Green fees are $13.50 plus tax daily, twilight, senior and junior discounts given. Carts are $17 plus tax. These courses are always busy but are busier on weekends and after 5 p.m. on weekdays. Tee times should be reserved one day in advance for weekdays and one week in advance for weekends.

The two Lake Hefner Golf Courses are scenic courses. The south course, built in 1965, has a total yardage of 6305, with a par 70. Its slope rating is 111, and its USGA rating is 67. Although this course is lined with water and trees, it is a mostly flat course, offering fun for the beginner as well as the more advanced player.

Opened in 1994, the north course is surrounded by Lake Hefner. It is a lake-style design with water-and-tree-lined fairways, and it was voted the fourth best golf course in the state of Oklahoma by Golf Digest. Total yardage is 6970, with a par of 72, slope rating of 128, and a USGA rating of 74.2. Amenities at these courses include putting greens, driving and practice ranges, a three-hole Academy course (Par 3), clubhouse, snack bar, pro shop, and restaurant.

Lincoln Park Golf Courses

4001 N.E. Grand Boulevard, (405) 424-1421. From I-35, exit at N.E. 36th Street. Go west one-half mile to Grand Boulevard then turn north and travel about one block to the clubhouse. Daylight to dark, weather permitting. Weekend and weekday rate $13.50 plus tax. Inquire about junior and senior discounts. Carts are $17 plus tax. For weekend tee times, call the previous Saturday. For weekdays, call one day in advance.

Lincoln Park offers both an East and a West Course. Both municipal courses have good character and they are kept in excellent condition for year-round play. The East eighteen-hole course has a combination of rolling hills and many tree-lined fairways. There are several water areas, and sand bunkers exist on every hole. The par 70 course has a total yardage of 6508, a USGA rating of 70, and a slope rating of 120. The West course, also an eighteen-hole course, has rolling to hilly terrain with trees, sand and water. The total yardage is 6508, with a par 70, USGA rating of 70.7, and a slope rating of 121. Facilities include a clubhouse, snack bar, restaurant, practice bunker, putting green, locker rooms, driving range, and putting range.

Silverhorn Golf Club

11411 N. Kelley Avenue, (405) 752-1181. From I-35 north, exit at Hefner and go west to Kelley. Turn north on Kelley and go one half mile. The Silverhorn gate is on the west side of Kelley. Open daily, daylight to dusk. Weekdays: $29 with cart, $21 to walk. Twilight, junior and senior discounts are given. It is recommended to get tee times one week in advance for weekends and one day in advance for weekdays.

Silverhorn is a well-maintained, fairly new course that is kept in excellent condition. The eighteen-hole course has creeks and trees bordering nine holes and a lake alongside the other nine. A par 71 course, it has 6768 total yards, a slope rating of 128, and a USGA rating of 73.4. Facilities include a driving range, a putting green, a clubhouse, and a restaurant.

Trosper Park Golf Course

2301 S.E. 29th Street, (405) 677-8874. Take I-35 south to S.E. 29th, then go east for 1.25 miles. Trosper Park Golf Course is on the north side of the street. Open daily, daylight to dusk. Daily green fees are $13.50 plus tax; twilight, junior and senior discounts are given. Carts are $17 for eighteen holes, $9 for nine holes. Call for tee time one week in advance for weekends, one day in advance for weekdays.

Trosper Park is a classically-designed course with wooded, rolling fairways and a creek meandering through the middle. This eighteen-hole course has a beautiful scenic setting with long, flat greens. Total yardage for the par 71 course is 6118. Slope rating is 125, USGA rating is 72.2. The facilities include a new clubhouse, a new practice facility with driving and putting range, a restaurant, and locker rooms.

Dining

Allisha's 'A Touch of Class' Tea Room $

9501 N.W. Council Road, (405) 722-9661. Located in the Northwest Shopping Center at N.W. Expressway and Council. Monday-Saturday 11-3.

Opened in the fall of 1994, this Tea Room is something special. Decorated with lace, ribbons and fresh flowers on every table, Allisha's provides menu items from recipes gathered over the past twenty-five years. Be sure to try Allisha's top-selling chicken salad and the Chocolate Italian Cream Cake.

Bricktown

Located in downtown Oklahoma City, (405) 236-8666. From I-40 west, exit Harvey and go north to S.W. 2nd Street. Go east to E.K. Gaylord, then north to Sheridan. At Sheridan turn east. From I-40 east, exit at Robinson and stay in the left lane that leads directly to S.W. 2nd. Turn north on E.K. Gaylord, then east on Sheridan.

Bricktown dates to the 1890s and was once Oklahoma City's prime industrial area, housing hardware, farm implements, groceries, print shops, hotels, and more. Manufacturing businesses were also here, including among others the Bunte Candy Company and the Oklahoma Furniture Manufacturing Company.

Although once a deteriorating area, the charm of the many brick buildings, its ideal location, and a concentration of shopping and fun eating establishments have brought crowds of people back to the area. Bricktown is THE place to be, whether it's for night-life entertainment, a downtown business lunch, or an after-the-game dinner.

There's more to Bricktown than just food and music. The stores in Bricktown cater to the discriminating shopper of art, antiques, architectural antiques, gifts, china, and more. Most of the shopping is located at or near 100 E. Main in the Bricktown Mercantile building. Hours vary with each store.

Bricktown also sponsors several events, with more being added each year. Put on some "green" and enjoy the St. Patrick's Day Parade on or around March 17th. Many activities for families are scheduled for the Bricktown Fourth of July celebration. The December Festival of Lights Parade ends in Bricktown, where Santa arrives and delivers candy to the children. For celebrating the New Year, you can't find a better party than at Opening Night, held in downtown OKC and Bricktown.

Getting to Bricktown and finding parking is now easier than before; the Downtown Bricktown Shuttle trolley runs from various stops in downtown Oklahoma City to Bricktown. Hours on weekdays are 11 a.m.-2 p.m., on weekends are 6 p.m.-2 a.m. The shuttle costs $.50 each way. As a restaurant patron, you may get a free return fare token.

Abuelo's *$, $$*

17 E. Sheridan, (405) 235-1422. Sunday-Thursday 11-10, Friday-Saturday, 11-11.

Authentic Mexican dishes–all served in large portions, on large plates– await you at Abuelo's. A thirty-five foot fountain gives the huge open room a feel of the outdoors, a welcome ambiance whether it's 100 degrees in the shade or 20 below with blowing snow. Try their shrimp and steak dishes prepared "south of the border" style! Cantina available.

Between the Bread Cafe *$,$$*

100 E. Main, (405) 232-2256. Monday-Saturday 11-3, Wednesday-Saturday 5:30-9. Closed Monday, Tuesday night and Sunday.

Fresh, homemade food is the highlight at this cafe. The menu includes pasta dishes, salads, sandwiches, steak, chicken, and fish. Enjoy coffee and occasional entertainment after your meal.

Boomerang Grille *$, $$*

103 E. California, (405) 272-0770. Monday-Thursday 11-8, Friday-Saturday 11-10, Sunday noon-3.

Enjoy a "retro" experience daily at this bar and grill. Jukebox music from the 1950s to 1970s adds to the ambiance as patrons enjoy the Boomerang's specialty–burgers and onion rings! Warm up your vocal chords on Friday nights; karaoke plays from 9 p.m. to 1 a.m. Patio seating is available.

Bricktown Brewery *$-$$$*

1 N. Oklahoma Avenue, (405) 232-2739. Sunday-Thursday 11 a.m.-midnight (serving until 10 p.m.), Friday-Saturday 11 a.m.-2 a.m. (serving until midnight).

One of the first and biggest restaurants in the area, the Brewery is known for its micro-brewery (ask for a tour anytime), their outstanding food with specialties of baby back ribs and grilled top sirloin, and their wide variety of live entertainment on every Friday and Saturday night. Check out their large upstairs recreation area, complete with billiards.

Bricktown Charley's *$, $$*

1 E. California, (405) 236-1116. Monday-Sunday 11:30 p.m.-2 a.m.

Live bands on Friday and Saturday and blues on Wednesday are the highlights at this club. Serving burgers, sandwiches, quesadillas, and fried foods in "Harley Davidson" decor, Bricktown Charley's also provides a jukebox, darts, pool tables, and outdoor patio.

Bricktown Joker's Comedy Club *$*

229 E. Sheridan, (405) 236-JOKE. Shows are held Wednesday-Saturday, with occasional special shows on Monday and/or Tuesday. Cover charge ranges from $5-7 plus a $4.50 minimum order charge.

Get your laughs in Bricktown at the Comedy Club. Previous comedians featured here include Bob Zaney, Jeff Dunham and Thea Vidale. Food served includes appetizers, hamburgers, onion rings, and more. Ask about smoking and nonsmoking showtimes.

Cafe Ole' *$, $$*

201 E. Sheridan, (405) 236-8040. Monday-Thursday 11-2:30 and 5-9, Friday-Saturday 11-2:30 and 5-10. Closed Sunday.

This small, intimate restaurant serves Santa Fe-style Mexican food. They're known for stacked, blue corn tortillas and a full bar with fresh-squeezed lime margaritas.

Chelino's *$, $$*

15 E. California, (405) 235-3533. Monday-Thursday 11-10, Friday-Saturday 11-11, Sunday 11-9.

This two-story, award-winning Mexican restaurant features fajitas and homemade tortillas as their specialties. Its lively and festive atmosphere is occasionally complemented with live music and folkloric dancers on Friday nights. In nice weather, enjoy the large outdoor seating area on the balcony.

Crabtown *$-$$$*

303 E. Sheridan, (405) 232-7227. Monday-Thursday 11-10:30, Friday-Saturday 11-

11:30.

Specializing in crab and seafood dishes, this restaurant also serves steak and chicken. Off-track betting is available.

Rocky's Music Hall

225 E. Sheridan, (405) 239-6060 for concert information. Concerts are typically held only on Friday and Saturday nights. $10 cover charge.

This hall features all-acoustic, traditional music concerts in a unique wood-and-brick setting. Especially take note of the 1910-era, thirty-six foot bar from England. Specialty coffees and deli sandwiches are made available during the performances.

Spaghetti Warehouse *$, $$*

101 E. Sheridan, (405) 235-0402. Sunday-Thursday 11-10, Friday-Saturday 11-11.

This family-friendly restaurant features Italian dining in a festive atmosphere and outstanding service. Their fifteen-layer lasagne is their signature menu item. Check out their delicious desserts, including New York cheesecake, carrot cake, and tiramisu.

Studio 310 Dance Club

310 E. Sheridan, (405) 236-3107. Wednesday, Thursday, Sunday 9 p.m.-2 a.m. Friday, Saturday 8 p.m-2 a.m. Typically there is a $5 cover charge.

Divided into several areas for dancing, this club plays "progressive" dance music and has pool tables and electronic darts.

Uncommon Grounds *$*

10 E. Main, (405) 236-5282. Monday-Thursday 7:30 a.m.-10 p.m., Friday 7:30 a.m.-midnight, Saturday 10 a.m.-midnight, Sunday 11 a.m.-9 p.m.

Enjoy your coffee and pastry on the patio, or have an Italian soda and bagel. This coffee shop occasionally hosts poetry readings.

Varsity Sports Grill *$-$$$*

115 E. Sheridan, (405) 235-5525. Sunday-Tuesday 11 a.m.-midnight, Wednesday-Saturday 11 p.m.-1 a.m. Also located at 1140 N.W. 63rd (842-0898) and 1732 S. Meridian (685-7715).

This grill is known as much for their baby-back rib dinners and grilled chicken salad as for their outstanding coverage

of sporting events worldwide via satellite television. Bingo is played on Wednesdays from 9:30 p.m.-midnight.

Windy City Pizza $, $$
27 E. Sheridan, (405) 236-0999. Sunday-Thursday 11-10, Friday-Saturday 11-11.

Chicago-style pizza is the highlight at this black-and-white-tiled pizzeria. Choose from artichokes hearts, sun-dried tomatoes, and many other more-or-less traditional toppings. If you don't feel like going out, call for delivery (limited delivery areas).

Oklahoma City Night Life
by Jay Porter

Bricktown is a great place for night life in Oklahoma City. Here are some other fun night-life restaurants and clubs to try in the capital city.

Boar's Head Restaurant and Club
2820 N.W. 63rd in the French Market Mall, (405) 842-2729. Call for cover charge information.

Offering good food and an eclectic roster of live music, the Boar's Head is a unique addition to Oklahoma City's nightlife. All ages are welcome until 8:30 p.m., after which it becomes a 21-and-over establishment only. A full menu is served until 1 a.m., so patrons can graze all night long.

Blue Note Lounge
2408 N. Robinson, (405) 524-5678. Located just west of I-235 at 23rd Street. Must be 21 or older.

With its great lineup of live blues, jazz and rock acts, the Blue Note has been pleasing ears in Oklahoma City since 1954.

Medina's on Paseo
3004 Paseo, (405) 524-7949. Open to those 18 and older, Medina's is closed on Monday.

Though its smoky atmosphere may be a bit too authentic for some, Medina's is the epitome of the Paseo's "downtown" style and is a great place to check out current works by local artists. In addition to a light menu, Medina's delivers strong coffee, liqueurs, wine, and beer. Live music and performance acts pack the house on the weekends, when there is generally a cover charge. Wednesday's "open mic." poetry night is free–and uninhibited.

TapWerks Ale House and Cafe
5700 N. Western, (405) 842-6769.

WIth over sixty-three varieties of specialty beer, fine cigars, and a great cafe menu, TapWerks is one of Oklahoma City's trendiest new destinations. Occasional live music adds to the ambiance, making TapWerks a great place to relax and chat with friends old and new.

VZD's Restaurant and Club
4200 N. Western, (405) 524-4203.

A subdued burgers-and-salad spot by day, VZD's is also one Oklahoma City's live-music institutions. This 21-and-over club features local and regional bands Thursday through Saturday. Rocking yet respectable, VZD's is definitely an uptown venue with lots of Oklahoma City's young professionals in the crowd. Several other clubs in the neighborhood serve up live music as well, but none serve up a full menu until 11 p.m., as does VZD's.

Waterford Lounge
6300 Waterford Boulevard (N.W. 63rd and Penn), (405) 848-4782.

Located in the Waterford Marriott Hotel, this 21-and-over bar and restaurant serves a full menu until 11 p.m. in one of the city's loveliest settings. Couples can always dance cheek to cheek on the parquet; there is occasional live music as well as a series of summer jazz parties on the verandah. For a "swellegant" evening, the Waterford is a delightful choice.

Applewood's 𝔖, 𝔖𝔖

4301 S.W. 3rd, (405) 947-8484. Exit I-40 onto Meridian, travel north to 3rd Street. Turn east and find Applewood's on the north side of 3rd at the end of the street. Monday-Thursday 11-2 and 5 -10, Friday and Saturday 11-2 and 5-11, Sunday (Country Buffet until 2:30 p.m.) 11-3 and 4:30-10.

No dress code or reservations are required for this award-winning, popular restaurant. The individual pot roast, apple cider baked pork chops and apple fritters are their specialties; they are also known for their delicious steaks, chicken, and homemade dinner rolls. Applewood's is American cuisine at its best!

Billy Balloo's

8371 N. Rockwell, (405) 728-7760. Exit I-44 at Northwest Expressway and travel west four miles to Rockwell. Turn into the Rockwell Plaza Shopping Center on the southwest corner. In the far southwest corner of the shopping center is a 54,000 square foot building with a neon sign announcing the restaurant. Sunday-Thursday 4 p.m.-midnight, Friday-Saturday 11 a.m.-2 a.m. Food service ends at 10 p.m.

Billy Balloo's goes the extra mile in combining food with entertaining activities. Patrons enjoy a room full of the finest billiards, electronic darts, and shuffleboard tables, a full service sports bar, a restaurant with a climate-controlled patio, an extensive arcade area, a regulation length in-line skate and roller hockey arena, and private rooms for most any occasion. Enjoy the pasta, pizza, salads, sandwiches, and burgers; then try the many activities that abound here. You might even play hard enough to work off the extra calories from your meal! Billy Balloo's is an excellent place for family fun, birthday parties, and company gatherings.

Boston Tea Party Tea Room 𝔖, 𝔖𝔖

116 N.W. 51st, (405) 842- 3477. Exit I-44 at Western and travel south to 51st Street. Turn west; the restaurant is located at the east end of The Colonies building. Tuesday-Friday 11-2 , Saturday 11-3.

This popular, quaint tea room transports visitors back in time to our country's beginning in New England. In a relaxed atmosphere, enjoy the excellent fresh chicken or tuna salads on a buttery croissant, whole wheat bread, or leaves of lettuce. Strawberry nut bread, sweet, frozen raspberry mousse, salads, soups, and chili are just some of the other items available for indulgence. Save room for a huge array of desserts, from peach cobbler to Rum Cream Pie topped with pistachio nuts.

Cattlemen's Steak House 𝔖𝔖, 𝔖𝔖𝔖

1309 S. Agnew Avenue, (405) 236-0416. From I-40, go south on Agnew. The restaurant is on the west side, past Exchange Avenue. Sunday-Thursday 6 a.m.-10 p.m. Friday and Saturday 6 a.m. til midnight. Handicapped accessible. No reservations are required, and casual dress is expected. Cattlemen's is open for breakfast at 6 a.m. and serves lunch specials as well.

Opening its doors in 1910, Cattlemen's is more than an Oklahoma tradition–it's an institution. With rich wood interior and pictures of western scenes and celebrities, the restaurant helps you to step back in time to experience the Old West. T-bones, filets, ribeyes, and lamb fries are specialties here. Come to Cattlemen's hungry; having served cowboys and even heads of state such as President George Bush, the chefs know how to satisfy hungry appetites.

Coach House 𝔖𝔖, 𝔖𝔖𝔖

6437 Avondale Drive, (405) 842-1000. Exit I-44 onto Western. Go north on Western to Avondale, which is one half block north of 63rd. Coach House is in Nichols Hills Plaza on the northwest side of Western. Monday-Friday 11:30 a.m.-2 p.m. Monday-Saturday 6 p.m.-10 p.m. Handicapped accessible. Reservations are recommended. Dress is formal.

Furnished with antiques, flowers and candles on every table, this small, intimate restaurant is the perfect place for couples to experience a night of romance. Coach House is known for its outstanding menu of gourmet delights. Grilled Veal Ribeye with Mushroom and Pinenut-Bocchinni Tortelinni are but two items from their constantly-changing menu.

Cowboy Bob's All-American Sports Grill and Museum $, $$

800 W. Memorial Road, (405) 752-8888. Located just east of the intersection of Western and Memorial in north Oklahoma City. If you are traveling on the Kilpatrick Turnpike, exit on Western, travel north a short distance to Memorial, then turn east. The restaurant is on the south side of Memorial. Sunday-Thursday 11-9, Friday-Saturday 11-10. Reservations are accepted. Handicapped accessible. 🖏

What started as a simple hobby of a young sports fan has turned into a lifelong interest for restaurant owner Robert Linley. Between his interests in sports memorabilia, great food, and fun dining experiences, Linley has developed a unique restaurant for his guests. Much of his rare sports collection focuses on Oklahoma and major college sports teams of the 1890s to the 1950s, but it also includes items from the Olympics. The information is arranged by decade, with the "artifacts" imbedded under clear lacquer on the tables. The memorabilia always seems to encourage interesting dinner conversation. A map of the tables and their respective decades is available if diners are interested in a particular time period. The food is as interesting as the atmosphere. The extensive menu includes delicious wood-burning, brick-oven pizza, fresh salads, pasta dishes, barbecue, and steak. Cowboy Bob's is enjoyable for all ages!

Eddy's Steakhouse Restaurant $$, $$$

4227 North Meridian, (405) 787-2944. Located about one block north of 39th Expressway on the west side of Meridian. Monday-Saturday 5-10. Weekends until 11 p.m. Reservations are not required. Dress casual. Handicapped accessible.

Since 1967, Eddy's has been a restaurant tradition in the Oklahoma City area. Owned and operated for 29 years by the Elias family, the restaurant continues to serve loyal patrons and to make new ones. Guests can relax and enjoy a quiet candlelight dinner in a homey atmosphere. Specialties are steaks and seafood, and Lebanese appetizers add a special and delicious touch to the meal.

Haunted House Restaurant $$, $$$

7101 North Miramar Boulevard, (405) 478-1417. Exit I-44 at Martin Luther King Avenue, travel one-half block north to the access road. Turn east and go three blocks to Miramar Boulevard, just west of Thompson's School Supplies. The Haunted House Restaurant is at the end of Miramar. Dress is dressy/casual. Reservations are required. Handicapped accessible.

Built in 1935, this old country estate has a haunted past. For the past thirty-three years, the Haunted House has been a popular choice for special-occasion dining. The restaurant specializes in beef, lamb steaks, lobster, and shrimp.

High Noon Saloon $-$$$

1323 South Agnew Avenue, (405) 239-7716. Exit I-40 south onto Agnew. High Noon Saloon is located in Historic Stockyards City, next door to Cattlemen's Cafe. Monday-Thursday 11 a.m.-9 p.m. Friday-Saturday 11 a.m.-10 p.m. Closed Sundays. Handicapped accessible.

Dine in an old western atmosphere, patterned after the movie High Noon. Barbecue ribs, smoked turkey and chicken, jalapeno sausage, and pulled pork are the specialties. Live country music is played Thursday through Saturday evenings.

Junior's $$, $$$

2601 N.W. Expressway, (405) 848-5597. Exit I-44 at Northwest Expressway, then travel west about one and a half mile. Junior's is located on the ground floor of the Twin Towers Oil Center Building, just west of the Charcoal Oven. Monday-Saturday Lunch 11:30 a.m.-2 p.m. Dinner 6 p.m.-2 a.m. Covered parking is provided. Reservations are welcome, but not required. Dress is casual. Two private dining rooms are available. Call in advance to reserve. Handicapped accessible. ▯

In addition to a delicious menu, Junior's provides guests with many extras. From the red wall paper and chairs to its sunken bar, piano bar, and postage stamp dance floor, Juniors offers a sophisticated evening experience with live music six nights a week. Specialties are lobster tail, steaks, shrimp, and marinated chicken breast. Order a Caesar or Syrian Salad and watch as it's made at your table. Junior's has daily lunch specials, and takeout orders are available.

Kamp's Grocery and Deli $

1310 N.W. 25th Street, (405) 521-2251. Located near Classen and 25th not far from downtown Oklahoma City. Monday-Saturday 7 a.m.-6:30 p.m., Sunday 9-5. Lunch is served 10:30-2:30 daily. Non-smoking. Credit cards accepted. Handicapped accessible.

Kamp's has been an Oklahoma City institution since 1910 when Kamp's Dry Goods Store set up shop on the fringes of the bustling new capital. The Kamp family still plays a big role in the operations of the grocery store and the newly-refurbished deli. Serving home-style favorites and wonderful fresh-baked pastries and breads, Kamp's attracts many loyal customers for breakfast and lunch. Guests can enjoy a peppered pork loin sandwich, and a variety of great salads.

Yippie Yi Yo, one of Oklahoma City's pioneering coffeehouses, shares Kamp's deli space and provides gourmet coffee treats as well as super-healthy juices and fruit smoothies. Best of all, diners enjoy their selections in an exquisitely-restored Art Deco dining area with original tin ceilings, bakery bar, and globe lanterns.

Lido's $$, $$$

2925 W. Britton Road, (405) 749-1413. Exit I-44 at May Avenue, traveling north to Britton Road. At Britton, turn west. Lido's is located about one block on the north side of Britton in the Britton Square Shopping Center. Other locations are 2518 N. Military Avenue and 2703 Villa Promenade. Monday-Thursday 11-9:30, Friday 11-10. Saturday 4-10 p.m., Sunday 4-9 p.m. Handicapped accessible.

A popular and unique restaurant, Lido's serves Vietnamese specialties such as fried spring rolls on vermicelli, Chinese specialties such as Chow Mein, and French specialties such as diced filet mignon. Frog legs, squid, Cornish hens, lobster, pork chops, and tofu are among some of the items that are on Lido's extensive menu. Don't miss this decidedly-different and very delicious experience.

L'Indochine $$$

1600 N.W. Expressway, (405) 848-6603. Take the Northwest Expressway exit from I-44. L'Indochine is located in the Richmond Suites Hotel, which is at the intersection of N.W. Expressway and Blackwelder (straight ahead and a little to the east after the exit). Monday-Friday, lunch 11:30-2. Monday-Thursday dinner 6-9:30 p.m., Friday and Saturday 6-10 p.m. Closed Sunday. Reservations are preferred. Dress is formal. Handicapped accessible.

The distinctive and delicious combination of Asian and French cooking techniques provides patrons with many savory delights at this warm and elegant restaurant. Grilled salmon, Asian chicken salad, filet mignon, and sauteed breast of duck are just a few of the delectable entrees. Equally wonderful are the many desserts. This is a "not-to-be-missed" Oklahoma City dining experience.

Old Germany Restaurant $$

15920 S.E. 29th in Choctaw, (405) 390-8647. Take I-40 east and exit at Choctaw Road. Go north (under the freeway) three miles to 29th Street. At 29th Street, go east one mile; the restaurant is located on the south side of the street. Tuesday-Saturday 11 a.m.-2 p.m., 5-9 p.m. Old Germany has another location in Norman at 3750 W. Robinson, Suite 106. (405) 321-6565.

For over twenty years, the Turek family has been serving authentic German cuisine. Immigrating from Germany to the United States in 1974, the family brought with them an entrepreneurial spirit and great German recipes. As the winner of numerous awards, including the Award of Excellence for their wine list from *The Wine Spectator* in San Francisco for nine years in a row, Old Germany

Octoberfest at Old Germany.

Restaurant is an entertaining and quality dining experience. The outstanding weiner schnitzel, bratwurst, cevapcici, German Beer, and more will make sure that your trip to Choctaw is one you'll want to repeat.

Old Germany Restaurant sponsors several events throughout the year. Their biggest event is **Oktoberfest,** held for three days in late summer or early fall. The festival features plenty of German food, beer, wine, and Gemuetlichkeit. Call for more information and exact dates.

Rose Garden Tea Room *S, SS*

4413 N. Meridian, (405) 495-2252. Exit I-44 onto 39th Expressway. Go west to Meridian then turn north. The eatery sits on the west side of Meridian, just north of the Antique House. Monday-Friday 11-2:30. Extra parking is available in back. Reservations appreciated.

Everything is pink and burgundy at the Rose Garden. Enjoy the homemade fare served on china and the delicate scent of roses in the air. From the ham and mushroom quiche to the pink-colored water, the Rose Garden Tea Room is a delight for the senses.

Ted's Cafe Escondido *S-SSS*

2836 N.W. 68th, (405) 848-8337. From Northwest 63rd Street and May, go 1/4 mile north. Turn east at 68th Street and travel one block. Look for the restaurant on the south side of the street. Monday-Thursday 11 a.m.-10 p.m., Friday-Saturday 11 a.m.-10:30 p.m., Sunday 11 a.m.-9:30 p.m. Parking is available across the street from the restaurant.

The crowds are always thick at Ted's, and for good reason–the food is outstanding! Known for their fresh Mexican food, Ted's specializes in marinated beef and chicken fajitas. Guests will also enjoy unique items such as spinach enchiladas, beef and chicken tamales, and the combination plates. Lite portions are available with many menu items.

Expect a long wait on Friday and Saturday nights, or try going on late Sunday afternoons when the restaurant is less busy. While you are waiting, watch the experts make flour tortillas. The extra time spent at Ted's is worth it!

The Wild's Restaurant *S, SS*

Located on Britton Road between Highway 81 and Piedmont Road, (between Yukon and El Reno), (405) 262-7275. Wednesday-Saturday 5-10, Sunday 12-8. All You Can Eat Buffet is featured on Friday, Saturday, and Sunday.

Completed in August, 1983, The Wilds Restaurant was built with an 1880s theme in mind. The 4000-square-foot dining area with hand-cut and stripped cedar logs, handhewn cedar booths, and old wagon wheel chandeliers create a rustic, Old West frontier atmosphere. Patrons choose from farm-raised channel catfish to juicy T-bone steaks, tender chicken to surprisingly-delicious buffalo. The covered wagon salad bar provides a delicious complement to the meal.

The Wilds offers more than a good meal. Stroll the grounds and see an authentic 1854 water-powered grist mill, a restored covered bridge, Texas longhorns, and a working barn. The Wilds host socials, picnics, dinners, and banquets. Call for more information.

Shopping

Casady Square

Located on three corners of North Pennsylvania Avenue and Britton Road. Call individual stores or (405) 843-7474 for information. Hours vary by store.

Forty stores are located in this one-stop shopping area. The more interesting shops include specialty clothing stores, a fabric shop, and **Greg Burns Studio**. An award-winning and popular Oklahoma artist, Burns paints detailed scenes familiar to Oklahomans, as well as Southwest scenes. Besides original art, the studio offers prints, cards, framed Christmas pieces, and more. Stop by to view beautiful artwork and to enjoy a visit with the artist.

Choctaw Trading Post

1520 N. Portland, (405) 947-2490. Exit I-44 at N.W. 10th and travel west to Portland. Turn north on Portland; the store is a few blocks ahead on the east side. Monday -Saturday 10-6, Sunday 1-5.

Oklahoma City

A tradition in Oklahoma City for many years, this store features authentic Native American items such as blankets, leather purses, moccasins, art work, and jewelry.

Across the street from the Choctaw Trading Post is another Native American store, **Inter-Tribal Designs** (405-943-7935). Products at this store include kachinas, pottery and beadwork.

The Colonies and other antique shops

Located between Western and Classen on N.W. 51st, (405) 842-9093 or (405) 842-1279. From I-44 east: Exit Western and turn south. Go to N.W. 51st and turn west. The Colonies is the blue two story colonial houses on the south side of 51st. Off-street parking is located behind the buildings.

Thirty-five antique shops are located here, offering antiques and collectibles such as quilts, furniture, military collectibles, and books. Shoppers can even sign up for a chair-caning class, or they can get their clock repaired here. When you tire of shopping, refresh yourself at the Boston Tea Party Tea Room.

While visiting The Colonies, be sure to pick up the Antique Guide to Oklahoma City. Other antique shops to explore in Oklahoma City are **Antique Alley**, Northwest 51st and Classen, (405) 840-3514; **The Antique Alley**, 1433 N.W. Expressway, (405) 943-4670; **Apple Tree Antique Mall**, 1111 North Meridian, (405) 947-8999; **Heartstrings Antique Mall** (has a tea room), 4600 Northwest 10th, (405) 948-8282; **The Sampler**, 9201 N. Western, (405) 848-7007; **Bricktown Antiques**, 100 East Main Street, 2nd Floor, (405) 235-2803.

Crossroads Mall

Located near the intersection of I-35 and I-240, (405) 631-4421. Monday-Saturday 10-9, and Sunday 10-6.

One hundred forty retail stores and four major department stores are found at Crossroads Mall. Several restaurants are located here, and an eight-screen cinema theater is located nearby. Strollers and wheelchairs are available.

50 Penn Place

Located on the southeast corner of Northwest Expressway and Pennsylvania Avenue, (405) 848-7940. Monday-Saturday 10-6, Thursday 10-8, Sunday 12-5.

The mall has twenty-five upscale stores such as Talbots, Laura Ashley, Balliet's, and Old School Clothing Company. Try the Belle Isle Brewery for hand-crafted ales and good grill food. Strollers are available.

Heritage Park Mall

Located on the northwest corner of Reno and Air Depot in Midwest City, (405) 737-1472. Monday-Saturday 10-9, Sunday 12-6.

Seventy-five stores, an arcade, a cinema, restaurants, and a food court are located here. Strollers and wheelchairs are available.

Nichols Hills Plaza

Located at Avondale (one fourth block north of Northwest 63rd) and North Western. (405) 842-3324. Hours vary by business.

This shopping area has forty-five businesses, including a tailor's shop and specialty stores featuring fine linens, upscale designer men's and women's clothing, and needlepoint supplies. The Plaza area has six restaurants and an upscale supermarket.

In September, area merchants sponsor the **Plaza Arts Festival**, which features work by Oklahoma artists. Admission is free. Special **Christmas lights** add to the holiday ambiance from Thanksgiving through New Years Day.

Penn Square Mall

Located on the northeast corner of Northwest Expressway and Pennsylvania Avenue. (405) 842-4424. Monday-Saturday 10-9, Sunday 12-6. Parking is sometimes difficult to find; there is a multi-level parking garage in the northeast corner near Foley's.

Built in 1960 as an outdoor mall, Penn Square is the oldest shopping center in Oklahoma

255

City. Now enclosed, the beautiful mall has four large department stores, 140 specialty stores, an arcade, a ten-screen cinema theater, the award-winning Pepperoni Grille restaurant, and a food court. Strollers and wheelchairs are available.

Quail Springs Mall

Located in Northwest Oklahoma City on Memorial Road between North May and Pennsylvania, (405) 755-6530. Monday-Saturday 10-9, Sunday 12-6. ⬚

Quail Springs is known as an over one-million square foot super-regional mall with 130 specialty stores and Dillard's, Foley's, J.C. Penney, and Sears. Highlighting the specialty stores are Disney, Gap/Gap Kids, Gymboree, Limited, and Victoria Secret. A full-service restaurant and a food court provide refreshment to shoppers. Quail Springs is located in a thriving retail area with several restaurants featuring ethnic and American foods. Strollers and wheelchairs are available.

Accommodations

Country House Bed and Breakfast

10101 Oakview Road, (405) 794-4008. The Country House is situated on five beautiful acres, one mile from Lake Stanley Draper. Single $60, Double $70. A two-night minimum stay is required. Reservations are required one week in advance. Children are allowed with supervision. Not handicapped accessible.

Nineteenth-century antiques and country collectibles furnish the romantic Country House. Two suites, each with a large, private bath, include the Balcony Room (with its own private balcony) and the Whirlpool Suite (with a large, red, heart-shaped whirlpool tub). A delicious, homemade breakfast is served at your convenience. Ask your hosts for information about the activities available at nearby Lake Draper.

The Grandisson at Maney Park

1200 N. Shartel, (405) 521-0011. From I-40 take the Classen Boulevard exit north to North-west 10th Street. Go east for two blocks to Shartel, then turn north one block on Shartel. The Grandisson is on the east side of Shartel. $75 to $150; ask about their packages and discounts for senior citizens and extended-stays. Call for information about the Grandisson's facilities for business meetings, weddings, receptions, anniversaries, and dinners. Reservations are necessary. Call ahead if possible; however, rooms are occasionally available for the following night. Handi-capped accessible. All major credit cards are accepted.

Built by wealthy railroad executive James W. Maney in 1904 and conveniently located in downtown Oklahoma City, this historic Victorian home was recently transformed into a beau-tiful bed and breakfast. Guests are first impressed with the beautiful entry featuring lighted stained glass, a curved hallway, and original mahogany woodwork throughout. Nine bedrooms are available, each featuring varying themes, antique furnishings, and full private baths. Two suites and seven rooms include queen- and king-sized beds, and seven have two-person jacuzzi tubs. A Continental-Plus Breakfast Buffet is served during the week, with a more complete break-fast served on the weekend. Other amenities at the Grandisson include two parlors, a refresh-ment center, a laundry facility, and a gift shop with handcrafted items, collectibles, and Made in Oklahoma products.

The Medallion

1 North Broadway, (405) 235-2780. From I-40, exit at Walker and go north to Sheridan. The Medallion is on the northwest corner of Broadway and Sheridan, directly across Sheridan from the Myriad Conven-tion Center. Weekend nightly rates are $84. Concierge level rooms are $155 nightly. A night's stay always includes a continental-style breakfast. Ask about their special occasion packages.

The 396-room Medallion hotel recently completed an eight million dollar renovation project, and now offers guests the ultimate in luxurious accommodations. Marble from Italy and beautiful carpets from London have added beautiful elegance to this downtown luxury hotel. The most interesting part of the renovations are the two floors of beautifully-appointed rooms, completely dedicated to providing guests with the utmost in security and VIP service. From the Crabtree and

Evelyn bath accessories and robes in luxurious bathrooms, to all-day concierge service and twice-a-day maid service, the level of service and attention to detail are unsurpassed. For breakfast, lunch and dinner, the Aria Grill provides American cuisine in Mediterranean-style decor.

Nelson's Homestay Bed and Breakfast

315 E. Wade, El Reno, (405) 262-9142. Call for directions. $45-95. Special occasion packages available. Reservations are required. Not handicapped accessible. Major credit cards accepted.

This Georgian colonial home was built in 1906 by Tom Jensen as a wedding present for his bride, Minnie. Opened as a B&B in 1995, the historic home has three guest rooms with shared baths. Sadie's Room, named after the owner's grandmother, is decorated in colonial antique walnut. The Deloss Nelson Room, named for the owner's great grandfather, is decorated around a Chisholm Trail theme with red cedar, a hand-constructed, four-poster bed, and an antique cedar chest. The "Grandmother's Dream," room features soft pink roses, floral bouquets, and all-white furnishings painted in ribbon and rose designs. A full gourmet breakfast is served each morning; specialties feature herbs grown in the innkeepers' special garden. A garden hot tub and a common room with cable television and phone are among the amenities.

Oklahoma City Marriott

3233 Northwest Expressway, (405) 842-6633. From I-44, take the Northwest Expressway exit and go west about two and a half miles. The Marriott sits on the north side of the Northwest Expressway, across from Baptist Hospital. Regular weekday rates are $139 (single); Honeymoon package is $115 per night; Two for Breakfast package is $98 per night (package prices include tax).

A combination of marble, natural light, and stunning crystal chandeliers add to the beauty of this luxury hotel. Conveniently located for sight-seeing and shopping, the Marriott also offers an indoor pool, hot tub, health club, two restaurants, and a popular lounge. For dining, try JW's Steakhouse featuring tenderly-aged steaks and seafood, or Allie's American Grille with its family-style dining. Russell's Lounge offers dancing nightly.

The most extensive weekend package is called the Honeymoon and features champagne, chocolates and an all-you-can-eat breakfast either through room service or at the restaurant. A weekend package called Two For Breakfast includes a breakfast buffet for two in Allie's Grille or a room service breakfast (limited to $17).

The Waterford Marriott

Northwest 63rd and Pennsylvania, (405) 848-4782. Traveling west on I-44, exit on to Northwest Expressway. Go west one half mile, turn north at Pennsylvania Avenue and continue to N.W. 63rd Street. The Waterford is located on the southeast corner. Regular room rates $149-750; Bed and Breakfast Weekend $99-139; The Waterford Weekend $185-225. 🅑

Completely renovated in 1996, The Waterford Marriott offers guests an English country decor and excellent service. A beautiful combination of hardwood and marble floors and columns, gorgeous flowers and dark wood furniture create an elegant ambiance in the lobby area of this luxury hotel, the only four-diamond hotel in the Oklahoma City area.

Two restaurants are located in the hotel, and both are known for their gourmet delights. Enjoy breakfast and lunch from The Veranda, or dinner from The Waterford Dining Room. Take advantage of The Waterford's special Sunday Brunch buffet, complete with live jazz music and champagne. Other amenities include a lounge, an outdoor swimming pool, a full-service athletic club, and a staff of massage therapists to help guests unwind during their stay.

Two weekend packages are offered year round. The Bed and Breakfast Weekend for two includes a one-night stay

Waterford Marriott

The elegant Waterford.

and breakfast for two, served either in The Veranda or in your room. The Waterford Weekend includes a three-course dinner for two in the Waterford Dining Room or delivered to your room, overnight accommodations, and breakfast for two. When making reservations, inquire about seasonal packages that may be offered.

Willow Way Bed and Breakfast

27 Oakwood Drive, (405) 427-2133. Located in the Forest Park area of Oklahoma City; call for directions and rates. Not handicapped accessible. Willow Way can host meetings, weddings, and receptions for up to seventy-five guests.

Four suites await visitors at this lovely, two-story tudor-style home. Situated on beautiful grounds, complete with wispy willow trees and plenty of wildlife, this in-the-city B&B gives a feel of being in the country. Each suite has its own bathroom and is tastefully decorated. The most unique room is Pleasant Under Glass, located in a former greenhouse. Three dining areas are available, and a cozy fireplace feels especially nice on chilly evenings. Breakfast is catered to guest's preferences and includes Willow Way's own sweet scones.

Events

An Affair of the Heart

Held twice a year for three days in February and three days in October at State Fair Park. From I-40 west, exit May and go north. From I-40 east, exit Portland and go north. At Reno, turn east. For date and brochure, call (405) 632-2652. $4 admits individuals for all three days. Watch the news media for discounts that are offered. NOTE: An Affair of the Heart is also held in July at Tulsa's Expo Center.

Billed as the largest arts and crafts festival in the country, An Affair of the Heart attracts numerous crafters and other merchandisers. The crowds of people who attend this event enjoy a large selection of American country, Southwest and Victorian arts, crafts, antiques, and collectibles. Dolls, handiwork, wooden crafts, clothes, baskets, blankets, folk art, jewelry, holiday items, and much more are available for purchase. Come with time and money to spare; there's much to select from, and lines can be long. If you love shopping for the unique and different, this is one "affair" you won't want to miss!

Red Bud Classic

Usually held on a Saturday and Sunday in mid-April in Nichols Hills, Oklahoma City, and Jones. For date and brochure call (405) 842-8295. Races start at Northwest 63rd Street and Pennsylvania Avenue at the Waterford Complex. Preregistration and release form with waiver must be filled out and signed. 10K and Two Mile events $15, Bicycle Tour $15, both events $25. Parking is available at the Waterford Complex (63rd and Pennsylvania) on race day before 1 p.m. Additional Parking is available at Penn Square Mall and the Glenbrook Center, across from the mall. Bicycle tour entrants must be at least twelve years old. All riders must wear a helmet. Handicapped accessible for most areas, the Red Bud also includes a wheelchair event.

The community comes together to promote good health and fitness and to celebrate the return of spring during the Red Bud Classic. Whether running, walking or bicycling is your favorite, the Red Bud Classic has a competition for you. The ten, thirty, and fifty-mile bicycle tour starts early on Saturday morning. The SCORE Children's Fitness Run starts at noon on Saturday at Nichols Hills Plaza, near the corner of Northeast 63rd and Western. After the run, entertainment continues for young and old alike—clowns, costumed characters, refreshments, pony rides, and live entertainment add to the fun. Pasta on the Pond at the Waterford Complex refreshes athletes and spectators. On Sunday, amateur athletes participate in the 10K and Two-Mile Runs, the Citizen's Walk and the Costume Category. The Red Bud Classic is two days of sporting fun and festivities for everyone!

Festival of the Arts

Held for about six days near the end of April at the Myriad Gardens and Festival Plaza. For date and brochure, call the Arts Council of Oklahoma City at (405)270-4848. From I-40 west, exit Walker

Oklahoma City

The Festival of the Arts.

and go north. From I-40 east, exit Robinson and go north. Parking is located between Reno and Sheridan. Free; but plan to pay for parking, food, and children's activities. Handicapped accessible; to avoid stairs, use the east-west sidewalks along Sheridan.

Since 1967, the Festival of the Arts has been one of the city's most anticipated festivals of the year. Noted as one of the top ten outdoor festivals in the country, the festival's main attraction is a juried art show and sale, with about 140 outstanding artists traveling from around the nation to exhibit at the festival. Entertainment is presented on several stages and includes musicians, theatrical groups, storytellers, magicians, and more. Many Oklahoma City residents will tell you that spring has not arrived until they've eaten their favorite foods from the popular international food booths–a tradition at the festival. This area is always crowded with patrons enjoying delectable treats such as Strawberry Newport and Indian tacos. Children's activities abound, from hands-on art projects to a special area to purchase inexpensive art.

If at all possible, try to go on a weekday. The festival is very crowded on the weekends and during the lunch hour as downtown office workers head to the food booths for a midday treat. Also keep an eye to the sky; April can bring wet and windy weather conditions. Purchase a festival program to keep abreast of the many performances and to get information on the artists.

Okla-Hoe-Down

Held in Joe B. Barnes Regional Park in Midwest City on the second Saturday in May. From I-40, exit at Douglas and go approximately 3.5 miles to Reno. At Reno, go west. The park will be on the south side of Reno. For date and brochure, call (405) 739-1293. Admission is free until 6 p.m., at which time anyone over the age of eighteen must have an arm band ($2) to remain.

At this western heritage festival, visitors can have their picture taken with a 2000-pound longhorn steer, cheer on the cowboys in the bull riding competitions, and watch the dance steps of the precision horse drill team. Other features include arts, crafts, and concessions, children's entertainment, Native American dancing, a chili cook-off, a car show, a petting zoo, and pony rides. End your day by listening to a fantastic evening concert.

Israeli Festival

Held the third or fourth Sunday in May at Emanual Synagogue at 900 Northwest 47th Street. From I-235 exit at 50th Street. Go west on 50th to Western. Turn south on Western to 47th Street. Emanual Synagogue is on the south side of 47th. For date and brochure call (405) 528-2113. Free, but there is a minimal charge for the children's activity area.

Traditional Israeli foods, dances, magicians, clowns, arts and crafts are just some of activities at this festival. Be sure to attend the mock Jewish wedding and mock barmitzvah. Gifts from Israel will also be available for purchase.

Paseo Arts Festival

Held the last Saturday, Sunday, and Monday in May at the Paseo art and shopping district, Northwest 30th and Dewey, Oklahoma City. For date and brochure, call (405) 525-2688. Free.

This area has drawn a variety of talented artists and thousands of art lovers since 1929. Although the Paseo has been through many ups and downs in the past, it has in more recent years become a mecca for interesting art shops, coffee houses, and more. The area's annual art festival showcases the work of over one hundred artists displaying such works as paintings, photography, drawings, wood and clay works, jewelry, glass, collage art, and caricatures. Entertainment includes performances by musicians and dancers and a children's hands-on art area.

Fr ntier Country

Red Earth Festival

Held the second weekend (Wednesday through Sunday) in June at the Myriad Convention Center. For more information, call (405) 427-5228. To order tickets, call (405) 297-3000. From I-40, exit at Walker and go north to Sheridan. Turn east on Sheridan to the Myriad. Although many activities are ongoing throughout the day, the grand entry of dancers in full regalia starts at noon on Friday, Saturday and Sunday. Day events: Adults $6 per day, children under twelve free. All-day passes (which include night shows) for Friday and Saturday: adults $10, children under age twelve $5. Three-day passes are $25; group rates are available in advance.

With more than one hundred tribes from across the North American continent represented, the Red Earth Festival has grown to be one of the world's largest cultural events of its kind. Voted the 1996 Outstanding Event by the Oklahoma tourism industry, Red Earth is a "don't miss" experience. Over 150,000 people, including many from other countries, attend annually to watch as Native American artists and dancers share the richness and diversity of their culture and heritage. The festival keeps growing, and it now features over 1800 North American Native Americans who demonstrate their skills and talents in the art show and dance competitions.

Over 250 nationally-known artists display their works of basketry, jewelry, pottery, sculpture, paintings, beadwork, and more during the art show and sale. Visitors are also entertained by dramatic storytellers, and a children's area features hands-on art projects. On Friday and Saturday evenings, special shows featuring the more unusual Native American dances are presented. Through the colors, art, dances, sounds, and experiences, people of all ages learn to more fully appreciate and understand Native American traditions.

Aerospace America

Usually held on the third weekend in June at Will Rogers World Airport. From I-40, exit MacArthur and go south. Watch for policemen guiding traffic to the free parking areas. For date and brochure, call (405) 685-9546. Advance tickets: Adults $8, Children (six to twelve) $3. Tickets at the gate: Adults $10, Children (six to twelve) $6. Children under six are free. For an enjoyable time, be sure to bring blankets or lawn chairs, hats, visors, sunglasses, adequate sunscreen, and drink lots of water. Water fountains are available throughout the air show grounds. Be sure to wear lightweight, comfortable clothing and walking shoes. No coolers or ice chests are allowed. Souvenir and concession stands are plentiful. Advance discount ticket locations are Homeland stores statewide, Blockbuster Video and Music stores, Oklahoma Air National Guard, FAA Mike Monroney Aeronautical Center, Tinker Air Force Base, and OKC All Sports Association.

A wonderful celebration of aeronautics, Aerospace America is known as one of the best air shows in the world. Visitors enjoy constant entertainment, both in the sky and on the air-show grounds. In the sky are special demonstrations by world-renowned aerobatic pilots, wing walkers, sky writers, and parachute teams. Top flying teams like the United States Navy Blue Angels, the United States Air Force Thunderbirds, and the Royal Air Force Red Arrows perform to enthusiastic crowds each year. On the grounds, festival-goers climb aboard military planes to view their special features, peruse a trade show with almost two hundred booths, and see a large display of antique and specialty aircraft. On Friday night, many lighted air displays thrill the festival audience. Weather permitting, the night performance also includes a hot-air balloon glow.

Arts Festival Oklahoma

Held Labor Day Weekend at Oklahoma City Community College, 7777 South May Avenue. From I-44, exit at 74th Street and go east. OCCC is located on the south side of 74th Street. For more information, call (405) 682-7536.

Over 160 booths display arts and crafts such as pottery, paintings, jewelry, and more; these art works are found under huge open-air tents at this relaxing and enjoyable festival. Musical and dance performances continually entertain guests, and festival food is available. There is a well-staffed children's area. Saturday evening at the festival is special; it features fireworks and music from the Oklahoma City Philharmonic.

Oklahoma City

State Fair of Oklahoma

Usually held the last two weeks of September at the State Fair Park. From I-40 west, exit at May and go north. From I-40 east, exit at Portland and go north. At Reno, go east. For more information, call (405) 948-6700. Adults $4, children twelve and under, free. Free admission with a grandstand or arena show ticket purchased prior to the opening day of the fair.

Over one million people attend the State Fair of Oklahoma, making it one of the largest and best-attended fairs in the country. From ferris wheels to merry-go-rounds, cotton candy to corn dogs, the fair has something for everyone, regardless of age! Among the special exhibits at the fair are the Victorian Good-Holm Mansion; product and service displays featuring products from Oklahoma and many foreign countries; and the Oklahoma Department of Wildlife Conservation's educational exhibit about Oklahoma wildlife. Midway rides and carnival games are always popular, as are the Space Needle Tower and monorail rides. The Cottonwood Post holds shows and competitions and features the State Fair Plains Indian Dancers.

Don't miss the Walt Disney World on Ice performances, the PRCA Championship Rodeo, and the Ringling Brothers and Barnum & Bailey Circus. These spectacular shows will thrill the entire family. The Oklahoma State Fair is a family adventure you won't soon forget!

Parking is free. Watch for discount ticket information in local newspapers and on local television and radio. Try to attend on a weekday at the opening of the fair, when the grounds tend to be cleaner and less crowded.

Czech Festival

Held the first Saturday in October along Main Street in Yukon. From I-40, take Route 66 into Yukon. This road becomes Main Street. For date and brochure, call (405) 354-3567. Free.

The Czech Festival began in 1966 to preserve the area's Czech heritage through food, music, competitions, and a parade. This tradition has continued, and the festival continues to get bigger and more popular. The day starts with the Czech Parade which begins at 10 a.m. along Main Street. Later, enjoy ethnic food like kolaches and other Czech specialties, try the rides at the carnival, visit the car show, the local railroad museum, and an arts and crafts area. Complete your day

Fred Marvel/Oklahoma Tourism

Czech dancers.

by dancing in the street to lively polka music and buying a souvenir from Czechoslovakia.

Heritage Hills Home Tour

The tours starts at Overholser Mansion, N.W. 15th and Hudson, (405) 528-8485. Held the first weekend in October. Advance tickets $8. Tickets at the door: adults $10, children (twelve and under) $5. A trolley is available to shuttle people between the homes.

The over three hundred homes of historic Heritage Hills are located from Northwest 14th on the south to Northwest 20th on the north, bordered by Robinson on the east and Classen on the west. During the tour, five families open their private homes to let neighbors of the surrounding communities visit these historical and architectural gems. All the homes in Heritage Hills were built before 1930, and many leaders and influential people of Oklahoma have lived in this area. Past homes visited by the home tour are marked by flags. Sandwiches and refreshments are available for purchases on the Overholser Mansion Lawn.

NOTE: The Annual **Symphony Decorators Showhome** sponsored by the Oklahoma City

Orchestra League and held in the spring (usually early May), is another home tour event to enjoy. To be chosen as the showhouse, the metro-located home must be over eight thousand square feet in size and have historical significance. Call (405) 848-6787 for more information.

Festival of Lights Spectacular

Held from Thanksgiving night through December 31st (6-10 p.m.) at Joe Barnes Regional Park in Midwest City. Traveling east from Oklahoma City, exit I-40 at Douglas. Go north on Douglas to Southeast 15th. Turn west and go 1/2 mile to the stoplight at Ocama. Turn north at this street and continue until you reach the dead end. Turn right and follow the road to the park. For more information, call (405) 739-1293. Free; donations are appreciated.

Visitors get into the holiday spirit as they marvel at the beautiful lighted displays of this drive-through festival. Particularly noteworthy is the 118-foot lighted Christmas tree. All displays are sponsored by businesses and private citizens of the community.

Guests can enjoy the live music or tune their radios to carols and information on the displays (watch for more information on signs). A concession stand is available for those who forget their own hot chocolate and popcorn.

Mesta Park Home Tour

Usually held the first weekend of December, the tour encompasses the area north of Northwest 16th to Northwest 21st and from Western to Walker. For dates, information and tickets, call (405) 528-4104. Advance tickets are $8, at the door tickets are $10. Children ages six to twelve are $5. Children under age six are not generally allowed.

Listed on the National Register of Historical Places in 1983 and declared a Historic Preservation District in 1994, Mesta Park provides plenty to see for those interested in Oklahoma's historic architecture. Mesta Park was named for Mrs. Perle Skirvin Mesta, known in the city's early days as the "Hostess with the Mostest." While visiting the six historic homes placed on the tour, you will see that Mrs. Mesta's warmth and neighborly spirit is still alive today. The homes in Mesta Park are generally prairie-style, two-story homes. It's easy to understand how Mesta Park is as fashionable today as it was in the 1920s.

Opening Night

Held December 31st in downtown Oklahoma City and in nearby Bricktown. For more information, call the Arts Council of Oklahoma City at (405) 270-4848. A $5 button is required per person. Children under age five attend free. Admission buttons may be purchased at Opening Night, or you may purchase one beforehand from businesses around the Oklahoma City area. Parking is available for about $4 in the lots and garages located in downtown. Trolley service is available every ten to fifteen minutes from major parking areas to central downtown and Bricktown.

Expect to ring in the New Year in grand style at Opening Night. This fun and safe festival is hosted with families in mind. From a variety of musical entertainment to hands-on art activities, visitors find fun and exciting activities as they wait to celebrate the old and bring in the new. Indoor events and performances are held in several downtown buildings and in Bricktown. Most activities are within walking distance of each other. At midnight, visitors gather for the big end-of-the-year countdown and the fireworks display greeting the new year.

Seminole

The town of Seminole was named after the Indians who settled the area more than a century ago. The Seminoles were a tribe who parted from the Creeks after a conflict over slavery-related issues. In the late 1920s, Seminole became a boom town shortly after one of the biggest oil pools in the United States was discovered there. Almost overnight, a town of 750 people swelled; at the peak of the oil boom, more than 100,000 people received mail at the Seminole Post Office. Seminole commemorates the oil boom days with an annual "Gusher Days" celebration. Seminole is also known for their outstanding **Jasmine Moran Children's Museum**.

Located approximately fifty-six miles east of Oklahoma City, and about ninety miles south and west

Seminole

of Tulsa. From Oklahoma City, take I-40 east to the Highway 99 exit, then turn south. From Tulsa, go southwest on I-44, then take the U.S. 377/99 exit at Stroud and proceed to Seminole. Seminole Chamber of Commerce (405) 382-3640.

Seminole Historical Society Museum

1717 State Highway 9 West, (405) 382-1500. Monday-Friday 10-4, 1st and 3rd Saturdays 10-2. Closed Sunday and holidays. Free. Handicapped accessible.

Located across the street from the Jasmine Moran Children's Museum is the new home of the growing collection of the Seminole Historical Society. The bulk of the exhibits are from the antique tool collection amassed by a local cabinetmaker. Learn about Seminole and the surrounding area at this expanding museum.

Shopping

Visitors to Seminole will find interesting shops on Main Street, including the following. (Hours vary per store.) **The Line**, 215 N. Main, (405) 382-6872. Items include an eclectic collection of fine gifts, including new country-wood creations, candles, pictures, and wedding gifts. Handicapped accessible. **Hare Expressions**, 227 N. Main, (405) 382-8030. Merchandise includes country fabric bunnies and bears, as well as other gifts and antiques. Handicapped accessible. **Parks Drug Co.**, 330 N. Main (at corner of Main and Evans). Plan to stop in to have a vanilla or cherry Coke at an old-fashioned soda fountain.

Dining

Polo's $, $$

100 N. Main, (405) 382-8355. Monday-Thursday 11-9, Friday-Saturday 11-9:30, closed on Sunday. Handicapped accessible.

If you want good Tex-Mex food, visit Polo's at the old Rock Island Depot at the end of Main Street. Their specialty, beef and chicken fajitas, are nothing short of outstanding. This restaurant started in Ada, and it has now expanded to other Oklahoma towns.

Events

Gusher Days

Held the first weekend in June in downtown Seminole. Call (405) 382-2878 for more information.

This festival celebrates Seminole's oil history, and it includes a rodeo, arts and crafts displays, food booths, a carnival and parade, a street rod show, an air show, and a sports festival.

All-Night Gospel Sing

Held during the third weekend in August, Thursday-Saturday, at the Municipal Park on Milt Phillips Avenue. Performances begin at 7 p.m. and end at midnight. Three-day passes are $24. For more information, call (405) 382-8351. Handicapped accessible.

Well-known professional groups such as the Hoppers, Inspirations and King's Men have performed at this event. Sponsored by the Frank Arnold Ministries, Inc. and the Seminole Gospel Sing Association, the All-Night Gospel Sing has become a unique tradition over its twenty-five years.

Bring your own lawn chairs. Indoor seating is available in case of rain. Concessions provided.

In the Vicinity

Quasada Ranch Fishing Lodge

Located east and north of Seminole near Okemah, (405) 944-5421. Call for directions. Year-round rates are adults $60 per night, children (ages two to ten) $30 per night. Standard rates cover fishing, meals, and snacks (plus, the lodge will store your caught fish on ice for you). Corporate and group discounts are given. Handicapped accessible. Make reservations at least a week in advance. A half-mile air strip is available. Children are welcome. No pets. This country setting comes com-

plete with the usual assortment of crawling and flying critters; guests should come prepared with long pants and boots.

Quasada Ranch Fishing Lodge is a red brick, ivy-covered building constructed in the 1920s as a school. In the 1950s, it was converted to a home, and now every square inch is devoted to serving a constant stream of visitors. There are seven guest bedrooms of various sizes. Two are large family-sized rooms, and the other five have either a twin-or full-size bed. Guests share bathrooms. The lodge has a dining hall, a recreation room with a pool table and a large selection of games, and a large living room equipped with a big-screen television. After a long day of fishing, guests can splash in the pool or soak in the hot tub.

What the lodge lacks in glamorous luxury, it makes up for with simple, rustic charm. In this inviting and comfortable setting, you will immediately feel as if you belong to one big family. This atmosphere has been created by owners Myrl and June Ives and their daughter Debbie, who moved from the city to work the 150-acre farm.

There are nine fishing ponds and a twenty-acre lake. A small, well-stocked pond on the lodge's front lawn is accessible to children and the disabled. Most people who visit the Lodge are avid fishermen who bring their own equipment. The Ives do have fishing poles, but guests are encouraged to bring their own tackle.

Guests don't go hungry here; three daily meals include large country breakfasts, lunches and dinners. Vegetables are homegrown; desserts and breads are homemade. Snacks and soft drinks are provided throughout the day.

Shawnee

Shawnee was once part of Indian Territory, and five tribes continue to call the Shawnee area their home. In the 1891 Land Run, Shawnee's first postmaster, Etta Ray, drove her stake when the opening gun was fired. The town of Shawnee grew around her 160-acre tract of land and was incorporated as a town on July 4, 1895. The city has a rich mixture of Native American history, cowboy traditions, and a diversified corporate community. The city has a "suburb personality"– a bustling main street, a large mall located off I-40, and growing neighborhoods flanked by farmland.

Christian groups will be interested to know about a retreat center named **A Place Like Eden**. For information about group retreats and other activities at this lovely facility call (405) 273-1994. *From Oklahoma City travel approximately forty miles east on I-40. From Tulsa, travel approximately sixty-six miles west on I-44 to Highway 18 (Chandler exit). Continue twenty-eight miles south to Shawnee. Greater Shawnee Area Convention and Visitors Bureau (405) 273-6092.*

Mabee-Gerrer Museum

St. Gregory's College Campus, 1900 West MacArthur, (405) 878-5300. From Oklahoma City, take I-40 east to the first Shawnee exit onto Highway I-77. Travel south until you come to the MacArthur exit; turn left and continue approximately one mile. You will notice St. Gregory's College on the

north side of the road; its entry is lined with pine trees. From Tulsa, travel east to the Chandler exit. Travel south on Highway 18 into Shawnee. Highway 18 (Harrison Street) intersects with MacArthur Street, turn right and continue west until you see the entry drive. The museum sits on the southwest end of the campus. Tuesday-Sunday 1-4. Closed Monday and holidays. Free; donations are accepted. Handicapped accessible.

The museum was founded in 1915 by Father Gregory Gerrer, a Benedictine Monk of St. Gregory's Abbey. The beau-

Mabee-Gerrer Museum.

Shawnee

tiful building houses Egyptian mummies, Renaissance paintings, Native American art and American landscapes, as well as ivory and bronze artworks. In the past, special exhibits have featured the works of Raphael, Chase and Jerome. Some exhibits change every three months. Call one to two weeks in advance to make group tour reservations. Tours are one hour in length, and they are conducted by docents.

Santa Fe Railroad Depot

614 East Main Street, (405) 275-8412. From Oklahoma City, take I-40 east to the second Shawnee exit, Kickapoo Street. Turn south and travel until you reach Main Street, turn east and travel five blocks. The depot is easy to locate on the north side of the street. From Tulsa, travel east to the Chandler exit. Travel south on Highway 18 into Shawnee. At Main Street, turn west. Tuesday-Friday 10-4, Saturday-Sunday 2-4. Free. Tours are approximately one hour long. Call one week in advance for group tours. Handicapped accessible.

Apart from the unique and varied collection of artifacts and exhibits inside, the museum building itself is worthy of inspection. Built in the Romanesque Revival style of the late 1800s, the Santa Fe Railroad Depot has walls of Bedford rock, ceilings of boxcar siding, and and other unusual features. The building is crowned with a tower.

Begun in 1938 by the Pottawatomie County Historical Society, the museum collection was first displayed at the Friends Missions Church. In 1981, the items were moved to the Depot. Objects related to the history of the Santa Fe Railroad are in abundant display. Other holdings include a life-size model of a horse, antique dolls, toys, a Model T Ford, farm equipment, a doctor's medical equipment, and a pump organ that survived the Shawnee tornado of 1924. Among the Native American artifacts are a Sac and Fox eagle-feather headdress, an eagle-wing ceremonial fan, a doeskin wedding dress, war axes, arrowheads, and spear points.

Dining

Deem's Bean Scene $, $$

2033 North Kickapoo, (405) 275-5553. From I-40 east, take the second Shawnee exit onto Kickapoo Street; travel south. Monday-Thursday 7:30 a.m.-11 p.m., Friday-Saturday 7:30 a.m.-midnight. Handicapped accessible.

Sip a cup of tea or order up a European espresso while you listen to live entertainment on selected evenings at Deem's (call for a schedule of events). Breakfasts include bagels, croissants, and homemade granola cereal. On the lunch and dinner menu are healthy soups, salads and sandwiches. This is an excellent dining choice for vegetarians, or for anyone who likes fresh, distinctive flavors. On a summer day, take a fruit smoothie outside onto the deck. In the winter, warm yourself with a cup of coffee inside. The decor is trendy and, on the walls, the work of local artists is displayed.

Charlie's at Firelake $, $$

1901 S. Gordon Cooper Drive, (405) 275-5535. From Oklahoma City, travel east on I-40 to the second Shawnee exit (Kickapoo Street). Turn south on Kickapoo and travel to Main Street. From Main, turn east and travel to Beard Street. Turn south on Beard Street, also known as Gordon Cooper Drive. Go two miles. The restaurant overlooks Firelake Golf Course. Monday-Thursday 8-2 & 5-9; Friday-Saturday 8-2 & 5-10; Sunday 8-2.

This restaurant offers tasty food and attractive scenery. Ask to be seated on the enclosed balcony that overlooks the golf course. The menu has everything from hamburgers and salads to chicken fried steak and prime rib dinners. For light eaters and vegetarians, Charlie offers several delicious options. His menu includes Portabello mushrooms over pasta (some say this dish tastes like steak), beans and cornbread, vegetable burgers, and a garden steak dinner. Charlie's is also open for breakfast with a traditional breakfast menu.

Country Indulgence Tea Room and Bakery $, $$

12 East Main, (405) 275-4544. Tuesday through Saturday 11 a.m. to 2 p.m. .

The owners describe the restaurant as "fine dining in the atmosphere of Grandmother's parlor." Favorites include the chicken salad sandwich, the flavored coffees and teas, and the fruit salad. The decor is elegant Victorian lace and floral patterns. Bakery items are prepared fresh daily, and personalized cakes can be specially ordered. The tea room also sells gifts and baskets.

Jay's Classic Steak House $, $$

From I-40 travel south on 177 and turn west onto old Highway 270. Take an immediate right and travel 1/2 block to the restaurant. (405) 275-6867. Tuesday-Thursday 5-9, Friday-Saturday 5-10. Large groups are welcome, and reservations are not required. Handicapped accessible.

Relax in the old-fashioned setting as you bite into one of the best steaks in Shawnee. Paul Buckmaster's rustic cabin restaurant has been in Shawnee for ten years. The cabin has a cathedral ceiling, and it is decorated with Oklahoma heritage crafts. Filet mignon and twice-baked potatoes are two reasons why locals have flocked to Jay's Classic Steak House. Other popular menu items include fried chicken and lamb fries. While you are waiting for dinner, enjoy an appetizer plate of crisp raw vegetables.

Van's Pig Stand $, $$ and Charcoal Room $$, $$$

717 E. Highland, (405) 273-8704. Van's Pig Stand: Monday-Friday 11-9, Saturday 11-1l, Sunday 11-3. Charcoal Room: Monday-Friday 5-9; Saturday 5-10; closed on Sunday. Van's is handicapped accessible, but the Charcoal Room is not.

This unusual combination of restaurants gives diners a choice of luxury dining downstairs or a barbecue meal in casual surroundings upstairs. In the Charcoal Room, select among entrees such as filet mignon, marinated chicken breast, and seafood. On the floor above, Van's Pig Stand feeds its diners all the authentic, hickory-smoked barbecue they want, including ribs, chicken dinners, and chopped beef. The restaurant's award-winning sauce makes the barbecued meals particularly memorable. The owner of Van's (family owned and operated for over 66 years), Jerry Vandegrift, claims that it was his mother, Thelma M. Vandegrift, who developed the original twice-baked potato.

Shopping

Ann & You

118 E. Main Street, (405) 275-4970. From I-40 and Kickapoo Street turn south and continue to Main Street. Turn east; look for the shop on the north side of the street. Monday-Saturday 9-5:30. Handicapped accessible.

This gift shop has a long-standing reputation in the area for its elegant and practical wedding gifts, as well as its baby gifts, bath items, and gourmet cooking utensils. The owner, Ann Davis, greets each guest with an offer of complimentary cappuccino (which is also for sale).

The Groves

602 E. Highland, (405) 878-9919. Monday-Saturday 9:30-5:30.

This shop is wonderfully full and quaintly cluttered. There is something new to discover at every turn. The eclectic collection defies categorization; you'll find everything from antiques, country crafts, and sophisticated porcelain, to wall hangings and holiday decorations.

Events

Jazz Festival

Held on Main Street the first weekend of October. For more information, call (405) 878-5300. Free.

For more than five years, the Jazz Festival has spotlighted superb local and out-of-town musical talent. Various civic organizations have food booths that serve Indian tacos, strawberry crepes, hot dogs, and baked potatoes. In the evening, for about $6, you can indulge in some of the most delicious desserts made by talented local chefs.

Accommodations

Mayne Harbor Inn

2401 East Highland, (405) 275-4700. Call for directions. $75-175 per night. It is best to make reservations one week in advance. Children 12 and under accepted. No pets. One room is disabled accessible. Member of the Oklahoma Bed and Breakfast Association.

This colonial-style inn is serenely tucked away in a wooded, parklike setting, where guests can relax and be pampered by hosts Margaret and David Larson. The two smaller rooms include the "Jean Anne" with twin beds and the "Marjory" with a queen-size bed. Both rooms are decorated with family heirlooms and antiques. Guests in these rooms may share an adjoining bathroom, or choose to use a hall bathroom.

The larger rooms include the "Dorothy," equipped with a two-person jacuzzi and a four-poster, queen-size bed. It is the home's original master bedroom, and it is decorated in a soothing green and white striped wallpaper. The spacious room has a sitting area as well. The inn also has a honeymoon suite that comes with a wood-burning fireplace, a king size four-poster bed, a wet bar, a small dining area, pine-paneled walls, and nine windows that overlook the wooded lawn. The larger rooms have private bathrooms.

Known for her culinary skills, Margaret Larson eagerly prepares a large breakfast menu. Breakfast may include any of the following: French toast, eggs benedict, German potato pancake with hot, homemade apple sauce, and garden omelettes with a ring-shaped cinnamon roll laced with walnuts and raisins.

Stillwater

New Canaan, The Promised Land–these were the names used to describe the north central portion of what is now Oklahoma. Originally part of Indian Territory, this land was wrested from several different Indian tribes as a depository for future Indian resettlements. Called the Unassigned Lands, the two million-acre area was still unsettled after the Civil War. Railroad companies, aspiring businessmen, and fortune hunters all saw the Unassigned Lands as a mecca of potential wealth. By 1879, a class of professional promoters had emerged, with the sole purpose of opening the Unassigned Lands to white settlers. Prominent among these promoters was David L. Payne. He established a string of "Boomer" camps along the borders of the territory; Boomers regularly invaded the Unassigned Lands, establishing small towns. Here they stayed (illegally) until caught and escorted out by the U.S. Army. One Boomer group camped on the banks of Stillwater Creek and took the creek's name for their town. Although later escorted out of the territory, the Boomers and their ten-year crusade had drawn national attention. By 1889, Congress agreed to open the Unassigned Lands to white settlers in a most unique way–a land run! The Unassigned Lands opened on April 22, 1889, and numerous towns were suddenly populated, including Stillwater. The town was forever changed when chosen as the site for a state university, Oklahoma A&M, now known as Oklahoma State University.

Located approximately 65 miles north of Oklahoma City, and about 64 miles west of Tulsa. From Oklahoma City, take I-35 north and Highway 51 east. From Tulsa, travel west on the Cimarron Turnpike, then take either the Perkins Road exit (Highway 177) or the OSU exit south about ten miles. Stillwater Conventions and Visitors Bureau (405) 743-3697.

Oklahoma State University

(405) 744-5000 or (800) 233-5019. Web site: http://pio.okstate.edu. Begin your tour at the Student Union, located just north of the intersection of University Avenue and Hester. Visitor parking is available in the lot at the corner of this intersection or in the nearby Student Union parking garage.

The town's city leaders lobbied hard to establish the Stillwater location of the state's agricultural and mechanical college. When they succeeded, the leaders secured an excellent future for their town. The school was founded in late 1890, but when classes started a year later, there were still no buildings, no books, and no curriculum. In the past hundred years, the university has grown to more than 36,000 students on four campuses, offering bachelor's, master's, and doctor's degrees in a large number of fields, including Doctor of Osteopathy and Doctor of Veterinary Medicine degrees.

Despite its humble beginnings, the college, then known as Oklahoma A&M, built its first building in 1894. Called **Old Central**, this pink brick building is now listed in the National Register of Historic Places and is operated by the Oklahoma Historical Society as a museum showcasing the development of higher education in the state. The school's history is documented through exhibits, and some rooms resemble the first classrooms of 1894. Visitors especially enjoy the restored President's Office and the Student Night Watchman's Room. Usually open Tuesday-Friday 9-5, and Saturday 10-4, the museum is closed Sunday, Monday and holidays. A nominal admission fee is charged. Special tours and slide presentations are available for groups by appointment. Call (405) 624-3220.

The OSU campus is quite attractive. Many of the two hundred permanent buildings on this 840-acre campus are red brick, following a Georgian style architectural theme. Prominent among these are the Student Union, the Edmon Low Library, the Colvin Physical Education Center, the Bartlett Center for the Studio Arts, and the Seretean Center for the Performing Arts.

Visitors will want to start their unofficial tour of the University at the **Student Union** to "get a feel" for campus life. Unions first appeared on college campuses in the early 1800s as debate halls for university students. The idea for a common meeting ground has now evolved to encompass a place where students, faculty, staff, alumni, and guests can assemble in a friendly, casual atmosphere. Opened in 1950, the OSU Student Union was once called the "Waldorf" of student facilities. With more than 543,000 square feet, it is one of the largest student unions in the world. Basically self-supporting, the Union offers a number of amenities including an 81-room hotel, a bookstore, and a theater. A variety of lounges and food service companies are located here, as are a shopping mall, a recreation center, a post office, a travel agency, and many University offices.

Located on the west side of the Student Union building, the **Formal Gardens** provide students, faculty and staff a quiet and restful place to take a break from their daily schedules. Ablaze with the colors of seasonal plantings, the gardens bring nature to the very heart of the campus.

The **Edmon Low Library** is conveniently situated in the center of the campus. With over 1.7 million volumes, this library was one of the first to offer open stacks to its students. Technologically up-to-date, the library has a computerized information system called PETE. Students and faculty use PETE to search the library and several other bibliographic databases. The Library also has a World Wide Web site on the Internet. (http://www.library.okstate.edu). Web browsers will find information regarding the services and facilities of the Library, access to PETE, and links to national and international catalogues and databases. The **Map Room** contains more than 200,000 maps and aerial photographs of most metropolitan areas in the U.S. The library's **Special Collections** consist of rare books, photographs, and selected material on Oklahoma history (open Monday-Friday 8-5). The books and papers of Oklahoma historian Angie Debo are here, as are the papers of Oklahoma's former governor, Henry S. Johnston. There are also collections on soil conservation and water resources. At the east end of the second floor are the **University Archives**; materials here document the development of OSU.

Located eight miles west of Stillwater, **Lake Carl Blackwell** is owned by the university. The 21,000-acre site is used for recreation and research. OSU has the nation's first university-operated Wellness Center. The health-related programs include free wellness screening, education classes, and aerobics and weight training instructor certifications. Dedicated to developing contemporary health maintenance programs, the center also offers instruction in counseling, exercise science, nutrition, pre-physical therapy, and wellness.

The Bartlett Center for Studio Arts was originally built in 1910 as a women's residence hall. Originally named for Maude Gardiner, founder of the University's home economics program, the building was used in many different ways throughout the years. Renamed and renovated as a result of a donation by the F.M. Bartlett family, the building now houses eleven studios for the visual arts. Also located here is the **Gardiner Art Gallery**. Faculty and student work is exhibited at the gallery on a regular basis, and a number of national exhibitions have also been hosted. The gallery is open Monday-Friday 8-5, Saturday 9-noon, and Sunday 2-5. For information about upcoming events, contact the Department of Art at (405) 744-6016.

The Departments of Music and Theater are housed in the **M.B. Seretean Center for the Performing Arts**. Built in 1970, the well-equipped center has two auditoriums that serve as the focal point for all music and dramatic presentations at OSU. Four to six plays by OSU students and a number of productions by other universities are presented each year. Call the Theater Department (405-744-9203 or 744-9208) for a schedule of upcoming plays and ticket information.

Spectator **sporting events** include Cowboy football, basketball, baseball, golf, wrestling, soccer, and tennis. Cowboy football is played on Lewis Field, a prominent feature of the OSU campus. Cowboy and Cowgirl basketball is played from October through March in the small but exciting Gallagher-Iba Arena. Wrestling is also hosted here from November through March. Cowboy baseball is played at the Allie P. Reynolds Baseball Stadium from February to June. Golf tournaments, played throughout the school year, are held at various locations. The spring sports of tennis and track hold meets February through June. Track events are held at the K.B. Droke Track and Field Center. Call the Athletic Office at (405) 744-5745 for an up-to-date schedule of sporting events and current ticket information.

The **Oklahoma Gardening Studio Grounds** are located just west of town. Home to OETA's excellent show "Oklahoma Gardening," the gardens are one of the most-visited sites at OSU. Gardens showcased in the past include the Children's Rainbow Garden, the All-White Flower Garden, the American Indian Garden, and the Chocolate Garden. Tours are conducted April-October; walk-in visitors are welcome. Appointments for guided group tours can be made by calling (405) 744-5404. Open Monday-Friday 8-5.

Before ending your tour of the campus, take a few moments to wander over to **Theta Pond**. Now a landscaped park complete with seasonal plantings and benches, the pond originally served as the watering hole for students' horses. A favorite place of students, faculty and guests alike, this is one scenic and restful attraction you won't want to miss.

Pleasant Valley School

1901 S. Sangre. From Highway 51 (6th Street), go south on Sangre to 19th Street. The school is open by appointment only. Call the Stillwater Board of Education at (405) 743-6300 at least two weeks in advance to get names and phone numbers of Pleasant Valley School alumni who give tours. Free.

Relive the memories of Oklahoma's early settlers when you visit this one-room schoolhouse. Built in 1899 on a 2.5 acre lot purchased for $5, this school taught students of all ages in one room. Alumni from the school volunteer as teachers and tour guides. Listen closely as they relate stories about their experiences in this school. Learn how students contributed to the activities of the school by carrying wood for the pot-bellied stove and by bringing ingredients for stew to be enjoyed at lunch time. Bringing lunch pails and wearing period clothing, fourth graders from across the state can spend a day at the school; families and other groups are also encouraged to schedule tours.

National Wrestling Hall of Fame

405 West Hall of Fame Avenue, (405) 377-5243. From Highway 51 (6th Street) go north on Duck Street to Hall of Fame Avenue. The museum is located on the southwest corner of this intersection on the OSU campus. Free parking is available on the west side of the building. Weekdays 9-4, and weekends by appointment. Free.

Tracing its beginnings to the dawn of civilization, wrestling has been called the Oldest Sport. In fact, wrestling was introduced to the Olympic Games in 708 B.C. At the Wrestling Hall of Fame, the history of the sport and it's greatest achievers are prominently displayed. Exhibits feature numerous photographs, uniforms, awards and memorabilia. The Hall of Fame honors wrestling legends, celebrates current competitors, and inspires future participants.

Sheerar Museum

7th Street and Duncan, (405) 377-0359. Located in downtown Stillwater. Travel one block south

of 6th Street (Highway 51) on Duncan. The Museum is on the corner of Duncan and 7th. Tuesday-Friday 11-4, Saturday and Sunday 1-4. Closed Monday and major holidays. Free.

This small, well-organized museum provides visitors with a glimpse of life in Stillwater from the turn of the century to the present. Exhibits include information on the Land Run, Oklahoma A & M (now OSU), and famous individuals who have visited the town. However, the main emphasis of the museum is to illustrate the daily lives of Stillwater's pioneers. Arranged by decade, exhibits contain photographs, newspaper articles, and artifacts that describe life in this small but progressive town. Also housed here is the nationally-recognized button collection of Mrs. Lena Sheerar. Containing 3450 buttons dating from the 1740s to the 1930s, this collection is noteworthy for its diversity. A small gift shop is located on site.

Walking Tour of Downtown Stillwater

Begin your tour of downtown Stillwater at the Sheerar Museum at 7th and Duncan. Ample parking is available. A brochure for the walking tour can be picked up inside the museum. Free.

With photographs and commentary, the comprehensive walking tour brochure highlights about thirty historic buildings in downtown Stillwater and emphasizes the town's commercial development. With most of the buildings built prior to the Depression, visitors can learn about popular architectural styles of the early twentieth century. Amusing anecdotes are also related; one of the more humorous tells of college students exiting a ballroom through the windows to the roof in order to get a breath of fresh air. Developed by former OSU graduate student Donna K. Wallace, the guide also contains a locator map. Along the way, visitors may shop in the stores located in downtown Stillwater or dine in the town's cafes. For history buffs or small-town aficionados, this is an entertaining way to spend an afternoon.

Golf

Lakeside Memorial Golf Course

Located north of Stillwater on Highway 177, (405) 372-3399. Open daily from 6:30 a.m. to dark. Green fees are weekdays $12.96, weekends $15.12 (twilight fee discount given); golf carts are $8 for nine holes and $16 for eighteen holes.

This 6600-yard, par 70 course provides moderate challenges for golfers. Creeks and ponds provide water hazards. Tee times are recommended for weekend play; they are taken beginning Tuesday for the weekend ahead.

Cimarron Trails Golf Course

Located just north of Perkins. (405) 547-5701. From Stillwater travel south on 177 to Perkins, turn east on Highway 33; look for the course on the north side of the highway. Open daily. Green fees on weekdays $12, on weekends $17. Carts are $8.95 per person. Tee times are recommended and are accepted up to a week in advance.

This new golf course (opened in 1994) provides water hazards and occasional problems with wind. Conveniently located near Stillwater, Tulsa, and Oklahoma City, it has received rave reviews from golf enthusiasts. Two par-three holes have fairway shots over water. Some holes are tree-lined, some tees are elevated, and the par five number nine hole has water surrounding the green. Course yardage is 6959, USGA rating is 74, and slope is 124.8.

Dining

Eskimo Joe's $

501 W. Elm, (405) 372-8896. Located one block east of the OSU campus on Elm. Restaurant hours: Monday-Saturday 11 a.m.-10 p.m., bar 11 a.m.-2 a.m.; Sunday 11 a.m.-9 p.m. (restaurant and limited bar). Clothes Headquarters: Monday-Saturday 10 a.m.-9 p.m., Sunday 11 a.m.-8 p.m.

Originally started as a beer joint by two OSU graduates in 1975, this intriguing and fast-growing business now boasts a popular restaurant and a world-famous clothing store. Once a diner, the wood, stone and glass block building has been expanded over the years to include five dining areas that seat over two hundred patrons. The menu offers salads, burgers, sandwiches, and chicken, steak and pork dinners.

If not for its famous logo of Eskimo Joe and his dog Buffy, Eskimo Joe's might still have been a fun bar with write-on-the-top tables. Instead, the famous logo, created by a freshman graphics design student, has sold millions of T-shirts and is now printed on shorts, shirts, jackets, ties, watches, and bags. The T-shirts have been declared the second most popular in the world and have even been acknowledged as a world collectible by the television show "20/20."

Eskimo Joe's Clothes World Headquarters is located adjacent to the restaurant. Here the latest in Joe's merchandise is displayed and sold. Each year, to coincide with the annual birthday celebration, a commemorative design is created. Community-minded, Eskimo Joe's, led by owner Stan Clark, sponsors a golf tournament and 5-K run, and the company presents all babies born at Stillwater Medical Center with tiny Joe's T-shirts to wear home. Don't miss this outstanding Stillwater enterprise, a true salute to American ingenuity!

The Hideaway *

230 S. Knoblock, (405) 372-4777. From Highway 51 (6th Street) turn north on Knoblock. Sunday-Thursday 11 a.m.-10 p.m., Friday and Saturday 11 a.m.-11 p.m. Hideaway has two locations in Tulsa and one in Oklahoma City.

You haven't been to Stillwater if you haven't eaten at Hideaway Pizza. Started by OSU college student Richard Dermer in 1957, this pizzeria has a large and loyal following. Offering appetizers, salads, hot and cold sandwiches, and pasta, the house specialty is, of course, pizza. Olive oil, garlic and sun-dried tomatoes are the ingredients that blend together to make these pizzas great taste sensations. Unique toppings provide customers with delicious choices seldom found in larger chain restaurants. The outstanding reputation enjoyed by this restaurant was born in a relatively small space where, on most any night, the line to get in went around the block. The current cozy, 2000-square-foot dining room sports an interesting collage and many colorful kites on the walls. The open kitchen allows customers to see employees hard at work. The menu cover is a collage of photos. Look closely; you may see the original delivery fleet of Volkswagen "Bugs."

For those who have left the college town but still need to satisfy their pizza cravings, there's a delivery service that ships frozen Hideaway pizzas anywhere in the United States, including Alaska and Hawaii. Go on....treat yourself to one of Stillwater's greatest traditions!

Mexico Joe's **

311 E. Hall of Fame, (405) 372-1169. From 6th Street (Highway 51), turn north onto Main and continue to Hall of Fame. At this street, turn east. Open daily at 11 a.m., the restaurant closes at 10 every night except Sunday, when it closes at 9 p.m.

Another one of Stan Clark's successful restaurants, Mexico Joe's serves delicious Tex-Mex food. Enjoy chips and salsa before filling up on tacos, enchiladas, and burritos. Don't miss the side orders of tortillas, rice and beans.

Stillwater Bay **, ***

623 S. Husband, (405) 743-2780. On the corner of Husband and 7th Street, across from the Courthouse in downtown Stillwater. Open daily, lunch 11-2, dinner 5-10.

This is one of the places local residents go when they want to celebrate a special occasion. Offering seafood and steaks, the restaurant also has weekly specials. Try their excellent Sunday Brunch. Started by Stan Clark, the owner of Eskimo Joe's, this restaurant has a loyal following.

New York Bagel *

521 W. Elm, (405) 372-2435. From Highway 51 (6th Street), turn north onto Main, and after several blocks, turn west onto Elm. New York Bagel is next door to Eskimo Joe's. Hours vary by store.

This fast-growing specialty restaurant was started in 1986 by three transplanted New Yorkers who were hungry for a taste of home. In the early 1980s, college buddies Rob Gerresi, Vince Vrana and Paul Sorrentino noticed a lack of good bagels in Oklahoma. Although they

talked about the possibilities of a store at that time, they put their idea on hold until after all three had graduated.

With the discovery of the "perfect" location (next door to Eskimo Joe's), and some capital from their families and other sources, the three set up their first New York Bagel Shop. Growing ever since, the store began to offer franchises in 1993; there are now five stores in the Tulsa area and several in Oklahoma City. Plans are being made to expand as far away as Oregon, California and Texas. Featuring a wide variety of bagels, flavored cream cheeses, and sandwiches, this is one of the best and busiest places to enjoy the delicious taste of New York!

Shopping

Antique Mall of Stillwater

116 E. 9th, (405) 372-2322. From 6th Street (Highway 51), turn south on Lewis and travel three blocks to 9th Street. Monday-Friday 10-6, Thursday evenings until 8, Saturday 10-5, Sunday 1-5.

Originally the Stillwater Opera House, this 1903 building has been converted into a mall for Stillwater's antique dealers. The 14,000-square-foot building is stocked with furniture, vintage clothing, jewelry, coins, primitives, glassware, and linens from over 100 dealers.

Downtown Stillwater

Primarily located on Main Street between 6th and 9th Streets, the downtown Stillwater area offers a wonderful variety of specialty and gift stores. Antiques, clothing stores (including a wonderful outlet for Stillwater-based **Cottontail Originals** that makes and sells children's and women's clothing around the world), gift and book stores, restaurants, and coffee shops can all be found in this Main Street Project town. Hours vary by store.

Accommodations

Friend House Bed and Breakfast

404 S. Knoblock Street, (405) 372-1982. From Highway 51 (6th Street), turn north on Knoblock. Rates are $60 per night. Open all year, except for Christmas. Reservations and a deposit are required. Older children accepted. Not handicapped accessible.

Named for Alwaina Friend Phillips, who owned the home along with her husband Elmer, Friend House offers comfortable accommodations to Stillwater visitors. This B&B is conveniently located close to the OSU campus (only two blocks away), and is near many shops and restaurants. It is owned and operated by Mrs. Phillips' daughter, Lou Salyer, and her husband Ben.

Three antique-filled rooms with private baths are available for guests. The Primrose Room features antique furnishings, prints and fabrics with a delicate rose motif. The Marble Room has several marble-topped pieces of furniture, as well as a double bed with a brass antique headboard. The Phillips Room offers guests a brass bed, rocking chair, easy chair, and triple-mirror dressing table. A morning room, also located upstairs, is the perfect place to relax; coffee and tea are available here each morning. A continental breakfast is served daily from 8-10 a.m.

Thomasville Bed and Breakfast

4115 N. Denver, (405) 373-1203. From the intersection of Perkins and Airport Road, go east one mile on Airport Road. Turn north (left) on Jardot (there is no street sign). Thomasville is 1/4 mile north, on the right. Rates are $60 per night, with an advance deposit required. Open only on weekends; reservations should be made well in advance, by referral only.

Many Stillwater visitors have found their way to Thomasville, where they've spent a relaxed and quiet evening at the Thomasville B&B. Built in 1889, this colonial manor home is furnished with antiques and treasures from throughout the world. It also contains a library and study filled with papers and memorabilia from Stillwater's past. Mrs. Virginia Thomas, the gracious proprietor of the Thomasville B&B and a longtime Stillwater resident, has always enjoyed entertaining.

The B&B has four guest rooms, each with a different theme. The rooms are named the Edison Room, the Baby's Room, the Play Room and the Parent's Room. Each room sleeps two, with two shared baths at the end of the hall. Although each room is beautifully decorated, the extra amenities make the Thomasville special. From late afternoon and evening snacks to the beautiful robes that are provided, the hospitality is impeccable. A "continental plus" breakfast is served each morning between 8 and 10 a.m. Elegantly served on fine table linens with crystal and silver service, this meal features seasonal fruit, muffins, specialty dishes, and sweet rolls. Although the home has four rooms, the B&B accommodates only two house guests at any one time.

Events

Allied Arts

Performances are held throughout the year at the Seretean Concert Hall, on the OSU campus at the corner of Knoblock and Morrill. Call the Seretean Concert Hall at (405) 744-7509 for a brochure listing performance dates, times and prices. Tickets are generally about $10 per person. Group discounts are available for ten or more.

Allied Arts is the oldest continuously-functioning university-related performing arts series. Dedicated to providing the university community with quality, live performances, the organization has previously sponsored orchestras, choral groups, theatrical productions, opera, dance, and international and traditional ethnic arts performances. Past artists have included the Vivaldi Traveling Circus, the Harlem Spiritual Ensemble, the San Francisco Taiko Dojo (Japanese drumming), and the Best of Gilbert and Sullivan.

Run for the Arts

Usually held the third Saturday in April on the west lawn and parking lots of the Payne County Courthouse. The courthouse is located at the corner of Highway 51 (6th Street) and Husband, near downtown. For more information call (405) 747-8084. Free

Honoring the Land Run of April 22, 1889, this juried arts and crafts show features artists from a five-state area. Many different mediums are represented, including jewelry, woodworking, pottery, sculpture, and painting. Jazz bands perform throughout the day; food vendors provide welcome refreshments.

Stillwater Community Band Concerts

Performed every other Thursday evening in June and July. For concert dates and times call (405) 747-8003. Held on the south lawn of the Payne County Courthouse, 606 S. Husband Street, located at the corner of Highway 51 (6th Street) and Husband. Free.

Family summer fun is offered at these concerts held "under the stars." Adult volunteer musicians make up this talented community band. An informative and entertaining narrator provides commentary for the program. Ranging from patriotic to whimsical, musical selections delight the entire family. The informal setting encourages adults to relax and listen; young children often play quietly or dance. Audience members are encouraged to bring lawn chairs, blankets and picnic baskets. The concerts are occasionally moved to the Stillwater Community Center at Eighth and Duck Streets.

Jumpin' in July

Call the Chamber of Commerce at (405) 743-3697 for a calendar of events. Hours and admissions vary by event.

A number of different events are held during Stillwater's month-long celebration. To start things off "with a bang," join residents as they celebrate the Fourth of July at the **Boomer Blast**! Visitors to this evening-long event at Boomer Lake are treated to a Classic Car Show, a Boat Show, and a Bungee Jumping. Children's activities, bands, special entertainment, and food booths contribute to the day's success. Evening brings one of the state's largest and most impressive fireworks displays, reflected in the waters of Boomer Lake.

Also held at Boomer Lake in mid-July is **"Oklahoma's Largest Family Picnic"** and the "Not so Still-water" **Great American Duck Race**. Later in the month, OSU hosts its **Celebrity Alumni Basketball Classic**. OSU alumni, honorary coaches, and television personalities participate in

this classic basketball event. The Stillwater Water Garden Society hosts its summer **Water Garden Tour** in July. The gardens, which add color, sound, beauty, and movement to residents' yards, are the features of this tour. Krazy Daze is a city-wide retail promotion featuring sidewalk sales, food vendors, children's activities, arts, and entertainment. This two-day event brings shoppers some of the best retail deals of the year.

July is also the month that Eskimo Joe's celebrates its anniversary. Originally a street party, the birthday bash had grown to unmanageable proportions. Now the grinning, dog-hugging mascot celebrates by participating in the city's month-long party. Live bands and entertainment, food specials, and specialty sports nights are all featured events. Some evenings, discounts are given to patrons who wear the famous Eskimo Joe's T-shirts. July is a great time to visit this friendly college town!

Stroud

Whether just "passing through" on a tour of Route 66, or coming to experience a small town adventure, Stroud is a great place to visit. Named for a local merchant, this town has always been a trade center. Located in the "wet" part of the state where alcohol was legal, the town first prospered from the illegal sale of whiskey to the nearby Creek Indians. This profitable enterprise "dried up" with statehood in 1907. By the early 1920s, Stroud was enjoying new-found wealth from the newly-discovered oil fields. Most recently, Stroud has become a popular shopping destination, primarily because the Tanger Outlet Mall is located near the town along the Turner Turnpike, virtually halfway between Tulsa and Oklahoma City. Be sure to pick up a copy of the visitors guide at the Chamber of Commerce office or at the Tanger Outlet Center office. The guide includes a **walking or driving tour** of the town's older residences.

Stroud is located fifty miles west of Tulsa and fifty miles east of Oklahoma City on I-44, the Turner Turnpike. Stroud Chamber of Commerce (918) 968-3321.

Paramount Apparel Manufacturing

414 W. 4th Street, (918) 968-2279. From the Turner Turnpike, exit at Stroud and head south towards downtown. Turn east on 4th and look for the store on the right. Monday-Friday 7 a.m.-3:30 p.m.

Formerly a hosiery factory, this T-shirt manufacturer provides real bargains to shoppers at their outlet store. Visitors may purchase T-shirts, sweatshirts, baseball shirts, and sleep shirts for a fraction of the cost one pays in retail stores. Children can create their own shirts, choosing the color and transfer they prefer, usually for about $5. Call ahead to schedule group visits or to check on the arrival of holiday T-shirt transfers.

Stroud Lake

Located three miles north on Highway 99 and three miles east of Stroud. For more information, contact the Stroud Chamber of Commerce.

Stroud Lake offers 621 surface acres of water for boating, fishing, water skiing, camping, and swimming. The east side of the lake has picnic tables, barbecue grills, and a pavilion and boat ramp, while the west side features a pavilion, boat ramp and fishing dock. Seventy-two campsites, twenty-eight with electricity, are available on a first-come, first-serve basis.

Dining

Rock Cafe 𝒮, 𝒮𝒮

114 W. Main, (918) 968-3990. Take the Stroud exit from the Turner Turnpike and travel south into town. Turn east onto Stroud's Main Street (the old Route 66). The cafe is on the south side of the road.

A Route 66 landmark, this cafe offers Swiss and American fare.

Wright's Restaurant 𝒮, 𝒮𝒮

Located at the junction of Route 66 (Main Street) and Highway 99. (918) 968-3042. Monday-Saturday 6 a.m.-9 p.m., Sunday 6 a.m.-8 p.m.

Serving locals for over ten years, this typical small-town cafe features good diner food—burgers, T-bone steaks, catfish, fried chicken, and more, with side orders of potatoes and salad bar. Locals gather here for morning coffee and daily lunch specials.

Shopping

Tanger Outlet Center

Located on I-44 (the Turner Turnpike), east of Highway 99. (918) 968-3566 or (800) 4-TANGER to verify hours (subject to change depending on the season; they are open extended hours during the holidays). Open daily, 10 a.m.-9 p.m., Sunday noon-6 p.m.

Tanger Outlet Mall features over fifty brand name manufacturers' and designers' outlets. Shoppers find almost anything they want—men's, women's, and children's apparel, housewares and home furnishings, toys, hardware, gifts, books, fishing equipment, and more. Two fast food establishments are located on the premises, with other restaurants located in nearby Stroud. At the end of each major season, the center hosts bargain days sales.

NOTE: Bargains can also be found in downtown Stroud where merchants offer gifts, antiques and clothing in specialty **Main Street stores**. Hours vary.

In the Vicinity

Prague

Established in 1902 by mostly Czechoslovakian pioneers, Prague is a small, charming town on the edge of Lincoln County. Main Street craft and antique stores provide a peek into the past. Much of the merchandise sold reflects the heritage of the town's early settlers. "Old World" antique china and hand-embroidered dresser linens are among the special treasures found in these stores. Try to visit in early May when the community celebrates its Czech heritage during the **Kolache Festival**, a decades-old tradition. "Czech us out," is the slogan of the local Chamber of Commerce. Take them up on it; Prague is a fun town to visit.

From Tulsa, travel west on I-44 (Turner Turnpike) to Stroud, then go south on Highway 377/99 about nineteen miles to Prague. From Oklahoma City go east on Highway 62 about forty miles to Prague. Prague Chamber of Commerce (405) 567-2616.

National Shrine of the Infant Jesus of Prague

Located at St. Wenceslaus Catholic Church, Highway 99 south, (405) 567-3080, (405) 567-3404. Monday-Friday 9-3:30.

The shrine was reestablished here when the original shrine in Czechoslovakia fell into Communist hands after World War II. The nineteen-inch replica of infant Jesus was installed in 1949 and dedicated by Pope Pius XII in 1955 during special Christmas week services. The shrine also has a gift shop.

Prague Bakery

913 Broadway (on the main thoroughfare), (405) 567-3721. Monday-Friday 6 a.m.-4:30 p.m., with an early afternoon closing on Saturday. Closed every Sunday and the entire month of July.

Prague Bakery is locally-famous for its Czech foods. Owen Davis, owner since 1967, offers delicious Klobasnic sandwiches, Kolaches, and Black Forest and rye breads.

Ripley's Fillin' Station

919 W. Main, (405) 567-2525. Monday-Saturday 11-9, closed Sunday.

Diners will appreciate the relaxed atmosphere of this gas-station-turned-restaurant. Enjoy a sandwich or burger, and top it off with a piece of pie. The pies are homemade by Helen Hand, a Prague resident of over seventy years. As the mother of five sons, Ms. Hand developed a reputation for the best pies around. Stop by and see why.

About the authors and editor:

Editor and publisher **Sarah Lowrey Taylor** is a native of Woodward, Oklahoma, and is a Phi Beta Kappa graduate of the University of Oklahoma. As director of the Plains Indians and Pioneers Museum in Woodward, she developed a great interest in Oklahoma's history, geography and culture. This interest led her to edit and publish her first book, *Exploring Oklahoma with Children, The Essential Parents' Travel Guide*. Her company has also sponsored the "Exploring Oklahoma Contest" for fourth graders throughout the state and has produced a curriculum guide that is available in all Oklahoma elementary schools. Taylor, along with her husband John R. Taylor, and their children Kathryne, Reed and Zane, live in Edmond, Oklahoma and have enjoyed many hours *Exploring Oklahoma Together*.

Elaine Warner is a free-lance writer who, with her husband Jack, has lived in Edmond for twenty-five years. She writes a monthly column on Oklahoma travel for the *Edmond Evening Sun*. Four generations of her family live in Edmond, so her travels include a wide range of interests to accommodate companions from two years of age to eighty-nine!

A native of Tulsa and a graduate of the University of Tulsa, **Susan Hollingsworth** knows Tulsa and Northeast Oklahoma very well. For several years, she taught school then owned and operated her own business (Tulsa Tours). She and her husband Larry live in Tulsa and "Explore Oklahoma" with their three children, Scott, Erin and Jill.

Sarah Kobos is a native of Tulsa who has been exploring the back roads of America every since her car started shimmying at turnpike speeds. She received her BA in English from the University of Tulsa in 1990 and currently works for the Williams Companies as a Systems Analyst.

Deborah Bouziden is a freelance writer whose work has appeared in such magazines as *Writer's Digest, Woman's Day, Sunday Digest, Woman's Touch, Living With Teenagers, Romance Forever*, and many more. With a team of eight others, she wrote and edited stories for *In Their Name*, Oklahoma First Lady Cathy Keating's book about the Oklahoma City bombing. Bouziden explores Oklahoma with her husband, David, and their two children, Yolanda and Nathan. They are native Oklahomans and have lived in Edmond for thirteen years.

Taprina Milburn is a stay-at-home mom and free-lance writer residing in Shawnee. She and her husband, Kermit, have two children, Aubrey and Brenner.

Shana Marlow, writer of the "Tulsa Night Life" article, is a native Tulsan with deep family ties to the state. She is employed by Koll Management Services and is active with volunteer work, particularly at Woolaroc.

Back: Shana Marlow, DeborahBouziden, Elaine Warner, Melba Prior, Martha Jacobs, Sarah Kobos.
Front: Randy Yates, Taprina Milburn, John and Sarah Taylor.

Advertisers Index

Our sincere apprecition to the following businesses for their support of this book and their interest in helping Oklahoma travelers. We encourage our readers to patronize these businesses. Please let them know that you appreciate their support!

▲ indicates that a coupon or discount is offered in the ad.

Calendar of Events

The following Calendar of Events serves as a reference guide to the events highlighted in this edition of *Exploring Oklahoma Together*. Refer to this guidebook, get your Events Guide from the Oklahoma Department of Tourism, and watch your local paper for events in your area. *Enjoy!*

▲ indicates that the event is seasonal (season runs for more than one month).

JANUARY

Five State Quilt Show, Guymon, page 26
Eagle Watch, Tulsa, page 121

FEBRUARY

Tulsa Indian Art Festival, Tulsa, page 121
Winter Expo, Red Earth Indian Center, Oklahoma City, page 242
Chocolate Festival, Norman, page 226
Bob Lowe Memorial Toy Tractor Show, Chickasha, page 198
An Affair of the Heart, Oklahoma City, page 258

MARCH

Easter Pageant, Kenton, page 23
Easter Egg Hunt, River Parks, Tulsa, page 108
Public Bake Day, Fort Gibson, page 77
Scottish Games, Midwest City, page 125
St. Patrick's Day Parade, Tulsa, page 248
"Luck of the Irish" Restaurant Crawl, Tulsa, page 122
Fur Trade Rendezvous, Fort Washita, page 164

APRIL

Spring Arts and Crafts Show, Turner Falls, Davis, page 169
Montmartre Festival, Chickasha, page 198
Art Under the Oaks, Muskogee, page 73
Summer Season Celebration, OKC Zoological Park, Okla. City, page 237
Dogwood Days, Idabel, page 152

Azalea Festival, Muskogee, page 76
'50s Bash, Okmulgee, page 80
Rural America Celebration, Cordell, page 182
Medieval Fair, Norman, page 226
Cimarron Territory Celebration, Beaver, page 22
Zoofari, Tulsa Zoo, Tulsa, page 103
Antique Show, Guymon, page 26
'89er Celebration, Guthrie, page 216
An Herbal Affair, Sand Springs, page 131
Run for the Arts, Stillwater, page 273
Red Bud Classic, Oklahoma City, page 258
Ardmoredillo Chili Cookoff, Ardmore, page 161
Selenite Crystal Festival, Cherokee/Great Salt Plains Area, page 31
Rendezvous, Gilcrease Museum, Tulsa, page 100
Festival of the Arts, Oklahoma City, page 258
Tulsa Walk, Tulsa, page 122
▲ Tulsa Designer Showcase, page 122

MAY

Grovefest, Grove, page 69
Kolache Festival, Prague, page 275
Arts for All Festival, Lawton, page 193
Oklahoma Steam and Gas Engine Show, Pawnee, page 86
Okla-Hoe-Down, Midwest City, page 259
Rattlesnake Festival, Okeene, page 43
Mayfest, Tulsa, page 122
Herb Fest, OSU Horticultural Center, Oklahoma City, page 242
May Fair Arts Festival, Norman, page 227
Rooster Days, Broken Arrow, page 127
Israeli Festival, Oklahoma City, page 259
▲ Shakespeare in the Park, Edmond, page 202
Pioneer Days Celebration, Guymon, page 25
Iris Festival, Ponca City, page 38
Strawberry Festival, Stilwell, page 87
Armed Forces Day Military Timeline, Fort Gibson, page 78

Calendar of Events

Blue Grass Festival, Woodward, page 46
Italian Festival, McAlester, page 145
Symphony Decorators Showhome, Oklahoma City, page 261
AdaFest, Ada, page 159
Paseo Arts Festival, Paseo art district, Oklahoma City, page 259
Chuck Wagon Gathering, National Cowboy Hall of Fame, Okla. City, page 235
Howdy Pardner Children's Festival, National Cowboy Hall of Fame, Okla. City, page 236
Jazz Banjo Festival, Guthrie, page 216

JUNE

Sand Bass Festival, Madill, page 165
Gusher Days, Seminole, page 263
▲ Stillwater Community Band Concerts, Stillwater, page 273
Stockyards Stampede, Stockyards City, Oklahoma City, page 245
Ron Alexander's Car Show, Turner Falls, Davis, page 170
Red Earth Native American Cultural Festival, page 260
▲ River City Players, Tahlequah, page 90

Fred Marvel/Oklahoma Tourism

Jenks Country Fair, Jenks, page 130
Judy the Elephant's Birthday Party, OKC Zoological Park, Okla. City, page 237
Juneteenth, Tulsa, page 103
Route 66 Blowout/Juried Arts Show, Sapulpa, page 133
Aerospace America, Oklahoma City, page 260
Tulsa Powwow, Tulsa, page 121
Sunfest, Bartlesville, page 56
Annual Gas Steam Engine Show, Kingfisher, page 34
Kidfest, Woolaroc, Bartlesville, page 55
Creek Nation Festival and Rodeo, Okmulgee, page 80
▲ Pawnee Bill's Wild West Show, Pawnee, page 85
Biplane Expo, Bartlesville, page 56
▲ Discoveryland's "OKLAHOMA," Sand Springs, page 131
▲ Trail of Tears drama, Tahlequah, page 89
OK MOZART Festival, Bartlesville, page 57
I-Lon-Shka Dances, Hominy, page 66
▲ Picture in Scripture, "The Man Who Ran," through Labor Day, Disney, page 70
Owa-Chito Festival, Broken Bow, page 150
Pecan Festival, Okmulgee, page 80
Sandplum Festival, Guthrie, page 217
Jazz in June, Norman, page 227
Reggaefest, Tulsa, page 123
Route 66 Festival and Car Show, Clinton, page 179
▲ Oklahoma Shakespearean Festival, Durant, page 163

JULY

Annual Quilt Show, Grove, page 69
▲ Jumping in July, Stillwater, page 273
Libertyfest, Edmond, page 206
Bricktown Fourth of July, Bricktown, Oklahoma City, page 248
Boom River Celebration, Tulsa, page 123
Christmas in July, Foss State Park, page 181
Old-Fashioned American Celebration, Frontier City, Oklahoma City, page 233

Calendar of Events

Calendar of Events

NOVEMBER

DECEMBER

Index

Index

Index

Index

Index

Index

Index

Index

Index

Index

Index

Index

Come Discover Oklahoma With Us!

Join Jane Jayroe, Jim Buratti and roving reporter Steve Neumann every week as Discover Oklahoma explores the best flea markets, museum, family entertainment, diners, restaurants, concerts, festivals, theater events, sporting events, bargain shopping, and much, much more! We'll show you where to go and how to get there! Discover Oklahoma, **It's worth the trip!**

(Check your local listings for time period and channel)

295

Oklahoma City

Please send me a little more info about Oklahoma City.

Name _____

Address _____

City/State _____

Zip _____

Send to: Oklahoma City Convention & Visitors Bureau
189 W. Sheridan Avenue ..
Oklahoma City, OK 73102